STYLE AND MEANING IN LATE ANTIQUE ART

How do we best see and understand the art of late antiquity? One of the perceived challenges is that this is a period whose visual production has been defined as stylistically abstract and emotionally spiritual, and therefore elusive. But this is a perception that – in her pathbreaking new book – Sarah Bassett challenges, offering two novel lines of interpretative inquiry. She first argues, by focusing on the art of late antiquity in late nineteenth-century Viennese intellectual and artistic circles, that that period's definition of late antique form was in fact a response to contemporaneous political concerns, anticipating modernist thinking and artistic practice. She then suggests that late antique viewers never actually abandoned a sense of those mimetic goals that characterized Greek and Roman habits of representation. This interpretative shift is transformative because it allows us to understand the full range and richness of late antique visual experience.

Sarah Bassett is Associate Professor of Art History Emeritus at Indiana University Bloomington. She is the author of *The Urban Image of Late Antique Constantinople* (Cambridge University Press, 2004) and the editor of the *Cambridge Companion to Constantinople* (2022). Her research and writing interests include late antique urbanism, collecting and display in the ancient world, and the historiography of late antique and Byzantine art.

STYLE AND MEANING IN LATE ANTIQUE ART

ANCIENTS AND MODERNS ON SEEING AND THINKING

SARAH BASSETT

Indiana University Bloomington

CAMBRIDGE
UNIVERSITY PRESS

CAMBRIDGE
UNIVERSITY PRESS

Shaftesbury Road, Cambridge CB2 8EA, United Kingdom

One Liberty Plaza, 20th Floor, New York, NY 10006, USA

477 Williamstown Road, Port Melbourne, VIC 3207, Australia

314–321, 3rd Floor, Plot 3, Splendor Forum, Jasola District Centre, New Delhi – 110025, India

103 Penang Road, #05-06/07, Visioncrest Commercial, Singapore 238467

Cambridge University Press is part of Cambridge University Press & Assessment, a department of the University of Cambridge.

We share the University's mission to contribute to society through the pursuit of education, learning and research at the highest international levels of excellence.

www.cambridge.org
Information on this title: www.cambridge.org/9781009466325

DOI: 10.1017/9781009466356

When citing this work, please include a reference to the DOI 10.1017/9781009466356
First published 2024

Printed in Mexico by Litográfica Ingramex, S.A. de C.V

A catalogue record for this publication is available from the British Library.

Library of Congress Cataloging-in-Publication Data
NAMES: Bassett, Sarah, 1954- author.
TITLE: Style and meaning in late antique art : ancients and moderns on seeing and thinking / Sarah Bassett, Indiana University, Bloomington.
DESCRIPTION: Cambridge : Cambridge University Press, 2024. | Includes bibliographical references and index.
IDENTIFIERS: LCCN 2023058633 (print) | LCCN 2023058634 (ebook) | ISBN 9781009466325 (hardback) | ISBN 9781009466349 (paperback) | ISBN 9781009466356 (ebook)
SUBJECTS: LCSH: Art, Roman. | Aesthetics, Roman.
CLASSIFICATION: LCC N5763 .B37 2024 (print) | LCC N5763 (ebook) | DDC 709.37–DC23/eng/20240227
LC record available at https://lccn.loc.gov/2023058633
LC ebook record available at https://lccn.loc.gov/2023058634

ISBN 978-1-009-46632-5 Hardback

Tous les genres sont bons hors le genre ennuyeux.
Voltaire, *L'Enfant prodigue*

CONTENTS

FIGURES

ACKNOWLEDGMENTS

As anyone who has ever written a book can attest, there is a paradox at the heart of the enterprise. On the one hand, the project is a solitary one devoted to reading, thinking, and writing. On the other hand, no such venture sees the light of day without the aid of a supporting cast. As this project draws to a close, acknowledging the contributions of the many people who made up my supporting cast is among the most pleasurable of all duties.

I begin with my home institution, Indiana University. Over a decade ago, when I first began thinking about the materials that would become the subject of this book, seed money from the university's New Frontiers in the Arts and Humanities program helped to launch the inquiry. Two leaves moved the project forward, and a final round of support from the university's Institute for Advanced Study allowed me to make up for time lost to the Covid-19 pandemic during the second of those leaves. Within this larger context, special thanks must go to department chairs past and present, Diane Reilly and Julie Van Voorhis, both of whom have helped to clear administrative hurdles. Colleagues at Indiana's Jacobs School of Music also deserve my thanks. Thomas Mathiesen welcomed me into his graduate seminar on ancient music theory, and Giovanni Zanovello, whose musicological research has taken a similar turn to my art historical efforts, helped me to clarify much of what that seminar introduced.

External support has been no less important. A year as a member in the School of Historical Studies at the Institute for Advanced Study in Princeton was funded by the Andrew S. Mellon Foundation. I thank Yve-Alain Bois, then head of the art history seminar, for his confidence in the project, together with other members of my institute cohort: Gianfranco Agosti, Michael Kunichika, Jason Moralee, and Felipe Rojas. A semester as the Croghan Bicentennial Visiting Professor in Biblical and Early Christian Studies at Williams College was also instrumental in helping me to complete the work. I am grateful to the art department and my colleagues Guy Hedreen and Liz McGowan for both the initial invitation and the ensuing hospitality, as well as to the Sterling and Francine Clark Art Institute for the opportunity to present my work in a public forum.

I have also benefited from questions and comments at other lecture venues. Many thanks to the individuals who made these visits possible: Diliana Angelova at the University of California at Berkeley, Margaret Mullett and the senior fellows at Dumbarton Oaks, Cecelia Olovsdotter at the Swedish Research Institute in Istanbul, Amy Papalexandrou at the University of Texas at Austin, Sarah Peirce at Fordham University, and Alicia Walker at Bryn Mawr College. I also add thanks to the unknown audience members whose comments skeptical and supportive helped to move my thought process along.

At Cambridge University Press, my editor, Beatrice Rehl, remains unequaled for her efficiency and sense of humor. The manuscript's readers also deserve my thanks. I appreciate the time they gave to reading and commenting on the manuscript. I have taken their suggestions seriously and incorporated them to the best of my ability. On the production side, I would be remiss were I to fail to acknowledge the hard work of Liz Davey, Cara Chamberlain, and Marijasintha Jacob Srinivasan and her team. Many thanks to you all. The mistakes, of course, are fully mine.

Other individuals have aided and abetted the cause in ways large and small. Amelia Bienz and Alexandra Burlingame offered logistical support. Sarah Bidgood and Janet Kennedy provided Russian translations, and Diana Reynolds Cordileone came to the rescue with clarification on Viennese materials. Richard Bidgood slogged through a very bad draft of Chapter 4 and survived to offer constructive criticism. At the final stage, in a supreme act of friendship, Betsy Sears read every word of the manuscript with a thoroughness and patience that was nonpareil. At other moments Betsy Bolman, Dan Caner, Deborah Deliyannis, Jaś Elsner, Susan Harvey, Dale Kinney, Giles Knox, Michael Koortbojian, Noel Lenski, Henry Maguire, Jeffrey Saletnik, Dawna Schuld, Nancy Ševčenko, and Ann Steiner also lent their support. My thanks to everyone. Without you this project would never have seen the light of day.

Finally, the last shall be first. I reserve my most profound gratitude for my beloved, Brian Madigan, and with him the late lamented Rupert, greyhound extraordinaire. Many were the occasions in which this project took me to the brink. When I stared into the Slough of Despond, man and dog were ever-present, the one offering a martini, the other demanding a biscuit, together creating safe harbor. This book is theirs.

ABBREVIATIONS

AA	*Archäologischer Anzeiger*
ActaIRNorv	*Acta ad archaeologiam et artium historiam pertinentia, Institutum Romanum Norvegiae*
AH	*Art History*
AI	*Ars Islamica*
AJA	*American Journal of Archaeology*
AJNum	*American Journal of Numismatics*
ANRW	*Aufstieg und Niedergang der römischen Welt: Geschichte und Kultur Roms im Spiegel der neueren Forschung* (Berlin 1972–1999)
AntTard	*Antiquité Tardive*
ArtB	*Art Bulletin*
BJb	*Bonner Jahrbücher des rheinischen Landesmuseums in Bonn und des Vereins von Altertumsfreunden im Rheinlande*
BMGS	*Byzantine and Modern Greek Studies*
BSl	*Byzantinoslavica*
BurlMag	*The Burlington Magazine*
ByzZeit	*Byzantinische Zeitschrift*
CAH	*Cambridge Ancient History*
CahArch	*Cahiers archéologiques*
CI	*Critical Inquiry*
CIL	*Corpus Inscriptionum Latinarum*
CorsiRav	*Corsi di cultura sull'arte ravennate e bizantina*
CPh	*Classical Philology*
CQ	*Classical Quarterly*
CR	*Classical Review*
DOP	*Dumbarton Oaks Papers*
EAA	*Enciclopedia dell'arte antica, classica e orientale* (Rome 1958–1984)
FR	*Felix Ravenna*
FS	*Frühmittelalterliche Studien*
GBA	*Gazette des Beaux Arts*
HTR	*Harvard Theological Review*
IstMitt	*Istanbuler Mitteilungen*, Deutsches Archäologisches Institut, Abteilung Istanbul

JAAC	*Journal of Aesthetics and Art Criticism*
JartHist	*Journal of Art Historiography*
JbAC	*Jahrbuch für Antike und Christentum*
JbKSWien	*Jahrbuch der Kunsthistorischen Sammlungen in Wien*
JdI	*Jahrbuch des Deutschen Archäologischen Instituts*
JHistColl	*Journal of the History of Collections*
JHistIdeas	*Journal of the History of Ideas*
JHS	*Journal of Hellenic Studies*
JÖB	*Jahrbuch der österreichischen Byzantinistik*
JRA	*Journal of Roman Archaeology*
JRS	*Journal of Roman Studies*
JSAH	*Journal of the Society of Architectural Historians*
JThS	*Journal of Theological Studies*
JWarb	*Journal of the Warburg and Courtauld Institutes*
LSA	*Last Statues of Antiquity* website (http://laststatues.classics.ox.ac.uk/)
MAAR	*Memoires of the American Academy in Rome*
MDAI	*Mitteilungen des Deutschen Archäologischen Instituts*
New Pauly Online	Brill Online Reference Works (http://referenceworks.brillonline.com/browse/brill-s-new-pauly
NPNF2	*Nicene and Post-Nicene Fathers, Second Series*, 14 vols., edited by P. Schaff and H. Wace. Peabody, MA, repr. 1994 (1890–1900)
Öjh	*Jahreshefte des Österreichischen Archäologischen Institutes in Wien*
PAPS	*Proceedings of the American Philosophical Society*
PBRS	*Papers of the British School at Rome*
PLRE	*Prosopography of the Later Roman Empire*, 3 vols., edited by A. H. M. Jones, J. R. Martindale, and J. Morris. Cambridge: Cambridge University Press, 1971–1992
ProcBrAc	*Proceedings of the British Academy*
RACr	*Rivista di Archeologia Christiana*
REG	*Revue des études grecques*
RendPontAcc	*Atti della Pontificia accademia romana di archeologia, Rendiconti*
RepKunstw	*Repertorium für Kunstwissenschaft*
RM	*Mitteilungen des Deutschen Archäologischen Instituts, Römische Abteilung*
RQ	*Römische Quartalschrift für christliche Altertumskunde und für Kirchengeschichte*
StP	*Studia Patristica*
ThLz	*Theologische Literaturzeitung*
ZÄS	*Zeitschrift für Ägyptische Sprache und Altertumskunde*
ZSlPh	*Zeitschrift für slavische Philologie*

INTRODUCTION

In 1902, writing with characteristic intensity, the Viennese art historian Alois Riegl declared that the "problem of late antiquity" was the single most pressing concern in the entire history of mankind.[1] By any reckoning, this was quite a claim, one that came in response to the negative assessment, historic and contemporary, of the period's art. Ever since the sixteenth century, when critics such as Raphael and Giorgio Vasari had taken it upon themselves to pillory late Roman art for what they understood to be its complete disregard of the centuries-old classical representational canon in a blistering appraisal of the fourth-century reliefs on the Arch of Constantine,[2] references to late antique visual production had summoned thoughts of disintegration and decline. Riegl's immediate goal was to turn the tide of opinion by identifying and explaining the mechanisms behind late Roman visual production.

He had attempted to do just that in a recent publication, *Die spätrömische Kunst-Industrie* (*The Late Roman Art-Industry*).[3] Against the claims of contemporaries, who, in keeping with Raphael and Vasari, had ascribed the transformation of Roman art to decline attendant upon the influence of external, barbarian forces, Riegl argued that the period's process of artistic change was internally driven. The new style of late antiquity, which he characterized in formal terms as symmetrical, frontal, repetitive, static, and optic in contrast to the asymmetrical, animated, varied, and tactile forms of the earlier classical tradition, demonstrated the expression of a new attitude that had developed within the Roman Empire itself. Riegl saw this attitude and the style associated with it as deliberate and purposeful, a mode of expression that conveyed meaning through its appearances. Specifically, it represented access to the mind of late antique Rome, a mind that had turned away from the worldly engagement of classical culture to immerse itself in the concerns of magical transcendence.[4]

While the description and explanation of the logic of late antique art may have been his short-term enterprise, Riegl's long-term goal was altogether more ambitious and all encompassing. As he saw it, the true value of late Roman art lay in the fact that it had created the conditions that would necessitate the Renaissance and with it the flowering of modern civilization.[5] The real problem was to convince people of this truth. Although the aspiration to persuade viewers of late antique art's pivotal role as the springboard for modern civilization gained no traction and has long since been forgotten, Riegl's work did have profound and lasting impact. It effectively laid the foundation for what was to become an enduring interpretive paradigm for late antique art in scholarship and teaching.

That paradigm defines its materials in formal terms, arguing that Roman art in the period between the first century and the eighth follows a stylistic trajectory that moves from "naturalism" to "abstraction." In this context, the categories of naturalism and abstraction refer to visual style, that is, to the way in which line, color, and composition are manipulated in a work of art and are understood to denote, respectively, the imitation of the world as we see it and the simplified interpretation of that same reality. The comparison between the first-century-BC sculptured reliefs of the Julio–Claudian dynasty on the Ara Pacis Augustae (the Altar of Augustan Peace) in Rome (Figure 1) and the sixth-century mosaic of Justinian and members of his retinue in the church of San Vitale, Ravenna (Figure 2), first mooted in the early twentieth century, has come to represent the classic demonstration of the change.[6]

In the Augustan relief, the Julio–Claudians – male and female, young and old – process along the two long sides of the altar. Figures carved in varying levels of relief fill the frame in three superimposed ranks, creating the sense of spatial recession. The children and heirs to the dynasty stand at the front, most fully rendered. Behind them in lower relief are the family's major players. Still further back, merely sketched, are other, unnamed members of the procession. No two figures share the same pose, and the participants appear to shuffle forward, turn and converse, stop and start in the way of all such ceremonial events. The garments, wrapped and stretched in broad swaths and tight folds, interact with the bodies they clothe, confirming the sense of motion by creating a complex series of undulating lines that weaves in and out of the composition. With its emphasis on three-dimensional form, the appearance of spatial recession, and the sense of implied motion, the procession is seen to

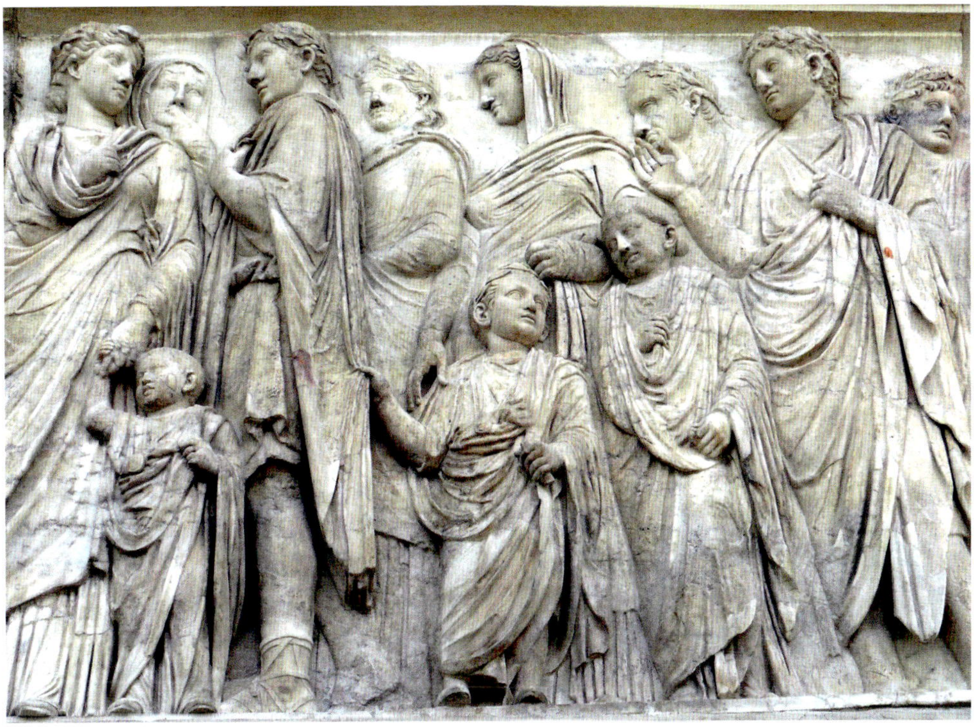

1. Julio–Claudian procession, Ara Pacis Augustae, Rome, 13–9 BC. Photo: S. Bassett

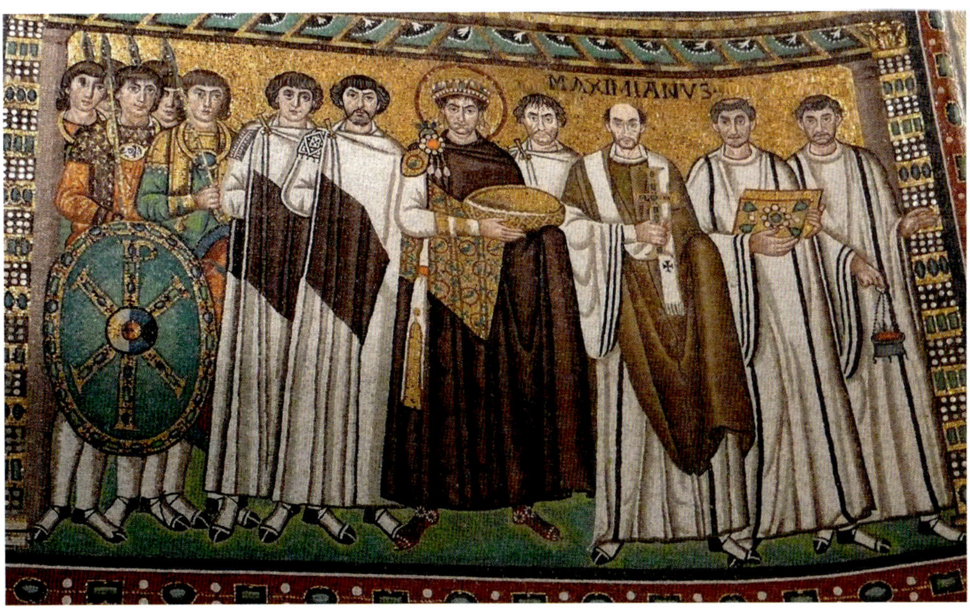

2. Justinian and his retinue, Church of San Vitale, Ravenna, mid-sixth century. Photo: S. Bassett

convey the look of the material world, and with it the experience of vitality and transience that stands at the heart of naturalistic representation.

The Justinianic mosaic, also depicting a procession, is a study in contrast. Justinian stands at the center of his retinue against a neutral green and gold ground. He carries a gold paten and sports the sartorial insignia of his office: the diadem, the purple chlamys with gold embroidered tablion, and jewel-encrusted red boots. A nimbus completes the look. To his left are members of the clergy; the bishop Maximianus, identifiable by inscription; and two deacons carrying objects for the celebration of the Eucharist: a censer and a codex. Court members appear to Justinian's right and left. Still farther to his right are soldiers. In direct contrast to the serried rows of richly sculptured figures in the Ara Pacis reliefs, these figures are laid out on a flat plane: There is no sense of depth, volume, or motion, an impression enhanced by the shift to the mosaic medium. Although the faces are individualized and costume distinguishes the participants' rank and status, each of the figures assumes the same frontal pose, confronting the viewer with only minor variation. The garments, which fall in wide blocks of color articulated by straight unbroken lines, not only underscore the planar composition but also create a sense of stasis. Further, the isocephalic arrangement of the heads and the compositional overlapping of figures who appear to collide and tread on one another's feet make any sense of volume, space, or directional movement ambiguous. It is not clear whether the group moves forward in a V-shaped configuration with Justinian at the apex or toward the emperor's left under the guidance of the clergy. These simplified, static forms, so planar and linear in their construct, define what is understood to be late antique abstraction.

Observing this shift is one thing, making something of it another. Following Riegl and his later interpreters, current understanding is premised on a formal polarity in which naturalism connotes the material world and rational thought, while abstraction conjures the immaterial world and spiritual experience. Correspondingly, this shift in appearances has been linked to a larger historical change, the turn from the polytheistic religious practices of Greco-Roman tradition to the monotheistic beliefs of Christianity, from antiquity to the Middle Ages.

As with all such generalizations, there is some truth to the observations of artistic form on which this broader understanding is based. From the late third century on, artists show a greater propensity for the use of this simplified manner of representation than they did in the first and second centuries, as demonstrated by a comparison of an early third-century image of the emperor Caracalla (Figure 3) and the porphyry portrait of a tetrarch from about 300 (Figure 4). The figures are similar in pose and iconography: In each, the head is turned sharply to the right, and both emperors sport the short hair and beard of a Roman military man. It is here, however, that the similarity ends. In the

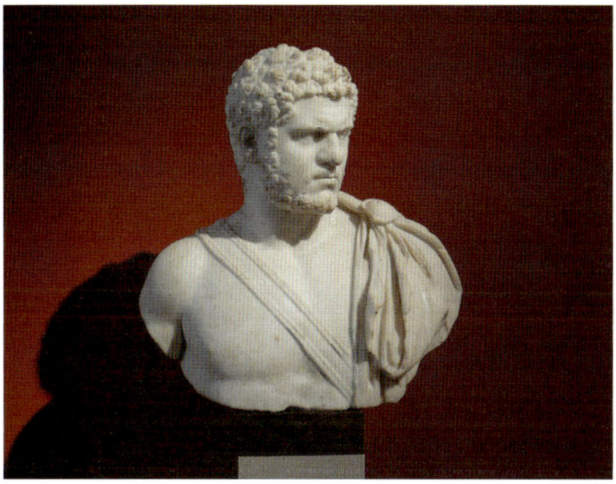

3. Caracalla, 212–217, Altes Museum, Berlin. Photo: S. Bassett

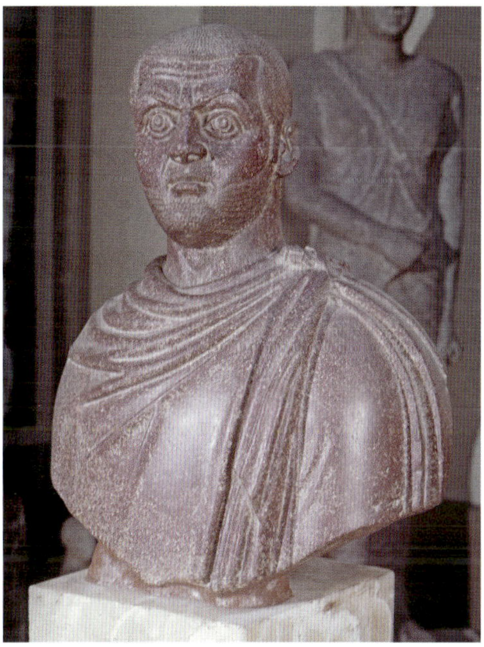

4. Portrait of a tetrarch, 284–304, Egyptian Archaeological Museum, Cairo. Photo: Borromeo/ Art Resource

Caracalla portrait, the artist marshals all of his skill to sculpture a figure that seems to imitate natural form and movement. The short hair and beard are rendered in three-dimensional waves of tousled curls to frame a square face carved as a series of modulated, merging surfaces that capture the texture of skin and the shape of its underlying flesh. A completely different sense of artifice regulates the carving of the tetrarchic bust where a bold interaction between mass, surface, and line characterizes the whole. Three clearly articulated but integrated masses – the head, the neck, and the shoulders – establish the visual field. The raised, uniformly stippled surfaces of hair and beard contrast with the regular contours of the polished face on which a series of sharp, but thick, projecting lines defines and emphasizes the eyes and brows. This stark treatment, together with the strange color of the porphyry medium eschews naturalistic observation for a type of representation so reduced and simplified that even basic identification of the figure is unclear.

While the Caracalla–tetrarch comparison confirms a shift from naturalism to abstraction, it tells only part of the story. For example, a portrait of the emperor Diocletian (284–304), the architect of the Tetrarchy (Figure 5), which dates to the same period as the porphyry bust, shows an altogether different stylistic sensibility, one much more in keeping with the kind of representational tradition manifest in the bust of Caracalla. Here the cubic structure of the porphyry image gives way to a more emphatically "naturalistic" depiction. The bearded emperor, lips tight and hair tidy under a massive diadem, casts what appears to be a quick glance to one side. The creased and undulating surfaces of skin suggest living flesh and blood.

There is, further, ample evidence of the persistence of naturalism well into late antiquity, as indicated, for example, by two later works broadly dated to the sixth century: a personification from the border of the peristyle mosaic of the Great Palace in Constantinople (Figure 6) and an icon of Christ from the Monastery of St. Catherine at Mt. Sinai (Figure 7). As pictorial images, both

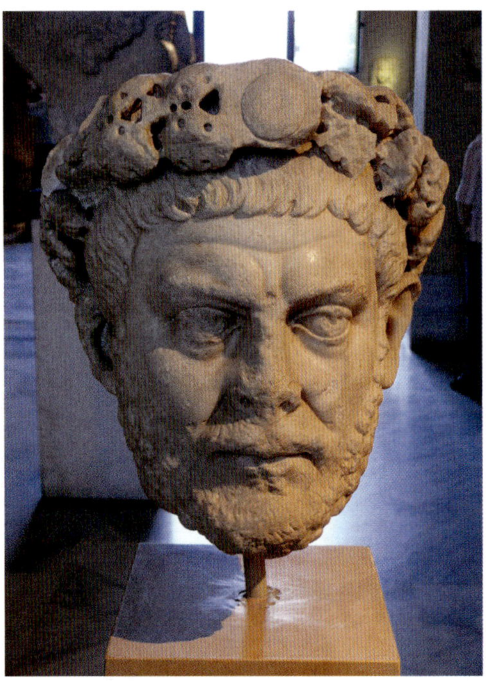

5. Portrait of Diocletian, 284–304, Archaeological Museum, Istanbul. Photo: S. Bassett

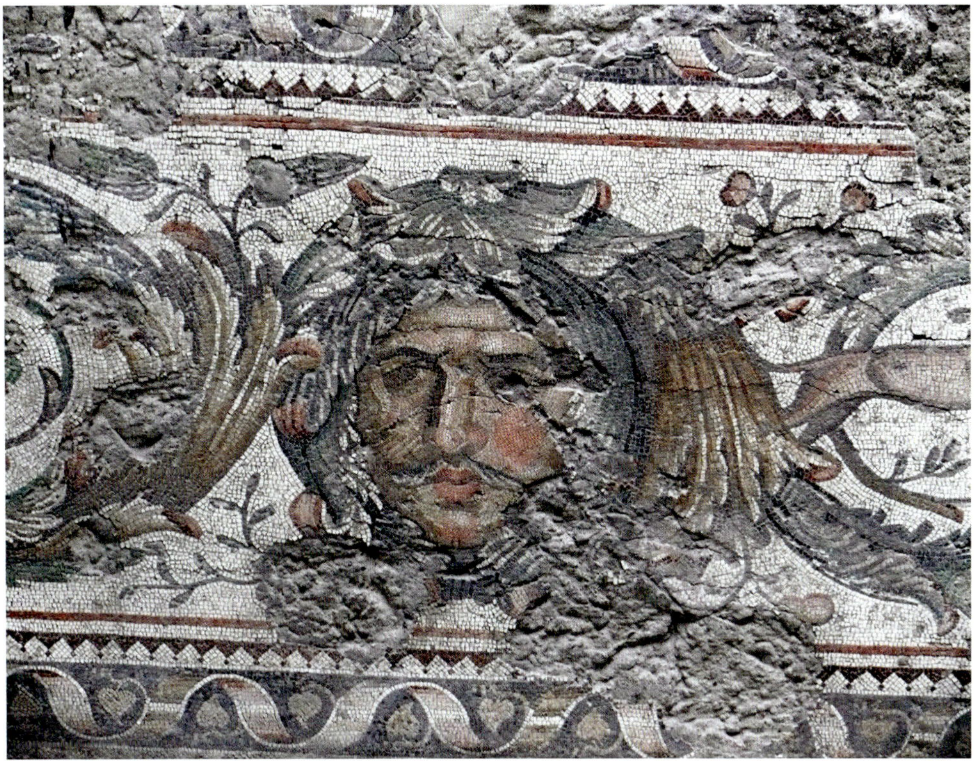

6. Head of a personification, Great Palace Mosaic, sixth century, Mosaic Museum, Istanbul. Photo: S. Bassett

the mosaic and the painting rely on two of the standard tactics of two-dimensional naturalistic representation: the modeling of figures in light and shade to create the illusion of three-dimensional form, what the ancients referred to as *skiagraphia*,[7] and a corresponding sense of space and motion. Finally, a comparison of the icon with a contemporary image from Sinai, the apse mosaic of the Transfiguration of Christ (Figure 8), demonstrates that the styles described as natural and abstract continue to coexist. Here bold lines and broad swaths of color replace the careful modulation of form seen in the icon. This coexistence of styles calls the current paradigm into question by pointing to a more complex visual culture than that expressed by the standard model of change. It also suggests that the established associations drawn between styles, meanings, and cultural conditions are neither obvious nor necessarily correct and that the concepts of naturalism and abstraction as currently understood should themselves be examined and placed in context.

Terminology also complicates the issue. While it is clear from literary sources that ancient viewers admired what we would call naturalistic effects and considered such representation as the end of art, there is no term for naturalism in the language of ancient art commentary. Instead, Greek and Latin authors speak of imitation (*mimesis/imitatio* or *emulatio*), and when they

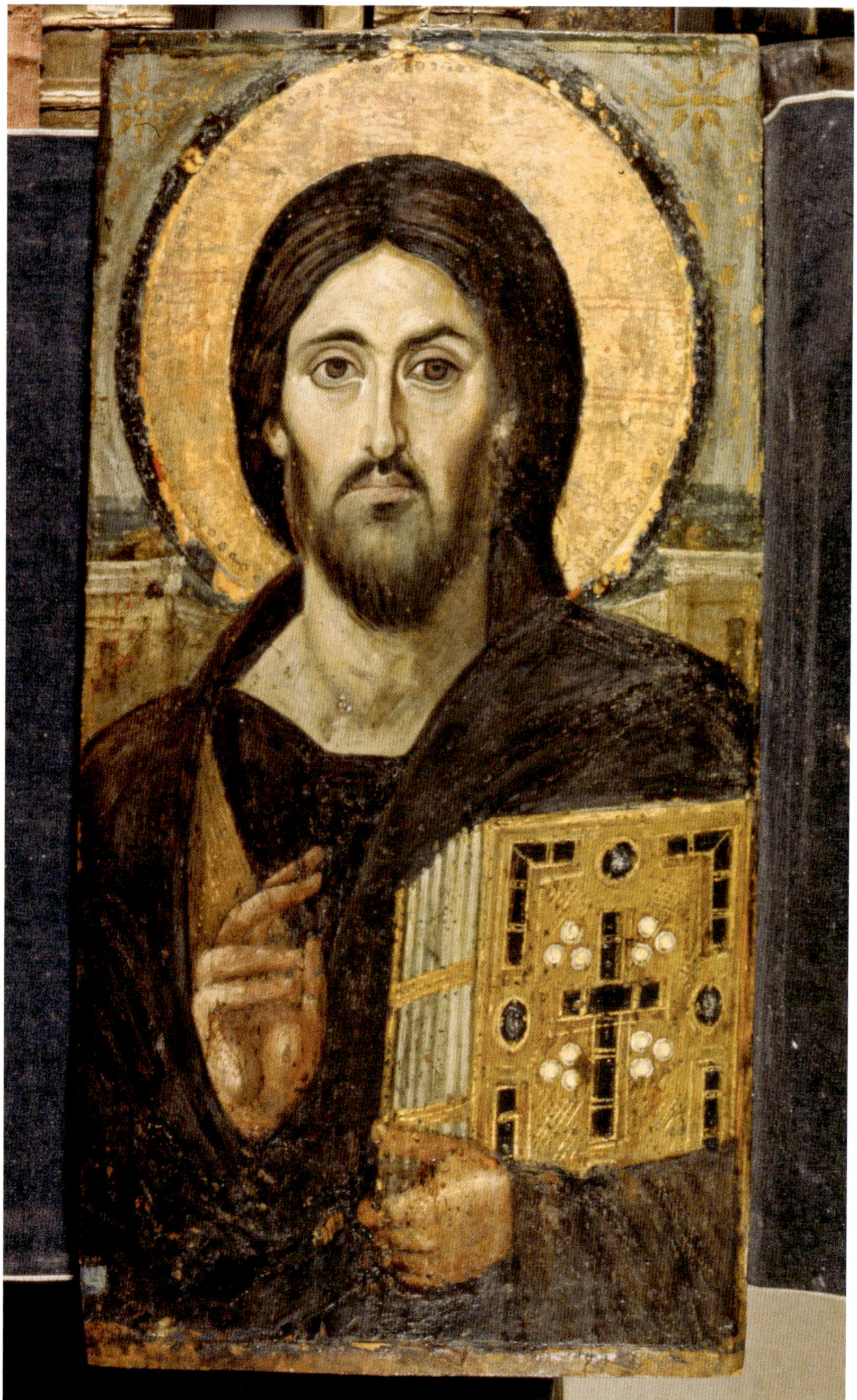

7. Christ Pantokrator, sixth century, Holy Monastery of St. Catherine, Mt. Sinai. Photo: By permission of Saint Catherine's Monastery, Sinai, Egypt. Photograph courtesy of the Michigan-Princeton-Alexandria Expeditions to Mount Sinai

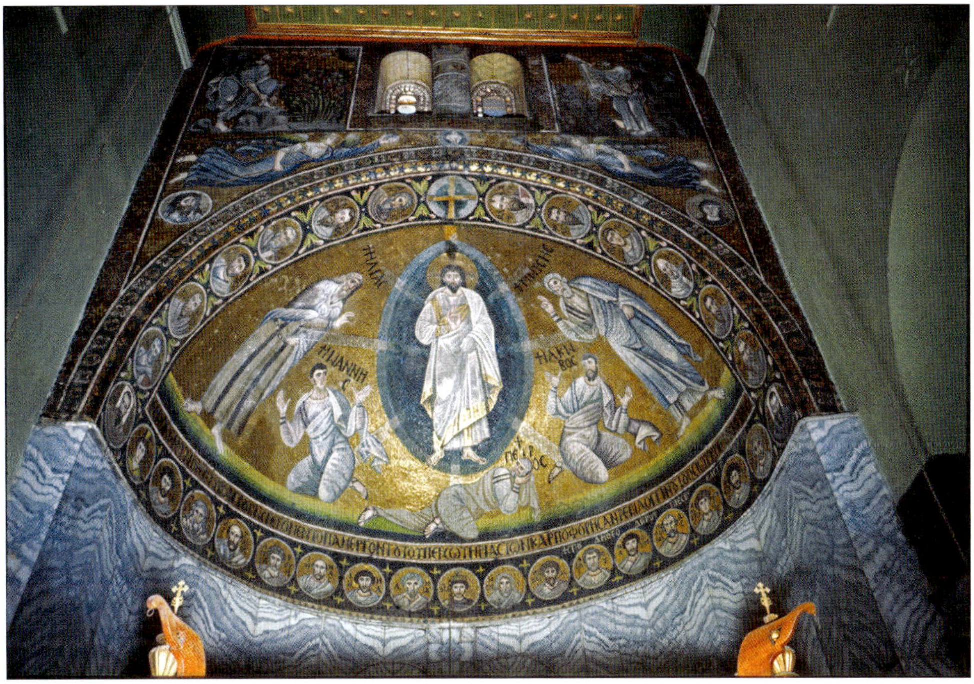

8. Mosaic of the Transfiguration, sixth century, Holy Monastery of St. Catherine, Mt. Sinai. Photo: By permission of Saint Catherine's Monastery, Sinai, Egypt. Photograph courtesy of the Michigan-Princeton-Alexandria Expeditions to Mount Sinai

do, it is not axiomatic that they refer to the illusionistic replication of the natural world, in that imitation may also refer to the copying of earlier artistic models. More problematically, neither language includes a word to convey the idea of visual abstraction: Imagination (*phantasia*), not abstraction, often stands in contrast to imitation, although even it relies on an idea of imitation for its definition.[8]

This absence of terminology does not, of course, mean that the stylistic effects modern observers describe as naturalistic and abstract were not recognized or valued. It does, however, suggest that ancient viewers approached style from a different position and with a different understanding. This book is an attempt to explore this understanding. It does so by following two different paths of inquiry. Part I considers why and how late antique art came to be associated first with abstraction and then with spirituality. It begins by examining the origins of the style's definition in fin-de-siècle Vienna. It then argues that before entering the mainstream, this particular understanding of the late antique style was conditioned by three factors: the contemporary politics of empire, the theory and practice of modern art, and a late-nineteenth-century interest in the occult sciences. Finally, it suggests that the formal definition of late antique style that emerged from Riegl's pen was a modernist construct that had little, if anything, to do with ancient ways of seeing, much less absorbing, the lessons of form. With this conclusion in mind, Part II pursues an alternative approach to the understanding of late antique style by turning to the evidence for ancient and late ancient thinking about formal value. In an effort to reconstruct a late antique "period eye,"[9] it harnesses the language of rhetoric, a discipline with a rich vocabulary of style. By drawing an analogy between visual and verbal form, it explores the ways in which varied approaches to form may have shaped late antique viewing habits and with them the response to the visual arts. As an approach, it builds on the belief that artists and their audiences were bound together in a reciprocal relationship forged by the universal traditions of Greco-Roman education (*enkyklios paideia*), traditions that shaped approaches not only to literary and visual understanding but also to the way of being in the world.

FURTHER DEFINITIONS

Two common but elusive terms, neither of which has a fixed definition, stand at the center of these discussions – *style* and *late antiquity*. Clarification is therefore in order. Definitions of *style*, also referred to as *form*, slide between descriptions that signal the ways in which such elements as line, color, and composition come together in a work of art, those that include materials and manufacturing techniques in the equation, and still others that incorporate considerations of iconographical content.[10] In this project, *style* refers to the formal aspects of a work of art, that is, to the manner of rendering form through the treatment of line, color, and composition. According to this definition, style can be associated with individuals, schools, and locations. With respect to the latter, it can be both local and universal. This choice reflects and is consistent with the definitions promulgated by ancient authors. It also reflects the emphasis on the formal understanding of style that guided the earliest discussions of late antique art.

The definition of *late antiquity* is equally mutable. Used first by Jacob Burckhardt to designate a span of approximately fifty years coeval with the third- and fourth-century reigns of the emperors Diocletian (284–304) and Constantine (305–337), its definition was dramatically expanded by the Viennese art historians studied here, first by Franz Wickhoff, whose nebulous references to late antiquity encompassed the Roman world of the later fourth and fifth centuries, and then by Riegl, who set the legalization of Christianity in 313 as its starting point and the coronation of Charlemagne as King of the Franks in 768 as its terminus.[11] The precision of Riegl's definition has never been equaled. Subsequent use of the term is often more in keeping with Wickhoff's looser definition and may refer to any one of a number of chronological variations. For some today, late antiquity begins in the second century and ends in the sixth. Others include only the fourth and fifth centuries in their definitions. Still others use the third through seventh centuries as the chronological frame. Most recently, late antiquity has been defined as the first millennium of the Christian era.[12] In this discussion, late antiquity indicates the period between the beginning of the fourth century and the end of the eighth century (300–800), a definition chosen for its consistency with Riegl's explorations.

STYLE IN LATE ANTIQUE ART: THE STATE OF THE QUESTION IN BRIEF

This project is hardly the first to tackle the question of style in late antique art. As the critiques by Raphael and Vasari indicate, the problem of assessing and explaining the stylistic shifts that took place in late antiquity was integral to the earliest art historical discussions. For both authors, the Arch of Constantine signaled decline because it was constructed from reused materials, and, although they readily admitted that some of these spoils were beautiful, their reuse stood as an indictment of the Roman artistic community. Effectively, the recycling of sculpture stood as evidence for the absence of competent artists in the city, a point of view confirmed by the fourth-century reliefs that had been made to complete the ensemble. They were, as Vasari put it, "*goffissime*," exceedingly silly.[13]

The scathing dismissal of the arch and with it the fourth-century reliefs guaranteed that the first serious consideration of late antique material would be a long time coming. In fact, it happened only in the late nineteenth century in the work of Franz Wickhoff and Alois Riegl. As had Vasari, both viewed late antiquity as a period central to the understanding of the history of art; however, in contrast to their predecessor they rejected the framework of decline. Broadly speaking, their achievement, which will be dealt with in greater detail in the first part of this study, was threefold. Wickhoff was the first to argue that the ostracized visual arts of late antiquity should be viewed as Roman, while Riegl laid the groundwork for a definition of late antique style as abstract and spiritual. Together, they confirmed the idea that late antique art represented a transition from antiquity to the Middle Ages, an epoch generating a style to be considered on its own terms.

That viewpoint, consolidated in the first decades of the twentieth century, in turn laid the groundwork for a different discussion in the overlapping disciplines of archaeology and art history, one that considered the question of stylistic origin. Some saw the genesis of abstraction in provincial art, but there was no consensus as to which provinces. Although most pointed to a vague and generalized East as the likely source of inspiration, there were also partisans for the West. Others considered the problem of style from a sociological point of view, arguing that abstract form had its genesis in non-elite plebian art.[14]

Tied into the question of origin was the issue of function. Once abstraction had been pinpointed as the characteristic mode of late antique visual expression, there was a further effort to explain its success. Ormond Dalton (1866–1945) and Charles Rufus Morey (1877–1955) agreed that the emergence of abstract form lay in its capacity to express spiritual transcendence and connected that ability to an eastern penchant for the mystical.[15] This type of generalized understanding was further honed. For example, André Grabar (1896–1990) modified the equation between abstraction and spirituality to explain the character of late Roman and Byzantine imperial images by arguing that the stylized, frontal depictions of later Roman emperors emphasized details of costume over individual physiognomy to create a detached and symbolic image of divinely bestowed imperial power.[16] In a similar vein, H. P. L'Orange (1903–1983) connected the forms of late third- and early fourth-century art and architecture to a contemporary spiritualization of ancient life.[17] Others understood the severity of third-century form less optimistically, arguing that the stylistic shift was an expression of anxiety.[18]

Although all agreed that late antique style was abstract, the question of naturalism continued to nag, if for no other reason than the fact that an ever-growing body of evidence indicated an enduring attraction to such form. In a scholarly world in which style was understood as a developmental phenomenon that proceeded from a baseline of abstract, primitive form through a rising arc of increasing naturalism that eventually returned to abstraction this persistence of naturalism required explanation. As a result, theories designed to account for its tenacity began to emerge, with some scholars arguing that it represented a survival and others seeing it as a revival. Whether favoring revival or advocating for survival, these theories introduced an important new wrinkle by specifically aligning naturalism with the classical or Hellenistic tradition. In this context, naturalism was often explained in sociological terms as the reflection of late pagan religious allegiance.[19]

There were no conclusive answers to any of these questions, but in spite of disagreement all participants came together on one issue, the nature of stylistic development. Whatever their stance, all argued from the point of view that visual style developed along a trajectory that moved inexorably from origins in primitive abstraction through a peak in naturalism that then unraveled into abstraction and decadence.[20] In other words, late antique art, a tradition in transit between antiquity and the Middle Ages, was going somewhere.

These debates were never firmly resolved, and questions of style continued to engage scholarly imagination until the mid-1970s when Ernst Kitzinger (1912–2003) and Kurt Weitzmann (1904–1993) produced two independently conceived overviews of late antique and early Byzantine art that seemed to offer the final word on the subject. The projects appeared at the same moment, in 1977. Kitzinger's came in book form as *Byzantine Art in the Making: Main*

Lines of Stylistic Development in Mediterranean Art, 2nd to 7th Centuries, while Weitzmann's took shape as an exhibition at the Metropolitan Museum of Art and its accompanying catalogue *The Age of Spirituality: Late Antique and Early Christian Art, Third to Seventh Centuries*. Both projects were the fruit of a lifetime's engagement with the visual material and the scholarly tradition interpreting it. As such, each represented a personal assessment of the state of inquiry into the matter of late antique stylistic development as it had played out over the course of the twentieth century. They also cemented the understanding of late antique art.

ERNST KITZINGER AND *BYZANTINE ART IN THE MAKING*

Byzantine Art in the Making represents Kitzinger's sustained meditation on the transformation of style in the passage from antiquity to the Middle Ages, a subject that had occupied his scholarly attention since his days as a graduate student in Germany in the 1930s.[21] Although he acknowledged the importance of iconographical research, his own proclivity was to approach late antique art through the matter of form. Thus, *Byzantine Art in the Making* puts style at the center of the conversation, identifying and analyzing its components, exploring its origins, considering its contexts, and examining its potential to generate meaning.

In many respects Kitzinger's work represents a summation of twentieth-century thinking. As had been the case in art historical circles since the publication of *The Late Roman Art-Industry*, Kitzinger identified the period as an age bridging the gap between the Greco-Roman world of classical antiquity and the Greek and Latin Middle Ages, a period of transition that ran between the third century and the seventh.[22] Its main stylistic components were two: the classical or Hellenistic style of Greco-Roman tradition, a manner of visualization rooted in naturalistic representation, and a non-classical, or abstract, style characterized by the schematic approach to form and space. Where Kitzinger differed from his predecessors was in his view of the relationship between these styles. While others saw stylistic development as a direct progression from naturalism to abstraction, Kitzinger presented the history of late antique form as one of interaction – what he referred to as a "dialectic" – between styles.[23]

This dialectical history begins with crisis: the collapse of the classical canon in the Tetrarchic and Constantinian art of the late third and early fourth centuries.[24] It then sees the revival of classical tradition in the later fourth century,[25] followed by the eruption of a new strain of abstraction in the decades framing the year 500.[26] A new wave of classicism washes over the abstract currents of the late fifth century to create a synthesis between these polarities in the sixth century;[27] however, this accord between opposites represents only a brief interregnum, and there follows a return to the polarization of classical and abstract forms around 600.[28] Finally, a second, enduring synthesis between Hellenistic and abstract form emerges in the mid-seventh century at the threshold of the Middle Ages.[29]

Kitzinger's primary effort was to explain the uses of style. To this end, he offered two interlocking proposals. The first was a theory of "modes." Drawing on the language of ancient, medieval, and Renaissance musical theory, which categorized sound according to harmonic and rhythmic structures that were themselves associated with ideas and emotions, Kitzinger observed the coexistence of two visual styles in late antiquity, describing them as modes. Each mode embodied its own stylistic conventions, conventions determined by subject matter and possessing the ability to describe different levels of existence.[30] Kitzinger's modes corresponded to the two established categories of modern analysis, the classical or Hellenistic style of Greco-Roman tradition and the abstract, nonclassical style that grew up alongside it. In this dualistic scheme, works associated with the classical canon embodied tradition and conveyed a sense of the ideal. The proper subject matter of the classical mode was mythology, but classical form could also be deployed for imperial portraits to evoke a sense of retrospection and, in a twist, would eventually be used to convey the spiritual transcendence of sacred figures in later Christian painting.[31] By contrast, the abstract mode, whose subject matter was imperial and religious, carried with it an emotional intensity, one that expressed everything from anxiety to superhuman imperial power to saintly otherworldly existence.[32] As these characterizations suggest, these definitions were not airtight, with the result that they sometimes bled into one another, allowing the modes to achieve similar ends.

Whatever its difficulties, the theory of modes represented the first serious attempt to explain the stylistic contradictions of late antique art. Unlike his predecessors, Kitzinger rejected the idea of a direct, teleological development. Specifically, he viewed the process of change as a conversation, in which classicism and abstraction coexisted and interacted. They did so in dialogue with one another across time and space, sometimes operating in independent states that challenged one another, sometimes coming together to complement each other in great moments of visual synthesis.

Among the problems that interested Kitzinger as he observed this interaction was the question of creative impulse. The theory of modes required the deliberate selection of specific stylistic solutions. As a result, it raised the question of artistic agency: In a world of modal composition, what say, if any, did an artist have in the creation of form? In search of an answer, Kitzinger turned to the language of modern sociology, borrowing two terms from the work of the sociologist David Riesman: *inner-directed* and *other-directed*.[33] Riesman had coined the terms to describe the mechanisms by which societies regulate behavior. Inner-directed behavior, characteristic of early modern, preindustrial society, was that in which individuals had so thoroughly internalized group values that they became their own. Other-directed behavior, evident in the modern industrial world, was that in which individuals looked outside of themselves for affirmation. Kitzinger modified these sociological definitions to describe the impulses directing artists. Inner-directed artistic form was that rooted in an internalized sense of the collective aesthetic. By contrast, other-directed artistic form resulted from the imposition of external will, such as the directives of a patron, upon an artistic project. In Kitzinger's scheme, inner-directed and other-directed behaviors were not mutually exclusive.[34] As with the styles themselves, each worked in dialogue with the other to shape the forms and directions of late antique art.

Kitzinger's developmental model was complex. Late antique art presented itself as a great double helix in which strands of classical and abstract form spiraled around a shared vertical axis, sometimes as distant threads, at other times intersecting points, and always linked by the horizontal bridges of the modes. What this solution offered was a revised sense of the passage from antiquity to the Middle Ages. Specifically, Kitzinger placed new emphasis on Hellenistic form in late antiquity, arguing that the dialectic between classical and abstract concluded with the emergence of an abstract and spiritualized classical style by the middle of the seventh century. Thus, the greatest achievement of the late antique transitional age was the preservation of the basic elements of classical form against the repeated onslaughts of nonclassical tradition.[35]

In restoring the preeminence of the Hellenic, Kitzinger offered a solution to a problem that had plagued scholarship ever since Riegl first took up the question of late antique style: the dissatisfaction with abstract form. Riegl had legitimated abstraction by describing it first as an internal development of Roman art and then as the visual manifestation of thought. Later scholars elaborated on this connection between form and meaning to make abstraction the vehicle for the expression of Christian spirituality. While this line of thinking may have explained what was understood to have been the dominant formal quality of late antique art, it did not make it lovable. Virtually every scholar grappling with the description of late antique art in the twentieth century lamented the passing of the classical tradition. Riegl himself found the material ugly,[36] and the American scholar Charles Rufus Morey, who did so much to advance the cause of late antique and early Christian art, was unequivocal in his conviction that the art of classical and Hellenistic Greece remained unsurpassed in human history.[37] His German contemporary Gerhard Rodenwaldt (1886–1945) looked longingly for classical renaissances,[38] and Kitzinger's own description of the interaction between classical and abstract form used the language of crisis and struggle to suggest distaste for the assault on classical style.[39] By observing and insisting on a role for Hellenic form in late antiquity's final synthesis, Kitzinger sought to reconcile the perceived tension between classicism and abstraction. Coming full circle from his introductory crisis, his was a restorative act, one that aimed to preserve the classical heritage and the values of truth, beauty, and reason associated with it in a changed world.[40]

KURT WEITZMANN AND *THE AGE OF SPIRITUALITY*

If *Byzantine Art and the Making* appeared as a capstone to twentieth-century thinking about late antique art in an academic context, it was an exhibition, *The Age of Spirituality* at the Metropolitan Museum of Art in New York, that brought the period stunningly to life for modern viewers. The exhibition, which opened in the fall of 1977, was the brainchild of Kitzinger's older contemporary, Kurt Weitzmann, who also had trained in Germany. Like Kitzinger, Weitzmann understood late antiquity as a transitional period that bridged the gap between pagan antiquity and the Christian Middle Ages. His purpose in the exhibition was to make that transition tangible. To that end, he and his colleagues brought together a staggering number of objects, 450 in all, from the former territories of the Roman world.[41]

The materials were organized in five thematic groups, or "realms," in order to convey the range of late Roman visual experience both synchronically and diachronically. The first, the "Imperial Realm," included 109 objects and concentrated on the display of official images, everything from monumental portraits in marble and bronze to small-scale ivory diptychs commemorating Roman officials. It also included scenic representations of imperial activities, among them depictions of ceremonies and warfare across a range of media monumental and minor.[42] The second, the "Classical Realm," included 248 objects associated with pagan mythology, science, and poetry.[43] The "Secular Realm" made up the third part of the exhibition with ninety objects, showing representations of daily life together with objects of daily use.[44] The "Jewish Realm," with eighteen objects, followed with a focus on representational art designed to provide a background for the fifth and largest of the groups, the "Christian Realm."[45] Here the display of 236 objects, with dates ranging from the third century to the seventh century, described the development of early Christian art. Sarcophagi, illuminated manuscripts, ivory carvings, and ecclesiastical plate documented the use of Old and New Testament themes as well as those with sources in apocryphal texts and traditions. The exhibition also considered varieties of representational strategies, narrative and iconic formats among them. Photographs of monumental apses and late antique holy sites were included in the exhibition, as were altar implements, reliquaries, and examples of church furniture.

While the make-up of the exhibition was chronological, numbers gave the visual narrative a particular slant, as did the nature of the themes treated and objects included within each of the realms. In terms of quantity, the Christian realm was by far the largest. Its story was also the most impressive. The display conveyed a sense of destiny, as humble objects, such as the modest lamps marked with Christian symbols that spelled out the first tentative beginnings of the faith, gave way to a range of small-scale luxury goods associated with the liturgy and the monumental mosaic programs of Christian churches designed to frame liturgical performance. By contrast, the arts of the imperial and classical realms could not hold a candle to those in the sphere of Christian production. Their numbers were smaller, and there was no sense of ongoing production. As for the secular and Jewish realms, the number of objects was negligible. Secular objects offered a contrast to Christian works, and works of Jewish manufacture were presented as the prelude to Christian production. As *The Age of Spirituality* made clear, late antiquity was the era of Christian triumph.

Style had its place in the march to Christian victory. Writing in the introduction to the exhibition catalogue, Weitzmann observed a centuries-long transformation of classical art according to a familiar formula: Between the third and the seventh centuries images passed from "the realism of bodily forms to the abstraction of more spiritual forms."[46] Abstract style, he opined, was not solely the stuff of "folklore and barbarians"; it was evidence of a desire to achieve a higher degree of spirituality than could be attained through naturalistic expression, and that desire was the hallmark of the period.[47] Late antiquity was, as the title of the exhibition proclaimed, the Age of Spirituality.

THE STAYING POWER OF AN INTERPRETIVE TRAJECTORY

Although it has been some time since the subject of style took pride of place in the study of late antique art, the imprint of this tradition remains visible. Jaś Elsner's influential study, *Art and the Roman Viewer: The Transformation of Art from the Pagan World to Christianity* (1995), published nearly two decades after Kitzinger and Weitzmann completed theirs, shares many of their basic assumptions. Elsner's aim was to understand late antique art and the changes in style that emerged in the Roman world from early to late, not by parsing visual form but by examining the "conceptual frames" that shaped habits of viewing. To this end, he argued that Roman literary sources described two different approaches to works of art – the "literal" and the "symbolic" – two paths to visual understanding that existed side by side throughout the course of Roman history, each reflecting the experience of a distinct representational style. Thus, literal viewing governed the response to naturalistic representation, symbolic viewing the approach to abstract traditions.[48]

Elsner recovered these ways of seeing through an analysis of two major sources, the descriptions of paintings by Philostratus the Elder (170/172–247/250) known as the *Imagines* and an anonymously authored text from the first or second century, the *Tabula* of Cebes. In the former, Philostratus describes a series of mythological paintings. In the latter, the anonymous author deciphers an allegorical representation of human life on a votive tablet. Elsner associates each of these texts with a type of viewing. Thus, Philostratus' description demonstrates the phenomenon of literal viewing, an experience of seeing in which the image is taken at face value and understood stylistically as a recreation of the natural world and its structure. By contrast, the *Tabula* of Cebes is an evocation of symbolic viewing, a habit of seeing that looked beyond actual appearances to see hidden truths in physical form. Implicit in the analysis of the *Tabula* is the sense of symbolic viewing as a response to abstract form. In addition, each of these viewing modes operates within a cultural context. Literal viewing is the province of secular engagement, while symbolic viewing aligns with the experience of the sacred. Finally, the traditions align with religious experience so that literal viewing becomes the perceptual frame of pagan tradition, symbolic viewing the matrix for Christian habits of seeing.[49]

Art and the Roman Viewer is not a book about style. Most of its discussion centers on the seeing and interpretation of iconography, and there is very little description or analysis of visual form in the manner of Riegl, Kitzinger, or Weitzmann. That said, the concept of style is ever present, hovering in the background of each discussion. What is interesting and important is the way in which Elsner understands this foundational concept. For him style is either naturalistic or abstract, and its individual visual dispositions correlate to meanings that can be associated with experiences of the secular or the sacred, the pagan and the Christian. Further, in common with his predecessors, Elsner understands that art in the period between the first and sixth centuries is moving along a visual trajectory that ends in abstraction.

Although different in kind, attempts to characterize late antique art emerge as strikingly similar in substance. All understand style as a dualistic phenomenon: naturalistic, on the one hand, and abstract on the other, a bifurcation of viewing habits that can be shown to have derived from nineteenth-century theoretical models.[50] Ideas about stylistic development are integral to this understanding. Even in the context of Kitzinger's dialectical approach, style moves along a developmental trajectory from naturalism to abstraction, antiquity to the Middle Ages. Because this is the case, style also functions as a chronological marker in which place is signified by the degree to which a work of art conforms to the tenets of one or another of the two poles. This model, which, as will be suggested, runs counter to the evidence of Roman art in general and late antique art in particular, perpetuates a belief in the perfectibility of stylistic development that ultimately can be traced to Vasari and his dictum that the arts "like human bodies are born, grow up, become old and die."[51] It is an uneasy fit.

NEW APPROACHES

This book is an attempt to tailor this ill-fitting suit. In an effort to refine the measurements, it sets aside the idea of late antiquity as the separate, transitional period it has become, to begin, as Wickhoff and Riegl did, by thinking about late antique art in the context of an ongoing Roman tradition. However, in contrast to their work, it acknowledges the pluralism of Roman tradition and the idea posited by Otto Brendel (1901–1973) that the simultaneous appearance of different styles in Roman art was the result of an association between form and meaning.[52] Subsequent studies by Tonio Hölscher, Ellen Perry, Michael Roberts, and Henry Maguire have refined this view by connecting first Roman and then Byzantine artistic production to literary understanding. As did Riegl and Kitzinger before them, all work from the understanding that form is a bearer of meaning. At the same time, these more recent scholars proceed with a different understanding of the relationship between appearances and expression. Whereas previous studies have presented style in terms of the imagined polarities of naturalism and abstraction, these studies open the door to a range of formal possibility and meaning.

Hölscher has described the Roman manipulation of style as a "semantic system" in which a broadly understood, ever-evolving set of forms marshaled different stylistic approaches to express different types of meaning as appropriate to the subject.[53] Derived from the Greek representational canon, those forms eventually took on an expressive life of their own within the Roman context. Thus, classical forms akin to the art of the Parthenon frieze or the Julio–Claudian processional frieze on the Ara Pacis represented a restrained, dignified style appropriate to state ceremonial,[54] while the more exuberant, densely packed style of a first-century BC copy of Philoxenus of Eritria's *Battle of the Issus* from the House of the Faun in Pompeii recalled late classical and Hellenistic styles and, through them, expressed the turmoil and pathos of battle.[55]

As Hölscher suggests, such visual usage finds parallels in ancient historiography and the genres of rhetorical declamation,[56] a proposal expanded upon in work by Ellen Perry, who takes on the problem of style in a discussion of the Roman practice of emulating works of Greek art. Using the evidence of literature together with treatises on rhetorical theory and practice, she develops a theoretical framework that describes the practice of emulation with reference to specific literary and rhetorical concepts. Specifically, she explains the plurality of styles in Roman art by observing that the concept of *decorum* (appropriateness) demanded a correlation between style and subject, a requirement that led artists to deploy a varied stylistic palette, one that had nothing to do chronology or with such modern organizing concepts as naturalism and abstraction.[57]

If Hölscher and Perry have made sense of the broad patterns of Roman style through the end of the early imperial period by looking broadly at the relationship between word and image, Michael Roberts has taken a similar approach with the art of late antiquity by drawing visual form into a relationship with late Roman poetry and poetics. Unlike Hölscher and Perry, Roberts does not concern himself with the phenomenon of stylistic plurality. Rather he explores one aspect of late Roman literary expression, the episodic structure of late Roman poetic narrative, and with it the taste for detailed exposition and diversion, a habit he links to contemporary practice in the visual arts.[58]

Finally, no discussion of the relationship between word and image in late antiquity can proceed without acknowledging the seminal work of Henry Maguire. Maguire has demonstrated the ways in which the sermons and hymns of the Orthodox tradition fed the imagination of artists across the span of Byzantine history. On a basic level, he has articulated how artists developed new iconographies in response to literary embellishments of bare-bones Gospel stories. In addition, he has argued that these images bear a more profound relationship with rhetorical tradition, one in which the visual solutions arrived at by artists share the narrative styles and structures of spoken and written language. Finally, by exploring these strategies, he has drawn attention to the aesthetic aspects of Byzantine art and the relationship between style and meaning.[59]

The impact of Maguire's work is evident in the flowering of studies devoted to the examination of the relationship between word and image that has come in its wake. The many essays by scholars such as Jaś Elsner, Liz James, and Ruth Webb have transformed the understanding of the rhetorical genre of ekphrasis.[60] Once disparaged as overwrought and uninformative, these descriptions are now seen more broadly as illustrative of late antique and Byzantine attitudes toward representation. Others, such as Antony Eastmond, have explored the evocations of rhetorical styles in individual works of art.[61] In short, Maguire's work has given rise to a new approach to and understanding of late Roman and Byzantine art.

The study of the relationship between word and image that has captured the interest of scholars in the fields of Roman and Byzantine art is part of a broader inquiry into the correspondences between verbal expression and visual form that has come to the fore in the last half century in ancient, medieval, and early modern studies. Spearheaded by the work of Michael Baxandall in the 1970s, this inquiry has made modern viewers cognizant of the ways in which the visual arts in any given period are embedded within an imaginative universe shaped by such diverse, yet interlocking, experiences as religion, trade, law, and education. Baxandall's exploration of the relationship between literary composition and pictorial representation in the work of the early Italian humanists and contemporary painters such as Gentile da Fabriano and Giotto articulated the correspondences between verbal and visual patterns of thought in artistic production, arguing that the similarities between them were the result of a common experience of language and the concepts it articulated.[62] His point was that learning shaped both the expectations of and response to the visual arts as well as the creation of the visual arts. Charles Radding and William Clark's joint study of the rapport between architecture and learning in the Romanesque and Gothic periods in western Europe followed a similar path by drawing analogies between developing conceptions of architectural design and intellectual argumentation in the eleventh and twelfth centuries.[63] Similarly, Mary Carruthers[64] and Paul Binski[65] have explored the relationship between the visual arts and rhetorical composition in the Gothic period, while Caroline van Eck[66] has extended these types of observations to the sixteenth and seventeenth centuries. In spite of their chronological range, all of these works build on the shared understanding that visual form is of a piece with a broad range of concepts that shape society and direct expectations.

Given the richness of these studies, a reader might reasonably wonder what this project adds to the conversation. To begin with, it clarifies the extent to which the reigning definition of late antique style was the product of a distinct historical moment. While others have connected Wickhoff's and Riegl's overall interest in the art of the later Roman Empire with Austrian imperial ambitions,[67] this study is, to the best of my knowledge, the first to suggest that the formal characterization of late antique style as abstract resulted from and was intended to support these ambitions.

Having observed the circumstances under which the interpretive model came into being, the book goes on to suggest a new critical language with which to examine late antique painting and sculpture, one consonant with the period itself. Building on the broad connections between verbal and visual form established in previous studies, this project proposes a more direct analogy between the two, for example, between verbal cadences and visual lines. In order to make these connections, it suggests that, given the status of rhetoric as one of the mimetic arts, the manifold and sometimes overlapping categories of style described in ancient rhetorical writing offer a language applicable to the discussion of painting and sculpture.

The point of exploring this language is to attempt to reconstitute a view of style that more closely approximates late antique understanding. That view saw style as something integral to the work of art. It was linked to subject matter, and, as ancient commentary makes clear, it operated within a mimetic framework in which the possibility for variation was enormous. By contrast, when Wickhoff and Riegl described late antique art, they understood style to exist independently of subject matter. It was a phenomenon that operated progressively within broad historical cycles that swung between the poles of naturalism and abstraction. For them, style was a unitary, autonomous expression of a cultural moment.

This project aims to recapture something of the ancient point of view. To do so, it relies on modern methods of formal analysis as a way into seeing beyond the customary categories of naturalism and abstraction. Such an approach is not without its critics. Initially developed as a neutral, "scientific" method to analyze works of art, formal analysis has been shown to have its own evaluative biases, and it is clear that the disinterested eye does not, and probably cannot, exist.[68] Moreover, it was exactly this kind of study that led Wickhoff and Riegl, pioneers in the enterprise, to their own conclusions. Allowing for these truths does not, however, invalidate the enterprise. However imperfect modern analytic practices may be, they allow the possibility of seeing style in new ways, and seeing style is no small thing. As the ancients understood, and as this book argues, style was an essential means of communication. Therefore, to understand late antique style is not only to understand more fully the meanings that surviving images were designed to convey but also to grasp the habits of mind that shaped late antique experience.

NOTES

1 Riegl 1902, nos. 93, 153. "*Das spätantike Problem ist meines Erachtens das wichtigste und einschneidendste in der ganzen bisherigen Geschichte der Menschheit.*" English translation, Schiff 1988, 173–90 at 173: "The problem of late antiquity is the most important and trenchant one in the entire history of mankind."

2 Visconti 1834, 20; Vasari 1998, 1: 224.

3 Riegl 1901; 1985 (English translation). All citations refer to the 1901 edition and the 1985 English translation by R. Winkes.

4 On the visual characteristics of late Roman form, see Riegl 1901, 46–49; 1985, 52–57. On the meaning of late Roman form, see Riegl 1901, 216–17; 1985, 231–33.

5 Riegl 1901, 6–7; 1985, 11.

6 Rodenwaldt (1928) makes the initial comparison.

7 Pollit 1974, 247–54.

8 Pollitt 1974, 37–41, 63–64 (relationship of mimesis to realism), 293–97 (*phantasia*), 53, 55, 99, ns. 13, 15 (mimesis and *phantasia* contrasted). Watson (1988) discusses the concept as it develops from its initial appearance in Platonic thought through its understanding by the Neoplatonists. Watson (1972) discusses the concept in the late Hellenistic period to early Neoplatonism.

9 Baxandall 1972, 29–108.

10 Important discussions of style include Schapiro 1953; Ackerman 1962; Bialostocki 1966; Gombrich 1968; Goodman 1975; Lang 1987; Sauerländer 1983; Summers 1989; Conkey and Haslof 1990; Van Eyck, McAllister, and Van de Vall 1995; Elsner 2003.

11 Wickhoff 1895; Riegl 1901, 10; 1985, 15; Burckhardt 1956.

12 Mazza (2005) offers a general discussion. For particular definitions, see Brown 1971 (second through eighth centuries); Kitzinger 1977 (third through seventh centuries); Fowden 2014 (first millennium).

13 Vasari 1998, 1:224
14 On the East-West dispute, see Brendel 1979, 38–47. Proponents of the East include Strzygowski 1902a; 1902b; Ainalov 1900 for Russian original; 1961 for English translation; Dalton 1911; 1925; Wulff 1914; Morey 1924. For the West, see Rodenwaldt 1921–22; 1944–45b. Bianchi Bandinelli (1970: 51–105) addresses plebian traditions.
15 Morey 1924, 38, 43, 47; Dalton 1925: 2.
16 Grabar 1936, 263.
17 L'Orange 1965; 1973.
18 Bianchi Bandinelli 1971, 1–21; La Rocca, Parisis Presicce, and Lo Monaco 2015.
19 Reinach 1926; Delbrueck 1929, 29–30; Rodenwaldt 1931.
20 Rumpf (1955) did not address the question of origins but rather established a firm developmental chronology.
21 Kitzinger 1934; 1940, 11–45; 1955; 1958; 1967. On Kitzinger, see Harley-McGowan and Maguire 2017.
22 Kitzinger 1977, 2–3. As he observed, 450 years represents a long transition.
23 Kitzinger 1977, 3.
24 Kitzinger 1977, 7–21.
25 Kitzinger 1977, 22–44.
26 Kitzinger 1977, 45–80.
27 Kitzinger 1977, 81–98.
28 Kitzinger 1977, 99–112.
29 Kitzinger 1977, 113–26.
30 Kitzinger 1977, 19.
31 Kitzinger 1977, 18 for form modulated according to content, 32–33 for classical style as retrospection, 113–16 for classical style as transcendence.
32 Kitzinger 1977, 16–18 for abstraction as anxiety; 14 for Roman spiritual crisis, superhuman imperial power, and the Constantinian friezes; 104 for saintly image.
33 Kitzinger 1967; 1977, 13. Riesman 1950, 14–17 for inner direction, 19–25 for other direction. See also McLaughlin 2001.
34 Kitzinger 1977, 124.
35 Kitzinger 1977, 126.
36 Riegl 1901, 46–51; 1985, 52–57.
37 Morey 1924; 1942, 4–5.
38 Rodenwaldt 1931.
39 Kitzinger 1977. The first two chapter titles – "Ancient Art in Crisis" and "Regeneration and Renewal of Classical Form" – reflect this point of view, as do references to the "collapse" of the Greek canon (7), and "jerky," "uncoordinated," and "trapped" forms (17).
40 Kitzinger 1977, 126.
41 The exhibit ran from November 19, 1977, through February 12, 1978. See Weitzmann 1979.
42 Weitzmann 1979, 2–123, nos. 1–109.
43 Weitzmann 1979, 126–268, nos. 110–249.
44 Weitzmann 1979, 270–364, nos. 250–340.
45 Weitzmann, 1979, 366–94, nos. 341–59 for the Jewish Realm, and 369–669, nos. 360–596 for the Christian Realm. Many of the objects included under the rubric of the Jewish Realm were not actually in the exhibition due to lack of portability.
46 Weitzmann 1979, xxii.
47 Weitzmann 1979, xxvi.
48 Elsner 1995, 1–14.
49 Elsner 1995, 15–48.
50 In addition to Riegl 1901, see Wölfflin 1915.
51 Vasari 1998, 1: 243. "*...come i corpi umani, hanno il nascere, il crescere, lo invecchiare ed it morire.*"

52 Brendel 1953; 1979.
53 Hölscher 2004.
54 Hölscher 2004, 47–57.
55 Hölscher 2004, 3–37.
56 Hölscher 2004, 113–24.
57 Perry 2005, especially 28–77 on decorum.
58 Roberts 1989, 66–121.
59 Maguire 1974; 1977; 1981; 1987; 1989; 1993; 1995; 1996; 1999; 2005; 2011a; 2011b; 2017.
60 James and Webb, 1991; Elsner 1996; 2007; Webb 1999; 2000; 2006; 2009; Elsner and Bowie 2009; Elsner and Meyer 2014; James 2007.
61 Eastmond 2010.
62 Baxandall 1971; 1972.
63 Radding and Clark 1992.
64 Carruthers 1990; 1998; 2007; 2010; 2013.
65 Binski 2004; 2014.
66 Eck 2007.
67 Olin 1994; Elsner 2019.
68 Donohue 2005; Kunze 2014; Neer 2010, 1–19.

PART I

MODERNS

ONE

EXPLORING THE "DARK CONTINENT"

Franz Wickhoff, Alois Riegl, and the First Definitions of Late Antique Art

IN THE MID-NINETEENTH CENTURY, THE IDEA OF LATE ANTIQUE ART AS A VIABLE subject of inquiry had no intellectual currency. As the discipline of art history began to take shape and the first universal histories of art began to appear on the shelves of German bookshops in the 1840s and 1850s, the visual world of the later Roman Empire had only a ghostly and maligned presence. Whether official or private, pagan or Christian, works of art from the later third through seventh centuries were examined cursorily, if at all, the accompanying discussions shoehorned into the last pages of chapters that discussed ancient art or the first paragraphs of those dealing with the medieval period. In these cramped quarters, major imperial monuments such as the fourth-century Arch of Constantine were held up as objects of ridicule, while the art of the earliest Christian communities, invariably represented by paintings from the Roman catacombs, was damned with faint praise as the pious if undistinguished predecessor of the great works created in Romanesque and Gothic Europe.[1] In this environment, late antiquity was, as Alois Riegl was to note when he came to the subject in the mid-1890s, the "dark continent of art historical inquiry," a period without name or date whose artistic identity summoned grim thoughts of decadence and decline.[2]

The lack of interest in or identification of a late antique art was in some measure a reflection of the status of Roman art. Although the evidence of Roman artistic production was acknowledged as monumental and magnificent, it also was dismissed as the poor and faded sister of Greek art. Moreover, not only was resistance to the very idea of an independent Roman art robust, but the Romans themselves were denied any but the most banal of artistic sensibilities. As the art historian Wilhelm Lübke (1826–1893) suggested, the Greeks were artists, the Romans bureaucrats. Evidence lay in the nature of their artistic production. While the Greeks produced sublime images of gods and heroes, Roman art was bombastic and official, its notable works the portrait statues, triumphal arches, and honorific columns of the imperial world. Worse yet, these monuments, although imposing, provided unequivocal evidence for the unraveling of classical standards of form and beauty.[3] Herein lay the rub: The real difficulty with Roman art was its style. With its odd systems of proportion, strange repetitions of form, and awkward spatial constructions, it was nothing if not ugly.

A further impediment to the development of the idea of a late antique art lay in the nineteenth-century approach to ancient Christian materials, the study of which took place outside the sphere of classical and art historical scholarship. In the great age of western European archaeological expansion, as governments poured funding into research and classical philologists and archaeologists from Europe's most prestigious universities attended the opening of schools and excavations across Greece and Asia Minor that were sources of national status and pride, the business of Christian exploration was in the hands of ecclesiastics, who operated with different ends in mind. Thus, while classical archaeologists recovered materials from sites such as Aegina, Pergamum, and Delphi in campaigns that gave physical life to the ideals of the classical civilizations understood to be the bedrock of the European intellectual tradition, Christian archaeologists excavated in places such as North Africa or the rocky uplands of the Syrian massif, providing material documentation for a different type of history, that of the early church, which in turn served as a platform for western missionary activity.[4]

Similar aims drove archaeological work in the city of Rome, a territory whose political agenda was as ambitious as its Christian archaeological patrimony was rich. As Italy moved toward unification in the mid-nineteenth century and the papacy's territorial holdings and political authority were increasingly circumscribed, the archaeology of Christianity took on new urgency. Investigation of the city's catacombs, which had begun in the sixteenth century but waned in the seventeenth and eighteenth centuries, once again came to occupy pride of place in the urban archaeological agenda as a means to enhance the spiritual authority of the Holy See in the face of its diminishing political heft.[5]

Given these unpromising conditions, it is remarkable and, in some respects, strange that there was, by century's end, a comparative explosion of interest in late antique art in, of all places, Vienna. Between 1895 and 1901, two major publications appeared that would give late antique art its definition: *Die Wiener Genesis* (*The Vienna Genesis*) by Franz Wickhoff and Wilhelm von Hartel and

Die spätrömische Kunst-Industrie (*The Late Roman Art-Industry*) by Alois Riegl. Working together, Wickhoff and Riegl aimed to shed light on works of art hailing from their dark continent of art historical inquiry.

DEFINING ROMAN ART: FRANZ WICKHOFF (1853–1909) AND *DIE WIENER GENESIS*

Two things were necessary before the study of late antiquity could be imagined: a definition of Roman art that would persuade contemporary viewers of its autonomy and creativity, and a demonstration of the continuity between pagan and Christian traditions. That project became the work of Franz Wickhoff,[6] who in the early 1890s divided his time between the Austrian Museum for Art and Industry and the University of Vienna. He took up this double-barreled task in an unlikely context, a publication devoted to one of the most well-known manuscripts in the Austrian Imperial Library, the codex known as the Wiener Genesis (Vienna Genesis).[7] The manuscript, which had been in the imperial library in Vienna since the seventeenth century, is an illuminated purple parchment codex that preserves an abbreviated version of the Septuagint Genesis text.[8] It survives incomplete, with twenty-four of an estimated ninety-six folios remaining. Each folio shares a standard format: Text written in large silver uncials occupies the upper half of the page, while an illumination related to the text is seen below. Although now dated to the sixth or even seventh century, earlier studies, Wickhoff's among them, assigned dates as early as the fifth century.[9]

At the time Wickhoff began his study, interest in the Genesis lay exclusively in the description of its miniatures. Earlier publications had presented these illuminations in isolation as a series of black and white engravings, and discussion had focused on iconography.[10] The new project, sponsored by the imperial library, was to take an entirely different tack, one that combined the latest photographic technologies with cutting-edge analytical methods to present the codex in a new light. For the first time, individual folios were reproduced complete and in color, recording each miniature and its allied texts in a single image. In addition, new forms of art historical inquiry were brought to bear on the manuscript's analysis. It was here that the publication made its most innovative intellectual contribution.[11]

Die Wiener Genesis, which appeared in 1895, was a collaborative venture. Wilhelm von Hartel, a classical philologist, took on the codicological and paleographic examination, Wickhoff the art historical assessment. They organized the results of their study in three parts. The first, by Wickhoff, offered a general art historical discussion; the second, by Hartel, provided the technical analysis; and the third, again by Wickhoff, described the iconography of each of the individual illuminations together with their stylistic characteristics.[12]

The conclusions were extraordinary. From his paleographical analysis Hartel observed, albeit incorrectly, that the manuscript was of fifth-century manufacture.[13] Wickhoff, following his colleague on date, identified the illumination's visual characteristics and described them as proper to Roman art.[14] These observations had important consequences: In the absence of any recognition of an autonomous Roman artistic tradition, much less a clear identification of its forms, they required Wickhoff to define what he meant by Roman art. That definition, as much as the analysis of the Genesis itself, stands at the heart of *Die Wiener Genesis*.

Wickhoff took on the definition in part one, centering his observations not, as was then the norm, on iconography but on style. Opening with a discussion of the Genesis illuminations, he isolated and described the manuscript's distinctive visual characteristics. These he identified as two: "continuous narration" (*die continuirende Erzählung* or *die continuirende Darstellungsart*) and "illusionist (or illusionistic) style" (*Illusionsstil*). The first, continuous narration, he described as an uninterrupted form of storytelling characterized by the repetition of a figure within a single visual field. The story of Rebecca and Eleazar at the well (Genesis 24:11–22) offers an example (Figure 9). Rebecca appears twice, walking toward the spring from which she will draw water and then slaking Eleazar's thirst with an offering from the well. According to Wickhoff, such repetition created a seamless flow of action in which no single event took precedence over another.[15] The second, illusionist style, he described as a coloristic means of representation designed to suggest rather than document form through the "impressionistic" (*impressionistischer*) manipulation of light, shade, and the physical medium of paint itself.[16] Wickhoff concluded by stating that, because both representational strategies were Roman, the Genesis must be considered a work of Roman art.[17]

These observations set the stage for Wickhoff's definition of Roman art. In the following three chapters, using the same observational tactics he had applied to the analysis of the miniatures, he discussed the nature of Roman painting and sculpture. In the second chapter, he mapped the relationship between Greek and Roman art in purely formal terms, beginning with a thumbnail sketch of the history of Greek sculpture from fifth-century BC Athens through second-century BC Pergamon and Alexandria. He then continued with a discussion of the sculptural production of Augustan Rome. The protagonists in this art historical survey were the Prima Porta Augustus, the reliefs from the Ara Pacis, and the Grimani reliefs, two sculptured wellheads that had recently come to the Kunsthistoriches Museum in Vienna, the one showing a ewe with a suckling lamb, the other a lioness and cub. Wickhoff observed a common style among all of these works, one that he characterized as a literal observation of nature, delicate and precise in its modeling, powerful in its relief. This, he noted, was "naturalism," a Hellenistic style used by Greek

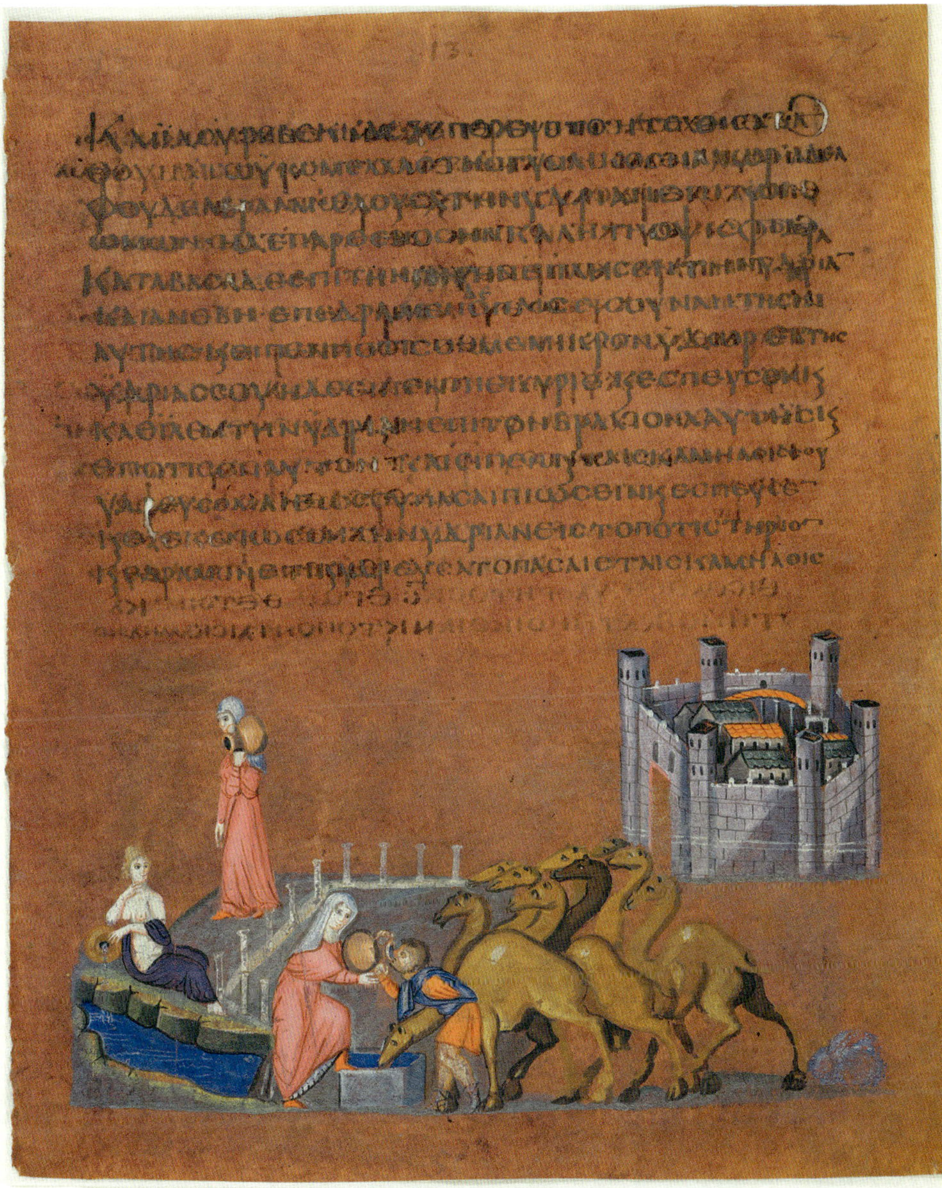

9. Rebecca and Eleazar at the Well, Vienna Genesis, sixth century. Österreichische Nationalbibliothek, Cod. Theol. Gr. 31, fol. 7v. Photo: Courtesy of the Österreichische Nationalbibliothek

artists in Rome for Roman patrons after Alexandrian models. It represented the last phase of Hellenistic and therefore Greek art and was the springboard from which all later Roman art would develop.[18]

Having established to his satisfaction that Augustan art was the last manifestation of the Greek tradition, Wickhoff continued in the third chapter with a description of Roman relief as it developed over the course of the first and

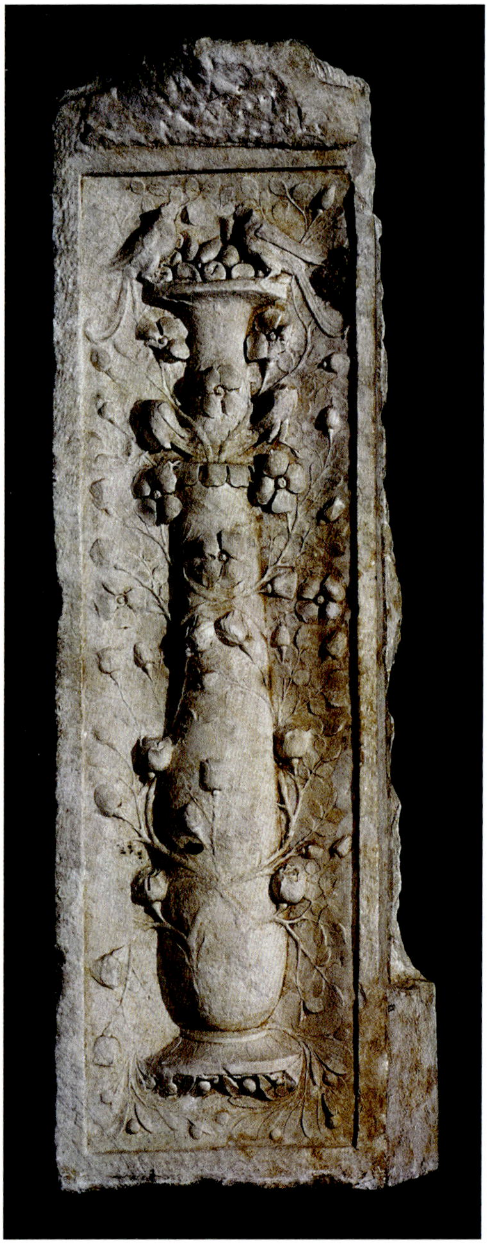

10. Floral relief from the Tomb of the Haterii, late first–early second century, Vatican Museums (Museo Gregoriano Profano). Photo: Album/ Alamy Stock Photo

second centuries. In a visual analysis of floral reliefs from the late first- or early second-century Tomb of the Haterii (Figure 10), he observed what he described as a new emphasis on modeling with light and shade in contrast to the precise, linear replication of detail seen in Augustan sculpture.[19] This new technique created what he considered an impression or suggestion of form, one that required the imaginative completion of the image by the viewer based on his or her experience of the world. He dubbed the style "illusionist" and argued that the approach was Roman, before going on to track its features at work in a series of first- and second-century examples, among them a first-century bust of a Flavian woman, the reliefs from the Tomb of the Julii at St. Rémy in France, and the Flavian panels on the Arch of Titus in Rome. Using the spiraling, historiated reliefs on the Column of Trajan as a further example, Wickhoff continued by arguing that this Roman illusionist style had its most characteristic expression when coupled with continuous narration, a phenomenon fully in evidence on the column.[20]

In the fourth chapter, Wickhoff traced a parallel course of development in Roman painting, arguing that the illusionist style replaced naturalistic representation in two-dimensional works of art over the course of the first century. Thus, the garden frescoes of Livia's villa at Prima Porta represented an analogue to the naturalistic reliefs from the Ara Pacis, while fourth-style wall painting from Pompeii corresponded to the illusionism of the Arch of Titus panels.[21] As in his analysis of sculpture, naturalism was understood as the documentary replication of natural form in all of its detail. Its means of expression was linear. By contrast, illusionism, best expressed through juxtapositions of color that capture not the minutiae of linear detail but the ephemeral effects of light and shade, suggested the nature of form rather than documenting it.[22]

Wickhoff defined this new Roman art in ethnic terms, as an amalgam of Greek and Latin, or Italic, traditions. The interest in natural form that stood at the heart of Greek art carried over into Roman production, where it was tempered by the illusionistic impulses and narrative techniques of a native Latin tradition.[23] Far from being an art of decline, Roman art was an art of new possibilities, one that flirted with the representation of nature, space, and time in different and exciting ways.

With Roman art defined, Wickhoff returned to the Genesis illuminations in his concluding chapter, recognizing in the execution of its surviving miniatures two types of style. The first style, which was linear, represented the work of artists trained in the book arts. The second, an illusionist style that was combined with continuous narration, derived from the brush of those with experience in the tradition of monumental painting. Although he felt that the execution in a good deal of the illusionist work lacked finesse, the issue of quality was ultimately of little import. What mattered most to Wickhoff was the combined presence of illusionist style and continuous narrative technique: With both in evidence, he claimed the Genesis for Roman tradition.[24] The implications were profound. In this single observation, he expanded the chronological frame of Roman art and drew Christian art into its orbit.

In its most basic sense, *Die Wiener Genesis* was an exercise in definitions: It articulated a concrete difference between Greek and Roman visual form and so gave shape and substance to the hitherto vague notion of Roman art both in terms of style and by extension chronology. By observing the emergence of the salient visual characteristics of Roman tradition in the art of the Flavian era, Wickhoff was able to place the emergence of what he felt to be a true Roman visual expression in the middle of the first century. By tracking the persistence of these traits as far as the Genesis, he extended the reach of this new tradition well into the fifth.

This seemingly straightforward act of definition had far-reaching consequences: Not only did it legitimate the idea of an independent Roman visual tradition, but it also revised the cultural context of that tradition. By describing the Genesis as Roman, Wickhoff transformed the idea of Roman art, broadening it from its official, imperial, and bureaucratic base to include works of Christian manufacture. This shift was significant. As an art that incorporated Christian images, Roman art now bridged the traditional historical chasm between antiquity and the Middle Ages. As such, it was, Wickhoff claimed, an art of transition.[25]

Although Wickhoff did not define a specific late antique art, he created the conditions for that discussion to happen. He did so most obviously by characterizing Roman art as a distinct phenomenon. Equally important was the method with which he arrived at that definition. Specifically, by treating visual materials as documents and placing the systematic observation of form at the center of study, Wickhoff established new criteria for art historical analysis. In this regard, he set himself apart from his contemporaries. Most nineteenth-century study pursued one of two paths: Either it approached a work of art from the point of view of a salon critic, pronouncing judgment in terms of positive or negative aesthetic value, or it concentrated on the identification and description of subject matter, a process that relied heavily on literary sources for understanding. By setting aside value judgment and iconographic description as the goals of art historical discussion, Wickhoff made the work of art a document in its own right, one that provided information in such formal elements as line, color, and composition. By isolating these characteristic features and compiling information about them, he was able to create something new, a history of visual form and with it a history of perception. In so doing, he set the stage for the work of his younger colleague, Alois Riegl.

LATE ROMAN ART: ALOIS RIEGL (1858–1905) AND *DIE SPÄTRÖMISCHE KUNST-INDUSTRIE*

While Wickhoff was working on the text that would become *Die Wiener Genesis*, Alois Riegl, then Wickhoff's curatorial colleague at the museum, was preparing material for an exhibition that would become the catalyst to the first sustained discussion of late antique art proper.[26] The Archaeological

Exhibition, held in 1893, brought together antiquities from Austrian private collections. Mounted in conjunction with the forty-second annual meeting of German Educators and Philologists which took place in Vienna that year, its purpose was to showcase Austrian holdings in ancient art. These holdings were overwhelmingly small in scale and included everything from practical objects such as cutlery and cooking vessels to prestige objects such as bronze statuettes of gods and heroes, arms, armor, and gold jewelry. Most of the items were of second- and third-century manufacture, but there was also a cluster of later materials listed in the accompanying visitors' guide that included works of "so-called barbarian enamel" of "late Roman manufacture." These were the works of Riegl's art-industry.[27]

Although only a small part of the exhibition, these objects captured Riegl's imagination, and when the Austrian Ministry of Education invited him to prepare the materials for publication, he accepted the invitation. Initially organized around objects first assembled for the Archaeological Exhibition, his study eventually expanded to include pieces from the Austrian imperial collections. *Die spätrömische Kunst-Industrie nach den Funden in Österreich-Ungarn im Zusammenhange mit der Gesammtentwicklung der bildenden Künste bei den Mittelmeervölkern* (*The Late Roman Art-Industry Based on Finds in Austria and Hungary in the Context of the Larger Development of the Fine Arts among the Mediterranean Peoples*) is the fruit of this labor.[28]

Riegl's title was in some respects misleading, for, although the materials of the art-industry were the *raison d'être* for the publication, they are by no means its actual subject. They represented, rather, one element in an ambitious study that Riegl imagined as a monumental two-part exploration of the visual arts in the "latest phase of ancient art."[29]

The Late Roman Art Industry was intended as the first part of this exploration. Its purpose was to examine the products of this art-industry in light of the Mediterranean artistic traditions that had given rise to their creation, and in so doing to discover the connections between Mediterranean art and the art produced by the Germanic peoples in the period between the fourth and the eighth centuries. Specifically, Riegl proposed to demonstrate that the development of this last phase of ancient art was beholden not to "barbarian" influence, as was generally supposed, but rather to changes generated from within the Roman world itself. Building on the work of the first part, the second part was to lay out the extent of the Germanic populations' contribution to the formation of the fine arts from the ninth century on. This second study was never completed, a casualty of Riegl's shifting interests and his untimely death in 1905.[30]

To identify and explain the nature of the latest phase of ancient art was thus the goal of the *Late Roman Art-Industry*. This was Riegl's dark continent: a place without date or name or visual characteristics. Accordingly, in an effort to illuminate the territory, Riegl opened with a definition of terms. He began by setting the dates, a task he undertook with astonishing precision. Late antiquity began in 313 with the legalization of Christianity and ended in 768 with the coronation of Charlemagne as King of the Franks, a 450-year span that Riegl characterized as an age of transition between antiquity and the Middle Ages.[31]

Next came the task of naming. Although he acknowledged the term "late antique" (*spätantike*) as appropriate, Riegl's preferred designation was "late Roman" (*spätrömisch*), a description that had the advantage of being simultaneously exclusive and inclusive. For Riegl, the weakness of "late antique" as a moniker was that it encompassed the art of all late ancient populations, Egyptian and Mesopotamian among them. Riegl saw his imagined community as distinct from the cultures of Egypt and the ancient Near East. The style under study was, he argued, a specifically Roman phenomenon, one associated not with the city of Rome or the Italic peoples but rather with the political enterprise of the Roman Empire and the cultural community it established across the time and space of the Mediterranean world. Riegl understood the uniform artistic tradition produced by and for this community as a kind of cultural glue that served the empire's varied populations, pagans and Christians among them. This phenomenon, enduring and cohesive, was distinctly Roman in the broadest sense of the word; therefore, he thought it fitting that this last phase of ancient art bear its name.[32]

With the chronological and titular scaffolding in place, Riegl then turned to building the larger program. The goal was to identify and describe what he referred to as "laws governing the development" (*Gesetze der Entwicklung*) of monuments in all media.[33] This was a two-pronged project. It demanded, first, that Riegl observe and characterize the formal qualities shared by the arts across media, and, second, that he explain the larger creative force shaping these laws, the phenomenon he referred to as *Kunstwollen*. According to Riegl, *Kunstwollen* governed not only the mind and hand of an individual artist, but also the society in which he operated. It thus conditioned both the creation of and response to artistic form. *The Late Roman Art-Industry* represents an effort to isolate and characterize the distinctive elements of a late Roman *Kunstwollen* as manifest in physical form.[34]

Riegl's second goal was to demonstrate how this late Roman *Kunstwollen* and the art to which it gave rise could and should be understood. Specifically, and against the prevailing opinion that artistic production from the fourth century on demonstrated the collapse of classical values in the face of barbarian influences, Riegl proposed that the last phase of ancient art represented the positive expression of a *Kunstwollen* that was the natural outgrowth of developments generated from within the Roman world itself.[35]

To demonstrate his point, Riegl cast his net wide. Following Wickhoff's newly expanded definition of Roman art and the methodological focus on formal analysis, he relied not only on the traditional sorts of monuments crucial to any study of Roman antiquity – portraits, triumphal arches, and sarcophagi – to build his argument but also on works of Christian art. Materials monumental and miniature were included in the discussion, everything from the fourth-century mosaics in the mausoleum of Constantia in Rome to sixth-century carved ivory panels. Riegl explored these materials in four chapters, each organized around medium. He began with architecture, continued with sculpture, and moved on to painting before coming to an examination of the small-scale works of the art-industry itself. The focus throughout was on form.

In chapter one, ostensibly on architecture, Riegl began once again with definitions, first identifying and describing the laws governing artistic production in all media, and then sketching their development from the Egyptian period through the Roman. Here he observed that the first goal of the visual arts throughout antiquity, whether among the Egyptians, the Greeks, or the Romans, was to imitate nature by representing figures and objects as recognizable material entities on a pictorial plane.[36] Further, it was his conviction that, although all art strives to meet these goals, individuals and, by extension, the historical periods in which they live have different ideas about what constitutes such imitation, based upon interlocking categories of conception and perception.[37]

For Riegl, three viewing traditions structured these categories: *Nahsicht* (near sight, or close viewing), *Fernsicht* (far sight, or distant viewing), and *Normalsicht* (normal sight, or normal viewing). Each term corresponded to a mode of perception and aligned with a moment in history. Riegl defined close viewing in terms of two dimensions. Its most characteristic manifestation was in the art of ancient Egypt, an art in which objects appear flattened and outlined within a single, two-dimensional plane, which he described as "tactile" (*taktisch*) and "haptic" (*haptisch*). This tactile essence constituted perception at its most basic and literal.[38]

Distant viewing, by contrast, was the representation of form in a spatial plane. Its most characteristic manifestation came in the fourth-century frieze that wrapped around the middle of the Arch of Constantine (Figure 11). For Riegl, the reliefs continued to represent figures within the plane, but they did so not on the two-dimensional surface but by isolating individual forms from one another within the plane's three-dimensional space, thus setting up an "optical" (*optisch*) contrast between light and dark. Here perception stepped back from the literal to become imaginative.[39] Like Wickhoff, Riegl understood this imaginative act of optical perception as a process in which an individual recognized and completed the forms represented from his or her own experience of the world.

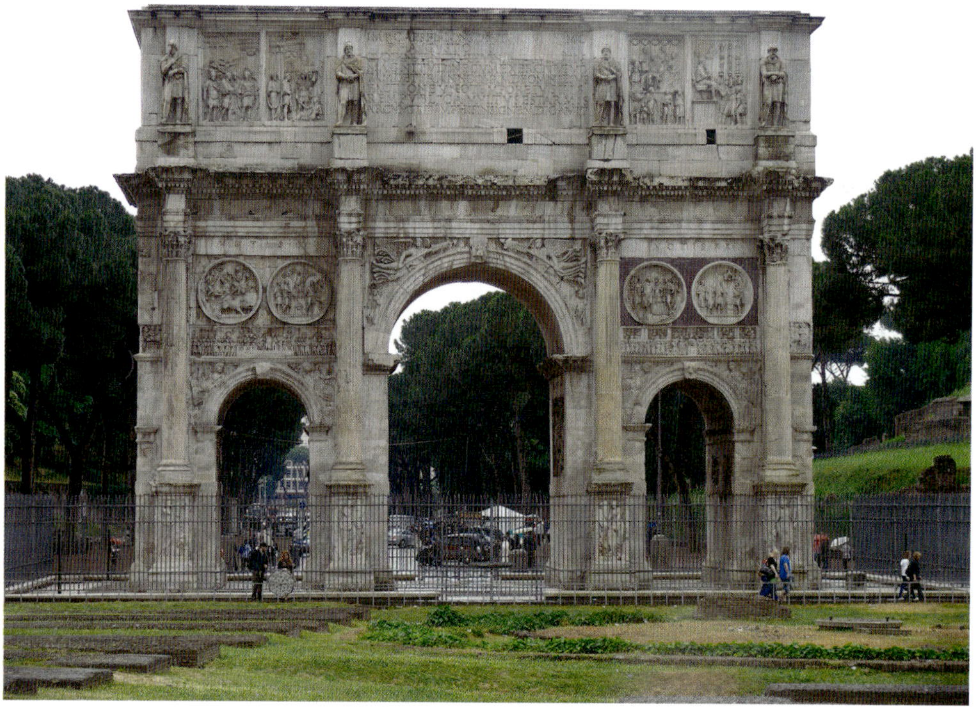

11. Arch of Constantine, Rome, 315. Photo: S. Bassett

Finally, between the poles of close and distant viewing stood the category of *Normalsicht* (normal sight or viewing). Normal viewing represented not only the balance between the literalness of close viewing and the imaginative play of distant viewing but also that between tactile and optical understanding. Its most characteristic manifestation came in the fifth-century BC reliefs from the Parthenon in Athens.[40]

In conjunction with the broad categories of close and distant viewing Riegl applied two other terms throughout his discussion, "crystalline" (*krystallinisch*) and "organic" (*organisch*). Although not directly defined, Riegl made it clear through usage that the terms characterized the formal qualities of representation. Thus, the term "crystalline" was used to describe works of art that emphasized symmetrical composition and two-dimensional, linear form, while the designation "organic" was applied to images that were asymmetrical and gave the appearance of three-dimensionality. Finally, he associated each of these visual values with a larger idea: Crystalline form embodied the immutable and eternal aspects of inorganic matter, while organic form expressed the accidental transience of nature and living beings.[41]

After defining his terms within the arc of a larger historical trajectory, Riegl then set about observing his laws at play in the various media. In a series of painstaking visual analyses, he identified and described the visual characteristics of late Roman art. Whether in architecture, sculpture, or painting, those characteristics included an emphasis on symmetrical, un-modeled shape, an interest in the repetition of form, composition within a plane, and, above all, the isolation of the figure in space, all characteristics of distant viewing. Riegl's most important identification of these characteristics occurred in the chapters on sculpture and painting. What he was eager to demonstrate in this analysis was not simply the nature of late Roman style but also the origin of that style in early imperial artistic production. To this end, each of the chapters offers a carefully orchestrated sequence of formal analyses designed to demonstrate the shift from normal to distant viewing that took place within the Roman context between the second and fourth centuries.

Chapter two, on sculpture, opens with a discussion of the fourth-century *largitio* relief on the Arch of Constantine in Rome (Figure 12). In it, Riegl characterizes the scene as one built up of individualized units in planar space. He observes that individual figures are separated from one another, surrounded by pockets of space, and that each figure stands within a larger symmetrical grouping around the central representation of Constantine. The relief represents, he states, the apex of symmetrical centralization.[42] Riegl then observes that modern viewers respond poorly to these qualities because they appear to reject the principles of animation and beauty that organized classical composition, with the result that the relief is understood as a monument of decline. Further, he notes that the decline itself is described either as the result of haste in manufacture or barbarian workmanship and influence. Riegl rejects these claims, arguing that the *largitio* frieze represents a new conception of naturalism and beauty rooted in principles of crystalline symmetry and optical composition that are, in reality, fully Roman.[43] The

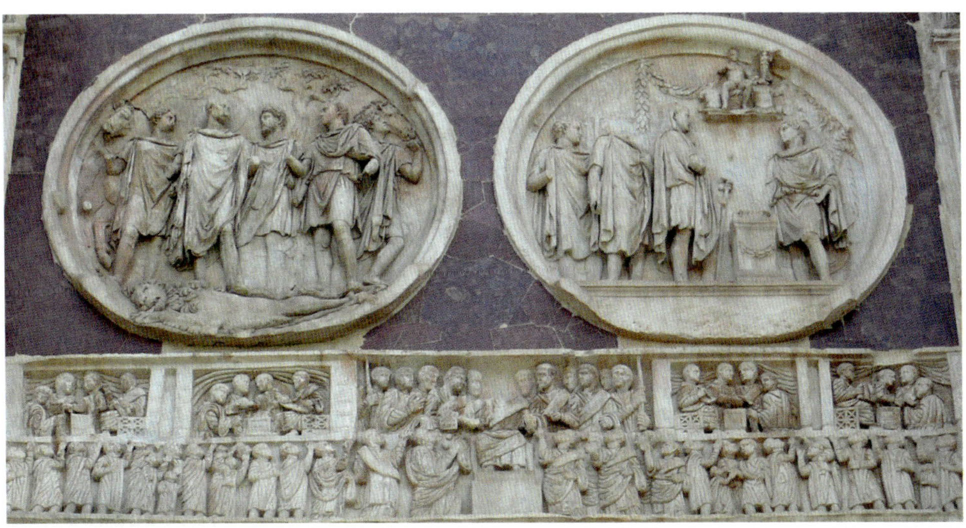

12. *Largitio* relief, Arch of Constantine, Rome, 315. Photo: S. Bassett

chapter goes on to demonstrate how this can be the case by tracking the development of form in Egypt, Greece, and early imperial Rome.[44] Having arrived at the second century, Riegl then settles in to the core of his discussion, an analysis of six sculptured reliefs ranging in date from the second half of the second through the early fourth centuries.[45] Here he not only maps the inexorable march to the Constantinian relief and distant viewing but also claims the latter as a purely Roman phenomenon. Having established both the aesthetic legitimacy and the Roman origins of the *largitio* frieze, Riegl then goes on to demonstrate the ways in which post-Constantinian sculpture in the later fourth, fifth, and sixth centuries – everything from monumental portrait busts to sarcophagi and small-scale ivory diptychs – derived from the style of the Arch of Constantine frieze. Implicit in this sequence of analyses was the claim that this later Roman art stood in a direct, internally developed line of descent from the classically based standards of the early Roman tradition.[46]

The subsequent chapter on painting follows a similar, if more circumscribed, logic. Mindful of the fact that the corpus of surviving Roman painting was small, limited at the time to the finds at Pompeii and the evidence of the Roman catacombs, Riegl made no attempt to discuss the evidence of the early imperial period. Instead, he began with the fourth century, noting how works such as the mosaics in the mausoleum of Constantia, which showed isolated figures against a neutral ground, were of a piece with the aesthetic standards of the Constantinian *largitio* frieze. Specifically, he saw the placement of individual objects against the neutral ground and the absence of cast shadow as indicative of a desire to isolate figures in space in a manner analogous to the composition of the frieze. He went on to observe the ways in which examples of fifth-century painting maintained this interest, before finally turning to what he considered the paradigmatic example of distant viewing in late Roman painting – the sixth-century mosaic of Justinian and his retinue from the church of San Vitale in Ravenna.[47]

The analysis of sculpture and painting in chapters two and three sets the stage for the book's raison d'être, Riegl's final observations about the works of the late Roman art-industry. Here he applied his analytical skills to the description and characterization of chip-carved metalwork, enamel, and garnet-inlaid jewelry, material dating from the fifth through the seventh centuries. He observed that this nonrepresentational art, which came largely from Austrian territory, not only used manufacturing techniques and decorative motifs that were of Roman origin but also adhered to the same laws of distant viewing that informed works of later Roman art. As a result, Riegl argued, these materials should not be understood as the products of barbarian ideation, as was customarily supposed, but as works participating fully in the *Kunstwollen* of the late Roman world.[48]

In the fifth and final chapter, Riegl stepped back from visual analysis to outline what he believed to be the fundamental characteristics of this late Roman *Kunstwollen*. He began by reiterating his assertion that all ancient art emphasized material appearance and natural imitation. To this statement he added the observation that in any given representational context, the aggregate of individual shapes used to achieve representation created a unity regulated by rhythm, and that, in the context of the later Roman world, that rhythm stressed uniformity and repetition through the use of rectangular, un-modeled shapes, planar composition, and isolated figures.[49]

To this point, Riegl's assessment of late Roman art had relied solely on the observation, description, and analysis of formal qualities. With those qualities established, he went on to introduce a new category of evidence, literary sources, calling upon the work of two authors – Plotinus (204/205–270) and Augustine (354–430) – to support his definition of a late Roman *Kunstwollen*.[50] Although he did not pursue the discussion of Plotinus, Riegl believed that he had found in Augustine an aesthetic theory to match his definition of the late Roman *Kunstwollen*, one that placed emphasis on complete shape and the creation of unity and rhythm via symmetry and proportion.[51] Finally, Riegl argued that distant viewing, with its isolation of forms in space, flickering optical qualities, and reliance upon the interpretive power of memory and imagination, corresponded to a particular late Roman worldview, one shared by pagan and Christian alike, that replaced reason with magic.[52]

By his own account, Riegl's project built upon and expanded Wickhoff's discussion of Roman art.[53] As had his colleague, he based his discussion on observation, description, and formal analysis with the aim of creating a scientific account of perception that could stand apart from what he felt to be the vagueness of aesthetic judgment. However, what no one would have suspected in reading his title is that its author, not one to think small, had gone well beyond Wickhoff in the service of this enterprise by outlining a theory and with it an entire history of visual form and human perception. What was important about this theory, among other things, is that it not only observed but also accorded meaning to style.

Under its terms, style, the visual manifestation of *Kunstwollen*, was the expression of a worldview and consequently subject to change. Thus, the ancient world, although consistent in its desire to represent objects within a plane, had three viewing phases, each tied to and expressive of a fundamental cultural ethos. The first – the literal, close viewing of Egyptian tradition – expressed an awareness of the arbitrary forces of nature to which human beings were subject. Its aim was to make those forces comprehensible through the structures of stylistic representation that Riegl defined as tactile, a method of representation that made the world tangible. By contrast, the second phase – normal viewing, the art of Periclean Athens, poised between close and distant viewing – expressed a binding and logical relationship between human beings and their environment. This was an art of cause and effect, of clarity and reason, a relationship expressed in the balance between the physical verification provided by tactile sensation and the imaginative input of optical experience. Finally, the third phase – the optical, distant viewing of the late Roman period that relied exclusively on the interpretive powers of imagination – expressed the sense of isolation and reliance upon magic to which people turned when cognizant of the imbalance between their own fragile existence and the power of nature. For Riegl, this distant viewing represented the visual corollary to the practice of Neoplatonic philosophy, syncretic pagan cult, and early Christian religion. This trajectory from close viewing to distant viewing, from tactile expression to optical expression, evinced neither advance nor decline. Rather, it mirrored and gave visual form to the shape of human experience, specifically the shifting balance in the relationship between human beings and their perception of their place in the world.

CONCLUSIONS

The work of Wickhoff and Riegl represented an initial foray into thinking about Roman art and with it the artistic production of late antiquity. As such, it focused on the basic task of definition, doing so primarily through the observation and analysis of visual form. Although Wickhoff and Riegl used different vocabularies to characterize form – *illusionism* for Wickhoff, *distant viewing* for Riegl – both agreed that the defining criterion of Roman art was its preference for rendering form through the manipulation of light and shade. Further, both understood this particular mode of representation in terms of habits of human perception. Specifically, each believed that forms created through the manipulation of light and shade demanded input from the viewer, a process that required the completion of the image from a personal stock of memory and experience. In essence, they saw Roman art, whether early or late, as an exercise in imaginative recreation.

To this formal definition, Wickhoff and Riegl added a second characterization, one that described their subject in terms of transition. For Wickhoff, this concept was rooted in the constancy of visual form. The persistence of the illusionism first seen in the Flavian Arch of Titus and later in the miniatures of the Vienna Genesis demonstrated the point. Its appearance early and late in works monumental and miniature offered visible proof of the link between pagan and Christian culture, antiquity, and the Middle Ages.

If it was Wickhoff who first mooted the idea of transition, it was Riegl who refined the concept, focusing first on the minutiae of form. In contrast to Wickhoff's general observations about the persistence of illusionism, Riegl made his case by tracking change within the larger illusionistic framework.

It was important to him that there were differences between a second-century sarcophagus relief and a fourth-century frieze on the Arch of Constantine. Far from demonstrating any break with Roman tradition, these differences documented the ways in which incremental changes within the larger framework of the Roman visual repertoire supported an idea of a representational continuum that was itself the manifestation of an internal transition.

To these observations about formal change, Riegl added the specificity of names and dates, a decision that bound his observations to time and place. His insistence upon the term "late Roman" established the focus of the discussion as western and imperial by connecting his materials to the city of Rome and its larger political enterprise, a stance underscored by the proposed chronological framework and the monuments chosen to illustrate his points. The chronology's circumscribing events – the victory of Constantine at the Milvian Bridge in 313 and Charlemagne's coronation as King of the Franks in 768 – established the period as the connective tissue between two of western Europe's defining imperial experiences, the Roman Empire of antiquity and the revived Roman Empire of the medieval and modern worlds. Moreover, as the choice of rulers and the moments emphasized suggest, these events placed a premium on the rise of Christian kingship.

The choice of monuments further buttressed this position. Following Wickhoff, whose discussion had circled around monuments from the city of Rome, Riegl based his own arguments on works of art and architecture of Roman provenance, arguing that, although there were other examples that might have suited his purpose, nothing that he had seen from territory outside of the West contradicted his basic conclusions.

Finally, Riegl offered what Wickhoff did not – an explanation. While Wickhoff had been content to observe the phenomenon of transition in its most general terms, Riegl felt it necessary not only to describe the particular nature of change but also to explain its meaning. He did so by suggesting an analogy between the late Roman visual imagination and the perceptions of such thinkers as Plotinus and Augustine, authors who stepped away from the clear light of reason into the flickering shadows of magical thinking.

In tackling the definition of Roman art, Wickhoff and Riegl created a new approach to the problem of how art might have a history. Their understanding grew not from the traditional descriptions of iconography or the assessment of form in terms of its relationship to an idealized Greek model; rather, theirs was a definition grounded in an analysis of visual style as a historical phenomenon. Thus, the lines, colors, and compositions of painting and sculpture represented historical data that in turn spoke of relations between people, places, and ideas. In the particular case of Roman art, stylistic analysis established continuities.

Wickhoff's illusionism linked the Arch of Titus to the Vienna Genesis, while Riegl's distant viewing allowed connections between second-century sarcophagi and the Arch of Constantine. Their combined efforts yielded three important conclusions: that Roman art constituted a discrete visual tradition whose visual legacy was as much Christian as pagan; that its forms were the result of internally generated change; and that it was, above all, an art of transition between antiquity and the Middle Ages.

NOTES

1 On early art historical texts, see Dilly 1979, 172–258; Schwarzer 1995. For an example of the discussion of Roman and early Christian art, see Schnaase 1842–1879, 2: 407, where the history of Roman sculpture ends in the second century with Hadrian and the Antonines. Schnaase (1842–1879: 3) discusses early Christian art in the context of Roman decline.

2 Riegl 1901, 2; 1985, 6.

3 Lübke 1885, 1: 271–75

4 On classical archaeology in the nineteenth century, see Dyson 2006 for the foundation of the German Archaeological Institute in Athens and the Olympia excavations (82–85), for the French at Delos and Delphi (117–21), and for the Austrians at Ephesos and the foundation of the Austrian Archaeological Institute (113–14). On the Austrians in Asia Minor, see Szmethy 2014. For German initiatives, see Marchand 1996, 75–115. On the history of Christian archaeology, see generally Deichmann 1983, 14–45, and Frend 1995. For the French in North Africa and Syria–Palestine, see Frend 1995, 51–76, 111–29, and Gran-Aymelian 1998, 239–45.

5 On Christian archaeology in Rome, see Frend 1995, 11–17, 76–83, 160–64. Antonio Bosio (1575/1576–1629) launched the first systematic investigation of the catacombs in the sixteenth century. See Bosio 1632. In the nineteenth century, Giovanni Battista De Rossi built extensively on Bosio's study when undertaking his own work on the catacombs. See Rossi (1864–1877), who is credited with establishing Christian archaeology as a rigorous scholarly discipline. He was also a faithful servant of the papacy and felt that the testament of Christian archaeology was a powerful weapon for the papacy against the errant tides of modern life. See Deichmann 1983, 21–23, especially 22, for his statements about the corrective potential of archaeological evidence.

6 On Wickhoff, see generally *EAA* 7:1218–19; Brendel 1979: 25–41; De Grummond 1996: 1192–93; Lachnit 2003.

7 Vienna, Österreich. Nbib, cod. theol. gr. 31.

8 Weitzmann 1979, 458, identifies the material as vellum; however, recent conservation has determined that it is parchment. See Hofmann 2020, 35–69.

9 On dating, Wickhoff and Hartel (1895:142) place the manuscript in the fifth century on the basis of paleographical analysis after reviewing arguments for dates ranging from the fourth to sixth centuries; Wickhoff (1900, 7, 172) confirms a fifth-century date. Earlier discussions include Lambeck and Nessel 1690; Kondakov 1886, 1:78–95; Garrucci 1872–1888, 3:29–43. Lambeck and Nessel dated the manuscript to the late fourth century. Kondakov, Garrucci, and Ainalov preferred the sixth century. Kondakov 1886–1891, 1:78–95; subsequent studies include Gerstinger 1931; Buberl and H. Gerstinger 1937–1938; Ainalov 1961,124–31 (for the original Russian publication, see Ainalov 1900); Mazal 1980; Zimmermann 2003; Hofmann, 2020.

10 Lambeck and Nessel 1690; Kondakov 1886, 1: 78–91, Garrucci 1872–1888, 3: 29–43

11 Wickhoff and Hartel 1895, n.p. See the foreward by the unnamed library administrators on the aims and aspirations of the publication.
12 Wickhoff and Hartel 1895. An edited English-language version (Wickhoff 1900) omitted Hartel's codicological analysis and Wickhoff's assessment of the individual miniatures, and subsequently was published in German (Wickhoff 1912).
13 Wickhoff and Hartel 1895, 142.
14 For the art historical date, see Wickhoff and Hartel 1895, 91; Wickhoff 1900, 172.
15 On continuous narration, see Wickhoff and Hartel 1895, 6–8; Wickhoff 1900, 8–13.
16 On illusionist style, see Wickhoff and Hartel 1895, 11, and Wickhoff 1900, 18. On the impressionistic aspect, see Wickhoff and Hartel 1895, 29–31; Wickhoff 1900, 48–53
17 Wickhoff and Hartel 1895, 12–13; Wickhoff 1900, 20.
18 Wickhoff and Hartel 1895, 25; Wickhoff 1900, 41.
19 Wickhoff and Hartel 1895, 29–31; Wickhoff 1900, 50–53.
20 On continuous narration, see Wickhoff and Hartel 1895, 59–61; Wickhoff 1900, 111–14.
21 Wickhoff and Hartel 1895, 68; Wickhoff 1900, 128.
22 On the difference between natural and illusionist form and the development of the latter in Roman painting, see Wickhoff and Hartel 1895, 64–87; Wickhoff 1900, 117–71.
23 On the transformation of Greek art into Roman, see Wickhoff and Hartel 1895, 28; Wickhoff 1900, 46.
24 Wickhoff and Hartel 1895, 88–92, 96; Wickhoff 1900, 172–82, 190.
25 Wickhoff and Hartel 1895, 96; Wickhoff 1900, 190.
26 The bibliography on Riegl focuses largely on his methodological role in the shaping of the discipline of art history. This discussion has a much more limited aim. Specifically, its purpose is to describe Riegl's definition of and approach to the period of late antiquity. For a more comprehensive investigation of Riegl's life and thought, see Olin 1992, Iversen 1993, and Cordileone 2014. See also Pächt 1963; Podro 1982, 71–97; Rampley 2013, 37–46.
27 For a general discussion of the exhibition, see Cordileone 2014, 187–93. For the objects, see nos. 256, 384, and 456–89 in the catalogue (Masner 1893b), which is basically a handlist.
28 Riegl 1901. The book was reissued as a trade publication in 1927. See Riegl 1927.
29 Riegl 1901, IV, 1; 1985, 4, 5.
30 Riegl 1901, 1; 1985, 5.
31 Riegl 1901, 10; 1985, 15.
32 Riegl 1901, 9–10; 1985, 14–15.
33 Riegl 1901, 1–2; 1985, 5–6.
34 On *Kunstwollen*, see Podro 1982, 95–97; Olin 1992, 71, 148–53; Iversen 1993, 1–18.
35 Riegl 1901, 4; 1985, 8.
36 Riegl 1901, 17; 1985, 21.
37 Riegl 1901, 17;1985, 21–22.
38 Riegl 1901, 20; 1985 24–25 (close viewing or near sight).
39 Reigl 1901, 21–22; 1985, 26–27 (distant viewing or far sight).
40 Riegl 1901, 20–21; 1985, 25–26 (normal viewing or normal sight).
41 Riegl 1901, 49; 1985, 55 (crystalline form). References to organic form as the approximation of organic nature appear throughout.
42 Riegl 1901, 46; 1985, 52.
43 Riegl 1901, 48; 1985, 55.
44 Riegl 1901, 51–72; 1985, 58–83.
45 Riegl 1901, 72–85; 1985, 83–95.
46 Riegl 1901, 85–123; 1985, 95–131.
47 Riegl 1901, 125–38, especially 132–33 for Justinian; 1985, 133–46, especially 139–40.
48 Riegl 1901, 139–207; 1985, 147–222.
49 Riegl 1901, 209–11; 1985, 223–25.

50 Riegl 1901, 211; 1985, 225.
51 Riegl 1901, 211–15; 1985: 225–30. Riegl did not quote directly from Augustine but instead relied heavily on a recent study of Augustine's aesthetic theory by A. Berthaud (1891). Especially important was Berthaud's second chapter, which focused on the ideas Augustine laid out in the now lost *De pulchro et apto*. Riegl (1901, 214; 1985, 229–30) stressed that Augustine's theories explained what modern viewers perceived as the ugliness of late Roman art as a matter of intervals of beauty.
52 Riegl 1901, 216; 1985, 232.
53 Riegl 1901, 6; 1985, 10.

TWO

ROME ON THE DANUBE

Late Antique Art and Austrian Identity

TO READ *THE VIENNA GENESIS* OR *THE LATE ROMAN ART-INDUSTRY* IS TO BE surprised. No one familiar with these studies can fail to have noticed that the lion's share of the discussion is directed not to the declared subjects of the titles but to the question of Roman art, its definition and history. Equally puzzling is the role that Wickhoff and Riegl played in these projects. Prior to these groundbreaking publications, neither author had evinced much interest in things Roman. Wickhoff had focused on the study of Renaissance art, work to which he subsequently returned, and Riegl's thinking on the matter had been limited to observations made in the context of his exploration of the development of the arabesque as a motif.[1] That the search for a definition of Roman art became the focus of their work in the last decade of the century is therefore noteworthy. As this chapter will argue, their shared interest in this new topic may best be understood in relation to their state-sponsored university education, employment in government institutions, and contemporary Austrian politics.

WICKHOFF, RIEGL, AND THE IMPETUS TO PATRIOTIC STORYTELLING

Both Wickhoff and Riegl attended the University of Vienna, each enrolling after an initial period of general liberal study in the two-year program at the imperially sponsored Institute for Austrian Historical Research (*Institut für*

Österreichische Geschichtsforschung). Wickhoff was a member of the institute between 1877 and 1879, Riegl between 1881 and 1883.[2] The institute itself was relatively new at the time, having been established in 1854 as part of a wholesale educational reform undertaken by the Austrian government. Its purpose was to train government workers, everyone from secondary school teachers and local librarians to archivists, university professors, museum curators, and high-ranking diplomats. To this end, the curriculum emphasized the study of diplomatics, that is, the critical analysis and interpretation of written historical documents.[3] Art history was also a feature of the course, the idea being that the painted, sculptured, and built patrimony of the Austrian state itself constituted a kind of historical documentation.[4]

In the course of their studies, students were introduced to the methodologies that would allow them to grapple with these materials. The early champion of art historical study in this context was Rudolf von Eitelberger, the university's first professor in the discipline. Initially appointed to the Faculty of Philosophy in 1852, Eitelberger moved to the institute in 1854, where he established the framework for the study of art history, one that would give pride of place to the type of analytical procedure that came to be thought of as the hallmark of the Vienna School. He did so by embracing an empirical approach that set the direct observation of individual works of art at the center of the discussion in a way that was analogous to the study of written primary sources. Thus, just as it was possible to examine a manuscript by noting its physical properties and observing its letter forms to come to conclusions about date and place of manufacture, it was also possible to observe a painting by documenting its material and visual characteristics.[5]

There was a larger purpose to Eitelberger's intellectual strategy. The institute aimed not simply to train its students in sound methodological procedure but to instill in them the sense that the study and interpretation of history was a patriotic duty, one that could legitimate Hapsburg rule by constructing inspirational narratives out of the raw materials of the Austrian state's archival and visual patrimony.[6] Eitelberger's own work offered a case in point. His studies of architecture in Dalmatia, then part of the Austrian empire, revealed similarities in construction techniques to buildings erected in the heart of imperial crown lands. As Mathew Rampley has shown, these observations allowed Eitelberger to argue that this peripheral area, which was clamoring for greater political autonomy, was integral to the Austrian state.[7]

As graduates of the Institute for Austrian Historical Research, Wickhoff and Riegl stood in a direct line of descent from Eitelberger. Their interest in promoting the work of art as a historical source, together with their adoption of methodological procedures based on direct, physical engagement with visual materials through formal analysis, makes that relationship clear, and, as the overwhelming emphasis on visual form guiding the work of *The Vienna*

Genesis and *The Late Roman Art-Industry* demonstrates, the institute endowed Wickhoff and Riegl with effective ways of looking at and analyzing works of art. It also appears to have left them with a keen, if less obvious, sense of imperial mission, one appropriate to their work as civil servants. That commitment had a profound impact on their work on Roman art, guiding the questions they asked, the observations they made, the goals they pursued, and the definitions at which they arrived. In no small measure, the choice, assessment, and interpretation of their materials was driven by the necessity of and the desire for patriotic storytelling. Thus, although there was no effort to construct a uniform history of Austro-Hungarian art, in ways overt and covert, the grand narratives about formal continuity and change that wind through Wickhoff's and Riegl's storytelling and make for such compelling methodological reading may also be understood as stories about Austrian imperial greatness.[8]

POLITICS IN FIN-DE-SIÈCLE VIENNA

The need for such storytelling had much to do with the contemporary fortunes of the Austrian state. Although its roots lay in the Middle Ages, the Austro-Hungarian Empire was a creation of the nineteenth century. In 1800, Austria was synonymous with the Hapsburg name, and the Hapsburg name with that of the Holy Roman Empire, territory that included not only Hapsburg dynastic lands in central Europe but also the Germanic states, the Kingdoms of Bohemia and Hungary, and a host of smaller principalities. Franz II Hapsburg (1768–1835) ruled this encompassing state from his capital at Vienna between 1792 and 1805, presiding over it as Holy Roman Emperor, an ancient title that carried with it the understanding that its holder wielded power inherited directly from the Roman emperors and with the approval of the pope. By 1806, in the wake of Napoleon's defeat of the Austrian armies at Austerlitz, that power had evaporated, and the Holy Roman Empire was defunct. Under the terms of the Treaty of Pressburg, its territory was dismantled, with the result that Franz abdicated the Roman crown to retrench and reign more modestly as Franz I, Emperor of Austria. At his death in 1835, his son Ferdinand (1793–1875) succeeded him. Suffering from a host of maladies, Ferdinand was ill-equipped to rule, and in 1848, in the face of revolution, he abdicated in favor of his nephew, the eighteen-year-old Franz Joseph (1830–1916).

In succeeding to the Austrian crown, Franz Joseph took control of the largest unified political territory in Europe after Russia, dismemberment of the Holy Roman Empire notwithstanding. With Vienna as its capital, its holdings stretched from the Russian frontier in the northeast to the German states in the west, and to Italy and the Adriatic coast in the south. Although expansive, it was a troubled state. Economically and politically underdeveloped by contemporary European standards, this polyglot, multiethnic empire saw nationalist factions representing various ethnic groups clamoring for political equality throughout its territories. In Vienna itself, a growing commercial and professional class agitated for political and social reform. Although the revolution of 1848 that had brought Franz Joseph to power was stifled by 1849, the emperor ultimately made concessions to these groups, his hand forced in the 1850s by economic crisis and a string of military defeats at the hands of his European rivals. Thus, 1860 saw the institution of a constitutional monarch and 1867 the creation of the Dual Monarchy of the Austro-Hungarian Empire. This arrangement, the *Ausgleich*, which offered greater autonomy to the Kingdom of Hungary, marked the end of Austria's claims to the status of Great Power in the Concert of Europe, a position it ceded to the German Empire.

Two issues dominated the Austrian political agenda after 1867. Internally, the question of nationalism remained one of the most pressing concerns for the imperial government as demands for recognition and autonomy by individual populations within the Empire – Czechs, Poles, and Slavs among them – continued with increasing urgency, threatening the stability of the monarchy and the state. Externally, the rivalry between Austria and the German states continued to rankle, as Austria watched its position on the international scene fade in the light of Germany's rise.[9]

The Vienna Genesis, The Late Roman Art-Industry, and Austrian Politics

Wickhoff and Riegl appear to have been drawn into this political project. There is ample, if oblique, evidence to suggest that their major publications, *The Vienna Genesis and The Late Roman Art-Industry*, spoke to this history and the contemporary political concerns it engendered by constructing a narrative about Austrian history from the evidence of its visual patrimony. The story of this enterprise begins in 1893 with the Archaeological Exhibition, an event that took the Viennese public by storm. Its goal, as stated by the museum's director Karl Masner was to showcase "the culture possessed by Austrian lands in Antiquity" by soliciting works of art from "the great art historical museums of the Austrian monarchy."[10]

The response to Masner's call was overwhelming, with over 1,600 objects contributed by private collectors and public museums to the cause. To make sense of the material, curators organized the contributions into three display groups. The first or "prehistoric" unit included fifty-nine objects, materials such as arrowheads, knives, and spears, which were shown together with Greek vases and Etruscan mirrors. The second and largest group displayed

918 Roman finds excavated from Austrian territory. For the most part, these artifacts were small-scale works of daily use, everything from household wares such as cooking pots and lamps to prestige goods such as bronze statuettes, arms, armor, and gold jewelry. The third section, made up of 670 Greek and Roman objects from Austrian collections, expanded the repertoire by adding late Roman textiles from Egypt, Greek vases, and sculpture.[11]

The Archaeological Exhibition lived up to Masner's claim, documenting Austria's rich ancient patrimony in physical terms and tracking it object by object from prehistory through the early medieval period. The physical evidence also made a larger statement about the cultural orientation of Austrian antiquity, one enhanced by the show's organization. The Roman objects dug from Austrian soil stood at the center of the exhibition where they made up the bulk of the display. In this way, organizational tactics and sheer numbers combined to make the evidence of the archaeological record clear: Whether utilitarian items or luxury goods, these objects spoke to a historic continuity between Rome and the culture of its northern frontier that was so complete that even the experience of daily living was fully Romanized; in other words, Austria was Rome. Further, as the presence of these same antiquities in modern Austrian collections demonstrated, that ancient culture continued to be an integral part of contemporary Austrian identity.

The Archaeological Exhibition bears witness to the Austrian urge to build a modern identity on the material culture of the past. This presentation of cultural patrimony with an eye to patriotic storytelling is of a piece with European scholarly practice. Across the continent, governments supported different strategies to engage with the material remains of the past and to articulate national identities. From as early as the eighteenth century, France did so by appealing both to its classical heritage and to that of the Middle Ages, that is, the Frankish legacy and the monumental testimony of the Gothic age.[12] In the German principalities, the emphasis was slightly different. As scholarship dedicated to the archaeological and philological legacy of ancient Greece and Rome unfolded with quickening intensity in the nineteenth century, the German states fostered a sense of pride and prestige based almost exclusively on an association with classical Greek traditions.[13] That the Roman focus of this particular Austrian project succeeded is clear from the response of the Viennese public, which flocked to its doors in such great numbers that the exhibition's run was held over beyond its projected three-month span into the following year.[14] Nor was its message limited to this one venture. *The Vienna Genesis*, published two years after the exhibition first opened its doors, was a product of this same moment, as was *The Late Roman Art-Industry*.

How Wickhoff came to the study of the Genesis codex is unclear, but the expansive discussion of Roman art and its definition in terms of one of the most precious manuscripts in the Austrian Imperial Library put it squarely in the moment. As with the Archaeological Exhibition, Wickhoff's aim appears to have been to connect the material holdings of the Hapsburg Empire with the legacy of Rome and perhaps even more specifically Christian Rome.[15] Riegl's involvement with his materials, which showed a similar impetus, sprang directly from the exhibition. A curator of textiles at the Museum for Art and Industry when the show was first suggested, he initially brought his expertise to bear on the textile displays.[16] When plans for a more lavish publication developed in the wake of the exhibition's popularity, Riegl was one of several curators seconded to the preparation and publications of works in metal.[17] Most of these objects were of second- and third-century date, but a small section of the Masner catalogue shows that there were one or two objects described as "late antique" and thirty-three objects listed as "so-called barbarian enamel of 'late Roman' manufacture."[18] These were the materials of Riegl's art-industry. Plans for the expanded publication eventually fell through; however, Riegl, who left the museum to join the university faculty, continued to study the materials on his own. *The Late Roman Art-Industry* is the result of his persistence.

At their most basic level, *The Vienna Genesis* and *The Late Roman Art-Industry* pursued the goals of the Archaeological Exhibition. As with the physical display, each study represented an exercise in cultural definition that aimed to bind the culture of Austria to the traditions of Roman antiquity; however, they did so by different means. The exhibition drew its persuasive power from the force of accumulation. The number of objects alone confirmed the Roman presence in historical Austrian lands. What that bursting display could not do, however, was document the inherent cultural connection between works of Roman manufacture and those produced in the Austrian hinterlands. It was one thing to observe that the objects found in Austrian territory were Roman, quite another to claim that works produced by Germanic peoples in these same territories at the end of antiquity were as well. Yet Riegl, arguing that late antique art was a purposefully Roman development, insisted that this was the case. His project was to dismantle the belief that late Roman style represented a decline of form foisted upon the Roman world at the hands of barbarian infiltrators. On this last point he was adamant: "To destroy this prejudice is the principal objective of all the research set down in this book."[19] The point was to demonstrate what others denied, that a shared *Kunstwollen* established a shared cultural connection between Rome and the populations of the Danube. This was a tall order, an end Wickhoff and Riegl realized through a painstaking analysis of material form that integrated contemporary historical thinking about late antiquity with a new kind of art historical approach that also happened to work in the service of the Austrian imperial agenda.

STRUCTURING LATE ANTIQUITY

Their first task in tackling this project was to develop a framework in which to discuss the materials. To that end, Wickhoff and Riegl looked to contemporary historical discussion for inspiration. Although Riegl is often credited with the initial definition of late antiquity,[20] his study was not the first to grapple with the concept. Instead, both *The Vienna Genesis* and *The Late Roman Art-Industry* represent a specialized, art historical arm of a larger body of nineteenth-century scholarship that focused on the late ancient world, an interest initially spurred by the work of the Swiss historian Jacob Burckhardt (1818–1897). Burckhardt's publication of *Die Zeit Constantins des Grossen* (*The Age of Constantine the Great*) in 1853, put the study of the later Roman Empire on the map, introducing the first definition of what he referred to as *die Spätantike*, the late antique.[21] Although he offered no precise chronological frame, indicating only that he saw the period as generally coterminous with the reigns of Diocletian (284–304) and Constantine (306–337), Burckhardt was clear on three major points: that late antiquity represented a discrete historical moment defined and set apart from the early imperial age by the definitive emergence of Christianity; that this new period was one of transition between antiquity and the Middle Ages; and, finally, that the transition itself was internal to Roman society, the result of cultural senescence.[22]

This definition became the scaffolding on which Wickhoff and Riegl hung their own discussions of Roman art. The inclusion of Christian art in their histories coupled with the insistence that developments in Roman style be seen as the product of internally generated change derive clearly from Burckhardt's observations. At the same time, they were no slaves to his conception, and both revised his thinking to suit their needs. Most notably, they transformed Burckhardt's chronological definition. Between the two of them, the fifty-year period that Burckhardt had associated with late antiquity became an 850-year affair, one that stretched from the Flavian era in the first century through the coronation of Charlemagne as King of the Franks in the eighth. As well, their preference for the term "late Roman" over Burckhardt's "late antique," suggested a more culturally specific understanding of the period, one supported by the use of western imperial monuments to argue their points.

This broad chronological definition, coupled with a tight geographical and cultural focus, allowed Wickhoff and Riegl to underscore two ideas that Burkhardt had championed but that the visual record seemed to challenge – continuity and transition. Each did so by observing style to construct a visual history of developing form that would emphasize continuity and transition over decline and rupture. As outlined in the previous chapter, Wickhoff found that continuity in the ongoing presence of illusionist form, while Riegl saw it in the qualities he associated with distant viewing. Between them, Wickhoff and Riegl – the one by focusing on illusionism, the other on distant viewing – created a seamless viewing history that linked first-century reliefs to those of the fourth century, and fourth-century reliefs to the sixth- and seventh-century materials of the art-industry to champion the notion of continuity over rupture.

The choice of monuments further refined this definition. In both studies, the great imperial monuments of Rome and the West represented the sum of Roman art: the Arch of Titus, the Column of Trajan, the Arch of Constantine, the imperial panels in San Vitale. There was no place for Republican art, nor was there any interest in the monuments of North Africa, Asia Minor, or the eastern Mediterranean littoral and its hinterland. This selection established the Roman project as western and imperial, a notion supported by the preference for the term "late Roman."

Finally, chronology confirmed this view. With its emphasis on the reigns of Constantine and Charlemagne, Riegl's treatment of the late period reconfirmed the western, imperial understanding of Roman history that also established Christianity as a defining feature. As Rome's first Christian emperor, Constantine created the framework for a Christian Roman Empire. In doing so, he set the stage for the emergence of Charlemagne. Crowned on December 25, 800, by the pope in Rome, Charlemagne became the heir to Constantine's Christian Roman imperium and the West's first emperor of Germanic stock. Thus, Rome passed its scepter to the Carolingian monarchs across the bridge of the later Roman age, creating a seamless transfer of power between Christian Rome and the Germanic north.

The claims for and arguments about visual continuity had three major implications. First, they allowed Wickhoff and Riegl to explain stylistic shifts as internally generated phenomena. This assertion, in turn, made it possible to classify works heretofore considered products of the early medieval migration period as works of Roman ideation. Finally, and perhaps most significantly, in making that classification they were able to suggest Austria's status as the natural heir to Roman tradition.

Together with the Archaeological Exhibition, *The Vienna Genesis* and *The Late Roman Art-Industry* spoke to this history and the contemporary political concerns it engendered. The projects did so by constructing a narrative about Austrian history from the evidence of its visual patrimony. The geographical and cultural identification of Austria with Rome not only reminded visitors that Austrian lands had constituted part of the Roman Empire but also facilitated a modern analogy between the multiethnic states of the new empire and the old that could play to both domestic and international audiences. For the domestic audience, it supplied a historic model for multiplicity within unity to which the varied populations of the Hapsburg Empire might aspire. For the international, and especially the German observer, it described Austria as the legitimate and unassailable heir to Roman culture and power in the nineteenth-century Concert of Europe.

In fashioning a new vision of Roman art, Wickhoff and Riegl recalibrated the understanding of medieval art and in so doing created the conditions for rethinking Austrian experience. When he defined the Genesis as Roman, Wickhoff not only demonstrated the transitional nature of Roman art but also offered a vision of empire that could serve as a metaphor for the Austrian imperial project. Just as Roman art, conceived for and represented by the great first-century monuments in the city of Rome, came to include different religions and cultures beyond the limits of the city, so Austria, from its capital at Vienna, extended its culture to the territories of its empire. When Riegl claimed the materials of the art-industry for Rome, he confirmed this very point. He also set new terms for understanding the nature of the modern Austrian state, casting aside its medieval, Germanic identity to brand it as ancient and Roman.

The use of the Vienna Genesis and the materials of the art-industry to spin a narrative about Austrian imperial power explains a good deal about the way in which Wickhoff and Riegl approached the definition of Roman art in both its historical and formal senses. Rome was the quintessential empire, the archetype for all modern imperial endeavors, the Austrian included. As such, it was a rich source of inspirational history. In addition, Rome had a special status for Austrians. Vienna had been founded and fortified by the Romans as the frontier settlement Vindobona, and Austrian territory south of the Danube had been an integral part of the empire. To tap into a Roman identity was to exploit an authentic pedigree established in the context of Rome's western imperial enterprise, a fact documented by one of the monuments at the heart of Wickhoff's discussion of Roman art, the Column of Trajan. Here in the great unfurling of the column's spiraling bands recording the emperor's actions on the Danube frontier, the history of Vindobona made its first appearance, demonstrating that from the start Austrian history and Roman history were one.

The argument that the Roman imperial period, from its earliest stirrings in the first century through to the late period of the eighth century, represented one prolonged transition also served these purposes. By extending the definition of Roman art and, by extension, Rome to Charlemagne's coronation as King of the Franks, Wickhoff and Riegl replaced the narrative of imperial collapse with a seamless connection between the ancient Rome of the Caesars and the medieval Holy Roman Empire that had given rise to Hapsburg dominance and Austro-Hungary itself.

Finally, and perhaps most significantly from the point of view of the historian of late antique art, the narrative task Wickhoff and Riegl set for themselves helps to explain the stress on "crystalline" style that emerged from

Riegl's account. If the broader argument about continuity were to stand up to scrutiny, the narrative required that late Roman style be abstract. It was not in the hazy illusionism of the Vienna Genesis but along the sharp edges of crystalline form that later Roman and early medieval art fit together. Whether manifest in the Arch of Constantine's *largitio* frieze or the individual works of the art-industry, crystalline form alone had the capacity to establish the stylistic continuity vital to Riegl's interests.

Whether Wickhoff and Riegl were successful in communicating these ideas is another question. If the remarks of their Viennese contemporary, Hugo von Hofmannsthal (1874–1929) are any index, their efforts appear not to have been in vain. Writing in his notebook, Hofmannsthal noted the following: "Wickhoff, Riegl, the Roman succession is alive in Austria!"[23]

NOTES

1 Wickhoff, whose dissertation was on Albrecht Dürer, ultimately wrote on a range of Italian artists that included Guido da Siena, Masolino, Michelangelo, and Venetian painters, among them Giorgione and Titian. For a selection, see Wickhoff 1913, Riegl 1891, 1893.

2 Ottenthal 1904, 69–70. Wickhoff appears as member number 80, Riegl as member 95.

3 Kölzer (2010) discusses the history and methods of the discipline of diplomatics.

4 Ottenthal (1904, 1–53) lays out the organization, methods, and purposes of the institute; Lhotsky (1954) examines the history of the institute. For the search for a national art history and the curriculum's political implications, see Rampley 2009; 2013, 74–95; Cordileone 2014, 50–57.

5 Rampley 2011.

6 Ottenthal 1904, 15–16; Lhotsky 1954, 1–30.

7 Eitelberger 1861. On Eitelberger, see Rampley 2009, especially 449–53.

8 Rampley (2013, 75) points out that there was no effort to construct a programmatic history of Austro-Hungarian art on the part of Wickhoff, Riegl, or any of their colleagues but rather a pervasive habit of oblique reference that could be construed as nationalistic and patriotic.

9 For an overview of Austrian imperial history from the late eighteenth century to 1918, see Macartney 1969; Rumpler 1997; Beller 2006, 85–196.

10 On the Archaeological Exhibition generally, see Cordileone 2014, 187–89. For the director's remarks, see Masner 1893a, 349–50; 1893b, iv and v.

11 See Masner 1893b, 1–5 (nos. 1–59) for the prehistoric finds; Masner 1893b, 6–74 (nos. 60–978) for the Roman materials; Masner 1893b, 75–134 (nos. 979–1649) for the remaining objects.

12 Montfaucon 1729–1734; Lenoir 1818; Viollet-le-Duc 1854–1868.

13 Marchand 1996.

14 Cordileone 2014, 187.

15 Elsner 2019.

16 Masner 1893b, v.

17 Cordileone 2014, 189.

18 Masner (1893b, catalogue nos. 456–89) listed enameled bronzes, which were described generally as "sog. Barbarenemail, spätrömisch." For late antique materials, see no. 256, a gold finger ring, and no. 382, a belt buckle attributed to the "Völkerwanderungszeit."

19 Riegl 1901, 4, "Dieses Vorurtheil zu brechen, ist das Hauptziel aller in diesem Bande niedergelegten Untersuchungen"; 1985, 8.

20 Bianchi Bandinelli 1973; Giardina 1999; Elsner 2002; 2019; Leibeschuetz 2005.

21 Mazza 2005: 591.

22 Burckhardt 1956, viii (on chronology and transition), 207 (on Christianity), 204–32 (on Rome's cultural old age). For discussion, see Mazza 2005, 591–93.

23 "*Die Nachfolge Roms in Österreich als liebendig (Riegl, Wickhoff).*" See Hofmannsthal 1979–1980: 10, 625. For discussion, see Olin 2000: 155.

THREE

EAST MEETS WEST

Archaeology, Art History, and the "Crystallization" of Late Antique Art

As Hugo von Hofmannsthal's aside suggests, Wickhoff's and Riegl's work did not go unnoticed. Yet, while his comment demonstrates a penetrating awareness of what the two were up to in an immediate political sense and suggests that, for better or worse, their interpretations hit home with the Viennese public, it stands in marked contrast to the long-term scholarly response of their contemporaries. In the years following the publication of *The Vienna Genesis* and *The Late Roman Art-Industry*, the archaeologists and art historians who were Wickhoff's and Riegl's immediate colleagues showed not the faintest awareness of the question of patriotic engineering. Far more important from their point of view were two issues, the one historical and the other theoretical. Initially questions of factual accuracy dominated the response. Eventually, these concerns proved incidental, as the innovative methodological questions and theoretical approaches that grounded their work, prime among them the concept of *Kunstwollen*, began to reshape the discipline of art history. Indeed, so great was the impact of these Viennese efforts that members of the next scholarly generation would describe their work as the "New Art History."[1] It was in this context that the visual definition of late antique art as abstract solidified. It did not do so without a struggle.

CRITICAL RESPONSES TO *THE VIENNA GENESIS*

As the first of the publications, Wickhoff's *The Vienna Genesis* occasioned the earliest response. An initial review by the philologist Karl Krumbacher in the recently launched *Byzantinische Zeitschrift*[2] did not stint in its praise. Krumbacher lauded Hartel's philological contribution together with the book's fine production values. In addition, intrigued by Wickhoff's stylistic approach and what he understood to be his rehabilitation of Roman art, he was fully supportive of the notion that the Vienna Genesis, and with it the whole of early Christian art, be understood within a Roman context. That said, Krumbacher was troubled by Wickhoff's understanding of the Roman materials. Specifically, he objected to the characterization of continuous narration and illusionist representation as Roman inventions, noting that both techniques had appeared in earlier works of ancient Mediterranean art. These reservations notwithstanding, Krumbacher was certain that Wickhoff's work would demand attention for years to come.

This assessment was prescient. While discussion of Hartel's contributions soon waned, interest in Wickhoff's waxed, so much so that his chapters appeared independently in an English-language edition of 1900. Translated by Eugenia Sellars Strong (Mrs. Arthur Strong) with Wickhoff's endorsement, the volume came out under the new title *Roman Art: Some of Its Principles and Their Application to Early Christian Painting*. As the revised title suggests, there was substantial editing. Hartel's dense codicological and paleographic analysis was eliminated, as was Wickhoff's own section on individual miniatures and artistic hands. Only the introductory chapters on Roman art survived.[3]

Whether responding to the initial Austrian publication or to the English-language edition, reviewers focused on Wickhoff's assessment of Roman art. The responses, which came from various sectors, were mixed. Positive reaction came from the art crowd, which appreciated the considerations of style. As one anonymous reviewer put it, *Roman Art* was a first in its "masterly exposition of the ancient painter's struggles with the problems of his art" and as such the most significant art historical study to have been written in years.[4] Wickhoff, it seemed, had brought Roman art to life, a fact that was not lost on the professional archaeological community. Percy Gardner also characterized Wickhoff's stylistic emphasis as a "great gain." In it he saw an approach that would encourage interest in the material in the way that dry-as-dust archaeological analysis could not.[5]

That said, Gardner's judgment was not ultimately sanguine. He lamented that Wickhoff, "misled by an imperfect acquaintance with antiquity," had not only failed to offer a systematic account of Roman art but had also made mistakes. In language familiar from Krumbacher's review, Gardner rejected Wickhoff's claims about the Roman origins of continuous narration and the illusionist form to which it was linked. Nevertheless, he was not categorically opposed to Wickhoff's thinking, and closed his review with the ambivalent observation, "Though I have no sympathy with Mr. Wickhoff's theory of art, I fully allow the suggestive and stimulating character of his essay. Perhaps it is the only existing book on Roman art which can claim these qualities; it is therefore likely to promote the study of the subject."[6]

JOSEF STRZYGOWSKI (1862–1941) AND *ORIENT ODER ROM*

The gracious reserve of these anglophone critiques was totally absent in the response of Josef Strzygowski, the man who was to become Wickhoff's most ardent critic. Strzygowski, who relented in his criticism of Wickhoff only when he turned his attention to Riegl, shared an intellectual pedigree with both. A fellow Austrian, he too had initiated his studies at Vienna; however, unlike his compatriots, who – save for brief periods of study in Rome – had kept close to Vienna, Strzygowski ventured farther afield. After his initial Viennese sojourn, he traveled to Berlin, where he studied with Herman Grimm, before moving on to Munich. There he completed his dissertation under the guidance of Heinrich Brunn and the Halle classicist Carl Robert. Strzygowski subsequently returned to Vienna, where he submitted his Habilitation and was appointed Privatdozent in 1887. In 1892, he joined the faculty at the University of Graz.[7]

Throughout this formative, peripatetic period, Strzygowski not only moved between institutions but also traveled widely. Visits to Rome between 1885 and 1889 found him studying Byzantine manuscripts and Renaissance drawings in the Vatican Library, together with the city's architectural patrimony and the monumental offerings in its major collections. In 1889 he set off for points east, traveling through Greece and Asia Minor in search of classical and medieval monuments with long stops in what was then Constantinople. January of 1890 found him in Russia for an archaeological congress, and between 1894 and 1895 he was in Egypt, writing a catalogue of Coptic materials for the Egyptian Museum in Cairo.[8]

These travels were crucial to the formation of Strzygowski's intellectual trajectory. On them, he first encountered the monuments that would claim his attention over the course of his long career. The journeys in Asia Minor took him to Etschmiazden and the Armenian materials that became his intellectual obsession. In addition, they afforded him the opportunity to meet scholars, such as Wilhelm Bode (1845–1929), with whom he would later collaborate at the Berlin museums, and to become aware of the work being done in scholarly centers outside of the German-speaking orbit, including Moscow and

St. Petersburg. Above all, they reveal a scholar of a very different temperament from his peers. Whereas Wickhoff and Riegl found their inspiration in the macrocosm of theoretical discussion, Strzygowski drew his nourishment from the microcosm of archaeological detail.[9]

Strzygowski laid these inclinations bare in *Orient oder Rom, Beiträge zur Geschichte der spätantiken und frühchristlichen Kunst* (*Orient or Rome: Contributions to the History of Late Antique and Early Christian Art*). Published in 1901, the book came as a direct challenge to *Die Wiener Genesis*. Strzygowski argued that the selective nature of Wickhoff's evidence together with his comparative strategies created a wholly misleading picture of Roman and early Christian art, one that failed to identify, much less answer, what he felt to be the question central to the understanding of Christian art, that of origin.[10]

Late nineteenth-century opinion placed those origins in the catacombs of Rome, the eastern origins of Christianity notwithstanding. With the great discoveries of Dura Europos decades in the future, there was, as far as most scholars were aware, little or no evidence for the origins of an early Christian visual tradition in the eastern Mediterranean. Further, the perceived aniconic bent of Judaism from which such a tradition would have emerged reinforced this thinking. As Wickhoff himself observed, the Old Testament prohibition of images established the Jews as an aniconic people, a status that implied that the earliest Christian art must have developed in communities beyond their sphere of influence.[11] At the time, because the painting and sculpture of the Roman catacombs provided the earliest known evidence for a Christian visual tradition, those communities were identified as Roman, a conviction summed up by the German cleric and scholar F. X Kraus (1840–1901) when he referred to Rome as the "cradle" (*Wiege*) of early Christian art in his 1896 publication *Geschichte der christlichen Kunst* (*History of Christian Art*).[12]

Strzygowski begged to differ. As his title suggested, he saw the options as two: the Orient or Rome. It was clear however, that he begged the question. Strzygowski's convictions were such that he knew full well that the true homeland of Christian art lay in the eastern regions of the Roman world. To set the record straight, he put aside the traditional evidence of the Roman catacombs to look for the origins of Christian art in materials from the territories of the East. Places such as Egypt, Syria, and Asia Minor – and with them the great cities of Alexandria, Antioch, and Ephesus – constituted Strzygowski's "Orient," a domain in which the formal and iconographic precepts of Hellenistic Greek art endured and mingled with the indigenous art of the Egyptian and Persian worlds to produce a successful new visual dynamic.

Strzygowski laid out this position in his introduction, questioning the idea that the city of Rome was the unique source of both Roman and Christian artistic traditions and challenging the work of the two most recent proponents of this errant logic, Wickhoff and Kraus. Although Wickhoff's *Die Wiener*

Genesis and Kraus's *Geschichte der christlichen Kunst* could not have been more different in aims and conception – the former using a new art historical methodology to establish the visual norms of an individual period in the history of western art, the latter offering a survey of Christian art from its first stirrings through the Renaissance – both shared a western focus that Strzygowski found galling.

Of the two authors, it was Wickhoff who most offended.[13] After an initial mention, Kraus's name never reappeared.[14] By contrast, Wickhoff's was everywhere, and Strzygowski saw no saving grace in his work. His methodology, his selection of evidence, and his conclusions all provoked criticism. To begin with, Strzygowski argued, Wickhoff's attempt to discuss the Vienna Genesis in the context of Roman art was misguided. Rather than take on a definition of Roman art, an exercise that he felt was completely beside the point, Strzygowski stated that Wickhoff should have looked directly for the origins of the codex's miniatures.[15] That this was precisely what Wickhoff thought he was doing is a point that seems to have eluded Strzygowski. This inability to see Wickhoff's purpose may well have been due to his own understanding of the nature of Roman art. In common with many of his contemporaries, Strzygowski felt that Roman art of the imperial age represented not a new, expansive wave of artistic expression but a last phase of Hellenistic art. For him, the city of Rome was only one of many artistic centers, among them Alexandria, Antioch, and Ephesus, each with its own tradition. It was therefore his contention that the material observed by Wickhoff, although imperial in content, was essentially a regional phenomenon, one that did not and could not stand for the art of the empire as a whole. Thus, Strzygowski countered, to understand Roman art fully it was necessary to consider evidence from the eastern territories of the empire.[16]

Wickhoff's formal characterization of Roman art also came under fire, as Strzygowski took issue with the claim that the use of continuous narrative and illusionist style were Roman inventions. To begin with, he agreed with Gardner and Krumbacher that continuous narrative was an invention of the eastern Greeks. He also considered it a technique absent from Roman painting. To bolster his critique he cited examples from the Hellenistic world, in particular the Telephus frieze from the Pergamon altar.[17] Strzygowski also dismissed Wickhoff's observations about illusionism, arguing, first, that there were no examples of illusionism in Pompeian painting and, second, that everyone paints by manipulating light and color.[18] He went on to note that this was especially true for artists in the East, using the recently discovered encaustic funerary portraits of the Wadi Fayum and icons from the Monastery of St. Catherine at Mt. Sinai as evidence.

Finally, Strzygowski objected to Wickhoff's comparative method, doing so on several counts. To begin with, he questioned the basic premise of comparing small-scale miniatures to monumental imperial sculpture, arguing that it would have been more appropriate to study the Genesis in light of similar codices, works such as the Rossano Gospels or the Codex Sinaiticus.[19] Further, as the manuscript comparanda suggested, there was the issue of cultural context. Wickhoff's decision to consider the Genesis, a Greek-language codex, outside of the eastern Mediterranean world that would have been its logical point of origin, baffled Strzygowski. In response, he suggested that the origins of the Christian visual tradition from which the manuscript sprang could be traced exclusively to the art of Alexandria.[20]

Having challenged Wickhoff on each of these points, Strzygowski then offered his own origin story. In chapter one, he examined third-century catacombs from Palmyra, arguing that the cruciform plans of the funerary chapels should be considered the source for later Byzantine church design. He also saw the iconography of the chapels' frescoes, specifically images of winged victories holding portrait medallions aloft, as precursors to angels bearing portrait medallions of Christ in such contexts as the church of San Vitale in Ravenna and the San Zeno chapel at Sta. Pudenziana in Rome.[21] Chapter two took up the question of sculpture by examining a series of Asiatic sarcophagus reliefs and arguing that the importation of such works into Rome had more bearing on the city's sculptured production than did indigenous traditions.[22] Chapters three and four addressed the contributions of Egypt, looking at woodcarving in the former and textile manufacture in the latter.[23] Finally, in chapter five, Strzygowski argued for a fourth-century, Constantinian dating of sculptured material at the Church of the Holy Sepulchre in Jerusalem, noting that its formal qualities set the stage for Byzantine tradition.[24] In short, whatever the medium, whether painted or sculptured, woven or built, Roman Christian art was a product of the East.

Orient oder Rom proved the first in a series of attacks that Strzygowski would mount as an advocate for the East. His next salvo came in response to Riegl and *The Late Roman Art-Industry*. The evaluation was no less tart. In a review in the *Byzantinische Zeitschrift* of 1902 he minced no words. Although characterizing Riegl as a respected colleague, he did not hesitate to declare outright that he was wrong. Strzygowski began by describing the title as a monument to false advertising: The book was not about the art-industry but about Mediterranean art in general. Further, Strzygowski noted that in dealing with this broad subject Riegl had fallen into an old trap. In common with everyone else, he assumed a progression of art from Egypt to Greece and thence to Rome without once stopping to consider the input of Mesopotamia and Syria. Finally, he took on Riegl's theoretical matrix. Strzygowski argued that iconographic analysis did not support Riegl's formalist claims, and that Riegl, well aware of this fact and eager to promote his own ideas, had concocted what he referred to witheringly as an "art historical system," a flawed analytical tool that should be seen as little more than the work of "modern art" and "psychologists."[25]

Not content with the stinging accusations of the review, Strzygowski continued his attack in a longer essay, "Hellas in the Embrace of the Orient" (*Hellas in des Orients Umarmung*), which appeared in the Munich *Allgemeine Zeitung* in February 1902. Here he took on Wickhoff and Riegl together, not only reiterating his previous points but also observing of Riegl that his was a theory without factual ground.[26]

Riegl did not take this onslaught lying down but parried with an astringent response of his own. "Late Roman or Oriental?" (*Spätrömisch oder orientalisch?*), which appeared in the *Allgemeine Zeitung* the next month, began by characterizing Strzygowski as "a man known for his combative and cutting manner,"[27] before dismissing his criticism as "theatrical clamor."[28] From there he went on to suggest that Strzygowski, in his relentless insistence upon the eastern origins of western art, was a one-trick pony who did not grasp the nature of the modern art historical endeavor, the desire to understand and explain the act of seeing. Moreover, he concluded, Strzygowski's observations were so generalized as to be meaningless. Never, stated Riegl, did his colleague offer examples to demonstrate his points. Implicit in the riposte was the sense that if ever there were a theory without factual ground it was Strzygowski's.

Its unorthodox insistence on the eastern origins of Christian art notwithstanding, *Orient oder Rom* expressed a deeply conservative outlook. Unmoved by the idea of an autonomous Roman tradition, Strzygowski built his argument on the then-common conviction that Roman art in the aggregate represented a last manifestation of Hellenistic art, one that played itself out in localized scenarios around the Mediterranean world.[29] Equally old-fashioned was his refusal to entertain the possibility that style could be used to analytical effect. In this regard, Strzygowski's orientation was fundamentally archaeological. His travels through North Africa and the eastern Mediterranean world had exposed him to an unparalleled range of monuments, and, although he was as much interested in the physical autopsy of works of art as Wickhoff, his interests lay less with questions of style and more with the identification of types and iconographies. At the very least, he appears not to have seen the point of Wickhoff's endeavors. Given his own disposition and interests, it is also possible that he did not understand them. Yet *Orient oder Rom* cannot be dismissed, for Strzygowski made an important contribution by insisting upon the recognition of the arts of the eastern Roman world. In so doing he threw open the door to a new body of evidence, creating a more inclusive and complex corpus for study. He was not, as it turns out, alone in these thoughts.

HELLENISTIC ORIGINS OF BYZANTINE ART

In championing the art and architecture of the eastern Mediterranean and western Asia, Strzygowski shared common ground with the work of his

Russian contemporary Dimitri Vlas'evich Ainalov (1862–1939), whose book *Ellinisticheskie osnovy vizantiiskogo iskusstva* (*Hellenistic Origins of Byzantine Art*) appeared in the *Bulletin of the Imperial Russian Archaeological Society* in 1900–1901.[30] It was thus contemporary with Riegl's *Late Roman Art Industry* and appeared shortly before *Orient oder Rom*. Ainalov looked to the traditions of the Greek East to explain the art of the Byzantine world, from its first flowering in the sixth century to the fifteenth century and beyond. For Ainalov, these roots were clearly recognizable, almost a given, and his review, in 1902, of *Orient oder Rom* expressed the view that most of what Strzygowski proposed had already been laid out in Russian scholarship.[31]

In fact, Ainalov's own work followed a trajectory set earlier in the century by his own teacher, the archaeologist and art historian Nikodim Pavlovich Kondakov (1844–1925), whose first major study, *Istoriya vizantiyskogo iskusstva ikonografii po miniatyram grecheskikh rukopsey* (*History of Byzantine Art and Iconography through the Miniatures of Byzantine Manuscripts*), had appeared in 1876 and was soon translated into French.[32] The book, which characterized Byzantine art through the study of manuscript painting, reflected its author's concern to develop a scientific method based on the factual evaluation of materials. Its principal interest lay in identifying the origin of a truly Byzantine art, a task he undertook through the description and comparative study of early Greek and Latin manuscripts, the Vienna Genesis among them.[33] A second major publication, *Russkiye drvnosti* (*Antiquities of Russia*), which appeared in six volumes between 1889 and 1899, examined materials of pre-Mongol date from within the confines of the Russian empire, many of which were of Greek or Roman manufacture and so, it was argued, connected Byzantine art, and through it the Russian empire, with the traditions of the Hellenistic East.[34] Thus, while the Austrians were struggling over a definition of late Roman and early Christian art, seeing developments almost exclusively in terms of Rome and the West, the Russians pondered the issue of Byzantine art in the context of the East. In both scholarly traditions, art took centerstage as the authors sought to construct an image of empire.

Strzygowski was certainly familiar with the work of the Russians. During his period of study in Rome, he had been introduced to Kondakov's *History of Byzantine Art* in its French translation.[35] Nevertheless, he made no mention of it in *Orient oder Rom*, perhaps because Kondakov's work, which began with the sixth century, picked up where Strzygowski's left off. It was with Ainalov that his interests intersected. The two shared common chronological ground and a similar outlook, a fact he acknowledged even as he lamented that his connection was doomed to remain superficial because his inability to read Russian limited his interaction with *Hellenistic Origins* to the illustrations alone.[36]

The language barrier notwithstanding, the Russians were not without their scholarly influence. Not only was Kondakov's work known through translation, but other German scholars, such as Oskar Wulff (1864–1946), were also influential in disseminating his ideas. Wulff, who studied with Strzygowski and spent the better part of his career at the Berlin museums, had been born and raised in St. Petersburg. He knew and maintained scholarly ties with Kondakov and his students throughout his career and was himself an untiring advocate for the eastern origins of early Christian and Byzantine art.[37] Thus, when Strzygowski took on Riegl, he did so with a cohort of intellectual allies.

Orient oder Rom was generally well reviewed, albeit with qualification. While the archaeological community took Strzygowski's general point, indeed welcomed his conclusions about the importance of the East, many were not willing to discount entirely the place of Rome in the development of Christian art. As more than one reviewer observed, the East may well have had its role in the development of iconography, but Rome was the fulcrum on which Christian art was introduced into northern and western Europe.[38] This stance reads less as a defense of Wickhoff and Riegl, who are almost never mentioned in the course of the reviews, and more as a desire to preserve Rome's time-honored role, not only as the birthplace of Christian art but also as a wellspring of western, humanistic civilization.[39]

TOWARD A PSYCHOLOGY OF LATE ANTIQUE ART: AUGUST SCHMARSOW AND WILHELM WORRINGER

The controversy sparked by Strzygowski represented an archaeological response to Wickhoff's and Riegl's work. Rooted in the evidence of objects and places, it fixed its inquiry on the pressing question of origins, either ignoring or overtly discounting the larger interpretive structures that Wickhoff and Riegl had put in place. This response represented but one point of view, however. In other sectors, Wickhoff's discussions of the mechanisms of illusionist form and Riegl's ideas about *Kunstwollen* and distant viewing proved the prompt to further academic inquiry. These discussions played out not only in the discipline of art history but in the allied disciplines of psychology and aesthetic philosophy, and it was in this intellectual vortex that the definition of late antique art received its fullest elaboration.

August Schmarsow (1853–1936) and the Empire of the Spirit

Perhaps the earliest contribution to this elaboration came from August Schmarsow, whose methodological study *Grundbegriffe der Kunstwissenschaft* (*Foundations of Art History*)[40] built directly on the foundations of the *Late Roman Art-Industry*. Observing that the study of early Christian art stood at the intersection of several different strands of scientific inquiry – the archaeological, the art historical, and the antiquarian[41] – Schmarsow proposed a corrective to Riegl that would modify the concept of *Kunstwollen* to better explain period style. Specifically, he argued that form was regulated by the laws of symmetry, proportion, and rhythm, and that each of these categories was, in turn, regulated by feeling (*Gefühl*).[42]

With this statement, Schmarsow made explicit what Riegl had only implied – the idea that form was an index of feeling.[43] Schmarsow understood form in two ways. On the one hand, it was a representational phenomenon that depicted the material world. On the other hand, it was the direct equivalent of style. In both instances, it had the capacity to reveal states of mind. Thus, in the early Christian world, the choice to depict figures with large eyes or elongated bodies revealed a concentrated and intense spirituality.[44] Similarly, manipulation of the visual aspects of representation made it possible to express psychological states, an idea that Riegl had explored only tentatively in his references to "magical thinking." Using the very examples chosen by Riegl – the fourth-century reliefs on the Arch of Constantine[45] and the Justinianic mosaic in San Vitale[46] –Schmarsow argued that the symmetry, proportion, and rhythm seen in these compositions enabled them to function as a direct expression of the "empire of the spirit."[47]

Schmarsow's fascination with Riegl had developed independently of any interest in the late Roman world. His own scholarship focused squarely on Renaissance Italy, and it was Riegl's method that captured his imagination.[48] Thus, the factual and archaeological issues that drove Strzygowski to distraction were of little consequence to Schmarsow, and his observations about such monuments as the Constantinian friezes and Justinianic mosaic came purely in the service of his own theory building.

Wilhelm Worringer (1881–1965) and Visual Abstraction

The disengagement from the nuts and bolts of later Roman art evident in Schmarsow's approach quickly came to characterize one arm of the response to Wickhoff's and Riegl's writings. Nowhere is this detachment more evident than in the work of Wilhelm Worringer. In 1907, Worringer completed his dissertation, *Abstraction and Empathy: A Contribution to the Psychology of Style* (*Abstraktion und Einfühlung. Ein Beitrag zur Stilpsychologie*), which he submitted to the faculty at the University of Bern after a peripatetic round of study at various German universities.[49] A year later, in 1908, it appeared as a commercial publication. As had been the case with Schmarsow, neither the book nor the thesis on which it was based was a study of late antique art per se. Rather *Abstraction and Empathy* was an essay in aesthetic theory that set out to explore the nature of human perception and the relationship between visual style and meaning. Specifically, Worringer's interest lay in defining the ways in which non-naturalistic styles reflected a worldview. In this context, the new descriptions of late antique art, especially those of Riegl, proved useful as a body of evidence from which to argue his case.[50]

Worringer's starting point was the aesthetic theory of the philosopher and psychologist Theodor Lipps (1851–1914). In *Foundations of Aesthetics* (*Grundlegungen der Aesthetik*), published in 1903, Lipps proposed that the psychological state of empathy (*Einfühlung*) offered the key to understanding aesthetic viewing pleasure. Defined in what was then the emerging discipline of psychology as the ability of an individual to understand or appreciate the feelings of another, the concept of empathy was understood largely in the context of human interactions. For purposes of aesthetic understanding, Lipps expanded its operative sphere by defining it as the ability to project human feelings into inanimate objects. As Lipps pointed out, objects cannot have emotions or project feeling. It is, therefore, the viewer who, in the act of observing, endows the object with these sensations on the base of his or her own experience. Thus, according to Lipps, someone who sees sorrow, rage, or joy in a portrait does not actually see any of those emotions. As fleeting psychological states produced only by living human beings, these feelings cannot exist in paint or stone. Rather, what the viewer sees are replications of the familiar visual manifestation of those states as envisioned by an artist: eyes swollen from weeping, a clenched jaw, a dazzling smile. These manifestations, in turn, trigger the viewer's own recollection of these emotions together with the emotions themselves, which then flow empathetically toward the object, allowing for its comprehension. For Lipps, this ability to identify and engage with an object was the source of aesthetic pleasure.[51]

Although Worringer found Lipps's theory interesting, he considered it incomplete, arguing that *Foundations of Aesthetics* examined empathy solely in the context of naturalistic representation, a fact that made it a creature of the classical art traditions of antiquity and the Renaissance. As such, he felt that empathy was bound to reflect a fully reasoned and happy engagement with the world, a restriction that meant that Lipps's theory was not and never could be a comprehensive aesthetic system because it failed to account for the full range of artistic production, specifically images produced at the non-naturalistic end of the representational spectrum.[52] Worringer's aim, therefore, was to engage this neglected end and create a complete viewing system. To do so, he turned to Riegl for help.[53]

Worringer began with Riegl's newly defined period of late antiquity and the stylistic categories of the organic and the crystalline. Then, following the example of Lipps, he continued by associating these styles with mental and emotional states. Thus, as Lipps had before him, he equated psychological empathy – the ability to identify and engage with the world – with the imitation of nature, a process he described using Riegl's term "organic." Hoping to complete what Lipps had left unfinished, he continued, arguing that Riegl's "inorganic" or "crystalline" style represented a visual corollary to another psychological state, abstraction, which he defined as a detached and intellectual attitude toward the world.[54]

Such an attitude expressed alienation from the material world, a rejection of physical reality in favor of inner, spiritual values that lead to transcendence.[55] To demonstrate his case he introduced the styles of the later Roman world, proposing that the rise of what he now referred to as "abstraction" in works such as the *largitio* frieze on the Arch of Constantine could be associated with the rejection of the material world and the rise of monotheistic Christianity.[56] In other words, and as Riegl had suggested, the isolated figures and repeating, geometric shapes of distant viewing had meaning beyond pure form. In this regard, Worringer, echoing Schmarsow's general feeling, also drew upon Riegl's belief that the simplified forms of abstraction should be allied with the kingdom of the spirit. Where he differed from both Riegl and Schmarsow was in the specificity of his claim. It was Worringer who tied the notion of visual abstraction directly to a specifically Christian spirituality. He brought the ultimately sketchy explanations of Riegl's final assessment of late Roman *Kunstwollen* to completion by directly connecting the style of the *largitio* frieze to "a new spirit which entered the Roman world through Christianity."[57] That spirit, according to Worringer, created a transcendental sensibility that found its expression in the form of visual abstraction.[58]

Having christened Riegl's inorganic, crystalline forms as abstract and described them as the visual expression of spiritual transcendence, Worringer then went on to explain their origins. Although he agreed with Wickhoff and Riegl that Christian art had been born in Rome and the West, he sided with Strzygowski on the matter of style. Worringer felt that because Christianity had been brought to the West from the East, its *Kunstwollen*, which was expressed by abstract style, was that of the Orient.[59]

Worringer's Orient, was, however, a far cry from Strzygowski's. While Strzygowski's East comprised Egypt and West Asia, Worringer imposed no such limitation. For him, the East included everything from the Mediterranean littoral to the shores of the Indian and Pacific oceans; that is, the entire continent of Asia. More importantly, his definition embraced far more than geography. For Worringer, abstraction carried with it an instinct for transcendence in life and religion. As he observed, the eastern penchant for abstraction in art represented an understanding of the limitations of sensory knowledge and intellectual rationalization in the face of the "unfathomableness of being."[60] Visually and emotionally, the Orient signaled pure transcendence.

The definition of late antique and early Christian art that emerged from Worringer's *Abstraction and Empathy* represented a synthesis of two very different strands of thinking. On the one hand, it embraced the gadfly Strzygowski's view that the visual traditions of the eastern Mediterranean were vital to the flowering of a late antique art. On the other hand, it understood and defined that flowering in the theoretical terms proposed by Lipps and Riegl. In the amalgamation of these points of view, it is striking that there is virtually no discussion of actual works of art, Worringer having limited specific reference to an example taken from Riegl, the *largitio* frieze from the Arch of Constantine.

PRACTICAL APPLICATIONS

It was only in the next scholarly generation that the practical implications of this theorizing made themselves known. A publication of 1925, *East Christian Art: A Survey of the Monuments* by O. M. Dalton (1866–1945),[61] keeper of early Christian and Byzantine antiquities at the British Museum, offers an example of how the new definition of late antique art came to color the response to actual works of art. The book represented a substantial revision of an earlier study from 1911, *Byzantine Art and Architecture*. As Dalton noted in his introduction, the availability of new materials for discussion together with new research and above all new theories for approaching them warranted the revamping. Thus, while *Byzantine Art and Architecture* had recognized the abstraction of late antique art and characterized it as a lamentable decline from classical standards, *East Christian Art*, echoing the sentiments of Riegl and his interpreters, rejected the idea of decadence in favor of historical and cultural change brought about by the rise of Christianity.[62]

According to Dalton, Christian art derived from two traditions: the naturalistic art of the Hellenistic Greek world and the abstract art of the Orient. Greek art was, he noted, "classical," "intellectual, "artificial," "secular," and "scholarly." While it was the perfect means for naturalistic representation, it was no vehicle for expressing the emotion attendant upon the transcendental drama of Christianity. For forms able to convey this expressive content, Christians therefore turned to the art of Syria, an art he described as "oriental," "emotional," "sincere," "religious," and "popular." This "Syro-Hellenistic" art became the foundation for the various traditions of Christian art that developed throughout the East.[63]

Dalton's eventual aim was to describe the origins of medieval art by tracking stylistic change using specific examples. His goal was shared by Charles Rufus Morey (1877–1955), a professor in the Department of Art and Archaeology at Princeton University.[64] Morey took up the project in an article, "The Sources of Medieval Style."[65] Borrowing from the disciplines of classical philology and archaeology, he identified two distinct late antique visual traditions – the "Neo-Attic" or "Asian" and the "Alexandrian" – both of which he traced to a common origin in Hellenistic art. Neo-Attic style, centered in Asia Minor, was evident in everything from archaistic sculpture of the second and first centuries BC to third- and fourth-century sarcophagi. As its name suggests, its origins were in Athens, and its character, which he described as academic and conservative, derived from the use of classic forms that favored flattened, linearly defined relief circumscribing a limited space. Although it spread to Rome in the Augustan age, its homeland was in the East, in the cites of Asia Minor and the Mediterranean littoral.[66] By contrast, Alexandrian art, associated with the eponymous Egyptian city, represented a progressive, impressionistic tradition built on light-and-shade modeling and with it the creation of three-dimensional space. Its sphere of influence encompassed Egypt, North Africa, and Rome. With the rise of Christianity, both Neo-Attic and Alexandrian art were transformed.[67] According to Morey, Neo-Attic traditions developed to become Byzantine art, and the Alexandrian traditions went on to shape the art of the Carolingian world and later western traditions.[68]

Morey restricted his initial observations about late antique style to a discussion of formal qualities. In two later works, *Early Christian Art* and *Medieval Art*, both of which appeared in 1942, he expanded the discussion to consider the relationship between style and meaning.[69] Specifically, he was interested in characterizing the impact of Christianity on essentially Greek traditions of art. Like Dalton and Strzygowski before him, Morey saw Christianity as a transformative force. Under its influence, Greek art, which he thought of as an expression of the Hellenic ability to bring the world under control by transforming the phenomena of nature into ideas, became "Orientalized," that is, rendered in a style that expressed emotional, spiritualized content. He described this change, which he observed equally in Neo-Attic and Alexandrian art, as a shift from naturalism to abstraction, and explained it as a rejection of "materialism" in favor of the "transcendental." In other words, style embodied what he referred to as a "point of view," what Riegl might have thought of as *Kunstwollen*.[70]

During the first three decades of the twentieth century, with the practical application of methodological and theoretical thinking about late antique style to the interpretation of actual works of art, late antique art achieved its definition. A basic chronological frame, stretching between the fourth and the eighth centuries, had been established, and there was an emerging sense that the focus of inquiry should include a full spectrum of works – pagan and Christian – from all the territories of the Roman world, Strzygowski's Orient included. There was also agreement about style. Symmetry, frontality, and linear emphasis were its hallmarks, together with the repetition of forms, planar composition, and the isolation of shapes in space. Integral to these observations was the consensus that these distinctive forms were bearers of meaning. Whether described as crystalline or abstract, late antique art had become the avatar of Christian transcendence.

NOTES

1 Rodenwaldt 1921–1922, 58. Rodenwaldt noted that there were three approaches to the study of late antiquity: as a classical archaeologist who saw in its products evidence of the decline of classical standards, as a Christian archaeologist looking for Christian monuments charting the rise of the new faith, or as a critic of the "new art history" (*die neuere Kunstgeschichte*), which saw the epoch as the gateway to the Middle Ages. Over twenty years later, he expressed the same sentiment: Rodenwaldt 1944–1945b, 81.
2 Krumbacher 1895.
3 Wickhoff 1900. These same chapters subsequently appeared as a stand-alone publication in a posthumous German edition of 1912. See Wickhoff 1912.
4 Brush and Pencil 1901.
5 Gardner 1901, 89.
6 Gardner 1901, 92. Subsequent commentary echoed this sentiment. A. M. Daniel (1911) characterized Wickhoff's discussion as "hardly more than a courageous attempt" to deal with the subject.
7 *EAA* 7: 522–23; De Grummond 1996, 2: 1061–62; Marchand 2009, 403–10; Sorensen 2022c.
8 Strzygowski 1904.
9 Strzygowski (1936, 11–14) details his early study and travels prior to the publication of *Orient oder Rom* in an autobiography. On Strzygowski, see Crum 1901; Dimand 1940; Herzfeld, Koehler, and Morey 1942; Marchand 1994; 2009, 403–410; Zäh 2012; Foletti and Lovino 2019.
10 Strzygowski 1901, 1 (corrective mission), 3 (origin of the Vienna Genesis and Christian art).
11 Wickhoff and Hartel 1895, 3–4; Wickhoff 1900, 2–3.
12 See his second chapter: "*Zweites Buch. Die Katakombe als Wiege der christlichen Kunst.*" Kraus 1896, 1: 30–57, at 30.
13 Elsner (2000) discusses Strzygowski's attacks on Wickhoff and Riegl.
14 Strzygowski (1901, 1) characterized Kraus's effort as a search for the origins of Christian art against Wickhoff's quest for the origins of Roman art.
15 Strzygowski 1901, 3.
16 Strzygowski 1901, 8.
17 Strzygowski 1901, 3–4.
18 Strzygowski 1901, 7.
19 Strzygowski 1901, 3.
20 Strzygowski 1901, 2.
21 Strzygowski 1901, 11–39.
22 Strzygowski 1901, 40–64.
23 Strzygowski 1901, 65–89, 90–126.
24 Strzygowski 1901, 127–50.
25 Strzygowski 1902a, 264–65 (Riegl's art historical system), 266 (modern art and psychologists).
26 Strzygowski 1902b. Elsner (2000) discusses Strzygowski's interactions with Riegl.
27 Riegl 1902, no. 93, 173: "*als kämpflustig und schneidig bekannten Gegner.*"
28 Riegl 1902, no. 93, 173: "*Theaterlärm*"
29 Strzygowski 1901, 8.
30 Ainalov 1961.
31 For translation and discussion of Ainalov's observations, see C. Mango (Ainalov 1961, x). For the original Russian citation, see Ainalov 1902, 139.
32 Kondakov 1877; French translation: Kondakov 1886. On Kondakov, see Lidova 2014; Taroutina 2021.
33 Kondakov 1886–1891: 1, 78–94.
34 For the six-volume Russian publication of *Antiquities of Russia*, see Kondakov 1886–1891. An abbreviated French edition (Kondakov 1892) was published as a single volume.

35 Strzygowski 1936, 11.
36 Strzygowski 1901, 43, n. 3.
37 Wulff 1903 contains a summary of *Hellenistic Origins*. His own magnum opus (Wulff 1914) was a two-volume study of early Christian and Byzantine Art. On Wulff, see Zaloziecky 1947.
38 Stuhlfauth 1901, 658; Marquand 1910, 365.
39 For a discussion of Strzygowski's loathing of Austrian and German Catholic humanist scholars and their championing of the West, see Marchand 1994 and Marchand 2009, 403–10.
40 Schmarsow 1905.
41 Schmarsow 1905, iv
42 Schmarsow 1905, 29.
43 Schmarsow 1905, 242.
44 Schmarsow 1905, 242.
45 Schmarsow 1905, 309.
46 Schmarsow 1905, 324.
47 Schmarsow 1905, 324: "Reich des Geistes."
48 Schmarsow published on artists such as Gherardo Starnina, Masaccio, Melozzo da Forli, and Federigo Barrocci and was also interested in Baroque and Rococo architecture. In 1888 he became the founding director of the Kunsthistorisches Institut in Florence where he lectured on Italian sculpture, Masaccio, and Masolino to students including Aby Warburg and Max J. Friedländer. Podro 1982, 143–49; Sorensen 2022b.
49 Another Bern dissertation, that of Heinrich Wölfflin (1886), also explored the psychological aspects of the human experience of art.
50 The publication history is complex. Worringer completed and published the dissertation in 1907 (Worringer 1907). The Munich publishing house R. Piper then acquired the text, producing a first edition in 1908. By 1910 there was a third edition. An English translation by Michael Bullock appeared as *Abstraction and Empathy: A Contribution to the Psychology of Style* in 1953 and was reissued in 1997. Editions cited here are the German publication of 1916 (Worringer 1916) and Bullock's translation (Worringer 1953).
51 Lipps 1903; 1906. On Worringer's assessment of Lipps, see Worringer 1916, 3; 1953, 4; Waite 1995, 21–29; Barasch 1998, 111–13. Waite is critical of Worringer's understanding of Lipps, arguing that he failed to grasp essential elements of his theory. My interest here is not in whether Worringer accurately represented the full range of Lipps's thought but rather in the way he used Lipps's writings to construct his own argument.
52 Worringer 1916, 8; 1953, 7–8.
53 Worringer 1916, 10; 1953, 9.
54 Worringer 1916, 3–4; 1953, 4–5.
55 Worringer 1916, 16–33; 1953, 13–24 on the two poles of naturalism and abstraction.
56 For example, he speaks of the "*Tendenz zum Abstrakten*" (tendency to the abstract). Worringer 1916, 125; 1953, 96.
57 "*Dass dieses Novum mit dem neuen Geist, der durch das Christentum in die römische Welt kam.*" Worringer 1916, 125; 1953, 96.
58 Worringer 1916, 135–36; 1953, 103–04.
59 Worringer 1916, 126; 1953, 102–03.
60 Worringer 1916, 63–64; 1953, 45–46.
61 On Dalton, see Hill 1945; Myres and Pottle 2004.
62 Dalton 1911 and Dalton 1925. On the revised approach to late antique and early Christian art, see Dalton 1925, v.
63 Dalton 1925, 3–6.
64 Lee 1955; Panofsky 1955; Smythe 1993; Sears 2017; 2022; Sorensen 2022a.
65 Morey 1924.
66 Morey 1924, 36–39; 1953, 16–28.

67 Morey 1924, 39–42; 1953, 40–41.
68 Morey 1924, 50 (for a diagram of Neo-Attic and Alexandrian style development).
69 For *Medieval Art*, see Morey 1942. *Early Christian Art* was published in 1942 and again in 1953; citations here refer to Morey 1953.
70 See generally Morey 1942, 21–92 ("Early Christian Art: The Transcendental Factor"). On orientalized, spiritualized content, see Morey 1942, 13. On the "denaturing of style," see Morey 1942, 39–40. For style as a point of view, see Morey 1942, 4.

FOUR

BUILDING VOCABULARY IN THE "EPOCH OF THE GREAT SPIRITUAL"

THE STUNNING REORIENTATION OF SCHOLARLY OPINION THAT TOOK PLACE between the publication of Wickhoff's *Die Wiener Genesis* in 1895 and Dalton's *East Christian Art* in 1925 put late antiquity on the art historical map, gave it time limits, a geographical frame, and, above all, a stylistic and cultural identity that eventually coalesced around the terms *abstract* and *spiritual*. Arriving at this terminology was no easy task. When Riegl and his cohort were writing the first descriptions of late antique art, there was no agreed-upon term to describe the forms that interested them. Images thought to deviate from the representational norms of the classical tradition were seen as failed or deviant. In a world in which the imitation of nature was entrenched as the unquestioned goal of representation, the idea of an art that veered from this path, whether historical or contemporary, was only beginning to be explored and remained to most an oxymoron. The approach to late antique art therefore represented a challenge. Not only was there the mandate to explain and legitimate the perceived peculiarities of its art, but there was also the problem of just how to do so. It was one thing to think that there was an argument to be made, quite another to attempt it in the absence of a developed language of description.

Needed was a vocabulary, free from pejorative connotation, that would signal the essence of the forms they were trying to describe. Initially, three terms vied for the honor: *crystalline*, *abstract*, and *inorganic*. Subsequently, *abstraction* and *stylization* entered the lexicon. These were not idle choices. Each word had a pedigree in scientific and philosophical discussion with well-defined associations that both reflected and shaped the understanding of late antiquity's visual habits.

CRYSTALLINE FORM

Throughout *The Late Roman Art-Industry*, Riegl used the term *crystalline* (*krystallinisch*) to characterize late antique style. When he did so, he borrowed from the language of the natural sciences to describe forms that were linear, planar, and symmetrical. The term initially appeared in the work of the French mineralogist Réné Just Haüy (1743–1822), who was the first to observe the regular geometrical structure of crystals and to describe it in mathematical terms.[1] Revealed as the product of immutable natural law, the regularity and consistency of crystalline structure soon became the very image of eternity. Hegel, for example, described the pyramids of Egypt as "prodigious crystals" embodying the idea of the eternal, the concept of the immortality of the soul, and the sense of the freedom of the spirit.[2] Later, crystalline form played a role in the work of Jacob Burckhardt and Gottfried Semper (1803–1879). Burckhardt believed the law of crystallization to be a constant in architecture and the foundation for composition in painting, and Semper saw it as a primitive form, basic to human experience.[3] Further, because of their regularity and transparency, crystals carried a long-standing historical association with divine revelation that had its roots in antiquity and the Middle Ages.[4]

THE ABSTRACT

As with *crystalline*, *abstract* as a descriptor of visual phenomena had its origins in scientific and philosophic language, particularly in nineteenth-century optics, then a branch of experimental psychology. In this context, abstract form was defined as nonrepresentational; that is, it consisted of lines, shapes, and colors that in and of themselves represented nothing. A blue rectangle, a yellow line, a smear of red constituted abstract form. As the examples suggest, the designation indicated not only the absence of subject matter but also detachment from concrete reality.[5]

Because of the lack of subject matter, a reference to abstract form initially suggested something very different from an allusion to crystalline form, a description that characterized the appearance of recognizable and definable things. Just what it hinted at was another question. Untethered from the appearances of the concrete world, abstract form presented a problem of interpretation. Specifically, it raised the question of whether line, color, and shape could have meaning outside of a representational context. Opinions were divided.

Hermann von Helmholtz (1821–1894), who explored the physiology of the eye and the philosophy of perception to posit that sight should be understood as a dynamic interaction between the physical operation of seeing and the elusive processes of memory and cognition, thought not. As Helmholtz argued, seeing represents a physiological response to the stimulus of light, but the understanding and interpretation of that stimulus represents the mind's response – perception. Perception itself is an interpretive act based on an individual's experience of the world and the memory of it. For example, someone recognizes a dog from a general experience of dogs, and the difference between Fido and Spot from the memory of individual dogs. Objects were therefore the necessary foundation to the construction of knowledge.[6]

Others were not so absolute in their assessment. Gustav Fechner (1801–1887), a physician turned psychologist, agreed with Helmholtz that subject matter was necessary if form were to communicate. At the same time, he remained convinced that line, color, and shape stimulated mental pleasure independently of subject matter and that, as a result, the contemplation of nonrepresentational form had the capacity to expand human consciousness and in so doing bring people into harmony with the cosmos. In this instance, abstract form, if not meaningful in its own right, pushed open a doorway to greater understanding.[7]

The question of how that doorway might be opened was taken up by others. Friedrich Theodor Vischer (1807–1887), who addressed the problem in a series of essays on aesthetic philosophy, saw the communicative potential of abstract form but agreed that it was difficult to understand how it could have meaning, given that it was not only nonrepresentational but also inanimate.[8] In pondering the issue, Vischer suggested that the answer lay not in form itself but in the human response to or perception of form, a process he referred to as "empathy" (*Einfuhlung*). Vischer described empathy as an involuntary psychological operation in which human beings instilled inert form with meaning by drawing on their emotional and intellectual experiences. As he saw it, "We attribute a mental disposition to the abstract forms of appearance so that our inner life appears to meet us in them."[9]

Vischer did not explain the mechanics of this empathetic interaction. That task was left to his son, Robert, who, in a manner reminiscent of Helmholtz, described its operation as a combination of physiological and psychological activity.[10] Focusing on emotional response, the younger Vischer argued that the fusion of physical and mental stimuli characteristic of the act of seeing[11] created a reciprocal relationship between the senses and the soul.[12] An initial ability to perceive what he called "spiritual value" or "vital force" within the world's phenomena set this process in motion,[13] while the empathetic projection first observed by his father constituted the final stage in the rapid-fire processing of sense data that involved the internalization of the objective world in the subjective body. Although Vischer thought that full union between subject and object could only take place between human beings,[14] he did allow that empathy had the power to energize the forms of the natural world.[15] There was a point to this process. The empathetic exchange between the individual and the object created a bond that fused the observer with the observed, thus unifying human beings with one another, with nature, and with the cosmos beyond.[16]

In the closing pages of his essay, Vischer took what proved to be an important turn by steering his discussion in the direction of the visual arts to argue that painting and sculpture, which he thought of in wholly representational terms, documented the human capacity for empathetic union with the phenomenal world and the universe of which it was a part. Each work of art, whether a sculpture such as the Farnese Hercules or a painting by Raphael or Dürer, stood as a permanent record of the creative act of human observation that constitutes the empathetic experience.[17] Within this discussion, Vischer offered two further definitions of abstract form that would have bearing on the visual arts.

The first defined all art as abstract form. Whether painted or sculptured, ancient or modern, art represented a stylization of chaotic nature that refined the appearance of individual objects by removing the extraneous detail impeding the perception of essence and highlighting the vital force within the material world. In its broadest sense, abstract form was thus simplified natural form.[18] A second definition linked abstract form to meaning. In surveying the material world, Vischer observed two types of form, the organic and the inorganic, the former corresponding to human sensuous nature and movement, the latter to human intellectual nature and stillness. Thus, organic form expressed the energy of a living act.[19] By contrast, inorganic form represented pure stasis and was what Vischer described as "abstract," adding that it represented the "harmony of the soul."[20]

With these observations, Vischer transformed the understanding of abstract form, first by connecting its definition to the recognizable shapes and structures of the material world, and then by linking it specifically to artistic representation, a context in which it came to have specific associations with two concepts: stasis and intellect. These proposals were foundational for the work of Theodor Lipps (1851–1914), whose interest in the psychology of art was, as noted previously, a spur to Worringer.[21] Lipps built his own study of aesthetics on Vischer's theory of empathy, arguing that empathy allowed an individual to become immersed in and appreciative of a work of art.[22] He also took on the question of abstract form, considering it in terms of expressive potential. Borrowing Vischer's language, Lipps observed that whether organic or inorganic, an underlying principle, the "abstract form," shaped every object. This abstract form was geometric and independent of natural form, an idea rather than an object.[23] Therefore, abstract form manifested a principle that was distinct from but revealed in the object. In this way, a straight line expressed the law of gravity, while a curving line visualized the geometry of the laws of undulation.[24] Further, as Lipps was quick to note, the response to these forms comes not as a rational, intellectual recognition of the laws of nature but as an encounter in which the viewer instantaneously distills the emotional and psychological implications of those laws. For example, the straight line evocative of the laws of gravity appears as if at complete rest, leaving the viewer at peace.[25] In this way, each geometrical representation expresses the essence of a particular mood.[26]

Over the course of the nineteenth century, the definition of abstract form underwent a sea change. A term that began life as a way to describe nonrepresentational line, shape, and color, and that was not even remotely associated with artistic practice, matured into a definition that could be applied to representation in the visual arts. Once tied to subject matter, the definition became more malleable. Abstract form was the simplification of natural form, a quality possessed by all works of art to the extent that all representation was based in nature. At the same time, in a world in which images were classified according to appearance as organic or inorganic, inorganic form came to be considered a specific type of abstract form. Finally, abstract form was an underlying, geometrically configured idea that expressed the essential mood of an object.

Increasingly prominent in this developing definition was the sense that there was a style to be associated with abstract form. The focus on inorganic form as a particular type of abstract form thrust the linear, symmetrical structures associated with crystalline form into the limelight with the result that *abstract* became a synonym for *inorganic* and *crystalline*. No less important was the association of these lines, shapes, and structures with ideas. Crystalline form took the lead with its intimations of immutability, permanence, and transcendence. With their associations with stillness and intellect, inorganic and abstract were not far behind.

ABSTRACTION AND STYLIZATION

As with abstract form, the understanding of abstraction fluctuated well into the nineteenth century, acquiring a synonym in the term *stylization* by century's end. Initially, abstraction referred to a mental process of selection and generalization from the particular. It was a way of organizing and controlling the influx of sense data, and as such a means of acquiring knowledge.[27] Eventually, abstraction was defined in the context of artistic practice. That definition, always based on the process of selection and generalization, had a range of meaning.

In its most straightforward understanding, abstraction was an act of simplification that reduced visible form to its most representative and essential elements.[28] Abstraction could also refer to a different kind of process, one involving the selection and recombination of elements from the natural world on the model of the ancient Greek artist Zeuxis, whose attempt to depict the surpassing beauty of Helen of Troy involved choosing the best individual features from five beautiful young women and combining them in a single image.[29] This process took place with the understanding that the goal of art was to create ideal beauty and in so doing articulate a noble idea.[30] Finally, abstraction indicated the invention of forms from imagination. Such creatures of human fancy as personifications or fairies and monsters – denizens of the world of the imagination – were products of abstraction. As always, such abstraction remained grounded in a naturalistically conceived, representational impulse that offered a variation on the Zeuxis tale: Fantastic though a centaur might be, he emerged from the conjoining of two known creatures, man and horse.

Although in some senses mutually exclusive, it was possible for these processes – abstraction from nature and abstraction from the mind – to exist side by side, as they served different situations and purposes. The former, which expressed the truth of pure reason, was the work of philosophers and the intellect, while the latter, which expressed the truth of imagination, was considered the provenance of poets and the heart.[31] In both instances, the working method allied the process to ancient tradition, making abstraction an ally of classical, academic form. Thus, in this context, abstraction implied the imitation of classical antiquity. Further, the process was understood as one that articulated an idea, whether noble or fantastical, through the activities of selection, organization, and recombination.

In these early definitions, abstraction always took place within a rigorously mimetic representational context, where it functioned as a kind of editorial activity, an interpretive process in which the artist took control of nature's text to reveal and clarify an object, and with it an idea. Its ultimate purpose was to create beautiful form that would engage intellect and emotion.

Both the understanding of abstraction as simplification and the understanding of abstraction as selection and recombination persisted into the nineteenth century. In the long run, however, it was the idea of simplification that gained the upper hand.[32] It was with this understanding that Robert Vischer and Theodor Lipps introduced the new term *stylization*. As with abstraction, stylization pursued simplification, what Vischer referred to as the "reshaping of natural forms" in a manner designed "to liberate and accentuate the essential and dominant aspect of the phenomenon."[33] Lipps offered a more expansive definition:

> To stylize means to make forms of reality detached from their concrete contexts in reality aesthetically intelligible. We do this when we successively disregard the characteristics which are peculiar to [the forms in their concrete reality] ... especially the many kinds of accidents which

> necessarily underlie [the forms] . . . What remains is a more or less general version of their existence, a more or less general law of shaping or formation, or a law of their becoming. To stylize we might therefore also say, means to release from the concrete forms of reality their more or less generally conceived law of shaping or formation and to visualize the law for itself . . . All types of geometrical forms can be obtained through this successive stylization. Inversely, we are forced to say that each geometrical form – the simple straight line not excluded – if not according to its historical origin, then according to its aesthetic essence is *stylized nature*.[34]

Vischer and Lipps defined stylization as a process applied to the objects of the natural world, which, if taken to its logical end, had the ability to reveal the geometrical essence of form and the laws governing its structure. As such, stylization clarified the definition of abstraction as simplification by stressing the idea that simplification facilitated the revelation of essence. Eventually, the distinction between abstraction and stylization fell away, and their meaning became elided. As Riegl put it, "Stylization often manifests itself as a decided and conscious abstraction."[35]

COSMIC ABSTRACTION

Consistent to all of these definitions was the idea that form had the capacity to reveal an essence, that is, the nature or character of a thing. This association of form with revelation was no less a product of the era. The definition that emerged in the nineteenth century grew out of discussion sparked by the work of G. W. F. Hegel (1770–1831) and Arthur Schopenhauer (1788–1860). These philosophers shared the conviction that there was an absolute principle operating in the world, an Idea that was present in nature, in human beings, and in that most distinctive of human endeavors, art. For Hegel, the Absolute, the essential meaning of the world, hovered below the surface of things, accessible to human beings, who were themselves an expression of the Absolute, through Spirit or Mind (*Geist*). Art, as the expression of this human Spirit, offered a concrete expression of the Absolute both in its general sense and as it was understood by human beings at a given moment in time; that is, as a depiction of the Absolute in its particular sense.[36]

Schopenhauer also created a role for art in human experience, arguing that it was a springboard to the understanding of and union with the cosmos by virtue of the fact that it distilled and revealed existential truth. He argued that every thread in the material world was part of the larger weave of the universal Idea. Each rock, tree, or cloud participated in and afforded a view into this transcendental realm, as every fragment of the material world, human beings included, participated in the essential Idea that informed existence. In consequence, sustained and focused aesthetic contemplation allowed an individual to recognize and consider the nature of matter and in so doing to become one with the single Idea underpinning the varied forms of visible reality. This process of recognition involved the stripping away of particulars to arrive at a kernel of essence. Thus, the contemplation of a particular tree in a particular garden at a particular moment could give way to a larger consideration of all trees, which in turn might give access to the understanding of all trees past and future, their arboreal essence, and, finally, the relationship between that essence and the universal Idea.[37] In the course of this act of contemplation, the viewer ultimately identifies the self with the object and the Idea within it, opening the path to union with the cosmos as the distinction between the viewer and the object of contemplation falls away.

These ideas also aligned with the nineteenth century's larger bent toward pantheism, the understanding that the divine is immanent in nature, a turn that grew out of the study of eastern religions, especially those of the Indian Vedic tradition. Hegel's general sense that the Absolute was immanent in nature participated in this trend, as did Schopenhauer's proposal that contemplation of material reality's forms could reveal the essence of the universe or Gustav Fechner's conviction that concrete matter might possess its own cosmic soul.[38]

Common to all of these proposals was the sense that, properly contemplated, matter, itself an expression of a universal idea, had the potential to reveal the workings of the cosmos and in so doing bring human beings into union with it. This understanding, which was present from the beginning in the definition of *crystalline*, gradually began to shape the general definitions of *form* that appeared in the nineteenth century. As Vischer's initial distinction between organic and inorganic form indicates, there was an effort to classify the varied forms of the material world and to consider how individual types might be understood. Originally directed toward an understanding of the natural world, his venture into categorization broadened to include artistic production, and it was in this context that the sense of abstract form as representational solidified, together with the understanding that it shared the essential qualities of inorganic, crystalline form. Here too was the idea that artistic form, whether organic or inorganic, became a potential locus of revelation, its lines, colors, and compositions laying bare the underlying structure of objects and with them the nature of the universe.

ART HISTORICAL USAGE

In the search for a definition of late Roman art, Riegl explored the applicability of these terms and the implications of their use as he mounted his own interpretations. He drew upon all three – *abstract*, *inorganic*, *crystalline* – at various points in his career. In his early publications *Altorientalische Teppiche* (*Antique Oriental Carpets*, 1891) and *Stilfragen* (*Problems of Style*, 1893), a study tracing the development of the arabesque from its origins in the Egyptian lotus capital through antiquity to its manifestations in Islamic art, he opted for *inorganic* and *abstract*. Later, in *The Late Roman Art-Industry*, he turned to *crystalline*. Subsequently, Schmarsow and Worringer, in projects that were less historically and more theoretically focused, retained the terms *inorganic* and *crystalline*, but reintroduced and preferred *abstract*. All three scholars also included *abstraction* and *stylization* in their dictionary.

As befit the exploratory sense of their work, these explanations were not fixed, and their usage often changed or acquired new shades of meaning. This was the case with abstract form. While Vischer's definition in terms of inorganic form held, the term *abstract* soon came to have associations with the East. Riegl used it in both *Antique Oriental Carpets* and *Problems of Style*, referring to "abstract directed tendencies,"[39] "abstract stylization,"[40] and "abstract laws."[41] These discussions established the properties of abstract style as linear and symmetrical.[42] Further, flat, abstract form stands in opposition to plastic perspective.[43] To this by-now standard usage, Riegl added the observation that abstract form had a distinct eastern flavor. There is, he observed in *Problems of Style*, "an oriental spirit of abstraction," which made it the property of Egyptian, Near Eastern, and Islamic art.[44]

With Riegl, *abstract* became *Oriental*, a conclusion he appears to have arrived at from his work with the textile collections at the Austrian Museum for Art and Industry and in *Problems of Style*. Although he made no direct statements about how this orientalized abstract form should be understood, preferring instead to dwell on formal issues, this association appears to have had implications for *The Late Roman Art-Industry*, where, in contrast to its consistent use in *Oriental Carpets* and *Problems of Style*, the term *abstract* all but disappears, replaced by the modifiers *inorganic* and *crystalline*. This shift may reflect the aims of the book. Insofar as its purpose was to locate the works of late Roman and Germanic manufacture within the classical orbit, an association with the abstract forms of the East would only have undermined the argument. As a descriptor, *crystalline* had the advantage in that it evoked the same formal associations and meaning without the perceived taint of the Orient.

When Schmarsow and Worringer took up the discussion they reinstated the concept of abstract form. Schmarsow used the term interchangeably with *inorganic* and *crystalline* without endowing it overtly with any particular Eastern emphasis. Worringer, expanding upon Riegl, also saw abstract form as synonymous with the Orient, arguing that it expressed a characteristically Asian sensibility, one given to reflection on and acceptance of the fragility of human existence within the overwhelming context of the cosmos.[45]

The authors also shifted the meaning of abstraction, making it as much the description of visual style as of artistic process. Riegl's reference to an "Oriental spirit of abstraction" appears to have referred to the process of simplification.

Worringer, expanding on Riegl and Lipps, introduced a two-pronged meaning: On the one hand, he associated organic form with empathy and a happy, pantheistic union with the cosmos, and, on the other, he allied inorganic form with mental abstraction and the sense of alienation from the world. In this context, abstraction became the style representative of this detached mental state, one that created a "resting point" in the visual landscape that offered refuge from the chaos of the world.[46]

While it is clear that Riegl, Schmarsow, and Worringer built their understanding of abstract form on the work of earlier nineteenth-century philosophers, they did so with a different remit, that of the historian. This difference was decisive. Once tied to history, the universal idea of abstract form that had been promulgated in scientific writing began to take on a more specific, cultural definition, one linked to time and place and, increasingly, to Christianity.

IN THE "EPOCH OF THE GREAT SPIRITUAL"

That late antique art should have come to be associated almost exclusively with abstract form and Christian spiritual transcendence within a decade of its initial description by Franz Wickhoff as illusionistic was by no means inevitable. As with the art of imperial Rome to which it was inextricably bound, the forms of late antique representation were many and diverse. For every Constantinian frieze there was an alternative – works such as the fifth-century mosaics in the church of Santa Maria Maggiore or the miniatures in the Vienna Genesis itself. That a definition rooted in abstraction and with it a distinct idea of spirituality emerged with such rapidity and such clarity is arguably a function of the intellectual moment in which the idea of a specifically late antique art was put forward. As Riegl himself observed, "In spite of its seemingly independent objectivity, scholarship takes its direction in the last analysis from the contemporary intellectual atmosphere."[47] Nowhere is this more evident than in the case of late antique art, a tradition that acquired its definition from a heady mix of conservativism and rebellion.

On the one hand, it was the conservative impulse that led Riegl to focus on inorganic, crystalline form. As circumstances surrounding the mounting of the Archaeological Exhibition suggest, this emphasis was necessary, as it allowed him to make the case for a direct connection between Roman imperial tradition and that of early medieval Austria. On the other hand, the understanding of late antique art that emerged from late nineteenth- and early twentieth-century Vienna was also a product of a more revolutionary spirit, specifically, the reaction against traditions rooted in classical and early modern habits of thought and practice that came to be known as "modernism."

As developed in the nineteenth century, the idea of modernism implied rupture with the past across the full range of human experience. In terms of art and the aesthetic questions aligned with it, modernism meant the rejection of the classical tradition and what was understood to be its emphasis on a literary canon that determined appropriate subject matter, theories that placed beauty at the center of the artistic endeavor, and a prescriptive approach to artistic practice. In place of these established values, artists and theorists proposed a new range of subject matter that would better reflect the exigencies of modern life, thus releasing them from the mandate to create beauty according to established norms and allowing them to develop new kinds of representational techniques and innovative theories of practice. In this context, the new studies in optics and perception that were so influential for Wickhoff and Riegl were marshaled equally by artists to explain how, in the absence of an established representational canon, art might be best understood.[48]

This rejection of the classical canon opened artistic practice to a range of possibilities, and there were, as a result, many modernisms: symbolism, fauvism, expressionism, vorticism, futurism, and suprematism to name but a few. While numerous and diverse, these projects shared common ground in the belief that art could and should reveal inner states of mind through the combined forces of subject matter and style, and that these inner states had something to say about the relationship between human beings and the universe. As Wassily Kandinsky remarked, this was the "Epoch of the Great Spiritual."[49]

There were of course various types of inner states to be evoked and an equally large number of strategies for achieving that end. Together they give a sense not only of the range of representational possibility but of the ways in which abstract form might be defined. For example, the French symbolist painter Odilon Redon (1840–1916) suggested the dream life of the unconscious in works such as *Guardian Spirit of the Waters* (Figure 13), an image that was both deceptively familiar in its use of naturalistic individual forms and perplexing in its juxtaposition of images and manipulations of space and scale. Redon's dreamy fictions contrasted markedly with work by artists such as Edvard Munch (1863–1944), whose painting *The Scream* (1893) defined the concept of expressionism (Figure 14). Munch also based his painting on the forms of visible reality, but, in contrast to Redon, he interpreted that reality by "stylizing" it through the extreme manipulation of line, color, and composition to upend representational conventions and capture the essence of a tormented psychological state.

Modernism also left its stamp on the Austro-Hungarian world in which Wickhoff and Riegl operated. In Vienna, modernist innovation coalesced around the movement known as the Vienna Secession (*Wiener Secession*). Known officially as the Association of Visual Artists (*Vereinigung Bildender Künstler*), the group, which was founded in 1897, set itself up as a challenge to the conservatism of the Austrian artistic community. A second group, the

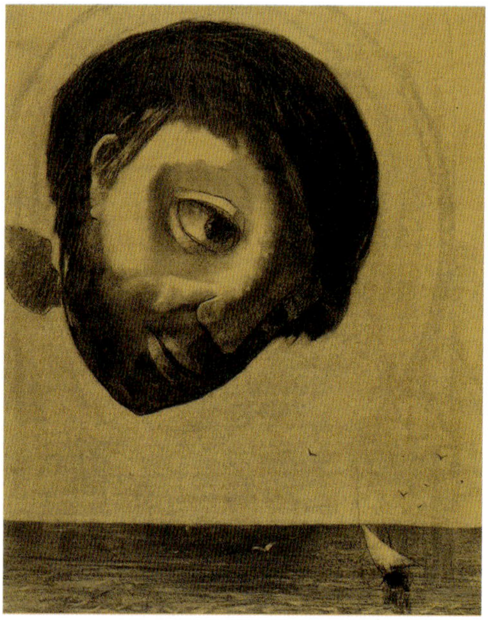

13. Odilon Redon, *Guardian Spirit of the Waters*, 1878, Art Institute of Chicago. Photo: Courtesy of the Art Institute of Chicago

Association for Arts and Crafts, also known as the Vienna Workshop (*Vereinigung für Kunsthandwerk, Wiener Werkstätte*), was founded in 1903 as an organ for promoting modern architecture and design.

Perhaps the best known of the original group of Secession artists was Gustav Klimt (1862–1918). Although he had trained with one of the most conservative and sought after of Viennese painters, Hans Makart (1849–1884), and had himself become a recipient of major public commissions for the Austrian state, Klimt eventually ran afoul of his patrons over a series of paintings executed for the Great Hall of the University of Vienna. Completed between 1899 and 1901, the Faculty Paintings, as they were known, were commissioned to commemorate the university faculties of Philosophy, Medicine, and Jurisprudence. In executing the work, Klimt took an altogether unorthodox line that left his patrons reeling. Instead of boiler plate images of classical personifications celebrating the individual faculties and their achievements, Klimt presented a series of disturbing tributes in which perplexing formal solutions veered dramatically from the traditions of academic painting to bolster strange, seemingly antagonistic iconographies. Philosophy, which the university commission had wanted to visualize the "Victory of Light over Darkness," showed a tower of figures drifting and twisting in ambiguous space in juxtaposition to a "globe of mystery," a lone light flickering at the bottom of the composition. Medicine, depicting the River of Life, complete with the skeleton of death, paid precious little heed to the idea of health, relegating the

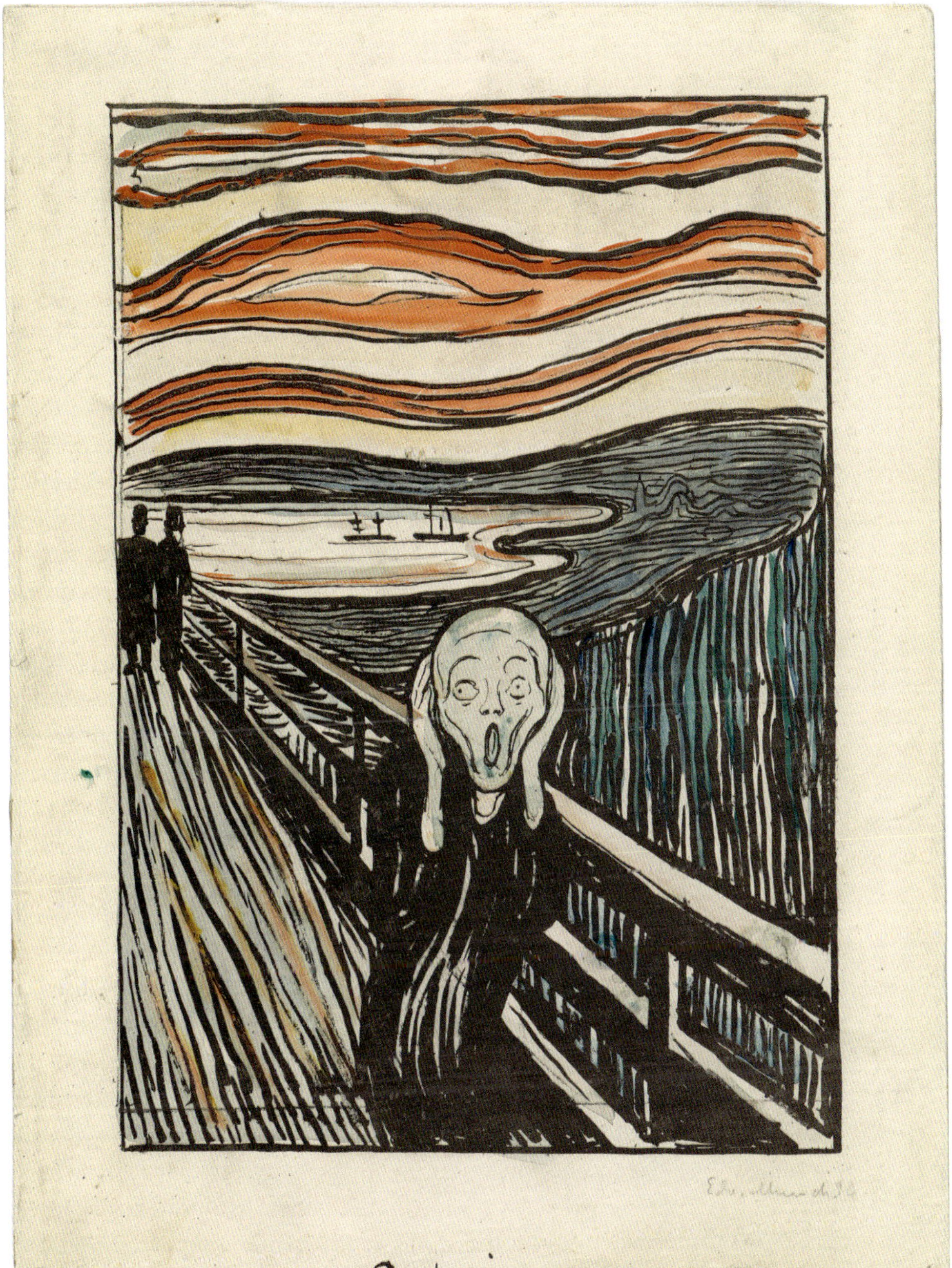

14. Edvard Munch, *The Scream*, 1895, Munchmuseet, Oslo. Photo: Courtesy of the Munchmuseet/O. Kvavik

goddess Hygeia to the bottom of the panel. There was nothing in the composition to suggest the preeminence of what was then one of the most accomplished medical faculties in the world. Jurisprudence offered a similarly unorthodox solution, showing a condemned man taunted by three female figures and a sea monster with personifications of Truth, Justice, and Law looking on from the background. The response was outrage. Newspapers of the day energetically tracked the dispute.[50] Eventually, eighty-seven members of the university faculty signed a petition for the removal of the images, a public prosecutor was hired, and the issue was debated in the Austrian parliament. Klimt, enraged, bought back the commission, and vowed never to work for the government again.[51]

It was in this lively, if contentious, environment, that Wickhoff and Riegl came to the exploration of late antique art. That they were aware of the artistic and philosophical currents swirling around them is clear. Indeed, Wickhoff himself waded directly into the fight as one of the few faculty members willing to rise to Klimt's defense. Addressing complaints that the paintings were ugly, stylistically incorrect, and immoral, he argued that it was necessary to see the work in light of the Secessionist argument that all styles have an equal claim to beauty.[52] In making his case, Wickhoff might just as easily have been championing the art of late antiquity. The logic used in defense of the Faculty Paintings was the logic that he and Riegl brought to bear on the problems of Roman and late antique art. It was in essence the argument of *Kunstwollen*. It was also the clarion call of the Viennese Secessionists themselves, a phrase emblazoned on the façade of their new exhibition hall: "To every age its art, to every art its freedom."[53]

That freedom followed from the conviction that form revealed inner truth. In and of itself, this idea was hardly revolutionary. As the early definitions of abstraction make clear, form's purpose was to express noble ideas. What was new in the modernist view, was the sense of form and the idea it expressed. Far from representing beauty and with it the noble idea, form now had the capacity to take unorthodox shape and in so doing to express individual, idiosyncratic states of mind. As the German expressionist painter Franz Marc explained, "We depend no longer on the image of nature, but destroy it, in order to show the powerful laws which reign behind beautiful appearances. As Schopenhauer put it, today the world as will is more important than the world as representation."[54]

As Marc's appeal to Schopenhauer suggests, the concerns of modernist art and the definition of late antique form sprang from a common source. It is in fact arguable that late antiquity's legitimacy as an artistic tradition was made possible as much by the emergence of a modernist aesthetic of abstract form as it was by developments in art history. To be sure, Riegl's notion of *Kunstwollen* created what he thought of as a scientific basis for the understanding of form that allowed late antique art its day in the court of historical inquiry, but modernism and its concerns contributed to the effort by creating the conditions that would allow those forms to make their visual appeal.

The idea of spiritual transcendence that late antiquity's abstract forms were said to reveal is of a piece with the modernist exploration of noncanonical visual form. In particular, the artistic urge to use visual form as a means to explore inner states of mind connects to a larger fascination with occult, esoteric, and spiritualist practice that took hold among artists and intellectuals. In the late nineteenth century, an interest in mysticism emerged as one of the responses to the industrialization and materialism that had so radically transformed modern life in the wake of the Industrial Revolution. This interest was expressed in a variety of ways: the study of such historical figures as the thirteenth-century theologian and mystic Meister Eckhart or his sixteenth-century counterpart, Jakob Böhme; a fascination with non-western religions such as Hinduism and Buddhism; and the development of new, esoteric organizations, among them the Rosicrucian Order and the Theosophical Society.[55]

Among these options, adherence to Theosophy was especially popular. The Theosophical Society, founded in New York in 1875 by Helena P. Blavatsky (1831–1891) and Colonel Henry Steel Olcott (1832–1907), was the most widely influential organization for the promotion of occult teaching in North America and Europe at the end of the nineteenth century and the beginning of the twentieth.[56] Its mission, promoted through local societies and the dissemination of the writings of Madame Blavatsky, was all-encompassing: to combat materialism in science and dogmatism in religion; to investigate the laws of the universe, including the concept of the fourth dimension, so as to develop the latent powers of human beings; to make known the esoteric teachings of the oriental religions; and to promote the brotherhood of humanity.[57] Especially interesting in these teachings was the belief that each human being generates a potentially visible aura, or thought-form, which reveals thoughts and emotion through distinctive patterns and colors. A second generation of Theosophists, Annie Besant and Charles W. Leadbeater, disseminated these ideas in two works, a joint publication, *Thought-Forms* (1901), and a single-author volume by Leadbeater, *Man Visible and Invisible* (1902).[58]

Theosophy was central to the development of the artistic ideas and attitudes that led to the development of non-objective painting across Europe in the first decades of the twentieth century in that many of the most influential modernist painters either peripherally explored or overtly embraced its tenets. While living in Munich, Kandinsky – a practitioner of yoga as early as 1900 – frequented a group interested in mysticism and is known to have read the writings of Blavatsky, Besant, and Leadbeater. Moreover, he paid tribute to Theosophical teaching when he noted that he wanted to depict the spiritual reality behind physical form as the world entered into what he referred to in Theosophical terms as the Epoch of the Great Spiritual.[59]

Seemingly different on the face of things, the study of empathy that emerged in scientific and philosophical circles in the last decades of the nineteenth century, the development of a modernist aesthetic in painting and sculpture, the interest in occult spirituality, and the art historical thinking that went into the definition of late antique artistic form share common ground. All built on the premise that it was possible to see and understand some sort of higher truth – the truth of human emotion or spiritual essence – through the objects of the material world. Riegl's contemporary intellectual atmosphere was indeed all pervasive.

Nowhere was this idea more evident than in the work of Wassily Kandinsky, whose treatise *Über das Geistige in der Kunst, insbesondere in der Malerei* (*Concerning the Spiritual in Art, Especially in Painting*) appeared in 1911. Kandinsky argued that form had the ability to convey spirit and mood through the manipulation of line, color, and composition. To illustrate his point, he included a series of illustrations, one of which was that of the sixth-century image of Justinian and his retinue from San Vitale, Schmarsow's quintessential image of the "Empire of the Spirit."

As the example of Kandinsky suggests, the idea of a spiritually infused modern art had no particular connection to Christianity. Rather, its origins lay in a generalized understanding of eastern philosophies – Buddhist and Hindu traditions, in particular – that could be traced to Hegel and Schopenhauer and the nineteenth-century pantheists. It was, as Worringer put it, the veil of the Hindu goddess Maia that cloaked abstract form in spirit.[60] That spirit, which became Christian by virtue of the images to which it was linked in historical discussions, was little more than an Orientalist fantasy, one that had nothing to do with Christian definitions of spirituality as they emerged first in the writings of the apostle Paul or in the later work of philosophers, historians, and artists. That this was the case is suggested by the vocabulary used to discuss the spiritual as it was manifest in the forms of nature and art.

SPIRIT AND SPIRITUAL

The terms "spirit" and "spiritual" as words connected with a human psychological disposition had their origins in Christianity, where they first appeared in the New Testament. The Pauline epistles refer to spirit, *pneuma*, and to the spiritual, the *pneumatikos*, using terms that subsequently were translated into Latin as *spiritus* and *spiritualis*. In both languages, *spirit* refers at once to the divinely generated force that reveals God's wisdom and to the human capacity to recognize and receive that wisdom.[61] In this context, the spiritual person is someone who attempts to live in the world under the influence of God. Such an individual stands in opposition to the worldly person, whose life is lived with the goal of personal gratification. Here the contrast is not between the material and the immaterial, the body and the soul, but between two different physically embodied ways of life.[62] This understanding prevailed until the twelfth century in the West. With the advent of scholasticism, a new layer of meaning was added, as *spirituality* came to refer to a distinction between rational humanity and nonrational creation. References to the "spiritual life" appear only at the end of the seventeenth century, after which time the term dies out. It resurfaces, always in a religious context, in late nineteenth-century France.[63]

In German, *spiritus* was translated as *Geist*. Throughout the Middle Ages, *Geist* referred either to apparitions or to the Holy Spirit (*Heilige Geist*), the third component of the Christian Trinity. In the eighteenth century, its meaning expanded to include mind-altering alcoholic spirits. Beginning in the nineteenth century, German began to make a distinction between sacred and secular in the matter of *Geist*. On the one hand, *Geist* preserved its Christian associations. In this context, its adjectival form became *geistlich*, religiously spiritual, that is, endowed with a Christ-like or sacred sensibility. Its antonym was *körperlich*, bodily or corporeal. On the other hand, *Geist* developed a philosophical meaning, one that referred consistently to the self-conscious human capacity for reason and understanding. In this sense, it is understood as mind or intellect, and the adjectival form is *geistig*, spiritual or intellectual, with emphasis on the latter. Paired with its antonym, *körperlich*, in the compound word *geistig-körperlich*, it refers to the whole nature of the person, that is, to the mind in tandem with the physical body.[64]

In discussions of abstract form, there is a consistent understanding of *Geist* according to its philosophical definition. Whether constructing a philosophical system, describing optical experimentation, considering the psychology of empathy, or discussing historical works of art, not a single author describes abstract form as *geistlich*. *Geistig* is, instead, the order of the day, even in discussions that describe abstract form as the agent of pantheistic union with the cosmos. What this usage suggests is that in references to "abstract spiritual form," *spiritual* refers to the Idea, the intangible essence of the concrete object that the process of abstraction was meant to reveal and the mind that facilitates its understanding. Abstract form also conveys a sense of harmony and repose, a feeling given life by the formal qualities of line, color, and composition. In short, the spirit embodied in abstract form represented a universal cosmic essence that transcended time and place. As such it served as a visual platform that offered human beings a contemplative focus that would allow them to connect to its universal nature.

When Riegl considered the matter of form, whether crystalline, inorganic, or abstract, he applied the philosophical understanding of *Geist* as idea or intellect to history and its objects. In so doing he linked the concept to the modern theories of perception first promulgated by Helmholtz, claiming that, in contrast to the tactile, material representations of Egyptian art, the optical, images of later Roman art represented an intellectualized rendering of physical reality that required imaginative reflection on form to achieve its full representational force.[65] In other words, for Riegl, later Roman art was intellectual to the extent that it required mental interpretation of representational form, the process of perception he described as distant viewing.

Riegl's understanding of intellect was not limited to the characterization of viewing habits. It also encompassed the forms of late Roman art that were the prompt to viewer response. The "crystalline" friezes on the Arch of Constantine were intellectual to the extent that they embodied the "first and eternal principle of form,"[66] that is, the idea of the thing represented.

Finally, Riegl considered these forms intellectual because they represented the visualization of a distinctive, historically based *Kunstwollen.* He found a general explanation for the period's *Kunstwollen* in Neoplatonism, syncretic religions, and early Christianity, intellectual systems he associated with a late Roman turn to magic against the rationality of earlier eras.[67] Riegl went on to establish the particular historical context with references to the work of Plotinus and Augustine, arguing that their thinking provided insight into the shape and structure of later Roman art. His use of these sources was, at best, superficial. There was no discussion of Plotinus, and references to Augustine were brief and indirect.[68] Riegl first appealed to Augustine's claim that there was no place for ugliness in God's creation. He then went on to argue that comments on unity, proportion, and symmetry in Augustine's general writings as well as his musical theory described the visual qualities of later Roman art.[69]

Riegl's goal in this discussion was not to establish the spirituality of later Roman art, but to find an explanation for the putative ugliness of such works as the Constantinian friezes by making an appeal to contemporary concepts of beauty. Nevertheless, it was with these observations that the correlation between abstract form and Christian spirit began to take hold, by virtue of the sheer force of connection of the late Roman *Kunstwollen* with one of the great early Christian thinkers.

It was left to Worringer to make that link explicit. He did so by observing that the Constantinian friezes embodied the "new spirit which entered the Roman world through Christianity."[70] Associating that spirit with the East and an age-old oriental disposition toward detachment and transcendence derived from Indian Vedic traditions that he saw as the antithesis of western rationality, Worringer found in abstract form the perfect avatar of psychological detachment. It was in his hands that abstraction became representative of the Christian search for otherworldly transcendence, an idea that would establish itself over the course of the following decade.

Although it has been noted that artists of the late nineteenth and early twentieth centuries took their cue from late antique and Byzantine traditions,[71] it might also be said that those same artists observed and imposed their own values on those traditions. The definition and understanding of late antique art that emerged during the last decade of the nineteenth century and early years of the twentieth century were shaped by the intersection of ideas from a range of scientific, historical, and theoretical study that was wholly modern. It was, to return to Riegl's observation that all scholarship is shaped by its circumstances, fully the product of its age. The understanding of late antique art that came to the fore in the early years of the twentieth century – in part a definition that served the political aspirations of the Hapsburg state and in part one that entwined with the concerns of avant-garde artistic practice – had as much if not more to say about the *Kunstwollen* of its own moment, it may be argued, than about that of the late antique world. If this is indeed the case, the implications for the understanding of late antique art are profound. Specifically, it raises the question of how best to understand the full range of late antique visual experience, everything from Wickhoff's illusionist form to Worringer's abstraction, with eyes more attuned to visual thinking in a late antique sense. That is the project of the next section of this book.

NOTES

1 Haüy 1784, for the mathematical basis. See also Haüy 1801; 1822.
2 Hegel 1975, 56. See also Gandelman 1982, 127.
3 Riegl 1966, 76; 2004, 125. For a discussion of Riegl's use of the term, see Rampley 2013, 156–57.
4 Bletter 1981; Prange 1994.
5 Morgan 1992b, 233.
6 For the treatise *Handbook of Physiological Optics*, see Helmholtz 1925, originally published 1856–57; a popular summary of his findings, *Recent Progress on the Theory of Vision*, appeared in 1868. Wickhoff used Helmholtz to develop his theory of illusionist form. See Gamwell 2002, 65–67, 94.
7 Morgan 1992b, 233; Gamwell 2002, 97–98.
8 Morgan 1992b, 233
9 Quoted in Morgan 1992b, 233. See 240, n. 28, for the original German and full citation.
10 Vischer made the case in his dissertation, *On the Optical Sense of Form: A Contribution to Aesthetics* (*Über das optische Formgefühl: Ein Beitrag zur Aesthetik*). See Vischer 1994. Malgrave and Ikonomou (1994, 17–29) and Barasch (1998, 99–108) discuss his contribution.
11 Vischer 1994, 92.
12 Vischer 1994, 116.
13 Vischer 1994, 102.
14 Vischer 1994, 103.
15 Vischer 1994, 105.
16 Vischer 1994, 109–10.
17 Vischer 1994, 117–20.
18 Vischer 1994, 119.
19 Vischer 1994, 121.

20 Vischer 1994, 119–20.
21 See Chapter 3.
22 Morgan 1992b, 234–35.
23 Lipps 1903, 225.
24 Lipps 1903, 226–28.
25 Lipps 1903, 227–35.
26 Lipps 1903, 250–54.
27 Morgan 1994.
28 Morgan (1996, 319) discusses the idea of generalization as it develops from Hegel's concept of the "universal idea."
29 Morgan 1992a, 674, 678.
30 Morgan (1994, 461–62 especially) discusses the matter with respect to Joshua Reynolds's *Discourses on Art*.
31 Morgan 1994, 450.
32 Morgan 1992b, 237, indicating that there were holdouts for a purely nonrepresentational definition.
33 Vischer 1994, 117.
34 Translated by Morgan 1992b, 234–35, from Lipps 1897, 25–26. Emphasis Lipps.
35 "*Die Stilisirung giebt sich vielmehr als eine ausgesprochene und bewusste abstrakte.*" Riegl 1923, 261.
36 Hegel 1971, 293, 297; 1975. For Hegel's debt to earlier ideas about abstraction, see Morgan 1996, 319.
37 Schopenhauer 1948, 1: 271.
38 See Fechner 1848; 1851; 1860. On pantheism, see Mander 2022 with bibliography and Gamwell 2002, 14–15.
39 Riegl 1923, XVII: "*das Abstrakte gerichete Tendenz.*"
40 Riegl 1891, 126, 161: "*abstrakten Stilisierung.*"
41 Riegl 1923, 3: "*abstrakten Gesetzen.*"
42 Riegl 1923, 5, 23: "*abstrakt-symmetrischen Gebild.*"
43 Riegl 1923, 240.
44 Riegl 1923, 267: "*orientalische Geist der Abstraktion.*"
45 Worringer 1953, 15, 46. Worringer's ideas on Asian religions are consistent with attitudes toward eastern tradition that began to be developed as early as the eighteenth century by thinkers including Voltaire and Diderot in the wake of European missionary activities. For discussion of early modern interactions with Asia, see App 2010. On German scholarship and the Orient in the nineteenth century, see Marchand 2009.
46 Worringer 1953, 103.
47 Riegl 1901, 2; 1985, 6.
48 It goes without saying that the bibliography on modernism is vast, encompassing not only the visual arts but also developments in literature and music. Studies focusing on the visual arts include Clark 1984, 1999, and Varnedoe 1990, both of whom deal with nineteenth- and early twentieth-century developments. For an overview in the range of disciplines, see Walz 2008 and Drucker 2014.
49 Kandinsky 1912, 125: "*Zum Schluß möchte ich bemerken, daß meiner Ansicht nach wir der Zeit des bewußten, vernüftigen Kompositionellen immer näher rücken, daß der Maler bald stolz sein wird, seine Werke konstruktiv erklären zu können (im Gegensatz zu den reinen Impressionisten, die darauf stolz waren, daß sie nichts erklären konnten), daß wir schon jetzt die Zeit des zweckmäßigen Schaffens vor uns haben und endlich, daß dieser Geist in der Malerei im organischen direkten Zusammenhang mit dem schon begonnenen Neubau des neuen geistigen Reiches steht, da dieser Geist die Seele ist der Epoche des großen Geistigen.*" See also Ringbom 1966, 393–402 for Kandinsky's relationship to the Theosophists.
50 For the collected commentary, see Bahr 1903.
51 Vergo 2015, 69–83; Schorske 2006.

52 Wickhoff's comments were delivered in a lecture to the university faculty. The text does not survive, but a summary appeared in the *Wiener Fremdenblatt*, May 15, 1900, 31–34. For excerpts, see Bahr 1903, 60–64. For discussion, see Simpson 2010, 5; Rampley 2013, 146–53.

53 "*Der Zeit ihre Kunst. Der Kunst ihre Freiheit.*"

54 Text and translation from Morgan 1996, 329.

55 On the various manifestations of the relationship between visual form and spiritual practice, see the essays in Tuchman and Freeman 1986.

56 On Theosophy generally, see Galbreath (1986, 388–89). On Theosophy and the occult, see Tuchman (1986, 17–61). On the relationship between art, the occult, and Theosophy, see Ringbom 1966; 1970; 1986.

57 Galbreath 1986, 388.

58 Galbreath 1986, 390; Ringbom 1986, 136–37, 149–50. Besant and Leadbeater 1901 was published by the Theosophical Publishing House, as was Leadbeater 1902. The popularity of Besant's work was such that it was subsequently reprinted in 1905 and 1925.

59 Ringbom 1986, 131.

60 Worringer 1997, 16.

61 1 Corinthians 2: 1–15; Romans 8:14–16.

62 Holder 2005: 1–5; Stewart 2005; Sheldrake, 2012: 4; 2013: 1–2.

63 Holder 2005, 1–5.

64 For the vocabulary's etymology and history, see Grimm and Grimm 1887, 2623–741 (*Geist*), 2777–786 (*geistlich*), 2771–775 (*geistig*).

65 Riegl 1901, 177–78; 1985, 188.

66 "*das erste und ewigste Formgesetzt*," Riegl 1901, 49; 1985, 55.

67 Riegl 1901, 216–17; 1985, 232–33.

68 Riegl set great store by Augustine's early work *De pulchro et apto*, a text rejected and destroyed by Augustine himself. He relied on Berthaud (1891) for the reconstruction of the text and citations in his own study: Riegl 1901, 211, n. 1; 1985: 225–26, n. 115.

69 Riegl 1901, 209–17; 1985, 223–34.

70 Worringer 1953, 96.

71 Greenberg 1961; Betancourt and Taroutina 2015.

PART II

ANCIENTS

FIVE

THE STYLES OF MIMESIS

In an ideal world, the question of how best to understand the interaction between late antique style and its viewers would be addressed by an appeal to contemporary critical writings on the visual arts, but the world, being imperfect, offers little such documentation. Apart from philosophical writings that provide general insights, this literature, which included technical, critical, and historical writing, hardly survives, making any such direct appeal limited. That such texts did once exist is certain from references in ancient authors. In the second century, Pausanias wrote tantalizingly of "those curious about the history of sculpture," suggesting a body of specialized, medium-specific writing about the history of art.[1] In the first century, Pliny, who claims to have collected no less than 20,000 noteworthy facts for the *Natural History* by reading approximately 2,000 volumes by 100 authors, was more precise.[2] Among the sources cited for sections dealing with the various forms of sculpture and painting are lost texts on metalworking and metal sculptors by Menaechmus, Xenocrates, Duris of Samos, and Menander; a text on Athenian votive offerings by Heliodorus; and a general discussion of painting by Fabius Vestalis. Pliny also credited artists' contributions: a text by the sculptor Pasiteles and works by the painters Apelles, Euphranor, and Parrhasius, for example.[3] Presumably, many of these sources discussed the technical and theoretical aspects of artistic production. Euphranor, for one, is known to have written a treatise on color.[4] Nor was Pliny alone in tapping into this literature. In the second century, the physician-philosopher Galen referred to Polyclitus' *Canon*, a treatise that addressed proportion.[5]

What, if anything, these authors had to say about style, is another matter. References are fleeting, their thoughts unknown except in the most general of senses. Despair is, however, unwarranted. In the absence of direct testimony, ancillary sources make it possible to consider the expectations with which late antique viewers approached images, whether painted or sculptured, and with them the ways in which they understood visual form, or style. Philosophical and scientific discussions outline the approach to and understanding of the basic aesthetic premises guiding ancient and late ancient artistic production. For purposes of approaching style, the most valuable resources are those related to the cognate arts of music, poetry, and rhetoric. Treatises, especially those addressing rhetorical practice, offer precise statements about style, both the manner of its use and its reception.

Given the ancient propensity to discuss the arts collectively as diverse manifestations of a single phenomenon, and the particular and enduring sentiment expressed by both Greek and Latin authors that painting and poetry share common techniques and purposes, the analogy between verbal and visual form made possible by such texts seems particularly apt. Most famously and succinctly summed up by Horace in the dictum, "Ut pictura poesis" ("as is painting, so is poetry"),[6] the comparison between the visual and the verbal remained a mainstay of ancient critical commentary well into the Byzantine period. Thus, in the sixth century, Prokopios of Gaza would remark, "Painting and poetry, the one with colors, the other with words – for words are the colors of poetry – imitate the figures of gods and men, their passions and their loves."[7] With this comment, Prokopios drew an analogy between the materials and structures of the visual and verbal domains that saw the painter's tools of lines and colors as the equivalent of the verbal practitioner's words and phrases.

The explicit articulation of the correspondence between these creative spheres opens an avenue to the understanding of visual style. Of particular importance in this regard is the literature of Greek and Latin rhetoric. Developed for the specific purpose of training students in the art of public speaking, this material elaborates a theory of verbal and aural composition that outlines procedural tactics and, with them, the categories and expressive capabilities of style. As such, it provides a useful model with which to approach questions raised by the visual styles of late antiquity.

Such an approach is not unfamiliar. As indicated above, Tonio Hölscher has proposed a similar, albeit less explicit, analogy for the art of the early imperial period, describing the Roman propensity to deploy multiple styles within a given period, or even a single work of art, as a "semantic system" in which, on the model of the rhetorical arts, certain styles were considered suitable for the representation of certain subjects. Thus, the overt realism of Hellenistic style appropriately rendered the pathos of battle scenes, while the classicizing forms of Attic tradition expressed the dignity synonymous with state ceremonial. Stressing the importance of *decorum*, or appropriateness, in representation, Ellen Perry has argued a similar point in her study of the Roman habit of sculptural emulation.[8]

Given that rhetorical practice continued to flourish into late antiquity and that artists were as much in the habit of using different styles as were their earlier imperial predecessors, these studies offer an important starting point for any inquiry into late antique style. Specifically, they lay the groundwork for thinking about late antique art by recognizing the connection between literary practice and visual production in the Roman world. Studies by Michael Roberts and Anthony Eastmond have done just that: Roberts has noted a correspondence between the aesthetics of visual and verbal composition, while Eastmond has drawn parallels between visual form and rhetorical styles in consular diptychs.[9] All of these observations have built on a line of comparison first explored by Henry Maguire in discussions of later Byzantine art.[10] Using this same premise as a starting point, this chapter argues not only that the perceived connection between media persisted in late antiquity but also that its stylistic categories –described in rhetorical texts – offer modern viewers a language with which to rethink the traditionally established polarity between naturalism and abstraction. In so doing, it pursues two goals. The first is to identify and describe the principles governing representational tradition together with the expectations artists and patrons had of representation. The second is to consider the place of style within this tradition.

MIMESIS

Mimesis stood at the heart of ancient artistic practice. Broadly speaking, it referred to representation, more specifically, and especially with respect to the arts, to imitation of the appearances, sounds, and actions that were part of human experience. These replications could take place in different ways. In large measure, they were understood to derive directly from the experience of the phenomenal world. The arts themselves were said to have had their origin in mimetic activity. Men learned to sing by imitating birds, to draw by tracing shadows. In this regard, mimesis signaled replication of the natural world. At the same time, however, mimesis was an act of creating worlds, of imagining plausible characters and convincing fictional situations and settings out of the experience of reality.[11]

That the visual arts of Greece and Rome had as their underlying aesthetic principle a fundamental commitment to the imitation of the natural world hardly needs to be pointed out. Even so, this commitment warrants discussion, for it is easy to forget that desire to replicate the naturally occurring features of the phenomenal world in two- and three-dimensional form was not necessarily so straightforward a project as it might appear. Ever since the fifth century BC when Plato and Aristotle initiated the philosophical discussion of artistic mimesis, identifying music, poetry, rhetoric, dance, mime, painting, and sculpture as the contexts in which imitation held sway, and in so doing establishing the category of the "mimetic arts,"[12] mimesis was understood as something other than the technical replication of the natural world. Whether as a reflection of reality or its invention, mimesis created the conditions for understanding human experience. It did so by putting experience on display.[13] As Plato saw it, it was the purpose of mimesis to "penetrate to the innermost part of the soul and most powerfully affect it."[14] Aristotle concurred, arguing,

> We enjoy contemplating the most precise images of things whose actual sight is painful to us, such as the forms of the vilest animals and of corpses. The explanation of this too is that understanding gives pleasure not only to philosophers, but likewise to others too, though the latter have a smaller share in it. This is why people enjoy looking at images, because through contemplating them it comes about that they learn and infer what each element means, for instance that "this person is so-and-so." For if one happens not to have seen the subject before, it will produce pleasure not as mimesis but because of its execution or color or for some other such reason.[15]

As Aristotle suggests, mimesis was something other than craft. Although the skill involved in producing the mimetic image could afford viewers pleasure, to think of it in such a one-dimensional manner falls short. Above all, mimesis appears to have been a representational process, the goal of which was to engage the mind and the emotions for the purposes of education.

That mimesis could take on this didactic role was based on the observation that imitation was a natural learning behavior. Children mimicked the sounds of their parents when learning to speak and emulated the behavior of their elders when beginning to make choices. In the process of learning to read and write, students copied the shapes of letters. In short, whether in the cradle or the schoolroom, mimesis was the path to understanding.[16]

Throughout the long history of antiquity and into the Byzantine Middle Ages, the idea that mimesis was a catalyst to knowledge persisted.[17] In the third century, Plotinus observed that the arts "do not simply imitate what they see, but they run back up to the forming principles from which nature derives."[18] That is, representational form – whether verbal or visual – derives from, depends upon, and demonstrates truth. This attitude endured into the later Byzantine period where it was expressed by the ninth-century patriarch of Constantinople, Photius, in a homily delivered at the inauguration of an image of the Virgin and Child in the Great Church, Hagia Sophia: "With such exactitude has the art of painting, which is a reflection of inspiration from above, set up a lifelike imitation." Here, mimesis allowed its viewers access to the truth of the incarnation.[19]

While philosophical discussion explored the basic concept of mimesis and its operative assumptions, it demonstrated little direct connection to contemporary artistic production. Individual artists are rarely mentioned and then only in passing. There was little or no commentary on actual works of art, only a theoretical understanding of the means and purposes of the mimetic arts in general, painting and sculpture in particular. In part, this has to do with the nature of mimesis itself. As understood in these texts, mimesis was seen less as a product than as an activity or a process. The arts, in other words, were born from mimesis, and it is this imitative process that lies at the heart of creative activity.

Discussions of mimesis often take place around this process, focusing on stories of technical mastery and working method. Pliny's report of an encounter between the painters Protogenes and Apelles in which the two match brushes in a battle of lines is one example. Eager to meet Protogenes, Apelles presented himself at the painter's studio. Finding him away, Apelles painted a fine line across one of the panels in his studio, leaving it as his calling card. Protogenes, upon his return, immediately recognized it as the matchless work of Apelles. In reply, he drew an even finer line on top of and within his visitor's, to which Apelles responded with an even finer line on top of Protogenes'. Admitting defeat in this linear exchange, Protogenes declared that the panel should be preserved for the masterpiece that it was. That the painting received its due is clear: It was brought to Rome, where it was displayed on the Palatine to much acclaim.[20]

Working method was also a focus. Galen's references to Polyclitus' lost treatise, the *Canon*, document the importance of establishing proper figural proportions in sculpture and suggest the role of mathematics in workshop practice,[21] while the well-known story of the painter Zeuxis' attempt to recreate the surpassing beauty of Helen of Troy by copying the best features of five separate models and recombining them in a new, ideal image that would capture Helen's loveliness in a way no single model could points to the ways in which artists both relied upon and selected from nature in the course of their work.[22]

Zeuxis' method offers a reminder that the way in which artists engaged with nature might be presumed to carry with it a dollop of invention. While mimesis indicated the direct copying of nature, it also allowed for the creative recombination of natural forms in the service of persuasive invention. This interplay between natural representation and invention was referred to as *phantasia* (imagination). *Phantasia* is often contrasted with mimesis in recognition of the fact that it conjures an image in the mind, while mimesis copies from models; however, this procedural distinction makes no differentiation between representational outcomes. An imagined image draws from the raw materials provided by nature and depends upon verisimilitude for its efficacy. In the first century, Apollonius of Tyana is said to have addressed the matter in a conversation with his companion Thespesion about the proper method of depicting the gods. Responding to Apollonius' criticism of the Egyptian habit of rendering the gods as theriomorphic beings, Thespesion asks in exasperation if we are to imagine that artists such as Phidias or Praxiteles made their way to Olympus to have the gods sit for their portraits. Apollonius dismisses the idea of direct mimesis, saying, "Imagination created these objects . . . a more skillful artist than imitation. Imitation will create what it knows, but imagination will also create what it does not know, conceiving it with reference to the real."[23] In other words, *phantasia* constituted a kind of recombinant mimesis.

Whether as an act of direct copying or imaginative recreation, mimesis had one obvious goal, persuasive representation. Nowhere is this more evident than in Pliny's famous account of the rivalry between the painters Parrhasius and Zeuxis:

> This last [Parrhasius], it is recorded, entered into a competition with Zeuxis, who produced a picture of grapes so successfully represented that birds flew up to the stage-buildings, whereupon Parrhasius himself produced such a realistic picture of a curtain that Zeuxis, proud of the verdict of the birds, requested that the curtain should now be drawn and the picture displayed; and when he realized his mistake, with a modesty that did him honor he yielded up the prize, saying that whereas he had deceived birds, Parrhasios had deceived him, an artist.[24]

What this story also makes clear is that the technical mastery fueling this contest was hard won. Mimesis, it seems, had a history. Quintilian describes the first tentative paintings of Polygnotus and Aglaophon as "rude" and credits Zeuxis and Parrhasius with major contributions to the conquest of mimesis, the rendering of light and shade, what the ancients referred to as *skiagraphia*,[25] and the mastery of line. Sculpture, which moved from the stiffness of such early artists as Callon and Hegesias through the craftsmanship and grace of Polyclitus to the skill of Phidias and Alcamenes before achieving perfection in the work of Lysippus and Praxiteles, shared a similar history.[26]

Pliny tells a parallel story. As the *Natural History* explains, representational traditions evolved between the sixth and fourth century BC to become ever more persuasive in their depictions of the phenomenal world, as one artist learned from and surpassed another. In the discussion of sculpture, for example, each artist plays a role in the developmental outline of its history. Scyllis and Dipoinus hold pride of place as the first to achieve fame by sculpturing in marble.[27] Following them, Phidias appears as the artist who revealed the possibilities of the sculptural medium. These possibilities were then taken up and elaborated by Praxiteles[28] before being perfected with the innovations of Lysippus.[29]

Quintilian and Pliny track the relentless pursuit of perfection. At the heart of their observations is a belief in the universality of naturalism as a point of visual reference, a sense of the history of the development of style as it works toward achieving this end, and a notion of artistic perfectibility. Historically speaking, that perfection was achieved for Pliny in the fourth century BC with the sculpture of Lysippus and the painting of Apelles and Zeuxis. Thereafter mimesis appears to have become as much a matter of imitating the works of accomplished artists and artistic traditions as it was of nature itself. Surviving statuary shows that already in the third century BC, artists began quoting from earlier works of art, a practice on which the Romans elaborated, thus giving rise to a dizzying array of styles that both coexisted with and followed upon one another – everything from the stiff patterns of archaizing form to fluid forms of baroque realism. Experience built upon itself, and, in this respect, mimesis was as much about copying from other artists as it was about relying on the example of nature. As Quintilian put it with respect to oratory, "It cannot be doubted that a large part of art consists of imitation. Invention of course came first, and is the main thing, but good inventions are profitable to follow."[30] The point in so doing, he continued, is not simply to copy, but to learn from and improve upon what has gone before in order to create ever more convincing and effective results.[31]

This procedure appears to have been followed by visual artists, as Pliny's account of Lysippus suggests. In observing the sculptor's innovative proportions, he remarked that Lysippus' system created an illusion of greater height when compared to the "*quadratas staturas*," the blockier proportions, of earlier artists, adding that Lysippus himself was reported to have said that his predecessors depicted men as they really were, while he represented them as they appeared.[32] Whether or not Pliny's report of Lysippus' estimation of his own achievements is accurate, this comment, which comes at the end of his historical summary of sculpture, is revealing for what it suggests about mimesis and the mimetic process. For Pliny, as for others, artists had always aimed for convincing naturalistic representation and continued to do so. It confirms that ultimately the means to achieve this end was seen to involve different, if related, processes: the direct imitation of nature; the emulation of accomplished works of art; and, as in the case of Lysippus' newly conceived proportional matrix, a healthy dose of *phantasia*.

Yet, for all the value placed on them, convincing representation, technical finesse, and the conquest of reality represented only one aspect of mimesis. Whether painted or sculptured, an image clearly was meant to be considered as more than an exercise in deceptive illusionism. Philostratus the Elder put it this way:

> Whosoever scorns painting is unjust to truth; and he is also unjust to all the wisdom that has been bestowed upon poets – for poets and painters make equal contribution to our knowledge of the deeds and the looks of heroes – and he withholds his praise from symmetry of proportion, whereby art partakes of reason. For one who wishes a clever theory, the invention of painting belongs to the gods – witness on earth all the designs with which the seasons paint the meadows, and the manifestations we see in the heavens – but for one who is merely seeking the origin of the art, imitation is an invention most ancient and most akin to nature; and wise men invented it, calling it now painting, now plastic art.[33]

As Philostratus observed, the imitation at the heart of painted and sculptured representation was the creation of wise men. Its techniques were rooted in observation and reason, and its results offered access to something greater and more profound.

Indeed, the consensus appears to have been that, whatever the art, mimesis was a process of revelation, one that laid bare intellectual and emotional states of mind.[34] Lucian (second century), in an essay on dance, observed, "To be sure it professes in the main to be a science of imitation and portrayal, of revealing what is in the mind and making intelligible what is obscure."[35] As often as not, that revelation dealt with character, as Plutarch's definition of poetry as "an imitation of character and lives" that brings out "indications of both vice and virtue" suggests.[36]

That the same goals were set for the visual arts is clear. Zeuxis is said to have painted an image of Penelope that represented "morality itself,"[37] and Euphranor's depiction of the Battle of Mantineia is said to have revealed the Athenians' "stout resistance abounding in boldness and courage and spirit." Plutarch, the author of these observations, noted that the underlying aim of imitation is to stir the mind and summon the emotions.[38]

THE STYLES OF MIMESIS

As these testimonia suggest, artists and their audiences were in accord with philosophers in that they viewed mimesis as a means to a revelatory end. At the same time, they leave open the question of what mimetic art looked like beyond the fact that it was persuasively natural. While all mimetic form took the natural world and the actions of gods and mortals as its subject, the visual rendering of such subjects could vary widely. As the range of stylistic possibility in the corpus of Greek and Roman art indicates, there was latitude in this definition. On the one hand, as in the case of Lysippus' sculpture (Figure 15), mimesis captured the look of the world. On the other hand, as archaizing statuary from the Augustan age (Figure 16) indicates, it could be an altogether different affair, a process that deliberately stood back from overt naturalistic representation to replicate formal values of an older age.[39]

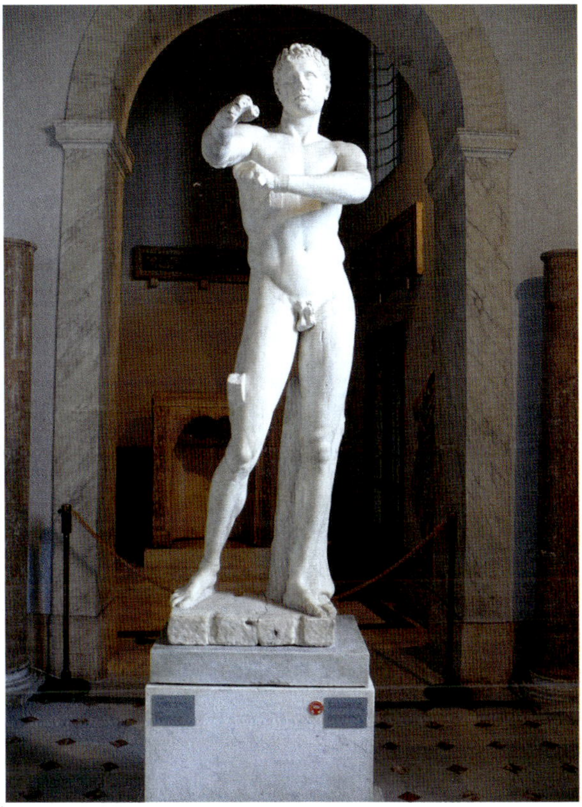

15. Lysippus, Apoxyonomus, Roman copy after bronze original of c. 330 BC, Vatican Museums (Museo Pio Clementino). Photo: S. Bassett

What guided the choice of style is therefore a question. To a certain extent, it was a matter of skill and disposition: Some artists were simply better at certain things than others. Commenting on the painter Nicophanes, Pliny observed, "although few can be compared for gracefulness" his "tragic feeling and weight of style is far from Zeuxis and Apelles."[40] Taste also played a role. Quintilian, writing on rhetorical style, draws an analogy between the work of painters and sculptors and the work of orators, noting,

> Now since Style is the product both of rhetoric and of the orator, and since there are (as I shall show) several forms of it, both the art and the artist are involved in all these, though they are all very different from one another, not only individually (as one statue differs from another, or one painting from another, or one pleading from another) but also generically, as Tuscanic statues differ from Greek or the Asianic speaker from the Attic. Now these different kinds of work of which I am speaking have each their own masters and indeed their own admirers; and the reason why the perfect orator does not yet exist (and why perhaps no art exists in perfection) is not only that different qualities predominate in different individuals, but that no single form has pleased everybody, partly because

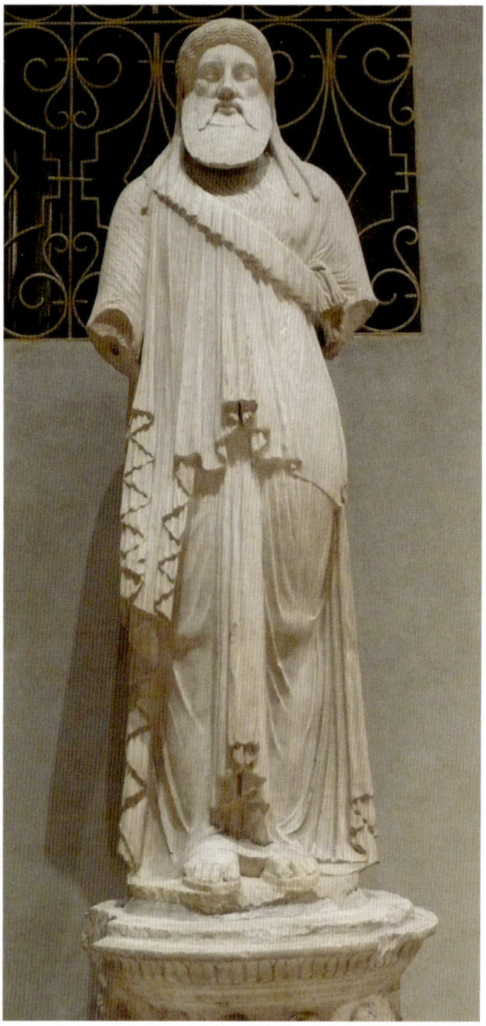

16. Archaizing statue of Dionysios, first century BC or later, Galleria Doria Pamphilj, Rome. Photo: S. Bassett

> of the conditions of particular times or places, and partly because of the tastes and aims of each person.[41]

He continues by considering the qualities of different artists, both in terms of formal mastery and the character of their style – the "accuracy" (*cura*) of Protogenes, for example, or the "craftsmanship and grace" (*diligentia et decor*) of Polyclitus.[42]

All of these discussions describe an awareness of and appreciation for the range of stylistic appearances that constituted mimetic representation. Archaeological finds support this idea. Sculptured installations of the early imperial period, such as those from a second-century house in Rome in which statues appear to have been installed with an idea to inviting formal comparisons between individual figures, give life to the idea of sensitivity to form. Four statues displayed in pendant pairs flanked doorways leading into the residence. An early second-century torso of a general rendered in a style reminiscent of fifth-century-BC Polyclitan form stood to the left of the first doorway across from another first-century figure, the representation of a faun in the fourth-century style of Praxiteles. At the next doorway, two statues of another fourth-century-BC sculpture, the *Pothos* by Scopas, one from the first century, the other from the second, flanked the entrance. Here the lack of any overt iconographic connection between figures suggests that the statuary was arranged specifically to call attention to form and in so doing invite identification and contemplation of individual styles.[43]

Nor were such exercises limited to the early imperial period, as a fifth-century collection of sculpture gathered by Theodosius II's court chamberlain Lausus indicates. The collection, which is said to have included works by such renowned ancient sculptors as Scyllis and Dipoinus, Phidias, Praxiteles, and Lysippus, appears to have been displayed in such a way as to describe a history of visual style, one that peaked, as noted by Pliny, in the fourth century BC.[44]

It is one thing to observe that Roman viewers were cognizant of style and another to consider the implications of their awareness. As Quintilian indicates, this appreciation was in part a matter of taste; however, if the evidence of the other mimetic arts is any index, it would be a mistake to view the issue solely as a question of connoisseurship and visual preference. In the case of poetic composition, for example, subject matter and genre governed the choice of style, and individual styles were developed according to standards that mandated structure, meter, and word choice. Thus, the great epic narratives unfolded in dactylic hexameter, a form synonymous with and suitable to the activities of gods and heroes, while lyric and tragic compositions deployed different structures, metrical systems, and vocabularies.[45] In each case, form at once derived from and signaled genre, its sounds and cadences enhancing and becoming a part of its meaning.

The same was true for musical composition, where the shaping of sound followed prescribed patterns that created distinct compositional modes, *tonoi* or *harmoniai*, each one of which had its appropriate uses and associations. The modes themselves were described by references to ethnic identity and geographical region, the most common of which were the Dorian, Ionian, Lydian, and Phrygian. The Dorian mode was associated with the western Greeks, while the remaining three took their names from populations in Asia Minor. Defined by pitch, rhythm, and harmonic structure, each *tonos*, of which theorists listed as many as fifteen,[46] expressed what was thought to be an *ethos*, or character, through the organization of sound. Dorian and Phrygian modes were suitable to the dignity and power of manly character, while Ionian and Lydian *tonoi* were associated with the relaxed and convivial lifestyle of women. Other modes, such as the hybrid Mixolydian, were considered dirge-like.[47]

The propensity to use style as an agent of meaning, to endow it with generally recognized connotations, is likely to have informed the arts of painting and sculpture in the same way as it did the other mimetic arts. That said, the question of how to understand its workings in the visual sphere is not readily answered, given the intermittent and generally opaque commentary on such matters in the available sources. For all the differentiation between styles, there is precious little direct information on how individual stylistic traditions were received, and the implications, if any, of these styles may be observed only obliquely. Passing remarks provide insight, such as Pliny's statement that Polyclitus' Doryphorus was "manly" (*virilis*) in its appearance,[48] an assessment that recalls the categorization of the Dorian mode. This similarity suggests common critical ground and in so doing invites understanding of the Doryphorus as a visual analogue to the somber, stalwart, even heroic virtues conveyed by the Dorian mode.

The descriptions of the Doryphorus and the Dorian mode offer fleeting glimpses of what might have been the outlines of a larger theory of style operating across the different media of the mimetic arts. At its core lay the idea that there was a rapport between the formal elements of style and the overall meaning and function of a work of art. That there was any such theory is of course open to question. Perhaps it is better to think in terms of a general understanding, one that relied broadly on established premises. One sector of mimetic tradition offers substantial clues as to what such understanding might have been – the literature of Greek and Latin rhetorical instruction, a long-lived body of writing that deals extensively with the issue of style, its forms, uses, meanings, and functions.

ARS RHETORICA AND THE MIMETIC ARTS

As was the case with the mimetic arts generally, the art of rhetoric conformed to a set of expectations regarding composition and performance. In much the same manner as poets or musicians, rhetors considered style an expressive tool, a force that not only was determined by subject matter but also shaped it. Thus, just as poets used lyric dactyls to express the hieratic stateliness of a character in preference to the more ordinary conversational rhythms of iambic trimeter, or musicians turned to the manly and serious Phrygian mode to gird men for battle, the rhetor composed orations using styles appropriate to subject matter and context. Its traditions are thus grounded in a shared understanding of artistic form and expression.

At the same time, however, rhetoric and its traditions stand out for the abundance of surviving documentation – practical, didactic texts that explain the logic supporting and the mechanisms facilitating stylistic expression in rhetorical composition. Nothing like this documentation survives for poetic or musical composition, where the extant literature is largely theoretical. As a result, the handbooks and exercises associated with rhetorical training offer an unparalleled view into ancient attitudes toward style, its selection, composition, and expressive possibilities, which, given the ancient propensity to view the arts as individual branches of a collective enterprise, can be used to work toward a fuller understanding of visual style and its operations. In addition, because of its penchant for systematic description and categorization of forms, the art of rhetoric offers a vocabulary for description that makes it possible to move beyond the modern categories of naturalism and abstraction to see late antique form in a different light. Specifically, it suggests that whatever the style, painting and sculpture in the late ancient world should be understood in terms of variation within the mimetic process. Finally, and perhaps most importantly, rhetorical literature affords an understanding of the imaginative world of late antique artists and their viewers in a way that no other material is able to provide. Embedded in the school curriculum, rhetoric shaped the intellectual habits and responses of its students through a course of training that, *mutatis mutandis*, remained fundamentally unchanged for hundreds of years.

Definition and History

Rhetoric, defined by the ancients as the "art of speaking persuasively" or the "art of speaking well," had its origins in the democratic societies of classical Greece, where it developed as the means to debate issues of public concern.[49] Although the great speeches attributed to the Homeric heroes in the *Iliad* and the *Odyssey* make it clear that oratory was an essential means of communication from the earliest periods of Greek history, it was in fifth-century-BC Sicily that the idea of rhetoric as a discipline operating according to established principles was said to have emerged in the work of two Syracusans, Corax and Tisias. Together they are credited with devising what was probably a system of legal argumentation. Later in the century, another Sicilian, the sophist Gorgias of Leontini, is said to have introduced the practice to Athens. Once introduced, it became established as an area of study, with the likes of Plato and Aristotle weighing in on its ways and means.[50] Having been established in Athens, the art of rhetorical declamation spread, over the course of the third and second centuries BC, to find new audiences and uses in the Hellenistic kingdoms of Asia Minor and in literary centers such as Pergamon and Alexandria. No longer limited to the courtroom or even to the civic arena, it became in these contexts a means to present all manner of ideas in public and private. As its purview expanded, rhetors spoke in praise of citizens and cities at public events, functioned as emissaries, and performed with equal fluency at wedding banquets and the salons of intellectuals. As a codified professional practice, it was omnipresent and pervasive, arriving eventually at the gates of Rome.

In the Roman world, where there had been a longstanding tradition of public speaking associated with legal, political, and military activities and such public occasions as funerals, the introduction of a standardized rhetorical practice came only in the second century BC. Taught by Greeks in Greek, rhetoric was viewed initially with suspicion; however, once Latinized, it became an integral part of the Roman educational system from the first century, thanks in no small measure to the impetus of Marcus Tullius Cicero (109–43 BC), who thought that its practice had intellectual and cultural value beyond the courtroom. By the period of the early empire, rhetorical training, which had by then become the hallmark of an elite education, offered an entrée into imperial service. With that, the place of rhetoric in the greater Roman world was secured, so much so that by the late antique period rhetors themselves enjoyed unrivaled status, not only as public voices but as citizens and intellectuals operating within a social network that shaped the individual fortunes of the late Roman cities from which they hailed and beyond them the destiny of the empire itself.[51] Rhetoric, in other words, was a force with which to reckon.

That rhetoric could create such a powerful and cohesive cultural framework was in large measure a result of the place it came to occupy in educational practice from as early as the fifth century BC, when it became a standard element in Athenian elite education.[52] From first youth, when schoolboys learned to read and write, through the more advanced training of adolescence that introduced them to the ways of argumentation, rhetorical training was a constant. For those who could afford it, the most complete educational course involved a two-phased curriculum. In the first, elementary phase, which began around the age of seven and continued for seven or eight years, students learned the basic skills of reading, writing, and oral recitation in a curriculum based on a stable of canonical authors, Homer foremost among them. With these skills under their belts, they then turned to these same texts to develop the ability for grammatical analysis and literary interpretation. When not busy with the business of language, they studied logic, geometry, astronomy, and music. There is also evidence that drawing was a feature of the curriculum. Aristotle, who observed that education should be systematic, universal, and publicly organized, allowed for the possibility of drawing in the curriculum, arguing that it was "useful for the purposes of life and very serviceable."[53] In other words, as much as literary or musical study, drawing was a means to train the mind.[54]

For most students, this basic course of study, which took place at the local level and could be completed to a greater or lesser extent in the absence of state-mandated learning, represented the sum of their education. For those who were inclined and had the means, a second phase provided more specialized instruction. Following such a course often demanded travel away from home for study at an established school in a large urban center such as Athens, Alexandria, or Antioch. Beginning around the age of fourteen or fifteen, these students were immersed for five or six years in the advanced study of grammatical rules, techniques for attaining compositional eloquence, and the in-depth analysis of the literary canon that had formed the bedrock of their training from the start. Their teachers were not only grammarians and rhetors but also, frequently, philosophers who trained them within the precepts of a specific philosophical system in acknowledgment of the understanding that there was as much a moral component to education and speaking as there was the straightforward acquisition of skills and knowledge.[55]

This course of study, which took place with admirable consistency in the towns and cities of the Roman world, had remarkable longevity. Although there was increasing standardization and elaboration of rhetorical theory first in the Hellenistic age and again in the later Roman period, the systems set in motion in the fifth century BC were fundamentally those of late antiquity and beyond. The consistency of instruction across time and space was not inconsequential. Whether in the Greek- or Latin-speaking world, the pagan or the Christian, mastery of rhetoric shaped the intellect, both individual and communal, and in so doing created a shared frame of reference and expectation that allowed members of the elite to recognize and interact with one another across the geographical extent of the Mediterranean world.[56]

A COMMONWEALTH OF STYLE

In molding intellectual habits, rhetorical instruction and its practice across time and space also created the conditions for a broader understanding of the mimetic arts, painting and sculpture included. Most immediately, it instilled in its students the understanding that speech could be classified, codified, and developed according to a set of rules. More broadly applied, it created a mindset that shaped not only the rules of human interaction on a grand and enduring scale but also those of a wider aesthetic understanding, one in which decorum demanded certain forms, appearances, and responses.

The idea that speech could be deployed in different ways for different purposes was basic to the enterprise, an idea recognized as early as the fourth century BC when Aristotle defined three categories of rhetorical declamation. To the initial genre of judicial or forensic declamation introduced by Gorgias, he added the deliberative and the epideictic categories, each geared to a specific purpose. Thus, forensic rhetoric continued its association with court proceedings. The deliberative genre was identified with public debate, and the demonstrative, or epideictic mode, expressed praise or assigned blame. This basic categorization of speech persisted into the Hellenistic age, albeit with growing elaboration within the basic genres of speech, a habit of multiplication and systematization within the original structure that continued into the Roman period and beyond. Eventually, each of these categories came to be associated with a particular way of speaking, or style. Touching on such matters as word choice, sentence structure, rhythm, volume, and pitch, style governed what to say and how to say it. Deployed properly, it was that which made speech persuasive.

As rhetoric flourished, a body of literature grew up to define its genres, explain its techniques, and facilitate its instruction. Preliminary exercises, or *progymnasmata*, formed the first line of instruction by providing students with preliminary exercises in composition. Surviving examples by authors such as Aelius Theon (first century) and Aphtonius (fourth century) include exercises in the composition of various types of rhetorical presentations, among them fable, narrative, moral anecdote, maxim, description, encomium, and the introduction of laws.[57]

There were, as well, treatises devoted to style. Perhaps the most influential of these texts was a work by the second-century rhetor Hermogenes of Tarsus, *Peri ideon* (*On Types of Style*). The text provides an explanation of the role of style and the means of its implementation together with an extensive descriptive vocabulary.[58] As Hermogenes informed his readers, it was the duty of an orator to consider, first, his subject matter and, second, the most compelling arrangement and presentation of material. The means to accomplish this goal was style. Hermogenes defined style as a quality based on ideas corresponding to certain, specified virtues. These ideas, or styles, were mandated by subject matter and to a large extent corresponded to genre. Within each genre, the manipulation of such elements as sentence structure, word choice, cadence, and rhythm defined the preferred speaking style. As a result, not only would a speech crafted for the courtroom have, by necessity, a very different style from one composed for a wedding, but, among courtroom presentations themselves, accusation was expected to have a very different tone from defense.[59]

Hermogenes identified seven basic speaking styles, each with its own subdivisions. These styles included Clarity, which was broken down to include Purity and Distinctness; Grandeur, with the subheadings Solemnity, Asperity, Vehemence, Brilliance, Florescence, and Abundance; Beauty; Rapidity; Character and its subdivisions Simplicity, Sweetness, Subtlety, and Modesty; and, finally, Sincerity, with its single subset Indignation. All these styles were grouped under the larger designation of Force, which the author defined loosely as the proper use of style. Finally, Hermogenes acknowledged four major stylistic groups: the Plain style, which corresponded to Clarity; the Grand style, synonymous with Grandeur and Beauty; the Middle style, based largely on Character; and the Mixed style, which, as the name suggests, combined all of these elements.[60]

In composing and delivering a speech, Hermogenes made it clear that no rhetor would adhere solely to one style throughout. Indeed, variation in style from line to line was often desirable, both as a means to more accurate expression and as a tactic for avoiding the pitfalls of too narrow an application of a single mode of expression. Given the possibility for the mixture of styles, what determined the ultimate tenor of a speech was the predominance of one mode over another.[61]

Hermogenes' influence was as widespread as it was long lived. Although he was a resident of Tarsus in Asia Minor, his work ultimately came to the attention of Latin speakers and writers. As the examples of Cicero and Quintilian indicate, rhetorical methods were as much a feature of the Latin tradition as the Greek, with the result that in the western territories of the Roman Empire Latin rhetors and their students were as eager to absorb rhetorical theories as any of the Greek-speaking denizens of the East. In his own lifetime, Hermogenes enjoyed the attention of Marcus Aurelius. By the sixth century, his work, or a tract considered to be his work, had been translated into Latin by Priscian,[62] and no less a thinker than Augustine of Hippo (354–430), who for all his intellectual prowess was no speaker of Greek, adhered to the basic precepts of Hermogenic theory.[63] His work also remained a mainstay of Greek rhetorical theory and practice as late as the eleventh century in the writings of the Byzantine scholar Michael Psellus.[64] Still later, in the thirteenth century, the emperor Theodore II Laskaris (1221/1222–1258) would refer to Hermogenes.[65]

The ways and means of rhetorical composition outlined in texts such as *Peri ideon* not only describe an approach to style, but also point to issues beyond the study of rhetoric itself. In their prescriptive nature they outline a way of understanding the mimetic arts and a larger process of artistic creation at odds with modern understanding. Rather than championing notions of renegade artistic genius and personal artistic expression familiar from early modern and modernist traditions, they describe systematically developed and universally agreed-upon practices that invited conformity and in so doing facilitated expressive communication. In this context, talent was manifest in the ability to operate creatively within the rules.

For as much as this thinking is alien to modern sensibilities, it is common to ancient understanding. Aristotle's *Poetics* represents what is probably the most familiar statement of this idea, but it is by no means the only example of this approach. Treatises by Aristoxenus (fourth century BC), Cleonides (second–third century), and Aristides Quintilianus (late third–early fourth century) laid out similar procedures for musical composition,[66] and it is a fair bet that such prescriptive recommendations represented a generally received understanding of artistic practice across media. References to lost treatises such as the *Canon* of Polyclitus or Parhassius' work on color suggest that similar regulatory practices governed the visual arts.[67]

At the same time that Hermogenes allows a view into the general principles of compositional practice, he also offers the possibility of thinking more precisely about the ways in which the works of art that were the end result of such procedures might have been received. To begin with, his stylistic categories together with his descriptions of their characteristics provide a template for understanding general principles. Consider the discussion of "Sweetness" (*Glykytes*), for example. As a category of style, Sweetness is designed to create the aura of pleasure. As such it is considered appropriate to mythical topics, as well as descriptions of things pleasing to the senses. Such descriptions may include, among other things, beautiful people and places; a sexual encounter between an amorous couple; or a stream rushing and bubbling beneath the bent bough of a blossoming tree. Sweetness is also the stuff of personification, as when Sappho appeals to her lyre to speak and be eloquent. The style of Sweetness is, above all, one of Purity (*Katharotes*) and Simplicity (*Apheleia*), values achieved by using the vocabulary of everyday language spoken in easy conversational rhythms and straightforward grammatical construction in which short clauses express complete thoughts.[68] As the recommendations make clear, style and subject were bound to one another in a symbiotic relationship, with subject mandating style and style elaborating and revealing the possibilities in a given subject.

Applied to surviving literary texts, these recommendations, eye-glazing to read, shed their prescriptive tedium. The mythological paintings described in the *Imagines* of Philostratus the Elder and his nephew Philostratus the Younger offer a case in point. The subject matter demands stylistic Sweetness, and the text obliges. As Hermogenes recommends, the diction and rhythm of the prose is conversational, unfolding with Clarity and Simplicity in straightforward clauses designed to engender feelings of pleasure and delight. The elder Philostratus' description of *erotes* (cupids) offers an example. Aphrodite's little henchmen gambol in a verdant landscape, some gathering apples, others cavorting amongst themselves:

> For here are four of them, the most beautiful of all, withdrawn from the rest; two of them are throwing an apple back and forth; and the second pair are engaged in archery, one shooting at his companion and the latter shooting back. Nor is there any trace of hostility in their faces; rather they offer their breasts to each other, so that the missiles may pierce them there, no doubt. It is a beautiful riddle; come, let us see if I can possibly guess the painter's meaning. This is friendship, my boy, and yearning of one for the other. For the *erotes* who play ball with the apple are beginning to fall in love, and so the one kisses the apple before he throws it, and the other holds out his hands to catch it, evidently intending to kiss it in his turn if he catches it and then to throw it back; but the pair of archers are confirming a love that is already present. In a word, the first pair in their play are intent on falling in love, while the second pair are shooting arrows that they may not cease from desire.[69]

Whether such descriptions describe actual works of art remains an open question. Whatever the answer, the issue at hand is the expressive tenor of the image, a quality conveyed not only in the careful description of the *erotes*' antics but also in a tactical manipulation of word choice and sentence structure designed to capture the essence of the subject matter. In the attempt to convey the painting's character in language, Philostratus offers a verbal simulacrum of the image that is more than a description of what he sees. His actual writing, the sweetness of his own style, not only is appropriate to his verbal exposition but also offers a corollary to, indeed translates, the sweetness of the painting's style for the reader. What is also clear from the description is that the image creates the context for understanding the larger lesson that is the goal of the mimetic process: The painting is, as Philostratus observes, a story about friendship.

In addition to identifying categories of style and describing their methods of composition, *Peri ideon* is useful for its descriptive vocabulary. The nouns and adjectives Hermogenes uses to define and describe style – words like *grandeur*, *simplicity*, or *charm* – often appear in descriptions such as those by Philostratus, indicating that they form part of a more widely recognized critical vocabulary. Philostratus suggests as much in the conclusion to a description of the Hours (*Horai*). "Perhaps," he says, "they permit us to weave a tale about the painter; for it seems to me that he, falling in with the Hours (*horai*) as they danced, was caught up by them into their dance, the goddesses perhaps thus intimating that grace (*hora*) must attend his painting."[70] The grace, *hora*, to which Philostratus refers is at once a pun on the name of the Hours, *horai*, and a characterization of the painting. As a descriptor it refers to a quality of style, Gracefulness (*Horaios*), that is itself associated with a particular kind of Sweetness and Simplicity. Such a reference indicates that descriptive vocabulary, far from being arbitrary, signals particular stylistic affiliations, thereby tapping into a broader vein of inference and understanding.

According to this logic, no style was an end in itself. Instead, each style conveyed moral and emotional associations signaling the virtues and vices of characters and actions depicted. In language, the easy flow of Sweetness with its intimations of grace, charm, and pleasure conveys the warmth of friendship and human interaction, while the sturdy, unadorned sentences that create Clarity embody the vapidity of the trite and commonplace,[71] and the stately cadences and elevated language of Solemnity evoke the majesty of gods and heroes, their dignity and virtue.[72] Philostratus the Younger suggests that the same function fell to style in painting:

> For instance, the poets introduce the gods upon their stage as actually present and with them all the accessories that make for dignity and grandeur and power to charm the mind; and so in like manner does

> the art of painting, indicating in the lines of the figures what the poets are able to describe in words.[73]

Noticeably absent from these discussions are references to naturalism or abstraction. These were not the categories used to evaluate and classify the formal qualities of works of art in an aesthetic culture that took the process of mimesis and the replication of visible phenomena as the starting point of any artistic endeavor. Instead, forms were observed with an eye to characterizing style on the basis of human attributes: grace, charm, grandeur, and the like. Those designations might refer to physical bearing, or they might acknowledge personality traits. In either instance, style was understood as an index of *ethos*, or character.

To observe parallels between Hermogenes' recommendations and Philostratus' prose is not to argue that Philostratus (or any other author) was working from a handbook but to call attention to two assumptions driving the larger literary and artistic culture in which they participated: that style and subject exist in a standardized, classifiable relationship, and that verbal and visual representations may be considered analogous not simply in terms of subject matter but also with respect to style. Given this relationship, it is possible to consider Hermogenes' text in a new light, to view it less as a handbook devoted to rhetorical composition and more as a guide to the range of possibilities in visual style. Specifically, by drawing analogies between visual form and verbal style and considering images with respect to Hermogenes' theoretical classifications it may be possible not only to categorize style in a manner more consistent with late antique understanding but also to understand the expressive implications of its form.

An example of fourth-century silver plate, the great circular dish from the Mildenhall treasure (Figure 17) suggests what such an approach might offer. The plate displays images in three concentric circles. The god Oceanus, bearded with seaweed, stares out from a central roundel. Nereids and tritons riding hippocamps swirl around him in the next band. On the outer circle, Dionysus, his leg propped on the haunch of an irritated panther, presides over a revel of dancing nymphs and satyrs, two of whom guide a drunken, staggering Hercules to the ground. Nymphs, some carrying drums, alternate with the satyrs as they trip around the outer ring, their bodies twirling, arms outstretched, and draperies flying, as the satyrs play musical instruments. Each figure strikes a unique pose and stands out clearly against the background, united with the others in the circular composition through a weave of undulating line established by the fluttering draperies and supported by gesture and glance.

Since its discovery in 1942, the Mildenhall plate has been discussed largely in terms of its date and iconography. When a late fourth-century date was

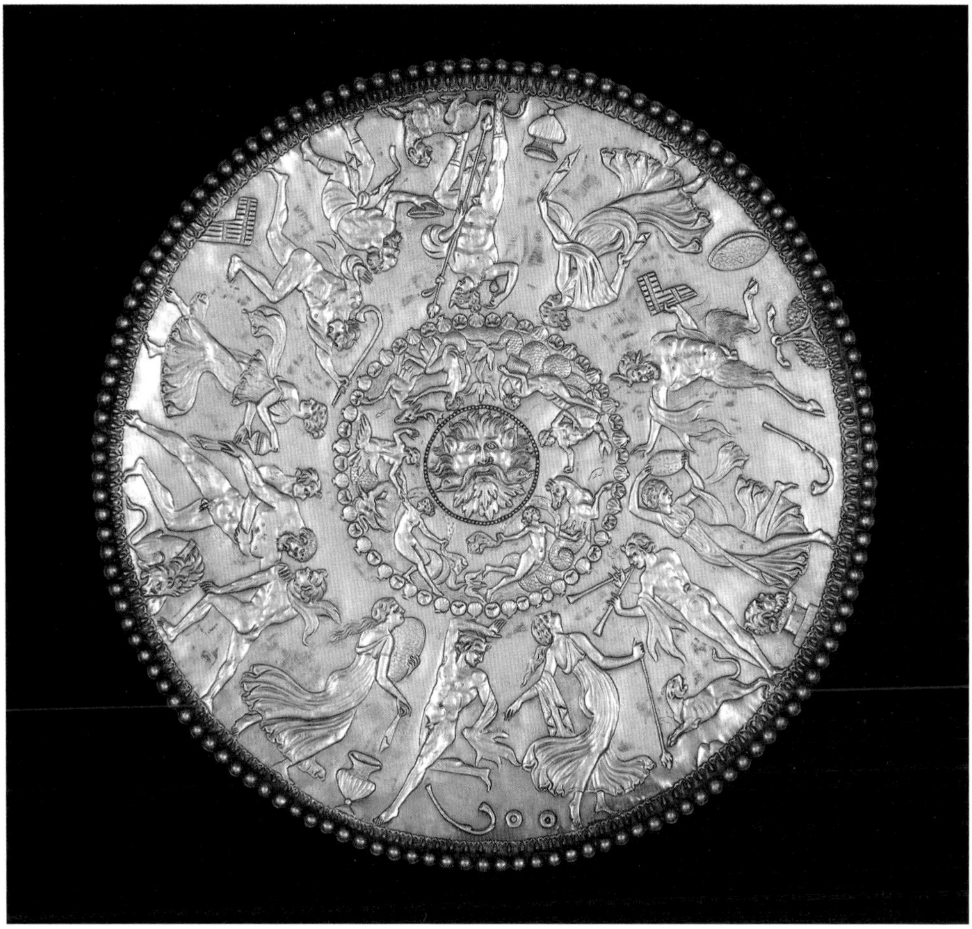

17. Great dish from the Mildenhall Treasure, fourth century, British Museum. Photo: The Trustees of the British Museum/Art Resource, NY

established on technical grounds, there was a stir, as the mythological subject matter seemed an anomaly in the context of Roman Christian culture. Accordingly, its ecstatic imagery initially was understood to document the religious affiliation of its owners, and the plate was marshaled as evidence for a fourth-century revival of pagan cult. Subsequently, the question of religious affiliation has been set aside and the plate has been seen as a document of aristocratic self-presentation, its mythological content understood generally as the visualization of the classical traditions of the *enkyklios paideia*, the general educational training built on the bedrock of rhetorical study.[74]

Very little has been said about style beyond the fact that the plate stands squarely in the classical tradition. Within this context, debate has centered on whether it represents a survival or a revival of classical form. In either case, the gamboling sea creatures and swirling revelers have been seen to fall short of the classical model, with criticism leveled at their anatomical inconsistencies.

As such, the plate is seen to document the diminished state of late fourth-century classical style.[75]

It is difficult to imagine that these are the terms the owners of the plate brought to bear on its appreciation. Material value aside, the dish must have been treasured for its craftsmanship and design. The composition is well thought out. Proportions are consistent, no two poses are the same, and individual figures, each one outlined against the ground, appear in loose, dynamically balanced configurations in which musicians and dancers on either side of a central figure mirror one another, some facing forward, others backward, their activity integrated into a single swirl of dance by the sweeping lines of limbs and drapery. A range of textures and coloristic effects achieved through mastery of metalworking techniques enhances their activity to capture the energy of the revel.

That style and subject matter complement one another is clear. Less evident are the implications of this synthesis. Hermogenes suggests a way to understand this relationship with the directive that the aspiring rhetor first pinpoint subject matter, the starting point of every rhetorical composition and the arbiter of style. The goal of stylistic selection is to facilitate mimesis; style captures the tenor of the event described in a formal manipulation of language that in turn stimulates analogous feelings in listeners, be they pity or rapture. In this instance, the mythological subject matter suggests two possibilities. Solemnity, which treats of thoughts concerning the gods, offers one option, and Sweetness, dealing with myth, fable, and legend, another. Of the two, Sweetness appears the better choice. As Hermogenes notes, a Solemn style is appropriate for speaking of the gods in their divine majesty. Such majesty is not, however, the stuff of the plate's far-from-solemn revelry. Far more suitable to this project is Sweetness, the same style used by Philostratus in his descriptions. Sweetness is, as Hermogenes observed, a style that expresses pleasure, both in the interpretation of the subject matter and in its ability to manipulate reader response.[76]

It is arguable that the Mildenhall plate offers an example of visual Sweetness. Its easily recognizable, clearly framed figures coupled with the straightforward compositional tactics suggest a visual analogue to Hermogenes' compositional recommendations and their verbal demonstration in Philostratus' description of the *erotes*. As in Philostratus' description, which moves easily from one group to the next as it documents the protagonists' actions, the Mildenhall plate makes a series of clear visual statements that depict the revelers in loosely affiliated groups following one after the next around the curvature of the plate. Within each group, supple, curving lines articulate the individual figures, suggesting the Simplicity and Purity integral to Hermogenes' definition of the style. In this easy progress from figure to figure, the plate not only envisions subject matter but also accomplishes an essential task of all mimetic art, the articulation of the larger sense of pleasure and delight and with it, once again, a sense of the rewards and virtues of community and friendship.

To approach the Mildenhall plate using the language of rhetorical theory makes it possible to set aside the notion of failed classicism and to examine the plate in a different light. This is not to unmoor the plate from the classical tradition to which it clearly belongs or to reject the idea that it be seen as an expression of the aristocratic cultural values rooted in the traditions of *paideia.* It is, rather, to refine the sense of what that tradition was and how its values were given visual expression, using Hermogenes' language as a point of access. With Sweetness recognized, the plate becomes more than a bland expression of aristocratic self-presentation. It appears rather as the perfect accessory for a convivial gathering, a plate whose particular stylistic affect captured and perhaps even stimulated the genial interactions between host and guest, and the delights of conversation that took place in the reflections off its gleaming surface.[77]

To suggest that a work of art such as the Mildenhall plate can be understood by analogy to rhetorical theory is not to imply that artists undertook the study of rhetoric or looked to well-thumbed handbooks to create their own work. It is, instead, to argue that handbooks such as *On Style* reflect an approach common to the mimetic arts with which painting and sculpture were classed. That approach not only regulated artistic practice but also responded to and structured viewer expectation and response within a shared aesthetic culture that was itself part of a larger worldview shaped by a centuries' long educational tradition that did more than train students in the practical matters of rhetorical declamation. It structured their minds and habits of thought, educating them in ways beyond the twists and turns of specific subjects to instill in them a common mental and emotional outlook, a way of giving and receiving information. That outlook produced and sustained the structures of everyday life in elite society. It also made possible and nurtured a common artistic culture of mimesis and its stylistic system of communication, creating what might be described as a commonwealth of style across the space and time of the Mediterranean world in which artists operated using the common currency of their shared artistic language.

Chapters 6, 7, and 8 explore this artistic language by examining works of late antique art using the recommendations of rhetorical composition and its stylistic classifications as a guide. In keeping with these guidelines, subject matter organizes the discussion. It does so around three broad topics: narrative, which includes both myth and history; ceremonial representation; and portraiture. Within these categories, the formal language of individual works of art and their implications for viewer reception will be examined. The goal is not to arrive at definitive answers but to propose a different way of thinking about the relationship between form, meaning, and function in late antique art independent of the categories of naturalism and abstraction. Specifically, it argues that it is important to understand late antique painting and sculpture and its stylistic variations within the context of that most enduring and pervasive of antiquity's cultural expressions, mimesis.

NOTES

1 Pausanias 1918–1935, 2: 496 (*Description of Greece* 5.20.2)

2 Pliny 1938–1962, 1: 12–14 (*Natural History*, preface, 17, and 21).

3 Pliny 1938–1962, 1: 144, 148, 152 (*Natural History*1: 33, 34, 35, 36) for complete lists. See Pollitt (1974, 73–81) on Pliny's sources.

4 Pliny 1938–1962, 9: 354 (*Natural History* 35.129).

5 Pollitt 1974, 14–22. On the *Canon*, see Tobin 1975, Stewart 1978, and Pollitt 1995. On Galen and Polykleitos, see Leftwich 1995.

6 Horace 1926, 480 (*Art of Poetry*, 361).

7 Procopius of Gaza 1963, 88. *Declamatio III (Venus)*, lines 1–3. "Γραφὴ καὶ ποίησις ἡ μὲν τοῖς χρώμασιν ἡ δὲ τοῖς λόγοις – λόγοι γὰρ τῇ ποιήσει τὰ χρώματα -μιμοῦνται δ' οὖν ἄμφω θεῶν τε καὶ ἀνθρώπων σχήματα, πάθη καὶ ἔπωτας."

8 Hölscher 2004; Perry 2005. See also Introduction.

9 Roberts 1989; Eastmond 2010. See also Bassett 2008, which argues the connection between rhetorical and visual styles.

10 Maguire 1981.

11 The modern literature on mimesis is extensive. Auerbach 2003 represents the classic literary study. More important for this discussion is Halliwell 2002. For a general account with bibliography, see Woodruff 2015.

12 Plato 2013, 1: 176 (*Republic* 2.373b); Aristotle 1995, 28–30 (*Poetics*. 1447a 13–28); Halliwell 2002, 153, 289.

13 Halliwell 2002, 5, 16, 23.

14 Halliwell 2002, 21, 23; Plato 2013,1:282 (*Republic* 401d).

15 Aristotle 1995, 36–38 (*Poetics*. 1448b 10–19); Halliwell 2002, 158.

16 Aristotle 1995, 36–40 (*Poetics* 1448b).

17 Halliwell 2002, 273.

18 Plotinus 1969–1988, 5: 236 (*Enneads*. 5.8.1). See also Halliwell 2002, 317–18.

19 Photius 1958, 290.

20 Pliny 1938–1962, 9: 320–22 (*Natural History* 35.36.81–82).

21 Galen 1981, 5:426; 2020, 95. For discussion of the *Canon*, see Pollitt 1974, 14–22; 1995; Tobin 1975.

22 Cicero 1949, 166–68 (*On Rhetorical Invention* 2.1.9).

23 Philostratus of Athens 2005, 154 *(Life of Apollonios of Tyana* 6.19).

24 Pliny 1938–1962, 9: 308–10 (*Natural History* 35.36.65–66).

25 Pollitt 1974, 245–54.

26 Quintilian 2002, 5: 282–86 (*The Orator's Education* 12.10: 3–10).

27 Pliny 1938–1962, 10: 8 (*Natural History* 36.4.9–11).

28 Pliny 1938–1962, 10: 14–18 (*Natural History* 36. 4. 18–25).

29 Pliny 1938–1962, 9: 172–74 (*Natural History* 34.61–5).

30 Quintilian 2002, 4: 322 (*The Orator's Education*, 10.2.1).

31 Clark 1957, 143–76 (the role of mimesis in rhetoric).

32 Pliny 1938–1962, 9: 174 (*Natural History* 34.65).

33 Philostratus 1931, 2 (*Imagines*. 1 [294K]).

34 Halliwell 2002, 16.

35 Lucian 1913–1979, 5: 246 (*The Dance*, 36).

36 Plutarch 1927–36, 1:136 (*How the Young Man Should Study Poetry*, 25C–26A).
37 Pliny 1938–1962, 9: 308 (*Natural History* 35, 63).
38 Plutarch 1927–36, 4: 500 (*On the Fame of the Athenians* 346F–347A).
39 Fullerton 1990.
40 Pliny 1938–1962, 9: 342 (*Natural History* 35.35.111).
41 Quintilian 2002, 5: 282 (*The Orator's Education* 12.10.2).
42 Quintilian 2002, 5: 282–286 (*The Orator's Education* 12.10.3–9).
43 Bartman 1988.
44 Bassett 2000; Bassett 2004, 98–120.
45 On the varieties of Greek and Latin meter and their uses, see Halporn, Ostwald, and Rosenmayer 1963.
46 Aristides. Quintilianus. *Peri musikes*, 15.1 in Mathiesen 1998, 59.
47 Cleonides, *Harmonic Introduction*, 12–14 in Mathiesen 1998, 44–46. Athenaeus, "Sophists at Dinner" (623e–28c) in Mathiesen 1998, 86–92. See also Pelosi 2020 on music and emotions; Schueller 1988, 39–44, 136–37 on music and *ethos*; D'Angour 2015, 188–202 on music and sensation.
48 Pliny 1938–1962, 9:168 (*Natural History* 34.19.55).
49 For the history and development of rhetoric and rhetorical study in the Greek and Roman world, see Kennedy 1963; 1983; 1999; Morgan 1998. For Byzantine traditions, see Hunger 1978, 1: 65–213. On rhetorical traditions and Christianity, see Cameron 1991. For the role of rhetoric in education, see Jaeger 1939; Marrou 1956; Clark 1957; Kaster 1988; Harris 1989; Brown 1992, 35–70; Cribiore 1996; 2001; Ford 2001; Morgan 2007.
50 Hinks 1940; Walker 2000, 17–41; Bons 2007.
51 For a general discussion of rhetoric in the Roman period, see Kennedy 1972; 2009, 102–256; Connolly 2007. For late antiquity, see Bowersock 1969, esp. 17–58; Watts 2006; Kennedy 2009, 257–84.
52 Morgan 2007, 305–08.
53 Aristotle 1932, 638–40 (*Politics* 1337b 23–1338a 20).
54 Seaman (2017, 19) discusses drawing in the curriculum. See also Seaman 2020, 13. Rouselle (2001) explores a broader role for images in education.
55 Watts 2006, 3–4.
56 Brown 1992, 35–70, esp. 38.
57 Corpus Rhetoricum 2008–2009. See Kennedy 2003 for English translation and commentary.
58 For the original edition by Hugo Rabe, see Hermogenes 1913. For the English translation by C. Wooten, see Hermogenes 1987. References refer to both editions.
59 Hermogenes (1913, 213–26, 383–95; 1987, 1–8, 110–19) addresses the different types of style and their uses.
60 Wooten (Hermogenes 1987, xi–xviii) outlines Hermogenes' approach to individual styles. On Force, see Hermogenes 1913, 369–80; 1987, 101–8.
61 Hermogenes 1913, 221–22; 1987, 5–6.
62 Kennedy 1983: 55, 58–59; 1999, 27, 205; 2003, ix
63 Kennedy (1999, 170–82) discusses Augustine and rhetorical principles.
64 See texts and discussions in Barber and Papaioannou 2017, 20–23.
65 Angelov 2019, 6.
66 For the treatises, see Mathiesen 1998, 35–66 and Jan 1895, 167–207. On Cleonides and Aristides Quintilianus, see Mathiesen 1999, 366–90; 521–83.
67 Galen discusses the *Canon* (1981, 5:426; 2020, 95), as does Philostratus the Younger (1931, 285) in his prologue to the *Imagines*. See Pollitt 1974, 14–22; 1995; and Tobin 1975 on the *Canon*. On Parhassius and other treatises, see Pliny 1938–1962, 1: 152–60 (*Natural History* 1.35–36).
68 On Sweetness, see Hermogenes 1913, 330–39; 1987, 75–81. On Purity, see Hermogenes 1913, 227–34; 1987, 8–14. On Simplicity, see Hermogenes 1913, 322–29; 1987, 71–75.
69 Philostratus 1931, 20–28 (*Imagines* 1.6).

70 Philostratus 1931, 268–70 (*Imagines* 2.34).

71 On subjects and thoughts appropriate to Sweetness, see Hermogenes 1913, 330–35: 1987, 75–79. On Clarity, see Hermogenes 1913, 226–41; 1987, 8–18.

72 Hermogenes 1913, 242–54; 1987, 19–26.

73 Philostratus 1931, 284–286 (*Imagines*, Prooemium [391K]).

74 Dohrn 1949; Brailsford 1955; Kent and Painter 1977, 33–39, nos. 54–79; Weitzmann 1979, 151–52 (cat. 130); Toynbee and Painter 1986; Kiilerich 1993, 165–67; Hobbs 2016, 18–62. On the connection between mythological silver and *paideia*, see Leader-Newby 2004, 141–60.

75 Brailsford 1955, 20–23, commented on the "pure classical style" and suggested a Mediterranean origin. Toynbee (1964, 309), Kitzinger (1977, 30 and 108), Kiilerich (1993, 180), and Hobbs (2016, 53) all observe the classicizing style.

76 On Solemnity, see Hermogenes 1913, 242–54; 1987, 18–26. For Sweetness, see 1913, 330–39; 1987, 75–81.

77 Hobbs (2016, 54–55, 273–87) sets the plate and its accompanying pieces in the context of a dinner party, arguing that they suggest plenty and status.

SIX

STORYTELLING AND THE "ILLUSIVE SIMILITUDE OF LIFE"

WHEN FRANZ WICKHOFF BUILT HIS DEFINITION OF ROMAN ART, HE DID SO ON an armature of stories, secure in the knowledge that narrative – the depiction of events unfolding in time and space – was integral to the experience of late antique art.[1] Whether in the open space of a major public venue or the intimacy of a domestic setting, narratives were omnipresent, and to his way of thinking they represented the quintessential Roman pictorial genre. It was not that the Romans had a monopoly on narrative: Egyptians, Mesopotamians, and Greeks all had tales to tell. What set the Romans apart was their method, or style, of storytelling. Wickhoff equated this style with his own definition of illusionist form, the technique of light and shade modeling that created "the effect of truth" by proposing an "illusive similitude of life" through a "progressive and increasingly thoughtful and accurate observation of nature." In other words, illusionist form established narrative as a mimetic exercise in truth telling.[2]

Wickhoff's focus on storytelling was not misplaced, as the abundance of narrative imagery in late antiquity indicates. Public monuments such as the Arch of Galerius in Thessaloniki (303) or that of Constantine in Rome (315) celebrated imperial wars and victories with sculptured records of military campaigns. In Constantinople, historiated columns dedicated to Theodosius I (395) and Arcadius (421) continued the tradition encountered on the second-century Roman columns of Trajan and Marcus Aurelius, while in the sixth century, mosaics at the entrance to the Great Palace of the Byzantine emperors documented Justinian's victories across the empire. In the domestic sphere, mythological tales unfolded in mosaics and frescoes adorning the walls and floors of elite residences. Textiles showing similar lore hung from doorways and intercolumniations, complementing these more permanent fixtures. Small-scale objects joined the assemblage: an illuminated manuscript of Homer or Virgil in the library, a silver platter with images of Achilles in the triclinium, an ivory pyxis with frolicking nymphs and satyrs in the boudoir. Nor was storytelling any less integral to Christian experience. On the small scale, narrative representations adorned sacred texts and all manner of liturgical equipment. Most impressive, however, were the monumental church interiors, where image cycles mapped the economy of Christian salvation.

Evidence also confirms Wickhoff's understanding of the aims of Roman visual narrative, as voices seconding Philostratus the Elder's reminder that painting encapsulated truth indicate.[3] For Eusebius of Caesarea, who clearly equated seeing with believing, "The witness of our eyes leaves no place for the instruction that comes through the ears."[4] Paulinus, Bishop of Nola, writing in the early years of the fifth century, echoed the sentiment. Commenting on a newly completed painting cycle for the church of St. Felix, he observed, "He who sees this [painting cycle], recognizing Truth in the empty figures, feeds his faithful spirit with a by no means empty image."[5]

Assumed, yet unspoken, was the look of truth. Wickhoff thought it a matter of illusionist form, of capturing the essence of the physical world using the techniques of visual mimesis. Yet, as ancient attitudes toward representation suggest, mimesis was a subtle, malleable phenomenon that took its cue from subject as much as from physical reality to extend the definition of truth into the intellectual and emotional realm. Nowhere is this proposition better demonstrated than in the visual narratives that captured Wickhoff's imagination, prime among them the miniatures of the Vienna Genesis. Using two miniatures from the story of Noah as a starting point for discussion, this chapter examines ancient ideas about narrative together with attitudes toward style to explore the ways in which formal choices helped viewers to understand the truths at the heart of late antique historical narratives.

THE VIENNA GENESIS

The two miniatures – folio 2v, a double-register representation of the departure from the ark and the sacrifice of Noah, and folio 3r, a single image of God's covenant with Noah – face each other on opposite pages. As with all the miniatures in the codex, the images give visual life to the text above. To do so, both adhere to the broader conventions of mimetic representation, simultaneously tailoring the use of line, color, and composition to direct the visual experience.

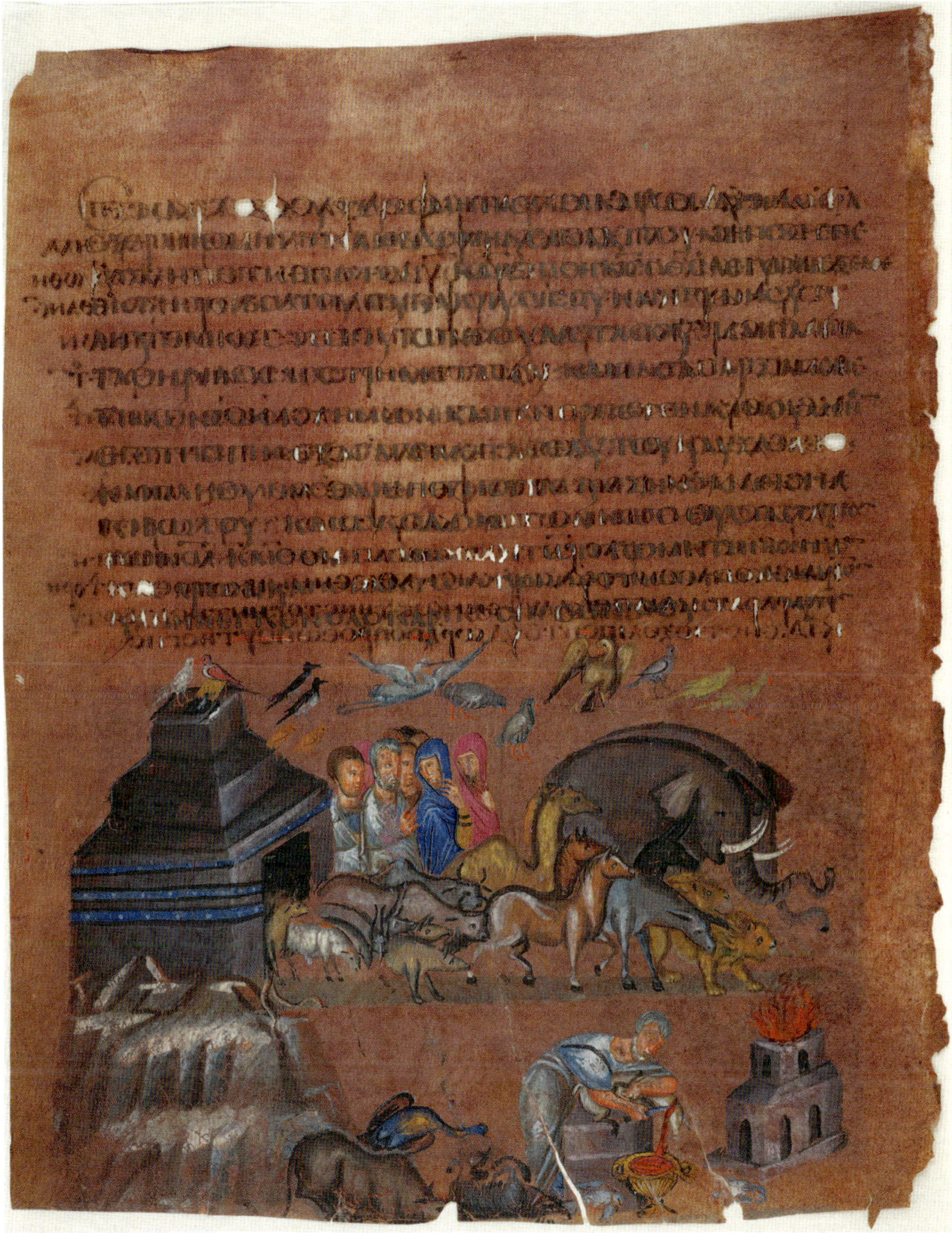

18. Departure from the ark and Noah's sacrifice, Vienna Genesis, sixth century, Österreichisches Nationalbibliothek, Cod. Theol. Gr. 31, fol. 2v. Photo: Courtesy of the Österreichisches Nationalbibliothek

Folio 2v (Figure 18) depicts two sequential moments in the life of Noah. The upper register illustrates the disembarkation from the ark:

> So Noah came out. Together with his sons and his wife and his sons' wives. All the animals and all the creatures that move along the ground

> and all the birds – everything that moves on land – came out of the ark, one kind after another.
>
> (Genesis 8:18)

The action, which uses the manuscript's purple-stained parchment as its background, begins on the left side, where the ark, shown in three-quarter view as a massive gray tower, sits lodged on Mount Ararat. Animals of all types – gigantic elephants with bright tusks and waving trunks; roaring, thick-maned lions; camels; and domestic cattle – spill across the page from an open door in the ark's side, as Noah and members of his family look on. Birds, some in seated pairs, others with their wings spread in flight, scatter above.

In the lower register, which again follows the biblical text, Noah offers a thanksgiving sacrifice:

> Then Noah built an altar to the Lord and taking some of all the clean animals and clean birds, he sacrificed burnt offerings on it. The Lord smelled the pleasing aroma and said in his heart: "Never again will I curse the ground because of humans, even though every inclination of the human heart is evil from childhood. And never again will I destroy all living creatures as I have done."
>
> (Genesis 8:20–21)

On the left, Ararat rises. At the foot of the mountain, dead cattle and birds, the sacrificial gifts, lie heaped on the ground. Toward the center of the composition, Noah leans awkwardly over a table as he pins down and slashes the throat of another victim, whose blood gushes into a golden vessel at the foot of the table. On the right, flames rise from an altar.

The facing page, folio 3r (Figure 19), illustrates God's covenant with Noah, the promise, guaranteed by the appearance of a rainbow, that he will never again destroy the earth by flooding:

> And God said, "This is the sign of the covenant I am making between me and you and every living creature with you, a covenant for all generations to come: I have set my rainbow in the clouds, and it will be the sign of the covenant between me and the earth. Whenever I bring clouds over the earth and the rainbow appears in the clouds, I will remember my covenant between me and you and all living creatures of every kind. Never again will the waters become a flood to destroy all life. Whenever the rainbow appears in the clouds, I will see it and remember the everlasting covenant between God and all living creatures of every kind on the earth."
>
> (Genesis 9: 12–17)

Noah and his three sons stand in a neat row along the groundline within a painted rectangular field. A blue sky with patchy pink clouds forms the backdrop, covering the purple parchment completely. Above them, a pink and green

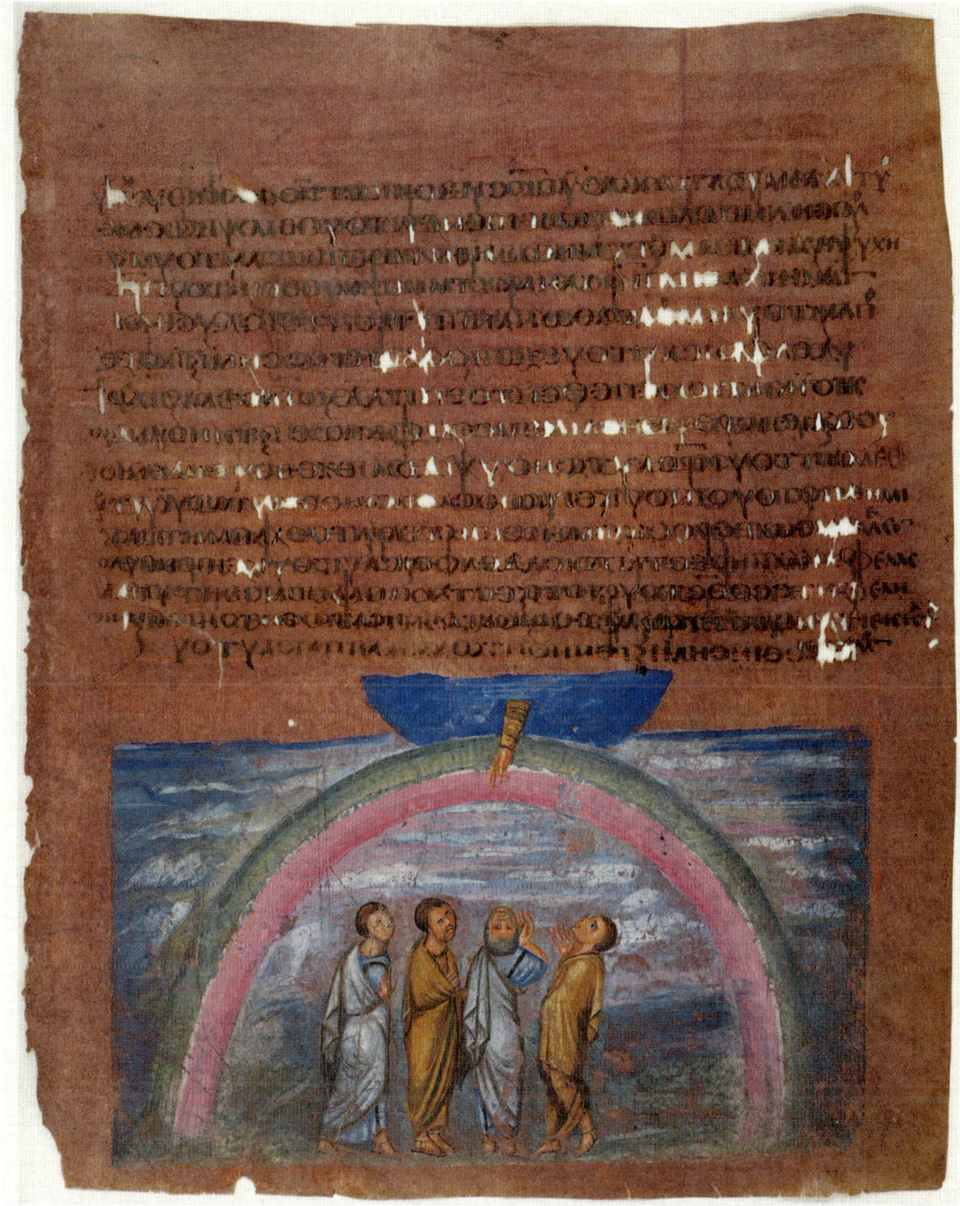

19. God's covenant with Noah, Vienna Genesis, sixth century, Cod. Theol. Gr. 31, fol. 3r, Österreichisches Nationalbibliothek. Photo: Courtesy of the Österreichisches Nationalbibliothek

rainbow stretches from one side of the composition to the other. In a lunette projecting from the rectangular field above the rainbow's apex, the hand of God appears, extending down across the colored arc in a gesture indicating speech. This is the moment in which God confirms his promise. The figures below respond, turning, lifting their eyes, and craning their necks, the better to see the rainbow and hear the voice of God. Noah, gray haired and bearded, wears a white toga and stands immediately below the hand of God, his back toward the viewer, his head thrown back, his right hand raised in wonder. Two sons flank him, each wearing long dark garments as they bend back to look to the sky. On the far left, the third son leans into the action. Clad in a white robe, he too turns his eyes heavenward, a hand raised in astonishment.

Wickhoff's own account of the miniatures was spare. Appearing as one of a series of descriptions in the general catalogue of the manuscript's images, it was limited to a basic description of the episodes.[6] Style was touched on only in the catalogue's prefatory remarks, where it was used as a diagnostic tool to assign artistic hands. Here Wickhoff noted that the Genesis was the work of several artists, some of whom had been trained in the manuscript tradition, others in workshops dedicated to monumental painting. To the former he ascribed a more linear style, to the latter more overtly illusionistic tendencies. In the course of this brief discussion Wickhoff assigned all but one of the first sixteen miniatures of the codex to the same painter, an artist he dubbed "the Miniaturist" as a reflection of his training in the manuscript tradition. The odd picture out was folio 3r, the covenant.[7]

Subsequent studies followed Wickhoff's lead, using stylistic considerations to address the interlocking questions of date, provenance, and artistic hands. Now recognized as a work of sixth-century manufacture, the manuscript was said to have a "classical" style that led Wickhoff and others of his generation to argue for an earlier date, in the fifth or even fourth century. Discussions of provenance then and now have assigned the Vienna Genesis unequivocally to the eastern Roman world, but there agreement has ended: Anatolia, Alexandria, Constantinople, and Syria have all been proposed as the manuscript's source. On the matter of hands, opinion has been equally varied. Kondakov and Ainalov attributed the codex to a single artist.[8] Others have argued for a division of labor, positing as few as six painters or as many as eleven. Whatever the verdict regarding numbers, all publications have steadfastly rejected Wickhoff's assessment and attributed the first eight folios to which the Noah miniatures belong to a single hand.[9]

For the most part, these assessments have been based on formal analyses. Compositions unfold within a single plane, with figures whose volume is expressed through modeling in light and shade dispersed along the ground line. Within these compositions, rich black lines articulate edges and borders. Details confirm these general similarities. The figures themselves are clearly related. Oval heads with large brows, full cheeks, and small, delicate features compressed into the center of the face characterize cranial structure. In the male figures, hair sweeps back in a neat, pomaded arc that springs from the center of the forehead. Hands are uniformly large with long, snaky digits. In both humans and animals, eyes are depicted using a sharp black dot that dominates the white.

Recent technical analysis supports these stylistic observations. The miniatures appear on the same bifolio, making it likely that they were painted by the same artist, identified in the recent restoration of the manuscript as Painter A. Pigment analysis confirms this supposition. Both the color palette and its chemical composition distinguish the work. The palette itself is restricted compared to that of other painters. Further, certain pigments or combinations of pigments are found only in the miniatures of the first eight folios.[10] These similarities notwithstanding, the miniatures approach the mimetic process from two very different points of view.

Folio 2v, the disembarkation from the ark and the sacrifice of Noah, offers an enthusiastic elaboration of these two sequential moments outlined in the accompanying biblical account. Iconography vividly augments the written story. While the text describes the departure from the ark by referring generally to "every living thing," the image does not hesitate to present a specific catalogue of what such creatures might be, everything from exotic elephants and domestic cattle to birds and snakes. In addition, Noah and the individual members of his family are precisely characterized. Noah appears in the white toga of a Roman citizen, his long white hair and beard describing his patriarchal status by borrowing from the imagery of philosophers.[11] His daughters-in-law, clad in brilliant tones of red and blue, confirm the elite association. Below, at the sacrifice, there is similar iconographic augmentation in the precise rendering of the slain beasts, Noah's straining pose, the gush of sacrificial blood, the flicker and glow of the altar's sacred fire.

Throughout the miniature, line, color, and composition enhance this development of the subject matter. In its account of the disembarkation, the upper register is as visually dense as the biblical account is verbally spare. From the massive block of the ark on the left to the delicate tips of the elephants' trunks on the right, people and animals fill the visual field, their overlapping forms differentiated from one another by short bursts of line and color. Alternating patches of color articulate the members of Noah's family, and animals appear in differing shades of brown and gray, their individual forms sharpened by daubs of paint and energetic, snaking lines that capture the sway of a back or the swell of a chest. Bright flecks of white describe the gleam of a tusk or the flash of light on a haunch. This vivid articulation of the scene with line and color uses formal variation to break up the visual field, an effect that captures the sense of motion as the figures burst from the closed quarters of the ark and surge forward, silhouetted against the manuscript's purple ground. This undulating profile further energizes the image. Rising on the left in a series of sharp angles, it gains the peak of the ark before descending in a like manner on the opposite side to meet the rounded forms of the human protagonists. Here it ascends again, outlining the curves of their heads and shoulders. On its descent the line joins and traces the rising and falling curves of the animals' bodies, before swooping over the massive backs of the elephants to end in a delicate flourish at the tips of the great beasts' trunks. At the bottom of the register, above the ground line, the legs and bellies of the animals create an equally complex profile.

The illuminator used many of the same tactics in the lower register, but with a more restrained hand. As in the disembarkation, an undulating profile sets the forms off against the purple ground. The line slides down the slopes of Ararat, traces the outline of the sacrificial beasts, and sweeps up and around the figure of Noah before cascading with the victim's blood into the sacrificial vessel where it stops, leaving the altar detached and isolated to one side. Less complex in its undulations and more restrained in its movement, the silhouette corresponds to the comparatively spare composition of the lower register where the crowded conditions of the upper scene give way to an open setting structured as a series of three separate pyramidal forms along the groundline: Ararat to the left, Noah in the center, the altar to the right. Within the individual areas, close attention is paid to expressive detail. Intricate lines sketch the heap of dead animals, the folds of Noah's garments, the shape of the vessel. Color complements the use of line. Concentrated in bright patches around the central figure of Noah, it calls attention to the patriarch and his actions. In contrast to the somber tones of the landscape, Noah's white robes gleam, as do the flow of blood, the golden receptacle, and the flames on the nearby altar. In combination, line and color focus attention on the individual groups, particularly that of Noah.

Folio 3r, God's covenant with Noah, offers a starkly different vision. The episode is depicted in a single frame, and there is scant elaboration on the biblical text. Only the protagonists, Noah and his sons – their costume and physiognomy consistent with that of the previous miniature – appear in a setting that includes nothing more than the spare ground, a bright, cloud-tufted sky, and an arching rainbow. Above, the hand of God signals the divine presence.

Style complements this reductive conception of the event. The horizontal ground line and the floating clouds, coupled with the discrete vertical forms of the standing figures, establish a subtle visual grid. The radiant pink and green rainbow anchors the composition as it stretches across this framework. Behind it, lush clouds, tinged with pink, merge evenly into a deep blue at the composition's edge. Beneath the rainbow, the vertical forms of Noah and his sons, each one isolated from the other, rise in monumental profile above the groundline. The alternation of white and brown garments articulates their separation. At the same time, details unify the group. Poses echo one another along the line to create a sense of cohesion. The figures on either end, one clad in brown, the other in white, turn toward the center, their stances and gestures mirroring one another. At the center, Noah and his son share the same contrapposto pose, the one seen from the rear, the other from the side. A spill of neatly folded drapery from Noah's shoulder overlaps with and merges into the line of his son's garment to bind the two together. Only the rocking form of the inverted lunette and the diagonally placed hand of God that erupts from it disrupt the structure, a visual formulation of the divine's jolting manifestation.

From one page to the next, magisterial stasis replaces vivid action, as the hurly-burly of the ark's unloading gives way first to pious devotion and then to divine revelation. This formal shift must have played no small part in Wickhoff's decision to assign the miniatures to different artists, yet as ancient discussions of narrative indicate, such stylistic changes had less to do with individual artistic preference than with the demands of subject matter. Artists, like rhetoricians, had a developed sense of what constituted proper narrative style.

ON SUBJECT AND STYLE IN ANCIENT NARRATIVE

The discussion of narrative (*diegesis/narratio*), which encompassed a range of subjects and genres that included poetry and prose, myth and history, had a long history in antiquity. First examined by Plato and Aristotle in the fifth and fourth centuries BC, and then by Greek and Latin authors in the Hellenistic and Imperial ages, it remained the subject of speculation over 1,000 years later, as indicated by the late commentaries of Greek and Latin scholiasts.[12]

Throughout this long period, one issue emerged early and remained a mainstay of analytical discussion: the relationship between content and form, that is, between the raw material of a story (*logos*) and its interpretive presentation, or style (*lexis*). As Dionysius of Halicarnassus observed, the same story in the hands of two different authors was likely to be told with different approaches and to different effect.[13] In other words, style mattered: It was *lexis*, not *logos*, that shaped a story and gave it resonance.[14]

This concept was as germane to history writing as it was to other literary endeavors, precisely because of its narrative content. As Lucian of Samosata (second century) observed:

> For all the body of the history is simply a long narrative. So let it be adorned with the virtues proper to narrative, progressing smoothly, evenly and consistently, free from humps and hollows. Then let its clarity be limpid, achieved, as I have said, both by diction and the interweaving of the matter.[15]

In other words, it was the historian's task to bring the past to life in a verbal style appropriate to the action. It was also the writer's duty to avoid bias, for history had but one task – to be a useful guide to the present, an end achieved only by telling the truth.[16]

The ability to achieve this end demanded the recognition of agreed-upon protocols, one of which concerned narrative's domain. Narrative was, first and foremost, the proper medium with which to explore everyday subjects, and those subjects, which included war, human relations, activities of the gods, events in the heavens and the underworld, and the origins of gods and heroes, required the use of everyday language.[17] Within this varied repertoire, the method of delivery, or "diction," might vary according to subject or speaker, but in doing so it always adhered to the conceit of the familiar.[18]

For historians, this mandate was especially important, for, as Lucian counseled, it was in straightforward, unelaborated speech that a writer found clarity:

> Now as to his language and power of expression, he need not at the beginning of his work sharpen his teeth to perfect proficiency in that vehement, sharp-fanged style that you know, packed with periods, and intricate with logical reasoning or other features of clever rhetoric. No, his tone should be more pacific, his thought coherent and well-knit, his language exact and statesmanlike, of a kind to set forth the subject with the utmost clarity and accuracy.[19]

Such clarity, in turn, represented the essence of truthful, unbiased expression:

> For just as we set free expression and truthfulness as the target for the historian's mind, so for his language this should be the first aim: to set forth the matter exactly and to expound it as lucidly as possible, using neither unknown or out-of-the-way words nor that vulgar language of the marketplace, but such as ordinary folk may understand and the educated commend. Then, let figures adorn the work that give no offence and in particular appear unlabored; otherwise, he makes language seem like highly seasoned sauces.[20]

For all its insistence on the necessity for clear, unlabored language, Lucian's discussion remained opaque about the details. His older contemporary, Hermogenes of Tarsus, had no such reserve. In the course of his musings on rhetoric, a category that overlapped with history, Hermogenes explained both the content and diction of everyday language. To begin with, it sticks to the facts, resisting the siren call of the extraneous. In addition, and in support of this basic content, it uses straightforward constructions in which nouns appear in the nominative case, short clauses deliver complete thoughts, and rhythms are conversational. For Hermogenes, this spare, unlabored language was the hallmark of a style he referred to as Clarity.[21]

To pursue Clarity in the sounds, structures, and rhythms of this daily speech was at heart a mimetic enterprise, one that had its counterpart in the world of visual representation in the straightforward depiction of the physical world that was visual mimesis's stock-in-trade. Pliny's tale of Zeuxis and Parrhasius suggested as much. The artists' two paintings – the one of grapes, the other of curtains – were nothing if not bare facts whose essential look was that of everyday reality.[22]

Clarity was not, however, static. Rather, it was a basic language that could be manipulated to expressive effect. In the verbal context, changes in word order, elaboration of sentences, and adjustments to vocabulary could embellish subject matter and in so doing tip the stylistic scales. Added information supplied parenthetically or in subordinate clauses might enrich a presentation. Conversely, pared-down phrases might drain it. Such manipulations of language built on the foundation of Clarity, their use dictated by their appropriateness to subject matter and context. Whatever the combination of styles, the goal was to direct listener response by using style to shape the presentation of basic facts.[23]

The miniatures in the Vienna Genesis, which were visualizations of sacred history, suggest an affinity with this approach to storytelling.[24] Individually and in tandem, the two scenes described above work from a baseline of visual Clarity to demonstrate the kind of lucid depiction of events expected of historical writing and, by extension, historical images. At the same time, each image builds on and transforms this basic formal model, the one by elaborating on form and content, the other by restricting it.

Elaboration governs both subject matter and style in Folio 2v, the embarkation from the ark and the sacrifice of Noah. The combination of the two scenes, and their distribution across two registers sets the tone with the creation of an elaborate panorama. Within each scene, a rich supply of anecdotal detail supplements the bare facts of the biblical account. In the upper register, the intricate use of line, variations in color, and compositional density complement and enhance the iconographic elaboration. In the lower register, the retreat from compositional crowding, together with a more restrained use of line and focused use of color, creates a calmer, more subdued, and deliberate image.

Hermogenes suggests some ways of thinking about this elaboration on the miniature's basic Clarity in his descriptions of verbal styles. Abundance (*Peribole*) or Fullness (*Mestotes*), characterized by the addition of information and the breakdown of a narrative into its constituent parts, finds a striking counterpart in the miniature's imaginative elaboration of content and the division of the composition into registers.[25] Further, the intricate treatment of line, color, and composition lends a feel analogous to a style known as Rapidity (*Gorgotes*). Recognizable verbally by the use of short choppy lines, Rapidity is designed to instill a speech with energy and vitality. In the miniature, the undulating lines of the cavalcade of animals coupled with changing flecks of color work to similar effect. Formal differences between the upper and lower registers also augment the sense of elaboration. The more subdued image of Noah's sacrifice plays off against the exuberance of the disembarkation, functioning as a kind of character study in contrast to the action scene above. Here the image suggests Sincerity (*Alethinos*).[26] Simple and without undue elaboration, the language of Sincerity is that of earnest, unadorned prayer, a sense of absolute devotion captured in the spare composition and focus on Noah as he leans into his awkward pose, the picture of pious concentration.

Contained within the framework of a single miniature, these contrasting episodes – the one expansive, the other focused – combine to reinforce an overall sense of Abundance. The point was not elaboration for its own sake; rather, Abundance served the specific end of instilling Clarity with a larger sense of what Hermogenes referred to as Grandeur (*Megesthes*), a broader stylistic interpretation that served an important end. If Clarity made clear what was happening, Grandeur impressed upon viewers the significance of what was depicted.[27]

On the opposite page, folio 3r, showing God's covenant with Noah, the artist takes a different tack, approaching the narrative not with the end of elaboration but with one of Severity. The single frame, sparsely inhabited, presents a very different picture than that of the boisterous eruption from the ark or Noah's absorbed act of sacrifice. The compositional grid, coupled with the bold arc of the rainbow, suggests a parallel with Hermogenes' description of Solemnity (*Semnotes*), a style characterized by direct, unambiguous statements made in steady unhesitating rhythms whose regular, uncompromising forms capture the sense of majesty appropriate to divine subjects.[28] At the same time, unusual details, such as the hand of God erupting from the inverted lunette and Noah's startling pose, offer relief from this formal intensity in a manner that suggest Subtlety (*Drimytes*), the use of unexpected diction.[29] If the Solemnity of the overall image creates the sense of grandeur and majesty appropriate to the divine, Subtlety makes manifest the uncanny nature of the event to charge the picture with a sense of new beginnings attendant upon the moment of divine revelation.[30]

Ultimately, the pair of images functioned as an ensemble that used the subtle instrument of style to shape not only the look of individual episodes but also the larger narrative trajectory. As the sequence suggests, style was conceived not as a unitary, unflinching formal solution but as a layered, evocative phenomenon whose shifting forms were designed to draw out the underlying import of the story, in keeping with the true aims of mimesis. Thus, in the passage from the exuberant release of the disembarkation through Noah's sacrifice to the awesome experience of the theophany, Abundance and Sincerity play off against Solemnity to create an overarching sense of Grandeur in the visualization of the portentous interactions that set the course for humanity's true and enduring relationship with the divine.

SANTA MARIA MAGGIORE

A century before the artists of the Vienna Genesis set to the task of illuminating the facts of biblical history in the intimate context of the codex, mosaicists at the church of Santa Maria Maggiore in Rome undertook a similar enterprise in the grand public venue of a papal building project (Figure 20). The church was completed during the pontificate of Sixtus III (432–440) as a three-aisled, wooden-roofed basilica with a projecting apse. Marble columns in the Ionic order surmounted by a molded stucco architrave separated the nave from the side aisles in an uninterrupted march from the western entrance to the eastern apse. In the clerestory, windows pierced the wall above each of the intercolumniations. Colossal Corinthian order pilasters in stucco framed the windows, rising from the nave arcade to the ceiling. Within this architectural setting, forty-two individually framed mosaic panels depicting episodes from the Old Testament books of Genesis, Exodus, Deuteronomy, and Joshua (twenty-one on either side) were mounted below the windows in stucco aediculae. Scenes from the lives of Abraham, Isaac, and Jacob occupied the south wall, episodes from the lives of Moses and Joshua the north.[31] Although construction in the building and restorations of the mosaics have altered the

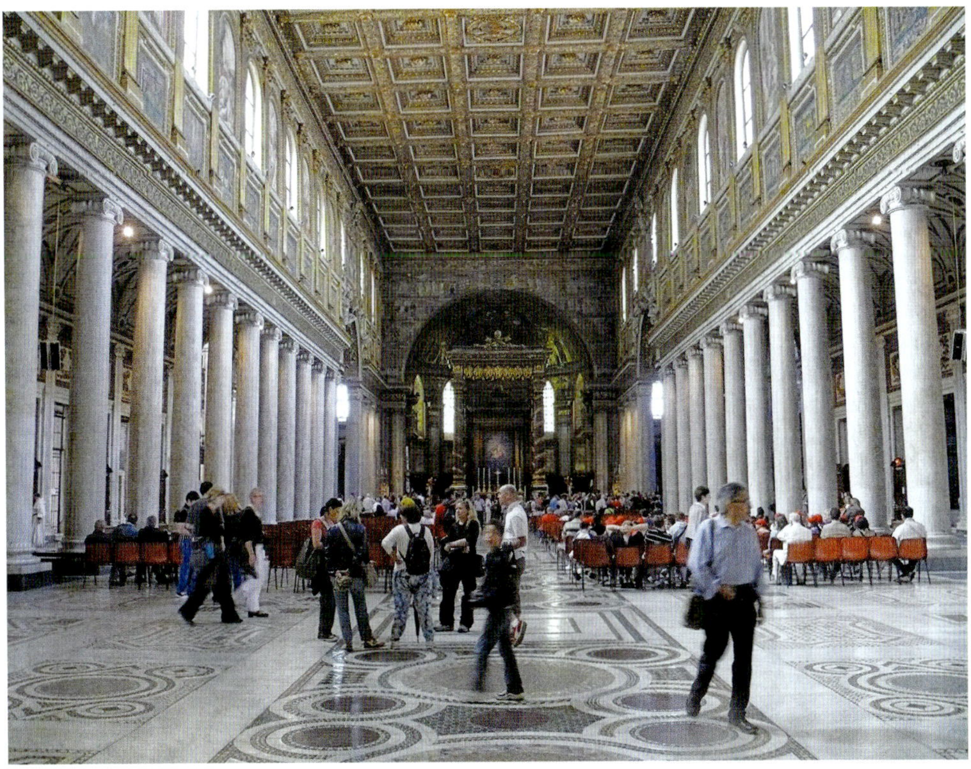

20. Nave, Santa Maria Maggiore, Rome, fifth century with later additions and restorations. Photo: S. Bassett

cycle over time, it nevertheless remains one of the most extensively preserved narratives from late antiquity. As such, it offers a monumental counterpart to the miniature painting of the Vienna Genesis.[32]

Ever since the nineteenth century, when the building's decor, which included both the nave and the triumphal arch mosaics, first began to be a topic of art historical appraisal, style has been at the center of the discussion. Nineteenth-century observers were struck by the mosaics' seemingly classical style, especially in light of the fifth-century date established by inscription in the mosaics of the triumphal arch. Manifest in atmospheric, spatially conceived compositions into which ponderated figures depicting standard types in the Roman repertoire were coherently integrated, this classicism was understood to be inferior to the efforts of the early and high imperial age, but it was impressive all the same.[33]

In the wake of Riegl's theories, the surety of this judgment changed. Having established that the operative style of late antiquity was crystalline, Riegl's thinking made a fifth-century date for such traditionally conceived images seem impossible. The solution was to re-date them. The impediment to doing so lay in the evidence of the arch inscription. In an effort to resolve this problem, it was decided that the two mosaic cycles – the one on the arch, the other in the nave – must be the result of separate, chronologically distant campaigns. Further, although previously understood as a stylistically coherent project, the mosaics were now seen to have radically different styles. As a result, the classicizing nave mosaics were assigned a date as early as the second century in some arguments, while the arch mosaics, newly defined as abstract and Byzantinizing, retained their fifth-century designation.[34]

Eventually, the mid-twentieth-century autopsy of the building together with restoration and study of the mosaics put paid to the idea of a chronological divide, and the Old Testament mosaics were reinstated as works of fifth-century manufacture.[35] Nevertheless, discomfort, owing to their style, remains. Ernst Kitzinger, for one, acknowledged their close relationship to classical precedent, while simultaneously arguing from the example of a single panel – the separation of Abraham and Lot – for their essentially abstract and expressionistic character.[36] It is, however, useful to see this panel, and others of its ilk, as products of the same system of stylistic understanding that produced the Vienna Genesis.

The separation of Abraham and Lot (Figure 21)[37] illustrates events from Genesis 13: 8–12 in which Abraham and Lot, in an effort to address overcrowding on the land, agree to go their separate ways:

> So Abram said to Lot, "Let's not have any quarreling between you and me, or between your herders and mine, for we are close relatives. Is not the whole land before you? Let's part company. If you go to the left, I'll

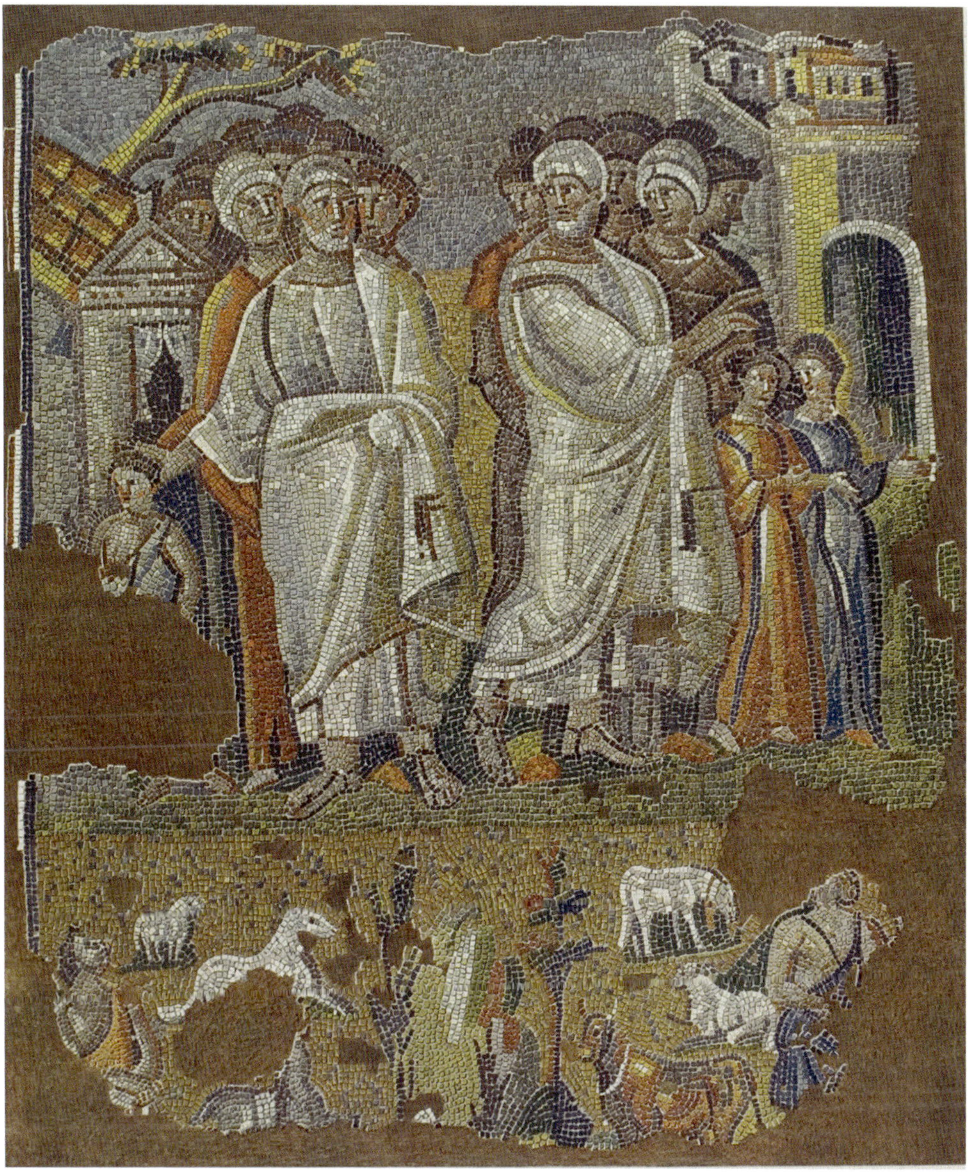

21. Separation of Abraham and Lot, Santa Maria Maggiore, Rome, fifth century. Watercolor record of the mosaic prior to its mid-twentieth-century restoration by J. Wilpert. After J. Wilpert, *Die römische Mosaiken und Malereien der kirchlichen Bauten vom IV. Bis XIII. Jahrhundert* (Friebürg im Breisgau, 1916): v. 3, plate 9. Photo: Courtesy of the Heidelberg University Library

go to the right; if you go to the right, I'll go to the left." Lot looked around and saw that the whole plain of the Jordan toward Zoar was well watered, like the garden of the Lord, like the land of Egypt. (This was before the Lord destroyed Sodom and Gomorrah.) So Lot chose for himself the whole plain of the Jordan and set out toward the east. The

> two men parted company: Abram lived in the land of Canaan, while Lot lived among the cities of the plain and pitched his tents near Sodom.

As is consistently the case with biblical passages, the description is spare. Apart from a glancing reference to the fertile Jordanian plain, appearances of people and places go unmentioned, making it the artist's task to envision the moment.

The image the mosaicist devised occupies the upper half of a two-register panel framed by a red, white, and blue border. In the lower portion, shepherds attend to sheep and cattle, their gazes turned to the action above, which takes place in a landscape constructed of three tiers: A verdant foreground on which the protagonists interact rises to meet a gold middle ground, which in turn gives way to blue sky. Abraham and Lot, each at the head of a group, dominate the composition. Abraham, on the left, appears with white hair and beard in the old-fashioned white *toga praetexta* of a Roman citizen of a bygone age.[38] He stands facing forward in a contrapposto pose, his lowered right hand reaching out to cup the head of a child, as he turns toward his left to look at his nephew. Behind him, largely concealed, stands his wife, Sarah, wearing an orange robe and white head covering. She too gazes toward Lot's group, locking eyes with her nephew's wife. A group of figures indicated by a cluster of heads, two of which exchange glances with one another, lines up behind her. A small building and a tree appear behind them. On the right, Lot – also depicted with white hair, beard, and toga – rotates away from Abraham, glancing back over his right shoulder toward his uncle. His right hand gestures across his body indicating the direction of his travel. Lot's wife, who wears a brown cloak and a white head cloth, stands behind him, returning Sarah's glance. His little daughters, their heads bare as an index of their youth, wear complementary blue and orange garments as they move in the direction of Lot's gesture. A cluster of heads behind them indicates a large group of travelers. Behind them stands a walled city, the Zoar of the biblical passage.

The composition's three tiers create a sense of spatial recession, and the two family groups balance the composition, filling it to nearly its full height as they recede into the background. Light-and-shade modeling gives weight, volume, and monumentality to Abraham and Lot, creating the sensation that the great swaths of cloth wrapped around their bodies respond to their movements. The bright upper edges of highlighted folds descend into shadowy recesses as fabric bunches around a hip or an arm at the grasp of a hand or the turn of a torso. Line also contributes to the sense of vitality, the undulating borders of the garments' edges suggesting the sway of fabric as it responds to bodily motion. Color enhances the sense of space and the compositional balance within the frame. A jagged cleft of gold tesserae at the center of the composition divides the two groups. On either side, the protagonists' white robes draw attention to the figures and their position at the front of the picture plane, while the warm colors of the women's garments and the dark figures behind them create the sense of recession within the landscape as they merge with the more subdued tones of the surrounding environment. Delicate color variations in the sky above and behind create an atmospheric quality. Although the two groups are clearly divided from one another, distribution of color binds the scene into a single whole. Abraham's white robes are mirrored by Lot's, and the oranges and blues of the secondary figures' garments are balanced across the composition.[39]

Surviving panels show similar characteristics. Throughout the nave, whether in double-register compositions or single-field representations, the same tripartite organization of the spatial setting predominates. Buildings and landscape elements anchor and frame complex groupings, and there is, throughout, an emphasis on balanced, lively composition, an effect achieved through the placement of forms and the distribution of color. Overall, the sense is one of stylistic Clarity. Yet within this homogeneous matrix, images also show individualized treatments that respond to the nature of their subject matter.

In the case of Abraham and Lot, iconographic and stylistic Abundance shapes the episode. With respect to iconography, the inclusion of landscape elements and the expanded cast of characters offer an inventive elaboration of the event. In contrast to the text, which refers only to Abraham and Lot, the mosaic envisions two complete households down to the details of individual appearance. The two protagonists, who are herdsmen, appear in white togas, the guise of elite Roman citizens of the early imperial period. This dress, antiquated by the fourth century, was, in the fifth century, associated with a golden age of virtue and simplicity.[40] Similarly, their white hair and beards summoned images of wise men or philosophers.[41]

Compositional solutions also support a style of Abundance, specifically, the division of the scene into two balanced groups in which line and color articulate individual elements within the whole. Line, created not only by outlining figures to set them apart from one another but also in the radiating drapery folds that shape the bodies of Abraham and Lot, further elaborates the scene, as do the application of varied patches of color to the individual figures and the treatment of proportion. Abraham and Lot are depicted using a Polyclitan proportional scheme, a choice that, coupled with the decision to show them in contrapposto poses, lends weight and gravity to their figuration.

As in the Vienna Genesis, these choices respond to the mandate that images offer a convincing approximation of the physical world with stylistic layering designed to direct viewers' understanding. Here Abundance enhances Clarity to lend a sense of Grandeur, which conveys the magnitude of the moment in which Abraham takes the first steps toward the realization of his destiny and Lot heads toward his destruction.

Across the aisle, in the south clerestory, scenes from the life of Moses show a similar propensity for Abundance as they elaborate on the terse biblical accounts of the prophet's life. They do so, however, in different ways, as the marriage of Moses and Sepphora (Figure 22) demonstrates. Mentioned only elliptically in the single sentence, "Moses agreed to stay with the man, who

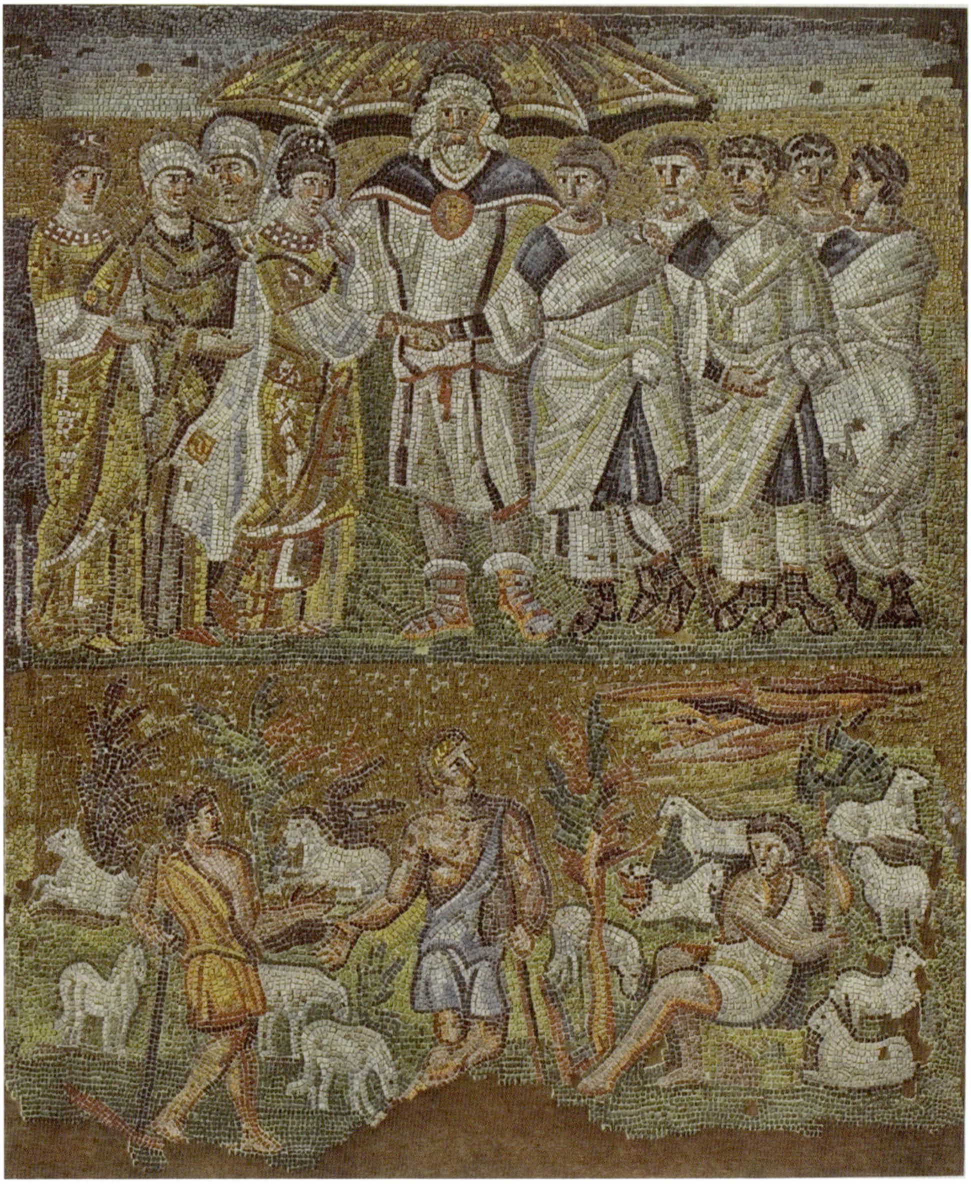

22. Marriage of Moses and Sepphora, Santa Maria Maggiore, Rome, fifth century. Watercolor record of the mosaic prior to its mid-twentieth-century restoration by J. Wilpert. After J. Wilpert, *Die römische Mosaiken und Malereien der kirchlichen Bauten vom IV. Bis XIII. Jahrhundert* (Frieburg im Breisgau, 1916): v. 3, plate 17. Photo: Courtesy of the Heidelberg University Library

gave his daughter Sepphora to Moses in marriage" (Exodus 2.21), the event receives elaborate treatment.[42] The setting is an open landscape. As in the separation of Abraham and Lot, figures stand along a green ground line, which rises to a golden middle ground before giving way to blue sky above. At the center of this atmospheric setting, three figures gather beneath a hovering golden canopy. In the middle, the towering figure of Jethro, the father of Sepphora and a Midian priest, dominates the composition. He faces forward, his arms outstretched to enclose the couple as he performs the ceremony. Sepphora, resplendent in a gold gown, stands on the left, and Moses, clad in the white toga of a late Roman consul, on the right. Each holds the right hand of the other. Attendants witness the celebration. Four men in similar dress stand behind Moses, and three sumptuously dressed women support Sepphora. On the far left, what appears to have been a fourth member of the female party is only partly visible, the tesserae having fallen away and been replaced in an incomplete manner.[43]

The elaboration of the subject matter draws on the iconography of Roman weddings. As they stand before Jethro with their hands clasped, Moses and Sepphora enact the *dextrarum iunctio*, the joining of right hands that represents the central act of union in Roman marriage ceremonial.[44] Dress also conforms to Roman standards. As in the separation of Abraham and Lot, Moses and his cohort wear the toga; however, they do so here in its late antique styling, known as the *trabea*. Characterized by stiff, flat bands that wrapped around both shoulders, it was associated with the magisterial class, suggesting the no-nonsense character of Moses and his companions. Correspondingly, Sepphora and her attendants wear the dress of late Roman aristocratic women. Architectural imagery also follows Roman models, with the canopy under which they stand represented as a segmented pumpkin dome.

In the same way that iconography suggests Abundance, so too do aspects of style. As in the separation of Abraham and Lot, the composition is divided into two contrasting groups, each of which is further broken down into its individual components. On the right, Moses and his cohort present a stolid, unified façade matched by that of the women on the left. The manipulation of line, color, and proportion differentiates the two groups. Among the men, light, shade, and line shape square, solid figures whose overlapping bodies stand in contrapposto poses, each straight leg creating a regular vertical pulse along the line. Dress solidifies the impression. The triangular shape of the diagonal fold of the *trabea*, the stiff cloth that wraps around the shoulders of each of the male participants, repeats itself down the row with minor variation. Below, narrow folds in the drapery echo the verticality of the straight leg, while even hemlines at knee and ankle introduce a stabilizing horizontal line. Isocephaly enforces the visual solidarity. In the female group, elongated proportions, coupled with the rich patterning of textiles and the fall of drapery in gently undulating diagonal lines, create a different look. The contrast between the male and female cohorts, between simplicity and elaboration, confirms the image of Abundance. It also suggests the use of two complementary stylistic strategies, Solemnity and Sweetness. Solemnity characterizes the sober, sturdy forms of Moses' group, while the treatment of Sepphora and her companions suggests Sweetness, a style associated with the decorative elaboration appropriate to pleasing subject matter.

Other formal tactics also help to shape the image. Specifically, symmetry, frontality, and hierarchy of scale give visual life to the idea of union at the heart of the episode's subject. Jethro's centrally placed figure acts as the compositional lynchpin around which the two figural groups balance. His frontal pose and commanding scale, which far outstrips that of anyone else, demand attention and indicate that he is the crux of the action. The two groups flanking him gather under the canopy, joined physically by the priest's encompassing embrace and the connective action of the *dextrarum iunctio*. Pose further cements the idea of union, providing a counterbalance to the stylistic distinctions introduced by the treatment of line and color in the individual groups. Moses and Sepphora step toward one another, the stance of the one mirroring that of the other. Figures to either side of the couple are arranged similarly, with the exception of the two male figures on the right who, as wedding guests are wont to do, turn and chat with one another, a charming detail that relieves the severity of the male line and enhances the notion of Sweetness.

Here, as in the Separation of Abraham and Lot, stylistic Abundance lends Grandeur to the episodes, thus underscoring the magnitude of events and transforming the ordinary into the extraordinary. At the same time, the recognizably different types of subjects – the one an action scene of separation, the other a ceremonial event of union – approach the treatment of Abundance in different ways. In the parting of Abraham and Lot, Abundance alone suffices to visualize the action. In the wedding of Moses and Sepphora, Abundance layered with Solemnity not only creates the sense of Grandeur, but also captures the majesty of prescribed, ritual activity.

Together the separation of Abraham and Lot and the wedding of Moses and Sepphora give a sense of the stylistic language adopted throughout the Old Testament cycle as a whole. As a matter of course, Abundance predominates and through it the sense of Grandeur. To the extent that every image in the nave represented an imaginative elaboration of a thinly worded biblical description, Abundance was of necessity an iconographic and stylistic given. It was not, however, a unitary proposition any more than mimesis itself, and further formal manipulation could easily alter the tenor of representation from one image to another. For example, a style referred to as Vehemence (*Sphodrotes*) was called forth in other scenes.

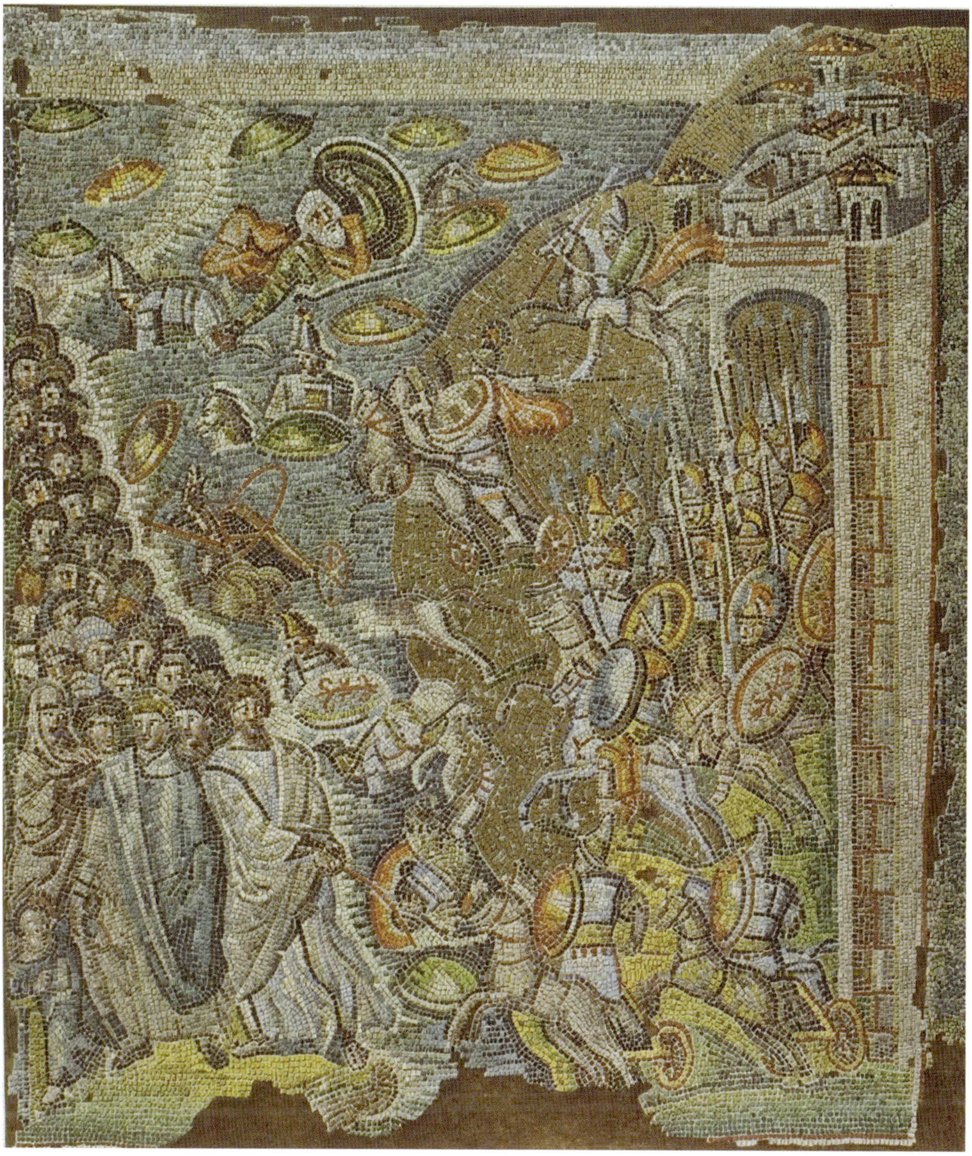

23. Moses and the Israelites crossing the Red Sea, Santa Maria Maggiore, Rome, fifth century. Watercolor record of the mosaic prior to its mid-twentieth-century restoration by J. Wilpert. After J. Wilpert, *Die römische Mosaiken und Malereien der kirchlichen Bauten vom IV. Bis XIII. Jahrhundert* (Frieburg im Breisgau, 1916): 3, plate 18. Photo: Courtesy of the Heidelberg University Library

The crossing of the Red Sea (Figure 23), an event that is given a blow-by-blow account in the biblical text (Exodus 14:1–29), offers a case in point. The scene depicts the cataclysmic moment at the end of the crossing in which the waters of the Red Sea engulf the Egyptian pharaoh and his army as the Israelites cross to safety:

> Then the Lord said to Moses, "Stretch out your hand over the sea so that the waters may flow back over the Egyptians and their chariots and horsemen." Moses stretched out his hand over the sea, and at daybreak the sea went back to its place. The Egyptians were fleeing toward it, and the Lord swept them into the sea. The water flowed back and covered the chariots and horsemen – the entire army of Pharaoh that had followed the Israelites into the sea. Not one of them survived.
>
> (Exodus 4:26–28)

On the left, Moses and Aaron march at the head of the Israelites, who appear behind them in an extended triangular formation as a series of neatly ordered heads. Moses, dressed as a Roman aristocrat, brandishes the staff that sends the waters tumbling in around the Egyptians. A towering palace rises along the right side, its gates opening to a bulging arc of golden sand. The pharaonic army departs from the gate. Within the walls, the troops march in order, their pikes erect. As they pass through the gate, their ranks dissolve as the blue waters of the sea crash into the golden desert, surrounding them and spreading mayhem. The waters themselves dominate the center portion of the scene, extending in an inverted triangle from a narrow band at the lower border to a wide swath at the top. Shields of varying colors scatter on the water's surface, while waves lap at the fallen horses and upended chariots. Pharaoh himself bobs in the water, soon to go under.

Style complements the visual description. Three sections, each demarcated by shape and color, structure the visual field: the marching Israelites led by Moses and Aaron, the swirling blue waters, and the castellated palace set in the golden sands. Within each area, a variety of forms – some ordered, others scattered – articulates the action. The regular series of the marching Israelites' oval, dark-haired heads contrasts with the haphazard distribution of the multi-colored shields and the angular forms of the Egyptians' broken chariots against the blue water. On the far right, the vertical pikes of the soldiers echoing the erect, towering walls soon give way to chaotic angular forms as the soldiers leave the safety of the royal confines.

Structured around the antithesis between order and chaos, the composition once again draws on Abundance to visualize the event, layering it with Vehemence.[45] Designed to express reproach, anger, and impatience, Vehemence is expressed verbally by the cacophonic sounds of short, jolting, arrhythmic phrases, sounds that find their counterpart in the dramatically fractured visual field, the irregular distribution of shape and color, the angled, unruly lines of spears, and the complex broken profiles of figures scattered across the scene. Such Vehemence serves a purpose. Together with Abundance, it adds Grandeur to the moment, but it does so in a novel way. Vehemence's task is to express displeasure with inferiors. Here it conveys the wrath of God brought down upon the Egyptians for their torment and pursuit of the Jews.

CONCLUSIONS

As the mosaics at Santa Maria Maggiore and the miniatures of the Vienna Genesis demonstrate, a common approach to narrative representation shaped storytelling in contexts monumental and miniature. Although continuous narration and an illusionistic rendering of form were sometimes in evidence as Wickhoff had observed, these were not the main criteria for successful storytelling. A figure might appear no more than once in a single frame or be rendered as convincingly with line as through the use of light-and-shade modeling. As the ability to move between line and color suggests, the principle of stylistic variation was far more important to the representational agenda. Working from a foundation of Clarity, artists used variations in line, color, and composition together with changes in proportion and scale to set the visual tone of an image and shape its meaning. This ability to manipulate style with such expertise was referred to as Force (*Deinotes*), "the proper use of style."[46]

Where Force really came into its own was in the structure of the larger story, as individual images, each fashioned according to its own stylistic needs, took their place in the visual line-up to shape the ebb and flow of narrative action. The paired miniatures from the Vienna Genesis make this clear, and the same was doubtless true for the mosaics at Santa Maria Maggiore, although lacunae and restorations make these narrative rhythms more difficult to establish and follow. By contrast, such rhythms are readily visible in a range of first- and second-century imperial monuments, suggesting that the tactics used in church and codex were following well-established traditions.

For example, the second-century Antonine altar from Ephesus, which celebrates the life of the emperor Lucius Verus (161–169), combines moments of action with those of ceremony in ways that presage the use of style in the later images.[47] Monumental reliefs from the U-shaped altar's podium include two reliefs to either side of the entrance staircase: the apotheosis of Verus on the left, Selene in her chariot on the right. Enthroned gods gather along either side of the stairway in the space in front of the altar. Outside, scenes depicting city personifications and an imperial adoption occupy the podium's long sides. A battle rages along the back. Two distinct styles were deployed to interpret these images. In the adoption scene (Figure 24), for example, the focus is on four figures at the center of a processional line. The emperor Hadrian (117–138) appears on the right, and his adoptive son Antoninus Pius (138–161) stands in the middle, flanked in turn by his own adoptive sons, Marcus Aurelius (161–180) on the far left and Verus, shown as a boy, to the right. The scene, which celebrates Antonine dynastic continuity, shares the

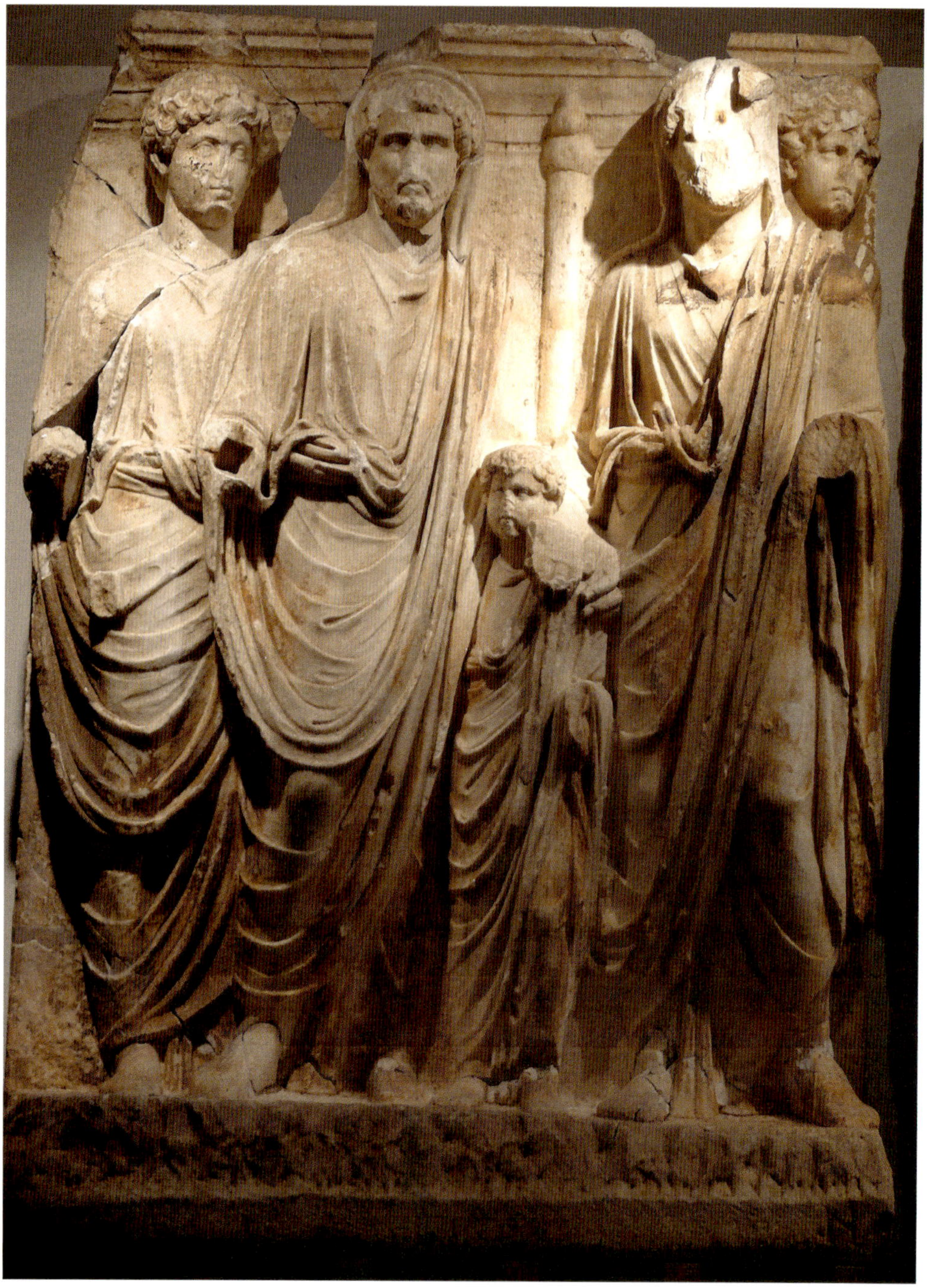

24. Adoption scene, Parthian monument, second century, Ephesus Museum Vienna. Photo: S. Bassett

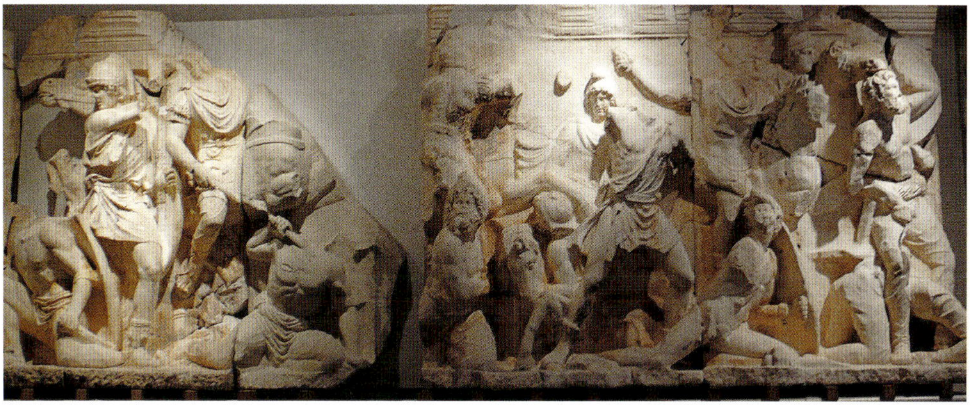

25 Battle scene, Parthian monument, second century, Ephesus Museum, Vienna. Photo: S. Bassett

properties of the ceremonial images in Santa Maria Maggiore and the Vienna Genesis, frontality and symmetry among them. The figures, which all face forward, fill the height of the relief. Distributed at regular, even intervals, they catch the light in such a way as to establish a stately vertical rhythm for the balanced, symmetrical composition, which is not unlike that of Moses and his cohort in the marriage scene. An elegant line, created by the fall of drapery, loops up and down to link the figures in a continuous visual chain. By contrast, the battle relief (Figure 25), which documents the Parthian wars in a series of crowded, frantic combat scenes, builds the composition from intersecting diagonals that create irregular, angled forms and deep, irregular pockets of light and shade, appropriate to the violence in ways familiar from the Exodus.

Similar distinctions appear on the historiated columns dedicated to Trajan and Marcus Aurelius, where mimetic form records the ebb and flow of events and action with scenes capturing both the ordered rhythms of military marches and the mayhem of battle through the strategic manipulation of line and composition.[48] Ordered ranks of troops march in neat, serried layers, their figures erect in parallel lines as they cross the Danube or advance across enemy territory. When these same troops undertake the daily work of conquerors, clearing forests or building fortifications, their forms bend and twist, the calculated angles of their bodies conveying a sense of disciplined action. In ceremonial scenes, as when the emperor offers a sacrifice, symmetrical compositions convey the solemnity of the occasion. Finally, in battle scenes, figures appear in broken ranks at uneven intervals, their limbs and torsos depicted in a variety of angled poses that convey the mayhem and anguish of war. Evidence for the historiated columns of Theodosius I and Arcadius in Constantinople suggests that such stylistic distinctions endured in the commemorative ventures that were heirs to the great Roman monuments.[49]

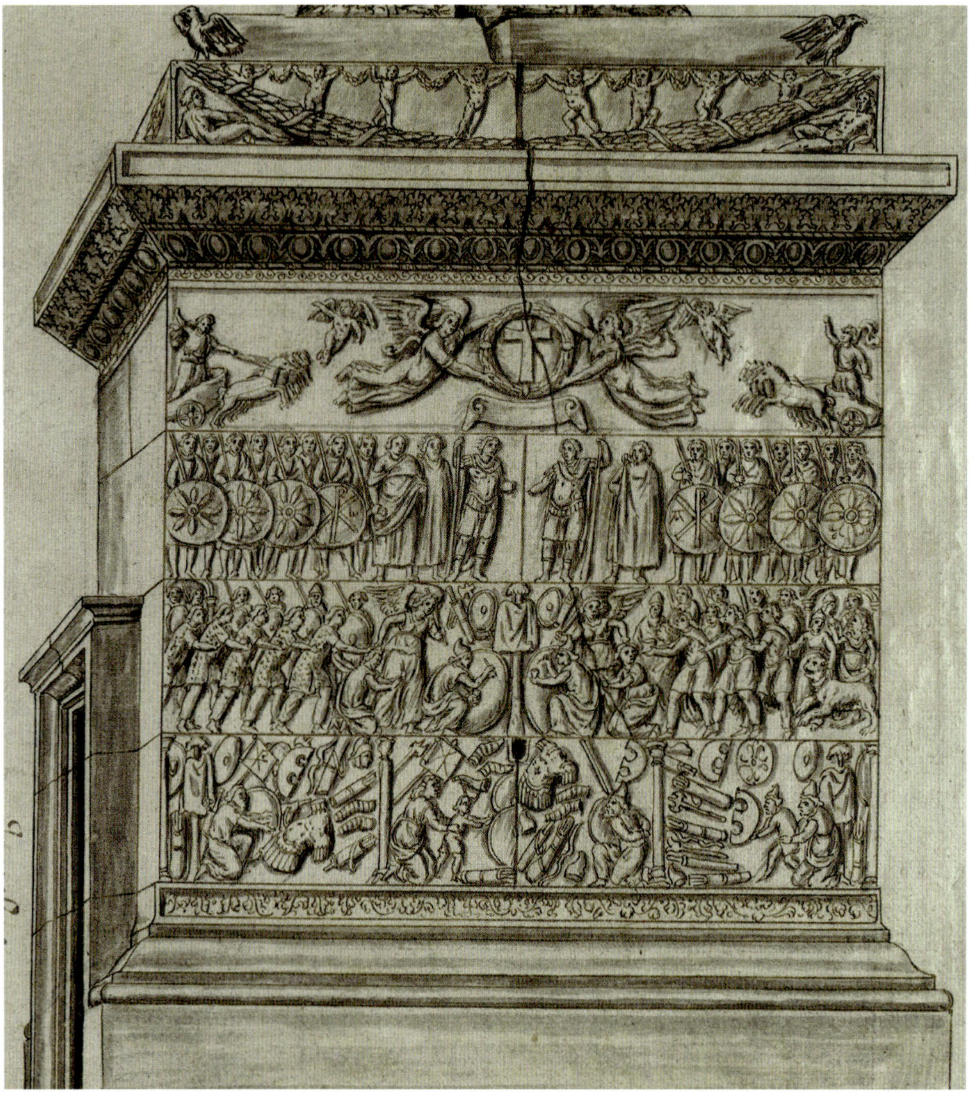

26. Drawing of the base of the Column of Arcadius, Freshfield Album, sixteenth century, Trinity College Library, Cambridge, Ms. O.17.2. Photo: Courtesy of the Master and Fellows of Trinity College, Cambridge

Sixteenth-century drawings of the now dismantled Column of Arcadius, which is thought to have commemorated the victorious campaign against Gainas and the Gothic federates (399–401), indicate that a variety of scenes appeared on the column, military processions, battle scenes, and imperial receptions included. On the base, reliefs depicted the celebration of an imperial victory and the concord between the reigning emperors Arcadius in the East and Honorius in the West (Figure 26). The scenes, which do not commemorate a historical event but represent rather a visual panegyric in praise of the emperors, appear on three sides of the base. On each side, highly regimented compositions are divided into registers, each of which is regulated by frontality and axial symmetry. On the rising relief, the narrative action, which includes military marches, battle scenes, and imperial reviews, unfolds in ways that follow a different stylistic mandate, one devoted to the documentation of events and action. In the lead-up to and aftermath of war, soldiers step out in regular, controlled columns, their individual bodies vertical against the long line of their neatly overlapping and carefully spaced horizontal rows. In the battle itself, this emphasis on order gives way to the use of dense, tangled compositions built up out of intersecting and overlapping diagonal lines. On the south side of the column, depictions of imperial ceremonial, similar to the compositions on the base, punctuate the action at regular intervals (Figure 27). Here, as in the Roman columns that are its predecessors, the Constantinopolitan relief deploys style with the same understanding of its interpretive potential.[50]

As records of Christian history, the mosaics of Santa Maria Maggiore and the miniatures of the Vienna Genesis shared the same sense of style as the great Constantinopolitan columns of their own age and the Roman monuments that came before. To make this observation is not to say that monuments created at different points over a three-hundred-year span were the same. Each was created within the stylistic boundaries of its own historical moment, meaning that circumstances of time, place, medium, and other aspects of manufacture inevitably resulted in formal differences; however, to the extent that these differences involved matters of taste, skill, and technique, they were largely superficial. What all of these monuments shared was an enduring conception of style and its mechanisms, one that placed mimesis at the heart of the representational enterprise, acknowledging as it did its range of formal possibility.

According to this understanding, two things took place simultaneously in the process of mimesis: representation and interpretation. Representation – the depiction of people, places, events, and things – required the Clarity integral to the accurate rendering of form. This was Wickhoff's "progressive and increasingly thoughtful and accurate observation of nature." By contrast, interpretation sought to render underlying meaning. It did so by marshaling the artifices of style. Thus, the frontality and symmetry governing the marriage of Moses and Sepphora pointed to the Solemnity inherent in the ritual moment, while the caustic imagery of Vehemence captured both the horror and the sense of relief implicit in the implementation of divine justice. Extended beyond individual image to narrative whole, the dexterous juxtapositioning of various styles made visible interior worlds, expanding the viewing experience to reveal the truth inherent in Paulinus' "empty image."

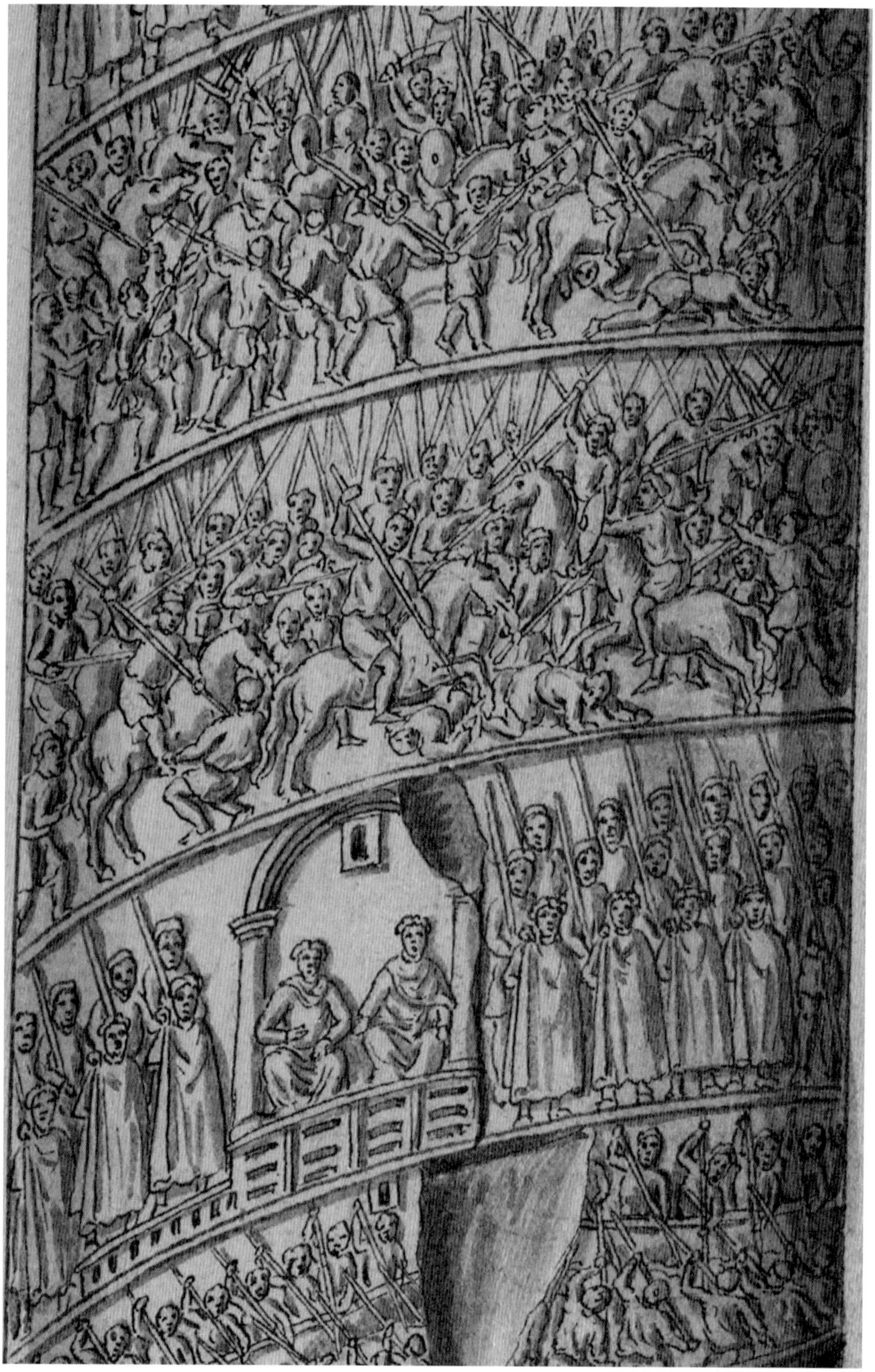

27. Detail of a drawing of the narrative reliefs on the Column of Arcadius, Freshfield Album, sixteenth century, Trinity College Library, Cambridge, Ms. O.17.2. Photo: Courtesy of the Master and Fellows of Trinity College, Cambridge

NOTES

1 Studies of narrative in Greek and Roman art include Torelli 1982; Brilliant 1984; Holliday 1993; 2002. These studies approach visual narrative by focusing largely on the structural and typological analysis of Greek and Roman narrative imagery.

2 On illusionist form, see Wickhoff and Hartel 1895, 28, 64; Wickhoff 1900, 46, 118.

3 Philostratus 1931, 1 (*Imagines* 1 [294K]).

4 Eusebius of Caesarea 1926–1932, 2: 424 (*Ecclesiastical History* 10.4.44)

5 *Carmina* 37.515–516, cited in Goldschmidt 1940, 60–61.

6 Wickhoff and Hartel 1895,146–47. This section was not included in the English translation.

7 Wickhoff and Hartel (1895, 144–45, 162–66) identify the individual painters as the Miniaturist, the Colorist, and three Illusionists. Ch. 5 addresses the intersection of miniature painting and monumental painting. See Wickhoff and Hartel 1895, 88–89, 96; Wickhoff 1900, 173, 189–90.

8 Kondakov 1886, 1: 78–95; Ainalov 1961, 124–31. Both thought that stylistic differences between miniatures could be accounted for by the fact that they were copied from different sources.

9 Wickhoff identified seven painters. Gerstinger (1931) and Hofmann (2020) follow Wickhoff's count. Morey (1929, 12) and Zimmermann (2003) identify six hands. Buberl (1936) proposed nine, and Mazal (1980) suggested eleven. In spite of this disagreement, all, save Wickhoff, attribute the two folios to the same artist. For a summary of the various positions, see tb. 1 in Hofmann (2020, 202–4).

10 On the folio structure, see Hofmann (2020, 35–69); on pigments and the identification of painters' palettes, see Hofmann (2020, 201–46).

11 On togas and dress, see Rothe (2020). On the implications of hair and beard in late antiquity, see Zanker 1995, 307–20; Bacci 2014, 212.

12 For general discussion of ancient narrative, see Russell 1981; Meiering 1987; Grethlein and Rengakos 2009; Nünlist 2009; Liveley 2019. For an initial definition of narrative, see Plato 2013, 248 (*Republic* 392d). Aristotle discusses narrative in the *Poetics*; however, the text does not appear to have been read widely in antiquity. On this point, see Liveley 2019, 54, 75. Contrast Russell (1981, 13), who points out that Byzantine scholars used the terminology of the *Poetics* to comment on novels. Writers of the Hellenistic and Imperial ages include the first-century BC Greek rhetoricians Hermagoras of Temnos and Dionysius of Halicarnassus. Horace weighs in in Latin with the *Ars Poetica*. See Liveley 2019, 83–88. For Greek and Latin scholiasts, see Meiering 1987, 54–98; Nünlist 2009; Liveley 2019, 77–83 (Homeric scholia), 89–96 (Servius and Latin commentaries).

13 Dionysius of Hallicarnassus 1974–1985, 2: 156 (*On Literary Composition*, 20).

14 Plato discusses the relationship between content and form, *logos* and *lexis*, in the *Republic*. See Plato 2013 1: 246–48 (*Republic* 392c–98b). For the forms of narrative, see especially 247. With some variation on the matter of content and form, Aristotle continues the discussion in *Poetics* and the *Art of Rhetoric*. He also notes the importance of identifying essential and inessential material and the matter of narrative cohesion, a point of view that later authors acknowledge either directly or indirectly. On the multiple ways to tell stories, see generally Dionysius of Hallicarnassus *On Literary Composition*. For discussion, see Halliwell (2009) in particular and Liveley (2019) in general, especially chs. 4 (on Horace) and 5 (on later critics). On ancient and late ancient criticism, see Meiering (1987) and Nünlist (2009).

15 Lucian 1913–1979, 6:67 (*How to Write History* 55).

16 On the usefulness of history and the unpleasing nature of bias, see Lucian 1913–1979, 6: 15–17 (*How to Write History* 9–10). On history as a guide, see Lucian 1913–1979, 6: 57 (*How to Write History* 42) – a view, as Lucian notes, also expressed by Thucydides (*History of the Peloponnesian War* 1.22.4).

17 On subjects appropriate to narrative, see Lively 2019, 13.

18 On narrative, see Plato 2013, 1:248–80 (*Republic* 392d–400e); Hermogenes 1913, 228; 1987, 9–10.
19 Lucian 1913–1979, 6: 59 (*How to Write History* 43).
20 Lucian 1913–1979 (*How to Write History* 44).
21 Hermogenes 1913,226–41; 1987, 8–18.
22 Pliny 1938–1962, 9: 309–11 (*Natural History* 35.65–66).
23 Hermogenes 1987, xvi.
24 On Christian conceptions of history, see the overview in Milburn 1954; Momigliano 1963, 79–99; 1990, 132–56; Chesnut 1986; Droge 1989; Adler 2008. On late antique historiography in general, see Croke and Emmett 1983.
25 Hermogenes 1913, 277–96; 1987, 41–54.
26 Hermogenes 1913, 352–63; 1987, 89–97.
27 Hermogenes 1913, 241–42; 1987, 18–19.
28 On Solemnity, see Hermogenes 1913, 242–54; 1987, 19–26. On association with the divine, see Hermogenes 1913, 243; 1987, 19.
29 Hermogenes 1913, 339–45; 1987, 81–84.
30 On new beginnings, see Hermogenes 1913, 266; 1987, 34.
31 For the church and its building history, see Krautheimer 1967, 1–67.
32 For a summary of the restoration history, see Spain 1983. Less exhaustive summaries appear in Richter and Cameron Taylor 1904, 403–5, and Brenk 1975, 5–8. For medieval restorations, see Bertelli 1955; Spain 1977. On modern restorations, see Giacomini 2005, 127. For the most recent interventions, which took place in two campaigns between 1929 and 1931, and 1936 and 1940, see Astorri 1934; Biagetti 1937; 1947; Bruyne 1938.
33 Early discussions include: Seroux d'Agincourt 1823, 2: 35–36; Schnaase 1842, 3:187–92; Garrucci 1872–1888, 4: 17–31; Kondakov 1886, 1: 95.
34 Richter and Cameron Taylor 1904; Wilpert 1916, 1: 412–500.
35 Deichmann 1948, 49–72; Cecchelli 1956; Künzle 1961–1962; Grabar 1968, 45–47; Brenk 1975; Kitzinger 1975; 1977, 67–80; Deckers 1976. Recent studies have focused on iconography: Spain 1979; Sieger 1987; Steigerwald 2000; 2007; 2010; Tronzo 2001; Geyer 2006; Martin 2010; Lidova 2015.
36 Kitzinger 1977, 71.
37 The panel is among the better preserved. Wilpert 1916, pl. 9, reproduced here, documents its appearance before the twentieth-century restoration campaigns. Tesserae are missing along the bottom edge, especially at the lower corners. There are lacunae throughout the lower half. In the upper portion, the child to Abraham's right is missing. In the twentieth-century restoration campaign these missing sections were integrated with modern tesserae.
38 Rothe (2020, 17–36) provides a brief history of the toga.
39 The color palette was extensive. See Astorri 1934; Brenk 1975, 6.
40 For the late antique understanding of the toga, see Rothe (2020, 149), who notes that at this late date, the toga had largely been replaced by the simple tunic known as the *paenula* for everyday wear even as it retained its symbolic associations with Roman identity.
41 For the image of the intellectual, see generally Zanker 1997.
42 Spain 1979 notes an emphasis on betrothals and weddings in both Old and New Testament imagery at Santa Maria Maggiore, which was designed to underscore God's essential promise that Abraham would become the father of a great people.
43 The panel is among the better preserved. Wilpert (1916, pl. 17, reproduced here) documents its appearance before the mid-twentieth-century restorations, showing limited loss of tesserae within the image. The most substantial lacunae appear along the edges where the red-, white-, and blue-striped border common to all images has been lost. A significant portion of the lower edge, now sketched in paint, has also fallen away. Along the upper left side, damage has been repaired by integrating tesserae; however, these do not reproduce the original figures.
44 Kitzinger 1975, 130.

45 Hermogenes 1913, 260–64; 1987, 30–32.

46 Hermogenes 1913, 368–80; 1987, 101–8.

47 On the altar, also referred to as the Parthian monument, see Eichler 1939, 488–94; 1971; Vermeule 1968, 95–123; Oberleitner 1978; Ganschow 1986; Engemann 1999; Landskron 2006; Siepel 2006; Faust 2012a; 2012b, 143–67.

48 On these distinctions, see especially Elsner 2000. On historiated columns in general, see Becatti 1960. On the Column of Trajan, see Lehmann-Hartleben 1926; Becatti 1960, 25–31; Steinby 1993–2000, 2: 356–59; Coarelli 2000. On the Forum of Trajan, see Steinby 1993–2000, 2: 348–56 ("Forum Traiani"). On the Column of Marcus Aurelius, see Becatti 1957; 1960, 47–84; Steinby 1993–2000, 2: 302–5; Deypeyrot 2010; Beckmann 2011; Griebel 2013.

49 The Column of Theodosius, which anchored the Forum of Theodosius, was erected between 386 and c. 393–394. Modeled on the Roman Column of Trajan, it commemorated the victorious campaigns against the Greutungi in a series of spiraling reliefs. The column itself fell during a hurricane in 1517. Until recently, surviving fragments were incastrated in the nearby Beyazit Hammam. Some fragments remain in situ. Others have been removed to the Istanbul Archaeological Museum. On the column and the forum generally, see Becatti 1960, 83–150; Müller-Wiener 1977, 258–65; Bauer 1996, 187–203. On the fragments, see Schede 1929, 332–36; Kollwitz 1941, 3–16; Schneider 1944–1945, 77; Eyice 1958; Becatti 1960, 104–50; Sande 1981; Fıratlı 1990, 27–30, nos. 55–60; Kiilerich 1993, 51–55. A drawing now preserved in the Louvre (no. 4951, 32264) may record the relief. There is, however, uncertainty as to whether it documents the Column of Theodosius or that of Arcadius. On the drawing, see Münz 1888; Kollwitz 1941, 21–22; Sande 1981, 73–78; Kiilerich 1993, 54–55.

50 In danger of collapse, the column was taken down in the eighteenth century. Its base, now almost completely eroded, remains in situ, wedged in between later buildings. Drawings preserve its original appearance. On the Forum of Arcadius, see Müller-Wiener 1977, 250–53; Bauer 1996, 203–12. On the Column of Arcadius, see Strzygowski 1893; Giglioli 1952; Becatti 1960, 151–264; Kiilerich 1993, 56–64; Bauer 1996, 209–11.

SEVEN

CEREMONIAL IMAGES AND THE "AMPLIFICATION OF GOOD THINGS"

ALTHOUGH WICKHOFF VIEWED NARRATIVE IMAGERY AS THE CENTERPIECE OF late Roman art, Alois Riegl had other ideas. For Riegl, a different type of image stood at the heart of the definition, the representation of ceremony. Prime among such images was the fourth-century *largitio* relief on the north side of the Arch of Constantine (Figure 12), the last section of a larger frieze showing Constantine's victory over his rival Maxentius, which wrapped around the arch at mid-level. Riegl argued that the relief, depicting the imperial distribution of largesse to the Senate and the Roman people, captured the essence of late Roman style in the planar, symmetrical nature of its composition, the frontal and repetitive use of figures – each one of which he saw as isolated in space – and the striking contrasts between light and shade created by undercutting and drilling that resulted in what he referred to as the "optical" character of the work. Above all, these forms, which repudiated natural observation, were "crystalline" and "magical," the stuff of dead matter and eternal transcendence. They were, likewise, inevitable. All sculptured relief from the second century on led inexorably to the *largitio*, and the *largitio* itself served as the springboard from which all later Roman art would be launched.[1]

Save for the superficial identification of the event and its participants, Riegl did not address subject matter. Instead, he relied upon his concept of *Kunstwollen* to describe and interpret the look and the meaning of images. Because *Kunstwollen* operated within a set of universal stylistic principles that not only correlated to specific states of mind but also operated cyclically, the trajectory of stylistic development and its attendant meanings was in no small measure preordained. Even more crucially, *Kunstwollen* relied upon homogeneity. It made no allowance for variation within a tradition, thereby ensuring a unitary style for each historical period.

The principles guiding the initial conception of the *largitio* relief could not, however, have been more different. As suggested previously, Roman art was rooted in the conviction that representation, whether visual or verbal, was a process rooted in and not rejecting mimesis. In addition, it proceeded from a sense of the inalienable congruence between style and subject that saw the former growing from and interpreting the latter according to a set of mutually agreed-upon conventions. As the discussion of mosaics at Santa Maria Maggiore and the miniatures of the Vienna Genesis in the previous chapter indicates, those conventions were crucial components in the interpretation of subject matter. The case of the *largitio* was no exception. Here style was cued by and worked in the service of a particular subject, the ritual of state ceremonial.

Roman state ceremonial covered a range of activity. Among other things, it included processions, sacrifice, and orations. Typical representations of such events include reliefs from the Altar of Augustan Peace (21–7 BC) (Figure 1), the Ara Pietatis (41–54), the Arch of Titus (after 81), the Arch of Trajan at Beneventum (109–14), and the Anaglypha Traiani (118–19).[2] These images, all of which date to the first two centuries of the imperial age, share a compositional logic that sets them apart from other types of narrative representation. Three basic characteristics have been identified with this visual paradigm: the planar arrangement of figures, the inclusion of backward-facing figures who chat with their neighbors in these planar rows, and the relaxed stance of individual participants.[3] Other common but by no means ubiquitous elements include the use of isocephaly and the tendency for figures to occupy the full height of the visual field. Modified according to the demands of contemporary marble-working techniques and period styles, these elements have been seen to have their origins in the classical style of the Parthenon frieze (447–32 BC). Their appearance in Roman relief is considered less a revival of Greek style and more an adaptation of its forms for the purpose of expressing the distinctly Roman qualities of *dignitas* and *auctoritas* inherent in such occasions. This paradigm became so ingrained that by the first century it existed independently of Greek models.[4]

That such elements could evoke this specific response was in part a matter of iconography: processional order, comportment, and dress codes, for example. At the same time, the response was also directed by stylistic choices. The planar arrangement of figures marked out a clear, ordered space within the frame, while the series of standing figures established a regular vertical rhythm. Enhanced by isocephaly – a device to stabilize the action and confirm horizontal unity – and varied by slight deviations in pose, this basic structure created a compositional grid that visualized the formality and solemnity appropriate to such communal events.

This chapter argues that the Constantinian *largitio* and other late antique images of its ilk – most prominently the sixth-century images of Justinian and Theodora in the church of San Vitale at Ravenna – continued the tradition. Far from deviating from this earlier, established formula, as has long been assumed, they operated within and elaborated upon the conventions of the Roman ceremonial paradigm to express not only the dignity of the event but also the character of its presiding emperor and, more broadly, the shared sense of Roman communal order. Further, they did so, not as isolated images, but as scenes that were integral to a larger narrative context.

THE *LARGITIO* RELIEF

The relief represents the imperial distribution of monetary largesse to the citizens of Rome, members of the Senate and the lower classes alike. Originally referred to as the *congiarium*, the ceremony was known by the second century as the *liberalitas* and referred to in the fourth century as *largitio*.[5] Whatever its name, the event was occasional, taking place in conjunction with such festivities as the accession of a *princeps*, the *tirocinium* (coming of age) of an imperial heir, or an imperial wedding. From the second century, it was allied closely with imperial victory celebrations, where it was the last in a series of events that included the emperor's formal arrival in the Roman Forum (*adventus*) and his speech to the population from the Rostra (*adlocutio*).[6]

Numismatic evidence indicates that during the *largitio* itself, the recipient of the benefit would step up onto a platform, register his name with an official, and then turn to receive the distribution from the emperor himself. Coins were inserted into hollowed-out depressions in a flat, rectangular tablet, which the emperor held up in his right hand before turning it over and allowing the lucre to fall into the fold of an outstretched toga or other garment. Because of the large number of people receiving the benefit, the event is likely to have taken place over several days and at multiple distribution points without benefit of the emperor's actual presence.[7]

The *largitio* relief depicts what would have been the central act of imperial largesse together with several subsidiary distribution scenes. The panel itself is rectangular and divided into two registers, each one corresponding to a level in a two-storied architectural setting that has been identified as the interior of the Basilica Ulpia.[8] Constantine, who sits enthroned on a dais at the center, cuts through both registers and dominates the visual field, filling the space from top to bottom. He is by far the largest figure in the composition by virtue of his actual size and his raised placement on the dais. He wears the toga and faces forward, his head now missing. Both feet rest on the ground, his left foot slightly in front of his right as he distributes coin from a rectangular distribution tablet with his right hand.[9] Behind him and set off by a balustrade, two staggered rows of senators, their scale slightly smaller than that of the emperor, stand to the left and right of the throne, their heads turned toward the center of the composition to observe the proceedings. At ground level, other senators flank the dais, some with their hands raised in acclamation, others with arms extended as they wait to receive their share. One in particular holds open the fold of his toga to catch the coin falling from the tablet. Behind them on either side, members of the general population stand in an extended line. Smaller again in scale than the senators, these figures include male citizens clad in tunics, some with children in tow. Poses vary slightly from one figure to the next, with some raising their hands in acclamation as others chat with their neighbors or hoist children onto their shoulders. For the most part, the figures are shown in either a side- or three-quarter view, as most turn toward the center of the composition, their heads in a single isocephalic line. To the right, a cluster of participants, adults and children alike, presents a notable exception to the larger central focus as they turn toward one another, look up, and gesture toward the register above. There, on the upper building level, in twin loggias opening to either side of the central imperial group, magistrates and other functionaries gather around tables, some standing, others sitting, all gesturing and speaking with one another as they oversee the distribution of coin in ancillary settings.[10] Throughout, whatever their size or pose, figures share the same blocky proportions. Many of them stand independently of one another, isolated against the dark background from which they appear to be detached by deep undercutting. Its folds created by drilling, drapery does little to articulate their summary anatomy, creating instead a web of sharp lines that cut into the relief's flat upper surface.

The composition is noteworthy for the diagrammatic treatment of the setting and the loosely symmetrical ordering of the figures within it. The towering, forward-facing figure of Constantine establishes the central axis, while the scene's players enhance the sense of balance through pose, gesture, glance, and the diminishing hierarchy of scale that spreads outward from the central pole. The two superimposed registers, one continuous below, the other segmented above, block out the architectural backdrop, creating a grid within which the participants operate. That said, the scene is not rigidly symmetrical. The emperor shifts almost imperceptibly in his seat. Within the larger, balanced framework, the figures, each one of which stands to the height of his register whatever his scale, take up a variety of poses, and the occasional drift in participants' attention on the lower level, together with the busy activity in the gallery above, lends a sense of motion and commotion to the proceedings. The undercutting enhances the feeling of activity by setting the relief's lighter upper surface off against the darker background. How the relief would have been altered by the addition of color, if any, is unknown.

Riegl's assessment of the *largitio* emphasized what he referred to as its planar composition and the symmetrical disposition of undifferentiated figures in frontal poses around the central imperial figure. He stressed the isolation of individual figures, a characteristic he linked to the contrast between light and dark, which he believed was intended to create a sense of infinite space. On the basis of these observations, he went on to argue that the *largitio* represented a deliberate turn from the traditions of classical art toward a new type of inanimate, crystalline beauty that had emerged from the traditions of Roman art over the course of the previous two hundred years, one that eschewed naturalistic imitation and in so doing reflected the late Roman dread of space and a habit of magical thinking.[11]

Riegl's discussion is noteworthy as much for the information it omits as for the information it includes. It does not mention the implied sense of motion in the seated figure of Constantine, nor does it note the substantial variations in pose among the participants. Thus, while the planar organization and general symmetry of the group are indisputable, the assertions that figures are isolated in space, that the composition as a whole is without movement, and that the relief should be understood as a new form of representation designed to create inanimate, crystalline forms alien to the classical tradition are, at the very least, open to question, as are the conclusions characterizing the collective Roman state of mind.

Riegl's view has nevertheless prevailed, with different aspects of his study provoking different responses among art historians and archaeologists. In art historical circles, the characterization of a late antique style rooted in the principles of a crystalline abstraction at odds with classical mimetic norms took hold, while among archaeologists the discussion generally focused on the question of stylistic origins. In addition to the diehards who continued to see the relief as a product of barbarian influence, there were those who took up Riegl's argument with Josef Strzygowski about whether the origins of late antique style lay in western or eastern traditions. Champions of western origins identified the relief's stylistic sources in either an indigenous Roman folk tradition or western provincial art, while promotors of the East looked to Parthian and Sassanian influence.[12]

The lone wanderer from the trail was Mrs. Arthur Strong (Eugenia Sellars Strong), Franz Wickhoff's translator. A proponent of Riegl's approach, Strong adopted his observational criteria and descriptive language in her own assessment of the *largitio*, agreeing with him that the isolation of figures in space created an optical sense of form. At the same time, however, she noted that this tendency to isolation, though well suited to the solemnity and dignity of the ceremonial subject matter, was less conducive to the interpretation of narrative action elsewhere on the Constantinian frieze. Strong did not develop these observations, however, and in a quick return to the Rieglian path she argued that the inanimate symmetry had a "spiritual side," which she connected ultimately to Christianity.[13]

Although Riegl's influence has proved tenacious, other approaches to the relief are possible. There is, for example, no reason to suspect that Roman viewers saw the *largitio* as something fundamentally different from other depictions of ceremonial occasions. It showed human beings from the emperor on down as they were engaged in one of the great and familiar activities of the Roman state. As such, it was mimetic. Moreover, many of its elements were consistent with those of earlier ceremonial relief, specifically, the planar composition and the configuration of the participants, several of whom face backward within the group, in isocephalic rows that occupy the full height of their register. In other words, in common with earlier depictions of ceremonial, the visual properties of the *largitio* not only represented the event but also used the regular vertical and horizontal rhythms of these forms to establish the tenor of the event and signal, as Mrs. Strong opined, the *dignitas* (dignity) and *auctoritas* (power) inherent in the action.

This observation is not to deny the differences between the *largitio* and earlier imperial reliefs. In particular, compartmentalization of the visual field, scale discrepancies between the figures, and a more rigid sense of symmetry distinguish it from its predecessors, as do such technical aspects of its manufacture as the preference for flat surfaces and their articulation by undercutting and drill work. Nevertheless, these elements are integrated into the ceremonial paradigm, suggesting not so much a break from tradition as its elaboration and intensification. These, then, are differences of degree and not of kind. This being the case, it is useful to consider how these integrated elements, old and new, made their collective impact.

Two sources, Hermogenes of Tarsus' *On Types of Style* and Menander Rhetor's discussion of the speech known as the "Royal Oration" in his larger treatise, *On Rhetoric*, suggest an approach. Hermogenes addresses the selection and creation of individual styles from a technical point of view, while Menander focuses on subject matter. Taken together, these texts offer a view into the logic driving the creation and reception of the *largitio*, both as a freestanding representation and as an image within the larger context of the fourth-century frieze of which it was a part.[14]

THE *LARGITIO* RELIEF AS VISUAL RHETORIC

As was the case with any representational image, the *largitio* demanded treatment appropriate to its subject, which was, broadly speaking, historical narrative. Two interwoven streams – the one formulaic, the other temporally specific – constitute the story. On the one hand, the central act of distribution focused largely on the centrally placed figure of the emperor represents a ceremonial event that had been established in tradition and was doubtless formulaic in its protocols. In this respect, the action upheld a practice that had been ongoing since time immemorial, giving eternal life to Roman custom. On the other hand, the presence of the particular emperor, Constantine, and the wealth of subsidiary activity surrounding the central and defining act of distribution – the participants' responses and the backroom activity in the loggia – suggest the energy of the specific event, together with its time and place. According to Hermogenes, such political subjects constituted a type of panegyric that demanded a narrative approach in the style referred to as Grandeur.[15]

As noted in the previous chapter, Grandeur had readily identifiable properties when deployed in the narrative context. Panegyric, itself a type of narrative, was no exception. As always, Grandeur emerged from a combination of styles, Clarity (*Saphneia*) foremost among them. Clarity, which stood at the base of any oration, was considered the most appropriate style for political subjects. Its function, here, as in other storytelling contexts, was to articulate a subject in the most lucid and straightforward manner possible by using a narrative approach that captured the language of everyday speech. At the same time, and because of these features, an excess of Clarity ran the risk of making a panegyric sound ordinary. It therefore needed an injection of other styles to create the requisite sense of Dignity and Grandeur. This fix was achieved by the use, singly or in combination, of various substyles – Solemnity, Asperity, Vehemence, Brilliance, and Abundance. Sweetness was also a desideratum, as was Beauty.[16]

Each of the styles capable of producing this effect had its properties and associations. Sometimes these qualities were distinctive. At other times, they intersected with those of other styles. Solemnity, which suggested thoughtfulness and moderation, was appropriate for occasions in which divine order was manifest in human affairs, for example, the dispensation of justice or the representation of sacrifice. Its approach was that of direct, unhesitating narrative. Low vocal pitch, broad sounds, slow cadences, and stately rhythms were central to its definition.[17] By contrast, Asperity and Vehemence, both of which signaled reproach – the former of inferiors, the latter of superiors – used the short phrases and clashing sounds that constituted the rough language of command.[18] Brilliance represented yet another possibility.[19] Its purpose was to temper harshness in a speech and to amplify the deeds of great men. The subjects of Brilliance were remarkable actions and noble sentiments, deeds that added luster to a career. Its approach, which avoided digression, was again narrative, its style that of Solemnity. The last of the types to produce Grandeur was Abundance.[20] Abundance elaborated upon a subject by introducing additional information, for example, the inclusion of not only an action but also its consequences. Reversal characterized its approach. Facts, for example, might be presented in reverse order, or the rationale for a statement prior to its supporting proof. Parallel statement was a preferred feature of its diction. Sweetness – a style appropriate to thoughts that give pleasure, praise of human beings among them – demanded a narrative approach with diction built around euphony, balanced clauses, and metrical rhythms.[21] Finally, there was the question of Beauty. Hermogenes did not consider Beauty a style in its own right. Instead, it was the process of polishing the whole, of reconciling the various threads of an oration, a task very often accomplished by the balance and symmetrical arrangement of elements to create a sense of order and harmony. When applied to a base of Clarity, any of these styles created a sense of Grandeur by adding weight and dignity to a speech.

Formal aspects of the *largitio* relief suggest an analogous approach. To begin with, the straightforward, almost diagrammatic presentation of the event created by the planar composition, the architectural frame, and the balanced, loosely symmetrical disposition of the participants around the central figure of Constantine bring to mind the unambiguous sounds and structures of rhetorical Clarity. At the same time, such time-honored features of ceremonial relief as the rows of standing figures create a regular vertical pulse evocative of the stately cadences of Solemnity, while the figures who break the line to interact with their neighbors and children alleviate the visual repetition to lend what would otherwise be a wholly sober and dogmatic narrative a pleasing anecdotal quality characteristic of Sweetness. There are also hints at the kind of narrative elaboration facilitated by Abundance. Hierarchy of scale amplifies discrepancies in the participants' social status, and the compartmentalization of the visual field allows elaboration of the subject matter by creating discrete spaces in which to document not only the distribution of largesse but also the behind-the-scenes activity of the bureaucratic state that made the larger event possible. Finally, the overall symmetry and balance of the composition suggest Beauty and its associations with order and harmony.

In the *largitio*, the established forms of ceremonial relief combined with newer features of symmetry, segmentation, and scale manipulation to create an image shot through with the sense of Grandeur appropriate to the event. The resulting image captured the dual nature of the event, its generic timelessness and its temporal specificity, to create a compelling record of the occasion in all its solemn majesty, together with a statement about the presiding emperor himself. Style, as Hermogenes noted, expressed character.[22] Accordingly, the Solemnity, Brilliance, and Abundance that glossed the *largitio* relief's basic compositional Clarity are likely to have expressed more than the generic dignity of Roman state ceremonial. As these individual styles coalesced and gave shape to the narrative, they also gave visual life to some of the emperor's defining qualities, among them the moderation of Solemnity and the luster of Brilliance. Above all, the refining polish of Beauty suggested the order and harmony inherent not only in the individual event but also in the broader promise of Constantinian rule.

THE *LARGITIO* RELIEF IN CONTEXT

Although Riegl discussed the *largitio* in isolation, it is, as is well known, part of an imposing sculptured ensemble that combined works of purpose-made fourth-century manufacture with reused reliefs from imperial monuments associated with Trajan (98–117), Hadrian (117–138), and Marcus Aurelius (161–180). Some have argued that the fourth-century frieze, either wholly or in part, may have been reused from a monument to Diocletian (284–304).[23] The purpose here is not to offer an exhaustive discussion of the arch and the full panoply of its sculptured installations, but to examine the style and content of the *largitio* within the context of the fourth-century frieze of which it was a part.

The frieze, which wraps around the arch at mid-level, consists of six individual sections. On the most generic level subjects include a marching army, the siege of a city, a river battle, the emperor's entry into Rome, an oration, and a distribution of imperial largesse. More particularly, the panels give visual life to the events leading up to and surrounding Constantine's defeat of his co-emperor and rival, Maxentius. In the spring of 312, Constantine, who was stationed in Gaul, crossed the Alps and descended into Italy, defeating garrisons at Susa and Turin before turning toward Milan. The city surrendered without a fight, Maxentius' troops having fallen back on Verona at the news of the Constantinian victories. Constantine then took Verona and Aquileia before turning south to Rome, where, on 28 October, he defeated Maxentius. The battle, which took place north of the city at the Milvian Bridge – the Tiber crossing on the Via Flaminia – gave him control of the capital. With battles to fight on the northern frontier, Constantine did not linger at Rome, and it was only upon his return in 315 that he celebrated the victory together with his *decennalia*, the tenth anniversary of his accession to imperial rule.[24]

The visual account of these momentous events begins on the short west side of the arch with the scene of the marching army, an episode generally thought to represent Constantine's departure from Milan (Figure 28). At the left, a cart loaded with passengers and accompanied by a column of infantrymen and cavalry riders passes through a city gate. At the center of the composition two transport animals – a mule and a camel – their minders, and an additional cluster of soldiers precede the cart. On the right, at the front of the line, soldiers carry standards of Sol Invictus and Victoria, as armored infantrymen lead the way.

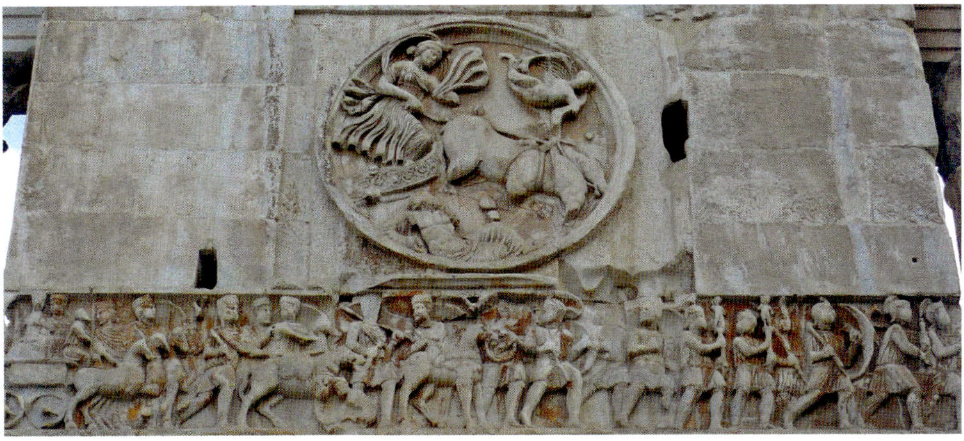

28. Departure from Milan, Arch of Constantine, Rome, 313. Photo: S. Bassett

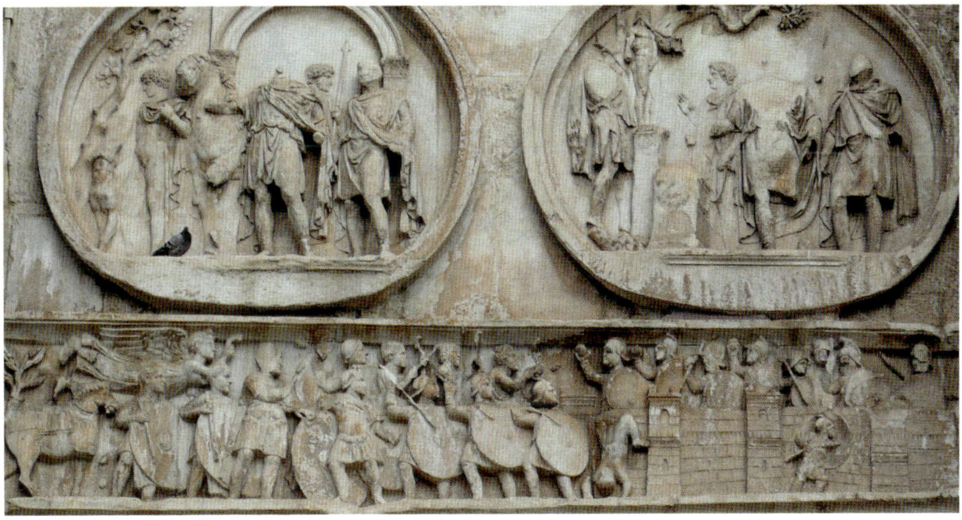

29. Siege of Verona, Arch of Constantine, Rome, 313. Photo: S. Bassett

The action continues on the south side, with two scenes of war, the siege of Verona over the left arch (Figure 29) and the battle at the Milvian Bridge over the right arch (Figure 30). In the former, the heavily fortified walls of the city dominate at the right side of the composition. A scout from Constantine's army passes in front of these walls, while the harried defenders are gathered inside, and a man plummets to his death from the battlement. To the left, Constantinian troops in full battle array stand poised for assault. Behind them, Constantine, who appears as a towering figure, directs the action under the guidance of a winged Victory, who hovers above him holding the crown of victory. In the battle of the Milvian Bridge, the now missing figure of the emperor stands on the embankment to the left,

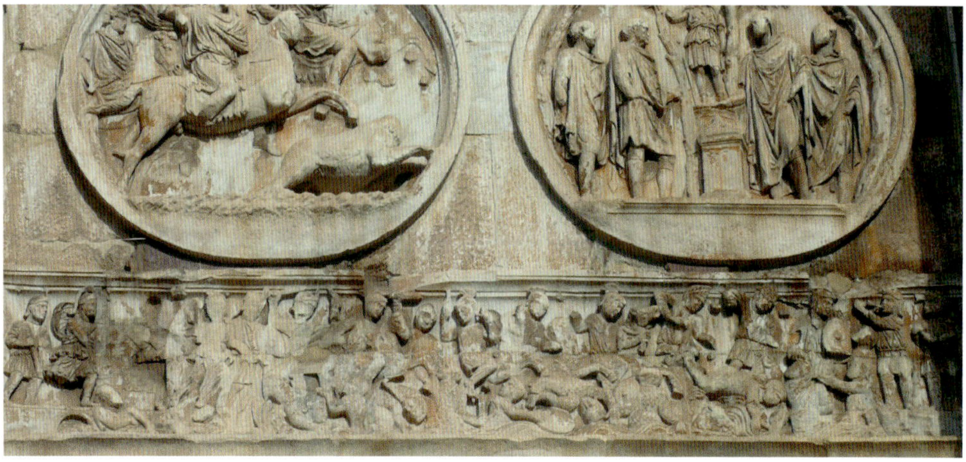

30. Battle at the Milvian Bridge, Arch of Constantine, Rome, 313. Photo: S. Bassett

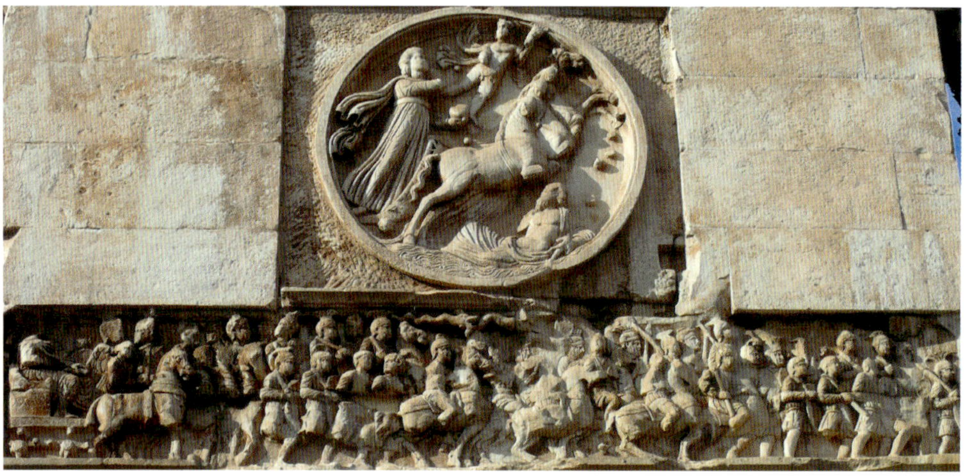

31. *Adventus*, Arch of Constantine, Rome, 313. Photo: S. Bassett

accompanied by personifications of Victory and Rome. A river god, Tiber, rises out of the water below him. At the center of the composition, troops fight both above and in the churning waters of the Tiber as Maxentius and his army go down in defeat.

Military action then gives way to ceremonial activity with a relief on the east side showing Constantine's *adventus*, his entry into Rome on the occasion of his *decennalia* (Figure 31). On the right, the now headless emperor rides in a jeweled cart as foot soldiers and cavalry lead the way. Finally, the action comes to rest in the two reliefs on the north side. The first, over the left arch, depicts the *adlocutio*, the emperor's address to the Senate and the Roman people in the Roman Forum (Figure 32). Constantine, again headless, stands at the center of

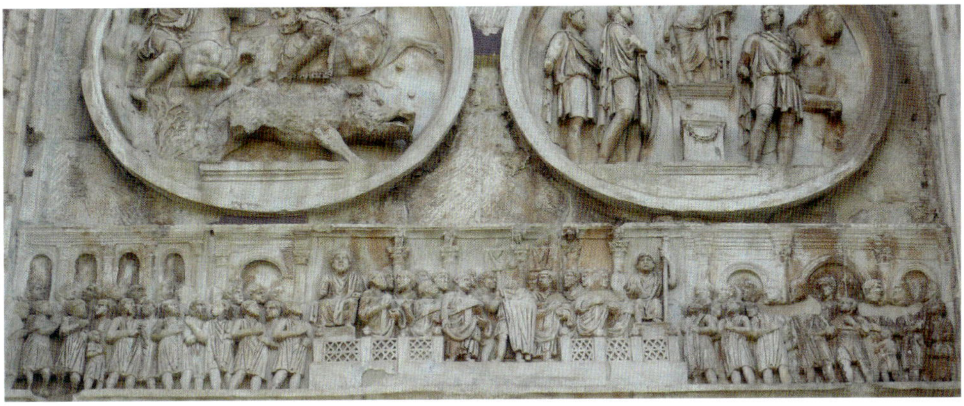

32. *Adlocutio*, Arch of Constantine, Rome, 313. Photo: S. Bassett

the composition on the speaker's platform, the Rostra, surrounded by members of the Senate. Two statues – one of Hadrian, the other of Marcus Aurelius – frame the group. Below, at ground level, the citizens of Rome gather to listen. The great monuments of the Forum form the backdrop: the Basilica Julia and the Arch of Augustus on the left, the Five-Column monument of Diocletian at the center, and the Arch of Septimius Severus on the right. The second and concluding image, over the right arch, is that of the *largitio*.[25]

Neither the *largitio* as a celebration nor its sculptured representation on the arch were ever intended to be experienced in isolation. In general, the distribution of largesse occurred as the culmination of a larger event, and it is evident that the actual Constantinian ceremony followed this protocol. Similarly, its sculptured depiction represented the prescribed conclusion to a sequence of activities. Thus, both the event and the relief derive their character from their place in the narrative order.

Although the subject had its origins in the historical events of the Constantinian campaign and the protocols governing imperial celebrations, the story's presentation was hardly that of an unedited news dispatch. The designers of the frieze shaped the narrative and its message through the choice of episodes and the style in which they were represented. In turn, this effort at selection and organization aligns with the conventions and structures of rhetorical composition. Nowhere is this similarity more clearly demonstrated than in a comparison of the frieze to the particular category of display rhetoric known as the royal oration (*basilikos logos*).

Such orations, classed under the general rubric of panegyric and known more particularly as encomia, had a specific purview. Their obvious and very practical aim was to showcase a ruler's good qualities. As Menander Rhetor noted:

> The imperial oration is an encomium of the emperor. Consequently, it will thus embrace a generally agreed amplification of the good things attaching to the emperor, but allows no ambivalent or disputed features, because of the extreme splendor of the person concerned. You should therefore elaborate it on the assumption that it relates to things universally acknowledged to be good.[26]

Those qualities were presented following a standardized format. The speaker began by acknowledging the enormity of the task before him together with his own limitations in the face of the challenge. Then, diving into the project, he continued by recounting the origin and lineage of the imperial subject, his nature and upbringing. There was a fair degree of flexibility allotted for the contents of this opening salvo. If, for example, there was nothing stellar about a ruler's genesis, these remarks could be cursory or omitted altogether. The second section, the core of the speech, included a discussion of the ruler's character traits and a description of the defining deeds of his career. Ideally, the latter touched upon the events of war before addressing those of peace. Throughout this section the speaker was expected to emphasize the ruler's favor with the divine and his command of the virtues essential to good rule: courage, moderation, justice, intelligence, and humanity. With these plaudits accomplished, the speaker then moved to the closing section of the address. This discussion might include comparison of the subject to previous rulers or references to offspring who would continue in his footsteps. Finally, the orator observed the prosperity and happiness of the state and its citizens before closing with an invocation for a long reign.[27]

Menander's instruction did not languish unheeded in the realm of the theoretical. Late Roman panegyric often follows this outline, nowhere more so than in two orations devoted to Constantine: an anonymously authored panegyric that was probably delivered at Trier sometime in 313 and a speech given at Rome by the orator Nazarius on the occasion of the emperor's *quinquinnalia* (fifteenth-year rule anniversary) in 321.[28] Nor, if the Constantinian frieze is any index, was this structure limited to oral presentations.

In the general narrative and the articulation of details, the frieze is consistent both with Menander's recommendations and their realization in contemporary panegyric. Three of the six panels focus on military activity – the departure from Milan, the siege of Verona, and the battle at the Milvian Bridge – an emphasis in keeping with the understanding that the real substance of an encomium lies in the description of military campaigns. Also, of a piece with this thinking is the careful documentation of detail. Different ranks of soldiers are depicted, along with animals and equipment, as are city gates, walls, and the Tiber itself. Further, the frieze shares the treatise's emphasis on the divine sanction afforded a just ruler, as indicated by the standards of Victoria and Sol Invictus and the personified Victory hovering above the troops as they press in on Verona.

The three remaining reliefs – the triumphal procession, the *adlocutio*, and the *largitio* – bring the military events to their close and shift the focus to the future and peace. Once again, the similarities to Menander's outline are striking. The interest in topographical detail seen in the previous reliefs continues, with settings in the Roman Forum and the imperial basilica clearly documented. These details also afford the opportunity for comparisons with previous rulers. In the *adlocutio* relief, the imperial statues on the Rostra and the monuments themselves encourage associations between Constantine and the architectural patrons who were his predecessors: Julius Caesar, Augustus, Hadrian, Marcus Aurelius, and Diocletian. Finally, although it does not directly address the question of Constantine's heirs, the *largitio* suggests Rome's happy and prosperous destiny not only through the distribution of largesse but also with the inclusion of the male children, Rome's next generation and the empire's future, in the proceedings.[29]

In the royal oration, the enumeration and description of the accomplishments documenting a royal curriculum served a larger goal. Directly correlated to mental ability and moral disposition, actions made clear the nature of a monarch's character. Their description thus served as the armature on which to build an evocation of a specific set of kingly virtues: courage, intelligence, justice, moderation, and humanity. In part, these virtues were implicit in the actions described. It was axiomatic that a scene of war would convey courage. But activities also needed elucidation, and it was the orator's duty to draw specific connections between an event and its implications: to underscore the emperor's courage, to point out the intelligence necessary for imagining and executing a military campaign, to call attention to the moderation shown in refraining from a city's sack, to underscore the sense of justice guiding legal action. The anonymous author of the panegyric of 313 did just that, emphasizing throughout the emperor's constant presence in the thick of battle, his shrewd planning and tactics, his clemency toward the fallen. Such direct observations were also enhanced by the choice of style, for example, the clashing sounds and quickening rhythms in descriptions of battle that gave way to the more stately cadences suitable to ceremonials such as the oration and the *largitio*.

The sculptured frieze has its parallels. The choice of subject matter balances evenly between scenes of war and scenes of celebration, with three scenes devoted to each. Further, the distribution of the scenes enhances the sense of order, with the two battle scenes on the south set off against the two scenes of celebration on the north and the two processional reliefs, the one on the west showing the emperor exiting the city of Milan, the one on the east depicting his entry into the city of Rome. Within this larger framework, the three scenes of war build to a crescendo as the departure from Milan leads inexorably to the disciplined attack on Verona before yielding to the frenzy of the Milvian Bridge and victory. Then events move toward their resolution, with the entry into Rome giving way to the paired scenes of celebration – the *adlocutio* and the *largitio* – and with them peace and prosperity.

Stylistic shifts, achieved through the manipulation of carving techniques and compositional tactics, enhance the narrative structure. In the departure from Milan, the row of figures, each heavily undercut and occupying the full height of the relief, is organized in clusters to create an irregular if unceasing pulse of light and dark that captures the jostling rhythms of the column's forward motion as the army moves out. The momentum changes in the following panel, the siege of Verona, where the horizontal block of the city with its thick walls punctuated by broad towers and vertical buttresses at the right side of the panel brings the forward motion to a halt. Within these walls, the defending soldiers turn and gesture, their arms and javelins raised at varying angles as they hurl rocks against their attackers. The irregular web of broken lines created by their gesturing limbs conveys the sense of fear and desperation. Outside, the mood is one of assurance as the ranks of identically posed soldiers present a uniform face, the regular rhythm of their round shields and the uniform diagonals of their bodies evoking energized and disciplined cohesion as they press their advantage. Behind them, occupying the full height of the register as he takes the stately contrapposto pose of heroes, Constantine, the architect of this victory, stands in isolation as he directs the action. Victory hovers personified above him, her grand scale and horizontal placement acting as a literal pointer calling attention to the emperor's tactical skill and favor with the divine. The sense of control and invincibility present in this scene gives way to mayhem at the Milvian Bridge, where, in this culminating event of the war, a frantic tangle of line created by the zigzagging forms of the choppy Tiber waters and the rectilinear protrusions of limbs – human and equine – encapsulate the brutality and the sense of struggle as Maxentius goes down to defeat. Turning the corner, time moves forward and the mood changes from horror to controlled exaltation, as ranks of infantry and cavalry lead Constantine in lively but disciplined configuration into Rome. Participants turn, talk, and gesture with one another in parallel rows of upright, overlapping figures. The woof and warp of the extended marching columns and the individual standing figures within them create a loose weave that stretches and compresses as the participants jostle one another while they make their way into the city. At the center, horses erupt into activity, their raised legs and rearing bodies lending variety to the movement. At the end of the procession, Constantine arrives, isolated in his majesty within the vertical and horizontal frame of his conveyance, a position that underscores his restraint and authority amidst the collective euphoria. Finally, in the last two panels, the *adlocutio* and the *largitio*, the action winds down in symmetrical and balanced compositions that evoke the sober, measured pace of the closing ceremonials.

As historical narrative, the frieze bears the imprint of the same sort of stylistic thinking that later shaped the Old Testament cycle at Santa Maria Maggiore and the miniatures of the Vienna Genesis. As was mandatory for such story-telling, the artist worked from a baseline of Clarity, depicting people and places in as straightforward and lucid a manner as possible. At the same time, the imaginative visualization of events eschewed the tedium of pure Clarity by calling on a variety of visual tactics to depict the ebb and flow of Constantine's historic march. The regular, repeating forms of Constantine's troops before the walls of Verona coupled with scale discrepancies emphasizing the emperor and his attendant Victory suggest the steady, stately repetition associated with Brilliance (*Lamprotes*), a style appropriate to the description of the deeds of great men, while the choppy chaotic tangle of the battle at the Milvian bridge evokes the harshness of Vehemence, that style used to express anger and condemnation. Together such styles express Abundance and through it the Grandeur appropriate to a recounting of the emperor's success. Nowhere is this more evident than in the *largitio* itself.

In the context of the Constantinian narrative, the *largitio* represented the formal end to a series of events that began in armed conflict. It was, however, more than a pro forma closing ceremony. If victory in battle demonstrated such imperial virtues as courage, moderation, and intelligence, then the *largitio*'s celebration added to the list by highlighting not only the emperor's generosity but also his justice and humanity, and the order synonymous with his harmonious rule. As such, the relief makes good on the dual claims of the arch, the inscriptions describing Constantine as "Liberator of the City" and "Restorer of Peace."[30]

The *largitio*'s style is nothing if not appropriate to this moment. As the final relief in the action sequence that the frieze represents, it brings events to their close in a manner at once solemn and pleasing. It does so by coupling the time-honored tactics of ceremonial relief with new strategies designed to strengthen the sense of grandeur appropriate to a scene that gives life to imperial virtue and the majesty of the person who inhabits them in what is ultimately a resolute expression of universal order, the power that brought it into being, and the promise of new beginnings.

CEREMONY AND STYLE IN SAN VITALE

The *largitio* relief is but one of a number of surviving late antique images to perpetuate the stylistic conventions associated with Roman ceremonial and its rituals. Examples from the decades leading up to the construction of the Constantinian arch include reliefs from the Decennalia Base in the Roman Forum – a dedication that originally formed part of the five-column monument offered to Diocletian in celebration of the tenth anniversary of his rule (294) – and the Arch of Galerius in Thessaloniki (298–303), which commemorated the Roman defeat of the Persians in 297. Later in the fourth century, the Missorium of Theodosius I (388) and reliefs on the obelisk base in the Hippodrome of Constantinople (390) continued the tradition, as did reliefs on the fifth-century base of the Column of Arcadius (408–421) and two sixth-century bases dedicated to the victorious charioteer Porphyrios. These conventions also became normative for depictions associated with Christian tradition, as in the case of the imperial panel of Justinian and his retinue in the church of San Vitale in Ravenna (c. 546).

Riegl included many of these monuments in his ongoing discussion of late Roman style, but arguably the most important for him was the image of Justinian (Figure 2).[31] The mosaic is set on the north wall of the apse, opposite a pendant image of the empress Theodora on the south wall and below a commanding image of the enthroned Christ in the semi-dome of the eastern end. Scenes based on Old and New Testament events blanket the chancel walls immediately in front of the apse (Figure 33). Completed shortly after the Roman reconquest of Ravenna from the Arian Goths in 546, it depicts the emperor with his retinue – an assembly of ecclesiastics to his left, court members surrounding him at the center, and a military guard to his right.[32]

All of the figures face forward, their heads at the same level and their forms overlapping with one another as their feet tread on those of their cohort. Although the members of the military guard are virtually indistinguishable from one another, the faces of the clergy and the courtiers are individualized, and costume distinguishes rank and status. The garments, which fall in wide blocks of color articulated by straight unbroken lines, underscore the planar composition. Further, the isocephalic arrangement of the heads and the overlapping of figures make any sense of volume, space, or directional movement ambiguous. It is not clear whether the group moves forward in a V-shaped configuration with Justinian at the apex or toward the emperor's left under the guidance of the clergy.[33]

If, as Riegl argued, the *largitio* represented the initial crystallization of a late Roman style at the crossroads of pagan and Christian experience, the mosaic was its chronological pendant, a marker demonstrating the culmination of that style in a fully Christian context.[34] Its planar composition and symmetrical organization stood in a direct line of descent from the *largitio* frieze, as did the frontality of the figures, the compositional emphasis on horizontal and vertical elements, and what he referred to as the complete isolation of figures in space. Riegl also saw the linear folds of the garments as the painted equivalent of drill work in sculpture and thought that the figures' slim proportions presaged developments in Byzantine art. Noting the individual portraits, he argued that the mosaic showed an undeniable interest in the material human being.

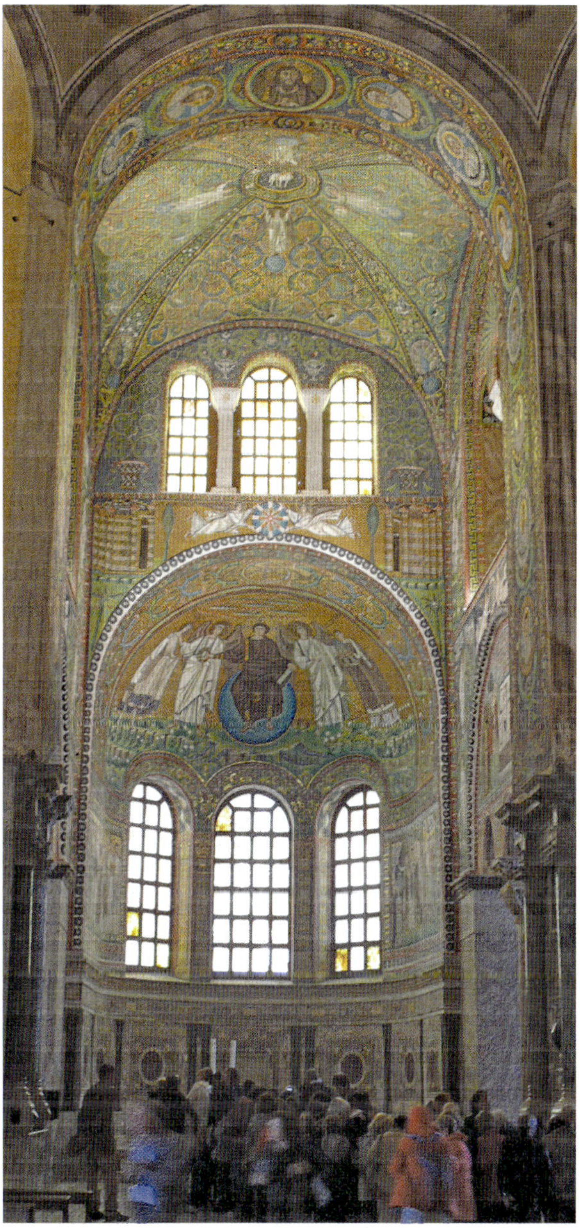

33. Chancel, Church of San Vitale, Ravenna, mid-sixth century. Photo: Courtesy of B. Madigan

Finally, he saw the whole composition as the perfect example of optical, distant viewing that captured the late Roman penchant for magical thinking.[35]

As was the case with the *largitio* relief, the response to Riegl's assessment varied. Those interested largely in his theoretical proposals embraced a spiritualized assessment of the image, most famously Wassily Kandinsky, who used it to illustrate his treatise *On the Spiritual in Art* (1912).[36] For those of a more historical persuasion the question again became that of stylistic origin.

Beginning in the nineteenth century, commentary had characterized the image as "Byzantine,"[37] implying a connection with the East. The nature of that connection was, however, left open, with some arguing for roots in the Parthian world, others the Constantinopolitan court. At the same time, there were others who saw the mosaics either as western, or as a hybridization of eastern and western traditions.[38]

The odd man out in this discussion was F. W. Deichmann, who, following the model of rhetorical theory, proposed that style should be understood not as a matter of workshop differences but as a representational choice conditioned by three factors: the placement of an image, its intended effect, and its function within the whole. Citing Cicero, Quintilian, and Augustine, each of whom acknowledged three rhetorical styles – the Plain, the Middle, and the Grand – he suggested that the image of Justinian be categorized as Grand.[39]

Deichmann did not pursue this discussion, thus leaving open the allied questions of why visual grandeur was appropriate to the subject, how it was achieved, and the nature of its effect. Once again, the subject itself yields some answers: The Justinianic mosaic, its content at once imperial and ecclesiastical, represents a ceremony. As such, it required the kind of solemn presentation appropriate to all such images, an end it achieved in part by drawing on solutions integral to the late antique ceremonial repertoire manifest in the Constantinian *largitio* relief: planar composition, the symmetrical disposition of the figures who take up the full height of the representational field around the central figure of Justinian, and isocephaly. These elements structured the composition, giving it the sense of Clarity foundational to any ceremonial image. At the same time, the emphasis on the figures and the diminished setting make the kind of unambiguous direct statement appropriate to Solemnity. The frontality of individual figures, their direct, piercing gazes, and their isocephalic arrangement underscore that statement, as do the limited range of color and the deliberate, stately rhythm established by the collection of figures and the columnar folds of their dress. An injection of Brilliance softens this sober mood. The division of the panel into three basic sections representing, from right to left, clergy, court, and military may be seen as a series of short, visual clauses that add complexity and luster to the processional structure. Abundance too is present. The individual groups offer the kind of repetitive, parallel structure that characterizes such verbal composition, while the overlapping feet and the spatial ambiguities they create may be considered analogous to the inversions of word order and the reverse presentation of facts that are among the features of rhetorical Abundance. Finally, the relationship between the generic and the specific in the portraits also may be considered an affirmation of Abundance. As an image of imperial power, the Justinian panel offers a series of stock figures, ecclesiastic, courtly, and military. At the same time, however, those same figures are treated as portraits: In addition to the emperor and his bishop, it is likely that the two subsidiary clergy and the court dignitaries are also portrait representations.[40]

As a representation of ceremony, the Justinianic panel shares many of the *largitio* relief's formal strategies. That said, its image of solemn majesty is also very different. In part, the distinction is the result of medium and the different interests, capacities, and aspirations of two- and three-dimensional representation. In other respects, it is a question of chronology. Just as the *largitio* reflects the introduction of new elements such as symmetry and balance to the ceremonial representational roster in the fourth century, so the Justinianic panel suggests the further adjustment and even hardening of those strategies by the sixth century. Specifically, the presentation of figures is more overtly and unvaryingly frontal, an effect that diminishes any sense of variety within the whole, thus intensifying the regular, vertical rhythms so crucial to the sense of solemn majesty. At the same time, the spatial ambiguity and complete lack of figural ponderation, techniques unknown in the Constantinian relief, introduce new strategies for further articulating that majesty.

The full implication of this majesty was made clear within the larger context. Just as the *largitio* owed its style to subject and the place of that subject within the expanded narrative of Constantinian victory, the Justinianic procession also saw its style conditioned by subject and context. Most immediately, this interaction took place with the pendant mosaic of Theodora and her attendants on the apse's south wall (Figure 34). The portraits face each other

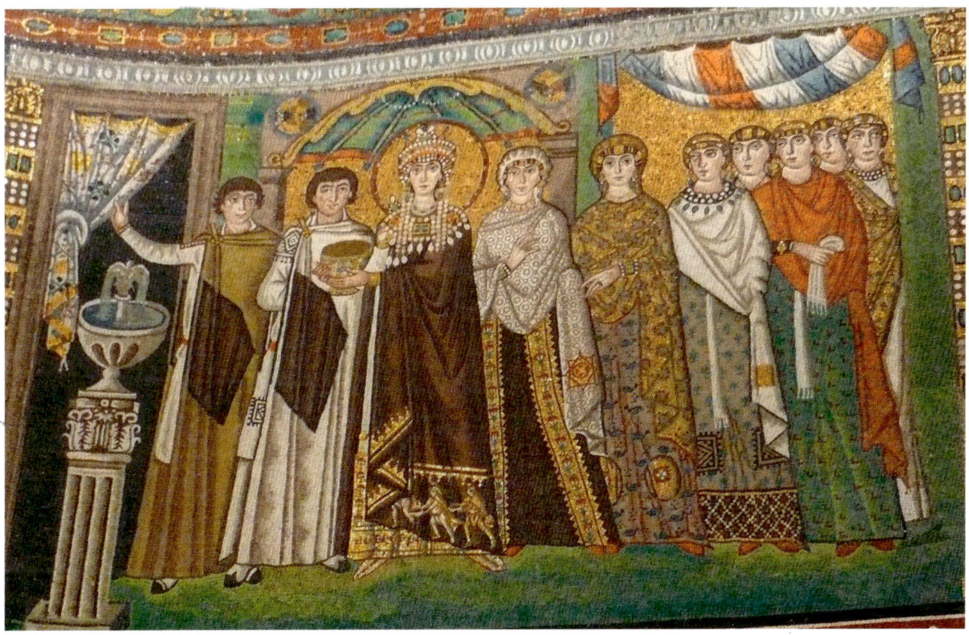

34. Theodora and her retinue, Church of San Vitale, Ravenna, mid-sixth century. Photo: S. Bassett

across the space, each within a jeweled border that abuts the similarly adorned frame of the semi-dome above. Theodora and her retinue stand against the same neutral green and gold ground used in the Justinianic procession. Similarly, the composition is divided into three segments. Theodora, identifiable by nimbus, crown, and purple chlamys, occupies the center ground framed by an apse as she carries a chalice in her extended right hand. Two courtiers, one male, the other female, share the space within the apse. To her left, beneath a tri-colored cloth of honor, gather her elegantly clad ladies-in-waiting, each one differentiated by costume and pose. To her right, a second courtier stands behind a fountain and gestures toward a doorway, his figure overlapped by that of the male courtier from the central section of the composition.

As pendant images, the panels use similar framing devices and background solutions. Compositional strategies are also shared. In both, the imperial figure occupies the central position. At the same time, there is a tripartite division within each group. Complex interrelationships between bodies in which figures overlap and collide are also common to both, as are the frontal disposition of the figures, a corresponding emphasis on vertical rhythms, isocephaly, and an interest in portrait representation. In these respects, the panels evince a visual coherence that not only links them visually but also suggests the imprint of the traditions of ceremonial representation.

There are also distinct differences between the two. In the Justinian panel the neutral ground is unelaborated, whereas in the Theodora portrait the same green and gold backdrop is broken up and arranged to include architectural features that suggest space and place. The figures set against these backgrounds also take on different airs. Those in the Justinian panel are proportionately larger and more robust with the result that they dominate the representational field, while those in the Theodora panel are smaller and more delicate, and occupy the middle ground. The characteristics of the larger groups are also evident in individual figures. The men in Justinian's retinue share poses and wear comparatively simple garments in a limited range of colors that fall in regular, columnar folds. In the Theodora panel, the female attendants strike a variety of poses, and no two garments are alike. Similar variety informs the images of the courtiers, who are themselves differentiated by pose and costume. Together with the elaboration of the architectural setting, this varied treatment of stance and dress creates a series of undulating lines across the surface of the composition that breaks up the visual field in a manner that contrasts with the steady, vertical rhythms of the Justinian panel.

This contrast is one of severity and elaboration. To a certain extent the differences are determined by sex and fashion: In the Roman world, women's costume tends to be more embellished than that of men. At the same time, however, this explanation does not account for the variation in dress extended to the male members of Theodora's retinue, much less the greater complexity of pose and setting that characterize that panel as a whole. Indeed, the extent to which variety permeates the entire scene seems purposefully at odds with the comparatively restrained treatment of the Justinian panel.

In this respect, the Theodora panel provides a welcome and necessary complement to the relentlessly solemn grandeur on display in Justinian's entourage. Here the large scale of the figures, frontal poses, and direct gazes are exchanged for a looser structure accompanied by proportionately smaller figures who display greater variety in pose, gesture, and glance. While the first two women in Theodora's entourage stare resolutely forward, those in the following group turn their gazes toward the center, and the last figure in the gathering, her attention wandering in a manner completely consistent with ceremonial representation, looks over her left shoulder to unseen activity taking place outside the scene.

These choices leaven the mood by varying the style to introduce the sense of charm and grace characteristic of Sweetness. Doing so unifies the images, adds depth to their message, and completes the ceremonial effect by bringing all the necessary expressive components into play. This juxtaposition of stylistic opposites underscores and highlights the characteristics of each. Thus, as the pendant to the Justinianic procession, the image of Theodora and her retinue sets the charm and grace of Sweetness against the weighty sobriety of Solemnity to create a more complete image of Grandeur. Doing so emphasizes not only the formal qualities of each style but also the virtues associated with them. In this instance, Solemnity and Grandeur, the perfect components of imperial majesty, bestow upon Justinian's retinue the sense of the moral authority of the emperor. By contrast, Sweetness, with its intimations of loveliness and pleasure, establishes Theodora as an imperial foil for that majesty. As Hermogenes himself remarked, it is the purpose of Sweetness to establish Solemnity.[41]

The symbiotic relationship between the two imperial panels extends to include interaction with the apse mosaic above, a representation of Christ with angels and saints (Figure 35). In this vision, Christ sits at the center of the composition, enthroned on the globe of the universe as it hovers above a verdant landscape fed by the rivers of Paradise. A gold sky striated with the colored lights of a new dawn illumines the background. His face clean-shaven and hair cut short, Christ presents a youthful figure. He wears a purple toga with gold clavi, and a cruciform, gem-bedecked nimbus surrounds his head. Standing angels, nimbed and clad in white togas with purple clavi, flank him, their brown, feathery wings tucked in behind. In turn, each angel presents a figure from the edge of the composition; Bishop Ecclesius, on the right, offers Christ a model of the church whose initial construction he oversaw, and San Vitale, on the left, leans in with covered hands to accept the martyr's crown

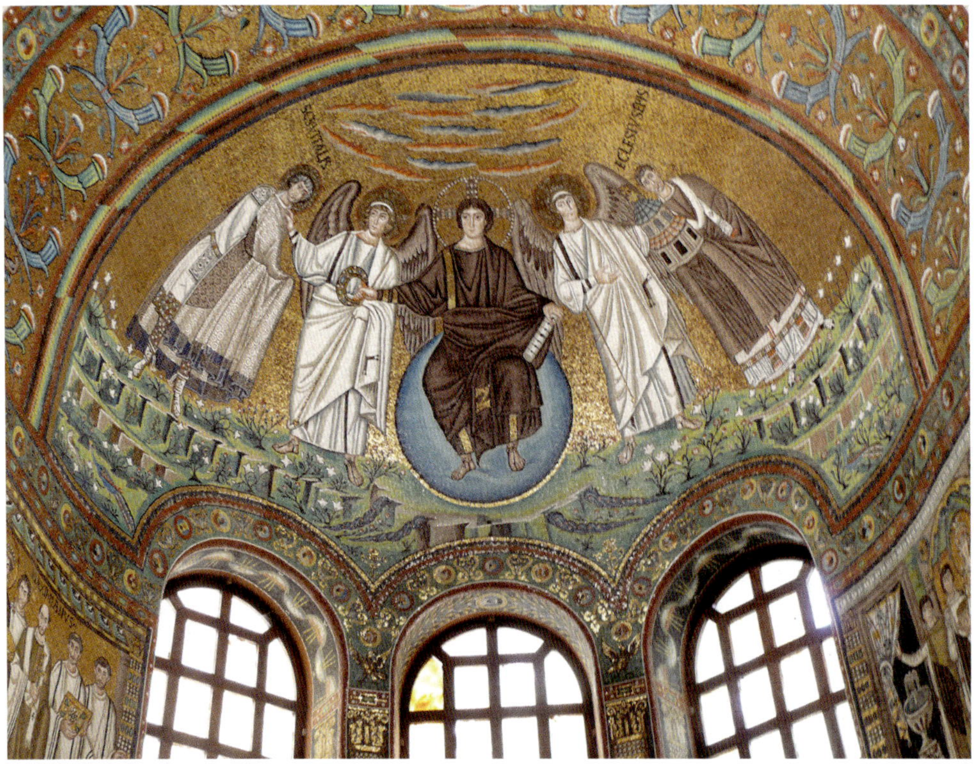

35. Christ enthroned with Bishop Ecclesius, San Vitale, and angels, Church of San Vitale, Ravenna, mid-sixth century. Photo: S. Bassett

from Christ himself. Ecclesius, bare headed, wears the garments of his office, while Vitale steps forward in his dress military costume, an elaborately embroidered white tunic and chlamys. An unadorned gold nimbus circles his head.

The figures stand in a single line against the gold ground, each form establishing a strong vertical axis within the composition's larger symmetry. A descending hierarchy of scale enhances the composition's balance: At the center, Christ is the largest of the group, followed by the angels, and, finally, the approaching figures of Ecclesius and Vitale. Color also plays a role, with Christ's garment, its broad purple field at once simple and opulent, drawing attention to the center. The white robes of the angels frame him, creating further balance, while the patterned garments of the earthly protagonists set them apart from the heavenly host. Isocephaly in the central group of Christ and the angels confirms the divide between heavenly and earthly participants: The heads of Christ and the two angels occupy the same line, while those of Ecclesius and Vitale are slightly lower. Although the central figures face forward, they are not strictly frontal. Christ extends his right hand toward Vitale, his gaze following, as he turns slightly on his throne. The angels, who stand in mirroring contrapposto poses, rotate away from the center as they turn toward their clients. Ecclesius and Vitale, whose poses also reflect each other, turn toward the center of the composition, each with arms outstretched – the former in order to give, the latter to receive.

The mosaic envisions a complex presentation ceremony.[42] At the same moment that Ecclesius steps forward to present Christ with his church, Christ, the pivot on which the action turns, offers Vitale his martyr's crown. To capture this moment in all of its ritual solemnity, this scene also relies upon the traditional tactics of Roman ceremonial imagery. Although spread across the curve of the apse, the composition is planar, with figures lining up in easy ceremonial stances. The participants, though few, show the same kind of vitality suggested by turning figures in larger groups such as those in the *largitio*. The angels rotate away from the central figure of Christ as they present their protégés. In turn, Ecclesius and Vitale, lean forward into the action, presenting and receiving their gifts across the space of the apse. Hierarchy of scale and isocephaly are integral to the scene.

Overall, the style demonstrates the combination of Clarity, Grandeur, and Sweetness proper to all such events. The straightforward disposition of the figures within the bloom of the landscape, and the corresponding pulse of their vertical forms, establishes Solemnity, an idea elaborated by the use of broad, unadorned fields of color for the garments of Christ and his angelic corps at the center of the composition and by the use of isocephaly in this focal group. The setting at once alleviates and enhances the image of Grandeur as the bright pinks and blues of the sunrise sky couple with the green, flower-studded folds of the craggy landscape to summon the idea of pleasure, an image confirmed by the elaboration of Ecclesius' and Vitale's costumes.[43]

Justinian and Theodora join in this ceremony from their subordinate positions within the apse, presenting their own gifts for Christ's table. As has often been observed, neither the emperor nor the empress ever visited Ravenna, with the result that the two processional images have often been understood to represent an imagined event that occurs independently of the action above. However, when viewed within the full context of the apse ensemble, they appear as participants in the larger ceremony unfolding above them, integrated into the activity by virtue of their placement within the apse's physical border, the ceremonial nature of their activity, and their shared style.

As in the *largitio* relief, this style both responded to and signaled the solemnity of the event itself and the majesty of its participants. It did so by appealing to an ingrained understanding of what such stylistic choices implied. As Hermogenes pointed out, the Solemnity at the heart of Grandeur was the vehicle for expressing thoughts concerning the divine.[44] Here, it created a vision of those thoughts in Christian terms to describe not only the event but also, portentously, a universal order in which the Roman emperor was an active and influential member of Christ's court. The inclusion of the imperial panels within the jeweled border of the apse establishes emperor and empress as members of the larger retinue, while their inferior placement makes clear the subsidiary rank of the imperial players within the hierarchy. At once favored and ordained by Christ, emperor and empress are also his servants, a fact underscored not simply by their position but also by their tribute-bearing activity. Following the lead of Ecclesius in the apse above, they continue the chain of offerings to Christ from their subsidiary position. Style confirms this vision, as the solemn cadences and harmonious balances of the individual compositions unite to celebrate the glory of God and the piety of his earthly servants.

In the same way that the Constantinian *largitio* represented the culminating act of the emperor's conquest of and entry into Rome, the imperial panels, together with the larger ceremonial ensemble of which they are a part, stand at the apex of a series of images in the chancel. Those images, which divide between portrait representations and narrative scenes, cover the walls and ceiling within a carefully articulated decorative framework. Medallion portraits depicting the apostles, Christ, and Saints Gervase and Protase line the intrados of the arch at the chancel entrance. Inside the sanctuary, the walls, which rise through two levels, show a variety of framed, interrelated images. On the south wall (Figure 36), a lunette collapses time to depict Abel and the priest

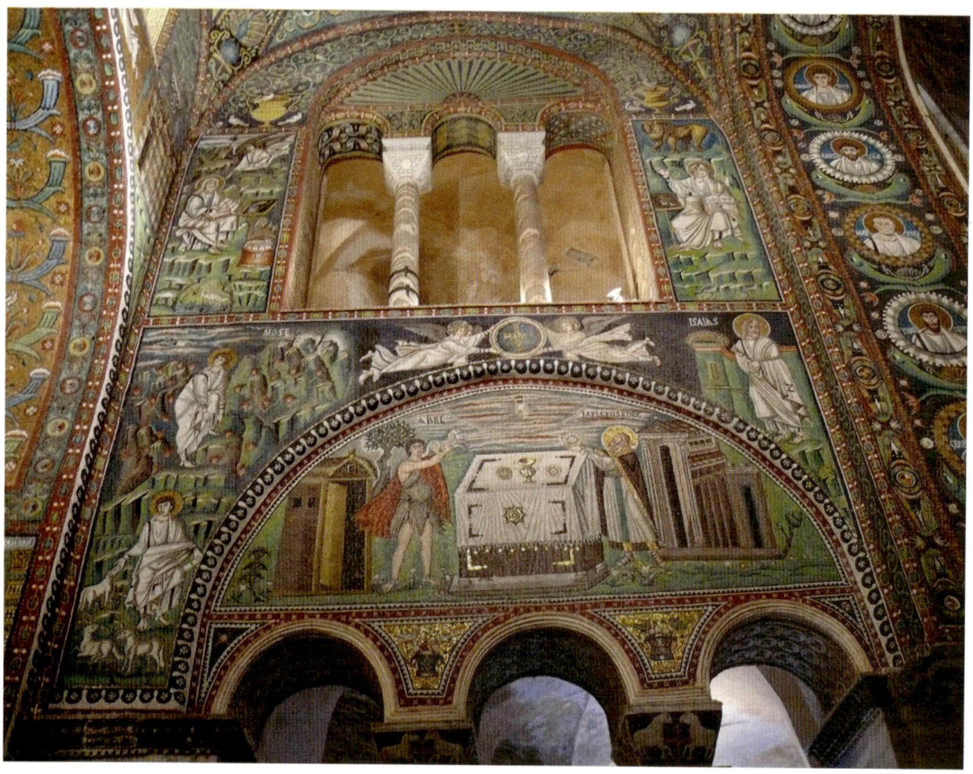

36. North chancel wall, San Vitale, Ravenna, mid-sixth century. Photo: S. Bassett

Melchizedek as they offer a sacrifice. In the spandrels above the lunette, Moses has his first encounter with God at the burning bush on the left, while the prophet Isaiah appears on the right. Between them, two hovering angels flank a radiant medallion. On the second level, to either side of a gallery opening, are full-length seated portraits of the evangelists Matthew and Mark, each with his signifying beast. Above them, a flourishing vine curves around the top of the arched window. On the north wall (Figure 37), a complementary set of images repeats the same pattern. The lunette, following the theme of sacrifice, combines two biblical episodes, the hospitality of Abraham and Abraham's aborted sacrifice of Isaac. The story of Moses continues on the spandrel's right side with the reception of the law, while the prophet Jeremiah occupies the left and the hovering angels hold the center ground. Above, the evangelists John and Luke take their places to the left and right of the gallery opening, as the vine motif unfolds above. On the eastern triumphal arch, the heavenly cities of Bethlehem and Jerusalem flank the opening to the apse, as another arching vine curves over a centrally placed window beneath the ceiling vault. This verdant motif continues on the vault, where four angels perched on transparent globes rising from the expansive tendrils of acanthus plants support an image of the paschal lamb at the center of a garlanded pergola.[45]

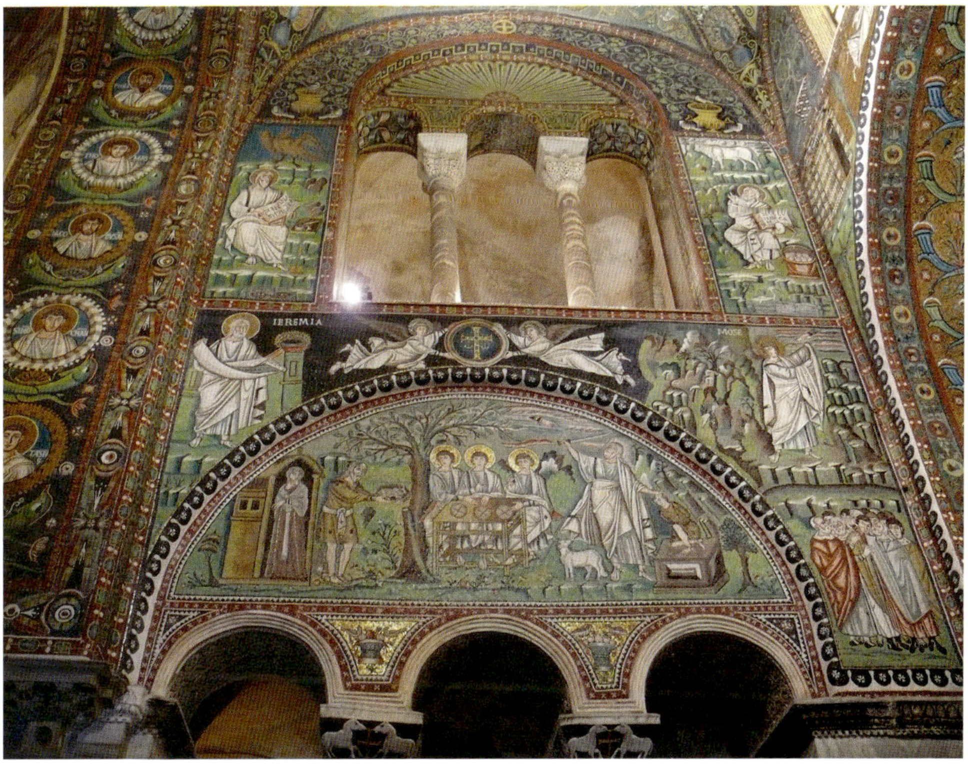

37. South chancel wall, San Vitale, Ravenna, mid-sixth century. Photo: S. Bassett

This dense, compartmentalized organization of the wall and the dazzling effect it produces has been described as the Jeweled Style.[46] It can also be said to offer a textbook example of Grandeur created by visual Abundance. As such it is consistent with the aims of the narrative sequence in Santa Maria Maggiore. The same is true of the individual images. Consider, for example, the calling of Moses on the south wall, the encounter in which God charges Moses with leading the Israelites out of Egypt:

> One day while Moses was taking care of the sheep and goats of his father-in-law Jethro, the priest of Midian, he led the flock across the desert and came to Sinai, the holy mountain. There the angel of the Lord appeared to him as a flame coming from the middle of a bush. Moses saw that the bush was on fire but that it was not burning up. "This is strange," he thought. "Why isn't the bush burning up? I will go closer and see." When the Lord saw that Moses was coming closer, he called to him from the middle of the bush and said, "Moses! Moses!" He answered, "Yes, here I am." God said, "Do not come any closer. Take off your sandals, because you are standing on holy ground. I am the God of your ancestors, the God of Abraham, Isaac, and Jacob." So Moses covered his face because he was afraid to look at God.
>
> (Exodus 3)

The action, which unfolds on two levels within the spandrel's irregular, curving shape, takes place in a craggy, if verdant, mountain setting, which rises from the lower edge of the composition to a deep-blue sky tinged with pink clouds at the top. There, the hand of God erupts from the clouds, gesturing toward a youthful, clean-shaven Moses who stands on the mountain below. Clad in the immaculate white toga of a Roman aristocrat, his head circled by a nimbus, he leans over to untie his sandals as bushes burst into crackling flame around him. Perched awkwardly on one foot, he turns his head toward the heavens. Moses appears again in the lower portion together with the sheep of his flock. He stands, facing forward, in a contrapposto pose, a scroll in his left hand, his right hand stroking one of the sheep.

As is the case with all such narrative images, both iconography and style build on a base of mimetic Clarity to offer a vivid elaboration of the spare biblical account in terms consistent with Abundance. The division of the image into two sequential events – one derived from the text, the other fully imagined – establishes the overall sense of this elaboration. Details of interpretation enhance this look, most notably in deviations from the biblical account. At the moment of his calling, Moses is confronted not with a single burning bush but with a mountainside erupting into flame, as no less than two dozen fires blaze around him. Further, in direct contradiction of the text, he turns toward rather than away from the voice of God. The pure invention of the second scene, which imagines Moses in the aftermath of his encounter, is of a piece with these choices, all of which are enhanced by details of costume and pose. In his early imperial dress and gleaming nimbus, Moses, transformed from a humble shepherd into a Roman aristocrat, summons the vision of a lost golden age in the archaizing style of his toga. His poses are also evocative. At the moment of his calling, the awkwardness of his rocking, one-footed pose implies his vulnerability. By contrast, the contrapposto stance he adopts below as he descends from the mountain to take up the mandate that he shepherd the Israelites to their freedom endows him with the look of the heroic. Conceived in wholly Roman terms, that mandate may be alluded to in the codicil-like roll.

Style supports this iconographic Abundance. The landscape, conceived as a series of interlocking horizontal and vertical forms, creates a complex, sometimes erratic, set of visual rhythms as the deep-green ground pushes back from the lower edge of the spandrel to meet a series of stacked horizontal platforms cut by dark, irregularly placed vertical clefts in the mountain. Color enhances these openings as the white highlights running along the upper edge of the clefts set off the dark, almost black, cuts in the green ground to create an irregular zigzagging pattern. Eventually, in the upper reaches of the composition, this horizontal organization unfolds into a set of vertically aligned peaks flecked with bright patches of yellow and red flame that in turn open out to the sky and the signaling hand of God. Moses stands out as a monumental figure within this structural grid, by virtue of his scale and the radiant white of his garments. His appearance, repeated in two separate poses, unites the two halves of the composition, not only through the duplication of the color on each of the levels but also by establishing a linear connection between the two episodes. Beginning at the lower edge of the composition, the line weaves over and around the backs of the sheep to connect to Moses' outstretched hand and through it to the vertical line of his body, which in turn connects to the curved outline of the balancing figure above.

The Calling of Moses is nothing if not Abundant, a sense conveyed not only by the iconographic elaboration of the episode but also by the particular qualities of the style. Throughout the composition, short segments of fluctuating line punctuated by bright fields and patches of color break up the visual field in a manner analogous to verbal Rapidity (*Gorgotes*). Characterized by the use of short clauses, Rapidity was designed to capture the swift pace of conversational exchange. Here, on the slopes of Sinai, the staccato imagery of the rocky clefts and fiery bushes conveys the urgency in the encounter between Moses and his God.

In its iconographic and stylistic Abundance, the calling of Moses captures the Grandeur of the events on Sinai. Other images in the chancel share the same tactics. Whether in the sacrifice of Abel and Melchizedek, the scenes from the life of Abraham, or the continuing story of Moses, the elaboration of iconography augments compositions, which are then further enhanced by variations in style. The image of Abel and Melchizedek relies on the tactics of Solemnity to convey the essence of sacrificial ceremony, while the intricate scenes from the life of Abraham summon Rapidity's sense of urgency in the service of their story.

The purpose here is not to discuss each image individually but rather to suggest the ways in which variations on the theme of Abundance enrich individual images to shape the sense of Grandeur appropriate to stories of interaction with the divine. That Grandeur, evident in individual images, is also present in the aggregate, that is, in the chancel's dense, tightly packed set of images. Here, as on the Arch of Constantine, style shifts in response to the needs of a narrative sequence, in this instance an accounting of significant moments of human interaction with the divine across the stages of sacred history. A similar shift takes place between the chancel and the apse, as the Rapidity of narrative interaction with the divine finds its resolution in the Solemnity of stately ceremonial. Against the close-knit imagery of the chancel walls, the stately, monumental forms of the apse ceremony express the virtues of the Christian monarch and the triumph of Orthodox Christianity.

CONCLUSIONS

When Riegl and his intellectual followers examined the fourth-century *largitio* relief and its sixth-century pendant the Justinianic mosaic as exemplars of late Roman art, they did so without recognizing that they represented but one type of image within a larger aesthetic system. Thus, instead of seeing the Constantinian *largitio* or the Justinianic procession as images in a sequence, Riegl viewed them in isolation, claiming for them qualities which they were never intended to express. Rather than describing a world of irrational thought and mystical longing, these images, which owed their formal logic to the traditions of ceremonial representation, envisioned the aura of dignity and authority surrounding such public ceremonial occasions as ritual sacrifice or public oration. In doing so, they at once shaped and reflected common agreement about the nature of such events. As elaborated in late antiquity, the forms in use spoke ever more explicitly to the understanding of the social order. The introduction of such new representational strategies as hierarchy of scale, or the more overt emphasis on symmetrical composition, created a diagram of communal order and the power relationships supporting it that underscored the essential role of the emperor in public life, whether, as in the case of Constantine, as a bringer of peace and a restorer of prosperity, or, as in the case of Justinian, as the advocate for the *res publica* with the divine.

Perhaps even more crucially, style also gave visible life to the virtues driving imperial success: courage, intelligence, moderation, justice, and, above all, *pietas*. As such, they were images of power.

NOTES

1 Riegl 1901, 46–51; 1985, 52–57.
2 Hölscher 2004, 55, for list; Torelli 1982, 89–109, on the Anaglypha Traiani.
3 Hölscher 2004, 50–51.
4 Hölscher 2004, 56.
5 On terminology, see Corbier 2006; Corbier and Schneider 2006.
6 On the *largitio* in Roman tradition, see Stylow 1972; on the integration of the ceremony into this sequence of events, see Torelli 1982, 107.
7 On the event and its equipment, see Beckmann 2015.
8 The major discussion of the *largitio* remains L'Orange and Gerkan (1939). For Basilica Ulpia as the traditional venue, see their discussion (1939, 1: 94–95).
9 On the tablets, see Beckmann 2015. L'Orange and Gerkan (1939, 1: 99) identified the pieces as tokens (*tessera frumentaria* or *nummaria*) to be cashed in.
10 Beckmann (2015) notes that the event probably took place over several days and required multiple stations, an understanding suggested by the use of the tablets in the subsidiary scenes.
11 Riegl, 1901: 46–51; 1985, 52–57. On magical thinking, see Chapter 2.
12 The art historians: Worringer (1908) used the relief as his main evidence for his theory of abstraction, arguing that its character was generally oriental. Morey (1924), Dalton (1925), and Grabar (1936) each took a similar view, as did Weitzmann (1974) and Elsner (1995). Among archaeologists, Rodenwaldt (1921–1922) favored the East, although he did not fully exclude the notion of a western provincial contribution. For a summary of earlier views, see L'Orange and Gerkan (1939, 1: 198–207).
13 Strong 1907, 332–40.
14 Hermogenes 1913; 1987. Menander Rhetor 1981, 77–94.
15 Hermogenes 1913, 241–96; 1987, 18–54.
16 On Clarity, see Hermogenes 1913, 226–41; 1987, 8–18, 242–96. On Dignity, Grandeur and their substyles, see Hermogenes 1913, 242–96; 1987, 18–54. On Sweetness. Hermogenes 1913, 330–39; 1987, 75–81. On Beauty: Hermogenes 1913, 296–311; 1987, 54–64.
17 Hermogenes 1913, 250–54; 1987, 23–26.
18 Hermogenes 1913, 255–60; 1987, 26–30.
19 Hermogenes 1913, 264–69; 1987, 32–36.
20 Hermogenes 1913, 277–96; 1987, 41–54.
21 Hermogenes 1913, 330–39; 1987, 75–81.
22 Hermogenes 1913, 320–22; 1987, 70–71. See also Menander Rhetor 1981, 77.
23 Wace (1907, 270–76), Knudsen (1989), and Rose (2021) argue that the fourth-century frieze traditionally attributed to Constantinian manufacture is also reused from a monument to Diocletian (284–304). Lenski and Koortbojian (2023) convincingly refute this idea. I thank the authors for sharing their work with me in advance of its publication.
24 Potter 2013, 137–44.
25 Holland (1946) identifies the arch.
26 Menander Rhetor 1981, 77.
27 Menander Rhetor 1981, 77–94.
28 Panegyrici Latini 1994, 211–53 (Panegyric 6).
29 An oration given before Constantine's father, Constantius, c. 298, addresses the importance of children. See Panegyrici Latini 1994, 140 (Panegyric 8.19.4). On the arch and its relation

to panegyric, see Rose (2021, 175), who acknowledges the general understanding of the arch's visual panegyric ever since L'Orange and von Gerkan (1939, 4–28, 161–91) first argued the point. In the same vein, see De Maria 1988, 203–11, 316–19, Peirce 1989, Elsner 2000, Carlson 2010, and Hughes 2014. Kuhoff (1991, 144–46) notes a specific connection between the siege of Verona and its visualization, as does Sandberg (2015).

30 The inscriptions, which are on the inside of the central arch above the Trajanic battle reliefs, are literally dedicatory: "Fundatori quietis" (to the restorer of peace) and "Liberatori urbis" (to the liberator of the city).

31 Riegl 1901, 132–33; 1985, 139–40.

32 The bibliography on the church and its mosaics is substantial. The standard work is Deichmann 1969–89, 1: 226–56, esp. 234–56; 2/2: 47–230, esp. 180–87.
On the imperial panels themselves, see Bassett 2008, from which this discussion derives, Nordström, 1953: 98–102; Stričević 1959; 1962; Grabar 1960; Manara 1983; Engemann 1984; Barber 1990; Andreescu-Treadgold and Treadgold 1997. The panels are also discussed in the following interpretive studies of late Roman and early Byzantine art: Simpson 1948, 27–39; Mathews 1971, 146–47; Kitzinger 1977, 81–88; MacCormack 1981, 259–66; Maguire 1987, 76–80; Elsner 1995, 177–89; Deliyannis 2010, 236–50. Most discussions focus on questions of iconography. The major exceptions are Andreescu-Treadgold and Treadgold 1997, which, although concerned with iconography, bases its arguments and conclusions on technical analysis of the mosaics, and Kitzinger 1977, which deals with questions of style.

33 A comprehensive restoration of the San Vitale mosaics was completed in 1990. For general publication of the materials, see Iannucci, Fiori, and Muscolino 1992. I. Andreescu-Treadgold's study of the Justinianic mosaic indicated that the mosaic was executed in two separate phases to accommodate changes in the city's episcopal leadership. The first phase was completed around 544, the second in 545. During this second intervention, the portrait of Bishop Maxentius and its accompanying inscription replaced that of his recently deceased predecessor, Victor, and the figure to the left of Justinian was added. There were also adjustments to Justinian's crown and his jewelry. These changes to iconography, although dramatic, do not affect the overall style of the mosaic. For complete discussion, see Andreescu-Treadgold 1995; Andreescu-Treadgold and Treadgold 1997.

34 Riegl 1901, 132; 1985, 139.

35 Riegl 1901, 132–33; 1985, 139–42.

36 Kandinsky (1912, 121; 1977, 57) used the mosaic to illustrate his text, presenting it as a simple "melodic" composition against later complex "symphonic" compositions. For equations between the mosaic and the spiritual, see Schmarsow 1905, 324.

37 Taine 1874, 221–25; Richter 1878, 72–92; Wulff 1914, 2: 361–62 and 421–24.

38 Kraus (1896, 1:440) saw the mosaics as western; Rodenwaldt (1928, 228–35) linked the mosaic to Roman ceremonial tradition but an orientalizing Parthian style. Later he expressed a change of heart, arguing that the mosaic mixed eastern and western styles: Rodenwaldt 1944-1945b, 10. Lazarev (1967, 80) characterized the style as local; Kollwitz (1965, 401–402) saw the mosaic as the product of a unique local workshop subject to eastern and western influences. Subsequent discussions posit a local workshop and two work phases, each with its own style. See Rizzardi 1988; 2005; Andreescu-Treadgold and Treadgold 1997, 715–16. For an assessment of individual artists and working techniques within the San Vitale workshop, see Andreescu-Treadgold 1992. For a discussion of the historiographical implications of the East–West issue, see Frantová 2019, 17–39.

39 Deichmann 1953; 1969–1989, 2/2: 190.

40 On the portraits and their identification, see Manara 1983; Engemann 1984; Andreescu-Treadgold and Treadgold 1997.

41 Bassett 2008.

42 For theories regarding the ceremony and discussion, see Stričević 1959; 1962; Mathews 1971, 146; Deichmann 1969–1989: 2/2, 189–90; MacCormack 1981, 260; Elsner 1995, 187; Deckers 2002; McClanan 2002, 128; Deliyannis 2010, 243.

43 See Andreescu-Treadgold (1995) on the medieval restoration and the resulting changes to the saints' costume.

44 Hermogenes 1913, 243–44; 1987, 19–20.

45 Autopsy of the mosaics indicates that they were executed in two phases after the completion of the apse. The first phase included the walls rising above the marble revetment to the springing of the vault. The second included the north and south tympana and the vault itself. See Andreescu-Treadgold and Treadgold 1997, 715–16.

46 Roberts 1989, esp. 66–121.

EIGHT

PORTRAITS CIVIC AND SACRED

NEITHER WICKHOFF NOR RIEGL HAD MUCH TO SAY ON THE MATTER OF portraiture. To the extent that such images made an appearance in their writing, it was to confirm their hunches on the nature of Roman style. Wickhoff, as might be expected, saw portraiture as an exercise in suggestive illusionism, as manifest early in the masterly sculptured representations of the Flavian era[1] and late in the newly discovered encaustic paintings from the Wadi Fayum, pictures that documented what he thought of as the Roman style's conquest of the East.[2] Riegl, unsurprisingly, stared into the same faces with a completely different understanding, describing both sculptured and painted work as "mask-like" (*maskenhafte*)[3] exercises in crystalline production whose goal was the expression of a spiritual life.[4]

It was Riegl's equation between crystalline form and spiritual life that took hold in the ongoing discussion. In 1905, five short years after the publication of *The Late Roman Art-Industry*, August Schmarsow, writing of the imperial portraits in San Vitale, would characterize such images as abstract and conclude that they represent "the kingdom of the spirit."[5] This understanding subsequently became the norm in discussions of portraiture, as the busts, shield images, and free-standing figures of the later Roman world all shook off the burden of earthly existence to wrap themselves in the mantle of otherworldly spirituality. H. P. L'Orange's discussion of the fourth-century portrait of the Roman senator C. Caelius Saturninus, better known as Dogmatius (Figure 38), is a case in point.

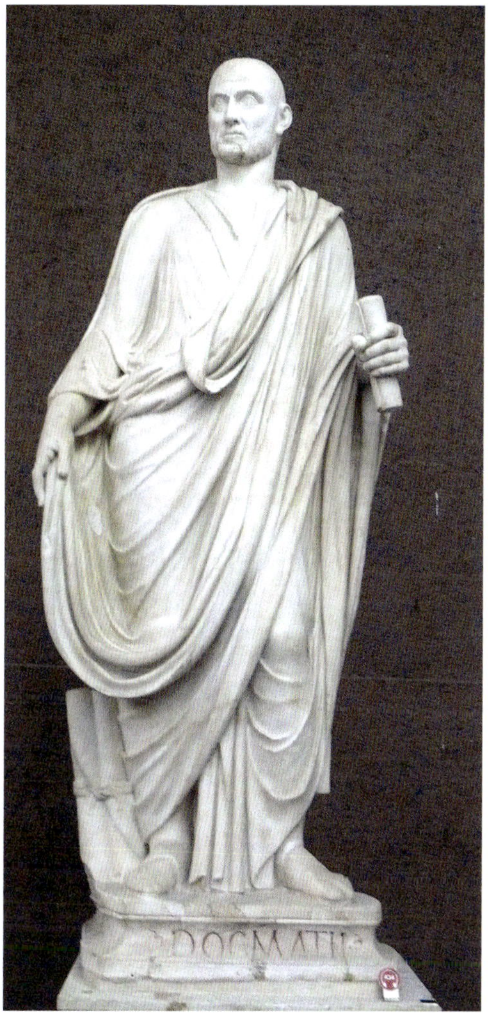

38. Statue of Caius Caelius Saturninus *signo* Dogmatius, 324–337, Vatican Museums (Museo Gregoriano Profano). Photo: S. Bassett

The standing marble portrait was created in the fourth century by repurposing two pieces from earlier statues: a draped statue body of the second century and a separately worked head of unknown date.[6] Dogmatius, identified by inscription on the statue's plinth and the accompanying base, wears the traditional toga of the early and middle empire. He stands in a contrapposto pose, his weight supported on his right leg. His right arm runs parallel to the side of his body as he holds the edge of the toga, which swoops across his body to wrap over his bent left arm, which projects from the body at a right angle. He carries a rotulus in his extended left hand, while a tidy bundle of scrolls rests behind his right ankle. His head and body turn to the right, an effect emphasized by the wide U-shaped folds of the toga as they move down the right side of his figure before sweeping across and up the left, directing attention to the

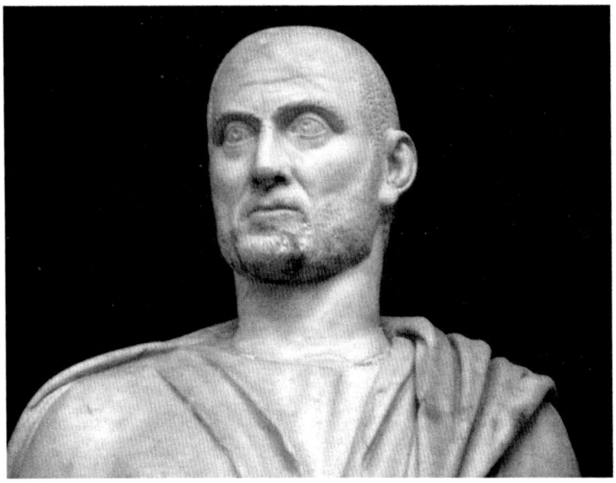

39. Head of Caius Caelius Saturninus *signo* Dogmatius, 324–337, Vatican Museums (Museo Gregoriano Profano). Photo: S. Bassett

head. The face itself (Figure 39) is lean, with prominent cheekbones; an aquiline nose; and large, deep-set eyes with drilled pupils and emphatic, bushy brows. Closely cropped hair recedes from a high, gently furrowed forehead, and a short, clipped beard articulates the taut line of his jaw. Fine lines indicate the nasolabial folds, and the lips are thin.[7]

L'Orange, who discussed only the head, responded to the lean countenance and emphatic eyes, describing the image as a "soul-portrait" whose features expressed a "pneumatic" sense of inner life that transcended the experience of the phenomenal world in a manner consistent with the teachings of the Neoplatonic philosopher Plotinus. Of this spiritualized expression, which he saw as a response to the crisis of the third century, he remarked, "Instead of the quivering life of the surface [seen in earlier portraits] we see a crystalline reflection of inner, abstract life. No longer the flashing play of features, but a permanent expressive mask."[8]

L'Orange was not the first to make such observations, nor was he the last, but, as R. R. R. Smith has observed, this blanket view of late Roman honorific sculpture is untenable. Built around a series of "false premises" – including the imposition of a unitary, teleological conception of formal development; analysis of works independent of context; the identification of unidentifiable subjects; and an anachronistic understanding of physiognomy – it misunderstands form and misrepresents the ways in which members of late Roman society wished to present themselves to both their contemporaries and posterity.[9] Specifically, the presumption that the simplification of form appearing at the end of the third century represents a turn from realism misrepresents the case. These images were nothing if not mimetic, and, as was always the case with the mimetic enterprise, the idea of imitation included both physical likeness and character. This chapter builds on these points to consider not only portrait sculpture but also early representations of the protagonists of Christian history, the images referred to as "icons."

PORTRAITURE IN THE LATER ROMAN WORLD

The Roman Empire was nothing if not portrait rich. In settings public and private, at scales monumental and miniature, images of men and women were a consistent feature in the visual landscape. In cities throughout the empire, whole sculptured populations took up residence, sharing space with a town's flesh-and-blood inhabitants. In the streets, forums, and public gathering places that shaped the urban environment, portraits of such local worthies as priests, magistrates, and provincial governors stood cheek by jowl with emperors and venerable historical figures. Installed initially to honor living subjects, with the passage of time, these statues also became tributes to the dead, and as such a visual manifestation of a distinct urban history. Nor was sculpture the only medium for such public recognition. As literary references and the scant remains of painted representation indicate, fresco and mosaic also played their part in the commemorative enterprise. Charioteers and other athletes might find their memory perpetuated in the mosaic floors of public baths, while emperors and their cohort appeared in the vaults and apses of palaces, temples, and churches.

Portraits also made themselves comfortable in the relative privacy of domestic and funerary settings. For example, the statue of Dogmatius, a gift from his son, appears to have been erected at his residence. Painted images may also have had their place amidst the roster of portraits in the family atrium, along with mosaic representations in the floor. Small-scale portraits were also fitting for these more intimate settings – the image of a woman and child in a gold glass medallion or an ivory diptych carved with a consular portrait. Finally, portraits were appropriate to the tomb, as indicated by the carved representations of men and women on sarcophagi or by painted portraits in catacombs.

The range of portraiture was extensive, its purposes and contexts diverse. Some types, such as the public honorific portraits, were of longstanding tradition. Erected in recognition of achievements, they included in their rank representations of poets, philosophers, and other culture heroes; emperors and other imperial office holders, such as prefects and provincial governors; and such local worthies as priests, magistrates, and other benefactors. These individuals were commemorated in various forms: the standing cuirass or toga statue, the bust, or the shield portrait. Other types, such as the commemorative diptych, gained favor only in the late empire. At small scale, their audience was restricted to circles of elite citizens who participated in an ongoing round of gift exchange. That said, surviving examples were dedicated to the same range of figures as their monumental counterparts: gods, emperors and members of their household, and high-ranking officials, most famous among them the consuls of the Roman Empire.[10]

Portraiture was thus a genre of tradition and invention. Uniting these efforts was a shared understanding of the aims of such representation and the means to achieve it. Whether monumental or miniature, the portraits of the Roman world served to honor their subjects. As such, they functioned as visual encomia, panegyrics designed to praise the living subject and enshrine his or her memory for generations to come. They did so using a widely understood language of visual communication that encompassed both iconography and style. Recent study has parsed this visual language of honor by focusing on the contexts and circumstances in which such statues were erected and the iconography of individual statues, such aspects of elite presentation as costume, hairstyle, and other elements of personal grooming.[11] The effect of these undertakings has been to restore an understanding of the ways in which these sculptured presentations operated within the competitive social context of the later Roman world to express ideas about status, character, and political inclination against the claims of spiritualized representation that have historically dominated the discussion. In pursuit of this goal, the discussion of the formal elements of style has received less attention.[12] Yet the manipulation of line, color, and composition was an equally vital component in these dedications, as formal choices worked hand in glove with iconography to enhance a statue's meaning. If the idea of conveying spirituality is now put safely to rest, it is appropriate to reexamine form and the strategies it embraced in the service of mimesis.

Consider again, Dogmatius or, more formally, C. Caelius Saturninus *signo* Dogmatius.[13] The statue offers a likeness of its fourth-century subject, whose *curriculum vitae* is outlined on the supporting base:

> In honor of Dogmatius. To Caius Caelius Saturninus, of *clarissimus* rank, enrolled by request of the Senate into the rank of *consularis*, count of our lord the victorious Augustus Constantine, deputy of the prefecture of the city, judge in the imperial court of appeal, twice deputy of the praetorian prefects: in the City of Rome and for the [provinces of] Moesia, financial inspector for Italy, prefect of the *annona* of the City, chief officer of the imperial patrimony, deputy of the chief officer of the imperial fisc, deputy chief officer of the imperial patrimony in Gaul, head of the census, deputy at the imperial council, head of the imperial records, head of the office of petitions, functionary of the imperial council receiving an annual salary of 200,000 *sestertii*, functionary of the imperial council receiving an annual salary of 60,000 *sestertii*, assistant functionary at the records office receiving an annual salary of 60,000 *sestertii*, advocate of the *fiscus* in Italy. Caius Flavius Caelius Urbanus, of *clarissimus* rank with the rank of *consularis*, [set this up] to his father.[14]

As the inscription makes clear, Dogmatius' was an illustrious career. Born into the equestrian class, he had been raised to the senatorial rank by the time of the dedication. Stints at court and in the imperial administration had earned him a series of increasingly illustrious positions and titles, among them some involving judicial and financial oversight. The commissioned statue, working in conjunction with the base, was tasked with giving visual life to the man behind this cursus in a manner suitable to his rank. To do so, it drew on well-established traditions of honorific representation.

The statue was in every respect familiar. As a freestanding *togatus*, it was a type long known from display in Rome and other cities of the empire, one that established the credentials of its honorand. Monumental scale contributed to its impact, as did the subject's pose. At 219 cm, the statue was imposing. Set atop its 84 cm base, it was even more commanding.[15] The contrapposto stance was of a piece with this magnitude. Although there is no direct ancient commentary on the use of contrapposto, and the ancient term, if there was one, has not survived,[16] visual materials suggest that as a formal and technical solution to figural composition it signaled the heroic. The earliest surviving uses of the pose date to the fifth century BC, when it appears in such Greek works as the Kritios Boy (c. 480 BC) and the Doryphoros of Polyclitus (c. 450 BC). Both statues suggest this association with heroic virtue in their subject matter. The Kritios Boy memorialized an Athenian youth, while the "spear-bearing" Doryphorus has been identified by some as Achilles. Quintilian's remark that the Doryphorus furnished an apt model for the representation of warriors and athletes supports this line of interpretation.[17] The consistent use of contrapposto in Roman honorific dedications suggests a similar, if expanded, application.

The iconography of dress also contributed to the statue's message. Dogmatius wears the traditional toga and tunic of the early and middle empire, together with *calcei*, the closed leather shoes of a member of the equestrian order.[18] This choice was significant. As reliefs from the late third-century Decennalia Base in the Roman Forum and the fourth-century reliefs on the Arch of Constantine attest, new togate fashions were coming into use among members of the Roman aristocracy at the time Dogmatius' statue was installed. Overwhelmingly, however, the old toga remained the costume of choice for individual honorific commemoration in the early fourth century, a choice that attested not only to its wearer's social status but also to his old school allegiances. Here was a man who embraced the *mos maiorum*.[19] Dogmatius' rotulus and the scroll bundle at his feet further support those ties by alluding to his education and with it his status as a cultured member of civil society.

As significant as dress was the iconography of the head, which drew on a package of standardized signs to shape the individual likeness. Dogmatius' cropped hair and beard had long been associated with the military, and in the early years of the fourth century, during the period of the Tetrarchy, the look had come back into fashion. By the time of the statue's dedication in the 320s, the style was already outdated in imperial portraits, when Constantine and his sons appeared clean-shaven and with more luxuriant hair in pursuit of a more idealizing look. It did however persist as an independent mode of representation for members of the elite well into the late antique period, where such representations identified their subjects as active citizens and tireless warriors for the state.[20]

Physiognomy complements this choice in grooming. The lean, bony face with its aquiline nose, high cheekbones, and deeply-set, drilled eyes coupled with the pronounced creases in the brow and the sharp lines of the nasolabial folds are of a piece with the short hair and beard. As R. R. R. Smith has observed of the portraits of other high-ranking officials from the period, this manner of depicting facial features represented a newly adopted way of emphasizing old virtues that had its roots in the Republican era, where the overall realism and plainness with which likenesses were rendered lent intensity to the face and suggested the virtues of *simplicitas* (candor), *veritas* (honesty), and *integritas* (truth).[21]

That a face could be instilled with such meaning rested on the common assumption that there was an equation between the outer physical form of the body and inner mental states.[22] In particular the face and, within the face, the eyes had the capacity to reveal the true nature of human disposition. Cicero[23] and Quintilian,[24] building on traditions of physiognomic analysis that could trace their origins to Aristotle, saw the eyes as the index of a man's mental state. Control of appearance was therefore essential. This view was seconded by the second-century physiognomist Polemon and his fourth-century epitomizer Adamantius, both of whom observed that the eyes revealed the soul. As Adamantius put it,

> And there are signs on the whole body of a man, and his voice and his breathing and his color contribute to practicing physiognomy. But many of the signs and the sum of them is located in the eyes, and the soul appears through these as if through gates.[25]

At first glance, such a remark might appear to confirm L'Orange's assessment of the portrait as an image of spiritual retreat; however, in reading on, it becomes clear that the soul to which the physiognomist referred is not the disembodied, otherworldly spirit envisioned in L'Orange's account. Rather, Adamantius, who went on to devote nearly a third of the treatise to discussion of the eyes, noted the myriad states of mind to be deduced from their shape and structure. As it turns out, the ocular gate might just as easily open onto the deceitful soul as the pure.[26] Dogmatius' own articulated gaze is consistent with the latter. Adamantius suggests as much with his own observation, "Eyes that are bright and shine like pools reveal good character,"[27] words that might easily describe Dogmatius' emphatically sculptured eyes – bright, shining pools that illuminate the face to create a mimetic representation in which the flesh and blood of human form express the virtue consistent with engagement, responsibility, and success in the world.

In short, the statue offered a visual encomium, a panegyric to the man and his qualities. Figure and base stood as an epitome of visual Clarity, with image and word presented as separable components that combined to articulate, reiterate, and summarize Dogmatius' *curriculum vitae* in a unified, readily understandable presentation. Within the whole, other stylistic devices generated the sense of Grandeur vital to the panegyrical enterprise. Specifically, the juxtaposition of straight and bent limbs introduced in the contrapposto pose lent an air of Abundance to the figure by creating a complex relationship between sculptured mass and its encircling space; this relationship built on a sense of antithesis to suspend the body paradoxically between stasis and motion. The sinuous, if restrained, figural profile that results from this pose, contributes further to this appearance, as do the long, elegant lines of the polished drapery, which sweep across the front of the torso, responding to the figure's torsion in an alternating set of dark troughs and bright ridges. The treatment of the head, with its sharp transitions between surfaces and the linear articulation of its details, offers yet another contrast. The clear, domical profile and the angular structure of the face stand out against the merging, undulating surfaces created by the easy torsion of the body and the drapery's rippling response. Short, stippled lines texture the hair, eyebrows, and beard, and each element of the face – from the nasolabial folds and the lips to the hairline and the beard line – is given sharp, linear articulation. Reminiscent of the kind of direct statement characteristic of Purity and Simplicity, this emphasis on line enhances the realism of the face, setting it off against the body's controlled, idealized elegance to inject the image with a dose of the Solemn.

The impact of the Dogmatius statue turns on a series of contrasts: between visual and verbal, straight and bent, light and dark, ideal and real. As such, it is a visual exercise in antithesis, itself a device of rhetorical style. Antithesis was at once simple and complex. Verbally, its basic tool was parallel construction, which it manipulated through complex changes of repetition and variation in long periodic sentences with the simultaneous, if contradictory, ends of clarifying and embellishing language. These verbal complexities in turn lent a sense of Grandeur to subject matter and speaker alike. The Dogmatius statue functions in a similar manner. Drawing on and combining the elegant formal trends of the middle imperial period with the unvarnished forms of a fourth-century realist tradition that had its roots in the Republican era, the statue described its subject as a worthy member of the senatorial class by using contrasting styles to create a sense of Abundance and, through it, the idea of Grandeur appropriate to the man and his accomplishments. At the center of this Grandeur was the contrapposto pose with its intimations of the heroic.

Further, in the concrete evocations of earlier historical styles, the statue engaged fully with the range of historical tradition, thereby establishing Dogmatius as an heir to the Roman past.[28]

The Dogmatius portrait is representative of its time. Across the late antique empire, efforts were made to honor worthy citizens in sculpture by conveying intangible qualities of character through physical form. Some statues showed a remarkable similarity to that of Dogmatius. Fourth-century togate statues of provincial governors C. Valerius Vibianus of Tripolitania and Virius Audentius Aemilianus of Campania combine reused second-century bodies with fourth-century heads to comparable stylistic effect.[29] Other images, such as that of Flavius Palmatus (Figure 40), provincial governor at Aphrodisias in the late fifth or early sixth century, show sculptors adopting allied but different approaches as they pursued the project of honorific representation.

The statue,[30] which was displayed in the Tetrastoon in Aphrodisias, is life size and, together with its inscribed rectangular base, stands over three meters

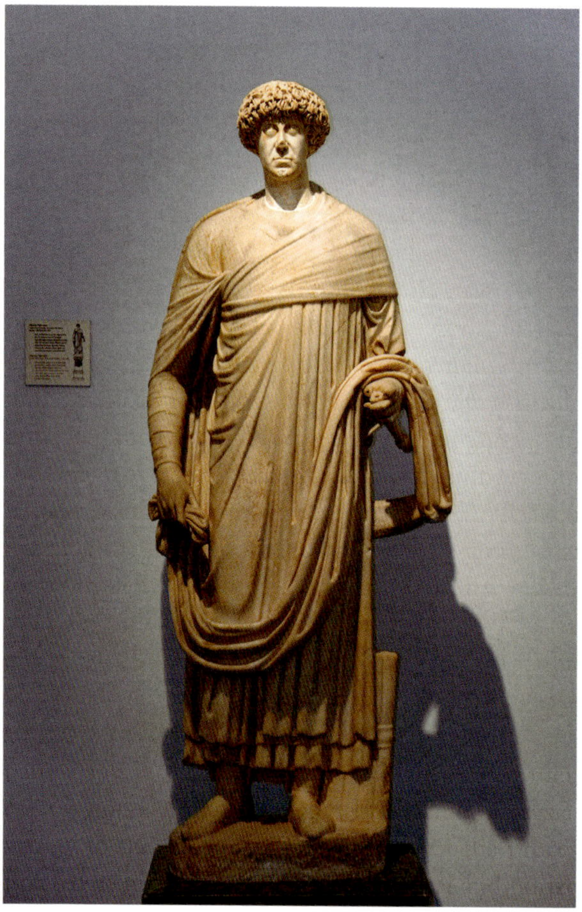

40. Statue of Flavius Palmatus, 450–535, Aphrodisias Museum, Aydin, Turkey. Photo: Images & Stories/Alamy Stock Photo

tall.[31] The inscription, which describes Palmatus as governor of Caria and vicar of Asia, offers a brief, if fulsome, dedication:

> To Good Fortune. The renewer and founder of the metropolis and benefactor of all Caria, Flavius Palmatus, *spectabilis* consular, also holding the position of the *magnificentissimus* vicar; Flavius Atheneus, the *clarissimus pater* of the most splendid metropolis of the Aphrodisians, set up [this statue of Palmatus] in gratitude.[32]

Palmatus stands atop the base, wearing the late antique toga – a two-layered, long-sleeved tunic over which a shorter, simplified toga is draped – together with strapped boots. He faces forward, his weight on his left leg and his right leg bent in a restrained contrapposto pose. A scroll bundle sits beside his left leg. He carries a scepter in his bent left arm, a *mappa* in his lowered right hand. The head, which was worked separately before insertion, is well preserved, save for a small break at the tip of the nose. Palmatus sports a curly mop of hair above a full face with a light, stippled beard and mustache. Shaggy eyebrows rise to meet bangs, which frame a deeply creased brow. His eyes, their lids and irises carefully detailed, stare straight ahead. Deep nasolabial folds emphasize his full face as they frame his thin, straight, closed lips.

The figure's iconography supports the contents of the inscription, which emphasizes Palmatus' imperial appointments, by presenting the governor in the latest Constantinopolitan fashion: Both the new toga and the coiffeur were the preferred look for members of the imperial court.[33] Thus, Palmatus stands above the provincial Tetrastoon as witness not only to his own ties to the center of power but to those of Aphrodisias as well.

As with the image of Dogmatius, style enhances this iconography. The pairing of physical portrait with verbal *curriculum vitae*, together with the statue's monumental scale, establishes Clarity, while other formal details, such as the use of contrapposto, suggest Abundance. The way in which those details are rendered is, however, a different matter. In contrast to the Roman senator, Palmatus squares his shoulders and sets his gaze directly before him, a choice with implications for the statue's larger impact. The pose shapes a contained, controlled relationship between mass and space, one in which Palmatus appears as if sandwiched between two horizontal planes, one in front of him, the other behind. Correspondingly, his profile is regular and contained, save for a swath of drapery that projects over his left arm. Within this frame, the drapery sets up a stabilizing, linear grid. On one side, the layered tunics fall in a set of unbroken, evenly spaced vertical pleats over his straight left leg. On the other, the garments, pulled by the wrap of the toga across the chest and shoulders, open out into a regular cascade of shallow, horizontally curving troughs that widen further in response to his bent right knee. Completing the look, the long U-curve of the toga sweeps down over the tunics from behind his shoulder to follow the line of his lowered right arm before turning to cross his torso in a series of neatly ordered folds. Alternations of surface depth are regular and slight, with the result that contrasts between light and shade are minimal. The tidy fall of drapery is interrupted only at the lower edge of the garment where lines established by the tunics' hems undulate gently across the front of the figure, creating a series of flat, overlapping folds and with them irregular patterns of light and shade that offer only a hint of motion.

The carefully circumscribed, regular rhythms of this formal presentation shape the figure, furnishing a sense of Sobriety. In this way, the statue's formal values accord with the even tenor of Palmatus' dress, pose, and facial expression. As with these iconographic elements, style suggests the stately demeanor of a seasoned and experienced member of the elite, a social stratum in which the appearance of emotional self-control and physical restraint functioned as nothing less than a manifestation of power.[34]

The statues of Dogmatius and Flavius Palmatus offer but two examples of the hundreds of honorific monuments that responded to and shaped the Roman sense of civic life. Although different in their details, both portraits are the product of a distinctive approach to the commemorative enterprise. Specifically, each statue pursues a fully mimetic representation, one that strives to capture not only physical likeness but with it the psychological essence of its subject. That a sculptor might achieve this goal depended not only on the ability to accurately reproduce a unique set of facial features but also on the skill with which he might conceive of and realize a psychological interpretation of his subject using the mechanisms of style. Style imitated the inner man, offering a visual validation of his character through the manipulation of line, color, and composition. Thus, just as each act of portrayal demanded the depiction of a unique set of physical characteristics, it also required the projection of a distinctive and recognizable character. In the case of Dogmatius, stylistic antithesis emphasized the tireless civic warrior. By contrast, Palmatus, a creature of compositional consistency, stood before the public of Aphrodisias as a sober representative of the state, a man of restraint and dignity in whom trust might be well placed.

If the statues of Dogmatius and Flavius Palmatus indicate the ways in which members of the elite wished to be presented across the time and space of the later Roman world, a late fourth-century toga statue of an emperor, also found in Aphrodisias, captures developments in the imperial sphere (Figure 41). The figure, which was found together with two inscribed bases – one dedicated to Valentinian II (375–392), the other to Arcadius (383–408) – stood outside the Hadrianic baths at Aphrodisias as part of a larger installation honoring members of the Theodosian house.[35] Identified both as Valentinian II and as Arcadius, the figure was carved from a single piece of white marble and stands 1.88 m high without its base. A plinth, which is integral to the piece, adds another

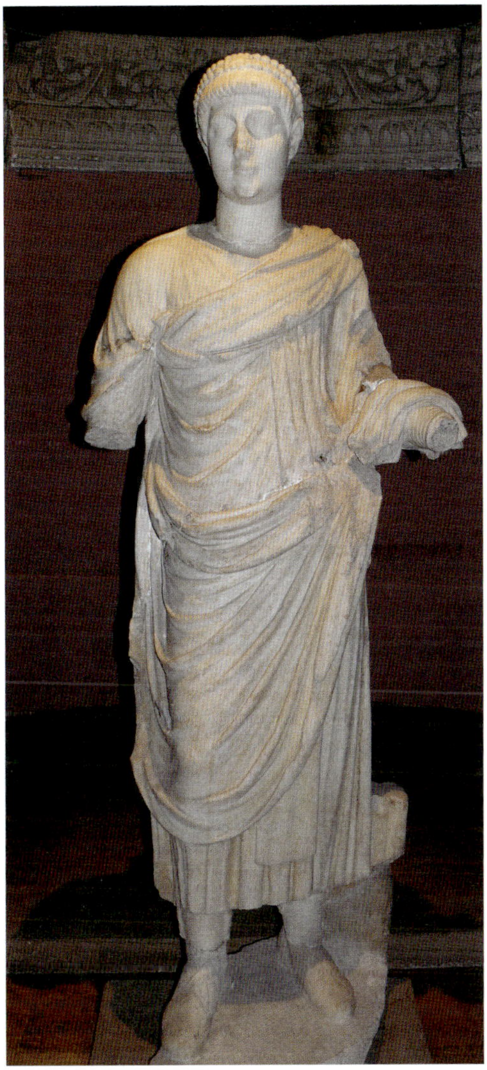

41. Statue of Valentinian II or Arcadius, 388–392, Archaeological Museum, Istanbul. Photo: S. Bassett

8 cm. The emperor is clad in the latest fashion, wearing the new style of toga and strapped boots. A diadem establishes his imperial status. He stands in a contrapposto pose, his weight resting on his straight left leg, as his body rotates to the right, his head following the turn. His left arm, extending from his body at a right angle, is broken at the wrist, while the right arm, which appears to have rested at his side, is missing from above the elbow. The missing hands may have held signs of power, a *mappa* and a scepter. The face is clean-shaven, its smooth, unblemished skin framed by thick, straight bangs that fall forward onto the forehead from beneath a pearl-encrusted diadem. Clearly articulated eyes with delicately circumscribed irises and drilled pupils gaze from beneath

the sharp arc of the brow. The long nose, broken on the left side, is straight and thin. A smile plays on the even lips above a rounded chin, which is also damaged.

The bases with which the statue was found are columnar and, at 0.88 m and 1.03 m, would have added substantially to the figure's height.[36] Their nearly identical inscriptions stress the honorands' universal dominion and victory. Perhaps as important is the equal space allotted to the devotion of Flavius Eutolmius Tatianus, the prefect who erected the images:

> With Good Fortune. The emperor of (all) the earth under the sun, and our victorious Master, Flavius Valentinianus the eternal Augustus. Flavius Eutolmius Tatianus, *clarissimus*, prefect of the sacred praetorium, dedicated [this statue] with the customary devotion, in the time of Antonius Priscus, *clarissimus praeses*[37]

and

> With Good Fortune. The emperor of (all) the earth under the sun, and our victorious master, Flavius Arcadius the eternal Augustus. Flavius Eutolmius Tatianus, *clarissimus*, prefect of the sacred praetorium, dedicated [this statue] with the customary devotion, in the time of Antonius Priscus, *clarissimus praeses*.[38]

As the dedications indicate, the two statues, which were doubtless as similar as their accompanying inscriptions, were erected by Flavius Eutolmius Tatianus during his tenure as prefect, a tour which took place between 388 and 392.[39] These images were visual encomia designed to honor imperial power, a concept whose reality was conveyed almost exclusively in visual terms.

The statue's iconography is familiar. The new-style toga establishes the emperor's civilian standing against the claims of military victory professed by the dedication. As the Latin panegyrist Pacatus indicated, arms may demonstrate power, but the toga increases the dignity of its wearer and those with whom he keeps company.[40] *Mappa* and scepter, if present, were likewise symbols of power and authority, in this instance that of the Roman consul, an office often assumed by the emperor. At the same time, the diadem confirms unequivocally the subject's imperial status, a testament to the dedicatory claims of universal dominion.

Sculptural style complements the iconographic description of elite status and power by drawing on the same framework of visual association that drove the creation of earlier tributes. As with the statues of Dogmatius and Flavius Palmatus, the combination of figure and base created Clarity, while the monumental scale, coupled with the play of straight and bent limbs summoned the idea of the heroic. Drapery enhanced the claim, its rich, three-dimensional folds carved with soft rounded edges that expanded and contracted in response to the figure's motion, emphasizing physical ponderation, shape, and structure. Together with the compositional solution of contrapposto, the bulk created by the drapery lent the statue a sense of monumentality that reinforced the heroic aura.[41] Finally, the antithesis integral to these choices endowed the statue with Abundance and, through it, Grandeur.

If such treatment of the body was familiar from the figure of Dogmatius and other statues of its kind, the head distinguished the statue by making manifest the exact nature of imperial Grandeur. The smooth, clean-shaven face with its full cheeks and lips together with the thick cap of hair projected an image of youth and well-being. In part, this iconography reflected the reality of the honorand's age. Whatever his precise identity, the emperor would have been somewhere between eleven and twenty-one at the time of the dedication.[42] At the same time, elements of style suggest an overt appeal to idealizing traditions of the past. In addition to the smooth, polished skin, the sharp line of the eyebrow above the eye socket and the precise linear treatment of the eyes and lids recall Polyclitan models perpetuated in statues such as the Doryphorus. This kind of stylistic retrospection was familiar in Roman art.[43] Absorbed into the Augustan imperial image and eventually that of Constantine, these formal choices conveyed an ideal of flawless, almost superhuman, beauty appropriate to the heroic universal ruler. Such was the sentiment of the anonymous author of a panegyric delivered before Constantine in 310, who compared the emperor to Alexander, observing,

> For it is a wonderful thing, beneficent gods, a heavenly miracle, to have as an Emperor a youth whose courage, which is even now very great, nonetheless is still increasing, and whose eyes flash and whose awe-inspiring yet agreeable majesty dazzles us at the same time as it invites our gaze. Such a man I conceive that great king to have been, such a man the Thessalian hero [Alexander], whose combination of supreme courage and beauty is celebrated.[44]

Indeed, such rulers appeared nothing short of god-like, as he noted when likening the emperor to Apollo, "You are, O Emperor, like he, youthful, joyful, a bringer of health and very handsome."[45] Later in the century, the orator Pacatus would praise Theodosius I (379–395) in similar terms. Speaking of the relationship between father and son, Pacatus admired the emperor's physical beauty, observing unstintingly,

> O nobility worthy of an Emperor, for a ruler to be the son of a man who should have been a prince himself, and who would have been equal to this very peak of power at Rome, not only because of his bravery and wisdom, but also because of the beauty of his body and his dignified bearing – just like this venerable beauty of yours, which is equal to its good fortune, and which, conspicuous far and wide, so graces imperial

> power that, to put it plainly, it is a moot point whether it is your courage which insinuates itself into our minds or your countenance into our eyes.[46]

Beauty, as the panegyric suggests, was an attribute of power. Its physical forms embodied courage, virtue, and wisdom. It was also an index of divine favor. The more splendid the physical form, the more clearly it made the workings of the heavens manifest in the affairs of men. Although unsure of how this happened – that is, whether the divine targeted a body for its innate beauty, whether the presence of the divine within the body made for beauty, or whether the development was symbiotic – Pacatus was certain that beauty was only appropriate for those with claims to universal power. As he remarked, "Such ought to be he who is adored by the nations, to whom private and public prayers are addressed over the entire world."[47]

While it is clear that beauty was observed as a late antique imperial attribute, its visual manifestation appears less obvious. In part, the smooth, taught surfaces of the Aphrodisias emperor's sculptured face, together with the clean, sharp transitions between planes and the precise delineation of line, conveyed the sense of beauty appropriate to the universal dominion alluded to on the base. There was, however, more. Slight, carefully implemented asymmetries were also a feature of the facial construction, beginning with the slight tilt to the left of the turning head. In addition, the diadem sits incrementally off-center, its squared central medallion tending to the left. Incongruously, nine pearls paired in a double row wrap around his head to the right, ten to the left. These nearly imperceptible imbalances are repeated throughout the head. The clearly delineated brows arch at different points. Below them, the right eye is slightly larger, its tear duct set slightly below that of the left. The irises are not quite centered, and their pupils are carved at different levels. The mouth, also slightly off-center, opens more on the left, although the lips are fuller on the right. A similar approach characterizes the treatment of the cheeks and jaw. Although there is youthful fullness throughout the face, the left cheek appears to be more rounded.

This attention to asymmetry had its purposes. Specifically, it was designed to instill the image with life by capturing the sense of motion. Symmetry (*symmetria*), or measure, was integral to the Polyclitan theory that produced the contrapposto pose. Based on the idea of the proportional relationship between parts, it was widely recognized as a key attribute of the beautiful.[48] There was, however, more to commensurability than measure. As the contrapposto pose implies, every motion creates its counter motion as one muscle relaxes and another flexes. Asymmetry was therefore as essential to the image of commensurability as was symmetry. The relationship between symmetry and asymmetry played out in the larger, antithetical structure of the contrapposto pose. In the head – where the representation of each element, from the mouth to the cheeks to the eyes and the forehead, represented a response to the head's larger motion and that of the body supporting it – this understanding of commensurability was manifest as a carefully crafted asymmetry that endowed a statue with the breath of life in the place where it was most fully and subtly expressed, the face.

This beauty, based on the finely tuned balance between measure and motion, had its counterpart in Hermogenes' critical language, where Beauty derived from a similar type of verbal balance. Likening speech to the body, he observed, "Beauty generally consists of symmetry and harmony and proportion in the various parts and limbs of the body, combined with a fresh and healthy complexion."[49] At the same time, the artificiality of perfect balance was undesirable, as it was unnatural and therefore unconvincing, thus subverting the orator's ability to persuade. Beauty, a carefully wrought style, was therefore a matter of artfully imbalanced balance, a question of polish.[50]

Paired with the heroic body made dignified by the adoption of the toga, the Aphrodisias emperor's head was nothing if not polished, his regular, harmonious features and smooth complexion inflected by slight imbalances conveyed the sense of youth and vitality appropriate to the ruler of the world. His was not an unfamiliar image. Surviving sculptured heads – among them the "Beyazit Head," a portrait identified variously as that of Arcadius or Theodosius II (Figure 42)[51] – render the idea of beauty in similar fashion, as do imperial representations on ivory diptychs, such as that of Honorius on the Probus diptych (406) or that of Anastasius (517).[52] This idealizing practice, which had its origins in the reign of Constantine, created a very different vision from that used to present Palmatius and members of his cohort. Vested in the head, it exchanged the image of the hardworking, sober citizen for the exceptional and dazzling look of the heroic that expressed the majesty of the imperial presence. As has been suggested, this differentiation between officials and emperors, which had its first stirrings in the early fourth century, represented a response to the profound changes in late Roman elite social practice. As the notion of the emperor as *primus inter pares* fell away to be replaced by an increasingly rigid sense of social hierarchy, the portraits of the elite, which had once taken their cue from imperial images, now developed a visual language that set them apart from the splendor of the imperial.[53]

These differences notwithstanding, the portraits of the later Roman world, whether of emperors or high-ranking officials, have a great deal in common. Both sets of images draw on the well-established language of the Roman visual repertoire. Working within the bounds of mimetic representation, they manipulate style to instill their subjects with the virtue appropriate to their status. Clarity, Sobriety, and Grandeur were not ends in and of themselves. They were the means by which character was revealed and the right to hold power was made manifest.

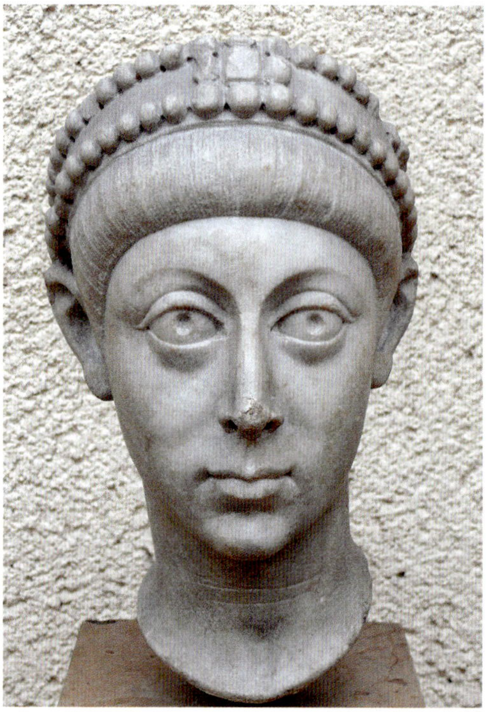

42. Head of Arcadius or Theodosius II, known as the Beyazit Head, late fourth or early fifth century, Archaeological Museum, Istanbul. Photo: S. Bassett

ICONS

Similar observations might be made of the painted likenesses of early Christian tradition, the representations of Christ, Mary, and the other protagonists of church history known to modern scholarship as icons. Similarities between icons and portraits have long been observed, and, as is the case with their sculptured relations, painted images have been understood as spiritualized images because of their formal qualities.[54] L'Orange himself was among the first to make such an equation, segueing from his analysis of Dogmatius into a discussion of a small, seventh-century portrait of Apa Abraham, Bishop of Hermouthis in Egypt and Abbot of the Phoibammon Monastery between 590 and 620 (Figure 43).[55] Painted in tempera on an acacia wood panel measuring 36.5 cm by 26.5 cm, the work shows the signs of age and use in cracks and abrasions, while four purposefully made holes in each of the four corners suggest that the painting was affixed to a wall or another surface. The figure – identified by an inscription divided between the upper right and left corners that reads "Apa Abraham Episk" (Apa Abraham, Bishop) – faces forward, holding a Gospel book in his left hand, to which he gestures with his right. He wears a deep-purple robe and the white omophorion of a bishop. A golden nimbus circles his head. White hair recedes from his forehead, and a

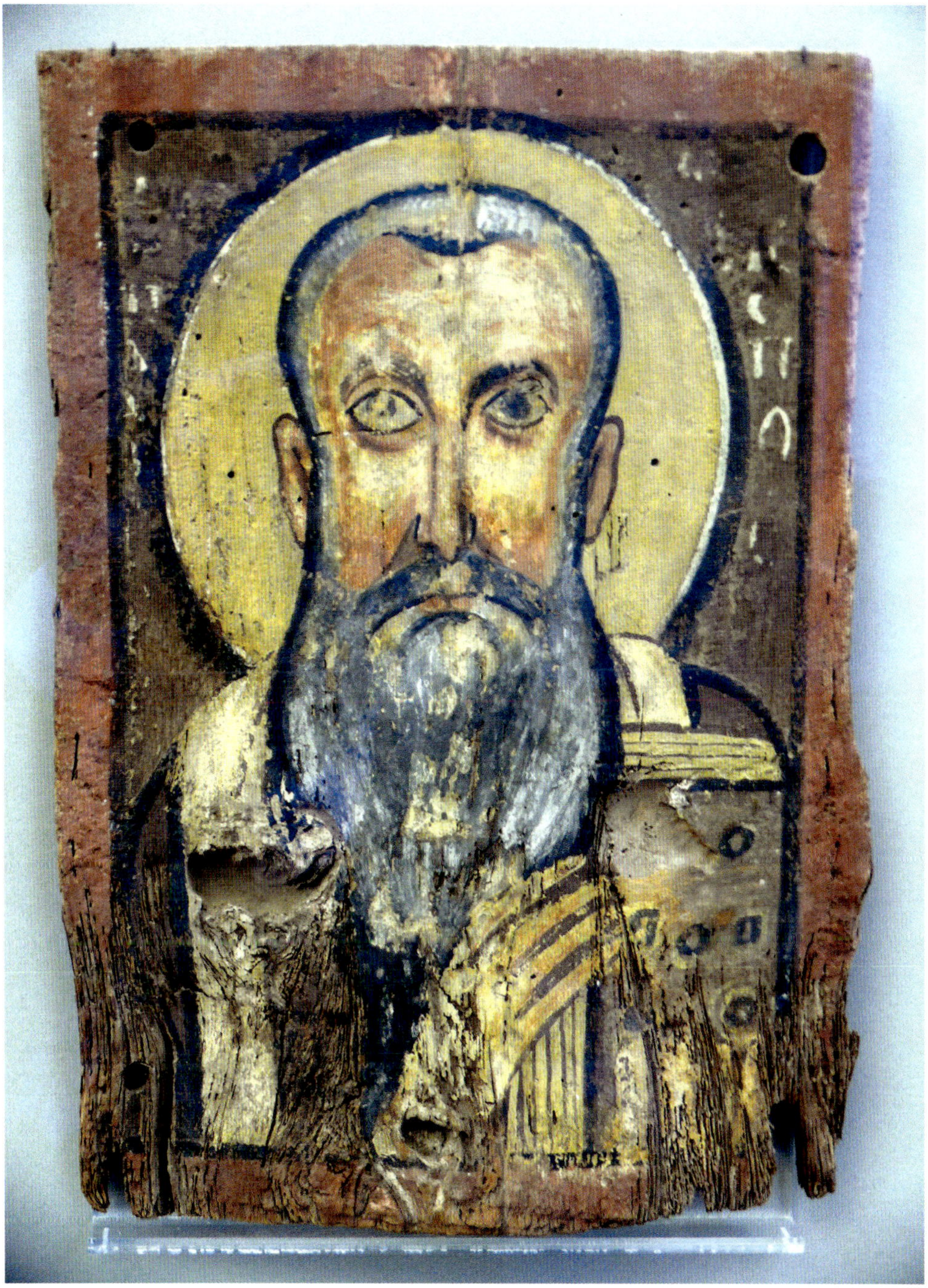

43. Portrait of Apa Abraham, early seventh century, Museum für Byzantinische Kunst, Berlin. Photo: S. Bassett

long beard flows onto his chest. He looks out, his eyes open, downturned lips pursed, ears protruding from his head. In terms of style, strong, black lines dominate the composition, outlining and accentuating the head and its surrounding nimbus. Broad, flat fields of color – purple and white for his garment, yellow for the nimbus, gray for hair and beard – complement the strong linear definition of form. Overall, the effect is one of spatially compressed, frontal composition that places the Apa Abraham's seemingly flat, unvolumetric figure along the picture plane.

L'Orange set this image in a direct line of descent from the sculptured portraits of the Roman world, emphasizing above all the way in which the style's linear emphasis imparted a spiritualized aspect to the subject akin to that of Dogmatius. "Here, more than ever," he wrote, "the expressional features have been abstracted from the physical and individual context of the head as though liberated from the body, from the corporeal man himself. They hover as a mere soul-picture in front of the material reality."[56] The essential features of L'Orange's interpretation have never been questioned. Yet aspects of Apa Abraham's iconography –the steady, intense gaze; the thin, down-turned lips; and the sharp definition of the nasolabial folds – invite comparison to images such as those of Dogmatius and Flavius Palmatus. Again, the blanket categorization of late antique images as spiritualized, disembodied representations is worth reconsidering.

Abraham's compressed, frontal presentation coupled with the picture's strong lines and flat, articulated fields of color recalls the containment of Palmatus' planar stance and with it the Clarity, Solemnity, and Grandeur of that statue. As in the marble portrait, these painted forms make visible the subject's virtues: the sobriety, dignity, and control characteristic of a distinctive image of power. Further, the visual elaboration of the gem-encrusted book cover and the gesture drawing attention to it add an element of complexity to the image that disrupts and so enhances the look of Solemnity by offering a visual gloss of Charm, which in turn lends Grandeur to Abraham's portrait.

Seen in this light, the Apa Abraham image may well have emphasized not the asceticism of a disembodied, "spiritual" character in retreat from the world but the dignified and forceful demeanor of a powerful community leader. Abraham was not a mystic or a hermit monk but a bishop and an abbot. He was a church leader whose power – public and active – was a function of his virtue and his possession of the Holy Spirit, a force that established him not only as a mediator between people and God but also as a community leader involved in the workaday business of pastoral care. As such, Abraham wielded a power that was as much temporal as spiritual.[57] As with Palmatus, iconography and style captured the moral rectitude and the accompanying sense of self-control necessary for an active man of the cloth, describing Abraham as a worthy possessor of power.

Such visual persuasion was not unique, as suggested by a group of sixth-century portraits from the Red Monastery church at Sohag in Upper Egypt. Integrated into the rich polychrome architectural décor of the rising walls of the church's triconch sanctuary, the portraits present a mix of bishops and monastics, among them the fourth- and fifth-century fathers of the White Monastery federation: Pcol, Pshoi, Shenoute, and Besa (Figure 44). The fathers appear in three-quarter-length portraits on the second level of the sanctuary's north lobe, each framed within an aedicula. Each member of the cohort stands facing forward, his identity and title inscribed in the upper right and left corners of the composition. All wear monastic garb and appear with the long tapering beard and receding white hair of a mature monk. Large ears project from the sides of their heads. The eyes, emphatically rendered, stare from beneath heavy eyebrows and high, furrowed foreheads. Their noses are sharp and straight above thin lips. The wide arc of a nimbus frames each of their faces. Stylistically, the emphasis is on linear form. A rich, black line outlines the faces, the nimbuses, and the bodies. At the same time, a schematized system of modeling suggests figural mass.

These features are by now familiar. The placement of the figures within the niches and their forward-facing poses put a premium on Clarity, while the clear black line that emphasizes, among other things, the bright, lucid gaze of

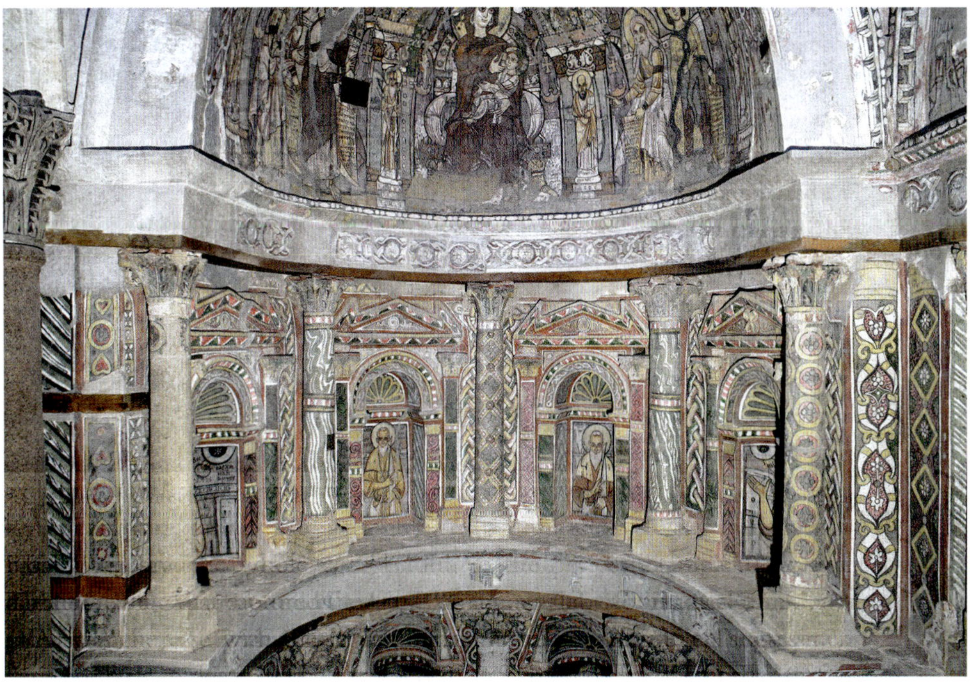

44. Images in the northern lobe, level II at the Red Monastery Church, Sohag, showing leaders of the White Monastery Federation, sixth century. Photo: Reproduced by permission of the American Research Center in Egypt, Inc. (ARCE). This project was funded by the United States Agency for International Development (USAID)

men of character endows the image with Solemnity and an accompanying sense of Grandeur, all forms that express the virtues appropriate to men of power. The architectural setting into which the images are integrated lends further support to this vision. The triconch's rising walls were of a piece with the elaborate "tabernacle facades" of Roman public architecture, display monuments whose grand scale and rich decoration spoke of order, wealth, and benefaction. Such theatrical structures served as backdrops to urban living. As such they were also the ideal setting for honorific sculpture: dedications to building patrons and other civic heroes. In the Red Monastery's triconch, the portraits of the monastic fathers occupied a similar place of honor, one acknowledging the importance and power of their benefaction.[58]

Similar Christian portraits were to be found across the Mediterranean world, sacred images that shared a vision of authority consistent with the norms of honorific sculpture and its display. In Thessaloniki, images of Saint Demetrios convey the same stately demeanor as do the images of the Egyptian monks and the Roman governor of Aphrodisias, or a mosaic of Saint Sebastian in Rome, now in the church of San Pietro in Vincoli.

While sober assessments of character achieved by emphasizing the values of Clarity, Solemnity, and Grandeur remained the most popular types of images in a society concerned with the proper exercise of authority, they were by no means the only type of representation. In the pursuit of effective character description, different styles could be used to different effect. This was the case with a late seventh-century depiction of John the Baptist (Figure 45).[59] The image, which measures 46.8 x 25.1 cm, is painted in encaustic, and the saint is rendered in a four-color palette of black/brown, blue, ochre, and white applied directly to the surface of a beech panel in pigment ranging from the fluid to the impasto. Although damage to the panel is considerable, the iconography remains legible. John dominates the composition, standing in a contrapposto pose at its center against a variegated blue and green background. Two medallion portraits that show Christ and Mary against ochre grounds occupy the upper left and right corners. John dresses in accordance with his biblical description, sporting a brown chiton cinched with a black, bezel-studded belt beneath an ochre himation flecked with white highlights. The woolly gray sheepskin, or *melote*, which constitutes his signature look, wraps around his right shoulder and knots at the front. A nimbus, long beard, and shaggy hair frame his face, which is distinguished by the dark color of its weather-beaten skin and bags under the eyes. John faces forward, his sandaled feet visible below the hem of his garment. At the same time, he turns his head upwards and slightly toward the right, his gaze directed toward Christ's portrait to which he also gestures with his raised right hand. In his lowered left hand, he holds an unfurled scroll documenting his own words: "Behold the lamb of God who takes away the sins of the world" (John 1:29).

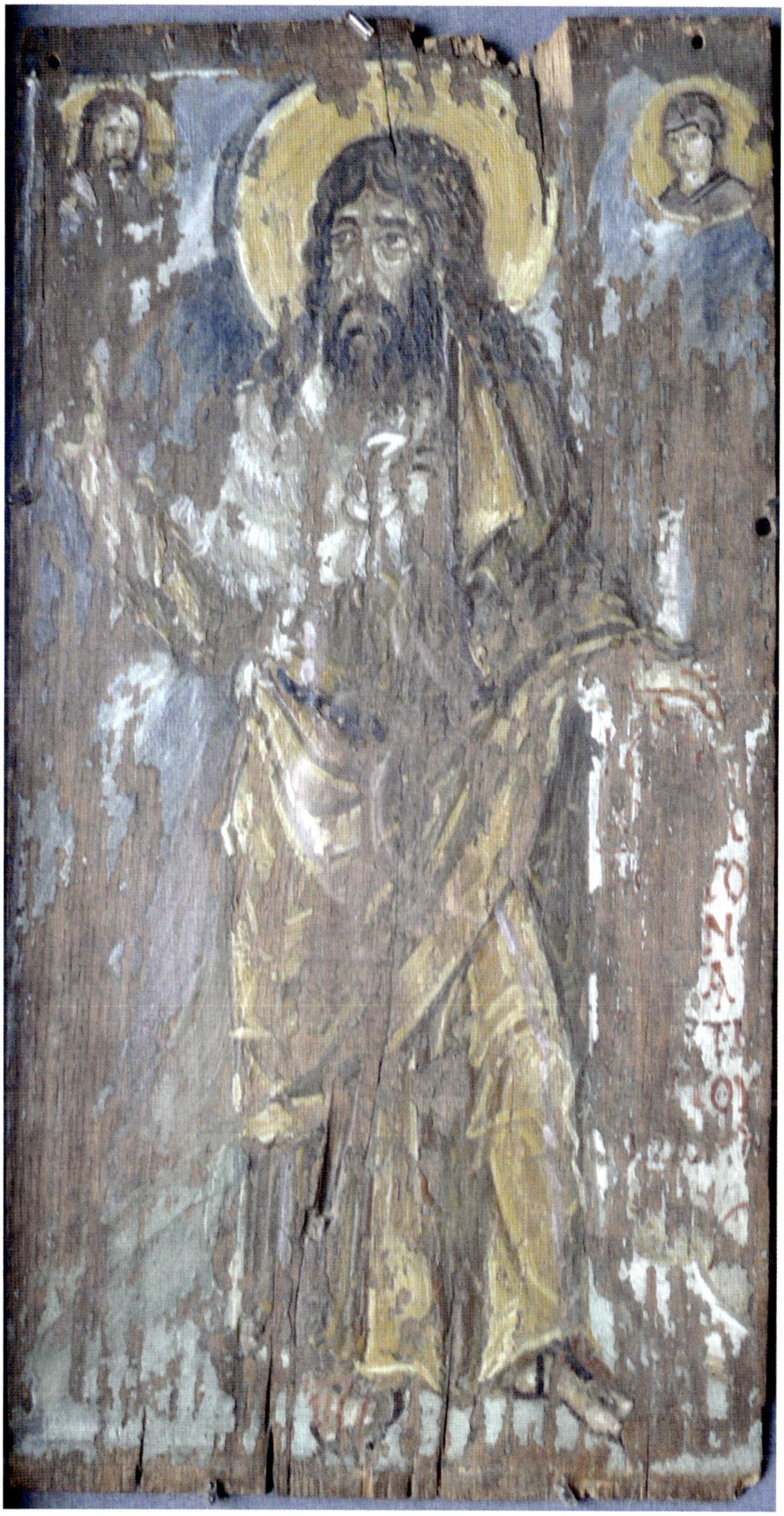

45. Icon of John the Baptist, seventh century, Bogdan and Varvara Khanenko National Museum of Arts, Kyiv. Photo: B. Madigan

In terms of style, three things characterize the image: the contrapposto pose, light-and-shade modeling, and an energetic use of line. Together, these devices structure the central figure and, by extension, the larger composition. Thus, the Baptist stands against the background, the dynamic use of contrapposto and line creating the sense that he is at once stable and in motion. The chiastic balance that emerges from the arrangement of straight and bent limbs anchors the figure in space. At the same time, this juxtaposition conveys a sense of motion by suggesting the figure's rotation, an effect enhanced by the upward gaze.

The play of light and dark complements the pose, establishing the figure's weight and volume by creating the illusion of massive drapery wrapping around and responding to the underlying body. At the same time, the contrasts of color, together with the modulation of the individual hues, create a series of lines that breaks up and enlivens the visual field. The ochre himation falls over the body as a net of sharp, splintered marks of varying length, width, and color, some light, some dark. Zigzagging diagonally across the torso, these lines expand and contract as if responding to the figure's shape and movement. Finally, the figure's elaborate snaking external profile complements this internal web of line, confirming the sense of motion.

The modeling of John's figure in terms of light and shade, together with the pose and its accompanying sense of torsion, creates a very different effect from that of the earlier seventh-century image of Apa Abraham with its broad fields of unmodulated color and accompanying linear emphasis. While these differences may be ones of date and provenance – that is, between early seventh-century Egypt and late seventh-century Palestine – it also is possible that they derive from subject matter.

The historical figure of John the Baptist, known also as the forerunner of Christ, appears in a variety of sources. All four of the synoptic gospels refer to him as a preacher from the Judean wilderness, who urges repentance and offers salvation through the cleansing act of a watery baptism. The gospels describe John's baptism of Jesus and with it his witness to the descent of the Holy Spirit, the revelation of Christ's divine nature. More specifically, Matthew (3.1–3), Mark (1.3), and Luke (3.1–4) identify him with the Old Testament and the prophet Isaiah's "voice crying in the wilderness" who "prepares the way for the Lord" (Isaiah 40:3–8). They thus see John as a precursor to Christ, the herald announcing the coming savior. The gospels also record John's death, with Matthew (14.1–6), Mark (6.14–26), and Luke (9.7) describing his run-in with Herod over his marriage to his brother's wife and the grisly demand of the king's niece and stepdaughter Salome for his head. They mention that many saw John either as the Old Testament Prophet Elijah or as a new prophet in the older figure's mold (Matthew 16.14; Luke 9.19). The first-century Alexandrian historian Flavius Josephus also referred to John's death, suggesting that the eventual defeat of Herod and his armies came as retribution for his killing of the Baptist.[60] Later, among the church fathers, John's baptismal role was fully acknowledged, together with his status as a prophet and forerunner of Christ.[61]

Gregory of Nazianzus' funeral oration for Basil of Caesarea offers some additional insight when he compares Basil to the illustrious figures of the New Testament, John among them, noting not only the Baptist's prefiguration of Jesus in every aspect of his life and death but also his asceticism and Basil's own imitation of these habits. On this last point Gregory observed, "It is no slight thing for the earnest to imitate the greatest of men, even in a slight degree."[62] As the comment suggests, John was enrolled among the biblical heroes.

A prophet, a witness, an ascetic, a hero: The icon presented some of these aspects of John's historical identity through iconography. The Baptist's costume, together with his unkempt hair and shaggy beard, established him as an ascetic in the manner of the great prophets Elijah and Isaiah to whom he was often linked in biblical and patristic commentary.[63] The message of the scroll also underscored his prophetic nature. This reference anchored the image at a specific moment in biblical time: John made the statement upon seeing Jesus before the Baptism, anticipating the descent of the Holy Spirit and the revelation of Christ's divinity. Finally, the Baptist's interaction with the medallion portraits of Jesus and Mary described his cognizance of Christ's human aspect – an identity fully entwined with his divine one – to establish his role as a witness to Christ's dual nature.

This iconography packed in a lot of information. In addition to the description of John and his witness of Christ's dual nature, it has also been seen as a response to events of the Quinisext council of 692, a gathering that forbade Christ's symbolic representation in the guise of a lamb on the grounds that it did not fully represent his human aspect. The portrait medallions, which show him together with his mortal mother, make that humanity manifest. They also have been seen as icons within the icon, representations that advocate for the legitimacy of image veneration at a moment when such practice was being called into question.[64]

For all of its density, there was one idea that eluded iconographic description – the intangible quality of heroic greatness referred to and so prized by Gregory. This is the moment where style came into its own, as the artist summoned the resources of line, color, and composition to convey the essence of John's character. As Hermogenes himself observed, it is the function of style to express virtue.[65] It did so in this instance by marshaling forces familiar from the portrait tradition, prime among them antithesis.

Contrapposto, together with light-and-shade modeling, gives form to the image. The juxtaposition of straight and bent limbs characteristic of the contrapposto pose establishes a sense of torsion and suspends its subject in the moment between stasis and motion, while the opposition of light and dark pigment complements the stance by creating the illusion of vibrant, three-dimensional matter. This is particularly true of the drapery. Gathered around him in massive folds, his clothing not only responds to and articulates his movements but also enlarges his body, lending it a sense of monumentality.[66]

The antithesis structuring John's physical form extends to the larger composition. Across a diagonal moving from the upper left to the lower right corner, the raised golden image of the medallion portrait proclaiming Christ's humanity plays off against the lower white surface of the unfurled parchment's rectangular shape and its witness to the divine word. Circle plays off against rectangle, upper against lower, visual against verbal, human against divine. The artist, in short, has marshaled the rhetoric of visual antithesis to create a heroic image. The unambiguous focus on the Baptist and the scale with which his image dominates the picture embrace Clarity and its ally Sobriety, while the combined use of contrapposto and chiaroscuro adds a necessary gloss of Complexity to create the Grandeur appropriate to the heroic content.

These tactics, familiar from the Roman portraits and the Egyptian icons, establish a baseline from which John's image is further elaborated by the use of line and color. The bending and projecting limbs join with the jutting drapery and the arc of the nimbus circling his head to create an extraordinarily active figural profile. Within the profile itself, waves of hair undulate against the blaze of the nimbus, and sharp splinters of light crack across the drapery as if to activate the figure. Color contributes to this sense, the yellow nimbus contrasting with the dark hair and beard, which in turn contrasts with the gray *melote* layered over the dazzling folds of the ochre himation. Optically, this vivid treatment of line and color is of a sort known to make the eye travel quickly across surfaces, energizing them and creating a sense of motion.

Unlike Apa Abraham, John was a missionary preacher, an uncompromising ascetic who demanded repentance and baptism in view of the approach of the kingdom of God. While his icon shares with Abraham's image the Clarity appropriate to a panegyric in the straightforward placement of the main figure and the balanced positioning of the roundels, the charged use of curved line and sharp color suggest a relation to Sincerity, a style designed to express oaths and pious statements and through them Character. Like Clarity, Sincerity results from direct statement; however, the choice of words and phrases within that statement can manipulate the sense of Character. Thus, short words and broken phrases, similar in the oral sense to the vivid web of broken line that depicts the drapery, suggest Asperity, a kind of speech appropriate to the no-nonsense demands of the Baptist's message.

Through the agency of style, John emerges from the background as a heroic figure consistent with his biblical persona. A prophet who was prophesied, a desert ascetic who returns to society to take up his mission of witness before meeting a martyr's death, John's physical representation embodies heroic antithesis. This stress on antithesis is also consistent with the Baptist's role as witness to the dual nature of Christ, an aspect of his life emphasized in the iconography. In the juxtaposition of straight and bent, light and dark, stasis and motion, and the unified presentation of these forms in the larger composition, visual antithesis makes the imponderable mystery of John's experience and with it the perplexing reality of Christ's own dual nature accessible to human perception and understanding.

PORTRAITS, ICONS, AND THE MIMETIC ENTERPRISE

Whatever their context or medium, surviving late antique portraits show a notable consistency in their approach to the project of representation. In figures painted and sculptured, sacred and profane, style served the end of honorific commemoration by shaping an image of what was regarded as the most telling aspect of an individual's appearance: character. Whether in particular representations, such as those of Dogmatius or Flavius Palmatus, or in more typical imaginings similar to those of the monastics, the elements of line, color, and composition breathed life into representation by creating visual evocations of the virtues driving human understanding, choice, and action. Integrated into the depiction of human form, styles as varied as Grandeur and Asperity conveyed not a denial of the physical body but a type of embodied representation consistent with a complete definition of mimesis as the imitation of physical and psychological states of being.

NOTES

1 Wickhoff and Hartel 1895, 37; Wickhoff 1900, 61–62.
2 Wickhoff and Hartel 1895, 82; Wickhoff 1900, 160–61.
3 Riegl 1901, 59–60; 1985, 68.
4 Riegl 1901, 110–11; 1985, 118–19.
5 Schmarsow 1905, 325: "es ist das Reich des Geistes."
6 The face's lack of depth, the flatness at the back of the head, and the long contour of hair on the neck all indicate a recutting. For the base and statue, see *LSA*–1266 (C. Machado), *LSA*–903 (J. Lenaghan).
7 C. Caelius Saturninus Dogmatius Rome, 324–37. L'Orange 1933, 64, 139, no. 92; Giuliano 1957, 81–82, no. 99; Blanck 1969, 34–35, no. A8; Bergmann 2005; Gehn 2012, 498–504, no. W3.
8 L'Orange 1973, 95.
9 Smith 1997, 171; Smith and Ward-Perkins 2016, 22–26. For further discussion, see Smith 1990; 1999; 2002.
10 Delbrueck 1929; Olovsdotter 2005.
11 Smith 1990; 1997; 1999; 2002; 2007; Smith and Ward-Perkins 2016, and the *LSA* website: http://laststatues.classics.ox.ac.uk.
12 Smith (1997; 1999; 2002) bases his discussions on the analysis of iconography, which he considers an aspect of style, and is less interested in the elements of line, color, and composition.

13 For the statue and base, see Musei Vaticani, Museo Gregoriano Profano, nos. 10493 and 10494. For the inscription: *CIL* VI 1704. Machado (*LSA*–1266) notes that the base and statue have always been considered part of the same monument, though there is some chance given the distance at which they were found from one another that they were not actually a pair. See also Machado 2021, 7.

14 Translation by C. Machado of *CIL* VI 1704: See *LSA*, no 1266.

15 For measurements, see *LSA*–1266 (C. Machado), *LSA*–903 (J. Lenaghan).

16 Pliny (1938–1962, 9: 169 [*Natural History* 34.55]) states only that Polyclitus had his statues "throw weight on one leg."

17 Quintilian 2002, 2: 465 (*The Orator's Education* 5.12.21).

18 Gehn (2012, 504) observes that the shoes may have been painted to represent senatorial footwear. Machado (*LSA*–1266) suggests they indicate that the statue refers to his status prior to elevation to consular rank.

19 On the toga, see Smith and Ward-Perkins 2016, 17–20. The second-century statue body is likely to have been chosen for reuse precisely because of the costume rather than economic necessity. Lenaghan (2016) notes that the traditional toga was considered most appropriate for honorific statues in the fourth century and that almost all reused togati were chosen because of costume, rather than to save on expense. Machado (2021, 658) concurs: "For members of the Roman elite, it was more important to be seen in a traditional costume than as embracing the new, probably court-oriented fashion." See Gehn 2012, 504 on *mos maiorum*.

20 On portrait styles and their implications, see generally Smith 1997; 1999; 2016, 22–26. For the expression of ceaseless vigilance, see Smith 1997, 198. On the iconography of the just governor, see Smith 1999, 185–88. On the stylistic relationship between imperial portraits and private portraits in late antiquity, see generally Kovacs 2014. Bergmann (2005) considers the military style a means of distinguishing sitters from the emperor. On Dogmatius specifically, see Gehn 2012, 498–504.

21 Smith 1999, 185–89.

22 On physiognomy generally, see Evans 1969 and Swain 2007.

23 Cicero 1942, 177 (The Making of the Orator 3, 221–22).

24 Quintilian 2002, 3: 49 (*The Orator's Education* 6.2.7).

25 Swain 2007, 497–99 (Adamantius, *Physiognomy*, A4).

26 Swain 2007, 497–99 (Adamantius, *Physiognomy*, A4).

27 Swain 2007, 499–515 (Adamantius, *Physiognomy*, A5–A23).

28 On the origins and implications of contrapposto, see Summers (1977), who discusses the equation between rhetorical ideas of antithesis and the formal solutions arrived at in the Renaissance with reference to ancient texts, especially Aristotle's *Rhetoric* and Quintilian.

29 For C. Valerius Vibianus, see *LSA*–2136 (J. Lenaghan), *LSA*–2178 (I. Tantillo and F. Bigi). For Virius Audentius Aemelianus, see *LSA*–41 (C. Machado, U. Gehn), *LSA*–46 (J. Lenaghan); Gehn 2012, 504–13, no. W4.

30 *LSA*–199; Smith 1999.

31 Statue: 201.5 cm; plinth: 11 cm; base: 145 cm. See *LSA*–198 (Smith), *LSA*–199 (J. Lenaghan).

32 Translation by C. Roueché. See *LSA*–199 (J. Lenaghan) and Roueché 1989, 102–3, no. 62.

33 Smith 1999, 176–85.

34 Brown 1988, 11–12; 1992, 48–58; Smith 1999.

35 Istanbul Archaeological Museum no 2264. *LSA*–163 (R. R. R. Smith); Mendel 1912–1914, 199–202, no. 506; Delbrueck 1933, 195–98; Inan and Rosenbaum 1966, 89–90, no. 66; Firatlı 1990, 6, no. 4; Smith 1999, 162, 182–83; 2007, 218–20, 228 (A37).

36 Arcadius: *LSA*–164 (J. Lenaghan). Valentinian II: *LSA*–166 (J. Lenaghan)

37 Translation by C. Roueché. See *LSA* 166, and Roueché 1989. No. 27. 49–52.

38 Translation by C. Roueché. See *LSA* 164 and Roueché 1989, no. 26, 48–52.

39 *PRLE* 1: 876–78 (Tatianus 5).

40 Panegyrici Latini 1994, 448 (Panegyric 2.1.2: Latinus Pacatus Drepianus on Theodosius).

41 Hallett (1986) discusses the ways in which Greek sculptors of the classical era increased the bulk of drapery to suggest monumentality.

42 Valentinian was born in 371, Arcadius in c. 377. The statues were dedicated between 388 and 392, which means that Valentinian would have been somewhere between seventeen and twenty-one, Arcadius between eleven and fifteen.

43 Idealizing forms represented one aspect of this retrospection, archaizing treatments that looked back to earlier Greek and Etruscan models another. For overviews and bibliography, see Fullerton 1990, Anguissola 2015, and Touchette 2015.

44 Panegyrici Latini 1994, 243 (Panegyric, 6. 17. 1–2: on Constantine).

45 Panegyrici Latini 1994, 455 (Panegyric 6.21.6: on Constantine). Smith (1997, 187, 194–201) discusses, respectively, the passage's Virgilian implications, and imperial images and the Latin Panegyrics.

46 Panegyrici Latini 1994, 455 (Panegyric 2.6.2: Pacatus on Theodosius).

47 Panegyrici Latini 1994, 455–56 (Panegyric 2.6.3–4: Pacatus on Theodosius).

48 Mathew 1963, 17; Plotinus, 1969–1988, 1:233–63 (*Ennead.* 1.6.1); Pollitt 1974, 17 22.

49 Hermogenes 1913, 297; 1987, 54–55.

50 Hermogenes 1913, 296–311; 1987, 54–64.

51 Istanbul Archaeological Museum, inv. No. 5028. Firatlı 1990, 7, no. 5.

52 Delbrueck 1929, 84–87 (Probus), 134, no. 21 bis (Anastasius); Olovsdotter 2005, 47–55, no. 11 (Anastasius).

53 Smith 1997, 179–87; Bergmann 2005; Bergmann and Kovacs 2016, 280–94.

54 For example, Kitzinger (1977, 65), who equates liner precision with spiritual intensity; Belting (1994, 26), who observes the conflict between a desire for individual likeness and an imperishable ideal; or Marsengill (2011; 2013, 16), who argues that Christian portraits become increasingly flat and abstract to suggest spirituality.

55 Berlin, Museum für Byzantinische Kunst, inv. Nr. 6114; Krause 1971; L'Orange 1973, 101; Zaloscher 1974, 147; Gustav-Lübke Museum der Stadt Haam 1996, 148, no. 110; Parlasca and Seemann 1999, 353; Zibawi 2003, 104.

56 L'Orange 1973, 101

57 See Rapp 2005 for the pragmatic, spiritual, and ascetic aspects of episcopal authority. On the relationship between bishops and monks, ministry and monasticism, see Rapp 2005, 137–52. On bishops and civic office, see Rapp 2005, 205–6. On the monk-bishop, see Rousseau 1971, 2010, 56–67, Chadwick 1993.

58 Kinney (2016, 47–49) discusses the implications of the architectural type. See also MacDonald 1986, 183–207, on the power of column displays and elaborated walls. On the Red Monastery generally, see Bolman 2016. Kinney (2016, 47–49) discusses the implications of the architectural type. See also MacDonald (1896, 183–207) on the power of the column displays and elaborated walls.

59 Originally at the Monastery of St. Catherine on Mt. Sinai, the icon is now at the Bogdan and Varvara Khanenko Museum in Kiev, inv. No. 113. Weitzmann 1976, 32–35, no. B11; Etingroph 2005, 543, no. 1. The major publication is Corrigan 1988. The following discussion derives from Bassett 2020.

60 Josephus 1926–1965, 8: 81 (*Jewish Antiquities* 18.2).

61 Gregory of Nazianzus 1894b, "Oration 39," 14–15, *NPNF2*, 7: 702–18 at 712–13.

62 Gregory of Nazianzus 1894a, "Funeral Oration on the Great Saint Basil, Bishop of Caesarea in Cappadocia," *NPNF2*, 7: 735–831 at 828.

63 Bacci 2014, 212.

64 Corrigan 1988, 3–4, 7–8.

65 Hermogenes (1913, 384–85; 1987, 110–12) on the expressive associations of different styles.

66 Hallett (1986) observes a similar phenomenon in the development of sculptured style in the fifth century BC.

CONCLUSION

The Arts of Persuasion

IN THEIR EXPLORATIONS OF LATE ANTIQUE ART, THAT "DARK CONTINENT OF ART historical inquiry," Franz Wickhoff and Alois Riegl came to two very different conclusions about the nature of later Roman style. For Wickhoff, its character was illusionistic. Riegl, by contrast, saw it as abstract and crystalline. This discrepancy proved a great problem for Riegl, who was at pains to demonstrate the error of his colleague's observations. It never occurred to him that both he and Wickhoff could be right, or that their different characterizations might be in keeping with late antique expectation. Yet, in fact they were.

While Wickhoff and Riegl worked from the assumption that style was an independent phenomenon that cycled through overarching phases of naturalism and abstraction, ancient viewers considered form in the context of individual images, assuming not only that it was mimetic by nature but that it operated according to the guiding principle of appropriateness (*decorum*) and an unshakable belief in the binding relationship between subject and style, *logos* and *lexis*. This being the case, style was by nature a malleable phenomenon, and viewers presumed, even demanded, stylistic variety.

This variety notwithstanding, certain features were common to all styles, and some styles came to predominate over others. For example, Clarity was crucial to any representational enterprise, be it the depiction of revelry on a silver plate or the formal protocols of ceremonial in monumental contexts. In each of these circumstances, the pursuit of Clarity directed the larger compositional structure, becoming the baseline to which variations as diverse as Sweetness and Solemnity could be applied. Abundance was also favored. As a means to elaborate and enrich a composition, it operated across a broad spectrum of subject matter. Achieved not through a single formula but through differing stylistic combinations, it could enliven sacred and secular subjects, narratives and portraits.

Although the array of styles was formidable, their combinations seemingly infinite, in practice the effects they aimed to achieve were applied carefully to conform to subject and occasion. Sweetness, with its intimations of pleasure, was overwhelmingly the favorite for intimate works associated with domestic living such as the Mildenhall Plate. It also had a place in the representation of women and children, as suggested by the representation of Theodora and her companions in San Vitale and the depictions of children on the Arch of Constantine. By contrast, Grandeur, arrived at through varying combinations of form, prime among them Abundance and Solemnity, was the effect sought in the public sector. In civic contexts, it helped to interpret the public persona of individuals such as Dogmatius. It was also a signpost of imperial virtue, as in the *largitio* relief on the Arch of Constantine. Similarly, in such ecclesiastical venues as Santa Maria Maggiore or San Vitale, Grandeur parsed the relationship between God and humanity. It was, in short, the ultimate image of power.

The verbal evidence of ekphrasis supports these observations. From the third-century descriptions of mythological paintings by Philostratus the Elder to the ninth-century patriarch Photius' observations about the image of the Virgin in Hagia Sophia, there is universal wonder at the mimetic persuasiveness of images. As Philostratus observed some centuries earlier,

> The painting gives the very image of things that are, of things that are taking place, and in some cases of the way in which they take place, not slighting the truth by reason of the number of objects shown but defining the real nature of each thing just as if the painter were representing some one thing alone.[1]

Within this general framework, descriptions use the vocabulary to evoke a range of visual styles. Philostratus the Younger praised an artist for the Charm and Clarity of his composition.[2] In another passage the elder Philostratus comments on a picture's fitness, or decorum.[3] Elsewhere, detailed enumerations of setting and participants summon the idea of visual Abundance. Here, a marsh teams with plant life and birds carefully observed.[4] There, dwarfs cavort around a personification of the Nile, each one striking a different pose, which in turn conveys a different mood.[5] Other descriptions summon the pleasure-making forms of Sweetness, as cupids tussle amicably with one another,[6] or Narcissus sits mesmerized by his reflection.[7] Within the whole, the allusions to specific rhetorical styles evoke the essence of place and make characters vivid. An image of the aging Daedalus is considered "Attic," that is, straightforward, simple, and wise in the unaffected manner of the Athenians,[8] while the youth and beauty of Pelops is described as "Lydian."[9] The Simplicity of a rendering of the young Critheis lends her the appropriate qualities of Charm and Grace and Beauty,[10] while a priestess of Dodona is Solemn.[11] Later observers were no less immune to the utility and power of this expressive language. Prudentius' descriptions of David, majestic in royal array on the walls of the basilica at Nola, suggest the guiding force of Solemnity,[12] and in the context of imperial panegyric, an emperor has the look of Dignity, itself an expression of justice.[13]

As these examples suggest, the correlation between visual and verbal styles was such that the verbal might evoke the visual, the visual the verbal. In both contexts style served a specific end: persuasion. When Aristotle described rhetoric as an art of persuasion, there is no evidence that he had any such visual analogies in mind. Five hundred years later, Quintilian's famous comparison of the styles of individual artists and orators[14] made it clear that such equations were both possible and meaningful. They suggest, as well, that visual styles, in common with their verbal counterparts, had the power to persuade.

Recognizing the capacity of painting and sculpture to demonstrate what might be thought of as visual eloquence has important repercussions. It implies that together with literature and music the visual arts were woven into the fabric of the *paideia*, that educational and cultural tradition that served as a universal frame of reference across the expanse of the later Roman empire. Nowhere is this claim more evident than in a comparison of works as distant from one another as a frescoed niche in the Egyptian monastery of Apa Apollo at Bawit (Figure 46) and the Justinianic panel at San Vitale in Ravenna, two images that share the same stylistic language.

The fresco, which dates to the late sixth or early seventh century, is divided into two equal registers. Above, against a blue ground, Christ appears as if at the Second Coming. He sits enthroned within a mandorla from which sprout wings adorned with the four beasts of the Apocalypse. Full-length figures of archangels Michael and Gabriel stand to the left and right of the central group. Below, an enthroned Virgin and Child sit at the center of the composition, beneath the upper figure of the returning Christ. Flanking them are figures of the apostles and local saints, each identified by inscription. The group lines up against a tripartite backdrop that rises from a baseline of brown through a middle strip of green to the pale blue of the sky. Mary and Jesus dominate the composition by virtue of their central placement and scale, and the deep color of the Virgin's garment. The flanking figures, which are differentiated in their facial features and details of dress, all face forward. Figures overlap, and some members of the cohort tread upon their companions' feet. Each stands to the same height, their heads and merging nimbuses at precisely the same level.

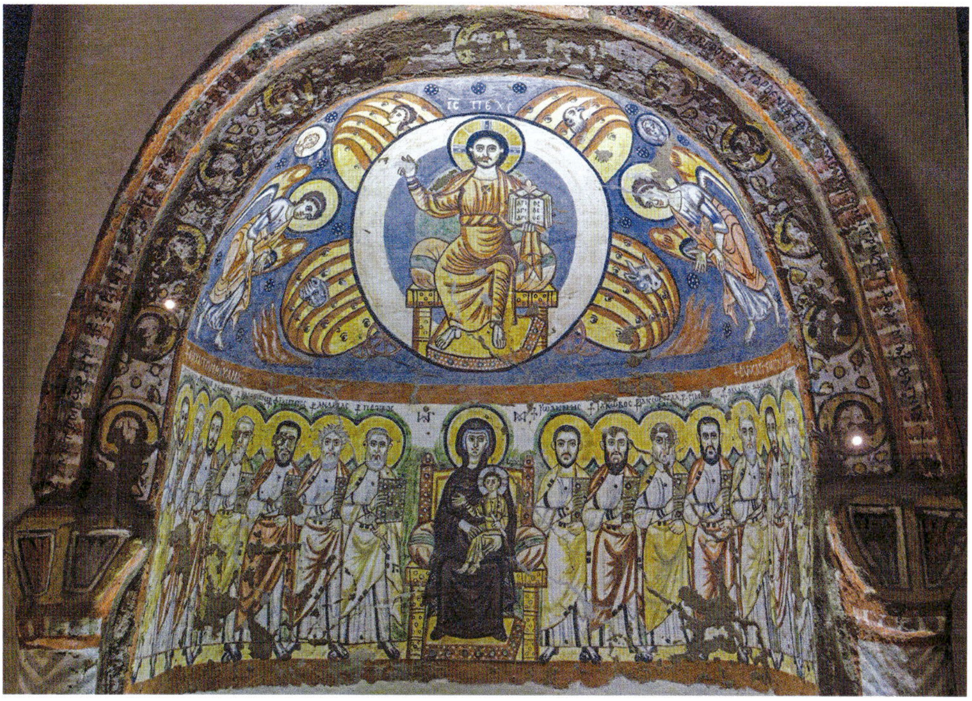

46. Apse fresco with enthroned Virgin and Child and the Ascension of Christ from Chapel 12, Monastery of Apa Apollo, Bawit, sixth-seventh century, now in the Coptic Museum, Cairo. Photo: B. O'Kane/ Alamy Stock Photo

The niche shares with the San Vitale chancel a penchant for the division of the composition into discrete, yet iconographically related sections, an effect that, together with the varied representations of the apostles and saints, establishes the general look of Abundance; however, and perhaps even more noteworthy, is the stylistic elaboration of the lower register that resembles the representation of Justinian and his entourage. As with the emperor and his retinue, a composition in which Justinian anchors the center, a centrally placed group – in this instance, the enthroned Virgin and Child – organizes the image, her steady, rectangular form establishing the essential Sobriety of the composition. Additionally, the surrounding figures demonstrate the same frontality, isocephaly, and illogicality in their relationships with one another as in the imperial panel. The techniques establish a sense of Abundance that further highlights the composition's essential Sobriety and in so doing lends it an appropriate air of Grandeur.

That the denizens of swampy Ravenna and the monks of arid Bawit could participate in such similar viewing experiences is a testament not only to the cohesiveness of late Roman visual experience across the geographical expanse of the empire but also to the enduring culture of the mimetic arts and the shared understanding of the styles that shaped them. As with the traditions of *paideia* with which they were allied, painting and sculpture worked with a universal mimetic language. In this instance, though the means of communication was visual, the goal was the same: to convey knowledge and reveal truth using styles that were neither natural nor abstract but Sober and Grand, Abundant and Sweet. In short, painting and sculpture, already classed with the mimetic arts, ranked also among the arts of persuasion.

NOTES

1 Philostratus 1931, 53–55 (*Imagines* 1.12).
2 Philostratus 1931, 299 (*Imagines* 3).
3 Philostratus 1931, 39 (*Imagines* 1.9).
4 Philostratus 1931, 35.
5 Philostratus 1931, 19–21 (*Imagines* 1.5).
6 Philostratus 1931, 21–29 (*Imagines* 1.6).
7 Philostratus 1931, 89–93 (*Imagines* 1.23).
8 Philostratus 1931, 65 (*Imagines* 1.16).
9 Philostratus 1931, 71 (*Imagines* 1.17).
10 Philostratus 1931, 163 (*Imagines* 2.8).
11 Philostratus 1931, 269 (*Imagines* 2.33).
12 Davis-Weyer 1986, 28–29.
13 Panegyrici Latini 1994, 140 (Panegirici Latini 8.19.4: Panegyric of Constantius).
14 Quintilian 2002, 5: 285 (*The Orators Education* 12.10.7–10).

BIBLIOGRAPHY

Ackerman, J. 1962. "A Theory of Style." *JAAC* 20.3: 227–37.

Adler, W. 2008. "Early Christian Historians and Historiography." In *The Oxford Handbook of Early Christian Studies*, edited by S. Harvey and D. Hunter, 584–602. Oxford: Oxford University Press.

Ainalov, D. V. 1900. "Ellinisticheskiia osnovy vizantiiskago iskusstva. Izsliedovaniia v oblasti rannevizantiiskago iskusstva." *S. Petersburg: Zapiski Imperatorskago Russkago Arkheologicheskago Obshchestva, XIII. Trudy Otdieleniia Arkheologii drevne-klassicheskoi, vizantiiskoi i zapadno-evropeiskoi, V.*

1902. "Review of Josef Strzygowski, *Orient oder Rom.*" *Vizantiiskii Vremennik* 9: 138–52.

1961. *The Hellenistic Origins of Byzantine Art.* Edited by C. Mango and translated by E. Sobolevitch and S. Sobolevitch. New Brunswick, NJ: Rutgers University Press.

Andreescu-Treadgold, I. 1992. "The Mosaic Workshop at San Vitale." In Mosaici a S. Vitali e altri restauri: Il restauro in situ di mosaici parietali. Ravenna, 13 ottobre 1990, edited by A. Iannucci, C. Fiori, and C. Muscolino, 31–41. Ravenna: Longo.

1995. "The Emperor's New Crown and St. Vitalis' New Clothes." *CorsiRav* 1995: 149–86.

Andreescu-Treadgold, I., and W. Treadgold. 1997. "Procopius and the Imperial Panels of S. Vitale." *ArtB* 79.4: 708–23.

Angelov, D. 2019. *The Byzantine Hellene.* Cambridge: Cambridge University Press.

Anguissola, A. 2015. "*Idealplastik* and the Relationship between Greek and Roman Sculpture." In *The Oxford Handbook of Roman Sculpture*, edited by E. A. Friedland, M. G. Sobocinski, and E. K. Gazda, 240–59. Oxford: Oxford University Press.

App, U. 2010. *The Birth of Orientalism.* Philadelphia: University of Pennsylvania Press.

Aristotle. 1932. *Aristotle Politics.* Translated by H. Rackham. Cambridge, MA: Harvard University Press.

1995. *Aristotle Poetics. Longinus on the Sublime. Demetrius on Style.* Translated by S. Halliwell, W. Hamilton Frye, D. A. Russell, D. C. Inneds, and W. Rhys Robert. Cambridge, MA: Harvard University Press.

Astorri, G. 1934. "Nuove osservazioni sulla tecnica dei mosaici romani della basilica di S. Maria Maggiore." *RACr* 11: 51–72.

Auerbach, E. 2003. *Mimesis: The Representation of Reality in Western Literature.* Princeton, NJ: Princeton University Press.

Bacci, M. 2014. *The Many Faces of Christ: Portraying the Holy in the East and West, 300 to 1300.* London: Reaktion Books.

Bahr, H., ed. 1903. *Gegen Klimt.* Vienna: J. Eisenstein.

Barasch, M. 1998. *Theories of Art, 3: From Impressionism to Kandinsky.* New York: Routledge.

Barber, C. 1990. "The Imperial Panels at San Vitale: A Reconsideration." *BMGS* 14: 19–43.

Barber, C., and S. Papaioannou, eds. 2017. *Michael Psellos on Literature and Art: A Byzantine Perspective on Aesthetics.* Notre Dame, IN: University of Notre Dame Press.

Bartman, E. 1988. "Decor et Duplicatio: Pendants in Roman Sculptural Display." *AJA* 92.2: 211–25.

Bassett, S. 2000. "'Excellent Offerings': The Lausos Collection in Constantinople." *ArtB* 82.1: 6–25.

2004. *The Urban Image of Late Antique Constantinople.* Cambridge: Cambridge University Press.

2008. "Style and Meaning in the Imperial Panels at San Vitale." *Artibus et Historiae* 57: 49–57.

2020. "An Icon of John the Baptist." In *The Eloquence of Art: Essays in Honour of Henry Maguire*, edited by A. O. Lamm and R. Schroeder, 18–28. Abingdon: Routledge.

Bauer, F. A. 1996. *Stadt, Platz und Denkmal in der Spätantike.* Mainz: P. von Zabern.

Baxandall, M. 1971. *Giotto and the Orators: Humanist Observers and Painting in Italy and the Discovery of Pictorial Composition, 1350–1450.* Oxford: Clarendon Press.

1972. *Painting and Experience in Fifteenth-Century Italy.* Oxford: Oxford University Press.

Becatti, G. 1957. *La Colonna di Marco Aurelio.* Milan: Editoriale Domus.

1960. *La Colonna Coclide Istoriata. Problemi Storici Iconografici Stilistici.* Rome: "L'Erma" di Bretschneider.

Beckmann, M. 2011. *The Column of Marcus Aurelius: The Genesis and Meaning of a Roman Imperial Monument.* Chapel Hill: University of North Carolina Press.

2015. "The Function of the Attribute of Liberalitas and Its Use in the 'Congiarium.'" *AJNum* 2.27: 189–98.

Beller, S. 2006. *A Concise History of Austria.* Cambridge: Cambridge University Press.

Beller, S., ed. 2001. *Rethinking Vienna 1900.* Oxford: Berghan Books.

Belting, H. 1994. *Likeness and Presence: A History of the Image before the Era of Art.* Translated by E. Jephcott. Chicago: University of Chicago Press.

Bergmann, M. 2005. "La ritrattistica privata di età costantiniana: l'abbandono del prototipo imperiale." In *Costantino il Grande. La civiltà antica al bivio tra Occidente e Oriente*, edited by A. Donati and G. Gentili, 157–63. Cinisello Balsamo: Silvana.

Bergmann, M., and M. Kovacs. 2016. "Portrait Styles." In *The Last Statues of Antiquity*, edited by R. R. R. Smith and B. Ward-Perkins, 280–94. Oxford: Oxford University Press.

Bertelli, C. 1955. "Un antico restauro nei musaici di S. Maria Maggiore." *Paragone* 6.63: 40–42.

Berthaud, A. 1891. *Sancti Augustini doctrina de pulchro ingenuisque artibus e variis illius operibus excerpta.* Poitiers.

Besant, A., and C. W. Leadbeater. 1901. *Thought-Forms.* London: Theosophical Publishing Society.

Betancourt, R., and M. Taroutina. 2015. *Byzantium/Modernism: The Byzantine as Method in Modernity.* Leiden: Brill.

Biagetti, B. 1937. "Intorno ai mosaici della navata centrale della basilica di S. Maria Maggiore." *RendPontAcc* 13: 101–16.

1947. "L'antica struttura della navata centrale della basilica di S. Maria Maggiore." *RendPontAcc* 22: 241–51.

Bialostocki, J. 1966. "Das Modusproblem in den bildenden Künsten: zur Vorgeschichte und zum Nachleben des 'Modusbriefes' von Nicholas Poussin." In *Bialistocki, Stil und Ikonographie. Studien zur Kunstwissenschaft*, 12–41. Dresden: VEB Verlag der Kunst.

Bianchi Bandinelli, R. 1970. *Rome: The Centre of Power. Roman Art to AD 200.* Translated by Peter Green. New York: George Braziller.

1971. *Rome: the Late Empire. Roman Art, AD 200–400.* London and New York: Thames and Hudson and George Braziller.

1973. "Spaetantike." *EAA* 7: 426–27.

Binski, P. 2004. *Becket's Crown: Art and Imagination in Gothic England, 1170–1300.* New Haven, CT: Yale University Press.

2014. *Gothic Wonder: Art, Architecture, and the Decorated Style, 1290–1350.* New Haven, CT: Yale University Press.

Blanck, H. 1969. *Wiederverwendung alter Statuen als Ehrendenkmäler bei Griechen und Römern.* Rome: "L'Erma" di Bretschneider.

Bletter, R. H. 1981. "The Interpretation of the Glass Dream – Expressionist Architecture and the History of the Crystal Metaphor." *JSAH* 40.1: 20–43.

Bolman, E., ed. 2016. *The Red Monastery Church: Beauty and Asceticism in Upper Egypt*. New Haven, CT: Yale University Press.

Bons, J. A. E. 2007. "Gorgias the Sophist and Early Rhetoric." In *A Companion to Greek Rhetoric*, edited by I. Worthington, 37–46. Oxford: Blackwell.

Bosio, A. 1632. *Roma Sotteranea*. Rome: G. Facciotti.

Bowersock, G. 1969. *Greek Sophists in the Roman Empire*. Oxford: Clarendon Press.

Brailsford, J. W. 1955. *The Mildenhall Treasure: A Handbook*. London: British Museum.

Brendel, O. 1953. "Prolegomena to a Book on Roman Art." *MAAR* 21: 7–73.

1979. *Prolegomena to the Study of Roman Art*. New Haven, CT: Yale University Press.

Brenk, B. 1975. *Die frühchristlichen Mosaiken in S. Maria Maggiore zu Rom*. Wiesbaden: Steiner Verlag.

Brilliant, R. 1984. *Visual Narratives: Storytelling in Etruscan and Roman Art*. Ithaca, NY: Cornell University Press.

Brown, P. 1971. *The World of Late Antiquity, AD 150–750*. London: Thames & Hudson.

1988. *The Body and Society: Men, Women, and Sexual Renunciation in Early Christianity*. New York: Columbia University Press.

1992. *Power and Persuasion in Late Antiquity: Towards a Christian Empire*. Madison: University of Wisconsin Press.

Brush and Pencil. 1901. Review of *Roman Art* by F. Wickhoff. *Brush and Pencil* 7.2: 128.

Bruyne, L. de. 1938. "Intorno ai mosaici della navata di S. Maria Maggiore." *RACr* 15: 281–318.

Buberl, P. 1936. "Das Problem der Wiener Genesis." *JbKSWien*, N.F.10: 9–58.

Buberl, P., and H. Gerstinger. 1937. *Der Wiener Dioskurides und die Wiener Genesis = Die Byzantinischen Handschriften*, vol. 1. Leipzig: Karl W. Hiersman.

Burckhardt, J. 1956. *The Age of Constantine the Great*. Translated by M. Hadas. Garden City, NY: Doubleday Anchor.

Cameron, A. 1991. *Christianity and the Rhetoric of Empire: The Development of Christian Discourse*. Berkeley: University of California Press.

Carlson, J. 2010. "Narrative Reliefs of the Arch of Constantine and the Panegyrici Latini." *New England Classical Journal* 37.3: 163–176.

Carruthers, M. 1990. "'Ut pictura poesis': The Rhetoric of Verbal and Visual Images." *Mentalities/Mentalités* 7.1: 1–6.

1998. *The Craft of Thought: Meditation, Rhetoric, and the Making of Images, 400–1200*. Cambridge: Cambridge University Press.

2007. "Sweetness." *Speculum* 81: 999–1013.

2013. *The Experience of Beauty in the Middle Ages*. Oxford: Oxford University Press.

Carruthers, M., ed. 2010. *Rhetoric beyond Words: Delight and Persuasion in the Arts of the Middle Ages*. Cambridge: Cambridge University Press.

Cecchelli, C. 1956. *I mosaici della basilica di Santa Maria Maggiore*. Turin: ILTE.

Chadwick, H. 1993. "Bishops and Monks." *StP* 24: 45–61.

Chesnut, G. 1986. *The First Christian Histories: Eusebius, Socrates, Sozomen, Theodoret, and Evagrius*. Macon, GA: Mercer University Press.

Cicero. 1942. *The Making of the Orator*, 2 vols. Translated by H. Rackham. Cambridge, MA: Harvard University Press.

1949. *On Invention. The Best Kind of Orator. Topics*. Translated by H. M. Hubbell. Cambridge, MA: Harvard University Press.

Clark, D. L. 1957. *Rhetoric in Greco-Roman Education*. New York: Columbia University Press.

Clark, T. J. 1984. *The Painting of Modern Life*. Princeton, NJ: Princeton University Press.

1999. *Farewell to an Idea: Episodes from the History of Modernism*. New Haven, CT: Yale University Press.

Coarelli, F. 2000. *The Column of Trajan*. Rome: Colombo, in collaboration with the German Archaeological Institute.

Conkey M., and C. Haslof, eds. 1990. *Uses of Style in Archaeology*. Cambridge: Cambridge University Press.

Connolly, J. 2007. "The New World Order: Greek Rhetoric in Rome." In *A Companion to Greek Rhetoric*, edited by I. Worthington, 139–65. Oxford: Blackwell.

Corbier, M. 2006. "*Congiarium*." In *New Pauly Online*, http://dx.doi.org/10.1163/1574-9347_bnp_e304050.

Corbier, M., and H. Schneider. 2006. "*Liberalitas, Largitio*." In *New Pauly Online*, http://dx.doi.org/10.1163/1574–9347_bnp_e703670.

Cordileone, D. 2014. *Alois Riegl in Vienna, 1875–1905: An Institutional Biography*. Burlington, VT: Ashgate.

Corpus Rhetoricum. 2008–2009. *Corpus Rhetoricum*, 2 vols. Edited and translated by M. Patillon. Paris: Les Belles Lettres.

Corrigan, K. 1988. "The Witness of John the Baptist on an Early Byzantine Icon in Kiev." *DOP* 42, 1–11.

Cribiore, R. 1996. *Writing, Teachers, and Students in Greco-Roman Egypt*. Atlanta: Scholars Press.

2001. *Gymnastics of the Mind: Greek Education in Hellenistic and Roman Egypt*. Princeton, NJ: Princeton University Press.

Croke, B., and A. M. Emmett, eds. 1983. *History and Historians in Late Antiquity*. Sydney: Pergamum.

Crum, W. E. 1901. "Communiqué on Strzygowski's *Orient oder Rom*, Leipzig, 1901." *CR* 15.4:232–34.

Dalton, O. M. 1911. *Byzantine Art and Archaeology*. Oxford: Clarendon Press.

1925. *East Christian Art: A Survey of the Monuments*. Oxford: Clarendon Press.

D'Angour, A. 2015. "Sense and Sensation in Music." In *A Companion to Ancient Aesthetics*, edited by P. Destrée and P. Murray, 188–202. Chichester: Wiley.

Daniel, A. M. 1911. Review of *The Art of the Romans* by H. B. Walters. *JRS* 1: 241–42.

Davis–Weyer, C. 1986. *Early Medieval Art, 300–1150*. Toronto: University of Toronto Press.

Deckers, J. G. 1976. *Der alttestamentliche Zyklus von S. Maria Maggiore in Rom*. Bonn: Habelt.

2002. "Der erste Diener Christi. Die Proskynese der Kaiser als Schlüsselmotiv der Mosaiken in San Vitale (Ravenna) und in der Haghia Sophia (Istanbul)." In *Art, Cérémonial et Liturgie au Moyen Âge, Actes du Colloque de 3e Cycle Romand de Lettres, Lausanne-Fribourg, 24–25 mars, 14–15 avril, 12–13 mai 2000*, edited by N. Bock, 11–57. Rome: Viella.

De Grummond, N. 1996. *Encyclopedia of the History of Classical Archaeology*, 2 vols. Westport, CT: Greenwood Press.

Deichmann, F. W. 1948. *Frühchristliche Kirchen in Rom*. Basel: A. M. Erbach.

1953. "Gründung und Datierung von San Vitale in Ravenna." In *Arte del Primo Milllenio. 2e Congrès International pour l'Étude du Haut Moyen Age, Pavia 1950*, 111–17, 188–90. Turin: A. Viglonglo.

1969–1989. *Ravenna: Hauptstadt des spätantiken Abendlandes*, 2 vols. Wiesbaden: F. Steiner Verlag.

1983. *Einführung in die christliche Archäologie*. Darmstadt: Wissenschaftliche Buchgesellschaft.

Delbrueck, R. 1929. *Die Consulardiptychen und verwandte Denkmäler*, 2 vols. Berlin: De Gruyter.

Deliyannis, D. M. 2010. *Ravenna in Late Antiquity*. Cambridge: Cambridge University Press.

De Maria, S. 1988. *Gli archi onorari di Roma dell'Italia romana*. Rome: "L'Erma" di Bretschneider.

Depeyrot, G. 2010. *La Colonne de Marc Aurèle*, 2 vols. Wetteren: Moneta.

Dionysius of Halicarnassus. 1974–1985. *Critical Essays*, 2 vols. Translated by S. Usher. Cambridge, MA: Harvard University Press.

Dilly, H. 1979. *Kunstgeschichte als Institution: Studien zur Geschichte einer Diziplin*. Frankfurt: Suhrkamp.

Dimand, M. S. 1940. "In Memoriam Josef Strzygowski." *AI* 7: 177.

Dodds, E. R. 1965. *Pagan and Christian in an Age of Anxiety: Some Aspects of Religious Experience from Marcus Aurelius to Constantine*. Cambridge: Cambridge University Press.

Dohrn, T. 1949. "Spätantikes Silber aus Britannien." *MDAI* 2: 67–139.

Donohue, A. A. 2005. *Greek Sculpture and the Problem of Description*. Cambridge: Cambridge University Press.

Droge, A. J. 1989. *Homer or Moses? Early Christian Interpretations of the History of Culture*. Tübingen: J. C. B. Mohr.

Drucker, J., et al. 2014. "Modernism." In *Encyclopedia of Aesthetics*, www.oxfordreference.com/view/10.1093/acref/9780199747108.001.0001/acref-9780199747108-e-507?rskey=HbhUpZ&result=1.

Dyson, S. 2006. *In Pursuit of Ancient Pasts*. New Haven, CT: Yale University Press.

Eastmond, A. 2010. "Consular Diptychs, Rhetoric and the Languages of Art in Sixth-Century Constantinople." *AH* 33.5: 742–65.

Eck, C. van. 2007. *Classical Rhetoric and the Visual Arts in Early Modern Europe*. Cambridge: Cambridge University Press.

Eichler, F. 1939. "Das sogenannte Partherdenkmal von Ephesos." In *Bericht über den VI. Internationalen Kongress für Archäologie*, 488–94. Berlin: De Gruyter.

1971. "Zum Partherdenkmal von Ephesos." *ÖJh* 49 Beihefte: 102–36.

Eitelberger, R. von. 1861. "Die mittelalterlichen Kunstdenkmale Dalmatiens in Arbe, Zara, Nona, Sebenico, Traù, Spalato und Ragusa, aufgenommen und dargestellt vom Architekten W. Zimmermann." *Jahrbuch der k. k. Central-Commission zur Erforschung und Erhaltung der Baudenkmale* 5: 129–312.

Elsner, J. 1995. *Art and the Roman Viewer. The Transformation of Art from the Pagan World to Christianity*. Cambridge: Cambridge University Press.

2000. "Frontality in the Column of Marcus Aurelius." In *La colonne Aurélienne. Autour de la colonne Aurélienne, geste et image sur la colonne de Marc Aurèle à Rome*, edited by J. Scheid and V. Huet, 251–56. Turnhout: Brepols.

2002. "The Birth of Late Antiquity: Riegl and Strzygowski in 1901." *AH* 25: 358–79.

2003. "Style." In *Critical Terms for Art History*, 2nd ed., edited by R. Nelson and R. Schiff, 98–110. Chicago: University of Chicago Press.

2007. *Roman Eyes: Visuality and Subjectivity in Art and Text*. Princeton, NJ: Princeton University Press.

2019. "The Viennese Invention of Late Antiquity: Between Politics and Religion in the Forms of Late Antique Art." In *Empires of Faith in Late Antiquity: Histories of Art and Religion from India to Ireland*, edited by J. Elsner, 110–27. Cambridge: Cambridge University Press.

Elsner, J., ed. 1996. *Art and Text in Roman Culture*. Cambridge: Cambridge University Press.

Elsner J., and E. Bowie, eds. 2009. *Philostratus*. Cambridge: Cambridge University Press.

Elsner J., and M. Meyer, eds. 2014. *Art and Rhetoric in Roman Culture*. Cambridge: Cambridge University Press.

Engemann, J. 1984. "Die religiöse Herrscherfunktion im Fünfsäulenmonument Diocletians in Rom und in den Herrschermosaiken Justinians in Ravenna." *FS* 18: 336–56.

1999. "Das Apotheosebild des Partherdenkmals aus Ephesos." In 100 Jahre osterreichische Forschungen in Ephesos: Akten des Symposions Wien 1995, edited by H. Friesinger and F. Krinzinger, 633–37. Vienna: Österreichischen Akademie der Wissenschaften.

Etingroph, O. E. 2005. *Byzantine Icons of the 5th to the First Half of the 8th Century in Russia*. Moscow: Indrik.

Eusebius of Caesarea. 1926–1932. *Ecclesiastical History*, 2 vols. Translated by K. Lake. Cambridge, MA: Harvard University Press.

Evans, E. 1969. *Physiognomics in the Ancient World*. Philadelphia: American Philosophical Society.

Eyice, S. 1958. "Neue Fragmente der Theodosiussäule." *IstMitt* 8: 144–47.

Faust, S. 2012a. "Prestige in der Provinz: Zum Bildprogramm des Partherdenkmals von Ephesos Munich." In *Ansehenssache.*

Formen von Prestige in Kulturen des Altertums, edited by B. Christiansen and U. Thaler, 319–52. Munich: Herbert Utz.

2012b. *Schlachtenbilder der römischen Kaiserzeit: Erzählerische Darstellungskonzepte in der Reliefkunst von Traian bis Septimius Severus*. Rahden Westf: Verlag Marie Leidorft.

Fechner, G. 1848. *Nanna oder über das Seelenleben der Pflanzen*. Leipzig: Leopold Voß.

1851. *Zend-Avesta oder über die Dinge des Himmels und des Jenseits*. Leipzig: Leopold Voß.

1860. *Elemente der Psychophysik*, 2 vols. Leipzig: Breitkopf und Härtel.

Fentress, J., and C. Wickham. 1992. *Social Memory*. Oxford: Blackwell.

Fıratlı, N. 1990. *La sculpture byzantine figurée au Musée Archéologique d'Istanbul; Catalogue revue et présenté par C. Metzger*. Paris: Librairie d'Amérique et d'Orient Adrien Maisonneuve, Jean Maisonneuve Successeur.

Foletti, I., and F. Lovino. 2019. *Orient oder Rom? History and Reception of a Historiographical Myth (1901–1970)*. Rome: Viella.

Ford, A. 2001. "Sophists without Rhetoric: The Arts of Speech in Fifth-Century Athens." In *Education in Greek and Roman Antiquity*, edited by Yun Lee Too, 85–109. Leiden: Brill.

Fowden, G. 2014. *Before and after Muhammad: The First Millennium Refocused*. Princeton, NJ: Princeton University Press.

Francis, J. 1995. *Subversive Virtue: Asceticism and Authority in the Second-Century Pagan World*. University Park: Pennsylvania State University Press.

Frantová, Z. 2019. *Ravenna: Sedes Imperii, Artistic Trajectories in the Late Antique Mediterranean*. Rome: Viella.

Frend, W. H. C. 1995. *The Archaeology of Early Christianity*. London: Geoffrey Chapman.

Fullerton, M. 1990. *The Archaistic Style in Roman Statuary*. Leiden: Brill.

Galbreath, R. 1986. "Theosophy." In *The Spiritual in Art: Abstract Painting 1890–1985*, edited by M. Tuchman and J. Freedman, 388–89. New York: Abbeville Press.

Galen. 1981. *On the Doctrines of Hippocrates and Plato*. Edited, translated, and commented on by P. De Lacy, 2nd ed. Berlin: Akademie Verlag.

2020. *On Temperaments; On Non-uniform Distemperment; The Soul's Traits Depend on Bodily Temperament*. Edited and translated by I. Johnston. Cambridge, MA: Harvard University Press.

Gamwell, L. 2002. *Exploring the Invisible: Art, Science and the Spiritual*. Princeton, NJ: Princeton University Press.

Gandelman, C. 1982. "Thomas Mann and the Theory of 'Crystalline Beauty'." *Orbis Litterarum* 37: 122–33.

Ganschow, T. 1986. "Überlegungen zum Partherdenkmal von Ephesos." *AA*: 209–21.

Gardner, P. 1901. "Wickhoff and Strong's *Roman Art*." *CR* 15.1: 89–92.

Garrucci, P. R. 1872–1888. *Storia della Arte Cristiana*, 6 vols. Prato: Francesco Giachetti.

Gehn, U. 2012. *Ehrenstatuen in der Spätantike. Chlamydati und Togati*. Wiesbaden: Reichert.

Gerstinger, A. G. 1931. *Die Wiener Genesis*. Vienna: Filser.

Geyer, A. 2006. "Bibelepik und frühchristlichen Bildzyklen: die Mosaiken von Santa Maria Maggiore in Rom." *RM* 112: 296–321.

Giacomini, F. 2005. "Considerazioni sul restauro dei mosaici delle basiliche romane nella prima metà dell'Ottocento: un punto di vista indulgente." *Arte Medievale*, n.s. 4.2: 127–36.

Giardina, A. 1999. "Esplosione di Tardoantico." *Studi Storici* 40.1: 157–80.

Giglioli, G. 1952. *La Colonna di Arcadio a Costantinopoli*. Naples: G. Macchiaroli.

Giuliano, A. 1957. *Catalogo dei ritratti romani del Museo Profano Lateranense*. Vatican City: Tipografia poliglotta vaticana.

Goldschmidt, R. C. 1940. *Paulinus' Churches at Nola: Texts, Translation and Commentary*. Amsterdam: N.v. Noord-Hollandsche utigevers maatschappij.

Gombrich, E. H. 1968. "Style." In *International Encyclopedia of the Social Sciences*. New York:

Macmillan. Republished in *The Art of Art History: A Critical Anthology*, edited by D. Preziozi, 143–49. Oxford: Oxford University Press, 1999.

Goodman, N. 1975. "The Status of Style." *CI* 1.4: 799–811.

Grabar, A. 1936. *L'Empereur dans l'art byzantin*. Paris: Les Belles Lettres.

1945. "Plotin et les origines de l'esthétique médiévale." *CahArch* 1: 15–36.

1960. "Quel est le sens de l'offrande de Justinien et Theodora sur les mosaïques de Saint-Vital?" *FR* 81: 63–77.

1968. *Christian Iconography: A Study of Its Origins*. Princeton, NJ: Princeton University Press.

Gran-Aymerian, E. 1998. *Naissance de l'archéologie moderne, 1798–1945*. Paris: CNRS Editions.

Greenberg, C. 1961. "Byzantine Parallels." In *Art and Culture: Critical Essays*, edited by C. Greenberg, 167–70. Boston: Beacon Press.

Gregory of Nazianzen. 1894a. "Funeral Oration on the Great Saint Basil, Bishop of Caesarea in Cappadocia." *NPNF2* 7: 785–831.

1894b. "Oration 39: On the Holy Lights." *NPNF2* 7: 702–18.

Grethlein, J., and A. Rengakos, eds. 2009. *Narratology and Interpretation: The Content of Narrative Form in Ancient Literature*. Berlin: De Gruyter.

Griebel, J. 2013. *Das Kaiser im Krieg: Die Bilder der Säule des Marc Aurel*. Berlin: De Gruyter.

Grimm, J., and W. Grimm, eds. 1887. *Deutsches Wörterbuch*, 10 vols. Leipzig: S. Hirzel.

Gustav-Lübke Museum der Stadt Haam. 1996. *Ägypten, Schätze aus dem Wüstensand: Kunst und Kultur der Christen am Nil: Katalog zur Ausstellung*. Edited by the Gustav- Lübke-Museum der Stadt Hamm and the Museum für Spätantike und Byzantinische Kunst, Staatliche Museen zu Berlin-Preussischer Kulturbesitz. Wiesbaden: Reichert.

Hallett, C. H. 1986. "The origins of classical style in sculpture." *JHS* 106: 71–84.

Halliwell, S. 2002. *The Aesthetics of Mimesis: Ancient Texts and Modern Problems*. Princeton, NJ: Princeton University Press.

2009. "The Theory and Practice of Narrative in Plato." In *Narratology and Interpretation: The Content of Narrative Form in Ancient Literature*, edited by J. Grethlein and A. Rengakos, 15–49. Berlin: De Gruyter.

Halporn, J., M. Ostwald, and T. Rosenmayer. 1963. *The Meters of Greek and Latin Poetry*. Indianapolis: Bobbs-Merrill.

Harley-McGowan, F., and H. Maguire, eds. 2017. *Ernst Kitzinger and the Making of Medieval Art History*. London: Warburg Institute.

Harris W. 1989. *Ancient Literacy*. Cambridge, MA: Harvard University Press.

Haüy, R. J. 1784. *Essai d'une théorie sur la structure des crystaux, appliquée à plusieurs genres de substances crystallisées*. Paris: Chez Gogué & Née de la Rochelle.

1801. *Traité des minéralogies*. Paris: Chez Louis.

1822. *Traité de crystallographie*, 2 vols. Paris : Bachelier et Huzard.

Hegel, G. W. F. 1971. *Hegel's Philosophy of Mind, Being Part Three of the Encyclopaedia of the Philosophical Sciences (1830)*. Translated by W. Wallace. Oxford: Clarendon Press.

1975. *Aesthetics: Lectures on Fine Art by G. W. F. Hegel*, vol. 1. Translated by T. M. Knox. Oxford: Clarendon Press.

Helmholtz, H. von. 1925. *Treatise on Physiological Optics*, 3 vols. Translated by J. P. C. Southall. Rochester, NY: Optical Society of America.

Hermogenes of Tarsus. 1913. *Hermogenis opera*. Edited by H. Rabe. Leipzig: Teubner.

1987. *Hermogenes on Types of Style*. Translated by C. Wooten. Chapel Hill: University of North Carolina Press.

Herzfeld, E. E., W. R. W. Koehler, and C. R. Morey. 1942. "Josef Strzygowski." *Speculum* 17: 460–61.

Hill, G. 1945. "Ormonde Maddock Dalton, 1866–1945." *ProcBrAc* 31: 357–53.

Hinks, D. A. G. 1940. "From Tisias to Corax and the Invention of Rhetoric." *CQ* 34: 61–69.

Hobbs, R. 2016. *The Mildenhall Treasure: Late Roman Silver Plate from East Anglia*. London: British Museum.

Hofmann, C., ed. 2020. *The Vienna Genesis: Material Analysis and Conservation of a Late*

Antique Illuminated Manuscript on Purple Parchment. Vienna: Böhlau.

Hofmannsthal, H. von. 1979–1980. *Gesammelte Werke in zehn Einzelbänden*, 10 vols. Edited by B. Schoeller and R. Hirsch. Frankfurt am Main: Fischer-Taschenbuch-Verlag.

Holder, A., ed. 2005. *The Blackwell Companion to Christian Spirituality*. Oxford: Blackwell.

Holland, L. B. 1946. "The Triple Arch of Augustus." *AJA* 50: 52–59.

Holliday, P. 2002. *The Origins of Roman Historical Commemoration in the Visual Arts*. Cambridge: Cambridge University Press.

Holliday, P., ed. 1993. *Narrative and Event in Ancient Art*. Cambridge: Cambridge University Press.

Hölscher, T. 2004. *The Language of Images in Roman Art*. Translated by A. Snodgrass and A. Künzl-Snodgrass. Cambridge: Cambridge University Press.

Horace. 1926. *Satires. Epistles. The Art of Poetry*. Translated by H. Rushton Fairclough. Cambridge, MA: Harvard University Press.

Hughes, J. 2014. "Memory and the Roman Viewer: Looking at the Arch of Constantine." In *Memoria Romana: Memory in Rome and Rome in Memory*, edited by K. Galinsky, 103–15. Ann Arbor: University of Michigan Press.

Hunger, H. 1978. *Die hochsprachliche profane Literatur der Byzantiner*, 2 vols. Munich: Beck.

Iannucci, A. M., C. Fiori, and C. Muscolino, eds. 1992. *Mosaici a S. Vitale e altri restauri. Il restauro in situ di mosaici parietali. Atti del Convegno nazionale sul restauro in situ di mosaici parietali, Ravenna 1–3 ottobre 1990*. Ravenna: Longo.

Inan, J., and E. Rosenbaum. 1966. *Roman and Early Byzantine Portrait Sculpture in Asia Minor*. Oxford: Oxford University Press.

Iversen, M. 1993. *Alois Riegl: Art History and Theory*. Cambridge, MA: MIT Press.

Jaeger, W. 1939. *Paideia, the Ideals of Greek Culture*. Translated by Gilbert Highet. Oxford: Blackwell.

James, L., ed. 2007. *Art and Text in Byzantine Culture*. Cambridge: Cambridge University Press.

James, L., and R. Webb. 1991. "'To understand ultimate things and enter secret places': Ekphrasis and Art in Byzantium." *AH* 14: 1–17.

Jan, K. von. 1895. *Musici Scriptores Graeci. Aristoteles, Euclides, Nicomachus, Bacchius Gaudentius, Alypius et melodiarum veterum quidquid exstat*. Leipzig: Teubner.

Josephus. 1926–1965. *Jewish Antiquities*, 8 vols. Translated by H. St. J. Thackeray, R. Marcus, L. H. Feldman, and A. Wikgren. Cambridge, MA: Harvard University Press.

Kandinsky W. 1912. *Über das Geistige in der Kunst*. Munich: Piper.

1977. *Concerning the Spiritual in Art*. Translated M. T. H. Sadler. New York: Dover Publications. Original English edition first published as *The Art of Spiritual Harmony*, London: A. Constable & Company, 1914.

Kaster, R. 1989. *Guardians of Language: The Grammarian and Society in Late Antiquity*. Berkeley: University of California Press.

Kennedy, G. A. 1963. *The Art of Persuasion in Greece*. Princeton, NJ: Princeton University Press.

1972. *The Art of Rhetoric in the Roman World, 300 B.C.–A.D. 300*. Princeton, NJ: Princeton University Press.

1983. *Greek Rhetoric under Christian Emperors*. Princeton, NJ: Princeton University Press.

1999. *Classical Rhetoric and Its Christian and Secular Tradition from Ancient to Modern Times*. Chapel Hill: University of North Carolina Press.

2003. *Progymnasmata: Greek Textbooks for Prose Composition*. Atlanta: Society of Biblical Literature.

2009. *A New History of Classical Rhetoric*. Princeton, NJ: Princeton University Press.

Kent. J. P. C., and K. S. Painter. 1977. *Wealth of the Roman World: Gold and Silver AD 300–700*. London: British Museum.

Kiilerich, B. 1993. *Late Fourth Century Classicism in the Visual Arts*. Odense: Odense University Press.

Kinney, D. 2016. "The Type of the Triconch Basilica." In *The Red Monastery Church: Beauty and Asceticism in Upper Egypt*, edited by E. Bolman, 37–48. New Haven, CT: Yale University Press.

Kitzinger, E. 1934. "Römische Malerei vom Beginn des 7. bis zur Mitte des 8. Jahrhunderts." Inaugural-Dissertation zur Erlangung der Doktorwürde der Philosophischen Fakultät (I. Sektion) der Ludwig Maximilians Universität zu München.

1940. *Early Medieval Art in the British Museum*. London: British Museum.

1958. "Byzantine Art in the Period between Justinian and Iconoclasm." *Berichte zum XI. internationalen Byzantinisten-Kongress*, München, 4.1: 1–50. Republished in *The Art of Byzantium and the Medieval West: Selected Studies by Ernst Kitzinger*, edited by W. Eugene Kleinbauer, 157–232; 391–93. Bloomington: Indiana University Press, 1976.

1967. "On the Interpretation of Stylistic Change in Late Antique Art." *Bucknell Review* 15.3: 1–10.

1975. "The Role of Miniature Painting in Mural Decoration." In *The Place of Book Illumination in Byzantine Art*, edited by K. Weitzmann, W. C. Loerke, E. Kitzinger, and H. Buchthal, 99–142. Princeton, NJ: Princeton University Press.

1977. *Byzantine Art in the Making: Main Lines of Stylistic Development in Mediterranean Art. 2nd–7th Centuries*. Cambridge, MA: Harvard University Press.

1981. "The Hellenistic Heritage in Byzantine Art Reconsidered." *JÖB* 31.2: 657–75.

Knudsen, S. 1989. "Spolia: The So-Called Historical Frieze on the Arch of Constantine." *AJA* 93: 267–68.

Kollwitz J. 1941. *Oströmische Plastik der theodosianischen Zeit*. Berlin: De Gruyter.

1965. "Ravenna zwischen Orient und Occident." In *Atti VI Congresso internazionale di Archeologia Cristiana, Ravenna, 1962*, 383–402. Vatican City: Pontificio Istituto di Archaeologia Christiana.

Kölzer, T. 2010. "Diplomatics." In *Handbook of Medieval Studies: Terms, Methods, Trends*, edited by A. Classen, 405–24. Berlin: De Gruyter.

Kondakov, N. P. 1877. Istoriya vizantiyskogo iskusstva ikonografii po miniatyram grecheskikh rukopsey (History of Byzantine Art and Iconography through the Miniatures of Byzantine Manuscripts). Odessa.

1886. *Histoire de l'Art Byzantin*, 2 vols. Translated by M. Trawinski. Paris: Jules Roam.

1889–1891. *Russkiye drvnosti v. pamiatnikoskh*, 6 vols. St. Petersburg: A. Benke.

1892. *Antiquités de la Russie Méridionale*. Paris: Ernest Leroux.

Kovacs, M. 2014. *Kaiser, Senatoren und Gelehrte. Untersuchungen zum spätantiken männlichen Privatpörträt*. Wiesbaden: Reichert.

Kraus, F. X. 1896. *Geschichte der Christlichen Kunst*, 2 vols. Freiburg im Breisgau: Harder'sche Verlagshandlung.

Krause, M. 1971. "Zur Lokalisierung und Datierung koptischer Denkmäler. Das Tafelbild Bischofs Abrahams." *ZÄS* 97: 106–11.

Krautheimer, R. 1967. *Corpus basilicarum christianarum Romae. Le basiliche cristiane antiche di Roma (sec. IV–IX) = The Early Christian Basilicas of Rome (IV–IX cent)*, vol. 3. Città del Vaticano: Pontificio Istituto di Archeologia Cristiana.

Krumbacher, K. 1895. "W. Ritter von Hartel and Frs. Wickhoff, Die Wiener Genesis," *ByzZeit* 4: 639–43.

Kuhoff, W. 1991. "Ein Mythos in der römischen Geschichte: Der Sieg Konstantins des Großen über Maxentius vor den Toren Roms am 28. Oktober 312 n. Chr." *Chiron* 21: 127–74.

Kunze, C. 2014. "Formal Approaches." In *The Oxford Handbook of Greek and Roman Art and Architecture*, edited by C. Marconi, 541–56. Oxford: Oxford University Press.

Künzle, P. 1961–1962. "Per una vision organica dei mosaici antichi di Santa Maria Maggiore." *RendPontAcc* 34: 153–90.

Lachnit, E. 2003. "Franz Wickhoff," in *Grove Art Online*, https://doi.org/10.1093/gao/9781884446054.article.T091470.

Lambeck, P., and D. de Nessel. 1690. *Catalogus, sive recensio specilis omnium codicum manuscriptorum graecorum, nec non linguarum orientalium, augustissimae Bibliothecae caesareae Vindobonensis*. Vienna and Nuremberg: L. Voight and J. B. Endleri.

Landskron, A. 2006. "Antike Bildsprache und das sog. Partherdenkmal." In *Akten des 10. Österreichischen Archäologentages in Graz, 7.–9. November 2003*, 107–12. Vienna: Phoibos.

Lang, B., ed. 1987. *The Concept of Style*. Ithaca, NY: Cornell University Press.

La Rocca, E., C. Parisis Presicce, and A. Lo Monaco, eds. 2015. *L'Età dell'angoscia. Da Commodo a Diocleziano (180–305 d.C.)*. Rome: MondoMostre.

Lazarev, V. V. 1967. *Storia della pittura bizantina*. Translated by G. Fossati. Turin: Einaudi.

Leadbetter, C. W. 1902. *Man Visible and Invisible: Examples of Different Types of Men as Seen By Means of Trained Clairvoyance*. New York: John Lane.

Leader-Newby, R. E. 2004. *Silver and Society in Late Antiquity: Functions and Meanings of Silver Plate in the Fourth through Seventh Centuries*. Abingdon: Ashgate.

Lee, R. W. 1955. "Charles Rufus Morey." *ArtB* 37: ii–viii.

Leftwich, G. 1995. "Polykleitos and Hippokratic Medicine." In *Polykleitos, the Doryphoros, and Tradition*, edited by W. Moon, 38–51. Madison: University of Wisconsin Press.

Lehmann-Hartleben, K. 1926. *Die Trajanssäule. Ein römisches Kunstwerk zu Beginn der Spätantike*, 2 vols. Berlin: De Gruyter.

Leibescheutz, W. 2005. "The Birth of Late Antiquity." *AntTard* 12: 253–61.

Lenaghan, J. 2016. "Reuse in 4th-Century Portrait Statues." In *The Last Statues of Antiquity*, edited by R. R. R. Smith and B. Ward-Perkins, 267–79. Oxford: Oxford University Press.

Lenoir, A. A. 1818. *Atlas des monuments des arts libéraux, mécaniques et industriels de la France, depuis les Gaulois jusqu'au règne de François Ier*. Paris: J. Techener.

Lenski, N., and M. Koortbojian. 2023. "The Constantinian Frieze on the Arch of Constantine: The Weight of the Evidence." *RM*: 129. Forthcoming.

Lhotsky, A. 1954. *Geschichte des Instituts für österreichische Geschichtsforschung, 1854–1954*. Graz: Hermann Böhlaus Nachf.

Lidova, M. 2015. "The Imperial Theotokos: Revealing the Concept of Early Christian Imagery in Santa Maria Maggiore in Rome." *Convivium* 2.2: 60–81.

2019. "The Rise of Byzantine Art and Archaeology in Late Imperial Russia." In *Empires of Faith in Late Antiquity: Histories of Art and Religion from India to Ireland*, edited by J. Elsner, 128–60. Cambridge: Cambridge University Press.

Lipps, T. 1897. *Raumästhetik und geometrisch-optische Täuschungen*. Leipzig: Barth.

1903. *Ästhetik. Psychologie des Schönen und der Kunst, Grundlegen der Ästhetik*. Hamburg: Leopold Voss.

1906. *Ästhetik. Psychologie des Schönen und der Kunst. Die ästhetische Betrachtung und die bildende Kunst*. Hamburg: Leopold Voss.

Liveley, G. 2019. *Narratology*. Oxford: Oxford University Press.

L'Orange, H. P. 1933. *Studien zur Geschichte des spätantiken Porträts*. Oslo: H. Aschenhoug & Co.

1965. *Art Forms and Civic Life in the Later Roman Empire*. Princeton, NJ: Princeton University Press.

1973. "The Origin of Medieval Portraiture." In *Likeness and Icon*, 91–102. Odense: Odense University Press. Originally published in *Acta Congressus Maadvigiani. Proceedings of the Second International Congress of Classical Studies*, vol. 3: 53–70. Copenhagen: E. Munksgaard, 1957.

L'Orange, H. P., and A. von Gerkan. 1939. *Der spätantike Bildschmuck des Konstantinsbogens*, 2 vols. Berlin: De Gruyter.

Lübke, W. 1885. *Outlines of Art History*. Translated by E. L. Burlingame. New York: Dodd, Mead & Co.

Lucian of Samosata. 1913–79. *Lucian*, 8 vols. Translated by A. M. Harmon, M. D. MacLeod, and K. Kilburn. Cambridge, MA: Harvard University Press.

Macartney, C. A. 1969. *The Habsburg Empire, 1790–1918*. New York: Macmillan.

MacDonald, W. L. 1986. *Architecture of the Roman Empire, Volume II: An Urban Appraisal*. New Haven, CT: Yale University Press.

Machado, C. 2021. "The Statue Habit and Statue Culture in Late Antique Rome." *JRA* 34.2: 632–66.

McClanan A. 2002. *Representations of Early Byzantine Empresses: Image and Empire*. New York: Palgrave Macmillan.

MacCormack, S. 1981. *Art and Ceremony in Late Antiquity*. Berkeley: University of California Press.

Maguire, H. 1974. "Truth and Convention in Byzantine Descriptions of Works of Art." *DOP* 28: 113–40.

1977. "The Depiction of Sorrow in Middle Byzantine Art." *DOP* 31:123–74.

1981. *Art and Eloquence in Byzantium*. Princeton, NJ: Princeton University Press.

1987. *Earth and Ocean: The Terrestrial World in Early Byzantine Art*. University Park: Pennsylvania State University Press.

1989. "Style and Ideology in Byzantine Imperial Art." *Gesta* 28: 217–31.

1993. "Disembodiment and Corporeality in Byzantine Images of the Saints." In *Iconography at the Crossroads*, edited by B. Cassidy, 75–83. Princeton, NJ: Princeton University Press.

1995. "Two Modes of Narration in Byzantine Art." In *Byzantine East, Latin West: Art Historical Studies in Honor of Kurt Weitzmann*, edited by D. Mouriki, C. Moss, and K. Kiefer, 385–95. Princeton, NJ: Princeton University Press.

1996. *The Icons of Their Bodies: Saints and Their Images in Byzantium*. Princeton, NJ: Princeton University Press.

1999. "The Profane Aesthetic in Byzantine Art and Literature." *DOP* 53: 189–205.

2005. "Rhetoric and Reality in Byzantine Art." *Rhetorik. Ein internationales Jahrbuch* 24: 14–26.

2011a. "The Realities of Ekphrasis." *BSl* 69: 7–19.

2011b. "La rhétorique et l'esthétique de l'art byzantine." In *La rhétorique des arts : actes du colloque tenu au Collège de France*, edited by L. Pernot, 45–72. Paris: Presses universitaires de France.

2017. "Rhetoric and Artistry in Early Byzantium." In *Handbuch Rhetorik der bildenden Künste*, edited by W. Brassat, 185–206. Berlin: De Gruyter.

Malgrave, H., and E. Ikonomou, eds. and trans. 1994. *Empathy, Form, and Space: Problems in German Aesthetics, 1873–1893*. Santa Monica, CA: Getty Center.

Manara, J. E. 1983. "Di un ipotesi per l'individuazzione dei personnaggi nei panelli del S. Vitale a Ravenna e per la loro interpretazione." *FR* 4th series 125–26, 13–37.

Mander, W. 2022. "Pantheism." *The Stanford Encyclopedia of Philosophy* (Spring 2022 Edition), edited by Edward N. Zalta, https://plato.stanford.edu/archives/spr2022/entries/pantheism/.

Marchand, S. L. 1994. "The Rhetoric of Artifacts and the Decline of Classical Humanism: The Case of Josef Strzygowski." *History and Theory, Beiheft* 33: 106–33.

1996. *Down from Olympus*. Princeton, NJ: Princeton University Press.

2001. "German Orientalism and the Decline of the West." *PAPS* 145.4: 465–73

2009. *German Orientalism in the Age of Empire*. Washington, DC, and New York: German Historical Institute and Cambridge University Press.

Marrou, H. 1956. *A History of Education in Antiquity*. Translated by G. Lamb. New York: Sheed & Ward.

Marsengill, K. 2011. "Portraits and Icons in Antiquity." In *Transition to Christianity: Art of Late Antiquity, 3rd–7th c.*, edited by A. Lazaridou, 61–67. New York: Alexander S. Onassis Public Benefit Foundation.

2013. *Portraits and Icons: Between Reality and Spirituality in Byzantine Art*. Turnhout: Brepols.

Martin, J. 2010. *Der Weg zur Ewigkeit führt über Rom: die Frühgeschichte des Papsttums und die Darstellung der neutestamentlichen Heilsgeschichte im Triumphbogenmosaik von Santa Maria Maggiore in Rom*. Stuttgart: Steiner Verlag.

Marquand, A. 1910. "Strzygowski and His Theory of Early Christian Art." *HTR* 3.3: 357–65.

Masner, K. 1893a. "Archaeologische Ausstellung im K .K. Oesterr. Museum 1893." *Mitteilungen des k.k. Oesterreich. Museums für Kunst und Industrie* 88.331: 349–50.

1893b. *Katalog der archaeologischen Ausstellung, 22. Mai bis 31. August 1893*. Vienna: Verlag des K. K. Oesterr. Museums.

Mathew, G. 1963. *Byzantine Aesthetics*. London: J. Murray.

Mathews, T. 1971. *The Early Churches of Constantinople, Architecture and Liturgy*. University Park: Pennsylvania State University Press.

Mathiesen, T. 1999. *Apollo's Lyre: Greek Music in Antiquity and the Middle Ages*. Lincoln: University of Nebraska Press.

Mathiesen, T., ed. 1998. *Greek Views of Music*. New York: Norton and Company.

Mazal, O. 1980. *Kommentar zur Wiener Genesis: Faksimile-Ausgabe der Codex theol.gr. 31 der Österreichischen Nationalbibliothek in Wien*. Frankfurt am Main: Insel.

Mazza, M. 2005. "Spätantike: genesi e trasformazioni di un tema storiografico (da Burckhardt a Mickwitz e Marrou via Riegl)." *Mediterraneo antico* 7.2: 586–638.

McLaughlin, N. 2001. "Critical Theory Meets America: Riesman, Fromm and the Lonely Crowd." *American Sociologist* 32.1: 5–26.

Meiering, R. 1987. *Literary and Rhetorical Theories in Greek Scholia*. Groningen: E. Forsten.

Menander Rhetor. 1981. *Menander Rhetor: A Commentary*. Edited and translated by D. A. Russell and N. G. Wilson. Oxford: Oxford University Press.

Milburn, R. L. P. 1954. *Early Christian Interpretations of History*. New York: Harper.

Momigliano, A. 1963. "Pagan and Christian Historiography in the Fourth Century A.D." In *The Conflict between Paganism and Christianity in the Fourth Century*, 79–99. Oxford: Oxford University Press. Reprinted in *Essays in Ancient and Modern Historiography*, ed. A. Momigliano and A. Grafton, 107–26. Chicago: University of Chicago Press, 2012.

1990. *The Classical Foundations of Modern Historiography*. Berkeley: University of California Press.

Montfaucon, B. de. 1729–1734. *Les monuments de la monarchie françoise qui comprennent l'histoire de France, avec les figures de chaque règne que l'injure des tems a épargnées*, 5 vols. Paris: J. M. Gandouin and P. F. Giffart.

Morey, C. R. 1924. "The Sources of Medieval Style." *ArtB* 7.2: 35–50.

1929. "Notes on East Christian Miniatures." *ArtB* 11: 4–103.

1942. *Medieval Art*. New York: W. W. Norton.

1953. *Early Christian Art: An Outline of the Evolution of Style and Iconography in Sculpture and Painting from Antiquity to the Eighth Century*, 2nd edition. Princeton, NJ: Princeton University Press.

Morgan, D. 1992a. "Concepts of Abstraction in French Art Theory from the Enlightenment to Modernism." *JHistIdeas* 53.4: 669–85.

1992b. "The Idea of Abstraction in German Theories of Ornament." *JAAC* 50.3: 231–42.

1994. "The Rise and Fall of Abstraction in Eighteenth-Century Art Theory." *Eighteenth-Century Studies* 27.3: 449–78.

1996. "The Enchantment of Art: Abstraction and Empathy from German Romanticism to Expressionism." *JHistIdeas* 57.2: 317–41.

1998. *Literate Education in the Hellenistic and Roman Worlds*. Cambridge: Cambridge University Press.

2007. "Rhetoric and Education." In *A Companion to Greek Rhetoric*, edited by I. Worthington, 303–19. Oxford: Blackwell.

Müller-Wiener, W. 1977. *Bildlexikon zur Topographie Istanbuls*. Tübingen: Wasmuth.

Münz, E. 1888. "La colonne Théodosienne de Constantinople d'après les prétendus dessins de Gentile Bellini, conservés au Louvre et à l'Ecole de Beaux-Arts." *REG* 1: 318–25.

Myres, J., and Pottle, M. 2004. "Dalton, Ormonde Maddock (1866–1945), Classical Scholar and Medieval Archaeologist."

In *Oxford Dictionary of National Biography*, https:oxforddnb-com.proxyiub.uits.iu.edu/view/10.1093/ref:odnb/9780198614128.001.0001/odnb-9780198614128-e-32698.

Neer, R. 2010. *The Emergence of Classical Style in Greek Sculpture*. Chicago: University of Chicago Press.

Nordström, C. 1953. *Ravennastudien: Ideengeschichte und ikonographische Untersuchungen über die Mosaiken von Ravenna*. Stockholm: Almqvist & Wiksell.

Nünlist, R. 2009. *The Ancient Critic at Work: Terms and Concepts of Literary Criticism in Greek Scholia*. Cambridge: Cambridge University Press.

Oberleitner, W. 1978. "Das Partherdenkmal." In *Funde aus Ephesos und Samothrake, Katalog der Antikensammlung*, 2 vols., 2: 66–94. Vienna: Kunsthistorisches Museum Wien.

Olin, M. 1992. *Forms of Representation in Alois Riegl's Theory of Art*. University Park: Pennsylvania State University Press.

1994. "Alois Riegl: The Late Roman Empire in the Late Hapsburg Empire." *Austrian Studies* 5: 107–20.

2000. "Art History and Ideology: Alois Riegl and Joseph Strzygowski." In *Cultural Visions*, edited by P. Schine Gold and B. C. Sax, 151–70. Amsterdam: Rodopi.

Olovsdotter, C. 2005. *The Consular Image: An Iconological Study of the Consular Diptychs*. Oxford: John and Erica Hedges, Ltd., BAR International Series 1376.

Ottenthal, E. von. 1904. *Das K.K. Institut für Österreichische Geschichtsforschung 1854–1904. Festschrift zur Feier des fünfzigjährigen Bestandes*. Vienna: Adolf Holzhausen.

Pächt, O. 1963. "Art Historians and Art Critics, IV: Alois Riegl." *BurlMag* 105: 188–93.

Panegyrici Latini. 1994. *In Praise of Later Roman Emperors: The Panegyrici Latini*, edited by C. E. V. Nixon and B. Saylor Rodgers. Berkeley: University of California Press.

Panofsky, E. 1955. "Charles Rufus Morey," American Philosophical Society Yearbook, 482–91.

Parlasca, K., and H. Seemann, eds. 1999. *Augenblicke: Mumienporträts und ägyptische Grabkunst aus römischer Zeit*. Munich: Klinkhardt & Biermann.

Pausanias. 1918–1935. *Description of Greece*, 4 vols. Translated by W. H. S. Jones. Cambridge, MA: Harvard University Press.

Peirce, P. 1989. "The Arch of Constantine: Propaganda and Ideology in Late Antique Art." *AH* 12: 387–418.

Pelosi, F. 2020. "Music and Emotions." In *A Companion to Ancient Greek and Roman Music*, edited by T. Lynch and E. Rocconi, 337–49. Hoboken, NJ: Wiley-Blackwell.

Perry, E. 2005. *The Aesthetics of Emulation in the Visual Arts of Ancient Rome*. Cambridge: Cambridge University Press.

Philostratus. 1931. *Elder Philostratus, Imagines. Younger Philostratus Imagines. Callistratus Descriptions*. Translated by A. Fairbanks. Cambridge, MA: Harvard University Press.

Philostratus of Athens. 2005. *Life of Apollonius of Tyana*, 2 vols. Translated by C. P. Jones. Cambridge, MA: Harvard University Press.

Photius, Patriarch of Constantinople. 1958. *Homilies of Photius, Patriarch of Constantinople*, edited and translated by C. Mango. Cambridge, MA: Harvard University Press.

Plato. 2013. *The Republic*, 2 vols. Translated by C. Emlyn-Jones and W. Preddy. Cambridge, MA: Harvard University Press.

2022. *Lysis. Symposium. Phaedrus*. Edited and translated by C. Emlyn-Jones and W. Preddy. Cambridge, MA: Harvard University Press.

Pliny the Elder. 1938–1962. *The Natural History*, 10 vols. Translated by H. Rackham, W. H. S. Jones, and D. E. Eichholtz. Cambridge, MA: Harvard University Press.

Plotinus. 1969–1988. *Enneads*, 7 vols. Translated by A. H. Armstrong. Cambridge, MA: Harvard University Press.

Plutarch. 1927–1936. *Moralia*, 16 vols. Translated by F. Cole Babbit. Cambridge, MA: Harvard University Press.

Podro, M. 1982. *The Critical Historians of Art*. New Haven, CT: Yale University Press.

Pollitt, J. J. 1974. *The Ancient View of Greek Art*. New Haven, CT: Yale University Press.

1995. "The *Canon* of Polykleitos and Other Canons." In *Polykleitos, the Doryphoros, and Tradition*, edited by W. Moon, 19–24. Madison: University of Wisconsin Press.

Potter, D. S. 2013. *Constantine the Emperor*. Oxford: Oxford University Press.

Prange, R. 1994. "The Crystalline." In *The Romantic Spirit in German Art, 1790–1990*, edited by K. Hertley, H. Meyric Hughes, P. K. Schuster and W. Vaughn, 155–63. London: South Bank Centre.

Procopius of Gaza. 1963. *Procopii Gazaei Epistolae et Declamationes*. Edited by A. Garzya and R. Loenertz. Ettal: Buch-Kunstverlag Ettal.

Quintilian. 2002. *The Orator's Education*, 5 vols. Edited and translated by D. A. Russell. Cambridge, MA: Harvard University Press.

Radding, C. M., and W. W. Clark. 1992. *Medieval Architecture, Medieval Learning: Builders and Masters in the Age of Romanesque and Gothic*. New Haven, CT: Yale University Press.

Rampley, M. 2009. "Art History and the Politics of Empire: Rethinking the Vienna School." *ArtB* 91.4: 446–62.

2011. "The Idea of a Scientific Discipline: Rudolf von Eitelberger and the Emergence of Art History in Vienna, 1847–1873." *AH*: 54–79.

2013. *The Vienna School of Art History: Empire and the Politics of Scholarship, 1847–1918*. University Park: Pennsylvania State University Press.

Rapp, C. 2005. *Holy Bishops in Late Antiquity: The Nature of Christian Leadership in an Age of Transition*. Berkeley: University of California Press.

Reinach, S. 1926. "Courrier de l'art antique." *GBA, anno* 68.1: 175–191.

Richter, J. P. 1878. *Die Mosaiken von Ravenna*. Vienna: W. Braumüller.

Richter, J. P., and A. Cameron Taylor. 1904. *The Golden Age of Classic Christian Art*. London: Duckworth.

Riegl, A. 1891. *Alt Orientalische Teppiche*. Leipzig: T. O. Weigel.

1893. *Stilfragen. Grundlegungen zu einer Geschichte der Ornamentik*. Berlin: Siemens.

1901. *Die spätrömische Kunst-Industrie nach den Funden in Österreich-Ungarn*. Vienna: Druck und Verlag der Kaiserlich-Königlichen Hof- und Staatsdruckerei.

1902. "Spätrömische oder orientalisch?" *Münchner Allgemeine Zeitung. Beilag* 93–94 (23–24 April): 133–156 and 162–165. Translated by P. Wortsman as "Late Roman or Oriental?" in *German Essays on Art History*, edited by G. Schiff, 173–90. New York: Continuum, 1988.

1923. *Stilfragen. Grundlegungen zu einer Geschichte der Ornamentik*. Berlin: Carl Schmidt.

1927. Die spätrömische Kunstindustrie. Vienna: Österreichisches Staatsdruckerei.

1966. *Historische Grammatik der bildenden Künste*. Edited by K. M. Swoboda and O. Pächt. Graz: Böhlau.

1985. *The Late Roman Art-Industry*. Translated by R. Winkes. Rome: Giorgio Bretschneider, 1985.

2004. *Historical Grammar of the Visual Arts*. Translated by J. Jung. New York: Zone Books.

Riesman, D. 1950. *The Lonely Crowd: A Study of the Changing American Character*. New Haven, CT: Yale University Press.

Ringbom, S. 1966. "Art in the 'Epoch of the Great Spiritual': Occult Elements in the Early Theory of Abstract Painting." *JWarb* 29: 384–418.

1970. *The Sounding Cosmos: A Study in the Spiritualism of Kandinsky and the Genesis of Abstract Painting*. Åbo: Åbo Akademi.

1986. "Transcending the Visible: The Generation of Abstract Pioneers." In *The Spiritual in Art: Abstract Painting 1890–1985*, edited by M. Tuchman and J. Freedman, 131–53. New York: Abbeville Press.

Rizzardi, C. 1988. "Paradigmi ideologici ed estetici nei mosaici ravennati di età giustinianea." *FR*, 4a ser. 39: 37–61.

2005. "I mosaici parietali di Ravenna da Galla Placidia a Giustiniano." In *Venezia e Bisanzio. Aspetti della cultura artistica bizantina da Ravenna a Venezia (V – XIV secolo)*, edited by C. Rizzardi, 231–74. Venice: Istituto veneto di scienze, lettere ed arti.

Roberts, M. 1989. *The Jeweled Style: Poetry and Poetics in Late Antiquity*. Ithaca, NY: Cornell University Press.

Rodenwaldt, G. 1921–1922. "Eine spätantike Kunstströmung in Rom." *RM* 36.37: 58–110.

1928. "Ara Pacis und San Vitale." *BJb* 133: 228–35.

1931. "Das Problem der Renaissancen." *AA*: 318–38.

1939. "The Transition to Late-Classical Art." In *Cambridge Ancient History 12: Imperial Crisis and Recovery, AD 193–324*, edited by S. A. Cook, F. E. Adcock, M. P. Charlesworth, and N. H. Baynes, 544–70. Cambridge: Cambridge University Press.

1944–1945a. "Bermerkungen zu den Kaisermosaiken in San Vitale." *JdI* 59.60: 88–110.

1944–1945b. "Zur Begrenzung und Gliederung der Spätantike." *JdI* 59–60: 81–87.

Rose, C. B. 2021. "Reconsidering the Frieze on the Arch of Constantine." *JRA* 34: 175–210.

Rossi, G. B. De. 1864–1877. *Roma sotterranea cristiana*, 3 vols. Rome: Cromo-litografia pontificia.

Rothe, U. 2020. *The Toga and Roman Identity*. London: Bloomsbury Academic.

Roueché, C. 1989. *Aphrodisias in Late Antiquity: The Late Roman and Byzantine Inscriptions Including Texts from the Excavations at Aphrodisias Conducted by Kenan T. Erim*. London: Society for the Promotion of Roman Studies.

Rousseau, P. 1971. "The Spiritual Authority of the 'Monk-Bishop': Eastern Elements in Some Western Hagiography of the Fourth and Fifth Century." *JThS* n.s. 22: 380–419.

2010. *Ascetics, Authority and the Church in the Age of Jerome and Cassian*, 2nd ed. Notre Dame, IN: University of Notre Dame Press.

Rouselle, A. 2001. "Images as Education in the Roman Empire, 2nd–3rd c. CE." In *Education in Greek and Roman Antiquity*, edited by Yun Lee Too, 373–402. Leiden: Brill.

Rumpf, A. 1955. "Stilphasen der spätantiken Kunst." *Arbeitsgemeinschaft für Forschung des Landes Nordrhein-Westfalen: Geisteswissenschaften, Abhandlung* 44: 5–44.

Rumpler, H. 1997. *Eine Chance für Mitteleuropa. Bürgerliche Emanzipation und Staatsverfall in der Habsburgermonarchie*. Vienna: Ueberreuter Sachbuch.

Russell, D. A. 1981. *Criticism in Antiquity*. London: Duckworth.

Sandberg, M. 2015. "'Obsidio Veronae' und 'proelium apud Tiberim': Zum Selbstverständnis des spätantiken Kaisertums anhand der Schlachtenfriese des Arcus Constantini." *Potestas* 8: 105–47.

Sande, S. 1981. "Some New Fragments from the Column of Theodosius." *ActaIRNorv*, ser. altera 1: 1–78.

Sauerländer, W. 1983. "From Stylus to Style: Reflections on the Fate of a Notion." *AH* 6: 253–70.

Schapiro, M. 1953. "Style." In *Anthropology Today: An Encyclopedic Inventory*, edited by A. L. Kroeber, 287–312. Chicago: University of Chicago Press. Republished in *Aesthetics Today*, edited by M. Philipson, 81–113. Cleveland: World Publishing Company.

Schede, M. 1920. "Archäologische Funde, Türkei." *JdI* 44: 325–68.

1929. "Archäologische Funde, Türkei." *AA*: 340–42.

Schiff, G. 1988. *German Essays on Art History*. New York: Continuum.

Schmarsow, A. 1905. *Grundbegriffe der Kunstwissenschaft*. Leipzig: Gebr. Mann.

Schnaase, C. 1842–1879. *Geschichte der bildenden Künste im Mittelalter*, vol. 3. Düsseldorf: Julius Buddeus.

Schneider, A. M. 1944–1945. "Fund- und Forschungsbericht Türkei 1943." *AA* 1944.45: 71–81.

Schopenhauer, A. 1948. *The World as Will and Idea/Die Welt als Wille und Vorstellung*, 3 vols. Translated by R. B. Haldane and J. Kemp. London: Routledge & Kegan Paul.

Schorske, C. 2006. "Gustav Klimt's Faculty Paintings and the Crisis of the Liberal Ego." In *Gustav Klimt: The Beethoven Frieze and the Controversy over the Freedom of Art*, edited by Stephen Koja, 13–26. Munich: Prestel.

Schueller, H. M. 1988. *The Idea of Music: An Introduction to Musical Aesthetics in Antiquity and the Middle Ages*. Kalamazoo: Medieval Institute Publications, Western Michigan University.

Schwarzer, M. 1995. "Origins of the Art History Survey Text." *Art Journal* 54: 24–29.

Seaman, K. 2017. "The Social and Educational Background of Elite Greek Artists." In *Artists and Artistic Production in Ancient Greece*, edited by K. Seaman and P. Schultz, 12–22. Cambridge: Cambridge University Press.

2020. *Rhetoric and Innovation in Hellenistic Art*. Cambridge: Cambridge University Press.

Sears, E. 2017. "Under Miss Green's Watch: Three Decades of Art History at the Index of Christian Art." In *Tributes to Adelaide Bennett Hagens: Manuscripts, Iconography, and the Late Medieval Viewer*, edited by P. A. Patton and J. K. Golden, 15–37. Turnhout: Brepols.

2022. "Iconography and Iconology at Princeton." In *Iconography beyond the Crossroads: Image, Meaning, and Method in Medieval Art*, edited by P. A. Patton and C. A. Fernandez, 9–34. University Park: Pennsylvania State University Press.

Seroux D'Agincourt, J. B. L. G. 1823. *Histoire de l'art par les monuments depuis sa décadence au IVe siècle jusqu'au son renouvellement au XVI*, 6 vols. Paris: Treuttel & Würtz.

Sheldrake, P. 2012. *Spirituality: A Very Short Introduction*. Oxford: Oxford University Press.

2013. *Spirituality: A Brief History*. Malden, MA: Wiley-Blackwell.

Sieger, J. D. 1987. "Visual Metaphor as Theology: Leo the Great's Sermons on the Incarnation and the Arch Mosaics at S. Maria Maggiore." *Gesta* 26.2: 83–91.

Siepel, W., ed. 2006. *Das Partherdenkmal von Ephesos. Akten des Kolloquiums Wien, 27.–28. April 2003*. Vienna: Kunsthistorisches Museum, and Milan: Skira.

Simpson, K. 2010. "Viennese Art, Ugliness and the Vienna School of Art History: The Vicissitudes of Theory and Practice." *JArtHist* 3: 1–14.

Simpson, O. von. 1948. *Sacred Fortress: Byzantine Art and Statecraft in Ravenna*. Chicago: University of Chicago Press.

Smith, R. R. R. 1990. "Late Roman Philosopher Portraits from Aphrodisias." *JRS* 80: 125–55.

1997. "The Public Image of Licinius I: Portrait Sculpture and Imperial Ideology in the Early Fourth Century." *JRS* 87: 170–202.

1999. "Late Antique Portraits in a Public Context: Honorific Statuary at Aphrodisias in Caria, AD 300–600." *JRS* 89: 155–89.

2002. "The Statue Monument of Oecumenius: A New Portrait of a Late Antique Governor from Aphrodisias." *JRS* 92: 134–56.

2007. "Statue Life in the Hadrianic Baths at Aphrodisias, AD 100–600: Local Context and Historical Meaning." In *Statuen und Statuensammlungen in der Spätantike – Funktion und Kontext (Spätantike, Frühes Christentum, Byzanz: Kunst im ersten Jahrtausend)*, edited by F. A. Bauer and C. Witschel, 203–35. Wiesbaden: Reichert.

Smith, R. R. R., and B. Ward-Perkins, eds. 2016. *The Last Statues of Antiquity*. Oxford: Oxford University Press.

Smythe, C. H. 1993. "Concerning Charles Rufus Morey." In *The Early Years of Art History in the United States*, edited by C. H. Smythe and P. M. Lukehart, 111–21. Princeton, NJ: Department of Art and Archaeology.

Sorensen, L., ed. 2022a. "Morey, Charles Rufus." In *Dictionary of Art Historians*, https://arthistorians.info/moreyc.

2022b. "Schmarsow, August." In *Dictionary of Art Historians*, https://arthistorians.info/schmarsowa.

2022c. "Strzygowski, Josef Rudolf Thomas." In *Dictionary of Art Historians*, https://arthistorians.info/strzygowski.

Spain, S. 1977. "Carolingian Restorations of S. Maria Maggiore in Rome." *Gesta* 16: 13–22.
1979. "'The Promised Blessing': The Iconography of the Mosaics of S. Maria Maggiore." *ArtB* 61.4: 518–40.
1983. "Restorations of the Sta. Maria Maggiore Mosaics." *ArtB* 65.2: 325–28.
Steigerwald, G. 2000. "Zur Darstellung Jesus im Tempel an Triumphbogen von S. Maria Maggiore in Rome (432–440)." *JbAC* 43:187–99.
2007. "Neue Aspekte zum Verständnis der Mosaiken des Triumphbogen von S. Maria Maggiore in Rom." *RQ* 102: 161–203.
2010. "Die Rolle Mariens in den Triumphbogen Mosaiken und in der Weihenschrift der Basilika S. Maria Maggiore in Rom." *JbAC* 51: 137–51.
Steinby, E. M., ed. 1993–2000. *Lexicon topographicum urbis Romae*, 5 vols. Rome: Quasar.
Stewart, A. 1978. "The Canon of Polykleitos: A Question of Evidence." *JHS* 98: 122–31.
Stewart, C. 2005. "Christian Spirituality during the Roman Empire 100–600." In *Blackwell Companion to Christian Spirituality*, edited by A. G. Holder, 73–89. Malden, MA: Blackwell.
Stričević, G. 1959. "Iconografia dei mosaici imperiali a S. Vitale." *FR* 80: 5–27.
1962. "Sur le problème de l'iconographie des mosaïques impériales de Saint- Vital." *FR* 85: 80–100.
Strong, E. S. 1907. *Roman Sculpture from Augustus to Constantine*. London: Duckworth, and New York: C. Scribner's Sons.
Strzygowski, J. 1893. "Die Säule des Arcadius." *JdI* 8: 230–49.
1901. *Orient oder Rom. Beiträge zur Geschichte der spätantiken und frühchristlichen Kunst*. Leipzig: J. C. Hinrichs'sche Buchhandlung.
1902a. "Alois Riegl, Die spätrömische Kunst-Industrie nach den Fundenin Österreich–Ungarn, in Zusammenhange mit der Gesamtentwicklung der bildenden Künste bei den Mittelmeervölkern dargestellt." *ByzZeit* 11: 263–66.
1902b. "Hellas in des Orients Umarmung." Beilage zur Allgemeinen Zeitung 18 and 19 February: 313–17 and 325–27; reprinted as Sonderabdruck.
1904. *Koptische Kunst*. Vienna: A Holzhausen.
1936. *Aufgang des Norden. Lebenskampf eines Kunstforschers um ein deutsches Weltbild*. Leipzig: Schwarzhäupter Verlag.
Stuhlfauth, G. 1901. "Strzygowski, Josef, Orient oder Rom." *ThLz* 26.25 (7 December): 657–60.
Stylow, A. 1972. "Libertas und Liberalitas. Untersuchungen zur innenpolitischen Propaganda der Römer," Ph.D. dissertation, Munich.
Summers, D. 1977. "Contrapposto: Style and Meaning in Renaissance Art." *ArtB* 59.3: 336–61.
1989. "Form, 19th-Century Metaphysics and the Problem of Art Historical Description." *CI* 15: 372–406.
Swain, S., ed. 2007. *Seeing the Face, Seeing the Soul: Polemon's Physiognomy from Classical Antiquity to Medieval Islam*. Oxford: Oxford University Press.
Szemethy, H. 2014. "Archaeology and Cultural Politics: Ottoman-Austrian Relations." In *Scramble for the Past: A Story of Archaeology in the Ottoman Empire, 1753–1914*, edited by Z. Bahrani, Z. Çelik, and E. Eldem, 331–75. Istanbul. SALT/ Garanti Kültür.
Taine, H. 1874. *Voyage en Italie*, 2 vols. Paris: Hachette.
Taroutina, M. 2021. "From First Rome to Third Rome: Nikodim Kondakov and Late Antique Studies," in *The New Late Antiquity: A Gallery of Intellectual Portraits*, edited by C. Ando and M. Formisano, 595–608. Heidelberg: Universitätsverlag Winter.
Tobin, R. 1975. "The Canon of Polykleitos." *AJA* 79.4: 307–21.
Torelli, M., 1982. *Typology and Structure of Roman Historical Reliefs*. Ann Arbor: University of Michigan Press.
Touchette, L. A. 2015. "Archaism and Eclecticism," in *The Oxford Handbook of*

Roman Sculpture, edited by E. A. Friedland, M. G. Sobocinski, and E. K. Gazda, 292–306. Oxford: Oxford University Press.

Toynbee, J. M. C. 1964. *Art in Britain under the Romans*. Oxford: Clarendon Press.

Toynbee, J. M. C., and K. S. Painter. 1986. "The Silver Picture Plates of Late Antiquity, AD 300–700." *Archaeologia* 108: 15–65.

Tronzo, W. 2001. "The Shape of Narrative: A Problem in the Mural Decoration of Early Medieval Rome." In *Roma nel alto medioevo, 27 aprile–1 maggio 2000. Settimane di studio del Centro italiano di studi sull'alto medioevo*, 2 vols., 1: 457–87. Spoleto: Centro italiano di studi sull'alto medioevo.

Tuchman, M., 1986. "The Hidden Meaning in Abstract Art." In *The Spiritual in Art: Abstract Painting 1890–1985*, edited by M. Tuchman and J. Freedman, 17–61. New York: Abbeville Press.

Tuchman, M., and J. Freedman, eds. 1986. *The Spiritual in Art: Abstract Painting 1890–1985*. New York: Abbeville Press.

Van Eyck, C., J. McAllister, and R. Van de Vall, eds. 1995. *The Question of Style in Philosophy and the Arts*. Cambridge: Cambridge University Press.

Varnedoe, K. 1990. *A Fine Disregard: What Makes Modern Art Modern*. New York: Abrams.

Vasari, G. 1998. *Le opera di Giorgio Vasari con nuove annotazione e commenti,* 9 vols. Edited by G. Milanesi. Florence: Le Lettere.

Vergo, P. 2015. *Art in Vienna, 1898–1918: Klimt, Kokoschka, Schiele and Their Contemporaries*, 4th ed. London: Phaidon Press.

Vermeule, C. 1968. *Roman Imperial Art in Greece and Asia Minor*. Cambridge, MA: Harvard University Press.

Viollet-le-Duc, E. E. 1854–1868. *Dictionnaire raisonné de l'architecture française du XI au XVI siècle*, 10 vols. Paris: Morel.

Vischer, R. 1994. "On the Optical Sense of Form: A Contribution to Aesthetics." In *Empathy, Form and Space: Problems in German Aesthetics, 1873–1893*, edited and translated by H. Mallgrave and E. Ikonomou, 17–29. Originally published as *Über das optische Formgefühl: Ein Beitrag zur Aesthetik*. Leipzig: Hermann Credner, 1873.

Visconti, Cav. P. E., ed. 1834. *Lettera sulle antichitá di Roma scritta da Raffaello d'Urbino a Papa Leone X*. Rome: Giuseppe Brancadoro e Comp.

Wace, A. J. B. 1907. "Studies in Roman Historical Reliefs." *PBSR* 4: 229–76.

Waite, G. C. W. 1995. "Worringer's *Abstraction and Empathy*: Remarks on Its Reception and on the Rhetoric of Its Criticism." In *Invisible Cathedrals: The Expressionist Art History of Wilhelm Worringer*, edited by N. H. Donohue, 13–40. University Park: Pennsylvania State University Press.

Walker, J. 2000. *Rhetoric and Poetics in Antiquity*. Oxford: Oxford University Press.

Walz, R. 2008. *Modernism*. New York: Pearson Longman.

Watson, G. 1972. "The Concept of *Phantasia* from the Late Hellenistic Period to Early Neo-Platonism." *ANRW, II* 36.7: 4765–810.

1988. *Phantasia in Classical Thought*. Galway: Galway University Press.

Watts, E. J. 2006. *City and School in Late Antique Athens and Alexandria*. Berkeley: University of California Press.

Webb, R. 1999. "Aesthetics of Sacred Space: Narrative, Metaphor, and Motion in 'Ekphraseis' of Church Buildings." *DOP* 53: 59–74.

2000. "Ekphrasis, Amplification, and Persuasion in Procopios' 'Buildings'," *AntTard* 8: 67–71.

2001. "The Progymnasmata as Practice." In *Education in Greek and Roman Antiquity*, edited by Yun Lee Too, 289–316. Leiden: Brill.

2006. "The 'Imagines' as a Fictional Text: 'Ekphrasis,' 'Apate,' and Illusion. In *Le défi de l'art: Philostrate, Callistrate, et l'image sophistique*, edited by F. Graziani, M. Costantini, and S. Rolet, 113–36. Rennes: Presse Universitaires de Rennes.

2009. *Ekphrasis, Imagination and Persuasion in Ancient Rhetorical Theory and Practice*. Farnham: Ashgate.

Weitzmann, K. 1976. *The Monastery of Saint Catherine at Mount Sinai: The Icons*, vol. 1. Princeton, NJ: Princeton University Press.

Weitzmann, K., ed. 1979. *Age of Spirituality: Late Antique and Early Christian Art, Third through Seventh Centuries*. New York: Metropolitan Museum of Art and Princeton University Press.

Wickhoff, F. 1900. *Roman Art*. Translated by Mrs. S. Arthur Strong. London: Heinemann, and New York: Macmillan.

1912. *Römische Kunst: die Wiener Genesis*. Berlin: Meyer and Jessen.

1913. *Abhandlungen, Vorträge und Anzeigen*. Edited by M. Dvořák. Berlin: Meyer & Jessen.

Wickhoff, F., and W. Ritter von Hartel. 1895. *Die Wiener Genesis*, 2 vols. Vienna: F. Tempsky.

Wilpert, J. 1916. *Die römische Mosaiken und Malereien der kirchlichen Bauten vom IV.bis XIII. Jahrhundert*, 4 vols. Freiburg im Breisgau: Herder.

Wölfflin, H. 1886. "Prolegomena zu einer Psychologie der Architektur: Inaugural-Dissertation der hohen philosophischen Fakultät der Universität München zur Erlangung der höchsten akademischen Würde. Munich: Kgl. & Universitäts–Buchdrukerei von Dr. C. Wolf & Sohn.

1915. *Kunstgeschichtliche Grundbegriffe*. Munich: Bruckmann.

Woodruff, P. 2015. "Mimesis." In *A Companion to Ancient Aesthetics*, edited by P. Destrée and P. Murray, 329–40. Chichester: Wiley-Blackwell.

Worringer, W. 1907. *Abstraktion und Einfühlung. Ein Beitrag zur Stilpsychologie*. Neuwied: Heuser.

1908. *Abstraktion und Einfühlung. Ein Beitrag zur Stilpsychologie*. Munich: R. Piper.

1916. *Abstraktion und Einfühlung. Ein Beitrag zur Stilpsychologie*. Munich: R. Piper.

1953. *Abstraction and Empathy: A Contribution to the Psychology of Style*. Translated by M. Bullock. New York: International Universities Press.

1997. *Abstraction and Empathy: A Contribution to the Psychology of Style*. Translated by M. Bullock. Chicago: Ivan R. Dee Publishers.

Wulff, O. 1903. "D. Ainalov, *Die Hellenistischen Grundlagen der byzantinische Kunst*." *RepKunstw* 26: 35–55.

1914. *Altchristliche und byzantinische Kunst*, 2 vols. Berlin-Neubabelsberg: Akademische Verlagsgesellschaft Athenaion.

Zäh, A. 2012. "Josef Strzygowski als Initiator der christlich-kunsthistorischen Orientforschung und Visionär der Kunstwissenschaft." *RQ* 107: 249–92.

Zaloscher, H. 1974. *Die Kunst in christlichen Ägypten*. Vienna: A. Schroll.

Zaloziecky, W. R. 1947. "Oskar Wulff (1864–1946)." *ZSlPh* 19.2: 249–65.

Zanker, P. 1995. *The Mask of Socrates: The Image of the Intellectual in Antiquity*. Berkeley: University of California Press.

Zibawi, M. 2003. *Images de l'Égypte chrétienne: Iconologie copte*. Milan: Jaca Books, and Paris: Picard.

Zimmermann, B. 2003. *Die Wiener Genesis im Rahmen der antiken Buchmalerei*. Wiesbaden: Reichert.

INDEX

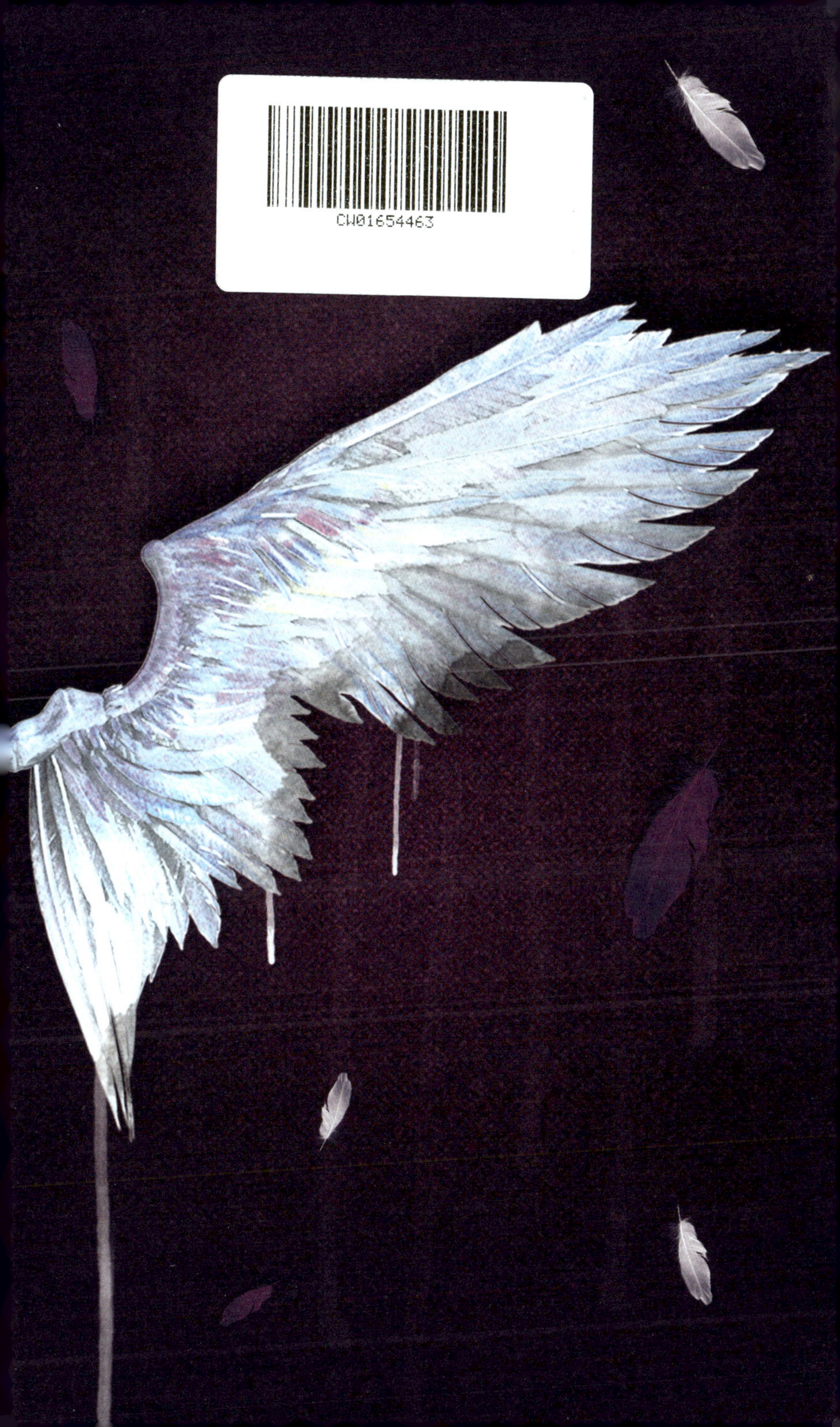

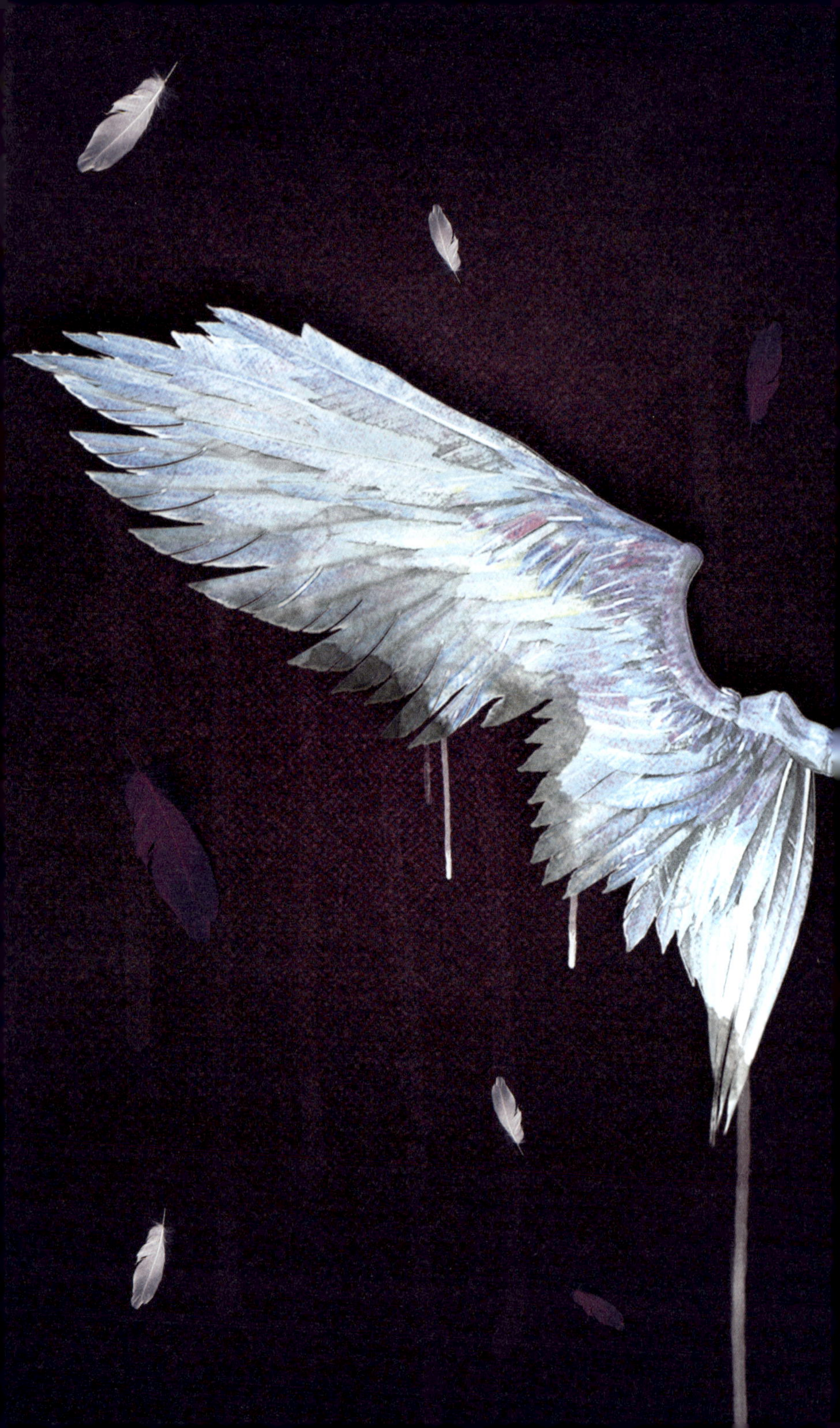

R. GAYE ÖNEL

Diriliş

ATEŞLİ KANATLAR SERİSİ III

DOKUZ

DİRİLİŞ

R. Gaye Önel

Türü Roman

Yayın Yönetmeni Ali Osman Başkuyu
Editör Aycan Sarıahmet
Redaksiyon Binnur Şafak Nigiz
Sayfa Tasarımı Vildan Yılmaz
Kapak Tasarımı Gizem Ulaş
İllüstrasyon R. Gaye Önel

1. Baskı Mart 2021, İstanbul

Yayınevi Sertifika No 46270
ISBN 978-625-7642-12-5

BASKI VE CİLT
MY Matbaacılık San. ve Tic. Ltd. Şti.
Maltepe Mah. Yılanlı Ayazma Sk. No: 8/F
Zeytinburnu / İstanbul
Tel: 0212 674 85 28
Matbaa Sertifika No: 47939

DOKUZ YAYINCILIK
Kitapyolu Basım Yayım Dağıtım Paz. San. ve Tic. Ltd. Şti.
Maltepe Mah. Davutpaşa Cad. Yılanlı Ayazma Yolu No: 8
Davutpaşa, Zeytinburnu / İstanbul
0212 640 00 35

R. GAYE ÖNEL

Diriliş

ATEŞLİ KANATLAR SERİSİ III

DOKUZ

Sonsuzluk ve ötesinde
yeniden kavuşana dek.
Atlas oğlum

"Yitip gittik diğer kayıp ruhlar gibi.
Şimdi diriliyoruz."

R. Gaye Önel

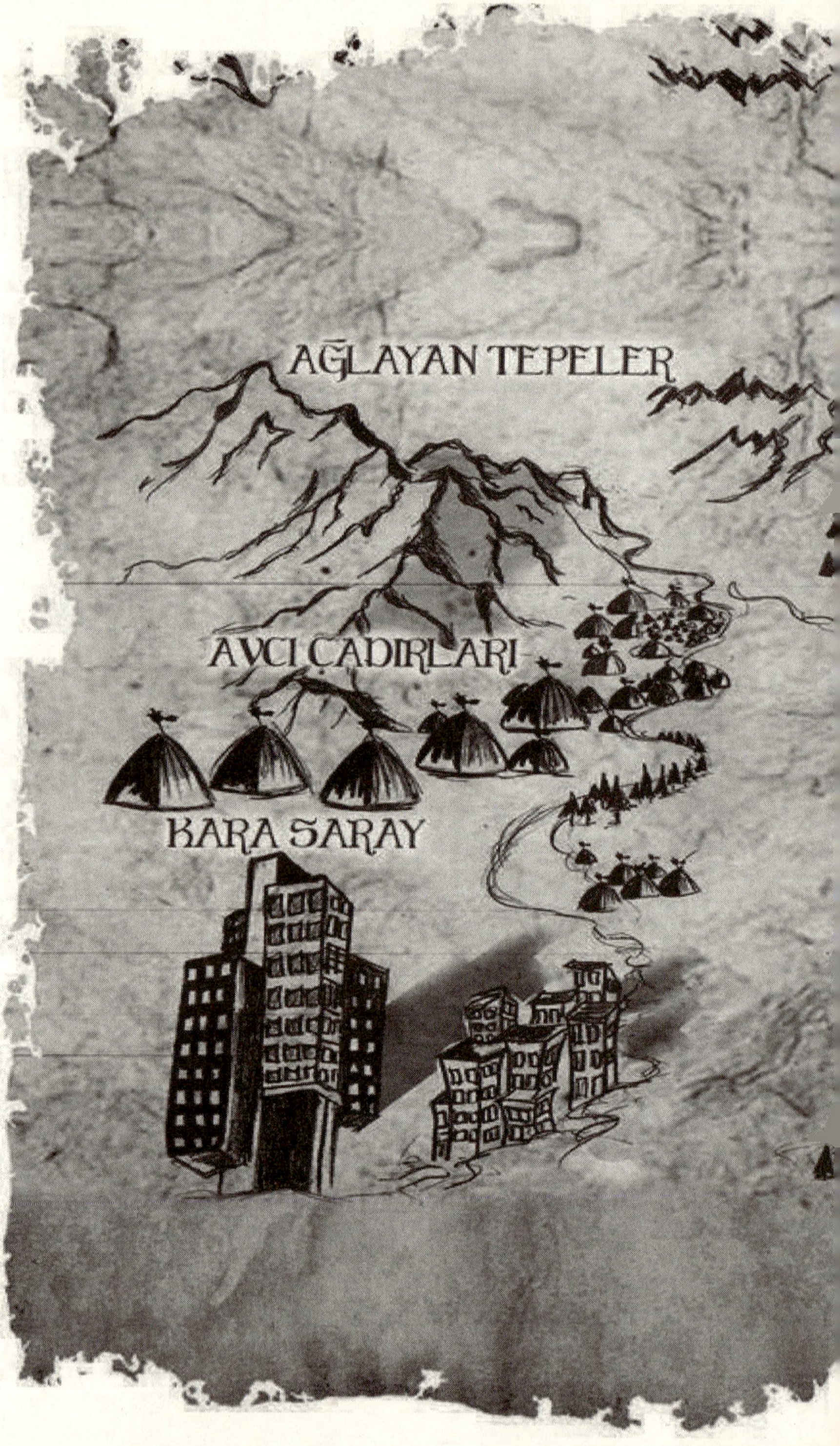
AĞLAYAN TEPELER
AVCI ÇADIRLARI
KARA SARAY

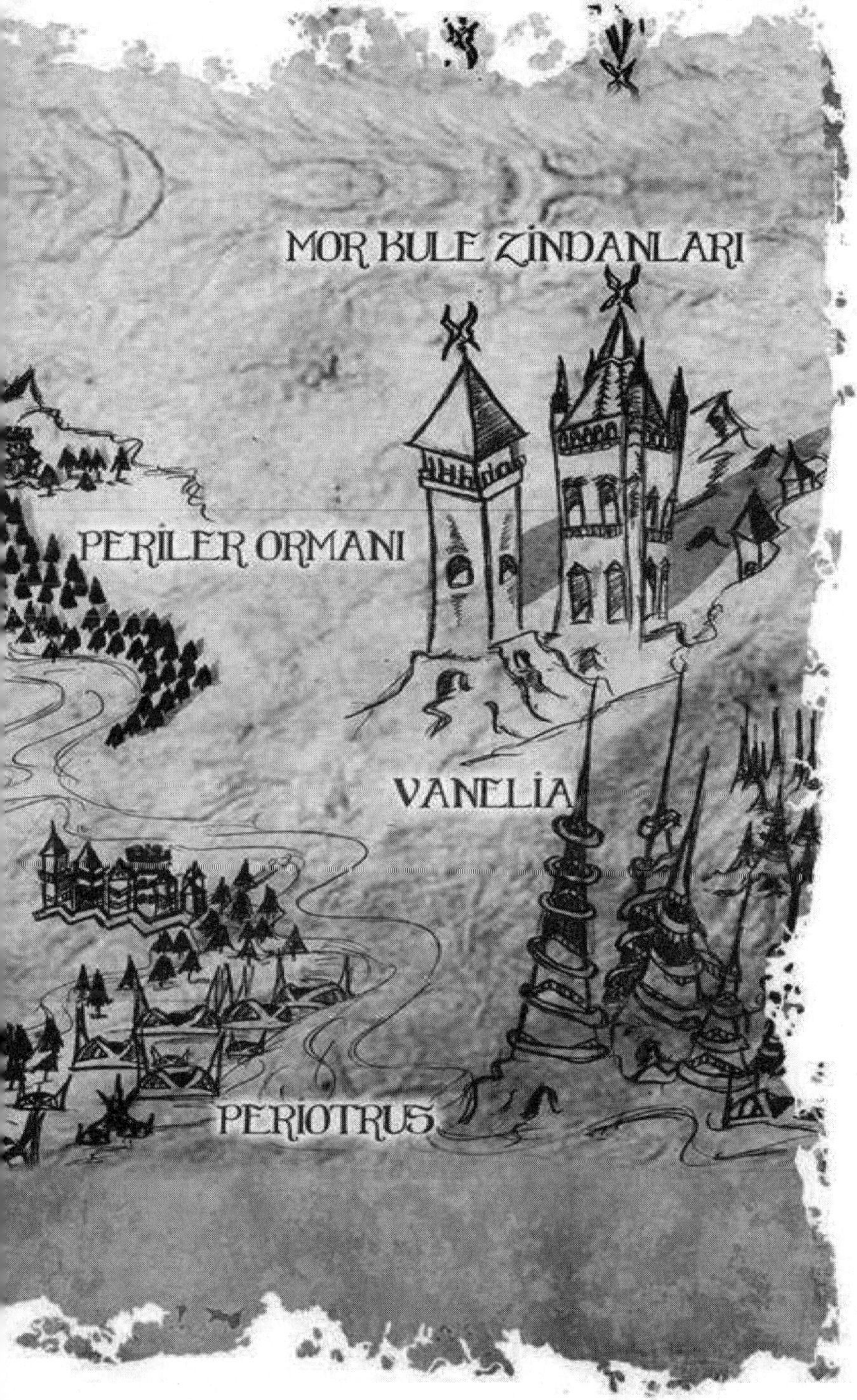
MOR KULE ZİNDANLARI
PERİLER ORMANI
VANELİA
PERİOTRUS

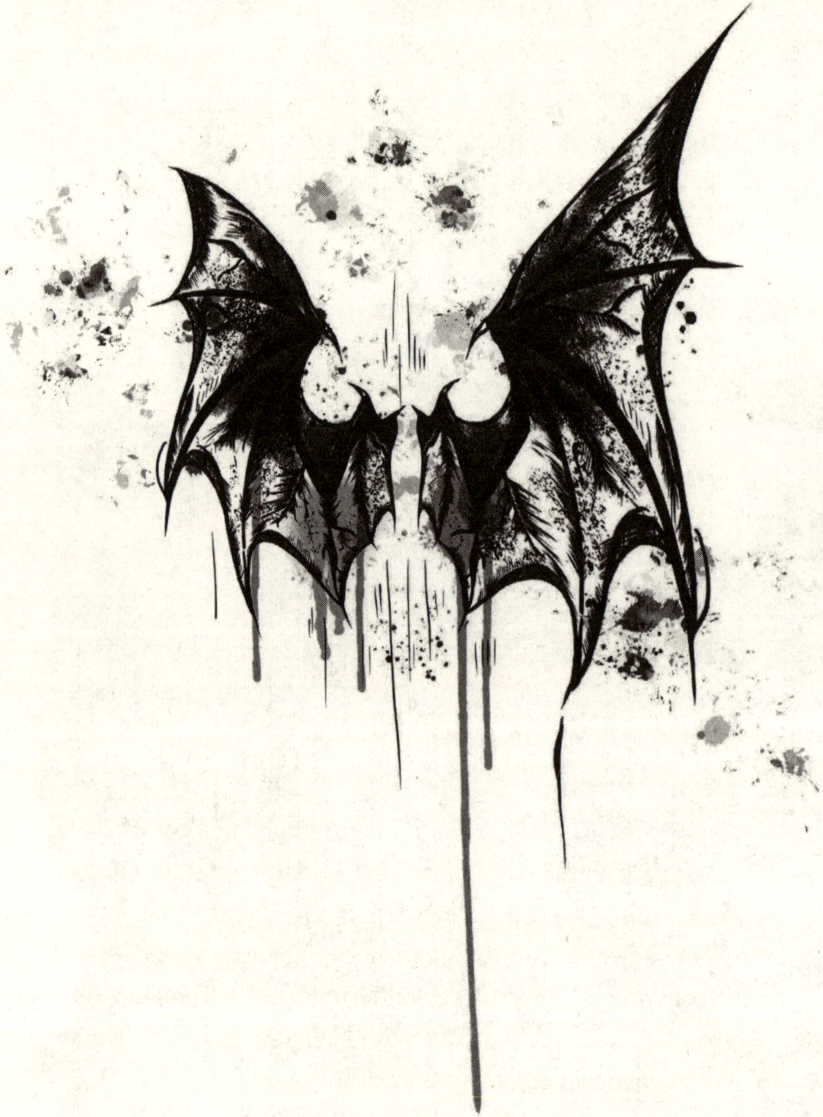

"Ey okur, kalk ve benimle yürü!"

ÖN SÖZ

"Daha fazla kötü ol.

Yeterince körleşirsen karanlığa, zifiri bile aydınlık gelir sana."

Alnımdan akan ılık kan damlaları gözlerime dolarken yutkundum. Neden canım yanmıyordu, ruhumun tamamen kararması insanlığımı da mı yanında götürmüştü? Artık canım yanmayacaktı, öyle mi?

Başımı tekrar vurdum demir tahta. Kan bu kez beraberinde bir çatırtı çıkararak saç diplerimden kaşlarıma doldu. Oradan yavaşça tenimi ıslatarak göz bebeklerime akmasını bekledim. "Yeniden iyileşecek olmana rağmen kendini neden paraladığını anlayamıyorum." Uğursuz kız kardeşimin sesi, çarpmanın etkisiyle çınlayan kulaklarıma dolarken gözlerimi kapadım. Kanın gözlerimi yakması gerekmiyor muydu?

"Orada kafanı oraya buraya geçirip kendine acımak istiyor olabilirsin ama yapmamız gereken şeyler var." Tuttuğum nefesimi bırakıp başımı kaldırarak ona döndüm. Turuncu saçlarını başının tam tepesinde örmüş, üzerine de her zamanki uyduruk, parlak elbiselerinden birini giymişti. Tüm hayatım mahvolurken onun bundan zevk almasına neden göz yumduğumu merak ettim.

Kız kardeşim gözlerini devirerek bana yaklaştı. "Artık kalpsiz bir pislik olman düşüncelerini herkese açmanı gerektirmiyor." Yanılıyordu, düşüncelerimi gizlemek için herhangi bir içsel dürtü hissetmiyordum.

Meredith hızlı adımlarla yanıma geldikten sonra elini bana uzatırken endişeli gözleriyle yüzümü taradı. "Kendine zarar vermeye çalışma." Sivri tırnakları alnıma değecekken kendimi geri çektim. "Zarar veremiyorum ki." Az önce onun dokunmaya çalıştığı yere uzanıp parmaklarımı hafifçe yaranın üzerinde gezdirdim. Çoktan iyileşmeye başlamış sert derinin üzerinde gezdi parmaklarım. "Belki de kalbimi çıkarmalıyım." İşaret parmağımı yavaşça kalbimin üzerinde gezdirdim.

Cadı kaşlarını çatarak ukalâ bir ifadeyle ellerini beline koydu. "Hiçbir şey bitmedi Cassandra." Yanılıyordu. Her şey bitmişti. Tüm hayallerin sonu gelmişti. Başımı olumsuz anlamda sağa sola sallayıp somurttum. Bunun üzerine Meredith cüret ederek elleriyle kollarımı tuttu. Elimi çekmeye çalıştıysam da bırakmadı. İri yeşil gözlerini kocaman açarak dikkatle suratıma baktı. "Pes mi ediyorsun?"

Bunu düşündüm. Pes mi ediyordum? Başımı bir robot gibi indirip bileğimi kavrayan parmaklarına baktım. "Pes etmiyorum," dedim sadece. Ardından ellerimi çekip tahtıma yöneldim. Demir taht şu an her zamankinden daha tiksinç görünüyordu. Bunun sebebi üzerindeki şekilsiz büyülü motifler değildi, kol kenarlarındaki bordo renkli kanların kuruduğu oluklar da değildi, sebebi benden önce üzerinde oturmuş kişiydi.

Oturduğumda başımdaki yaranın çoktan kapandığını biliyordum. Başımı bir yerlere vurarak kırsam bile kendime zarar veremiyordum.

"Kanatlarını geri istiyor musun?" Onu duymazdan geldim çünkü saçmalıyordu. Kanatlarım zaten benimleydi. Dirseğimi tahtın koluna yaslayarak derin bir nefes aldım. Ona bugünlük defolmasını söylemek üzere dudaklarımı araladım.

"Beyaz kanatlardan bahsediyorum." Bir anlık bile duraksamadım. Bu hiçbir şeyi değiştirmezdi. "Kanatlarımdan memnunum." Katran rengi, parlak, dev kanatlarım vardı ve beni hiç yarı yolda bırakmıyorlardı, onlardan memnundum. Beyaz olanlar için kılımı kıpırdatmama gerek yoktu.

Ama anlaşılan bu yanıt Merr cadısının hoşuna gitmemişti. Daha da diretti. "Peki ya Aidan?"

Kalbim ufacık bir an için ritmini kaçırdı, ardından tekrar eski hâline döndü. "Ne olmuş ona?" Meredith'e bakmıyordum ama sırıttığını görebiliyordum, kendince ruhuma dair ufak bir sızıntı buldu sanıyordu.

"Ona yeniden kavuşabilirsin." Nefesimi bırakarak geriye yaslandım. Gözlerimi kapatırken alnımdaki yaranın kanaması tamamen sona ermişti. "Bu neyi değiştirir?"

Cadıdan birkaç saniyeliğine cevap gelmedi. Onu şaşırttığımı hissedebiliyordum ama bunu onu şaşırtmak için yapmamıştım.

"Aidan'ı diyorum, şu asi çocuğu. Yeniden kavuşabilirsin belki de." Gözlerimi açmadım. Merr'in vızıldamaları bugün de son bulmayacak gibiydi. O ve ahmak hayalleri canıma okuyordu. Durmadan gerçeküstü fanteziler peşinde gezinen bir kaçıktı o.

Beni eski hâlime döndürmek istediğini biliyordum. Ben eskisi gibi olamayacağımı biliyordum ama o bilmiyordu. Aidanhell'in artık umurumda olmadığını bilmiyordu.

"Eğer onu bulursan..." duraksayıp düşündüm, *selam söyle mi* diyecektim. Ona artık ne diyebilirdim ki? Aidan benim dünyama gelemezdi, ben de onunkine gidemezdim. "Bulursan," dedim bir kez daha gözlerim yavaşça kararırken. "Öldür ki onu düşünmek zorunda kalmayayım."

BÖLÜM 1

Her zaman kana susamış bir kaçık değildim.

Yani bazı zamanlar kana susamış gibi davranıyordum ama bunun sebebi atalarımın yaptığı gibi şeytanların peşinden gitmekti.

Bana öğretilen gibi şeytanın peşinden onu alt etmek için gitmiştim ama öldüremediğim yetmezmiş gibi bir de ona âşık olmuştum.

Eh, hâl böyle olunca da artık *kaçık* diye adlandırılmam doğaldı. Doğal olmayan şey ise aslında hiçbir zaman kim olduğumu bilmememdi.

"Kim olduğunla ilgili tüm o varoluşsal sancılarını daha sonraya bırakabilir misin?" Başımın üzerinden geçen ok *viyuvv* sesleri ile havayı yararken gözlerimi kırptım. Meredith kızıl saçları havalanırken elindeki kılıçla çığlık atarak bana doğru koşuyordu. Aslında bana doğru sayılmazdı, önümdeki avcıyı hedef almıştı.

Dediğim gibi her zaman böyle değildim ama hayat beni buna mecbur etmişti. Kılıcımı kınından çekerken kan ve kir kokulu savaş alanından derin bir nefes aldım. Bana şeytan atalarım gibi güç ya da melek atalarım gibi huzur miras kalmamıştı.

Bana kalan şey, kan ve küldü.

***

"Pazartesilere bayılıyorum." Omzumun üzerinden, hâlâ yere eğilmiş olan kardeşime baktım. Baygın bir avcının üzerini arıyordu. Pek çok özelliğinin yanı sıra Merr tam bir ganimetçiydi. "Pazartesi günleri her zamankinden daha aptal oluyorlar. Bodoslama üzerimize geldiklerini gördün." Çamurlu elleri hâlâ avcının iç ceplerindeyken başını kaldırıp hayretler içerisindeki parlak yeşil gözleriyle bana baktı. "Şu kızıl olan baltasıyla geliyordu Cass." İşaret ettiği yerdeki avcının cansız bedenine baktım. Elindeki baltayı hâlâ sımsıkı tutuyordu ama ruhu çoktan bu diyardan göçüp gitmişti.

Pekâlâ, bazı şeyleri masaya yatırmak gerekirse kalpsiz bir katil değildim. Aslında kalpsiz ve katildim ama ikisi beraber değildi. Öldürürken bundan inanılmaz bir zevk almıyordum. Öldürebiliyordum çünkü karşılık vermemek aptalca olurdu. Bethany benim ne olduğumu biliyordu, yıkım getirenlerin kulağına çalınan dedikodularını ise sadece hayal edebilirdim. Ama avcılar o kadar inatçıydılar ki hâlâ bana sataşmaya devam ediyorlardı.

Pekâlâ, ikinci bir gerçekliği masaya yatırmak gerekirse beni öldürmek öyle kolay değildi. Beş milyar kıç bir araya gelip kıçlar korosu eşliğinde beni öldürebilecek kadar sıkı olduklarını söyleseler dahi, hiçbir faninin beni öldüremeyeceğini biliyordum. Oysa Meredith, tüm o kötü ününe, çarpık bir şekilde işleyen zihnine ve de ön görülemez hareketlerine rağmen tanıdığım insana en yakın olan varlıktı. Öldürülebilir birini yanımda taşımak da aklımın olup olmadığını sorgulatıyordu.

Sahi! Nerede benim aklım?

Aklım, kanatlarımla beraber yeryüzündeki en yakışıklı adamın bir iblis olarak verdiği son nefesiyle uçup buharlaşmıştı. Ama ben zaten çok zeki olduğumu hiçbir zaman iddia etmemiştim.

Meredith, elinde bazı incileri yer yer kırılmış renkli iki bilezikle bir zafer kazanmışçasına sırıtıyordu. Muzır gözleri gözlerime değince gülüşü yavaşça solup yerini şüpheciliğe bıraktı. "Suratında yine şu her şeyi çözmüş bilge kadın ifadesi var."

Omuz silkerek söylediklerini görmezden geldim. "Benim için çarşambaların pazartesilerden bir farkı yok. Haftanın her günü aptal olabiliyorlar." Kanla lekelenmiş olan gömleğime bakıp hoşnutsuzlukla dudaklarımı büzdüm. "Marr ve Anton'u bulduğumda onlardan birer tane gömlek isteyeceğim, bu hafta dördüncü gömlek bu." Meredith'in arkamda bir yerlerde kıkırdadığını duydum. O iki bileziğin içinde zehir olduğunu biliyordu ve çoğu insanın dokunmaya bile çekineceği küçük toplar kız kardeşimi heyecanlandırıyordu. Aile genlerimizde ciddi sıkıntılar olduğunu çok önceden anlamıştım. Annem -ki cehennemin en deli ve güçlü leydisi Lilith oluyordu bu- bizi doğururken genlerimize kendine has deliliğinden bol miktarda akıtmıştı. Meredith üzerindeki tozları temizlerken daha önce dile getirdiğim şeyi düşünüyordum. Delilikler bana, memeler ise Meredith'e kalmıştı. Kılıcımı belime yerleştirirken kana bulanmış kâküllerimi temiz serçe parmağımla kulaklarımın arkasına ittim.

Avcılar ya da artık yeni yozlaşmış gruplarına taktıkları isimle yıkım getirenler peşimizi bırakmıyordu. Aslında bunun destansı ironisi bu hastalıklı ruh hâlimle gülmeme sebep oluyordu. Çünkü ben de onları arıyordum. Aniden aklıma gelen bir şeyle kaşlarımı çatıp kardeşime döndüm. "Kediler gibi koku bırakıyorsun değil mi? Her seferinde bize gelmelerinin başka bir açıklaması olamaz."

Kardeşim başka bir avcının boynundaki zinciri çekerken bir anlığına duraksadı. "O dev kanatlarından kül yağıyor. Kör bir dev bile seni takip edebilir." Tekrar önüme dönüp kanatlarıma baktım. Normal zamanlarda, yani silahla vurulmadığım, balta ile kesilmediğim ve kıçıma ok yemediğim, isle kaplanmadığım, kanla cilalanmadığım, sadece sessizce yasımı tuttuğum o zamanlarda kanatlarımdan kül yerine parlak tozlar yağardı. Beni meleklere yakın kılan tek şey buydu. Diğer zamanlarda hayatımda gördüğüm en ürkütücü varlıktım. Meredith için ise durum farklıydı. O beni büyüleyici buluyordu, tüm o kızıl kıskançlığına rağmen.

"Hiç kör bir dev gördün mü?" Yanıtını beklemeden adımlarımı çıkmaz sokağın tek yönüne doğru çevirdim. Beş avcı yaşanmamış seneleri, zoraki cesaretleri ve iflah olmaz kibirleriyle çıkıp geldiklerinde barda Max'e yardım ediyordum. Apar topar elimizde kılıçla bardan ayrılırkenki tuhaf suratını düşününce içimdeki gülme isteğine zar zor engel olabiliyordum.

Bir avcıyla mantıklı cümle kurabilecek kadar hareketsiz duramıyorduk. Ben onları aradığımı söyleyemeden bana saldırmaya başlıyorlardı. Aklı başındaki tek bir insan ile karşılaşsaydım her şey daha farklı olabilirdi.

İnsan bazen keçileri temelli kaçıracağını düşünüyor ama hayat her zaman sizin ona bağlandığınız şeylerle övünür. Ve ben acınası hayatımda birçok şeye bağlıydım. Ne yazık ki aşk bunlardan biri değildi.

Artık o lükse sahip değildim.

Derin bir nefes alıp caddeye çıkarken kanatlarımı içime çektim. Kaburgalarımı onlar âdeta bana söverken esnetip büktüm. Kanatlarım son tüylerine kadar vücuduma saklandığında bu kez de ben sövdüm. İblis kanatları, sergilenmek için yanıp tutuşuyorlardı. Benim onları sakladığım her seferinde canıma okuyorlardı. Gerçi bunun başka bir sebebi vardı. Şeytan cehennemden uzaklaştıkça güçleri azalırdı. Hikâyenin bu bölümü size fazlasıyla tanıdık gelebilir.

Şeytan yeryüzüne uygun değildi. Bizler insan bedenleri, ciğerleri ve hatta damarlarında kötülük akan karanlık kalbimizle bile bu diyara uygun değildik. Aldığım canlar pelerinim, işlediğim günahlar gölgem olmuş, oradan oraya savrulurken bile bunu düşünüyordum. Cehenneme de ait değildim.

Orayı terk etmiştim.

Işıkların altında durup arabaların geçmesini bekledim. Bir araba su birikintisine batıp botlarıma çamur sıçrattığında eğilip baktım. Damlacıklar bile birbirini kolluyordu. Biri nereye diğeri oraya. Benim neyim vardı? Ait olamayan bir ruh ve sayısız laneti. Ve lanetli yoldaşları.

"Yine kendine acıyorsun değil mi?" Meredith koşa koşa yanıma geldi. Yüzündeki kurumuş kan lekeleri ve darmadağın olmuş kıymetli saçlarına rağmen gülümsüyordu. Lanetli yoldaşlarımın en lanetlisi sanırım Meredith'di. "Draza'ya kocaman bir kargo yaptırsaydın." Sırıtarak çapraz taktığı çantasını arkasına aldı. Hırsızlık yapmış olduğu gerçeğine mi yoksa benden saklama çabasına mı gülsem bilemedim. *Ganimetçi Merr.*

"Cehennemi terk ettiğinde kelle avcısı olacağını sanıyordum. Bir kurye değil," dedi dudaklarını hoşnutsuz bir ifadeyle bükerken. Sönük sokak lambalarının loş ışığının izinde beraber karşıya geçerken söyleniyordu. "Ben kelle avcısıyım sen de kurye. Makul bir görev dağılımı." Kaldırımda yürürken diğer insanlar yanımızdan geçip gidiyor, rüzgâr kanlı kâküllerimi gözlerime çarpıyordu. Kimsenin bana tuhaf tuhaf bakmamasının sebebi ise Meredith'di. Yarıya kadar açtığı göğüslerinin üzerine düşen turuncu-kızıl saçları ile fazlasıyla dikkat çekiciydi. Eğer bu yetmiyorsa kaşlarından ve çenesinden kan sızan ürkütücü bakışlarına da odaklanabilirdiniz.

"Draza'ya bu ay gönderdiğimiz dördüncü avcı grubu. Ve ne aileni ne de Bethany'i bulabildik. Bu iş için buraya gelmenin sebebi Draza'dan önce onları bulmak istemendi. Hedefe yaklaşamadığımız gibi..."

Bıkkınlıkla nefesimi bıraktım. Ellerimle saçlarımı dağıtıp yolma isteğime zar zor söz geçirebiliyordum. "Bethany saklanıyor, bu yüzden onun bizi bulmasını bekliyoruz." O bir yanıt veremeden gözlerimi kısarak yüzüne baktım. "O kör devlerin görebildiği külleri bırakışımın sebebi bu. Bethany bir şeytanın izini sürebilir."

Kız kardeşim homurdanırken dikkatim dağıldı ve kaldırımda yolunu şaşırmış iri bir taşa takılıp tökezledim. Hemen toparlanırken göz ucuyla cadıya baktım. "Gülersen o güzel burnunu dağıtırım." Kız kardeşim morararak sustu. Nihayet köşeyi döndüğümüzde Max'in barı ışıklar içindeydi. Saat gece yarısını çoktan geçmişti ama sarışın barmen bizim dönmemizi bekliyordu. Barın önünde park edilen bisikletlerin arasından geçerek kapıya uzandım.

"Hey, selam uzaylı!" Max, tezgâhtan çıkıp kocaman açtığı mavi gözleriyle önce bana sonra kız kardeşime baktı. Ardından gözleri tekrar bana kaydı. "O üstündeki kan senin mi?" Bakışlarını takip edip üzerime baktım. En iyi deyimle kan gövdeyi götürüyordu. "Cıks."

Barmen rahatlayarak nefesini bırakırken tezgâha tutundu. "Kızlar, bu kez gerçekten öldüğünüzü düşündüm."

Anlamayarak Meredith'e baktım. "Ölemeyeceğimizi söylemedin mi?"

Kız kardeşim sırıtarak Max'e sarıldı. "Böyle daha çok seviyor bizi. Senin de bildiğin üzere insanlar kaybedebilecekleri şeyleri severler, onlara bağlanırlar. Ölümsüzlük senin ve benim daha az büyüleyici olmamıza sebep olur."

O an üzülmemeliydim. Sanki ağır bir lafın altında kalmış gibi ruh hâlim düşmemeli, auram kararmamalıydı ama onun yerine omuzlarım düştü ve bir kez daha gerçeği hatırladım. *Kaybedilebilecek bir şeyi sevmiş, bağlanmış ve en sonunda da kaybetmiştim.*

"Ben yatmaya gidiyorum." Tezgâhın altından anahtarı alıp barın arka tarafına doğru yola çıktım. Binayı saran merdivenlerden yukarı çıkarken gökyüzündeki tüm yıldızlar tarafından gözetleniyor gibiydim. Kollanıyormuş gibi değil de her an canımı alacaklarmış gibi parlıyorlardı. *Seni izliyoruz Cassandra, tek bir hatanda seni yiyip bitireceğiz,* der gibi. "Ne zaman bu kadar düşman olduk?" Yıldızlar yanıt vermedi.

Çatı katının kapısını aralayıp ışığı açınca kendimi son iki aydır yaşadığım odamda buldum. Kendimi çarşafını en son ne zaman değiştirdiğimi hatırlamadığım yatağa bir çuval gibi bırakırken kafamdaki tilkiler dans ediyordu. Bethany ile görüşmeliydim çünkü nasıl yaptığını anlamadığım şekilde avcıların sayısı hızla artıyordu. Karargâhlarında dev avcı tavukları olup kuluçkaya yatmıyorlarsa eğer tek bir açıklaması olabilirdi, insanları avcılara dönüştürüyorlardı. Avcıların sayı artışı da hırsız iblisleri tetikliyordu. Cehennemden yeryüzüne bitmek bilmeyen bir göç söz konusuydu. Hırsızlar ve vampirler dünyaya iniyorlardı. Cehennemde çoktan dünyanın besin yönünden çok zengin olduğuyla ilgili dedikodular yayılmıştı. Bu yüzden birinin ben hayatın neresindeyim, neden var oldum dramını bırakıp yeryüzüne inmesi gerekmişti.

Marr ve Anton'un onlarla olmadığını biliyordum. Kalbimin derinliklerinde bir şey bana bunu hissettiriyordu. Gerçi kalbimin derinliklerinde hissetme lüksüne sahip bir parça var mıydı emin de olamıyordum. Işığı kapatıp ay ışığının tekinsiz gölgeleri tavanımda oynaşırken ailemi düşündüm. Dediğim gibi her zaman kana susamış bir kaçık değildim ama hayat beni buna mecbur etmişti.

BÖLÜM 2

Boğazıma dolan kanla sıçrayarak uyandım.

Gözlerim deli gibi yanıyor, metalin iğrenç tadı burnumu ve ağzımı yakıyordu. Öksürerek ağzımdaki kanı çıkarmaya çalıştım. Sorunu anlamadığım için şaşkındım. Tehlikeyle yüzleşmek için elimi yastığımın altına atıp bıçağımı çıkardım. Burnumdan kanlar akarken elimdeki bıçakla karanlığı yardım. Kimse yoktu. Nefes sesi duymaya çalışıyorsam da başaramıyordum. "Ah..." Canım yanıyordu. Kanlı parmaklarımla el yordamıyla şifonyerin üzerindeki ışığı bulup açtım.

Kanlı öksürüklerim ve uğuldayan kulaklarıma rağmen ayak seslerini seçebiliyordum. Biri delicesine koşuyor, olduğum yere varmaya çalışıyordu. Öksürerek yatakta iyice doğruldum. Sırtımı yatak başlığına dayayıp burnumu parmak uçlarımla tıkadım.

Meredith odanın kapısını kırıp yıldırım gibi içeri dalarken öksürüklerim dinmemiş, aksine şiddetlenmişti. "Ne oluyor be?" Yanıma varıp bir eliyle omzumu tutup diğeriyle alnımdaki saçları geriye yatırdı. Göz bebeklerimi görmeye çalışırken küfrediyordu. "Ayın daha ikisi. Daha şimdiden yoksunluk çekiyorsun." Bir öksürük krizi daha gelince ellerinden kurtulup yatağın üzerine kustum. Bu kez kardeşim ne kadar iğrenç bir görüntü olduğuna dair mırıldanıyordu.

Büyük bir patırtı eşliğinde Max odaya girerken bir kez daha kusmamak için yanağımın içini dişliyordum. Barmen çocuk aceleden kayıp düşerek Meredith'in hâlihazırda kırdığı kapıya kafasını geçirdi. Kaybettiği birkaç saniyeyi telafi edercesine uzun bacaklarıyla neredeyse yuvarlanarak yanıma geldi. Mavi okyanus rengi gözlerinde yaşlar birikmiş bir hâlde, dağınık görüntüsüyle yanı başımda diz çöktü. "Ölüyor mu?" Gülmek için ağzımı açınca tekrar öksürmeye başladım. *Öldüğüm falan yok, amma abarttınız,* diyecekken daha fazla konuşamadım.

İstemsizce kürek kemiklerim önce içe sonra dışarı bükülerek kanatlarımı sırtımdan çıkardı. Gözlerim kayıp giderken kanatlarımın komodini, üzerindeki eşyalarla beraber devirdiğini gördüm.

Hiçliğe sürüklenirken artık öksürmediğim için memnundum. Bu kez biri tarafından kucaklanmamış, kaldırılmamış, kurtarılamamıştım.

Bu kez Aidan yoktu.

"Cassie, uyan." Soğuk parmaklar göz kapaklarımı zorla aralarken görüntü yavaş yavaş yerine geldi. Max, hâlâ karşımda dağılmış bir hâlde ağlıyor, Meredith ise antik dildeki büyüleri sıralıyordu. Nefes almadan hızla okuyordu, ne kadar süredir yaptığını bilmiyordum ama kan kırmızısı dudakları çatlamıştı. Aralarda anlayabileceğim şekilde konuştuğu da oluyordu. "Aç gözlerini seni pislik şeytan, gitmene izin yok," demişti bir kez. Sanki bu diyardan çekip gidebilirmişim gibi.

Nihayet çarşafın kandan bir balçıkla sırılsıklam olan yerini Max çekip aldığında, Meredith beni yere indirdi. Elleriyle ıslak saçlarımı geriye atarak büyüsünün son sözlerini fısıldadı. Dudaklarından birkaç parlak alev fırlayıp yüzüme ulaştığında kendimi daha iyi hissediyordum. Gözlerimi zar zor açarken konuşmaya çalıştım. "Aidanhell ben ona müdahale etmeseydim bunları mı yaşayacaktı?"

"Şşş, sessiz ol! Bunları yarın konuşacağız. Ayrıca Aidanhell'in benim gibi akıllı bir rehberi yoktu. Bundan benim sayemde kurtulabildiğini biliyorsun." Terli saçlarımı alnımdan çekerek dikkatlice yüzüme baktı. Konuştuğunda sesi az önceki kadar öz güven dolu değildi, bir fısıltı gibi çıkmıştı. "Birkaç cana mâl olsa bile."

Elleriyle beni dengede tutarak sırtımın tamamını duvara yaslamama yardımcı oldu. Az ileride Max'in kırılan camları süpürdüğünü ve sümüğünü çekiştirdiğini görebiliyordum. "Ben ölürsem tek ağlayacak olan Max." Meredith sözlerim üzerine düzeltmekte olduğu saçlarımdan bir tutamı huysuzca çekti. "Sana bayılmıyorum ama ölmen işime gelmez." Omuz silkmek için yaptığım hareket kaburgalarımın ağrısıyla son buldu.

"Ayda bir can almamız yetmiyor. Artık her hafta birini kurban edeceğiz." Başımı kaldırıp gözlerine baktım. Ne düşündüğünü bu hâlde anlayamıyordum. Ama tahmin edebilirdim. Max bizlerin normal olmadığını biliyordu ama tüm detayları anlatarak onu çıldırtmak istememiştik. Deli bir arkadaş şu an ihtiyacım olan son şeydi. Bu yüzden Meredith komşu binalardakilerin duyabileceği bir sesle saçmalarken Max'e doğru döndüm. "Bahsettiği şey tam olarak fanileri öldürmek değil, bunu biliyorsun." Max'in soluk beyaz elleri tuttuğu süpürgeyi daha sıkı kavradı. Başıyla onaylarken bana çok da inanmadığını hissedebiliyordum.

Şeytan cehennemden uzaklaştıkça güçsüz düşerdi ancak bir şekilde bunu önleyebilirdi. Cehenneme kurban verirsek yeryüzünde gezinebiliyorduk, sürekli bir durum değildi ama gerektiğinde yardımcı oluyordu. Her şey katran karası boka dönmeden önce neden bunu akıl edemediğimizi düşündüm milyonuncu kez. Aidan'ı bir kefaret ödemekten kurtarabilir miydik? Eğer zamanında bunu denemiş olsaydık belki de…

Kız kardeşimin yardımına gerek duymadan ayağa kalkarken derin bir nefes aldım. Bana baktığındaki yüzü endişeden kırışmıştı. Yeniden auraları görmek birkaç günümü alacaktı. Konuştuğumda hâlâ ne zaman yere yığılacağımı bekler gibi bir hâli vardı. "Ee, bu kez kimi öldürüyoruz?"

***

Etik kurallar konusundaki anlaşmazlığımız, benim bu gece kriz geçirip neredeyse sona yaklaşmama kadar devam etmişti. Şimdi ise tek anlaşmazlığımız kötüleri mi yoksa ölecek olanları mı öldürmemiz gerektiği konusundaydı.

Meredith suçluları öldürerek daha büyük miktarlarda güç sağlayabileceğimi düşünüyordu. En kötülerden akan kötülük beni besleyebilirdi, dünyada kalma süremi uzatabilirdi. Öte yandan kötü birini arayacak vaktimiz de yoktu. Denk gelmediğimiz sürece birini öldürmek için hastaneye gidiyor, orada ölüm döşeğindeki birine yaklaşıyorduk.

Daha önce birkaç kez avcıların enerjisinden beslenmeye çalışmıştım ama ruhlarından akan cılız güç bana sadece bir hafta yetebilmişti. Daha sonra Merr'in yardımıyla bir tecavüzcüyü indirmiştim ve bu bana düşündüğümden daha uzun süre yetmişti. En sonlarda ise hastaneye gitmeye başlamıştık. Yoğun bakım ünitesinin açık büfe oluşuyla ilgili ahlaki bir sıkıntı yaşamayı ikinci seferimde bırakmıştım.

Gerçi işler burada biraz garipleşiyordu. Çünkü Meredith'in söylediğine göre kurbanların ruhları bedenlerinden çıkıp beni çevreleyip beslerken ben gülümsüyordum. Gülümsediğimi hatırlamıyordum ama sorun değildi. Marr, Anton ve Jo için bir süre daha burada kalmam gerekiyordu ve gereken enerjiyi nasıl sağladığımın hiç ama hiç önemi yoktu. İçimdeki cılız bir ses *tek kalma sebebin bu değil*, diyordu. O tahta dönmek istemiyordum. Bunu denemiştim, aylarca o karanlık tahtta oturmayı denemiştim ama bu herkes için pek çok açıdan kötü sonuçlanmıştı. Birkaç ay önce ben… Şu anki gibi değildim.

Dün geceden bu yana Max ve Meredith bana uygun bir kurban bulma umuduyla arayışa çıkmış, Max de barı bir arkadaşına emanet etmişti. Odamda yatağımın üzerinde uzanırken saatime baktım. Öğleden önce gelmeleri gerekirken hâlâ yoklardı. Anlaşılan ölmeye meraklı birini bulamamışlardı. Tecrübelerime göre kolay kolay kimse ölmek istemiyordu. Yaşama tutunmak, iblisler için olduğu kadar insanlar için de değerliydi.

Meredith ortadan kaybolduğunda hep yaptığım gibi telefonumu çıkarıp Jo'yu aradım. Telefon birkaç kez çaldı, çaldı ve tekrar çaldı. Yanıt veren olmayınca kapatıp çekmecemin içine koydum. Yatağa uzanıp sancıyan göğsümü görmezden gelerek kolumla gözlerimi kapadım.

Herkesi kaybetmeye ne kadar yakındım her şeyi kazandığımı zannederken.

Max'in arkadaşı bardaki müziği değiştirip yavaş ritimli bir şarkı açınca kalbimde bir ağrı hissettim. Bunun sebebi güçlerimin azalması ya da zayıf kalmam gerçeği değil, Aidanhell ile dans etmenin anısının kalıntılarıydı. "Sanki üzerinden milyonlarca sene geçmiş gibi."

O ne yapıyordu? Hiçbir fikrim yoktu.

Başlarda, bir iblis olarak nefes almayı yeni öğrendiğim karanlık zamanlarımda, onu birkaç kez düşünmüştüm. Ama sonra bunun beni kaosa sürüklediğini fark etmiştim.

Lanetli bir varlığın kutsal bir şeyi düşünmesine izin var mıydı? Yoksa cüretkârlık şeytanın özelliklerinden biri miydi?

Birkaç zilin birbirine çarparak çıkardığı sese benzer bir çınlama havaya karışınca kırık kapıya baktım. Gölge, yavaşça hareket edip kapıyı araladı. "Kim var orada?"

Önce parlak tozlar, ardından mis gibi bir tarçın kokusu odayı doldurunca gülümsedim. Hâlâ gülümseyebildiğim için minnettar hissettim. "Turuncu kafa?" Bunun üzerine kırık kapım bir gıcırtı eşliğinde açılarak misafirimi odaya aldı. Peri çocuk her zamanki somon-yeşil renk tuniği, daha koyu pantolonu ve perilere has zarif çantasıyla odaya girerken şaşkınca kırık kapıma bakıyordu. "Burada ne oldu?"

Yatakta doğrulup ona gelmesini işaret ettim. "Her zamanki şeyler." Yeşil Çamların son veliahtı Urange yanıma yaklaşmadan hemen önce tek kaşını kaldırarak yüzüme baktı, bu yanıttan hoşnut değildi.

"Biz burada otururken çığlık atarak gelen, kafayı yemiş bir grup avcı yok değil mi?"

Sırıttım. "Hayır, sadece Meredith gelecek."

Urange irkildi. Şimdi kararsızca kapı eşiğinde dikiliyordu. "O sanki onlar kadar tehlikeli değilmiş gibi söyledin bunu." Tekrar sırıttım. Perilerin espri anlayışı en karanlık zamanlarda dahi beni güldürebilen bir uyuşturucu gibiydi.

"İçeri gel." Ayağa kalkıp ona doğru yürüdüm. Tarçın kokusu eşliğinde eşikten geçip yeşil bez çantasını girişin sol tarafındaki kıyafet tepeciğine bıraktı. Doğrulurken turuncu buklelerini eliyle geriye itip derin bir nefes aldı.

"Seni görmek güzel."

Çoktan yanına varmış olduğumdan ellerimi tuttu ve eğilerek dudaklarını ellerime değdirdi. "Seninle yeniden karşılaşmak bir onur, Majeste." Ellerimi çekip ona sarıldım. Şimdi tarçın kokusunun bulanmadığı tek bir toz zerreciği kalmamıştı.

"Bana artık Majeste demiyorlar." Yeniden ayrılırken ekledim. "Tabii bunun tahtı reddedip dünyaya inmemle bir ilgisi olabilir."

Urange dudağını dişleyerek bunu düşünüyormuş gibi yaptı. "Muhtemelen öyle bir şeyle ilgilidir." Ardından yanımdan geçip yatağımın yanındaki eski sandalyeye yürüdü. Başka bir erkeğe sarılmak bana normalde olmadığı kadar Aidanhell'i hatırlatıyordu. Ne tarçın ne de başka bir koku Aidanhell'i tamamlayamazdı. Gerçi artık nasıl koktuğundan emin değildim, o bu diyarlara ait değildi.

Beni daldığım rüyadan kendime getiren Urange'ın oflaması olmuştu. Sandalyeye güvenmemiş olacak ki yerdeki cam parçalarına dikkatle basıp zıplayarak komodinimin üzerine oturdu. Hançerlerimin ikisini orada bıraktığımdan emindim ama görünen o ki Urange'ın herhangi bir yerine saplanmamışlardı.

"Aileni bulabildin mi?" Olumsuz anlamda başımı sallayıp yanına gelerek kendimi dikkatlice yatağa bıraktım. Bir süre boyunca ikimiz de konuşmadık. Ben ışığın aydınlattığı havada uçuşan toz tanelerini izlerken Urange da beni izliyordu. "Bizler gibi görmüyorsun değil mi?"

"Neyi?" Gözlerimi kaldırıp ona baktım. Beni incelemeye devam ediyordu. Eliyle önce gözlerimi sonra çevremi işaret etti. "Her şeyi. Kırmızı gördüğünü söylemişlerdi."

Sırıttım. "Hayır, her kim söylediyse hayal gücü bayağı genişmiş." Ardından aklıma gelen bir şeyle durdum. "Aslında sanırım," dedim, ara verip dudaklarımı ısırdım. "Sanırım iki kez kırmızı gördüm ama bunun şeytanlıkla ilgisi yok, sadece gözüm dönmüştü."

Urange yine tek kaşını kaldırdı. O böyle şeyler yapmaya devam ederse Aidanhell'i hayatımdan çıkarma planlarım zarar görecekti. Onsuzlukla onsuzluğa alışmak arasında derin bir fark vardı. Eksikliğine karşı koyabilirdim, sadece ona tekrar kavuşacaksam. Ama bu hâlde eksikliğin bir ebediyet süreceğini bilmek... Bu her şeyi değiştiriyordu.

"Aloha nasıl?" Urange'ın rahat bakışları değişerek yerini karamsarlığa bıraktı. Eliyle alnındaki parlak buklelerini düzeltmeye çalışır gibi yaptı. "Pek iyi gitmiyor ama sen bunları kafana takma. Zamanla düzelebilir." *Ebilmek* kelimesi hâlihazırda kaçmış olan keyfimi daha da kaçırdı. Katze, strigoilerin bir ruhu olmadığını söylemişti.

"Bir ruhu yoksa ve ruhu gerçekten de gitmişse nasıl eski hâline dönebilir?"

Peri çocuk üzerinde düşünmeye tenezzül bile etmeden yanıt verdi. "Bunun bir yolu olsaydı pembe ağaçlarımız olmazdı." Anlayıp anlamadığımı ölçmeye çalışır gibi şüpheyle gözlerime baktı. "O ağaçları unuttun mu? Hayalarımı tekmelediğin gündü."

Neredeyse kahkaha attım. O günü o kadar iyi hatırlıyordum ki. Şimdi bile ilk uçuşumda rüzgârın tenimi keserkenki hâlini hissedebiliyordum. Bir insan bedeninde nefes alamamış, rüzgârdan kaçınmaya çalışmıştım. Hatta düşmüştüm ve Aidan beni cezalandırarak bir daha yalnız uçmamı yasaklamıştı.

Ah Aidan, şimdi her gece yalnız uçuyorum. Ve sen yoksun.

Ceza verebilecek, kızacak tek bir kimse bile yok.

"Daldın gittin."

İrkildim. "Zor zamanlar geçiriyoruz." Anlamayarak bana baktı. Ne dediğimi düşününce saçmaladığımı fark ettim. "Her neyse," dedim elimle konuyu dağıtmak için havayı âdeta tokatlayarak. "Buraya neden geldin?"

Ve Urange sonunda oturuşunu düzeltip derin bir nefes aldı. Bana söyleyeceği şeyden önce gözleri, hâlâ eşiğin yanında duran çantasına kaydı. "Aslında sana bir şey getirdim. Bekle." Kalkarak çantasını aldı. Tekrar yanıma geldiğinde içinden bir harita çıkarıyordu.

"Haritayı masa örtüsü olarak kullandınız herhâlde." Elindeki buruşmuş kâğıda baktım. "Ya da küllük," dedim tek kaşımı kaldırarak. Tanrım, berbat hâldeydi! İşin daha berbat olan kısmı ise benim o harita ile ilgilenecek vaktimin olmamasıydı. Tükenmek deyiminin canlı örneğiydim. Öyle hızlı tükeniyordum ki görüşüm bulanıklaşmaya başlamıştı.

Urange'ı severdim ama durumumdan ona bahsetmek istemiyordum, ne de olsa periler dedikoduculukları ile de ünlülerdi. İnsanların benim gücüm hakkında saçmalamasını istemiyordum. Tahtı kısa süreliğine vekile vermem zaten yeterince dedikoduya sebep olmuştu. İblisler diyarı artık bana *hilekâr,* diyordu. Ailemi, arkadaşlarımı, eski ırkımı yarı yolda bıraktığım yetmezmiş gibi şimdi de onları yarı yolda bırakmıştım. Bana ihtiyaçları olduğunu düşündükleri kritik zamanlarda tüm cehenneme siktiri çekip toz olmuştum. Böyle biliyorlardı. İşin aslı ise daha karmaşıktı. Cehennemin sakinleri huzurlu yaşantılarına geri dönmek istiyorlarsa dünyaya bulaşmayı bırakmalıydık ve bu iş de cehennemden yönetilemiyordu.

Peri çocuk nihayet haritayı açıp zayıf dizlerinin üzerine koydu. Kalemi ağzına sokup kapağını çıkardı. "Çok pis görünüyor çünkü pis."

Ah, aydınlandım!

"Yani," dedi kapağı kalemin arkasına takarken. "Uzun senelerdir ellenmemişti ben arşivlerden bulana kadar." Kendiyle gurur duyduğunu belli eden ukalâ bir sırıtışla çilli yanakları sıkıştı.

"Şimdi de bunun neden önemli olduğu bölüme mi geliyoruz?" dedim gözlerimle kucağını işaret ederek. "Ah, evet." Kırmızı mürekkep kalemin ucuyla kahverengi haritadaki bir tepeciği işaretledi. "Lilith burada kalıyor." Başını kaldırıp merakla gözlerine baktım.

"Ve bu beni ilgilendiriyor. Çünkü..."

"Çünkü o kadın her şeyin anahtarı. Dünyanın en iyi kadını olmayabilir ama sana yardım edebilir." İşte şimdi kahkahalarla gülüyordum. Hatta öyle bir kahkaha atmıştım ki biraz daha abartırsam kırık camları titreteceğimi biliyordum.

Neredeyse gözlerimden yaşlar akarken kendimi durdurup periye baktım. Suratı asılmış bir ifadeyle elindeki haritayla bana bakıyordu. "Lilith öyle yardım isteyebileceğin bir tip değil, üstelik annem olması onu daha az kötü biri yapmıyor." Ellerimle kendimi gösterdim. "Bu hâlde olmamın tek sorumlusu da o. Yani ondan bir konuda yardım istersen sonuçlarına katlanırsın." Bir dahaki sefere bu kadar şanslı olmayabilirdim. Artık Lilith'e rehin verebileceğim tek şey aldığım nefesti.

"Son yardımını istediğimde içimdeki tüm iyiliği kaybettim. Bir dahaki sefere kalan bölümlerimi de kaybedebilirim." Aidanhell'i kurtarmıştım ama sadece bu kadardı. Bu hikâyede kazanan taraf yoktu. O ya da bu şekilde eski hayatıma dair bir şeylerin bitişiydi bana ettiği yardım. O yoğun aurası, zehirli kelime oyunlarıyla dişi şeytan kâinatta bulaşılmayacak kadınlar arasında ilk beşteydi.

Urange sözlerimden hoşlanmayarak kaşlarını çattı. Ben ağzını açıp bir sonraki gün doğumuna kadar kafamı ütüleyeceğini düşünürken o hiçbir şey söylemedi. Ayağa kalkıp kirli haritasını katlayarak çantasının içine koydu. Ağır adımlarla kapıya yürüdükten sonra eşikte durup son bir kez bana döndü. Bir şeyler söylemek için dudaklarını açıp sonra vazgeçip kapatıyor gibiydi.

"Aidanhell'i onun sayesinde kurtardın. Sev ya da sevme, o senin annen. Ve sevdiğin adamı kurtardı." Ardından donuk bir şekilde bana bakıp evimden çıktı. Arkasından seslenmek istemiştim ama gücüm yoktu. Gitmesine izin verdim. Tahtta oturduğum ilk zamanlar sırf şaka yapıyor diye öldürülmesini emretmiştim ve Urange peşine yolladığım kara bölük askerlerinden çok zor kurtulabilmişti. Urange dirilen bebek bir iblis olduğum için bazı şeyleri görmezden gelse de aramız eskisi gibi değildi.

O gittikten çok sonra bile hâlâ boş bir şekilde odamın kapısına baktım. Sevdiğim adamı kurtarmak her şeye mâl olmuştu.

Meredith yanında Max ile çatı katı merdivenlerinden çıkarken yaptığım fedakârlığı düşünüyordum.

Hiçbir şey bitmemişti.

Her şey yeni başlıyordu.

Ve cadı elinde kocaman, rengârenk poşetlerle odama girip, "Sana bir kurban buldum," dedi.

Hayatım böyleydi. Pes etmenin kıyılarında gezerken yeniden aydınlanan yollardı benim devam etmemi sağlayan. Ayağa kalkıp yastığımın altındaki bıçağa uzandım. Kemerime koyarken artık ne için savaştığımı düşündüm.

Lilith'e kaptırmak istemediğim kalan son nefesimi, uğruna feda edecek neyim vardı?

BÖLÜM 3

Telefonum titreşince uğruna nefes alacağım şeyin beni aradığını gördüm.

Hayat savaşmak anlamına gelirdi, sadece kazanmak için de değil, devam edebilmek için.

Cep telefonumu açıp arayana baktım. Arkadaşlarımın peşi sıra merdivenleri hızlıca inerken telefonu kulağıma koydum. “Bücür.” Karşı tarafta kardeşim homurdandı.

“Geçen hafta geleceğini söylemiştin.” Gözlerimi devirdim. Tam zamanlı bir ergen olmadan önce Jo, çok daha çekilebilirdi.

“Ailemizi bulmaya çalışıyorum.” Ve kardeşim bir kez daha homurdandı.

Barın atıklar ve belâ arayanlar için kullandığımız yan kapısını açarak bizden ayrılan Max’e el salladım. Dudaklarını oynatarak “Dikkatli ol.” ya da “Siktir git, ölme.” demişti. Emin olamıyordum.

Bu yüzden sadece, “Sen de,” deyip bardan çıktım.

Yağan yağmuru görüp bir adım gerileyince kapüşonlu bir hâlde yarı kör gezen kız kardeşime çarptım. “Şu kılıç az önce böbreğimi çıkarıyordu.” Elindeki kılıcı abartılı bir hareketle gösterip ardından kemerine taktı. *Sanki kılıcı kullanabilirmiş gibi.* Ne kadar eğitirsem eğiteyim bizim gibi olamıyordu. Ben tombul ellerimle tahta kılıçlarla savaşçılık oynarken o, oyuncak bebeklerini zehirlere batırıp çıkarıyordu. Ne diyebilirdim ki, uzmanlık alanlarımız başkaydı.

“Konuşacak mısın?”

Öksürdüm. Ben öksürünce Meredith gece karanlığına rağmen parlayan yeşil gözlerini yüzüme sabitledi. Bir anda ölüp gitmemi bekler gibi bir hâli vardı. “Evet, anlat neredesin?” Ve Jo konuşmaya başladı. Bir yandan anlattıklarına odaklanmaya çalışıyor bir yandan da yağmurun altında bir çekirge edasında neredeyse uçan kardeşimi yakalamaya çalışıyordum. Gittiği ara sokağı biliyordum ama o kadar yorgundum ki onsuz gidemeyeceğimi de biliyordum.

Yağmur taneleri arabaların farlarıyla aydınlanan ışıltılı caddelerde tişörtüme düşüyordu. Kulağımda kardeşimin heyecanlı sesi, önümde hızlıca dalgalanan kızıl saçlar ile birkaç gün daha güçlü kalabileyim diye birini öldürmeye gidiyordum.

“Beni özledin değil mi?”

Bir yağmur tanesi burnuma düştü. “Tabii ki bücür. Çok özledim.” Hattın diğer ucunda Jo’nun gülümsediğini hayal ettim. Bir abla olarak yanında olamıyor ancak telefonlarda onunla görüşebiliyordum, üstelik ne zaman kanatlarının çıkacağını da bilemiyorduk. “Kanatların çıktığında yanında olacağım. Sana dediğim yerde kal. Şimdi kapatmam gerekiyor. Seni seviyorum ufaklık.” Jo kendime dikkat etmemi söyleyip telefonu kapattı.

Bethany ile topluluğa ihanet eden bir grup avcı buradan kaçıp gitmişti. Onlar giderken Beth ile iletişim kurup kardeşimin onlar tarafından eğitildiği enstitüden çıkarılmasını istemiştim. Bethany isteğimi yerine getirmişti ve bu avcıyı son görüşüm olmuştu. Ondan bir daha haber alamamıştım.

"Neredeyse geldik." Bir araba yanımızdan geçerken oluklarda biriken suyu ayakkabıma sıçrattı. Kardeşime yetişmek için adımlarımı hızlandırdım.

"İki işiler, aynı yerde takılıyorlar."

"Hırsızlar mı?"

Meredith'den bir süre yanıt gelmedi. "Pek sayılmaz, daha çok tacizciler. Bir kez tecavüz, birkaç kez gasp ve şiddet eğilimi. Bahse girerim tacizlerine karşı koyan çocukları da öldürmüşlerdir. Yani katiller." Ona inanmadım, umutsuzca birini öldürmemi istediği için beni gaza getirmeye çalışıyordu. Ama yine de takip ettim.

Yağmur şiddetlenip şehrin asfaltını çamura bularken ayakkabılarımız sırılsıklam olmuş hâlde koşuyorduk. Kardeşim hızlı koşarsak daha az yağmura yakalanacağımızdan neredeyse emindi. Ama ben doğru olmadığını biliyordum. Her an tabutu açıp içine giriverecekmiş gibi olduğum gerçeğiyle baş etmeye çalışıyordu. Zamanın azaldığıyla ilgili mırıldanıp duruyordu.

Meredith karşıdan karşıya geçerken elleriyle saçını ensesinde toplamaya çalıştı. Onu izlerken tıpkı onun gibi dağınık saçlarımı hizaya getirdim. Kâküllerim ise ayrı bir konuydu. Onları kesememiş ama uzatamamıştım da. Görüntüm konusunda en bariz şeylerden biri buydu. Ve memnundum. Bir yıl önceki Cassie ile şu anki Cassie arasındaki en büyük benzerlik buydu. Gözlerim aynı değildi. Burnum birkaç kez kırılıp yeniden iyileşmişti, belki aynı görünüyor olabilirdi ama ben aynı olmadığını biliyordum. Dudaklarım ise tam üç kez bir yumruğun etkisiyle patlamış, bir kez ise paramparça olmuştu.

Tüm bunların yanı sıra ufak tefek çiziklerim de vardı. Kaşımın ortasından geçen dikenli bir yara izi edinmiştim. Bu diğerleri gibi iyileşmemişti, sebebini ise bilemiyorduk. Aidanhell'i iyileştirirken olmuş olması gerekiyordu. Avuç içlerim de Aidanhell'i iyileştirirken zarar gören yerlerimden biriydi. Yanmışlardı. Ve şimdi artlarında parlak beyaz-kızıl izler bırakmışlardı.

Sol dizim Aidanhell'in beni mağaramıza götürdüğü gün iyileştirdiği yerlerimden biriydi ve kemik bir kez deriyi yırttığı için orada silik uzun bir iz bırakmıştı.

Bir sene öncesiyle aynı değildim. Ve değişen şeyler sadece fiziksel değildi. Bir yıl önce çok çalışmaktan sızlanan, yatağa girdiği an horuldayarak uyuyan gamsız bir kızdım. Hayatla tek alıp veremediğim şey tatil günlerimde kamptan uzaklaşmak için aileme yalvarmamdı. Şimdiyse… Ne tatil günüm vardı ne de kamp. Onlara sızlanıp şımarabileceğim bir ailem de yoktu.

"Geldik mi?" dedim tereddütle. Gözlerim kız kardeşimin hareketsiz duran sırtındaydı. Elimi hızla cebimdeki hançere attım. Meredith omzu üzerinden bana kaçamak bir bakış atıp tekrar önüne döndü. Aramızdaki mesafeyi azaltarak yanına sokuldum.

Sesleri duyduğumuzda yağmur azalmış, hava daha da kararmış, tüm o fantastik hikâyelerde anlatılan puslu caddeler çoğalmıştı. Öldürülemez olduğum gerçeği kalbimdeki korkuyu silip götüreli çok olmuştu. Ölmüyorsanız kolay kolay korkmuyordunuz.

Ama bilge bir adamın dediği gibi, ölümden beter şeyler vardı. Ve Meredith'e göre ben bu şeyleri öğrenme konusundaki aşırı hevesim sayesinde sonuma bayağı yakındım.

"Şu ceketi çıkar da ne çaldığımıza bakalım."

Histerik bir öksürük adımımı yavaşlatmama sebep oldu. "Seni orospu çocuğu, hani öldürmeyecektik?" İki kişiydiler. Meredith silüetlere en yakındaki binanın yanına eğilerek yavaşça başını uzattı. Ben de üst taraftan bakarak konuşanları görmeye çalıştım. Siyah kapüşonlu bir adam elinde iki çantayla yere çömelmiş, bir şeyleri ayıklıyordu. Bir sis tabakası hemen üzerlerinde yükselirken gözlerimi kıstım. Diğeri kusuyordu.

Bir hamle yapmak için öne atılınca Meredith kolumu tutup beni gizlendiğimiz yere çekti. "Şşş," dedi azarlar gibi. Dudaklarım sinirden çizgi hâlini alırken kendimi zapt ederek duruşumu bozmamaya gayret ettim.

"Öldürmedik ki. Biraz pekmez akıttık." Tanrım, iğrençlerdi!

Bir de bize şeytan diyorlardı, herhangi birini kötülük yapması için ikna etmediğimi biliyordum. Kimsenin özellikle cehenneme gitmesini istiyor değildim. Herkesin kendi cehennemi vardı. Hepimiz kendi cehennemlerimizde layığı olduğumuz cezayı yaşıyorduk.

Faniler tek derdimizin onları kötü yola sürüklemek olduğu konusunda kendilerini ikna etmiş olabilirlerdi ama esas kötülük içlerindeydi. Kimse kimseye zorla zorbalık yaptıramazdı.

Yere eğilmiş olan diğeri kusarken onunla bir kez daha dalga geçti. Meredith'in bugünkü kurbanın hangisi olduğunu söylemesine ihtiyacım olmadığını fark ettim. "Burada bekle," dedim sessizce. Kardeşim ayağa kalkınca geriledim. Bana döndüğünde suratında tuhaf bir ifade vardı.

"Burada kalayım ve bütün eğlenceyi kaçırayım öyle mi?"

Ters ters ona baktım. "Bak bu gereklilik." Tekrar başımı hafifçe uzatıp adamları gördüm. "Keyfi işkenceci değiliz." Cadı ukalâ bir tavırla omuz silkip tekrar onlara döndü. Sırtının yavaş hareketinden nefes aldığını anlayabiliyordum.

"Tüm *o ben aslında kimse için endişelenmem* tavırlarını kapıda bırakıp gerçekliğe dön. Benim için endişelenmene gerek yok. Ben bir büyücüyüm." Elini görebileceğim şekilde havada tutup parmağını şıklattı. Ufak parlak bir kıvılcım işaret parmağı ve başparmağı arasında gidip gelirken bana gördün mü dercesine göz kırptı.

"Herkes kendi kıçından sorumlu o hâlde," dedim doğrularak. İşte başlıyorduk. Tüm o kaostan sonra bile hayatım uğursuzluklar silsilesine tutturulmuş bir ataç gibiydi. Boktan uzaklaşamıyordum, aksine daha da çok batıyordum. Kardeşim dirseğini geriye büküp kendi kılıcına uzanırken bokta tek başıma yüzmediğim için memnundum. "Yine de sen arkamda dur." Bu bir rica değildi, elimin tersiyle onu iterek kendimi açığa çıkardım. İksirler, kara büyüler ve hatta uğursuz dilekler konusunda Meredith bir uzman olabilirdi ama iş kılıçlara geldiğinde beş para etmezdi.

"Hey, selam!" Arkamda bir homurdanma duyuldu.

Ben onlara seslenince ayakta olan adam küfredip geriye sendeledi. Ben iki adım daha atınca bir kez daha sövüp kaçmaya çalışırken tökezledi. "Ben değildim. BEN DEĞİLDİM!" Bir kez daha tökezleyince Meredith'in homurtusunu daha net duymuştum.

Ve onun defolmasına izin verdim. Art arda yeminler edip tökezleyerek uzaklaşmaya çalıştı. Diğeri ise korkmamıştı. Doğrulurken arkadaşının arkasından bağırıyordu. "Seni salak. Şu kızdan mı korktun?"

Şu kız?

Cehennemin leydisi demek istedi herhâlde.

"Şimdi öleceğin bölüme geçiyoruz. Yani bir yarım dakika sonra yalvarmaya falan başlayabilirsin."

Kapüşonunu çıkarıp dövmeli kel kafasını kaşıdı. "Sen gerçekten deliymişsin be." Ardından geğirdi. Havadaki sıcaklık hızla düşerken neredeyse gülecek olduğum gerçeği beni şaşırtmıştı. Ölüm geliyordu ve bu sırf kaçınılmaz olduğu için, ihtiyacım olduğu için geliyordu.

Pislik torbasını öldürmek için hançere ihtiyacım yoktu. Hem Meredith herifi ölmeden saniyeler önce ona teslim etmem gerektiği konusunda sonu gelmez bir nutuk atmıştı. Bu yüzden ona yaklaşırken ve dişlerimi gösterecek şekilde kocaman sağlıksız bir sırıtışla suratına bakarken öldürmemem gerektiğini unutmamaya çalışıyordum.

Öldürme ama ağzını burnunu dağıt piçin. Elimi kaldırıp saldırganın kapüşonuna uzandım. Adam bir küfürle elimden kaçmaya çalışıp geriye atlayınca ben de üzerine yürüdüm. Savurduğu tekme dizime çarpınca içimden kahkahalarla gülmek geçti. Marr'ın bir zamanlar mutfak masamızda elinde tuttuğu çatalı sallarken dediği gibi, "Yemeğinle oynama Cass."

Dizime savurduğu tekmenin ardından yumruklarını hizalayıp aptal küçük zaferinden zevk alan adama baktım. Ardından yüzüne tükürdüm. Bu da benim daha yaratıcı bir küfürle ödüllenmemle sonuçlandı. Eğer Draza gibi zehirli bir dile sahip olsaydım şu an suratında küçük, sevimli, su dolu kabarcıklar oluşurdu. Bunun yerine milyonuncu kez küfür dinliyordum. Sanki bu kulaklar daha fazla küfrü kaldırabilirmiş gibi.

"Bu daha sürecek mi?" Meredith'in sesi sıkılgan geliyordu. Soğuyan hava ile sis bulutu dağılmış, ara cadde gözler önüne serilmişti. Eğer bunu yapacaksam birkaç fazladan gözün önünde yapmam gerekecekti. Kaybedecek bir dakikam daha olmadığı için yumruklarını hizalamış saldırganın üzerine atladım. İki elimle bileklerini tutup karnına tekmemi geçirdim. O da boş durmamaya çalışıp bana kafa atarken tırnaklarımı etine geçirdim.

Sersemlemedim, aksine daha da sinirlendim. Art arda karnına tekmeler atıp iki büklüm bir şekilde geri gitmesini sağlıyor, bir yandan da sağ elimle onun sol elindeki küçük parmağını çekiştiriyordum. Birkaç saniyenin sonunda parmağını kırıp dişlerimi adamın boynuna geçirdim. İğrenç leş gibi bir koku burnuma dolunca geri çekildim. Adamın ağzımdaki iğrenç kanını tükürmeye çalıştım ama metal tat bitmiyordu. "Seni kaçık. Seni kaçık. Seni deli sürtük!" Beni bırakıp elini beceriksizce bastırarak boynunda açtığım yarayı kapamaya çalışıyordu.

"Şimdi onu bana bırak." Meredith yanıma gelirken onu dinlemeden bir kez daha ileri atılıp ayağımla pisliğin dizine vurdum. Kemiğin deriyi yırtan sesi kulaklarıma dolarken memnuniyetle geri çekilip adamın yerde kıvranan bedenine baktım. Meredith onaylayan bir ifadeyle bana baksa da yere oturup çantasından eşyalarını çıkarmaya başladı. "Atar damarını iyi kemirmişsin," dedi adamı üstünkörü incelerken.

Başımı kaldırıp ara sokaktaki binaları taradım. Işığı yanan bir ev görmeme umuduyla göz gezdirirken derin nefesler alıyordum. "Fazla zamanımız yok," dedim hâlâ evleri tararken. Eğer şimdi gücümü yenileyemezse cehenneme dönmem gerekecekti ve tecrübelerime göre cehenneme hemen dönmem işe yaramazdı. Aidanhell'de yaramamıştı. Gerçi o çukurdan sevilesi kardeşi Draza'yı çıkarabilmek için kefaretini ödüyordu. Eğer kara büyü kefareti gerekmiyorsa bir şeytan güçsüz düştüğünde başına ne gelirdi bilemiyordum.

Işıklar açık değildi. Bu kez sokağın tek girişini kontrol ettim. Kimse yoktu. Ellerimle kollarımın tersini sıvazlayarak kardeşimin yanına geldim. "Fazla zamanımız yok derken şaka yapmıyordum." Hani aç olmadığınız hâlde koca bir hamburgeri yedikten sonra üzerinize çöken o ağır his vardır ya, onu binle çarpın.

"Tamam, burada işim bitti. Gel." Elimi tutup beni boynundan hâlâ kanlar akan adamın yanına oturttu. Ben oturunca hızla kalkıp parmaklarını adamın boynundaki yaraya sokup daha fazla kan akıttı. Saniyeler içinde asfaltın üzerinde çevremize bir daire çizmeye başlamıştı. İşini bitirip gelene kadar adamın nabzı azalıyordu. Nihayet oturduğunda saldırgan neredeyse ölmek üzereydi. Bir pentagramın şeytan köşesi olmaya bayılmıyordum ama birazdan canlanacak olmanın verdiği huzur şimdiden beni sarmalamıştı.

Daha fazla zaman, daha çok zaman. Belki bir şeyleri yeniden akla mantığa uydurmak için gereken tek şey zamandı.

Elim hâlâ kız kardeşimin soğuk avucunun içindeyken dizlerimin üzerinde yere çöktüm. Adamın kanı boynundan asfalta akarken kız kardeşim boşta kalan eliyle kanayan yaraya bastırdı. Merr pek çok şey olabilirdi ama bir doktor değildi. "Adamı öldürüyorsun," dedim biraz panikle. Eğer bu adamı ölmeden kullanamazsam mahvolmuştum. Oysa kız kardeşimde azıcık bile panik yoktu.

"Şş," dedi sessizce. Ardından elini çekip bana uzandı. Kanlı işaret parmağıyla alnımı çizerken gözlerimi kırpmadan ona baktım. Bir büyü okuyordu. Şeytan dilinde.

Her şey çok çabuk olmuştu. Bir elma kabuğuna giren bıçak misali pek pürüzsüz bir işlem değildi, acı da veriyordu ama çok çabuk bitmişti. Meredith ruhumu yarıyordu.

Ruhunuzun yarılması, başınıza gelmeden kolayca anlayabileceğiniz bir durum değildi. Hayatımda yaşadığım her acı verici tecrübede daha çoğunun olmayacağına kendimi inandırmıştım. Bunda ölümsüz olmanın da büyük bir payı vardı.

Fakat her zaman unuttuğum bir şey vardı. Ben asla standartlara uyan bir tip değildim. Ölümsüzken bile acı çekebiliyordum. Ruhum olmadığını düşündüğümde bile ruhum yanabiliyordu. Bu yüzden Meredith yanı başımda iki elimi sertçe tutmuş beni zapt etmeye çalışırken çok şaşırmadım. Aklım sadece ve sadece bedenimin içinden geçen o alevlerdeydi.

Alevlerin nereden geldiklerini bilmiyordum. Nerede bittiklerini de bilmiyordum. Alevlerin geçtiği yolu biliyordum. Boğazımdan, kalbimden ve karnımdan geçiyorlardı.

"Gözlerim!" dedim çığlık çığlığa bağırırken. "Yanıyor!" Alevler gözlerime ulaştığında nefes alamıyordum. "Bu neden oluyor?!"

Çığlıklarımın arasından Meredith'in haykırışlarını duyabiliyordum. "O ölmemiş. Ruh kopmamış. Tanrım, Cass hâlâ burada! Ve artık fiziki boyutta yer almıyor. Onu öldürmem lazım. DAYAN!"

Alevler yavaşça sönükleşip yerlerini öldürücü bir soğuğa bırakırken bir kez daha bağırdım. Meredith'in saldırganı öldürmek için yaptığı her hamle canımı yakıyordu. Ruhlarımızın bağlı olduğunu hissedebiliyordum. O adama yaptığı tüm işkenceler benim de bedenimde gezinirken acıdan aklımı kaçırmamaya çalışıyordum.

Aşk, iyi ya da kötü değildir.

Aşk, kaderdir.

Bir kalp atışı süresinde gözlerim hafifçe açıldı.

Aşk, kaderdir.

Gözlerim aralanırken bakışlarım ayaklarımın altındaki saldırgandan, onun başında kan ter içinde büyü yapan kızıl saçlı cadıdan çok uzaklara kaydı.

Bakışlarım orada duran ama asla orada olamayacak olan tek şeye takılmıştı.

Sadece bir an için bedenimdeki tüm acıları görmezden gelip yutkunarak ona baktım. Bir ışık huzmesi havada süzülerek yavaşça zemine inerken artık yutkunamıyordum.

Işık havada spiral oluşturarak üzerime doğru gelirken gözlerim yanmaya devam ediyordu. Artık acı hissedebildiğimden emin değildim.

Meredith saldırganı doğrarken yüzüme sıçrayan kanları önemsemedim. Havada metalik koku, rüzgârla yüzüme yapışan kanlı kâküllerim, bedenimi açıp içine kor atılmış gibi hissettiren acım… Hepsi durmuştu. Tek gerçeklik oradaydı.

Ve üzerime geliyordu.

Işık havada yayılıp saldırganın bedenine girerken bir koku benliğime çarptı.

Aşk kaderdir.

Gözyaşlarım gözlerimi yakarken nefes alamadım. Dudağımı ısırıyordum. Kan dudağımdan akıp yere düşüyordu.

Ağlıyordum.

Ağlıyordum.

Aşk bir kaderdir.

İyi ya da kötü değildir.

Işık adamın bedenine girip kaybolana dek ona baktım. Görüntü yaşlardan bulanıklaşıncaya kadar gözlerimi kırpmadım. Nefes almadım. Sadece ağladım.

Birkaç dakika sonrasında hâlâ ağlıyordum. Meredith tereddütle omzuma dokunduğunda dönüp ona bakmadım. Elinin tersiyle burnumun üzerindeki kanları silerken de ona bakmadım. "Adam öldü. Ona ne olduğunu bilmiyorum. Ruhu bir anda kayboldu. Sanki alınıp götürüldü. Sanki… Sanki…"

"Sanki ölüm meleği alıp götürdü gibi mi?" dedim çatallaşan sesimle. Bunun üzerine Meredith ellerimi tutarak karşıma geçti. Onu görmek istiyordum ama gözlerim hâlâ ışığın az önce dalgalandığı yerdeydi. Hâlâ o kokuyu düşünüyordum.

"Cass, ne oldu?"

Ona baktım. Dehşete kapılmıştı. Pislik içindeydi, acınası bir hâldeydi. Benden daha iyi durumda olabilirdi. "Onu gördüm," dedim sessizce.

Beslenmediğim için vücudumun tükenişini hissedebiliyordum. Hayatım damarlarımdan çekilip gidiyordu. Ama gidemezdim! Onu şimdi bulmuşken gidemezdim! Kanlı bir öksürük ciğerimi yakarken başımı sağa sola salladım. "Olmaz olmaz olmaz, zamanı değil! Başkasını bulalım. Burada kalmam lazım."

Meredith anlamıyordu. "Zamanımız kalmadı, birini bulabilmek günlerimizi alır. Günlerin değil saatlerin bile yok."

"Hayır!" Dişlerimi sıkıp ağzımdaki ılık kanı yere tükürdüm. "Onu kaybetmeyeceğim!" Meredith'in görüntüsü tiyatro sonlarında kapanan perdeler gibi siyah bölmelere ayrılırken ayakta kalmaya çalıştım. "Olmaz, kaybedemem." Beni sarsıyordu, belimi tutuyor saçlarımı yüzümden çekiyordu. "Sakin ol. Kimden bahsediyorsun? Halüsinasyon görüyorsun. Sakin ol."

Ve o an idrak ettiğim gerçekle kalbim sancılandı. Gözyaşlarım yeniden yanaklarıma akarken ayakta durma yetimi kaybettim. Haykırmak istiyordum! Bu diyarı yakmak istiyordum ama onun yerine tek yaptığım ellerimle beceriksizce Meredith'e sarılmaktı. "Onu gördüğümü sandım. Aidanhell'i gördüğümü sandım. O… O, melek olmuştu. Onun gibi kokuyordu."

Kız kardeşim saçımı okşarken bana daha sıkı sarıldı.

"Ama o olamaz. Çünkü o yok. Çünkü ben asla onu hak edemem. Çünkü ben aşağılık bir varlığım, o ise bir melek." Hıçkırıklar boğazımı yakarken bir kez daha gözyaşlarımın akmasına izin verdim. "Onu gördüğümü sandım."

Ve kötülük bir kez daha kazanmıştı. Şeytan hilekârdı. Kendi kendimi kandırmıştım.

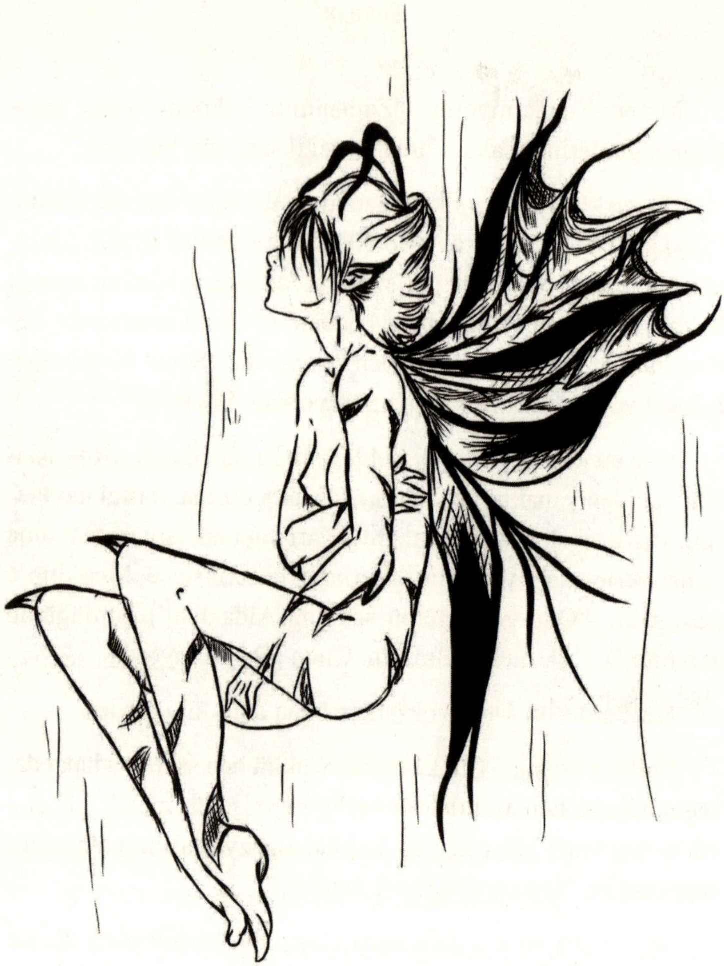

"Ve sonunda karanlık bile
beraberinde getirdiği gölgeleriyle
gizleyemediği her günah için
af diledi."

BÖLÜM 4

Draza

Tüm hayatım boyunca başıma birden fazla imkânsız olay gelmişti.

İlk olarak bir cadıya âşık olmuştum. Ki bu sanırım tüm yaşadıklarım içinde en imkânsız ve akla uymayanıydı. İkinci olarak kara elfe dönüşmüştüm ve Tanrı biliyor ya artık sevmediğimi iki sivri kulağım vardı. Sonra ise ölmüştüm.

Gerçi içinde bulunduğum durum göz önüne alınırsa belki de ölüm benim için kısa bir tatildi. İçinde bulunduğum konumdan kastım ise yeniden dirilip bir strigoiye bebek bakıcısı olmaktı.

"Bak, o sikik hayatın umurumda sanıyorsun, değil mi?" Bok kokulu zindana yaklaşıp ellerimle paslı demir parmaklıkları tuttum. Biraz daha yaklaşarak strigoinin bakışlarımı görmesini istiyordum. Ama o benden tarafa bakmıyordu bile. Bu yüzden gözlerimi devirerek bir kez daha denedim. "Cassie'ye sana bakacağıma söz verdim."

Zindanda ufak bir hareketlenme olunca doğrulup birazcık geriledim. İblisçe hareket etmişti. Tam olarak söylemek gerekirse kirden keçeleşmiş saçları başının yukarı doğru süzülmesiyle havalanmıştı. Ve bu zindanın içinden daha fazla bok kokusu gelmesi dışında hiçbir şey sağlamadı. "Pek söz tutan birine benzemiyorsun."

"Şuursuzca kıç emen bir vampir mi söylüyor bunu?" Parmaklarımı soğuk demirlerden çekip avuç içlerimi üzerime sildim. "Bak," dedim milyonuncu kez sabrım tükenirken. "Burayı sevmiyorsun. Yarasalarla arkadaşlık etmek hoşuna gitmiyor olsa gerek. Sana benim neyin hoşuma gitmediğini söyleyeyim." Kaşlarımı çatarak ona döndüm. "Saraydaki tüm gardiyanları gebertmen." Bunun üzerine Aloha başını hafifçe sağa yatırıp tuhaf tuhaf bana baktı.

Varlığının kimyasını sorguluyor gibiydim, kabul ama zaten adam sıkıntısı yaşadığımız boktan bir zamandaydık. "Whydar'dan aldığım geri zekâlı kurtların sana yem olmaktan daha kutsal bir görevleri vardı." Ve iblisçe sırıttı. Aramızdaki iki metre mesafeye rağmen dişlerinin kızıllığını ve dudaklarındaki kurumuş yara kabuklarını görebiliyordum. "Vekil kral kutsallık hakkında ne biliyor? Sen ve senin soylu kıçından emir almıyorum."

Sorun da buydu. O, hiçbir şeyden emir almıyordu. Herhangi bir vampir topluluğun üyesi falan da değildi. Sadece var olmuştu ve onu öldürmemem gerekiyordu, söz vermiştim.

"Söz verdiğim kişiye borçluyum," dedim somurtarak. Cassandra su katılmamış bir salak olmasaydı bu tahta sahip olamazdım. Tüm yetkilerinden vazgeçip dünyaya gitmeseydi şu an Aloha'nın söylediği gibi soylu kıçım demir tahtta yayılmazdı. "Tam olarak üç kurt adam ve beş tane peri öldürdün."

"Altı."

Bir şeyler mırıldanmıştı. "Ne dedin?"

"Altı tane peri öldürdüm." Ayağa kalkarken zindandaki lavabonun kenarına tutundu. "Ve için rahat olsun, bu sadece başlangıç."

Bana doğru yaklaşırken gözlerindeki ölümcül parlaklık heyecanlanmama sebep oldu. Henüz çukura atılmadan önceki ruh hastası zamanlarıma benziyordu. Onda kendimi görmüştüm.

İblisçe bana daha da yaklaşırken göz ucuyla koridorun sonundaki bir çift zindana baktım. "Sıkıldığını biliyorum," dedim yeniden ona dönerken. "Şu tarafta eski dostun Ahmet var."

İblisçenin az önce parlayan gözleri tereddütle donuklaşırken parmaklıklardan yarım metre daha uzaklaştım. "Rohan burada mı?" Başımla onayladım. "Kuzeye bakan zindanda uyukluyor olmalı. Eğer cici bir vampir olursan ona sağladığım bazı imtiyazları sana da sağlarım."

Bunun üzerine vampir kahkaha atarmış gibi ağzını açtı ama çıkan ses daha çok boğulan bir gergedandan geliyor gibiydi. "Aidan sana sik kafalı derken yanılmıyormuş. Sen gerçekten tanıdığım en boş şeysin. Ayrıca ne olduğun da belli değil, o kulaklar ne öyle?"

Kirden kararmış işaret parmağını kulaklarıma doğrultunca kaşlarımı çattım. "İblisler dünyasının son modası. Ama şimdi yeni bir şey var. Herkes kıçına kuyruk taktırıyor. Eğer çeneni kapatmazsan senin üzerinde denerim."

Aloha teslim olurmuş gibi ellerini kaldırarak ağır adımlarla parmaklıklara yaklaştı. "Buraya gelip konuşmak isteyen sensin." Keçeleşmiş kahverengi dalgalı saçları sağ gözünü kapatmıştı. "Geliyor, küfrediyor ve gidiyorsun. Benden ne istiyorsun?" Aramızda kalan yarım metre boyunca ağzındaki leş kokusu havada süzülüyordu. Kurt adamların siyah kanı dudaklarını ve göğsünü boyamıştı. Ona büyükbaş hayvanlar getirmiştik ama o hiçbirini istememişti. Doğaüstü kanı konusunda saplantılı bir tutumu vardı.

"Senden bir değil birkaç şey istiyorum."

İblisçenin gözleri şaşkınlıkla irileşince söyleyeceklerimi bir kez daha düşündüm. Belki de onu dünyaya göndermek iyi bir fikir değildi.

"Bu zindandan çıkmak istediğini biliyorum ve sana istediğini vereceğim. Ama karşılığında casusum olacaksın. Tabii önce birkaç gün seni gözlemlemem gerekiyor." Derin bir nefes verip ekledim. "Yani artık benimsin."

Deli vampir boğulur gibi bir ses çıkarıp gülmeye başladı. Birkaç saniye güldükten sonra elleriyle gözlerindeki yaşları silip, "Ben kızlardan hoşlanıyorum," dedi. Başımı yan çevirip aptal suratına bakarken ekledi. "Yani erkeklerle bir sorunum olduğundan değil. Gerçi şu aralar sekste de gözüm yok. Sadece öldürmekle ilgileniyorum."

Gözlerime baktı. "Senin şu avcı kızı öldürmemi istiyorsan o zaman başka tabii."

"Ne saçmalıyorsun sen?" Zindanlardan bir adım uzaklaştım. Uzun saatler uyumayınca insan diyalogları kafasına göre kurguluyordu herhâlde. Aksi takdirde kaçık iblisçenin bana böyle bir şey diyemeyeceğini biliyordum. "Ne avcısı?"

Ama iblisçe gülüyordu. "Sarışın olan. Şu seni çukurun dibine yollayan. Ama hakkını vermek lazım, esaslı kızmış. Senin o soylu kıçını şeytanların cehennemine göndermek cesaret ister."

Ben yanıt veremeyince ekledi. "Ben bir vampirin kötü hâli değilim, iblis. Ben bir vampirin evrimleşmiş hâliyim. Düşünceleri duyabilirim." Kırmızı derin kor rengi gözleriyle gözlerime baktı. "Bir iblisin içini okuyabilirim." Bunu bilmediğim için kafamı taş duvarlara vurmak istiyordum. Cehaletimi çaktırmamak için kaşlarımı daha da çatıp kollarımı göğsümde birleştirdim.

"Hımm evet," dedim anlamsızca.

Bunun üzerine iblisçe gülümsedi. "Bana vampirlerin tanrısı diyebilirsin sevgili Draza ve artık senin hizmetkârınım."

***

Sonunda kafayı sıyırıyor olduğum gerçeği içimde kahkahalarla gülme isteği uyandırıyordu. Sonunda gerçekten sıyırmıştım ve bu konuda ne çokbilmiş periler, ne destansı cadılar ne de herhangi bir doğaüstü psikolog bir şey yapabilirdi. Kafayı yemişliğimle kimse ilgilenemezdi.

"Acaba ben mi kafayı daha çok yedim yoksa Aloha mı?"

Odada tek başınaydım. Komikti. Her şey komikti. Bu kez kendimi bırakıp kahkahalarla güldüm. Düşündükçe daha komik olduğuna karar veriyordum. "Bir boka yaramıyorum," dedim kahkahalarımın arasından. Ailemi koruyamadım, kardeşimi... En yakın arkadaşımı.... Sevdiğim adamı.

"Ben ne boka yarıyorum?"

Uğruna kehanet yazılacak bir insan değildim. Bir ucubeydim. Bir ucube kraliçesi. Ve şimdi deliliğim artık halüsinasyon görmemle yeni bir boyut kazanmıştı. Artık reddedilemez bir şekilde deliydim.

"İnsanları korkutuyorsun." Meredith kapıyı tekmeleyerek açıp elindeki tepsiyle içeri girdi. Kızıl kirli saçlarını başının tepesinde toplamıştı.

"İnsanları korkutmamdan hoşlanacağını düşündüm." Bunun üzerine kardeşim omuz silkerek yatağıma oturdu. Tepsiyi bacağımın yanına koyarken konuşmaya başladı. "Benim için sakıncası yok. Max müşteriler kaçıp giderse Cassie'nin yara bantlarını nasıl alacağız tribine girdi. Yani insanları kaçırma. Bazılarımızın hâlâ para kazanması lazım."

Doğru duyup duymadığımdan emin değildim. "Bazılarından kastın senin dışındaki beş milyar insan herhâlde." Bunun üzerine kız kardeşim tepki vermeden gömleğimin eteklerini tuttu. Yukarı kaldırıp katlarken canım yanıyordu. Karnımdaki yarayı açıkta bırakıp tepsideki şişeyi aldı.

"Senden iyi hemşire olurmuş." Şişeyi karnıma boca etti. Canımın yanması artık nefes almak kadar alışıldık gelmeye başlamıştı. Bu yüzden sadece dişlerimi sıkıp karnımı bükerek pamuğu yarama sürmesini bekledim.

"Kendi karnını parçalarken ne düşünüyordun?" Pamuğu tırnaklarımla açtığım yaraların üzerinde gezdirirken dişlerimi daha da sıktım. "Zevkine canımı yakma Meredith. Hadi bırak artık." Eline uzandığım sırada gözlerini devirerek pamuğu karnımdan çekti.

Hatırlamıyordum. Kendi bedenimi neden parçaladığım hakkında bir fikrim yoktu. "Belki de sonunda delirdim. Aloha'dan mikrop kapmış da olabilirim. Tam bir strigoi gibi davranıyorum."

Meredith inanamayarak bana baktı. Elleriyle gömleğimi yeniden kapatırken belli belirsiz gülümsüyordu. "Strigoilik bulaşabilecek bir hastalık değil."

"Hmm. Oysa yüzüme hapşırdığından emindim. Yani düşünsene o devasa heriften kocaman bir mikrop yüzüme yapışmış olabilir."

Max, kız kardeşimin açık bıraktığı kapıdan girerken, "Kim hapşırdı?" diye soruyordu. Ardından ayakucuma geldiğinde durdu. İri mavi gözlerinin daha da büyümesini izledim. "Ne oldu size?" Kız kardeşim önce esneyip ardından sırtı tutulmuş gibi kürek kemiklerini esnetti. Ben ise sadece baktım.

Sessizlik devam ederse Max'in kafayı yiyeceğinden korktum ve yanıt vereye karar verdim. "Ben delirdim ama onun ne yaptığını bilmiyorum." Meredith ters ters bana bakıp ayağa kalktı. "Birini öldüremedik. Ne olduğunu bilmiyoruz."

Aslında çok minik bir parçamın ne olduğuyla ilgili bir fikri vardı. Derin bir nefes alıp onlara bundan bahsetmek için dudaklarımı araladım. Oysa ben konuşamadan Merr araya girdi. "Herif önümüzdeydi fakat Cassie tam o an durdu." Konuşmasını hızla kesip benim az önceki hâlimi taklit etti.

Max sırıtırken Meredith taklidine devam etti. Gözlerimi kısarak ona baktım. Pekâlâ, sopa yutmuş gibi dikilmediğimi biliyordum. "Orada," dedim devamını nasıl getireceğimi bilmediğimden susarak. "Orada başka bir şey oldu."

Meredith duymazlıktan gelip kollarını göğsünde kavuşturdu. "Bir dahaki sefere bu kadar şanslı olmayacağız." Bahsettiği şeyin şansla en ufak bir ilgisi yoktu.

Yatakta geriye sürünüp hafifçe doğrularak sırtımı Max'in eski yatak başlığına yasladım. Bir süredir o ânı düşünüp tartıyordum. Gücümü toplamak için geçen saatlerim boyunca bunu onlara anlatabilmenin yollarını aramıştım. Olası tüm senaryolar acınası bir şekilde bitiyordu. Yani sonuçta şey diyemezdim,

"Hani bir daha asla göremeyeceğim yakışıklı melek var ya, hah işte orada göründü ve bana selam çaktı."

Semavi varlıklara bulaşmak mı? Daha neler Cassie!

Düşüncelere öylesine dalmıştım ki Max'in yanıma gelip oturduğunu fark edememiştim. Kalçasıyla ayrık bacaklarımı ittirerek kendine yer açmıştı. Mavi gözleri yüzümde şüpheyle gezinirken konuştu. "Bizden bir şey saklıyorsun."

Vay canına!

Hiçbir şey söylemedim. Bir şeytanla uğraşmaları yeterince zorken bir de deli bir şeytanla uğraşmalarını istemiyordum. "Draza'dan haber var mı?" diye sordum bakışlarımı onlardan kaçırıp. Ama kız kardeşim attığım yemi yemedi.

O bilmiş, meraklı insanı fıtık eden iri parlak gözlerini üzerime dikti. "En son bir şey sakladığında sonunda kendini kafeste bulmuştun. Sence benden bir şey saklamak akıllıca mı?"

Omuz silktim. Muhtemelen değildi.

"Gerçekten dinlenmek istiyorum ben aslında…"

Meredith diretiyordu. Bu kez konuştuğunda sesi fısıltıdan ibaretti. "Eğer bir şey saklıyorsan yemin ederim…" Sonraki kısmı Max'in duymadığına sevinmiştim. Meredith bazen ağzı bozuk çatlak bir cadıya dönüşüyordu. "Bir kız varmış," dedi cebinden ekranı kırık telefonunu çıkarırken. Benimle konuşurken tuş kilidindeki şifresini giriyordu. "O da bir cadı ama bizim gibi değil. Zebanileri duydun mu?"

Başımı olumsuz anlamda salladım.

Gözlerini devirirken söylendi. "Önceki hayatında avcı yerine bir su samuru olmadığına emin misin? Max bile senden daha bilgili." Max uyarıcı olacağını düşündüğü çimdiği Merr yerine benim bacağıma yapınca çığlığı bastım. Hızlıca özür dilerken eliyle çimdiklediği yeri ovuyordu. Cehennemden uzaklaştıkça güçsüzleşiyordum ve bu artık beni bayağı sinirlendiriyordu.

"Cehennemde cadılar vardı Cass. Onlar kötü ruhları cezalandırır, onlarla beslenirler. O cadılar insanlara baktıklarında günahlarını görürlcr." İlgimi ekmişti. Yani hâlâ bunun benim şu an sönmekte olan yaşam enerjime nasıl bir fayda sağlayacağını bilmiyordum ama dinlemeye devam ettim.

Meredith ekranda bulduğu resmi yakınlaştırıp kırık telefonunu karnıma bıraktı. Telefonu kaldırıp objektife yansıyan, gözleri gümüş renkteki kıza baktım. "Tuhaf görünüyor."

Meredith telefonu geri alıp Max'e uzatırken sırıtıyordu. "Öyle. Onlardan pek fazla yok, başka bir gezegenden geldiler. Neyse, bu kız şu an başka bir eyalette ama onu bulabilirim. Üstleriyle konuşup buraya gelmesini sağlayacağım. Bizim için gerçekten günahkâr birkaç insan bulabilir."

Dudaklarımı yanıt vermek için aralayıp hemen kapattım çünkü Max neşeli kahkahalar atmaya başlamıştı. "Bu kızıl popo her durumdan nasıl kurtulacağını gayet iyi biliyor." Bakımlı parmaklarıyla Merr'in yanağından makas aldı. "Eğer kız kardeşin olmasaydı çoktan bir rögar kapağının altını boylamıştın kızım." İrkildiğimi belli etmemeye çalıştım. İnsan tam zamanlı bir şeytana dönüştükten sonra kimseye ihtiyacı kalmayacağını düşünürdü ama işte buradayım. Kollarımda yaralar, ağzımda bitmcyen bir metal tadı ve çevremde iki endişeli dost.

Gerçi Meredith dost değildi. Aslında... İnsan da değildi.

"Neden devamlı içinden bana sayıyormuşsun gibi hissediyorum?" Neredeyse öksürecektim. Meredith gözlerini kısmış şüpheyle bana bakıyordu. "Öyle değil," dedim hemen. "Yani her zaman değil. Tamam, hadi artık gidin." Max itiraz edecek gibi olduysa da Meredith onun koluna yapışıp yatağımın ayak ucundan kaldırdı.

Onlar gittikten çok sonra bile bugünü düşünüyordum. Bir serap görmüştüm. Bu adil değildi. Umudun artık dünyamda daha fazla yer tutmayacağını düşünmüştüm. Umut etmeyi bırakmıştım. O hâlde bu içimde filizlenen aptal şey neydi?

Tuttuğum nefesimi bırakıp sıkıcı tavanı incelemeye devam ettim.

Düşünüyordum da keşke o dev beni yeseydi. Belki o gün orada beni yese ya da çiftleşse ve ben de huzur içinde ölseydim. İşte o zaman bu olanlar hiç yaşanmayacaktı.

Hiç meleze dönüşmeyecek, şeytan olmayacak, sevdiklerimi tehlikeye atmayacak, can almayacak ve âşık olmayacaktım.

Kalbimdeki sızı dediklerimi onaylarcasına şiddetini arttırdı. Acaba o devi geri bulmakta çok mu geç kalmıştım?

"Aman be, sikerler." Kolumla gözlerimi kapatıp içimde fokurdayan dayanılmaz acıya rağmen uyumaya çalıştım.

❋❋❋

Max'in rutubet kokan banyosunda duş alıyordum. Alnımı buharlı fayansa koyup sıcak suyun altında iyice kendini bırakan yarama dokundum. Kendi kendini parçalamak hakkında ne derler bilirsiniz. Sonunda canınız çok yanar, tecrübeyle sabit.

Parmaklarımı henüz minik kabuklar bağlamış yaramdan çekip kafamda gezdirdim. Su faturası ya da o tarz fani bir gereksizlik yüzünden haftanın her günü yıkanamıyorduk. Bugün banyo günümüzdü. Bir dünyanın kraliçesiyken diğer dünyanın hiçbir şeyi olabiliyordum. Öte yandan Meredirth her iki dünyada da işini halletmenin yolunu daima bulurdu.

Banyonun dışından sesler gelince bıkkınlıkla nefesimi bıraktım. Suyu kapatırken sessizce sövmeye başlamıştım. Banyo keyfi buraya kadardı işte.

"Umarım havlunu yanına almışsındır. Misafirimiz var." Kapının diğer ucundan kız kardeşimin boğuk sesi geliyordu. Saçlarımdaki suyu sıkıp kabinden çıktım. Aynaya bakmadan havluyu alıp bedenime sardım. Bir saniye sonra kapıyı açmıştım.

Meredith kızı getirmişti.

Kız da kızdı hani. Açık, altın sarısı parlak saçları, resimdeki gibi olmayan mavi gözleri ve kâğıt gibi beyaz teniyle ilgi çekiciydi. Boyunun benden biraz uzun oluşuna anında gıcık olmuştum. Bir şey demeden yanlarına gittim.

"Bu bahsettiğim kız, Misha."

Genç cadı elini uzatınca ıslak avuçlarıma rağmen sıktım. "Kız kardeşim olayı anlatmıştır," dedim yanlarından ayrılıp diğer odaya geçerken.

Üstümü değiştirdikten sonra yanlarına döndüm. Cadı, mavi gözlerini merakla üzerimde gezdirdi. Ben de ona bakıyordum. Bir saniye sonra ise göz gözeydik. Ve ben, o an insan olmadığını net olarak anlamış oldum. Göz bebeklerinin hemen yanında kırmızı haleler vardı. Ve o haleler canlıymış gibi hareket ediyorlardı.

"Çok dikkatli bakmasan daha iyi olur," dedi kız cılız bir sesle. Bunun üzerine gözlerimi kırpıştırdım. Kız gözlerini kapatıp dudaklarını belirli belirsiz kıpırdatacak şekilde bir şeyler fısıldadı. Ardından koyu kahve kirpiklerinin gölgelediği gözlerini açtı. Artık tıpkı resimdeki gibi bakıyordu.

"Vay anasını!" Omzumun üzerinden Meredith'e baktım. Kayıtsız bir şekilde omuz silkip cadıya döndü. "Gözlerin bu şekilde olduğu zaman günahkârları görebiliyorsun değil mi?" Cadı sessizce başını salladı. Bakışları tuhaf bir şekilde hâlâ üzerimdeydi.

Dikkatini çeken şeyin ne olduğunu anlamaya çalışırken bakışlarım kardeşimle cadı arasında gidip geldi. Misha, kız kardeşime bakmıyordu. Anlaşılan ona tek tuhaf gelen bendim.

Zebani bile beni gördüğünde garipsiyordu. Kız, omzuna astığı maun rengi çantasını ayaklarının dibine bırakıp gözlerinin önüne gelen saçlarını kulaklarının arkasına sıkıştırdı. "Normalde insanların günahlarını görürüm." Eliyle havada hayali bir daire çizdi. "Tam bu şekilde ince televizyonlar gibi görünürler." Meredith'e kaçamak bir bakış atınca onun da bana bakmakta olduğunu fark ettim.

Aynı şeyi düşünüyorduk. Vah vah! Hayat onun için çekilmez olmalıydı, gerçi ben kimdim de böyle bir yargıya varabiliyordum? Cadı bizden bir ses çıkmayınca devam etti. "Çoğu günahkârı bu şekilde buluyorum. Ama sende bu günah hololarından yok."

Bir an için şaşırdım. Ardından çenemle kız kardeşimi işaret ettim. "Ya onunkileri görüyor musun?" Cadı olumlu anlamda başını salladı.

Tüm ölümsüz yaşantısı boyunca Meredith'i utandıran herhangi bir şey olmadığına emindim. Ama bu kez kız kardeşim kızarmıştı. Tabii ona bunu sorarsanız size çilleriyle ilgili bir şeyler saçmalardı ama ben sebebini anlamıştım.

Ağrıyan karnıma rağmen sırıttım. "Hey, morardın! Misha eğer senin gelmiş geçmiş tüm günahlarını görüyorsa başı dönmüş olmalı."

Meredith bir an irkilir gibi oldu. "Sen kendinle ilgilen." Bakışları keskin bir şekilde karnıma kaydı. Göğsünde birleştirdiği kollarını çözüp, "Pansuman zamanın mı geldi?" diye sorarak bana doğru yaklaştı. O endişeli bir şekilde hareket ederken Misha bir adım geri çekildi.

Elimle bana gelişini durdurdum. "Gerek yok, birkaç saat daha idare edebilir."

Kız kardeşim emin olamazmış gibi yarama baktı. "O iyi. Ama birini bulmazsak kötü olacak."

"Haklı," dedim atletimi indirirken. Pamuğun dışına kan sızmadığı için iyi olduğumu düşünüyordum. Hemşirelik becerilerim avcılık yeteneklerimle kıyaslanamazdı, felakettim.

Aslında şeytan olan bir şeytan avcısı olduğumu düşünürsek hangi meslekte daha kötü olduğumu bilmiyordum. Olabileceğim her şeyin en kötüsüydüm herhâlde.

Platin saçlı cadı bileğini ters çevirip başparmağının hemen altındaki damarlarına dokundu. Önce sağdan sola, ardından yukarıdan aşağı bir artı işareti çizdi. Bir saniye sonra bileğinin yaklaşık on santim üzerinde beyaz-mavi bir görüntü titreşti.

Gördüğüm şeyi ifade etmem gerekirse... Eh nasıl ifade edeceğimi bilmiyordum. Ama Misha neye baktığından son derece emindi. Sonrasında konuşmaya başladı. Bu şu çok sevdiğiniz hit yabancı şarkıların nakarat kısmındaki anlamsız sözlere benziyordu.

"Latin büyüsü," dedi kız kardeşim yanıma sokulurken.

Gözlerinde gördüğüm şeyin kıskançlık olduğunu fark edince sırıtmaktan kendimi alamadım. "Onun büyülerini bilmediğini söyleme bana." Kız kardeşimin yeşil gözlerinde bir ışık titreşti. "Seninle ilk karşılaştığımızda Draza bir cadıya büyü yapmanı istemişti ve o büyü Latinceydi." Meredith'in gözlerinde gördüğüm ışık kendini karanlığa bırakırken kız kardeşim elleriyle önüne düşen saçları kulaklarının arkasına tıktı. Aura görüşüm için odaklanmak üzere nefesimi tutup ona baktım. Aurası üzüntü doluydu.

Bu ani değişiklik bende olmasını beklemediğim bir farkındalık yarattı. "Bunu konuşacağız," dedim tırnağı boğuşurken kopmuş işaret parmağımla havada anlamsız bir hareketle onu işaret ederek. Başıyla sessizce onayladı ama gözleri ve aklı hâlâ benden uzaktaydı.

"Hadi başlayalım." Misha ağır bir hareketle havayı yararken kendimi yaptığımız şeye odaklamaya çalıştım. Ama cadı etrafında şiddetli bir rüzgâr estirince bu mümkün olamadı. Havada çırpınan kâküllerim deli gibi gözlerime çarparken bir adım geriledim.

Misha'nın platin sarısı saçları tutamlar hâlinde havalanıp renklerini siyaha bürümeye başladılar. Bir an sonra rüzgârın şiddeti azalmaya başladı. Alnımın önüne siper ettiğim elimi indirip ondaki değişimi daha iyi görmeye çalıştım.

Karşımdaki kız artık o değildi. Siyah saçlı, gümüş renginde ürkütücü gözlü ve birkaç yaş daha büyük bir versiyonuydu. İçimdeki bir ses ondaki değişikliklerin sadece fiziksel olmadığını söylüyordu.

Nitekim Meredith arkamdan yaklaşıp uzun parmaklarıyla koluma yapıştığında bir şeylerin beklenildiği gibi olmadığını anlamıştım. "Şimdi dikkatli ol Cass. Artık bilinmeyen topraklardayız." İçimden dediklerini tekrar ederken cümlenin saçmalığını düşündüm. *Bilmediğim ne kaldıysa artık.*

Genç kız uzun ince kollarını bedenine sarıp hafifçe gerindi. "Ahh, dünya gibisi yok," dedi karanlık, yapışkan bir eko bırakan ses. Cadı kollarını yavaşça çözüp yüzünü kaplayan siyah saçlarını omuzlarının arkasına attı. "Ah Majeste, ne büyük onur!"

Meredith ile birbirimize baktık.

"Sen iyi misin?" dedim temkinli bir şekilde cadıya yaklaşırken. Ama Meredith tişörtümün arkasından tutup beni geri çekti.

Cadının iri gümüşi gözleri bu küçük hareketliliği fark edince zekâyla parıldadılar. Ah evet, ilkel olabilirdi ama aptal değildi. Keşke aptal olsaydı. Nedense tanıştığım her varlık benden daha zeki gibi geliyordu.

Cadı ben ona yaklaşmayınca bana doğru hamle yaptı. Dostane ya da düşmanca değildi.

"Bücür beni pek sık çağırmaz."

"Bücür?" Cadının bakışları salisenin onda biri gibi bir zamanda önce karardı sonra tekrar berraklaştı. "Sarı saçlı cadı. Misha. Ben isim kullanmayı doğru bulmuyorum ama o Misha adını kullanmakta ısrarcı."

Şüphelerimde haklıydım. O Misha'nın bedeninde yaşayan misafir bir cadıydı. Ben henüz bunları düşünmeye başlamışken cadı histerik bir kahkaha attı. "Misha'nın bedeninde ondan önce ben vardım. O ve ben biriz." Pekâlâ, hâlâ deli insanları ayırt edebiliyorsam demek ki ben deli değildim. Yani bu varsayımımın tek dayanağı deliliğin dereceleri olmadığıydı.

Cadı elime uzanıp parmaklarımı porselen rengi, soğuk avucunun içine aldı. "Beslenmemiz lazım." Gözlerini kapatıp gülümsedi. "Bu şehrin karanlık sokaklarında çok fazla günahkâr var."

Bana fazlası değil, sadece bir tanesi lazımdı. Ona bunu aynen ilettim.

Bunun üzerine cadı gözlerini kapatıp tekrar Latince fısıldadı. Bu dil eski cadıların diliydi. İlk cadılar şifacıydı. Günümüzde tıp terimlerinin Latince oluşunun da sebebi buydu, gerçi bunu faniler pek bilmiyordu. Peh, onlar birçok şeyi bilmiyordu zaten.

Karnımdaki acıyı görmezden gelmeye çalışırken dudaklarımı ısırdım. Dünyada sadece öldürebilir olmuyorduk. Acı da çekiyorduk. Ki bu cehennemde hüküm sürdüğüm geçtiğimiz aylar boyunca hiç olmayan bir şeydi. İnsan olmaktan vazgeçtiğim gün, acı çekmeyi de bırakmıştım.

Cadı bir gözünü açıp bana baktı. Eğer bir insan olsaydım şu an bütünüyle tüylerim diken diken olurdu. "Henüz uyanışın gerçekleşmemiş." Kılımı kıpırdatmadım. Kastettiği şeyi biliyordum, Lilith söylemişti.

Benim küçük güzel kâhinim, melekliğinden vazgeçmiş olabilirsin ama benliğini kucaklamazsan kalan yarına da sahip çıkamayacaksın. Bir şeytan olmak sandığın kadar kötü değil.

Anının verdiği tiksinti duygusu ile yerimde rahatsızca kıpırdandım. Tabii ya, şeytan olmanın nesi kötü olabilirdi ki?

"Birini öldürüp uyanmak gibi bir şey bu sefer," dedi ortak dilde. Ardından uyuz bir gülümseme ile yaptığı işe döndü. Arkamda bir yerlerde Merr'in kaskatı kesildiğini hissedebiliyordum. Ama şu an daha önemli işlerimiz vardı.

"Birini buldum. Billhouse hastanesine gitmeliyiz." Yatağımın yanına gidip komodinin dibine bıraktığım siyah sırt çantamı aldım. Yatağımın altındaki hançerimi de fermuarını açtığım çantanın içine attım.

Meredith ise kredi kartını bulamadığı için hayıflanıyordu. Kendi çantasını takan Misha'ya bakarken Meredith'e kızdım. "Kredi kartını ne yapacaksın?"

"Çikolatalı keklerden alacağım." Yemin ediyorum cadı bile bir an ona baktı. Ben ise masa lambamı alıp kız kardeşimin kafasına geçirsem yine de savaşabilir mi diye düşünüyordum.

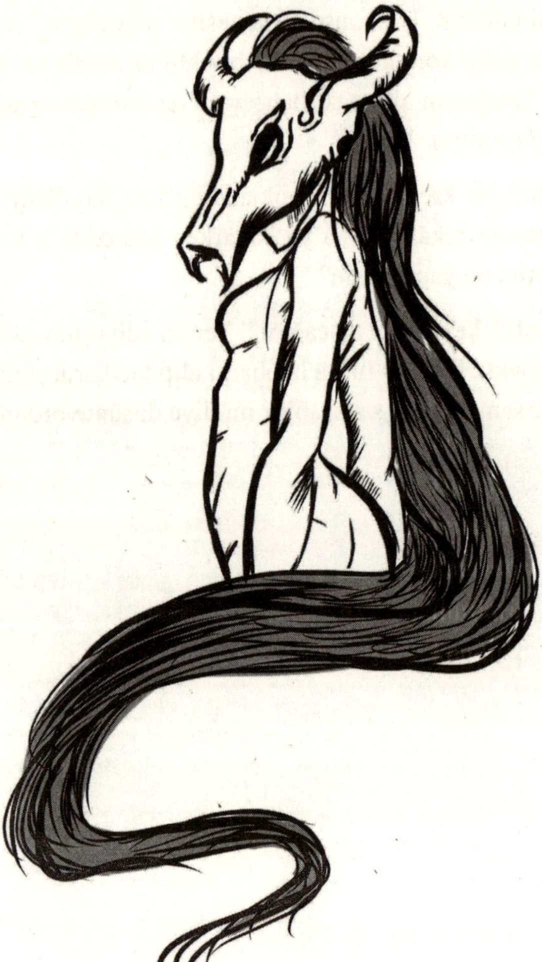

"Şeytan hilekârdır.
Sözleri kalbinizi zehirler."

BÖLÜM 5

2 AY ÖNCE

Beyaz bir kar tanesi zarifçe havada süzülüyordu. Dairesel hareketlerle gökyüzünde yüzerken hiçbir şey ona engel olamıyordu.

Öyle özgür ve güzeldi ki... O minicik hâli ile dokunulmazdı.

Kar tanesi havada süzülüp rotasında ilerlerken saklandığım gölgelerden çıkıp göğe baktım. Ona ulaşabilmek için parmak uçlarımda yükselip göğü kucakladım. Avuçlarıma bir şey konunca gözlerimi kırptım. Kâküllerim gözlerimi kapatırken öne eğilip ellerimi açtım.

Bu bir kar tanesi değildi. Bu küldü.

Kül tanesi avucumun içini ısıtırken gözlerimi kapadım. Öyle günahkâr ve kötücül gözlere sahiptim ki, saf bir kar tanesini bile küle çeviriyordum.

❊❊❊

Bardak parmaklarımdan kurutulup taş zemine düşerken yerimde sıçradım. Gözlerim aralanıp beni gündüz gördüğüm kâbuslardan uyandırırken kırılan cam parçaları taklalar hâlinde dağılıyordu.

"Hedrick," dedim neredeyse fısıltıyla. Hedrick'in beni duyabilmesi için bağırmama gerek yoktu, o ve ben Meredith'in yaptığı bir büyü sayesinde iç seslerimizle dahi konuşabiliyorduk. Baş kara iblis saniyeler içinde yanımda bittiğinde tahtımda rahatsızca kıpırdandım.

"Ne istemiştiniz majesssteleri?" Elimle yerdeki cam parçalarını gösterdim. İblis başıyla onaylayıp gözden kayboldu. Son günlerde pek fazla konuşmama gerek yoktu. Hatta nefes almama da gerek yoktu. İstediğim kadar nefesimi tutabiliyordum. Gözlerimi kırpmasam da olurdu. Hatta yutkunmasam bile olurdu. Ama yutkunmazsam kendimi devamlı olarak sarhoş edemezdim. Ağır hareketlerle ayağa kalkıp sunağa doğru yürüdüm. Tanrılara kurban için hazırlanan sunağın hemen bitişiğine kocaman bir ziyafet masası hazırlanmıştı. Herhangi bir şeyi kutlamıyorduk, sadece bu masa artık hep böyleydi, hazır olmasını istiyordum. Birileri gelebilirdi… O, gelebilirdi. Ve geldiğinde Meredith ne derse desin çok acıkmış olacaktı.

O, yaşıyordu.

Ben yaşıyordum, teknik olarak.

İhtiyacım olmasa da derin bir nefes alıp masadaki şarap şişesine uzandım. Kapağını fırlatıp yeni bir kadehi doldururken gözlerim karıncalanıyordu. Kırmızı görüşü açmak için dayanılmaz bir istek duyuyor, bununla nasıl savaşacağımı bilmediğim için her seferinde görmezden geliyordum. Şişeyi bırakıp dolu bardağı dudaklarıma yaklaştırdığımda gözlerim hâlâ hissettiğim karıncalanma ile kapanmıştı.

Ağır, yapış yapış, baharatlı bir koku havaya usulca dağılırken bardağı tutan parmaklarımı sıkılaştırdım. Kendinden önce o berbat kokusu geliyordu.

"Yine mi içiyordun?" Meredith kafasının üzerinde âdeta yeni bir baş gibi pörtlemiş olan topuzunu hiç bozmadan yanıma gelmişti. O kadar hızlı hareket etsem kafamı yarabilirdim, zarafet meziyetlerimden biri değildi.

Kız kardeşim elimdeki bardağı çekince avuç içime bir boşluk hissi yayıldı. "Arkadaşın Aloha seni çağırıyor." Ben yanıt vermeyince yeşil gözlerini gözlerime dikti. "Gitgide daha da vahşileşiyor. Ona katlanamıyorum." Üst dudağım keyifle kıvrıldı. Meredith bizi anlayamazdı. O kötüydü ama kötülüğü hiç anlamamıştı. O bir seçim sebebiyle kötü olmamıştı, böyle doğmuştu, iyiyi ve kötüyü tercih etmediği için bilemiyordu. Ben biliyordum. Ne anlama geldiğini bile bile seçmiştim kötüyü.

Ben hâlâ yanıt vermeyince Meredith gözlerini devirdi. "Kanatlarını kemirip atacakmış." Güzel gözlerini kısıp kuşkuyla yüzüme baktı. "Hâlâ onunla satranç oynamak istediğine emin misin?"

Şimdi düpedüz sırıtıyordum. "Eğer o olmasaydı sıkıntıdan ölürdüm." Kardeşimin koyduğu bardağı alıp kafama diktim, ardından masaya bıraktım.

Çoktan taht odasının kapısına yöneldiğimde Meredith'in arkamdan mırıldandığını duydum. "Sanki ölebilirmiş gibi."

Başımı sağa sola sallayıp onu duymazdan geldim. Geniş koridorlar ve daha az önce cilalanmış gibi duran mermer zemini arkamda bırakırken cüppemin etekleri ayaklarıma çarpıyordu. Birbiri ardına gelen ihtişamlı koridorlar bittiğinde, şatonun nispeten daha karanlık olan bölümüne gelmiştim. Muhafızların bu bölümde durmasına gerek görmediğim için aydınlatma yoktu. Şeytanın şatosu el değiştirdiğinden beri burada birtakım değişiklikler olmuştu. Öncelikle şu deli saçması meşaleleri söktürüp yerine son model sensörlü lambalar taktırmıştım, ki bu pek çok açıdan kötü bir karardı. Sensörler hareket eden her şeye parlıyorlardı ve bir zaman sonra lambalar neredeyse sönmemeye başlamıştı. Meredith bunun sebebinin atalarımın -şeytan olanlar- öldürdüğü hayaletlerin hâlâ şatoda gezmesinden kaynaklanabileceğini düşünmüştü.

Ben ise birilerinin beni kızdırmak için yaptığına neredeyse emindim. Gerçi bir bakıma amaçlarına ulaşmışlardı. Geçtiğimiz hafta zindanların kapısındaki lambayı söküp onu oraya koyan yarı fani işçinin kafasına fırlatmıştım. Eğer Meredith ve o cehennem fenası büyüleri olmasaydı lambacı adam çoktan ölmüş olacaktı.

Onun için üzülmezdim. Kötü biriydi, kötüler ölürdü. Aslında bir düşününce... İyiler de ölürdü.

Konu neden hep ölüme geliyordu?

"Buraya geleceğinizi söylememişlerdi." Yaşlı Rohan nefes nefese bir şekilde karanlıktan çıkıp doğruca yanıma geldi.

Yan yan ona baktım. "Birilerine haber vermem genelde." Hafif bir esinti bedenimden yayılınca sakinleşmek için yutkundum. Rohan gözlerini kocaman açmış şaşkınca bana bakıyordu. Öyle çok şaşırmıştı ki gözlerinin etrafındaki kırışıklıklar kaybolmuştu. Avuç içlerimi pelerinimin eteklerine silip önemsiz bir şeyden bahsedermişçesine konuştum. "Bu son zamanlarda oluyor. Önemsiz bir şeydir muhtemelen." Yaşlı iblişçenin yavaşça inip kalkan göğsünden derin bir nefes aldığı anlaşılıyordu.

"Bana çok eski bir şeyi hatırlattın," dedi sadece. Ardından başıyla selam vererek geldiğim aydınlık koridorlara doğru yol aldı.

İnsanlara bir şeyleri hatırlatmak konusunda iflah olmaz bir yeteneğim vardı. Kendimi süresi geçmiş antika bir alet gibi hissediyordum. Bozuk bir televizyonu tekmeleyince çalışması gibi bir yerlerime bıçak sokup kalbimi filan sökmeye çalışırsanız ancak çalışıyordum.

Öte yandan vücudumdan çıkarabildiğim tek şey hava akımları değildi. Olur olmaz zamanlarda avuç içlerim yanıyordu. Bazen çok çok minik kıvılcımlar bile görüyordum. Ve bazen tamamıyla aklımı kaçırıp ormana kaçmadan hemen öncesinde kana susuyordum. Kan isteği diğer şeylere pek benzemiyordu, durdurulamaz ve yakıcıydı. Şeytanlığa geçişimin ilk haftası kendimi her gece ormanda buluyordum. Her saraya dönüşümde hizmetkârlar ellerinde havlularla avluda beni bekliyor oluyordu. Çırılçıplak titreyen bedenimi havluya sarıp doğruca banyoya götürülüyordum.

Bir keresinde tırnak diplerimdeki kanları geçirebilmek için Katja'nın bana hançerlerle manikür yapması gerekmişti.

Her uyandığımda karşımda Merr'i buluyordum. Elinde bir şişe suyla daima saklandığım yerde beni bulurdu. O iri yeşil gözleriyle tepeden bana bakar, dizlerinin üzerine eğilip şişenin kapağını açarak bana uzatırdı. Ben ise görüş alanıma giren kanlı parmaklarımla şişeyi kavrardım.

"Birini öldürdüm mü?" Ona bu soruyu defalarca sormuştum ama tek bir yanıt bile alamamıştım. Birini öldürsem bana söylerdi değil mi? Söylerdi, Merr böyle bir şeyi gizlemezdi.

İblişçenin açık bıraktığı kapıdan içeri girip arkamdan kapattım. Mahzenin uzayıp gittiği koridorlar boyunca aklım ilk haftalardaki vahşiliğime gitmişti. Aidan görseydi… Eh iyi ki görmemişti. Eğer görseydi… Benden tiksinirdi.

Ben kendimden tiksiniyordum.

"Ben de senden tiksiniyorum balım." Adımlarımı durdurup geldiğim hücrenin parmaklıklarına baktım. Aloha suratında kocaman gerçek bir sırıtışla orada duruyordu. Kirli parmakları demirleri sıkı sıkı tutmuştu. Suratında, özellikle ağzında doğal olmayan bir şey vardı, bir şeyler fena hâlde ters gidiyordu.

"Strigoi güçlerin gitgide ilerliyor ha?" Meredith'in kanatlarımı sökmekten bahsettiği kankam Aloha'ydı. En deli ve manyak olan güya oydu ama ben kendimi en çok ona yakın hissediyordum.

Gülümseyişine karşılık verirken parmaklıklara yaklaştım. "Kanatlarıma dokunmak yok. Uslu bir vampir ol da satranç takımını getireyim." Vampirin gözlerinden bir an için gölgeler geçti. Yine o çok acıktığı zamanlardan birine denk gelmiştik. Bıkkınlıkla nefesimi demirlere doğru üfledim. "Bak, çok sıkılıyorum. Koca bir köyü yakıp kül etmek istiyorum. Her şeyden nefret ediyorum." Vampir şüphe ile kırmızı günahkâr gözlerini kıstı. Bir süredir kimse onu yıkamaya çalışmamış gibiydi. Koyu kahverengi saçları topaklar hâlinde kafasına yapışmıştı. Bir zamanlar kütüphanecilik yapan o umursamaz güçlü adamı özlemiştim. Tüm evren kafayı sıyırmadan önce o ve ben çok iyi birer dosttuk.

Elimi uzatıp kilide dokundum. Anahtarı takıp çevirince büyük bir *tak* sesiyle hücrenin kapısı açıldı. İtip içeri girince Aloha omzunun üstünden bana baktı. Kapıyı tekrar kapatıp kilitleyerek anahtarı cüppemin cebine koydum. "Kaçsan bile burada dişlerini geçirebileceğin leziz bir şey yok. Sadece çoktan ölmesi gereken tipler var. Bir de kokuşmuş kara iblisler." Bir an bunu düşündüm. Yere eğilirken konuşmaya devam ettim. "Gerçi Rohan da kokuşmuş sınıfına giriyor. Uzun zaman önce ölmeliydi." Cüppemi dizlerime toplayıp bacaklarımı esneterek yere oturdum.

Aloha parmaklıklardan ayrılıp hoş olmayan gözlerle beni süzdü. Ağır hareketlerle tam karşıma geçip sırtını parmaklıklara verdi. Gözleri üzerimdeydi. "Buraya geliyor ve zırvalayıp duruyor. Sanki dedikleri bir şeyi değiştirecekmiş gibi."

"Bana da aynısını yapıyor," dedim huysuzca. "Lider olmak istemedim." Başımı kaldırıp gözlerine baktım. Kızıl gözlerinin eski kahverengi hâlinde olmasını isterdim. Eski Aloha bana bir fikir verebilirdi.

Bunun yerine yeni Aloha konuştu.

"Ama oldun. Ve şimdiden elini kana buladın." Merak duygusu içimi parçalarken hâlâ gözlerine bakıyordum. Şimdiki ifadesini anlamak biraz zordu. "Dünyaya saldığın hırsızlar sadece çok kıymetli meleğini aramıyor, fanileri de öldürüyorlar. Benim içim hava hoş gerçi." Elinin tersiyle akan burnunu sildi. "Ben bir hırsız iblis olsaydım meleği aramak şöyle dursun, her gün bir faniyle işi pişirirdim. Ve sonra da öldürürdüm."

Çevremdeki herkes saplantılı bir şekilde ölüme bağlıydı.

"Demek istediğin şeyi anladım." Bacaklarımı uzatıp başımı geriye atarak duvara yaslandım. "Hırsızların ne yaptığı pek önemli değil. Bir süredir pek bir şey hissedemiyorum."

Aloha sırıtıyordu. Onun olduğu yerden gelen keskin koku yüzümü buruşturmama sebep oldu. Burada işim bitince bir kara iblisi onu yıkaması için görevlendirecektim. "Evrimini çok güzel tamamlıyorsun o hâlde. Bir sonraki aşama merhametini yitirmek olacak. Bu olduğunda sen ve ben daha çok vakit geçireceğiz."

Sıkılmıştım. Doğrulup cüppemdeki tozları temizlerken ona baktım. "İple çekiyorum."

Zindanlardan ayrılıp da merkez koridorun ışıkları gözüme çarpana kadar uykuda gibiydim. Merhametimin bir kısmının bende olmasının bir zamanlar melek filan olabileceğimle ilgili olduğunu söylemişlerdi. Gerçi Lilith dahil hiçbir büyücü çağrılarıma dönmüyordu ama yine de Meredith'e sahiptim, şimdilik.

Merhametsiz.

Peh, sanki çok ihtiyacım vardı.

"Yer cüceleri akşına! Deve boku gibi görünüyorsun." Meredith abartılı bir hareketle gözlerini kocaman açarak yanıma koşturuyordu. Aynı metrekareyi paylaşacak kadar yanıma sokulduğunda beni koklamaya başladı. "Kan mı emdin?"

İnanamayarak ona baktım. "Yok artık."

Erkeksi bir kahkaha havayı delerken ikimiz de arkamızı döndük.

Güzelliğin erkeksi hâli, beyaz bir pantolon ve beyaz bir gömlekle kendini bir hediye paketi gibi süslemiş, kömür karası ürkütücü gözleriyle bizi izliyordu. Bazen bu güzelliğin Draza'da boşa harcandığını düşünüyordum. Bir elf iblis için, hatta bir erkek için bile fazla güzeldi.

Fani kızlarının dizlerini titrettiğine emin olduğum içten bir gülüşle yanımıza yaklaşıyordu. Adımları Urange'ınkiler gibi zarifti. Draza âdeta havada kayarak yanımıza geldiğinde Meredith çoktan susmuştu. Draza'ya bakışlarını yakalıyordum. Ve bu nadir minik anlarda içimdeki bir parçam -narsist, geri zekâlı ve Pollyanna'nın amca kızı olan küçük parçam- Meredith'in pişmanlık hissettiğini söylüyordu.

"Hey Draza. Özür dilerim, babanla yatarken niyetim senin duygularını incitmek değildi."

Meredith ölse, tekrar dirilse ve tekrar ölse de yine de bu cümleyi dile getirmezdi ama ben anlıyordum. Bunu o rengârenk ışıkların devamlı olarak hareket ettiği cadı gözlerinde görebiliyordum.

Elf yanımıza yaklaşınca gözlerim omuzlarının hemen üzerinde olması gereken kanatları aradı. Yoklardı. Kanatlarını özleyen bir iblise göre kanatsız gezmesi komikti. Ben bile çoğu gece içime çekmeyi unutuyordum. Ömrümün on yedi senesi kanatsız olduğum düşünülünce kuyruğa da ayak uydurabileceğimi fark ettim. Tabii ki bir kuyruk istemiyordum.

"Bethany'i yine bulamamış gibisin." Meredith özür dilemekte kötü olmasının yanı sıra insanı sinir eden, âdeta kriz geçirten bir gıcıklığa sahipti. Ölümsüz hayatın en büyük laneti Meredith ile beraber olmaktı.

"O kızı asla bulamayacaksın." Meredith'in dolgun üst dudağı keyifle kıvrılırken, yeşil gözleri parladı. Beth'e ölüyor falan değildi. Sadece Draza'nın mutlu olmasını istemiyordu.

Elf ondan tarafa bakmadan bana döndü. "Bu tahtı hak etmedin. Burada oturuyor olmayı kardeşime borçlusun. Eğer onu öldürmeseydin..."

"Cassie kimseyi öldürmedi. Aidan meleğe dönü-" Elimle Meredith'i durdurdum. Draza'ya döndüğümde içimde bir şeylerin alevlendiğini hissettim. Sinirlere hâkim olmakla sakin olmak arasındaki fark, damarlarımda gümleyen bir nabız gibiydi.

"Tahtı mı istiyorsun? O beyaz elf kıçın bu tahta oturmayı göze alabilecekse gelsin." Meydan okurcasına suratına baktım. Bazen avuçlarım yerine gözlerimden ateş çıkarmak istiyordum. Sanırım bu açık ara beni hayattaki en ucube şey yapardı, Meredith'den sonra elbette.

Elf hoşnutsuzca suratıma bakarken aklından tarttığını görebiliyordum. O uğursuz kara gözlerinde ihtimallerin birbiri ardına aktığını görebiliyordum. "Aura görebildiğimi biliyorsun değil mi? Korkuyorsun, hatta altına işeyeceksin." Yalandı. Draza korkmuyordu, kararlıydı ve en son isteyeceğim şey birinin var olan düzenimi değiştirmesiydi.

Dakikalar gibi geçen birkaç saniyenin sonunda elf konuştu. "Bir gün bunları yaptığın için pişman olacaksın. O tahtı kazanmak için kan akıttığını sanıyorsun değil mi?" Durup hastalıklı bir şekilde güldü. "O tahtta oturabilmek için her dakika kan akıtıyorsun. Zamanı geldiğinde Lucifer'dan bile daha çok leşin olacak. Sırf o Tanrıların belâsı inadın yüzünden." Arkasını dönüp giderken sinirle saç tokasını çıkarıp gümüş rengi parlak saçlarını omuzlarına saldı.

Omzumda hissettiğim el ile irkildim. "Onu takma. Salağın teki. Bugün yapman gereken şeyleri konuşalım. Süvariler geldiğinde son ateşkesin iptalini isteyecekler, yani bunun ne demek olduğunu biliyorsun Cass. Birinin ordunun başında durması lazım." Yanıt vermeden hafifçe silkinerek elini omzumdan çekmesini sağladım. Hâlâ Draza'nın bizi bıraktığı yerdeydik.

"Onun beyaz elf kıçına ben de ölmüyorum ama elimizdeki en iyi komutan o. Ve duymak istemediğini biliyordum ama adamlar onu dinliyor. Onu seviyorlar."

Meredith'in söylemediği iki kelime zihnimde benimle alay eder gibi oynaştı.

Seni sevmiyorlar.

Aslında çok uzak alternatif bir yaşamda bana itaat etmesi gereken askerlerin beni sevmeyişine içerleyebilirdim. Ama o an hissettiğim içerleme değildi. Sıkılmıştım.

Bu nasıl mümkün olabilir bilmiyordum ama başıma bir ağrı saplandı. İki elimin başparmakları şakaklarımı ovarken tahtıma yürüdüm. Soğuk metali sırtımda hissedinceye kadar geriye yaslandım. Ellerim hâlâ başımın iki yanındaydı.

"Tüm bunları istemedim." Kız kardeşim yanıt vermedi. Meredith hakkında pek çok şey söylenebilirdi. İki yüzlü, kaltak ve daha birçok şey. Ama o bilgeydi. Bir yanım annemden miras kalan bilgeliği onun alışını kıskanıyordu. Ben ne almıştım? Kin ve nefret mi? Yoksa ölüm mü?

"Yine uyumayacaksın değil mi?" Bunun üzerine ona döndüm. Yeşil gözlerinin çevresi endişe ile kırışmıştı. "Son sefer," dedi biraz duraksayarak, "zincirleri zamanında getirememiştik." Elimi kaldırıp onu susturdum.

Pekâlâ, işte geliyor.

Yeni mükemmel hayatımın birtakım eksikleri vardı. Bunlardan biri Aidanhell'i kurtarırken balataları yakmış olmamdı. En iyi tabirle uykuya daldığım an çığlıklar atarak ortalarda geziniyordum. Ve genelde bu olduğunda tek çığlık atan ben olmuyordum.

Birileri ölebiliyordu.

Gözlerimi kapayıp yüzümü ekşittim. "Kimse sarayda bir kurt adam olduğunu söylemedi." Betayı öldürmüştüm, aslında öldürmek biraz basit kalıyordu. Kanatlarımla kafasını kafesleyip koparmıştım. Ciddi anlamdaki tek suçu ise karanlık koridorda bana rastlamasıydı. Ardından gözlerimi açıp kendimi haklı göstermek istercesine direttim. "Ayrıca kim alfa kurdun betaya âşık olduğunu bilebilirdi ki?"

Küçük çıldırmalarım sonucu betasını kaybeden alfa kontrolden çıkmıştı. İttifakı bozup bizimle çalışan tüm kurtları geri çekmişti.

Meredith sakin görünmeye çalışıyordu. Aslında tam böyle, gerginliğin insan suretinde aramızda gezindiği vakitlerde sakinleşebilmemiz için Rohan odanın çeşitli yerlerine kokular koymuştu ama bu ironik biçimde neredeyse her şeye alerjisi olan cadı kız kardeşimi daha da kızdırıyordu.

Kız kardeşimin hâlâ bana baktığını fark edince onu sinirlendiren şeyin iblisçenin ahmakça yerleştirdiği kokular olmadığını fark ettim. Doğrudan bana bakıyordu ve ifadesi tam anlamıyla suçlayıcıydı. "Geceleri ortalarda dolanıp birilerini öldürüyorsun ve konseyden dünyaya gitmeyi talep etmişsin."

Talebimi yapalı iki ay olmuştu ama kimse bana dönmemişti. Benimle kimse doğrudan karşılaşmak istemiyordu, hakkımda çoktan söylentiler yayılmıştı. Şimdi bile araf süvarilerinin toplantıya geç kalma sebebi buydu. Beni görmek istemiyorlardı. Ben Lucifer'ı öldürüp Aidanhell'i meleğe dönüştürmüştüm. Onların gözünde insanken de şeytana evrilmiştim, yani olabilecek en kötü şeydim, tahmin edilemez, saptanamaz bir şeydim. Kim bilir onlara neler yapardım?

Tabii olaylar aslında böyle şekillenmemişti.

"Kabul etmişler mi bari?" Sanmıyordum. Konsey beni burada istiyordu. Hırsızlar dünyaya indiği için bu diyardaki dengeyi sağlamam gerekiyordu. Konsey pek çok şey istiyordu. Sorun şu ki ben istemiyordum. Ben kişiliğini kaybetmiş deli bir rakun gibi geziniyordum.

Meredith sinirle turuncu saçlarını geriye attı. Kaşları öyle çok çatılmıştı ki hayali kırışıklıkları belirginleşmişti. "Etmişler."

Ve işte o an bu deli rakunun geleceği belli olmuştu. Tabii kabul edildiğimi duyduğumun iki ay sonrası, kendimi kan kaybından eski bir yatakta ölürken bulacağımı düşünmemiştim. Geleceğe dair daha umutluydum.

"Öyle hemen sevinme Majeste. Ben de seninle geliyorum." Kız kardeşim ben yerimden kalkıp kara askerlere onu köpek balıklarına yem etmeleri emrini vermeden önce ekledi. "Krallığı bir süreliğine Draza idare edecek. Vekil kral artık o."

***

Hastaneye girmek sandığımdan kolay olmuştu. Nedense birinin bu ucube kızlar üçlüsünü durduracağını düşünmüştüm. Ama ne yanından geçtiğimiz güvenlik görevlileri ne de lobide çarpıştığımız doktorlar bizi durdurmamıştı.

Şehrin hemen dışındaki hapishanede yangın çıkmıştı. Dakikada bir ambulanslar sirenleriyle şehri inleterek buraya geliyorlardı. Bizim böylesi yoğun bir zamanı seçmemiz tesadüf değildi. Misha -dönüşüm geçirmiş hâli pek Misha gibi durmuyordu- hapishanede tam ağzımıza layık -bunu gerçekten söylemişti- adamların olduğu konusunda diretmişti.

Yanık et kokusunun nispeten daha az olduğu acilin sonundaki koridorlarda ilerlerken Meredith'in yanımızda olmadığını fark ettim. "Onu gördün mü?" Misha başını olumsuz anlamda sallayıp arkasına dönerek geldiğimiz yere baktı. Kardeşim görünürlerde yoktu.

Soğuk eli kolumu tutunca telaşlı arayışımı bıraktım. "Zaman kaybediyoruz. Seremonine ben yardım ederim." Ruhu bedenden çıkarabilmem için bir cadıyla beraber olmam gerekiyordu. Benim kendi cadım görünürlerde olmadığı için istemeyerek de olsa Misha'nın teklifini kabul ettim.

Beş dakika sonra Misha yataklardan birinin önündeki perdeyi çekip beni kendisiyle beraber içeri aldı. Orada yatan adamın başına gidip serumun borusunu kolundan çekti.

Adamın sağ kolu ve bacağının yan tarafı yanmıştı. İlk müdahalede temizlenmiş, üzerine ağrı kesici krem sürülmüştü. "O baygın." Eh bu kabul edilebilirdi. Üçüncü derece yanıklarla uyanık bir şekilde durmak istemezdiniz.

Adamın sağlam kolu ve ayak bileğindeki kelepçeye baktım. Birkaç dakika sonra bir daha bunları kullanmayacaktı. Tereddüt, gece karanlığındaki bozuk bir lamba gibi zihnimde yanıp sönüyordu. Öldürmeliydik, değil mi?

Misha tereddüdümü hissetmiş gibi adamın üzerine eğilmiş hâlde dururken başını hafifçe yan çevirip bana baktı. "O merhameti hak etmiyor."

Sanki buna herhangi bir canlı karar verebilirmiş gibi.

"Merhamet değil," dedim hemen. Ardından ne zaman kemirmeye başladığımdan emin olamadığım başparmağımın tırnağını azat ettim. "Suçu neydi?" Cadı tekrar adama dönüp mahkûmun yüzüne düşen siyah saçlarını üfleyip dağıttı.

"Ailesini öldürmüş."

"Neden?"

"Kollarına bak." Baktım. Damarları kararmıştı. Tüm kolu boyunca zehirlenmiş dallar gibi yayılıp gidiyordu.

"Bağımlı."

Cadı başını onaylarcasına salladı. "Durup daha fazla sohbet etmek isterdim ama," dedi bıkkınca sonra hemen ekledi. "Küçük erkek kardeşini ekmek bıçağı ile doğradığını bilmek belki seni daha iyi hissettirir."

İrkildim. Bunun beni daha iyi hissettirdiği falan yoktu. "Seni piç!" Suratına tükürmek istedim.

Bizim hakkında küfürler savurduğumuz piçimiz ise her şeyden habersiz yatıyordu. Onu pişman edecektim! Onu. Onu...

"Gel, hızlıca ölmesini sağlayacağım. Hazır mısın?" Onun için istediğim ölüm bu değildi ama vücudum bir an önce bir ruh alamazsam yaşamamın imkânsız olduğunu bağırıyordu.

Misha'nın yanına gidip yatağa oturdum. Cadı adamın sağ tarafına geçip işaret parmağının tırnağıyla boynunu gösterdi. "Parçalayacak mısın, boğacak mısın?" Seçimi bana bırakması hoşuma gitmişti.

Beyaz gömleğimin kollarını katlayıp caninin üzerine eğildim. Terliyordum. İki elimle boynunu kavradım. Yapacağım cinayete odaklanmadan önce başımı kaldırıp cadının gözlerine baktım. Yavaşça gözlerini kırpıp dudaklarını araladı. Büyüye başlamıştı.

Var gücümle adamın boğazını sıktım. Misha, yandaki monitöre bağlı olan kabloları çektiği için adamın nabzını göremiyorduk ama cadının yaptığı büyü sayesinde ruhun bedeninden dışarı çıktığını görebiliyordum. Beden bu dünyadan göçüp giderken ben daha fazla sıkıyor, daha da fazla terliyordum. Alnımdaki ter gözlerime iniyor, onları yaşartıyordu. "Öl artık," dedim dişlerimin arasından. Karnımdaki dikişlerin bir bir açılışını da hissediyordum.

Ruh bedeni tamamen terk ederken ellerimin ayalarını okşayıp titreşti. Parmaklarımı adamın boğazından çekip derin nefesler almaya çalıştım. Havada asılı kalan benliği bedenime girerken tüm iç organlarım sancıyordu. Gözlerimin içi yanıyordu. Sanki aynı anda hem yaşıyor hem de gidiyordum, ki bu diyardan gittiğim onca ânı düşünürsek... Ölüyor gibi değildim. Ölümden çok daha mahrem bir şeydi bu.

Orada kendi iç savaşımı verirken cadının sesli bir şekilde nefesini tuttuğunu gördüm. Baktığı yöne bakmak için yerimde hafifçe dönerken bile her yerim az önceki deneyimin farkındalığını yaşıyordu. Hem uçuyor hem yüzüyor gibiydim.

Ve gözlerim cadının gördüğü şeye takıldı. Perdenin önü ışıldıyordu. Bu öyle bir ışıltıydı ki kalbimi durdurmuştu. Aciz kalbim durmuştu. Ben de durmuştum, evren de durmuştu.

"Onu görüyor musun?" diye fısıldadım.

"Orada bir ışık huzmesi görüyorum."

Misha görmüyordu. Bir ışıktan daha fazlasıydı. Bir ışığın kömür karası siyah saçları olmazdı. Işığın güzel tatlı kahverengi gözleri de olmazdı. Işığın güzel gözlerinden bir damla yaş çıkık elmacık kemiklerine düşmezdi. Gerçi herhangi bir insan da zaten bunu bu şekilde göremezdi, anlaşılan uydurmuştum. Hâlâ elinde bıçağıyla gezinen deli bir rakundum.

"Aman Tanrım!"

Az önce öldürdüğüm adamın ruhu bedenime tamamen dolduğunda ışık yavaşça titreşti. "Ah, hayır hayır hayır!" Hızla yerimden fırladım. "Hayır, ne olur hayır!" Titreşen ışığa dokunmaya çalıştım. Tanrım, görüntü bulanıyordu!

Siyah dalgalı bir saç teli rüzgârla yerinden oynadı.

Uydurmamıştım, bu oydu! Bu o!

Ellerimle deli gibi solup giden ışığı tutmaya çalışıyordum. *Tanrım, lütfen gitme!* "Aidan lütfen! Hayır!" Işık kaybolmadan önce zarifçe elini uzattı. Ardından görüntü bir daha gelmeyecekmişçesine silinip gitti. Kollarımla kendimi kucaklamış bir şekilde yere düştüm.

Ağlıyordum. Şoktaydım. Güldüm. Kahkaha attım. Sonra tekrar ağladım.

"Buradan gitmeliyiz." Cadı üzerime eğilip ellerini omzuma koyarken yerdeki çılgın ritüelimi tekrarlıyordum. "Oymuş," diyebildim sadece. Ardından Misha beni kaldırdı. Kolunu omzuma atarken sarı saçları yüzüme çarptı. İnsan hâline dönmüştü.

Bir elimi sırtına doladım. Az önce çok güçlü hissediyordum, şimdi ne olmuştu? Ne olmuştu da her şey Aidanhell'i gördüğüm bir salise içinde tuzla buz olmuştu?

Tekrar kahkaha atınca Misha omzumdaki eliyle bana bir çimdik attı. "Şurada yatan ölü adamı kontrole gelen olmasa bile deli gibi davrandığın için insanlar bize bakacak. Şimdi sakin ol." Ardından boşta kalan eliyle soluk mavi hasta perdesini çekti. Çevredeki kargaşa hâlâ devam ediyordu. İnsanlarla dolu, metal ve kan kokusunun harmanlandığı koridorlardan geçerken adımlarımı hızlandırmaya çalıştım.

Gelirken döndüğümüz son köşeyi de geçince kızıl saçlar görüş açıma girdi. Elinde torbalarla kız kardeşim bize doğru koşar adım geliyordu. Misha durup kardeşimin bize katılmasını bekledi. Dizinin birini büküp destek alışı gözümden kaçmadı. Kaç kiloydum ki ben?

Kız kardeşim nefes nefese yanımıza vardı. "Hey," dedi derin bir nefes almadan önce. Bakışları sarışın cadı ile aramda gidip geldi. "Sanırım bitirmişsiniz." Gözleri üzerimde fazlaca durdu.

O ölmemiş seni salak.

"Elindekiler ne?" Misha, kardeşimin elindeki torbalara bakıyordu. Bir hemşire yanımızdan koşup geçerken Meredith parmağını dudaklarına götürdü. "Şş, sessiz olun! Dışarıda söylerim." Sonra Misha'nın koluna dokunup beni işaret ederek, "Onu ben hallederim," dedi. Bir saniye sonra omzumda kız kardeşimin eli vardı. "Sana söylemem gereken bir şey var Merr."

"Bu bekleyemez mi?"

Başımı sağa sola salladım. Hastanenin geniş kapısından çıkarken Misha bize önderlik ediyordu. "Misha'nın koruması bizi almaya geldi. Onun yanında konuşmak istemezsin herhâlde." Bunu düşündüm. Eve gidince söylemeye karar verdim.

Motosikletlerin park alanına varınca kardeşim beni kaldırıma oturttu. O ânı düşünüyordum. Onu. Güzel kahverengi gözlerini. Ve o gözlerin sulanışını.

Elimi kalbime götürdüm. Hâlâ atıyordu. Hâlâ hissediyordum. Ben hâlâ biraz bendim.

Parlak far ışığı gözlerimi kör edince elimi gözlerime siper ettim. "Geldi." Kendiliğimden ayağa kalkıp kardeşime tutundum. Merr koluma girdiğinde arabaya doğru yürümeye başladık. Misha ön koltuğa yerleşirken bize döndü. "Sizi aldığımız yere bırakacağız."

Peşi sıra arabaya girdik. Meredith başımı omzuna yasladı. Doğrulmak yerine derin bir nefes aldım, kendimi kız kardeşimin cılız bedenine bıraktım. Tanrım, öyle yorgundum ki... Ayakta durabilmem bile bir mucizeydi.

Şu ana dek gördüğüm en parlak mavi gözler dikiz aynasından bize bakınca dikkatim dağıldı. "Ben Khandar," dedi mavi gözlü adam. Ardından koltukta yan dönüp omzunun üstünden bize baktı. "Aidanhell'i tanırdım."

Nefesim içime kaçtı. Meredith hemen müdahale etti. "Ee, şey biz ondan şu sıralar pek bahsetmiyoruz." Gözlerini kocaman açarak beni işaret ettiğinden neredeyse emindim. Bunun üzerine mavi gözlü Khandar mahcup bir şekilde kekeledi. "Bilmiyordum."

Bir süre bana baktı. "Hilekârla sonunda tanıştığım için memnunum." Yavaşça başımı salladım. Ardından yola çıktık.

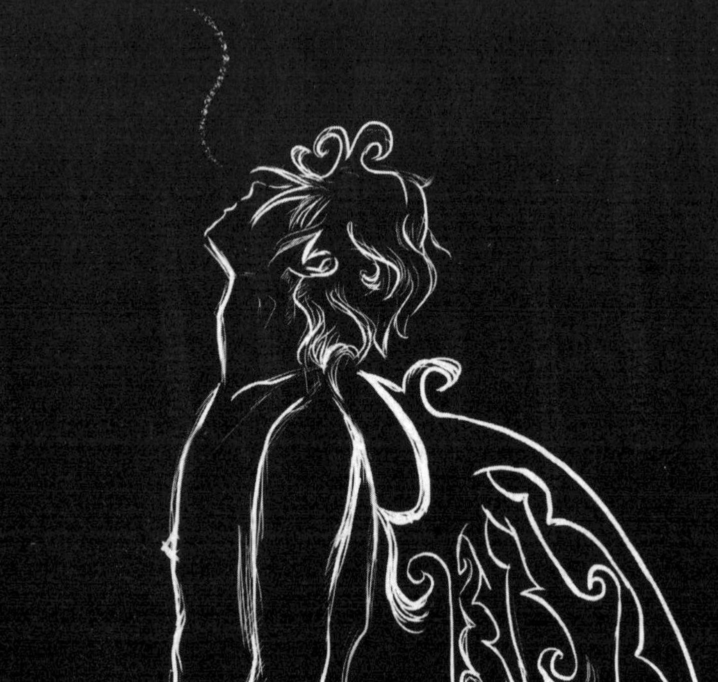

"Ruhumun olması gereken yerde
Koca bir karanlık var. Ben iyi biri değildim.
Ama bu kez...kötü olmaktan da öteyim."

BÖLÜM 6

"Ne saçmalıyorsun?"

Eşyalarımı topluyordum. Bunun için de Max'ten aldığım bavulu kullanıyordum. Pek bir eşyam yoktu. Birkaç iç çamaşırı, bir bot, eski bir spor ayakkabı ve ölü kızın boynundan aldığım madalyonla annemin günlükleri.

Aslında Max'in telefonundan ben hazırlanırken bana eşlik etsin diye Misuguns'ın Armegeddon'unu açmasam daha az hastalıklı bir durum gibi görünebilirdi bu. Ama her neyse.

"Bunu daha ne kadar sürdüreceğiz." Sıra hançerlerimdeydi. Fermuarı çekip bavulu askısından tutarak kız kardeşime döndüm. "Ben hazırım. Gidelim."

Önümden çekilmeyince çevresinden dolanıp kapıya ilerledim. "Bir yere gitmiyorsun." Peşim sıra gelirken gözleri bavulumdaydı. "Hem Lilith'in dünyada olduğunu sana kim söyledi?" Cevap vermek için dudaklarımı aralayınca samimi, çocuksu bir ses odayı doldurdu.

"Ben dedim. Selam Cass." Yüzüme çarpan parlak peri tozları sebebiyle neredeyse hapşıracakken periyi selamladım. "Bir asır oldu sanki görüşmeyeli." Urange odanın diğer tarafındaki selamladığı Meredith'i un gibi görünen peri tozuyla kaplanmış şekilde bırakıp bana koştu.

Bana sarılırken geçen seferki soğuk Urange'dan eser yoktu. Neredeyse kemiklerimi kıracaktı. "Senin için endişelendik. Draza herkesin ağzına sıçıyordu."

"Sen kimsin ve geçen günkü periye ne yaptın?" Urange mahcup bir ifadeyle omuzlarını düşürürken dünyada bipolar perilerin de var olabileceği gerçeğini kabul ettim.

Sırıttım. Bu krallığı gayet iyi yönettiği anlamına geliyordu. Kendimi kollarından kurtarıp geçen gün yapamadığımı yaptım. Ona adamakıllı baktım. Burnunun üzerindeki çiller çoğalmış, turuncu bukleleri de uzamıştı. Onunla ilk uçtuğum gün bir asır önce gibiydi. "Seninle geliyorum."

Sırıtmaya devam ederken kız kardeşime döndüm. "Birileri hâlâ bana sadık anlaşılan." Meredith huysuz çocuklar gibi yüzünü ekşiterek kollarını göğsünde topladı.

"O salak bavulun ve acınası silahlarınla annemize gitmiyorsun!" Yüzündeki peri tozlarını atmadan kızıl saçlarını savura savura üzerimize yürüdü. Elimdeki bavulu alıp odanın diğer tarafına fırlattı. "Seni aptal! O Aidan değildi! O gitti, anlıyor musun?"

Kaşlarımı çattım. Urange aramızdan çekilince Meredith ile aramda esen sert rüzgâr tarafından kuşatıldım. "Gözlerime inanıyorum." Meydan okurcasına çenemi dikleştirdim. "Eğer hastanenin içinde dolanmasaydın, sen de pekâlâ görebil-" Kız kardeşim uyuzca kahkaha attı. "Bir dakika bir dakika! Dolanmak mı? Devamlı olarak kendini yaraladığın için ilaç çalıyordum!"

Ardından pes edermiş gibi avuç içlerini kalçasına vurdu. "Lanet olsun, seninle gelmeyeceğim! Yeter!"

Bir süre kimse konuşmayınca Urange öksürerek boğazını temizledi. "Şey, Cass gideceğini öğrenince yardım gerekli olur diye düşündüm...Ve elbette destek için..."

Meredith'in ürperdiğini görünce gelenin Draza olacağını düşündüm ama bu saçma olurdu. Onu geride krallığımı korusun diye bırakmıştım.

Odaya dolan orman kokusu ile gözlerim kocaman açıldı. "Yoksa?" Urange sırıtıyordu. Marcus geniş omuzları ile kapıdan girerken kendimi uzun zaman sonra ilk kez sevinçli hissediyordum. "O kaltağa bensiz kurabiye ziyareti yapacağınızı duyduğumda çok kırıldım. Hey sis, selam, beni özledin mi?" Meredith'e muzipçe göz kırptı. O ikisinin arasının asla düzelmeyeceğini biliyordum.

Koşup ona sarıldım.

Bir parçam Jo'nun da bize katılabilmesini çok ama çok isterdi. Jo'yu düşüncünce içinde olduğum durum mutluluk vermeyi bıraktı. Güzel anları bok etme konusunda iflah olmaz bir yeteneğim vardı. Ondan ayrılırken konuşmaya başladım. "Neredeydin?"

Marcus'un kehribar rengi parlak gözleri Meredith'in üzerindeydi. "Yanıt vereceğim ama önce ablam benim üzerimde büyü yapmayacağına söz verecek."

Meredith orta parmağını gösterince Urange tıksırarak güldü.

"Bari yakınımda olmasın." Durup üşürmüş gibi yaptı. "Brrr tüylerimi ürpertiyor." Omuz silkerek kız kardeşime döndüm. Ben herhangi bir şey diyemeden başını eğip hepimizi kasıp kavuracakmış gibi yanan gözlerini bizden esirgeyerek hızlı hızlı odayı terk etti. “Ben Max’e bir bakayım,” dedi mırıldanarak.

O gidince Marcus çocuk gibi tuttuğu nefesini bıraktı. “Asırlar geçse bile o cadı beni ürpertmeye devam edecek. Beni bir Trex’in evine anadan doğma biçimde terk etmişti. İnsan kıyafetleri giyebilir, öyle davranabilir ama size söylüyorum,” deyip az önce kız kardeşimin hiddetle çıkıp gittiği kapıyı işaret etti. “O asla bir insan değil, olamaz. Şeytan bile değil. Ya ne bileyim, çok kötü biri.”

İşte buna gülerdim. Kanatlarımın dibi de onun sözlerine gülmek istercesine sırtımda karıncalandılar. “Geç otur.” Omzuna hafifçe vurup çenemle pencerenin önündeki koltuğu işaret ettim. Marcus gözlerini kısıp koltuğa kötücül bir bakış attı. “Iyy, yok sağ ol. Dizanteri olmak istemiyorum.”

Koluna vurup somurttum. “Dizanteri su ile bulaşıyor ve koltuk o kadar pis değil.”

Urange gidip koltuğa oturunca ben de yatağa geçtim, Marcus ise duvara yaslandı. “Katze ile beraber Vanelia’daydık.”

“Balayı mı?”

Kardeşim gözlerini devirdi. “Ya tabii. Sanki evlenmemiz mümkünmüş gibi.” Bunu mümkün kılamayan yüzlerce sebep vardı. Ve bir melez doğurarak krallıkları birbirine katmak bunlardan sadece biriydi. Marcus dalıp gidince onu uyandırdım. “O nasıl?” Yüzüne kocaman bir gülümseme yerleşti. “İyi. En yakın zamanda görüşeceğinizi umuyormuş.” Bakışlarımı kucağımda birleştirdiğim ellerime diktim. Katze son seferimizde bana vurmuştu ve bana vurduğu için onun boynunu dişlemiştim. Bu ilk şeytan olduğum o karanlık altı aylık dönemde gerçekleşmişti.

Canını yakmadığım tek bir dostum kalmamasına özenle dikkat etmiştim.

"Vampirleri hallettik."

Bu söylediğine kendisi de inanamıyormuş gibiydi. Kollarımı göğsümde kavuşturup şüpheli bir ifadeyle ona baktım. "Draza'dan aldığım son rapora göre vampirler başıboş bir şekilde yeryüzüne iniyormuş." Gözlerimi önemini vurgulamak istercesine kocaman açtım. "Hem de kitleler hâlinde. Yani gerçekten insanların bu aptalca hareket eden toplulukların farkında olamayacak kadar gerzek olduklarını mı söylüyorsun?"

Urange koltuğumda rahatsızca kıpırdanınca ona döndüm. "Bana yalan söylemeyin bir daha." Birbirlerine kaçamak bakışlar attılar. Zihnim hâlâ dün olanlarla kaynarken burada durup kriz yönetimi yapacak hâlde değildim. Ah Tanrım... Keşke her şeyi başa sarabilseydim.

"Cass, her zamanki gibi sana yardım edeceğiz. Biliyorsun." Başımı kaldırdığımda erkek kardeşimin anlayışlı, kehribar rengi gözleriyle karşılaştım.

Ben bana yardım edeleri harcarım. Öldürür, un ufak ederim. Aloha gibi, Aidan gibi. Ve bana güvenen, bir zamanlar dostum olan tüm o geri zekâlı avcılar gibi. Lütfen bana inanmayın, benimle birlikte savaşmayın.

Bunun yerine isteksizce mırıldandım. "Teşekkür ederim." Marcus gülerken sabahın erken ışıkları altın sarısı saçlarına düştü. Bu saçlar bana meleği hatırlatmıştı. Eh artık onu göremediğime göre endişelenmeme de gerek yoktu. Bir ölüm meleği şu an için listemin sonlarında bile değildi. Kıçımı yakmak isteyen meşaleleri tutacak oldukça hevesli bir kalabalık vardı.

"Sizinle geleceğim." Sırtımı dikleştirip *puffy* yorgandaki oturuşumu değiştirdim. "Oraya dönüp tüm kafayı yemiş şeytan kastlarıyla uğraşmam gerektiğini biliyorum."

Urange hemen söze girdi. "Hayır, hepsiyle değil. Gitmeden önce perileri ve süvarileri halletmiştin." Durup bir saniye perinin söylediklerini düşündüm. "Yetmez. Elfler var, kurtlar ve vampirler. Tanrım, hiç bitmeyecek gibiler!"

Duruşumu bozmamak için nefes almayı bıraktım. Kararlı görünmeye çalışıyordum. "Burada yarım kalmış bir işim var." Arkadaşlarım Aidan ile ilgili olan son olaylardan habersizlerdi.

Sormalarını, diretmelerini bekledim ama bunun yerine ikisi de ayaklandılar. "Sen işlerini hallet, biz takılıyor olacağız." Kaşlarımı çatıp yataktan kalktım. "Bir kurt ve peri nerede takılabilir ki?"

Marcus kıs kıs gülüyordu. "Urange ile geldiğim için yolda bayağı kustum." Geçmişi hatırlayınca yüzüm istemsizce asıldı. Marcus yolculuğa dayanamıyordu, özellikle de peri tozlu olanlara.

"Midemi doldurmam gerekiyor."

"Pizzacıya gidelim. Biri var, pardon bir yer var, güzel yapıyorlar," dedi Urange hemen. Bu telaşlı hâline anlam veremesem de onlara arkamı dönüp az önce hazırladığım bavulumdan cüzdanımı çıkardım. Sahip olduğum tüm parayı onlara verirken çar çur etmemeleri için tembihliyordum.

Onlar gittikten sonra Marcus'un dizanterili dediği koltuğa oturup bacaklarımı çapraz yaptım. Güneş havada tembelce yükselirken geleceğimi düşündüğümü fark ettim. Geçmişin hesabı kesilirken geleceği düşünmem sadece aptallıktı.

Pantolonumun ön cebinden telefonumu çıkarıp Jo'yu aradım. Telefon ikinci çalışta açıldı. "Selam böcek."

"Selam abla." Şükürler olsun ki birimiz neşeliydi. "Ee, nasıl gidiyor?"

"İyi. Birileri üzerinde deneme yapabiliyorum," dedi hızlıca. Şimdi ise fısıldıyordu. "Bethany'e söylemedim ama avcıları tekmelemek süper eğlenceli." Kahkaha attım. İşte benim küçük bücürümsü yaramaz kardeşim.

Gözlerim doluyordu. Kirpiklerimin hemen bitimindeki gitgide şişen gözyaşı damlasını parmağımın ucuyla aldım. Damla bütünlüğünü koruyamayıp parmağımı boydan boya ıslattı.

Lilith görülerimden birinde şeytanların gözyaşı dökebileceğini söylemişti. Ağlamak için iyi biri olmama gerek yoktu. Sevgi yeterdi. İşte bu yüzden sevgi iyi ya da kötü değildi. Herkes severdi, sevgi sevgiydi.

"Seni ellerinden alacağım. Beth ile güvendesin ama ilk fırsatta yemin ederim seni kurtaracağım."

Hattın diğer ucunda kardeşim yavaşça nefesini bıraktı. "Cass. Kurtarılmaya ihtiyacım yok, bunu konuşmuştuk. Artık on dört yaşındayım ve kendi seçimlerimi yapabiliyorum. Ben şeytan olmak istemiyorum." Kalbimi tekmeleyen iri su samurlarını görmezden geldim. "Jo. Anlıyorum." *Anlamıyordum.*

"Şimdilik orada güvendesin." Radikal bir grubun Jo'nun peşine düştüğünü öğrendiğimde onun tanıdığım en güçlü kadınla gitmesine izin vermiştim. Beth kardeşime bakıyordu ama onu aynı zamanda bir avcı olarak yetiştiriyordu. Kraliçenin erkek kardeşinin yakalanıp zindanlarda olgunlaşmasını sağlamak isteyen faşist bir grup vardı, benimle güvende olamazdı.

"Burada güvendeyim abla. Benim için endişelenme, seni seviyorum." Gözlerim yanarken elimi yumruk yapıp ısırdım. "Ben de ufaklık." Telefon kapandığında bir süre yanağımdan indiremedim. Gözlerimi kırpıp gözyaşlarımı davet de edemedim. Sadece bekledim, neyi beklediğimi bilmeden.

"Ben fena hâlde lanetliyim." Meredith'in geldiğini biliyordum. Bir süredir kapı aralığında durmuş beni izliyordu. "Uygun bir zaman olmadığını biliyorum ama seninle konuşmam gerekiyor."

Telefonu komodinin üzerine koyduktan sonra iki elimle koltuğun kollarına ağırlığımı verip ayağa kalktım. "Benim de seninle görüşmem gerekiyor. Bir kez daha deneyeceğim."

Kız kardeşim anlamayan gözlerle yüzüme baktı. "Beslenecek misin?"

"Hı-hı." Elimin tersiyle gözlerimi sildim. "Buna mecburum. Bir kez daha deneyeceğim ve eğer bu kez onu göremezsem söz veriyorum gideceğim." İçimden sessizce ekledim, *Lilith'e gidip soracağım.*

O şeytandan asla vazgeçmeyeceğim.

"Sen ne diyecektin?" Meredith önemsiz bir şeymiş gibi elini salladı. "Boş ver, sonra konuşuruz." Gözleri az önce hazırladığım bavula kaydı. "Hastaneye gidiyoruz değil mi?" Bavulun ön yüzünden hançerlerimi çıkarıp kemerime taktım. "Taksiye binmiyoruz. Kimse uyanık değildir bu saatte. Yolda Misha'yı ararsın."

Kız kardeşimin uçmaktan daha az sevdiği bir şey varsa o da telefonla konuşurken uçmaktı. Ama karşı çıkmadı. Kapıyı açıp sabah güneşini içeri aldı. Çatının kenarına yürüdüğünü biliyordum. O beni beklerken hızla temiz bir gömlek giyip atkuyruğumu sıkılaştırdım.

Yanına vardığımda bir adım geri çekilip kanatlarımı açmamı bekledi. Kadife kanatlarım sırtımı yavaşça yarıp hızlı çekimde büyüyen bir filiz gibi havada ilerledi. Simsiyah kanatlar göğü kapladığında Meredith'e yaklaştım. Kollarını boynuma sardığında iki adım koşup hızımı alarak kendimi çatıdan aşağı bıraktım.

***

Dün canını aldığımız adamın yerinde şimdi bir başkası vardı. Perdenin yarısı açık olduğundan içeriyi görebilmiştim. Oldukça ihtiyar bir kadın yatakta yatarken üzerine eğilmiş orta yaşlı kadın da ağlıyordu. Meredith gerekli araştırmayı yapmadan ortaya atlayan tiplerden değildi. "Onlar nasıl sence?" dedim fısıldayarak başımla kadınların oturduğu yeri işaret ettim.

Kız kardeşim bir eliyle omzumu tutup baktığım yere uzandı. "Olabilir. Nasıl olsa ölecekmiş gibi görünüyor. Ama kötü birilerine benzemiyorlar."

Güvenlik ilk günkü gibi değildi. Her iki mahkûma bir güvenlik görevlisi gelecek şekilde her yer üniformalı adamlarla doldurulmuştu. Bu sıkıyönetim canımı sıktı. "Sana kötü birini bulmada bol şans." Kollarımı huzursuzca göğsümde birleştirdim.

Tüm bu çabayı cehenneme gidene kadar tok kalmam gerektiği için sarf etmiyordum. Eh bence hikâyeye dâhil olan herkes benim kim için orada olduğumu bilebilirdi.

"Psikiyatrideki bir hasta fenalaşmış."

Genç, siyah saçlı bir doktor erkeklere has o kalın sesiyle koridorda bağırdı. Ardından gözden kayboldu. "Bize deli değil kötü birileri lazım." Meredith yanıt olarak sadece omuz silkti. Farklı şekillerde yetişmemize rağmen çoğunlukla birbirimizi anlıyorduk. Bu durumun benim şeytana dönüşmemle de bir ilgisi olabilirdi tabii ki. Ne de olsa ben avcıyken Meredith ile karşılaşmıştık ve o karşılaşmada birbirimizi neredeyse öldürecektik.

Telefon çalınca dikkatim dağıldı. Önemli olabilme ihtimaline karşı arka cebimdeki telefonu çıkardım. Arayan Misha'ydı.

"İkinci kat, numara dokuz." Ardından telefon kapandı. Kız kardeşime döndüm. "Az önce konuştuğum normal olan mı yoksa kafayı yemiş olan cadı mıydı emin değilim. Beni takip et." Kız kardeşim rengârenk giyimine zıt kuru kafalı sırt çantasının kollarını düzeltip beni takip etmeye koyuldu.

Merdivenleri hızla çıkarken kalbimin atışı neredeyse duyuluyordu. Midemin tam ortasında alevden bir top zıplıyor gibiydi. Top her çepere çarpışında tek bir ses çıkıyordu. *Aidan... AİDAN!*

Sırtıma sert bir şey çarpınca tökezledim. "Hey, ne yapıyorsun?" Hışımla arkamı döndüğümde Meredith'in alnını tutup sıvazladığını gördüm. "Neden durdun öyle birden?" dedi cadı sanki benim suçummuş gibi. Gözlerimi devirdim. "Bu geceki işi berbat edersen bir başka hakkımız olmayacak. Bu sikik yerdeki son gecem bu."

Derin bir nefes aldım. İşaret parmağımı keten gömleğinin yakasına koyup dürttüm. "Bunu berbat etme Merr." Deli kız kardeşimin yeşil gözlerinde şimşekler çaktı ama yine de başını hızlıca sallayıp onayladı. Ben ve dörtnala koşan kalbim arkamızda deli cadıyla beraber kalan merdivenleri çıktık.

Numara dokuz, koridorun sonundaki beyaz kapılı bir odaydı. Odaya en yakın yer numara sekiz ve kuzey cephesindeki yangın merdiveniydi. Burada birilerinin canını aldıktan sonra ateş almış gibi kaçacağımız için gözlerim devamlı olarak yangın merdivenindeydi.

"Buradan kaçacağız." Kız kardeşime merdiveni gösterdim. "Cehennem cadıları ışınlanabiliyor ama sen bir bok yapamıyorsun." Kız kardeşim yanıt vermedi. O an kendisinin de bunu düşündüğünü fark ettim. Bu yeni, tuhaf farkındalığımı başka bir zaman düşünmek için beynimin bir köşesine itip koridoru kontrol ettim. Uygun zaman geldiğinde numara dokuzun kapı kolu avuçlarımın içindeydi.

Bir saniye sonra ise içerideydim.

Meredith arkasından kapıyı kapatınca yeni kurbanımla odada üçümüz kalmıştık. Kurbanım yirmili yaşların sonunda, sarı saçlı bir kızdı. Birkaç adım yaklaşınca onun sarışın değil de peruk olduğunu gördüm. "Yok, hayır bu ne?" Meredith tek adımda yanıma gelip omzumun üzerinden yatağa baktı. Kızı görünce benzer bir reaksiyon verişini izledim. Cep telefonumu çıkarıp son aramalara girdim.

"Alo?"

"Ne oldu?" Cehennem cadısının kaygısız sesi kaşlarımın titreşmesine sebep oldu.

"Ne mi oldu? Bu kız kanser." Son kelime odanın sessizliğini birkaç oktav arttırmıştı. Eğer yavru bir sinek odada uçmaya karar verirse kanat seslerini duyabilirdiniz.

Cadı yanıt vermeyince söylenmeye devam ettim. "Kötü biri istiyorum demiştim. KÖTÜ. Büyük K ile." Bir elimle şakaklarıma bastırırken hastaya arkamı döndüm.

"Biliyorum. Sakin ol şeytan. Kız da biliyor, bunu kendisi istedi. O gördüğünüz kanser hastası olan bir cehennem cadısı."

Hoparlörü açıp söylediklerini tekrar etmesini istedim. Meredith hastane odasının içinde yankılanarak eko yapan sesi dinledikten sonra şaşkınlıktan küçük dilini yutmuştu. Bir yorum yapamıyorduk.

"Siz kanser olabiliyor musunuz?"

Hattın diğer ucundan bir süre ses gelmedi. Tam ben yeni bir şey söyleyecekken Misha konuştu. "O bu diyarda olmaması gereken bir şey. Size direnmeyecektir."

Gözlerimi kapadım. "Anlaşmamız bu değildi." Cadı histerik bir kahkaha atınca kulağıma ağrı saplandı. "Şeytanla yapılan anlaşmalar genelde düşünüldüğü gibi ilerlemez, ha?"

"Kötü biri miydi bari?" Şimdi ilerleyip ayakucundaki demiri tutuyordum. Aldığım kararların beni getirdiği nokta her zaman hastalıklı bir şekilde tuhaf oluyordu. Eğer bir kitap karakteri olsaydım beni kaleme alan ruh hastasını bıçaklardım!

Lanet olsun!

"Kötü biriydi." Telefonu kapayıp arka cebime koydum. Alnımdan akan huzursuz ter damlalarının dünyada olmamadan mı yoksa eski insansı alışkanlıklarımdan mı kaynaklandığını bilmiyordum. "Bir saniye ver bana." Son banyomun üzerinden iki gün geçmişti. Elimi başımın iki yanına aldım. Yağlı saç tellerim parmak aralarıma dolunca onları tutup çektim. Şımarık küçük bir çocuk gibi tepinmek istiyordum.

Bir süre öyle kaldım. Sonra aklıma yeni bir şey geldi. "Onun acı çekmemesi için bir büyü bul."

Meredith gülümseyince doğruldum. "Bunu diyeceğini biliyordum." Ardından beni ittirip yatağa yaklaştı. Yatan kızın çarşafını tutup aşağı çekti.

Kız çok çok zayıftı. Uçurumdan itilişimden sonraki günlerimi hatırlatıyordu. Gözlerinin altı yaşamı unutmuş bir zombi gibi mosmordu. "Büyü ile kanseri iyileştiremezler mi?" Meredith kızın ayakucuna oturdu. "Cehennem cadılarının büyüleri bizimkiler gibi değil. Hoş bizimkiler de senin düşündüğün gibi işlemiyor zaten. Herkes kendi çöplüğünün efendisidir Cass. Burası dünya." Ardından kızın ayak bileğine dokunup büyüsünü fısıldamaya başladı.

İşini bitirmesini beklerken gözlerimi kızın yanındaki kabloların bağlı olduğu monitörden alamıyordum. Tık tık tık tak tık tık tak... Nabzın sesi soğuk odayı doldururken tırnaklarımı avuç içlerime geçirdim. Kendisi ölmek istemişse yapacak bir şey yoktu, değil mi?

"Gelebilirsin." Yaslandığım duvardan uzaklaşıp kardeşimin yanına geldim. Hasta kız gözlerini aralamıştı. "Sen şeytan kraliçe olmalısın." Ne diyeceğimi bilemeden orada öylece durdum.

Kız zoraki bir şekilde gülümseyince ben de kendimi gülümsemeye zorladım, sanki birazdan onu öldürmeyecekmişim gibi.

"Pek kraliçeye benzemiyorsun."

İşte buna gerçekten sırıttım. "Sen de bir cehennem cadısına benzemiyorsun." Kızın yüzündeki gülümseme silininince kendi dudaklarımı büzdüm. Koca ağızlı şapşal ben... "Öyle demek istemedim, yani..."

Kız zayıf parmaklarını kaldırdı. "Sorun değil. Hastalanmamın sebebi buraya ait olmamam. Beni ait olduğum yere götürecek diyarlar arası bir kurye yok. Yani buradan kurtulmamın tek yolu ölmem. Eğer sen yapmazsan zaten bir süre sonra öleceğim."

"Neden intihar etmedin?" Meredith'e inanamayarak baktım. Koca ağızlılık ailemin geninde vardı herhâlde.

"Bizler intihar edemeyiz." Kollarını kaldırıp beyaz gecelik içindeki cılız bedenini gösterdi. "Bu can bize ödünç verildi." İki kolunu yanlarına uzatıp gözlerini birkaç kez kırptı. Meredith'in büyüsünün işe yaradığını görebiliyordum. "Ancak bir başkası beni vahşice öldürürse bu benim sorumluluğum dışında gerçekleşmiş olur." Bana bakıp içten bir şekilde göz kırpınca aynı gün içinde ikinci kez ne yapacağımı bilemedim.

"Bir şey hissetmeyeceksin." Başucuna ilerleyip soğuk yatak başlığını tuttum. "Adın neydi?"

"Lisa," dedi kız yavaşça.

"Lisa. Şimdi gözlerini kapat ve ona kadar say, tamam mı?" Cadının dudaklarına rahatlamış bir ifade yayıldı.

Ölümden korkmak ya da ölümü yaşamak birbirlerinden tamamen ayrı şeylerdi. Pek çok varoluş ölümden korkardı. Ama sadece bazıları ölümün ne demek olduğunu bilirdi.

Ben ölümün ne demek olduğunu bildiğimi düşünüyordum. Aidan'a içimde kalan tüm o kırıntıları gönderirken, geride sadece kırık bir kabuk bırakacak kadar kendimi bitirdiğimde öldüğümü düşünmüştüm. Meredith ise gerçekten de ölmüştü ve en az ölüm kadar sarsıcı olan yeniden dirilmeyi yaşamıştı.

Ama Lisa'nın gözlerinde daha önce pek çok kişide gördüğüm o şey vardı. Onun bu diyardaki savaşı bitmişti, geri de gelmeyecekti.

Cehennem cadısının soğuk parmakları elime değince irkilerek daldığım düşüncelerimden sıyrıldım. Cadının sağlıksız bir şekilde moraran ince dudakları aralanıp esaretinden kurtulmuş bir fısıltıyı dışarı çıkardılar. "Teşekkürler." Ardından cadının içindeki parıltı titreşerek dışarı çıkmaya başladı. Lisa'nın göğsü yukarıya kalkıp da nefesini dışarı bırakır bırakmaz parıltının şiddeti arttı. Elini bırakmadan tüm o ruhunu kabul ettim.

Orada yalnız değildik.

Ensemde hissettiğim karıncalanma merakımı ele geçirerek bakışlarımı odanın kapısına kaydırmama sebep oldu. Gördüğüm şey...Cadının elini bıraktım.

"Aidan?" Dışarıdan çıldırmış gibi görünebilirdim ama umurumda değildi. Bir elimi uzatıp kapının önündeki parıldayan şeye doğru yürüdüm. Işık topu bir anlığına öne atılınca soluğumu tuttum. Tanrım... Sanki beni tanımış gibiydi! Tüm bunları uyduruyor olamazdım!

"Aidan?"

Işık topu bir an için söner gibi olunca olduğum yerde kıpırdamaktan korkar hâlde dikilmeye devam ettim. Sonra ışık topları birbirinden ayrılıp bir silüet oluşturunca kalbimin çok ama çok hızlı çarptığını fark ettim. Nabzım kulaklarımda atarken ona bakmakta olduğumu fark ettim. Gerçek ona.

O simsiyah dalgalı saçları, altın bir toz perdesinin ardından bana gülümsüyor gibiydi. Gözlerim yanıp da yaşları serbest bırakınca bir kez daha öne atıldım. Bu kez omzumda bir el beni durdurdu. "Gidiyor," dedi kardeşim yavaşça. Ve haklıydı. Işık topları başta iki tane oldular, sonrasında daha da çoğaldılar. Öyle bir hızla gittiler ki göz bebeklerim odanın karanlığına alışamadı. Önümde dev parlak noktacıklar görüyordum.

"Bu kez sen de gördün," dedim kız kardeşime dönmeden. Görüntü hâlâ yer yer parlak ve baş ağrıtıcıydı. Şu an sevdiğim adam burnumun ucunda olsa bile göremeyebilirdim.

"Gördüm. O sanırım Aidan'dı." Ve aylar sonra ilk kez nefes aldığımda ciğerlerim yanmadı. Kocaman umut dolu bir nefes alıp kız kardeşime döndüm. "Bunun anlamı ne peki?" Meredith'in yeşil gözlerinde tereddüt titreşti. "Bunları ben bilemem," dedi bakışlarını benden çekerken.

Ardından omzumda duran elini hafifçe sıktı. "Ama bir yolunu buluruz, hep bulduk." Elimi elinin üzerine koyup kararlı bir şekilde başımı salladım. Yarım bıraktığım ruh emme işine gitmeden önce olduğum yerde durup derin bir nefes aldım. Nefes almasına gerek olmayan birine göre oldukça fazla soluklanıyordum. Lisa ben ona yaklaşırken tepki vermedi. Çoktan bu diyardan göçüp gitmişti. Ardında ise kanser olmayan bir beden ve cadı ruhunun güçlü kırıntılarını bırakmıştı. Yatağının önünde diz çöküp o ruhun parçalarını bir bir içime kabul ettim.

Lisa yok olduktan sonra soğuk hastane zemininde oturmaya devam ediyordum. "Birileri gelip bizi götürmeden kalk hadi." Meredith kızın üzerine kabloları yeniden yerleştirmek için komutumu bekliyordu. O, kabloları taktığı an nabzı hissedilmeyecek ve monitör dev bir şekilde ötmeye başlayacaktı. Hemşirelerin odaya kaç saniyede geleceği ise bilinmezliğini koruyordu.

"Bir konuda karar vermeye çalışıyordum," dedim yerimden kalkarken. Az önce bana eklenen ruh gücünden sonra bir süre beslenmesem bile olurdu. Zaten cehenneme dönüyordum ama yine de…

"Tanrım, o bakışlar ne?" Meredith abartılı bir ifade ile gözlerini devirip kollarını kucağında birleştirdi. "Her ne öneriyorsan hayır."

"Sen kabloları tak, ne düşündüğümü sana o ara söylerim." Kız kardeşim kollarını çözmeden önce gözlerini kısıp yüzüme baktı. "Sen dediğimi yap." Yavaşça kollarını çözüp Lisa'nın nefessiz bedenindeki kabloları yerlerine bantladı. Serumu yeniden taktıktan sonra monitörün tuşuna basıp açılmasını bekledi.

Üç saniye içinde buradan gidecektik.

"Onu tekrar göreceğim. Bu gece. İster gel ister gelme."

Ardından monitör ötmeye başladı.

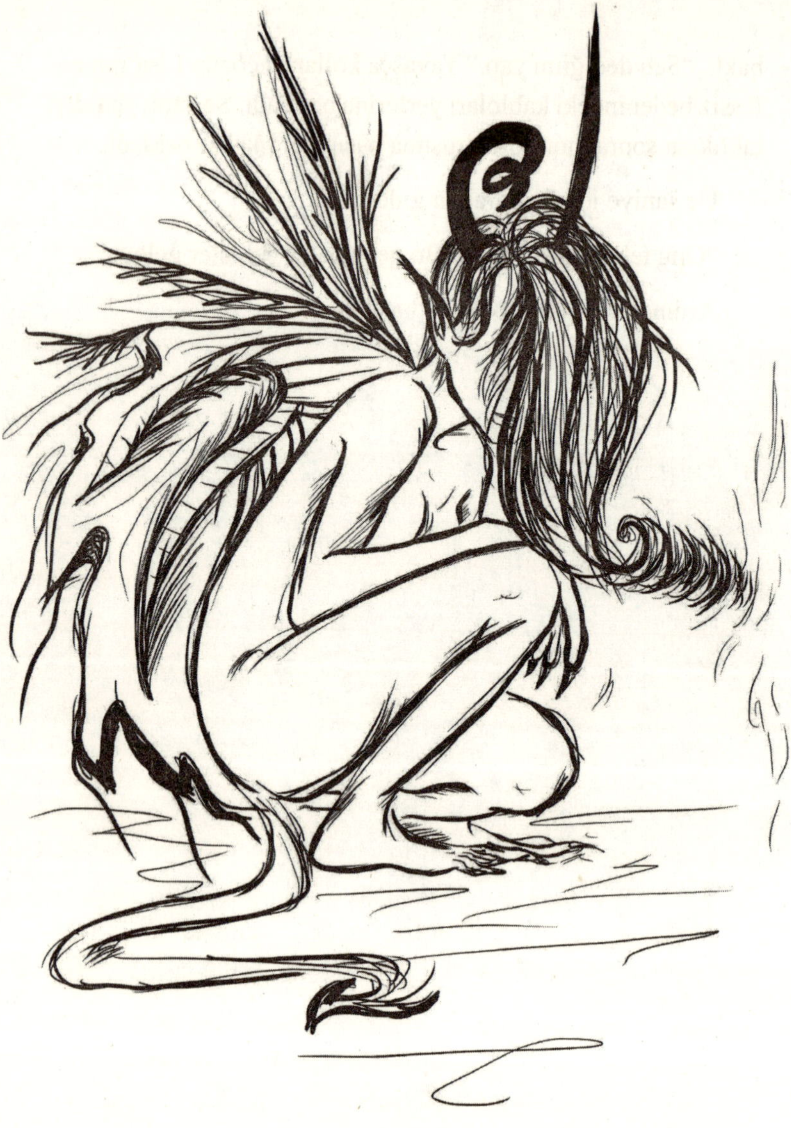

"On yedi senedir ölüsün Cassandra,
yeniden doğmak için."

BÖLÜM 7

Melekler pek çok zaman yaptıkları gibi huzurlu evlerinde göğü izliyorlardı.

Zamanın olmadığı, yağmurun yağmadığı o evrenin en dibi ve en yüce mekânı olan yerde, her şeyden uzak, tüm o eril ve dişil kimliklerinden sıyrılmış bir hâlde boşlukta yüzüyorlardı. Sadece bir tanesine tüm bu sessizlik gereksiz ölçüde boğucu geliyordu. Ve sadece bir tanesi kalbinde dinmeyen bir sızı hissediyordu. Uyuyordu, uyanıyordu ama hep eksik bir şeyler olduğu hissinden kurtulamıyordu.

Melek sızıyı anlayamıyordu. *Sızı* diye tanımladığı şey göğsünün orta yerindeki bir ağırlıktı meleğin. Diğerlerine -ustasının izin verdiği ölçüde görüşebildiği diğer meleklere- sızıyı sormuştu ama hiçbirinden doyurucu bir yanıt alamamıştı. Melek dünyaya indiği son seferlerde bir hayal görmüştü ve sızının kaynağı da o hayaller olmalıydı.

İlk uyanışında -usta melek ona böyle demişti- bazı şeyleri hatırlamaması doğaldı. Zamanla tüm anılar yerine gelecek demişti ustası. Ama başmelek aynı zamanda önceki hayatının hatırlanmaya değer olmadığını da belirtmişti. Simsiyah zift gibi kanatların vardı, demişti meleğe. *Günahkâr bir varlıktın önceden ve bu senin tek kurtuluş yolun.*

Yine de melek kendini geçmişi düşünmekten alıkoyamıyordu. Eksik hissetmek boynunu büküyordu. Benliği cevaplanmamış binlerce soruyla doluydu ve çevresindekilerin beklentisi de onun sormaması yönündeydi. Bir şeyler yaparken hatırlayacağını umuyordu ama bir şey yapamıyordu ki. Sadece o dağ eteğindeki ahşap, minik kulübesinde uyanıyor, kendine yemek yapıp yiyor, bulaşığını yıkıyor ve büyük daire şeklindeki penceresinin karşısına geçiyor, kır havasını içine çekip masasında oturuyordu.

Sonrası ise rutindi. Usta melek ona parıl parıl parlayan incecik bir kalemle siyah kapaklı eski bir deri defter vermişti. Kalemin ucu deftere değdiğinde sayfaların üzerinde melek dilinde isimler ve doğum tarihleri yazardı. Başmelek her gece yatmadan hemen önce defterlerin olduğu dosyayı verir ve kontrolleri yapmasını tembihlerdi. Melek, o zaman dosyada isimlerin sol yanında yeni rakamların yazdığını görürdü.

Uyanışından birkaç hafta sonra ustasının kim olduğunu anlamıştı.

Pek çok isminden sadece biriydi Azrail.

İnsanlar ona farklı şeyler söylerdi. Melek de ona usta diyordu. Bazen başmelek dediği de oluyordu ama genellikle o altın sarısı saçlı, zarif, uzun boylu ve özenle yontulmuş bir heykeli andıran keskin yüz hatları olan melek, onun ustasıydı.

Bir gece yüzünde kanlar ile gelip ona dosyayı uzattığında, melek onunla gitmek istediğini söyledi.

"Sıkıldım. Ben de gelmek istiyorum." Can almaya hevesli miydi bilmiyordu, sadece yola devam etmek, bir şeyleri hatırlamak istiyordu. Hatırlamak önemliydi, değerliydi. Melek hayatında değerli bir şeyler olmasını arzuluyordu.

Tanrım... Bir şeyler fena hâlde yanlıştı. Çok büyük bir şeyi unutmuş gibiydi. Sanki unutursa öleceği bir şeyi zihninden silmişlerdi. O kimdi? Ailesi var mıydı? Evli miydi? Sevgilisi... O, sevebilir miydi?

Melek o gün bir şey yemedi. Evinden çıkıp kutsal kanatlıların cennet dedikleri o inanılmaz güçlü enerji akımına doğru adım attı. Kanatlarını kürek kemiklerinin arasına doğru içine çekti ve cennetinin kokusunu ciğerlerine gönderdi.

Hüzünlüyken hüznün sebebini bilmemek tuhaftı.

Ve ustası geldi. Ona bu kez beraber gideceklerini söyledi. İki melek kollarının arasında defterlerin neredeyse taşacağı dosyaları ve bembeyaz takım elbiseleri ile sınırın başladığı büyük perdeye doğru uçtular.

Dünya meleklerin gelişine pek çok kez şahit olmuştu. Ama şansa bakın ki dünya dilsizdi. Kimseye o gece iki meleğin sırtlarında parlak dev kanatlarıyla yeryüzüne ayak bastığını söyleyemezdi.

Melek çıplak ayakları asfalta değdiğinde dayanamayıp derin bir nefes verdi. İçi titriyordu. Her daim ruhunu kemiren o eksiklik duygusu şimdi kabararak ruhundan taşmış gibiydi. Bir adım daha atınca yerdeki su birikintisi meleğin beyaz pantolonunun bakir paçalarını ıslattı. Başını eğip baktı. Bu kirler bile ona tanıdık geliyordu. İçten içe hiçbir zaman beyaz giyen, düzgün, temiz biri olmadığını hissetmişti. İlk beslenmesi ve uyanışına yardımcı olan ustası dışında gördüğü diğer melekler de ona bu konuda bir şey anlatmamışlardı. Herkes onun için önemli olanın şimdiki zaman olduğunu söylüyordu. Birileri o bu konuma gelebilsin diye çok fazla şey feda etmişti.

Bunu söyleyen melek ise Azrail'in baş çırağıydı. Nathaniel tıpkı Azrail gibi altın sarısı saçlı, karizmatik bir melekti. Ustaları gibi pek konuşmaz, sadece işini yapardı. İşini yapmadığı zamanlarda ise asla ortalarda görünmezdi. Melek çoğu zaman onu görmezdi. Dosyaları bazen Nathaniel getirirdi ve o zamanlarda bile iki melek asla sohbet etmezdi.

O günden sonra hep bunu düşündü. Birisi o böyle yaşayabilsin diye bir şeyleri feda etti. Böyle dememiş miydi altın saçlı melek?

"Nereye gidiyoruz?" diye sordu melek diğerine. Sarışın melek akşam melteminin kâküllerinin kaşlarına vurmasına müsaade etti. Uzaklara bakıp düşündü. "Bir hastane. Birileri yaralanmış. Görevimiz gidip ruhunu toplamak." Durup diğerine baktı. "Vakit geldi. Vakti gelen her şey bir gün gider."

Melek bunu düşündü. Bu mantıklıydı. Başını eğip diğeri gibi kanatlarını tekrar sırtından çıkardı. Birlikte yükselirken kanatlarına değen sert rüzgâr meleğe yeniden yaşadığını hissettirdi.

İnsanlar, tepeden bakıldıklarında komikti. Oradan oraya koşturan küçük, sevimli karıncalar gibiydiler. "Kanatlarını görmesinler. Şuraya ineceğiz." Azrail anatomi atlasından fırlamış gibi duran, son derece kibar ve ince parmaklarıyla bir binanın çatısını işaret etti. Rüzgâr iki meleği de kucaklarken dev hastanesin çatısına indiler.

"Beni takip et ve gerekmedikçe kimseyle konuşma." Melek, ustasının emrini sessizce başıyla onayladı. Heyecan içini kemiren bir fare gibiydi. Kalbi hiç olmadığı kadar hızlı atıyordu. Bugünün diğer günlerden farkı neydi bilmiyordu ama eksiklik duygusu kilolarca anının arasından sıyrılıp yüzeye çıkabilmek için can çekişiyordu.

Beraber çatıdaki kapıyı açıp merdivenlerden inmeye başladılar. Azrail birden durunca melek de durdu. "Her zaman bunu yapmamıza gerek yok. Duvarların içinden geçebilirsin ama şu an için sana bunu öğretemem, çok erken. Öyle zamanlarda direkt olarak ışınlanırsın. Bir diğer yol ise eğer kimsenin seni görmesini istemiyorsan zamanı yavaşlatırsın." Azrail işaret ve başparmaklarını kaldırıp birbirine bastırdı. Sonra bir saatin akrep ve yelkovanıymışlar gibi hareket ettirdi. Zaman önce yavaş, sonra ağır ve keskin bir ivmeyle durdu. "Bunu henüz yapmayacaksın. Eski usul devam edeceğiz." Azrail ellerini çözünce zaman akışına kaldığı yerden devam etti. Usta melek tekrar konuşmaya başladığında koridorda ilerlemeye başlamıştı. "Birinin canını alırken insansı formumuzdan çıkarız. Olması gerektiği gibi ışığa dönüşürüz. Ki ışığa dönüştüğünde biraz miden bulanacak. Görüşün biraz azalabilir, bunlara hazır ol." Devam etmek için köşeden dönmeden önce Azrail duruverdi. Gözlerinde insanoğlunun anlamlandıramayacağı bir şeyler gizliydi. "Birini tanıdığını sanırsan eğer, sakın durma. Bu seni yanıltır. Sen bu dünyaya ait değilsin. Bölük pörçük anılarını değil beni, ustanı takip edeceksin."

Ve bir kapının önünde durdular.

Kapı açıldığı an melek nefes almayı unuttu. "Bu da ne böyle?"

"Bunun böyle olmaması gerekiyordu." Azrail odaya dalıp meleğin görüşünü kapatmıştı ama melek onun hemen peşinden içeri girdi. İlk başta ne gördüğünü anlayamadı melek. Az önce tehlikeli bir hızla çarpan kalbi sanki aniden duruvermişti. Onu bu denli sarsan, yatakta yatan ve sarımsı ruhu bedeninden yarı yarıya koparılmış ölmekte üzere olan insan değildi. Onu sarsan insanın başında duran diğeriydi.

Güzel ela rengi gözleriyle yatakta yatan adama bakıyordu. Melek içeri dalınca kızın dikkati dağıldı ve dönüp meleğe baktı.

Dolgun, güzel kırmızı dudakları aralandı, ardından tekrar kapandı. Melek onun enerjisinin neredeyse sönmek üzere olduğunu görünce sebebini bilmediği bir korkuya kapılıp öne doğru atıldı. "Sana geride dur dedim." Azrail güçlü kolunu kaldırıp meleği geriye savurunca kız ufak bir çığlık attı.

"Hayır hayır hayır! Bu gerçek olamaz!"

Melek, ışık formuna dönüştüğünü hissedince ağlamak istedi. Çaresizdi. Kıza uzanmak istedi ama yapamadı. Elleri yoktu, gözleri yoktu, ona seslenebileceği bir ağzı yoktu. Ama kızın vardı. Kız tüm o yitip giden enerjisine rağmen ağır ağır ayağa kalktı. Kahverengi kâkülleri gözlerinin önüne düşüp güzel gözlerini gölgelerken, bir eliyle yatağa tutunup diğeriyle meleğe uzandı. "Aidan," dedi güçsüz bir sesle.

Ve Azrail, meleği hiç ağırlığı yokmuşçasına kucaklayıp odanın dışına çıkardı. İnsan zamanıyla bir saniye sonra cennetin soğuk çiğlerinin oynaştığı çimlerdeydiler. Aidan insan formuna dönerken yerde cenin pozisyonunu alıp yumruklarını sıktı. Gözlerini açamıyordu.

O içinde var olduğunu bildiği eksiklik artık somuttu. O kızdı. Kız eksiliğiydi. Kız, Aidan demişti. Adı buydu.

Aidan.

Adı bile eksik gibiydi.

Aidan, hiçbir şeyi bilememenin verdiği acizlik duygusuyla çırılçıplak bir şekilde çimlere uzandı. Azrail onu çimlere bırakıp bir anda kayboluvermişti, öyle ki Aidan olanlar hakkında ustasına soru bile soramamıştı.

Uyandığında hâlâ çimlerin üzerindeydi. Gözleri iri gövdesinin ezdiği çimlerin üstündeki ıslaklıkla bir olmuştu. Kirpiklerini elinin tersiyle silip doğruldu. Çırılçıplaktı ama üşümüyordu. Tuhaf duygular bedenini sarmıştı. "Aidan," kelimesi döküldü dudaklarından. "Aidan."

Ufak bir çatırtının ardından biraz hışırtı ve çağlayan dereler gibi berrak bir ses kulağına geldi. "Evet, adın bu." Aidan başını kaldırıp meleğe baktı. Mükemmel kelimesi melekler için bulunmuş olmalıydı çünkü aciz lügatında Azrail'i tarif edebileceği tek şey buydu. O, ihtişamlıydı.

Ama içinden bir ses, en derinlerdeki hastalıklı, cılız bir ses ona kendisinin de bir zamanlar ihtişamlı olduğunu söylüyordu. Bunun üzerine Aidan kendi bedenine baktı. Çıplak karnına, kollarının kaslı kıvrımlarına, gözlerinin önüne düşen simsiyah kömür karası saçlarına baktı. Hâlâ ihtişamlı sayılırdı. Üstelik bembeyaz, gür, kuvvetli kanatları vardı.

Azrail güzeldi ama Aidan kendini güzel hissedemiyordu.

"Geçmişimi öğrenmek istiyorum." Bunun üzerine aylardan beri ilk kez değişik bir şey oldu. Melek güldü. Bembeyaz inci dişleri pembe dudaklarında parıldadı. "Sizler hiç değişmiyorsunuz." Sizler derken kastettiği şey boşlukta, havada asılı kaldı. Aidan öyle çok meleğe benziyordu ki kendini dışlanmış hissedemedi.

Aidan içinde kavrulan kibri gözlerinden görünmesin diye başını eğdi. Hissettiği şey kibirdi. Ve bedeni içindekini istemeyip dışarı kusmak istercesine eğilip büzülüyordu. Aidan var oluşuna sövüyor gibiydi.

"Geçmişime ihtiyacım var."

Azrail zarif elini kaldırarak onu susturdu. "Burada sana verilenlerden başka bir şeye ihtiyacın yok."

Aidan, meleğin ihtiyaç kelimesinin anlamını bilip bilmediğinden emin değildi. Ağır hareketlerle dikkatlice yerden kalktı. Haftalardır kirlenmeyen dizleri çim ve toprağın kucağında lekelenmişti. Kızarmış dizlerinin üzerindeki parçalanmış toprağı elinin tersiyle silkeledi. "O kız kimdi?"

Aidan o an meleğin gözlerinden geçen anlık karartıyı uydurmuş olabileceğini düşündü.

"Hiç kimse." Aidan gözlerini şüpheyle kıstı, buna inanmadı. Hiç kimse size adınızı söylediğinde kalbiniz teklemezdi.

"Oraya geri dönmem gerek." Yürümek için davranınca Azrail görülmemiş bir zarafetle kayarak önüne geçti. "Onu tanımıyorsun. Tanımadığın biri için her şeyi riske atmaya değer mi?"

Yaşlı meleğin eski sözleri kulaklarında çınladı. *Biri senin için her şeyi feda etti.*

"Bir dahaki göreve yine seninle geleyim. Eğer o kız dediğin gibi *hiç kimseyse* peşini bırakacağım." Melek bilgelik akan safir mavisi gözleriyle uzun bir süre Aidan'a baktı. Ne düşündüğünü anlamak için ya çok zeki ya da çok semavi olmak gerekiyor gibiydi.

"Zaten onun peşini bırakacaksın. Melekler, melek dışında diğer hiçbir varlıkla iletişim hâlinde olamaz."

"Her gün yüzlerce insana dokunuyor, onların canını alıyorsun." Azrail ifadesiz gözlerle Aidan'a bakmaya devam etti.

"Bazen tüm bunların neden başına geldiğini merak ediyorum ama sonra seni izliyorum ve fark ediyorum. Melekler tarihindeki şahit olunabilecek en tuhaf şeylerden biri bu. Bu zamanda var olduğum için şanslıyım. Şimdi görelim bakalım şeytan kız ne yapacak?"

Ardından Azrail, Aidan'ı cennetin o açık yeşil sedir ağaçları ile bezenmiş tazecik ormanında bırakıp gitti.

O gittikten çok sonra Aidan meleğin dediklerine dikkat etti. Bir robot gibi duyduğu sözcükleri tekrarladı. "O şeytan kız."

Şeytan kız.

Aidan'ın adını bilen şeytan kız.

O kimdi?

***

Hastaneden çıkmanın pek çok yolu vardır.

Öncelikle herkes gibi kapıları kullanabilirsiniz ya da kafeteryanın açık havaya açılan kısmında sigara içen insanların toplaştığı yerden çıkabilirsiniz. Eğer bir suç işlediyseniz casus filmlerindeki gibi bir çalışanı bayıltıp kıyafetlerini ve kartını çalarak çıkabilirsiniz. Silahınız varsa ve kafanız iyi çalışmıyorsa ya da çaresizseniz birilerini rehin alabilirsiniz.

Ama asla ve asla pencereden atlamazsınız. Çünkü bu insanlar için hem saçmadır hem de çok can yakıcıdır.

Neyse ki insan değildim. Odaya yaklaşan adımları duyar duymaz Meredith'e sarılıp onunla beraber kendimi pencereden dışarı atmıştım. Tabii o an pencerenin sadece yarısının açık olduğundan habersizdim. Ben açık olan aralıktan kendimi bırakırken sırtımdaki Meredith hastane odasının camına kafasını gömmüştü. Bu sebeple ikimiz birlikte aşağı doğru düşerken bir yandan bana bağırıyordu. "Lanet olası, kafamı kırdın!"

Onu bedenimin ön tarafına alıp kanatlarımı açtım. Düşüşümüz yavaşlayıp ters yönde ivme kazanarak sonlandı. Kanatlarım bizi yukarı taşımaya başlamıştı. Ben yükselirken kız kardeşimin saçlarındaki cam parçaları boynuma çarpıyordu. Meredith bir eliyle kanayan başını tutuyor diğeriyle de omzumu sıkıyordu.

"Bir kez olsun bir şey yapmadan önce bunu düşün!"

Ama düşünemiyordum ki. Zihnim bomboştu. Aklım hâlâ dakikalar önce yaşadığım olayda kalmıştı. Yarım bir yıl boyunca asla olmayacağını düşündüğüm şey olmuştu işte. Annemin uğursuz kehaneti yarım yıl boyunca zihnimde dönüp durmuştu.

Ruhu tamamen kararmış olanlar melekleri göremezler.

Ama ben görmüştüm ve Meredith de görmüştü. Kız kardeşim kanayan başını tutmayı bırakıp turuncu saçlarını göğsüme gömerken elleriyle sırtımdaki tutuşunu sıklaştırdı. "Onu sen de gördün," dedim rüzgâr sesimi boğamasın diye bağırırken.

"Kulağımı sağır etmene gerek yok ve evet, gördüm." Saçları çeneme çarparken kanatlarımı daha hızlı çırpmaya başladım. Onu başka birinin daha gördüğü gerçeği keyfimi öyle yerine getirmişti ki damarlarım, içime pompalanan yepyeni bir enerjiyle dolup taşmaya başlamıştı. Durmadan gülmek istiyordum. Gökdelenlerin tepesinden siyah bir kartal gibi havayı yararak geçerken deli gibi gülmek, bu diyarı inletmek istiyordum.

"Yani deli değilim." Sırıtıyordum. Ve bunu durduracak gücü kendimde bulamıyordum. "Aidan'ı benim de görmem deli olmadığın anlamına gelmiyor. Sen hâlâ delisin," dedi kız kardeşim huysuzca. Sözleri kulağa boğuk geliyordu. Kafasını çok ciddi çarpıp çarpmadığını merak ettim.

Barın binası görüş alanıma girince daha da hızlandım. "Eğer bu çarpışma da kafanı kıramadıysa ne kırar bilmiyorum Merr." Kız kardeşim sadece homurdanınca başımı hafifçe eğip yüzünü görmeye çalıştım. "Üzerime kusarsan ben de kusarım ve uğruna servet akıttığın saçların mahvolur." Meredith yanıt vermek yerine belime doladığı kollarını biraz daha sıktı.

Çatı katına vardığımızda onu dikkatlice indirip uzaklaşarak kanatlarımı sırtımın içine çektim. Birkaç kanat darbesi çatıdaki hortumları hareket ettirince gürültü çevreye yayıldı. "Daha fazla dikkat çek. Şu birkaç bina bizi duymadı," dedi Meredith terslenerek. Eliyle başının arkasını tutuyor, gözlerini de sımsıkı kapatıyordu. Canının yandığını anlamak için kâhin olmama gerek yoktu.

"Urange seni iyileştirebilir," dedim tereddütle. Perilerin büyü yapabildiklerini hepimiz biliyorduk, sorun şu ki ne tarz büyü yapabildikleri hâlâ gizemini koruyordu. Urange pek çok şeyi yapabilir; uçabilir, öldükten sonra pembe bir ağaca dönüşebilirdi ama birini iyileştirmek söz konusu olduğunda... Eh, görecektik.

Meredith küfürle karışık bir şeyler homurdanınca gözlerimi devirdim. Kendisini pekâlâ iyileştirebileceğini biliyordum ama ne derlerdi, terzi kendi söküğüne yama yapamaz gibi bir şey. Ya da o tarz başka bir deyimdi işte. Tam onu azarlamaya başlayacakken Marcus ve Urange koşar adım yanımıza geldiler.

Kurt önce bana sonra Meredith'e baktı. Kız kardeşinin yanına giderken soru soran gözleri üzerimdeydi. Urange yanı başında bana yaklaşırken ellerimi avuç içlerimi gösterecek şekilde havaya kaldırdım. "Siz birini kurban etmeye gitmediniz mi? Max öyle demişti. Görünen o ki, biri sizi kurban etmiş." Marcus, saçlarına dokunmak için elini uzatınca cadı, kurdun eline vurdu. "Ben hallederim," dedi ters ters.

"Onun nesi var?" Urange, cadıdan hoşlanmazdı. Periler ve cadılar tam olarak bestie sayılmazlardı ama biz hepimiz artık tuhaf bir biçimde ekip olmuştuk. "Kafasını çarptı," dedim kız kardeşime bakarken.

Meredith hışımla bize dönünce çenemi kapadım. "Kafamı kırmaya çalıştı da başarılı olamadı diyelim." Öfkesinin tek sebebinin kafasını yaralamam olmadığını biliyordum. İçten içe Aidan konusundaki saplantılı davranışlarımı sorguluyordu.

"Urange, onu iyileştirebilir misin?"

Peri kafasını hafifçe yatırıp güz rengi saçlı kardeşime baktı. "İyileştirebilirim ama sadece uyumlu olursa," dedi şüpheci bakışları hâlâ cadının üzerinde gezinirken.

Meredith öfkeyle ellerini kaldırdı. "Boş versene," dedi kanlı avucunu bana gösterecek şekilde açarken. "Ben Max ile hallederim." Hemen yanında ona dokunmaya çalışan erkek kardeşine öldürücü bakışlar attı. "Benden uzak dur Marcus, ben hallederim dedim." Sonrasında tekrar bana döndü. "Sen de onlara erkek arkadaşını yeniden nasıl elde edebileceğinle ilgili planını anlatırsın."

Urange ve Marcus'un kafayı yemişim gibi bakışlarını görmezden gelerek, "Bir planım olmadığını biliyorsun," dedim sertçe. Oysa Meredith çoktan arkasını dönmüş, bana güzel kıçını göstererek çatı katı daireme doğru yürümeye başlamıştı.

O gittikten sonra Marcus ağır adımlarla yanıma geldi. Üçümüz sessizlik yemini etmiş gibi konuşmadan öylece dikiliyorduk. Rüzgâr terden ıslanan tenime çarparken içimi tatlı bir ürperti kaplıyordu. Tüm tatsızlıklara rağmen duyularımdaki coşkuya engel olamıyordum. Marcus ve Urange, Meredith'in az önce patlattığı erkek arkadaşını yeniden elde edebilmek ile ilgili mevzuyu açıklığa kavuşturmamı bekliyorlardı.

"Pekâlâ, rahatlayın. Auranız çok gergin, beni de geriyorsunuz." Marcus sanki hiç beklemediği bir anda kafasına kurtboğan katılmış su dolu balonlardan birini atmışım gibi şaşkınca bana baktı. Konuştuğunda iri kollarını göğsünde kavuşturmuştu.

"Sana ağabeylik taslamak haddim değil ama bildiğim tek erkek arkadaşın Aidan," dedi tereddütle. Sanki onun bilemediği bir şeyi Urange bilebilirmiş gibi soru soran gözleri periye çevrildi.

"Yemin ederim Cassie'nin yaptığı hiçbir şeyi anlamıyorum," dedi peri kendini savunarak. Sonra o da bana döndü. "Anlatacak mısın yoksa sen anlatana kadar kanadındaki tüyleri tek tek koparmaya başlayalım mı?"

Ürperdim. "Anlatacağım. Ama önce söylemem gereken bir şey var. Marr ve Anton'un izini bulabileceğiniz konusunda size güvenmeliyim. Onları güvenli bir yere taşıyın ve Jo ile telefonda konuşmalarını sağlayın. En azından bir konuyu halletmiş olayım."

Peri tek kaşı şüpheyle kalkarken yüzüme bakmayı sürdürdü. "Başka ne işin var peki?"

Marcus huysuzca ekledi. "Krallığını korumak dışında demek istedi."

Gözlerimi devirdim. "Lilith'i bulma konusu da ertelenecek," dedim kardeşimin sözlerini duymazlıktan gelerek. "Ama merak etme, vampirler ve hırsızlar konusuyla ilgileneceğim. Sadece bugün değil." Dudağımı huzursuzca dişlerken yaptığım şeyi fark ederek şaşırdım. Bir iblis olduğum aylar boyunca böyle sıradan insani hareketler yapmayı bırakmıştım.

"Peki bugün bunların hiçbirini yapmayacaksan ne yapacaksın?"

Başımı kaldırıp soruyu soran periye baktım. "Bugün Aidan ile ilgileneceğim. Sanırım onu görmenin bir yolunu buldum." Gülümseme yüzüme yayılırken Marcus ve Urange birbirlerine baktılar.

Bu kız kafayı yemiş, diye düşündüler.

***

Bana verilen tek gömleği yatağımın üzerinde katlanmış bir şekilde buldum. Şeytanların dünyasında biri eşyanızı aldıysa muhtemelen size büyü yapmak için almıştır ya da o tarz kötü bir niyet için. Ama meleklerde bunun anlamı sadece birinin temizleyip geri verdiğidir.

Şeytanlar mı? İyi de ben şeytanlarla ilgili ne bilirdim ki?

Gömleğimi giyip düğmelerini iliklemeye başladım. İlikten geçen her düğmeyle beraber kararlılığım artıyordu. Onu kesinlikle görmeye gidecektim. O kızı bir yerden tanıyordum ve tanıdığım yeri bulmaya niyetliydim.

Geçmiş, tozlu bir zeminin altındaki parlak mücevherler gibiydi. Sadece bulunmayı bekliyordu. Ben ise aylardır ilk kez yaşıyor gibi hissetmiştim. Bir hayaldi belki tutunduğum ama kendimi o hayale tutunmaktan geri alamıyordum.

Giyinip parmaklarımla saçlarımı taradım. Melekler ayna kullanmıyordu. Doğruyu söylemek gerekirse aynaya ihtiyaçları da yoktu. Hepsi mükemmel birer modeldi. Belki de kendimizi beğenip kibirlenmemiz için ayna yoktu ama eğer sebep buysa da kibri engellemek bu kadar kolay olmazdı.

Artık hazırdım. Derin bir nefes alıp odamın kapısını açtım. Cebimde silah olarak kullanacağım kalem *ben buradayım,* diye bağırıyor gibiydi. Bir silah kullanabilecek olma ihtimalim ne kadardı bilmiyordum ama bildiğimi sandığım dünyam saniyelerle değişirken her ihtimale hazır olmak istiyordum. Kapıyı itip dışarı çıktım.

Cennetin tazecik temiz kokusu ciğerlerime dolarken hayalimi düşündüm. *Hayalimin simsiyah kâkülleri yüzünde uçuşurken ufak, çekik gözleri parlıyordu. Tanıdık bir ifade dudaklarında oynaşırken ayağa kalkmaya çalışıyordu.*

Sonrası karanlık.

Elimi kalbime götürüp derin bir nefes aldım. Onu tanıyordum. Kalbim, avucumun içinde sıcacık atarken kalbimin de onu tanıdığının farkına vardım. Bu her ne ise daha önce olmamıştı.

Ayaklarım yere sabitlenmiş gibi kıpırdayamadım. Bu ben değilim. Böyle hissetmemeliyim.

"Selam melekçik." Elimi göğsümden çekip duruşumu sağlamlaştırdım. Sesin sahibini tanıyordum. Yukarı bakınca içinde kaldığım küçük kulübenin üzerinde onu gördüm. Bembeyaz takım elbisesinin içinde âdeta parlayan bir yıldız gibiydi. Yıldızların başçırak gibi altın sarısı saçları varsa tabii.

"Selam." Kalp atışım düzene girerken çenemi kaşıdım. Melek ise bu hareketime gözlerini kısarak baktı. Bir saniye sonrasında gülümsedi. "Bu tarz hareketleri sık sık yapmaya mı başladın?"

Onu anlamadım.

Melek kanatlarını sertçe çırpıp kulübeden atlayarak yanıma indi. Gömleğimin yakaları boynuma çarparken bir adım geriledim. Kanatlarımız güzeldi. Ama... Bir şeyler eksikti. Renklerinde beni rahat hissettirmeyen bir şey vardı.

"İnsansı hareketleri diyorum," dedi kibar eliyle çenemi işaret ederken. Parmaklarım istemsizce çeneme kayarken diğer meleklerin neden bir yerlerinin kaşınmadığını merak ettim. "Bir yere gidiyor gibiydin." Ona yanıt veremedim. Ne diyeceğim hakkında hiçbir fikrim yoktu.

Buna karşılık melek, yüzündeki parlak altın sarısı uzun bir saçı omzunun gerisine attı. O da tanıdık geliyordu ama kız kadar değil. Kız farklıydı.

"Ben..." Tam çırak diyecekken kızın sözleri aklıma geldi. "Adımı öğrendim Nathaniel. Aidan sanırım. Aidan." Meleğin gözlerinde bir parıltı yanınca dediğim şeyi düşünüp elimi çektim. "Ben iyi değilim." Elimle başımı gösterip parmağımla daireler çizdim. "Sanırım kafayı filan yiyorum ya da yedim. Ben..."

Melek elini kaldırıp beni durdurdu. "Hiç görmemen gereken bir varlığa maruz kalmışsın. Kafan karışmış. Sıfırlanman gerekiyor. Ama cennette bu tarz şeyleri yapan kişileri bulamazsın." Sözleri kafamı daha da karıştırıyordu. "Birkaç saat bekle. Ustan geldiğinde o sorularını yanıtlayabilir."

"O nerede?"

Melek başını yan yatırıp gerçekten de büyük bir merakla bana baktı. "Ruhları topluyor tabii ki." Nathaniel bu kez ellerini beyaz pantolonunun ceplerine koyup kamburunu çıkararak bana eğildi. Yüzüme çok yakın duruyordu. "Ah zavallı çocuğum, çok güçlü ve karanlık bir şeye bulaşmışsın." Uzun, beyaza boyanmış tırnaklarından biriyle gözlerimin önüne gelen saçımı kenara aldı.

Elimi yavaşça kaldırıp elini tuttum. “Benden sakladığınız bir şey var. Ben tam olarak ne kadar zamandır bura-” Durup başımı çevirerek içinde durduğum uçsuz bucaksız ormana baktım. “Cennetteyim?”

“Tam günü bilemem ama altı aydır buradasın.” Meleğin göz bebekleri büyüyüp arkamda bir yere odaklandı. Sesin geldiği yöne dönerken kalbimin atışına söz geçiremiyordum.

Tok, güçlü bir ses atmosferimizi âdeta değiştirirken meleğin bileğini bıraktım. “Benimle hiç sohbet etmedin ama Nathaniel ile konuşuyorsun.” Azrail kanatlarının hızını azalttı. Nathaniel ona hiç yakışmayan eğreti bir hareketle omuzlarını silkince şaşırmama engel olamadım.

Usta benim asla gösteremeyeceğimi düşündüğüm tarzda bir zarafetle yere inince kulübeye neden kapı koyduklarını anlamaya çalıştım. Çatıya açacakları dev bir kuş deliği iş görürdü. Bu gördüğüm en gereksiz şeydi. Hayır hayır hayır, böyle sözler saçmaydı. Bunlar kibirdi. Kibir… Burada yer almaması gereken bir şey.

Sanki kötü şeyleri üzerimden atabilirmişim gibi silkindim. Azrail sanki bunu her gün yapıyormuş gibi kaygısız bir şekilde Nathaniel’e dönüp konuştu. “Bir şeyler gördü. Önceki hayatından onu en çok rahatsız edecek şeyi desek daha doğru olur.”

“Kızı gördü demek. Bu zamana kadar denk gelmemeleri tuhaf olmaya başlamıştı.”

Kız, kız… Onu biliyorlardı.

İçimde kabaran duygu karşısında düşüncelerim darmadağın oldu. Kıskançlık mıydı bu? NE SAÇMA AMA!

Nathaniel ellerini ceplerinden çıkarıp göğsünde birleştirirken beni sıkı bir süzdü. "Ben gitsem iyi olacak. Gün batımına dek halletmem gereken çok şey var." Başıyla Azrail'i selamladıktan sonra yavaşça arkasını dönüp kanatlarını sırtından çıkardı. Gidişinin rüzgârı bize çarparken sorularıma yanıt alma umuduyla orada dikilmeye devam ettim.

"Bana her şeyi anlatman gerekiyor."

Ustam güldü.

"Azrail ile böyle konuşmak genç bir meleğe hiç yakışık almıyor." Dudaklarımı aralamışken beni susturdu. "Ama sen genç bir melek olmaktan daha çok yetişkin bir şeytansın." Kapıyı açıp beni çağırdı. "Gel Aidan, sana anlatacaklarım var."

Böylece Azrail benim için kapıyı açık tutarken derin bir nefes alıp içeri girdim.

BÖLÜM 8

Draza

Sular saçlarımı yıkarken başımı banyonun duvarına yasladım. Gözlerimi kapatıp olumlu bir şeyler düşünmeye çalıştığım her seferinde kulağıma su kaçıyordu. Hizmetçilerin pek çok kez ısrar etmesine rağmen küvet ve benzeri teknemsi şeyleri artık kullanamıyordum.

Mümkünse bir süre çukuru anımsatacak herhangi bir şeyi görmek istemiyordum.

Başımı kaldırıp suyun gözlerimin içine girmesine izin verdim. Sanki birkaç litre su simsiyah gözlerimi temizleyebilirmiş gibi. Bir daha asla doğduğumdaki gibi normal gözlerim olmayacaktı. "Siktiğimin..." Derin bir nefes alıp gözlerimi kapadım. Su, ufak ve hoş bir şiddette göz kapaklarıma vururken yerine getirmem gereken tüm o sorumluluklardan kendimi azat ettiğimi hayal ediyordum.

Tüm bunları kendim istediğim için yapmak başka, başkası için yapmak başkaydı. Gözlerimi açtım. "Tek bir şeye de ben karar verebilseydim." Ilık su dudaklarımdan boynuma, oradan da bedenimin inişli çıkışlı hatlarına akıp ağır ağır hareket ederken arkamda bir yerden hoşnut bir mırıltı duyuldu.

"Mmm."

Ellerimle gözlerimin önüne düşen gümüşi saçlarımı geriye atıp sesin kaynağına baktım. Tıpkı benim gibi beyaz saçları olan Luera yatağımda uzanıyordu. Üzerinde diğer tüm o peri kızlarında olan parlak, içi gösteren, kışkırtıcı kıyafetiyle davetkâr bir edayla bana bakıyordu. Konuştuğunda sesi âdeta en nadide ziller gibi çınlıyordu. Minik neşeli çanların eşliğinde bana cilve yapıyordu. "Hayatımda gördüğüm en yakışıklı şeysin." Sesi pek çok erkek gördüm der gibiydi.

Bir lastikle ıslak saçlarımı bağlarken yatağın üzerindeki çarşafa uzandım. Su sesi kesilmişti. Pietra ellerinde havlu ile bana gülümsüyordu. Luera gibi onun da üzerinde iri göğüslerini gösteren şeffaf bir elbise vardı. Pek çok gereksiz şey görmüştüm ama en salakçası şu elbiseler olabilirdi. İsraf gibi geliyordu.

Pietra havluyu bana uzatınca Rohan'ın ipek çarşaflarını geri yatağa bıraktım, satenlerini ıslatırsam o yaşlı çenesinden kurtulamayacağımı biliyordum.

Pietra havluyu almama izin vermedi. Aksine elinde havlu ile bana yaklaştı. Elleri bedenime değmeden önce iri gri gözleri ile gözlerime baktı. Gülümsedim.

Pietra'yı yanımda istememin sebebi çok becerikli bir peri olması falan değildi. Çok güzel oluşu da değildi. Tek sebebi ellerini iyi kullanıyor oluşuydu.

Havlu belimin çevresinde oyalanıp bacaklarımın arasını kurularken kendimi tutamayıp inledim. "Yavaş ol Pietra." Kendimi tek adımda yatağa atıp sırtüstü çıplak bir şekilde uzandım.

Kral olmanın en güzel yanlarından biri de buydu. Ara sıra ben bile ne istersem yapabiliyordum.

Ve şu an ne istediğini bilen büyük bir parçam canıma okuyordu. "Kızlar, gelin." Elimi onlara uzatıp gözlerimi kıstım. "Bu elf biraz oyun istiyor." Luera şeffaf kıyafetini omuzlarından aşağı kaydırırken Pietra çoktan kucağıma atlamıştı.

***

Kızıl saçlı fahişe, uzun ve beyaz tırnaklarını boğazıma geçirdiğinde öksürdüm. "Bunu fena ödeyeceksin!" Ve o daha da sıktı. Öyle ki geride bir boğaz bırakmayacak şekilde beni parçalamaya başlamıştı.

"Şu genlerin mükemmelliğine bak," dedi boğazladığı boynumdaki âdem elmasımı yalarken. "Seninle mükemmel bir çocuğumuz olacak."

"Hayır!"

Nefes nefeseydim. Yatakta oturuyor, gözlerimin karanlığa alışmasını bekliyordum. Göğsüm inip kalkarken tuzlu bir ter damlası alnımdan kayıp dudaklarımın üstüne düştü.

Kâbuslar... Ah, kahrolası kâbuslar!

Ellerimle yüzümü kapayıp sakinleşmeye çalıştım. O kaltak zebaninin kucağımda inip kalkışının görüntüsü içimde öğürme isteği uyandırıyordu. Olaydan sonra bir daha başka bir kadınla beraber olamamıştım.

Pietra ve Luera'yı göndermiştim. Onlarla birlikte olacakken anılarım boğazıma bağlanmış yağlı bir urgan gibi ruhumu sıkmıştı. "Acilen yapmam gereken bir şey var, çıkın lütfen," demiştim. "Ah, şapşal krallar aşkına!" Kendimi tekrar yatağa bıraktım. Terden sırılsıklam olmuş yastığım boynuma değince ürperdim. Kendi yatağımda güvendeydim. Ayrıca güvende olamasam bile bu geri zekâlı bir cehennem cadısının bana tecavüz etmesi anlamına gelmiyordu, en fazla kurtların gelip organlarımla taş kâğıt makas oynaması olurdu.

Eğer biri gelip bana "Bir cehennem cadısını sikmek mi istersin yoksa böbreğini mi sökelim?" diye sorarsa yanıtım belliydi. "Lütfen iki böbreğimi birden alın efendim."

Bir kadının sizi isteğiniz dışı günde yirmi kez erekte hâle sokup kendi kendini üzerinize atması ve sizin ona sahip olmadığınız her an kırbaçlanmasını sağlaması tecavüz değil miydi? Öyleydi.

İğrençti.

Öğürmemek için yanağımın içini ısırıp kolumu gözlerime kapadım. Kısa vadede onların elinden kurtulduğuma sevinmiştim ama uzun vadede geçmiş peşimi bırakmayacaktı.

Renkli geçmişim adlı öyküme bir yenisini daha eklemek beni heyecanlandırıyordu. "Tek bir normal gün," dedim sessizce karanlığa. "Sadece bir gün uyanıp yemek yiyeyim ve huzur içinde uyuyayım." Karanlık, uğursuz sessizliği ile âdeta bu dediğime kahkaha atıyordu.

Sanki biz şeytanların huzurlu günü olabilirmiş gibi. *Seni kafayı yemiş zavallı kara elf Draza. Doğduğun andan beri lanetlenmiş bir zavallısın.*

Kolumu, kapadığım gözlerimin üzerinden indirip tavana baktım. Yapılacaklar listesi… "Tüm krallık bir zamanlar istediğim gibi bende." Öyleydi. Bunun için bir kez ölmüş, tecavüze uğramış, kendi kardeşimi bıçaklamış olsam bile sonunda istediğim olmuştu. Aslında en başında babam krallığı bana bırakmış olsaydı tüm bunlara gerek kalmazdı. "Pehh!" Kendi kendime konuşuyordum.

"Hapa!" Yattığım yerden boğazlanmış bir aygır gibi bağırdım. "Buraya gel!" Ardından yatakta duruşumu düzeltip geriye yaslandım. Hapa aslında adı Hapa olmayan, kendi hâlinde bir kara askerdi. Ona böyle seslenmemin onu rahatsız edip etmeyeceğini sormuştum. Rahatsız olmuyordu. "Rohan'ı toplantı odasına götürün. Üstünü başını temizleyin." Kara asker başını eğerek odadan çıkıp karanlıkta kaybolduğunda kendimi yeniden çarşaflara bırakıp gözlerimi tavana diktim. Aidanhell burada olsaydı ne yapacağını bilir miydi? Sanmıyordum. Kardeşim pek çok şeyde bir numara olabilirdi ama krallığı yönetmek bunlardan biri değildi. Aidan bürokrasi kelimesini şişman bir domuz sanabilirdi. Politika ile arası ise hiç iyi olamamıştı.

Parmaklarımın sert eklemlerini oymak ister gibi gözlerime bastırdım. Ama onun normal gözleri vardı, hem de hep. Oysa ben lanetliydim. Bir çift renkli iris bana fazlaydı, öyle değil mi? Ne de olsa uğursuz Draza ne bilirdi ki? Onun talepleri olabilir miydi ki? O kimdi ki?

Vekil kralım. Sonunda kralım işte. Ve ilk kez kendimi kanıtlamam için elimde gerçek bir fırsat var. O fırsatı da çar çur etmeyeceğim, bir zamanlar cadıyla yaptığım hataya düşemem. Psikolojimin ne denli sikildiği de umurumda değil. Kötü şeyler sadece benim başıma gelmiyor.

Hapa yeniden eşikte belirince neredeyse oymak üzere olduğum gözlerimden parmaklarımı çektim. "Evet?"

"Efendi Rohan'ı yerleştirdik. Başka bir arzunuz var mı Majeste?"

Yatakta doğrulup ayakucumda tortop ettiğim gömleğimi üstüme geçirdim. "Mor kule zindanlarına bir elçi yolla. Hapishane başmüfettişini en yakın zamanda bekliyorum." Kara asker selamlayıp odadan çıktı. Gömleğimin düğmelerini iliklerken aynadaki aksime baktım.

"Elf olmakla lanetlendin," dedim kendi kendime. "Elf olmuş olman devamlı kendine acımanı gerektirmez. Ne olmuş işkenceye uğradıysan? Sen de başkalarına işkence ettin. O beyaz kemikli ellerin var ya… Onlarda kimsenin nefes aldığından haberdar dahi olmadığı fanilerin bile kanları var."

Odadan çıkıp toplantı odasına yürürken umutsuzluk, iblis kalbime bir taş gibi oturmuştu. İlk şeytan savaşlarından bu yana babam barışı sağlamak için neler yapmıştı acaba? O barışı sağlarken iki evladının da kadın peşinde koşması karşısında ne düşünmüştü ki?

Zemin kendini siyahtan solgun mavi bir mermere bırakırken, Aidan kadın peşinde koşuyor sayılmazdı diye düşündüm. O asla tek bir kadının peşinde koşmamıştı. Aslında bakarsak bir iblis olarak geçirdiği seneler boyunca Aidan asla bir kadının peşinden koşmamıştı.

Gerçi Cassie vardı. Onun peşinden dünyaya bile gitmişti, geri zekâlı.

Askerler kenara çekilirken kapıyı ittirip salona girdim. Oval masamız Rohan dışında bomboştu. İblisçe ise tedirgin duruyordu. Gözleri önündeki bir bardak su ile benim aramda gidip geliyordu. Ben yanına yaklaşırken iblisçe kalkıp tedirgin fakat kibarca selam verdi. "Majeste," dedi neredeyse fısıltıyı andıran yaşlı sesiyle.

Tam karşısına gözlerim kapıyı görecek şekilde oturdum. "Rahat ol Rohan, artık sana kızgın değilim." İblisçe tuttuğu nefesini bırakırken tek bıraktığı nefesi değilmiş gibi görünüyordu. Ruhu da dudaklarının arasından uçup giderek buharlaşmıştı sanki. Sandalyesine otururken gözleri hâlâ bendeydi. "Merak etme Rohan. İnsan korkudan kolay kolay ölmüyor. Bizzat tecrübe ettim. Çukurdayken ölmeyi deli gibi istediğim zamanlar olmuştu." Rahatsız edici görüntüler gözlerimin önüne doluşunca yüzümü ekşittim. "Hâlâ kral olmamı sorguluyor musun?"

"Asla," dedi yaşlı adam hemen. "Önceden de sorgulamamıştım. Sadece siz..." Elimi kaldırıp sözünü kestim. "Bak, muhabbet edecek adam arasaydım zindanlarla Aloha ile cehennem şarabında yıkanıyor olurdum. İyi fikirlerine hâlâ ihtiyacım var. Artık bir şeylere son noktayı koymak istiyorum." Dirseklerimi masaya dayayıp parmaklarımı birleştirdim. "Vekil kral olmanın pek önemi olmadığını düşünebilirsin," dedim sakince. "Bir şey demene gerek yok. Asla tahta layık olmadığımı düşündüğünü biliyorum. Ama Aidanhell'den daha çok hak ettiğim de ortada." Sustum o da sustu. Rohan konuşmadan önce uzun uzun düşünürdü. Bilgece laflar etmeye bayıldığından mıydı bilmem, sadece düşünüyordu işte. Bazen onun sadece morgain incisi taşıyan ölmüş bir paşa olması saçma geliyordu. Nedense her şeyi biliyor gibiydi, bunun bir sebebinin de biz serserilik peşinde koşarken onun tüm krallıktaki ihtiyarlarla tanışması olduğunu biliyordum.

Dedikodu basit ortamlarda zararsız ve zaman öldürücü olabilirdi ama cehennem krallıklarında dedikodu rüzgârın yönünü değiştirebilecek bir güce sahipti. Başta Aidanhell ve o aptal kızın kehaneti bile bir dedikoduydu. Ama bir de şimdi bakın... Kader ağlarını bir bir örüp ağa takılan her biri ruhu da emdi. Her şey her zaman olması gerektiği gibi oluyordu.

"Tek başıma yapamam." Gözlerimi gözlerine sabitledim. "Seninle de yapamam. Bana yardımcı gerekiyor. Mor Kule Zindanları'na bir elçi gönderdim. Kralı ve veziri buraya çağıracağım. Onlarla yaşadım. Beni tanıyorlar ve... Ahlaki yönden pek geçer not alamasalar bile savaşçılıkları konusunda onlara güvenebilirsin." Rohan bir şey demek için maruz kaldığı bakımsızlıktan çatlamış, yaşlı incecik dudaklarını araladığında aynı anda birkaç şey oldu.

Bir gürültü ayak tabanlarımı titreştirecek kadar zemini sallarken salonun iki kollu geniş kapısı bir grup kara askerin bağırtısıyla ardına kadar açıldı. Rohan ve ben yerimizden kalkıp depremi -ki cehennemde deprem olmazdı- algılamaya çalışırken askerler canhıraş bağırtılarla odaya daldılar. "Neler oluyor asker?" Hapa, simsiyah gözlerinin asla olamayacağını düşündüğüm şekilde daha da kararmış hâlde deli gibi çevresine bakınıyordu. Gördüğü şey her neyse, askerin zayıf deriden oluşmuş, cildinden fırlamış gibi duran gözleri yuvalarında huzursuzca dönüyordu. Benden daha fazla korktuğu şeyin ne olduğuyla ilgili çaktırmadan endişeye kapılmaya başlamıştım.

En fazla ne olmuş olabilirdi ki?

"Biri sikik aklını kaçırmadan önce bana ne olduğunu anlatabilecek mi?" Az önceki sarsıntı geçmişti ama zemin ve üzerindeki büstler hafifçe sallanmaya devam ediyorlardı. Tahtın iki yanındaki Gargoylelar birbirilerine dönüp kendi dillerinde fısıldamaya başlayınca sabır katsayımın daha fazla sınanamayacağından emin oldum. "Cehennem fili mi geldi, ne oluyor?" Panikten deliye dönmüş kalabalık yanıt vermeyince sakince derin bir nefes aldım. "Tamam, kızmayacağım, biri açıklasın yeter."

Hapa nihayet bozuk aksak konuşma yetisini henüz az önce kazanmış gibi art arda nefesler aldı. Sonrasındaysa bana döndü. "Üç büyük varlık," diyebildi kesilen, ıslık gibi çıkan harflerini birleştirerek. "Elçi de döndü."

Bahsettiği üç büyük varlığın elfler olduğunu düşündüm. "Bu kadar tantana kara elf kralı ve yardımcıları için miydi yani? Tamam, onları içeri al," dedim yeniden sükunetimi sağlamaya çalışırken. "Tapınak büyücülerine gidin. Sarsıntının sebebini öğrenmek istiyorum." Hapa önce kararsızca çevresine bakınsa da sonrasında emre itaat ederek selam verip kapılardan geri çıktı. "O kadar tantanayı hak edecek kadar gösterişli değiller inan." Rohan yanıt vermedi. Bir şeyin onu rahatsız ettiği zamanlardaki gibi huzursuz sükunetini sürdürüyordu.

"Elflerin gelişi depremi açıklamıyor," dedi bana değil de daha çok kendi kendine.

Yeniden tahtıma kurulurken, "Cehennemde deprem olmaz," dedim net bir dille. "Gerçi artık her boku da bekliyorum bu kokuşmuş yerden. Sen ve bende biraz akıl olsa zaten... Şu an diğerleri gibi siktirip gitmiştik. Yitip giden koca bir hayal kırıklığını sırtlanıyorum gibi geliyor." Başımı arkaya yatırıp derin bir nefes aldım. "Babamın aklı varmış Ahmet Paşa. Bak gitti, kurtuldu. Çukurun dibinde kim bilir üzerinde kaç tane zebani fahişesi varken onları döllemekten de çekinmiyordur. Keyfine düşkün adamdı, bilirsin." Gözlerimi kapadım. Zira acı verici bir anı gözkapaklarımı ucunu sivri mızraklarla dürtüp kendini göstermek istiyor gibiydi.

Meredith ve sevgili babamın hoş olmayan samimiyetteki görüntüleri beynime üşüşünce gözlerimi sımsıkı kapattım. Bir kadına kalbini verdin ve o da o kalbi aldı... Her neyse.

Kapı yeniden açıldığında artçı sallantılar da son bulmuştu. Eşikteki iki kara askerin ortasındaki elçi, sanki az önce hayaletler tarafından kovalanmış gibi bembeyaz bir suratla duruyordu. Hemen arkasındaki gümüş saçlar gözlerime ilişince yerimden kalktım. "Sonunda gelebildiniz. Hoş geldiniz kardeşlerim." Liderleri Farhand ve Vezir Konyak, elçinin yanından geçip odaya girdiler.

"Draza," dedi Farhand selam vermek için hafifçe eğilirken. Elflere has zarif suratında kuşku dolu bir ifadeyle bir bana bir de odaya baktı. "Çağrını duyunca hemen geldik ama yolda... Bir şeyler oldu."

Konyak selam verip koşar adımlarla yanıma yaklaştı. "Majeste, o gürültüyü duydunuz değil mi? Mor Kule'nin bile kulelerini hareket ettirmiştir. Yer yarıldı gibi bir sesti." Onay almak istercesine kralına baktı. Farhand düşünceli bir ifadeyle başını salladı.

"Buyurun," dedim masayı göstererek. "Herkes az önceki depremi konuşuyor. Büyücülere haber saldım. Ne olduğunu en yakın zamanda öğreniriz."

Farhand saçları kadar beyaz peleriniyle masadaki yerini alırken, "Cehennemde deprem olmaz," diye bildirdi. Rohan boğazını temizler gibi yapınca göz ucumla ona baktım. Yaşlı adamın ifadesi, kara elflerden bir bok olmaz şeklindeydi. Kibir tüm şeytanlara atfedilen bir özellik olabilirdi lakin en çok zarif kulaklı, oval yüzlü elflere yakışıyordu. O keskin çene ve burun hatlarının süslediği berrak parıltılı tene kibir yakışırdı elbet. Ama kibirli olmak çoğu zaman kişinin hatalarını görmesini de engelliyordu. Örneğin, beyinsiz biri kibirlenince komik duruma düşüyordu. Maske bir yere kadar kapatabiliyordu tabii.

"Bunun farkındayız," dedim yerime geçerken. Konyak ve Rohan yan yana oturunca bir an için ikisine baktım. "Sizi çağırdım çünkü güçlü müttefiklere ihtiyacım var." Konyak yerinde huzursuzca kıpırdanınca konuşmamı yarıda kestim. "Söyleyecek bir şeyin var gibi." Vezir, ben ve Farhand'a kıyasla koyu kalan gri saçlarını omuzlarının gerisine attı. Konuşmaya başladığında dik duruşunu korumaya çalıştığı her hâlinden belliydi.

Politika, dedi iç sesim, bazen çukurdan bile fena.

"Ana Saray'a yakınlığımızla biliniriz. Tüm kastların suçluları bizim zindanlarımızda barınır. Zamanın başından beri bir kez bile isyan etmedik. Lucifer bize kendi öz oğlunu kral yaptığında bile buna karşı çıkmadık." Şimdi direkt olarak bana bakıyordu. "Kimseye sorun çıkarmadık, savaş çıktığında bile uyumsuzluk yapmadık."

Sinirlerime hâkim olmaya çalışırken neredeyse seğiren gözümü elimin tersiyle kaşıdım. "Karşılığında ödüllendirildiniz. Farhand ve sen, bugün burada, oval masada oturabiliyorsanız bunu bana borçlusunuz." Farhand'dan zarif görüntüsüne tezat oluşturacak şekilde hoşnutsuz bir homurtu duyulurken kendime daha fazla hâkim olamadım. "Bakın uyumluyuz deyip duruyorsunuz ama uyumlu olduğunuz tek konu, zindanlardaki mahkumlara yapılan işkenceler. Yanımda duracaksanız bunu pasif olarak değil bizzat göstermeniz gerekiyor. Madem Ana Saray'a bu kadar bağlısınız, Mor Kule'yi Ana Saray'a bağlamak istiyorum. Farhand artık hem kulenin lideri hem de burada kralın yardımcısı olarak görev alacak."

Farhand koltuğundan sertçe kalktıktan sonra iki elini masaya koyup eğilerek gözlerime baktı. Konuştuğunda gümüş rengi saçları omuzlarından masaya düşmüştü. İfadesi de tıpkı diğer kara elflerin olduğu gibi tanımsızdı. Simsiyah gözleri gözlerime sabitlenmişti. "Majeste," dedi soğuk bir sesle. Ardından o cümleyi bitiremeden salonun kapısı ardına kadar açıldı.

Bir elfe dönüştürülüp Mor Kule'ye tekmelendikten sonra hayatın artık daha tuhaf olamayacağını düşünmüştüm. Sonrasında Aidanhell elinde deli saçması bir kehanetle çıkagelince hayatımı düzeltebilmenin bir yolunu bulduğuma emin olmuştum. Kanatlarımı geri almıştım. Ama tabii ki bu sikik diyarda beni devamlı olarak şaşırtacak şeyler olurdu. Örneğin kimse benim çukura gideceğimi öngöremezdi. Annem bir gün oğlunun çukura gönderileceğini ve babasının metresiyle neredeyse evlenecek olduğunu öğrenseydi, tekrar tekrar dirilirdi.

Ve eminim ki biri onu tekrar öldürmek için orada hazır olarak beklerdi.

Ki konumuz bu değil. Konumuz benim çürümüş hayatım ya da beyazlığını kaybetmiş zift rengi gözlerim de değil, hatta konumuz çukurdan sonra mahvolan ve kainattaki hiçbir şeyin asla düzeltemeyeceği mahvolmuş psikolojim de değil. Hayır, konumuz şu anda taht salonuma giren uçsuz bucaksız ışık topu.

Dev, parlak, göz alıcı bir ışık huzmesi salonu dolduruyor, odada tek bir karanlık zerreciğin kalmaması için çılgınca uğraşıyor gibiydi. Bu kadar parlak olabilecek pek az şey vardı. Lilith, diye düşündü zihnim. Lilith sonunda gelmiş olabilir miydi?

Elimin tersini gözlerime siper edip boşta kalan elimle kemerimdeki hançerime uzandım. "Kim var orada?" dedim gürleyerek. Kimdi bu gelen ve nasıl odaya dan diye girebiliyordu?

"Zemin sallanıyor," dedi Rohan ışıkla başlayan yoğun uğultunun içinde sesini duyurmak için neredeyse bağırarak.

"Göster kendini yabancı," dedim elimi indirip saldırı pozisyonumu alırken. Yabancı kendini göstermedi ama sallantıyı durdurdu. İki ayağımı da sağlam bir şekilde yere basıp sırtımı büktüm. "Geride dur Rohan," dedim gözlerim ışıktan dolayı neredeyse körleşmişken. Düşman Lilith ya da başka her neyse,

Rohan'ın yapabileceği hiçbir şey yoktu. Öte yandan ben güçlüydüm.

"Göster kendini dedim. Karşında cehennemin kralı Draza duruyor." Bu kez parıltı bir kez daha şiddetini arttırdı. Ardından yavaş yavaş kısılmaya başladı. Yabancı kendisini göstermeden önce son bir kez yaşayan her bir canlının duyabileceği şekilde derin bir uğultu çıkardı. Karşımda bir yaratık olduğundan son derece emin hâlde saldırı pozisyonumda kapıya doğru ilerledim. Kapıda kimse yoktu. Bir an eşiğe ve ötesine hızlıca baktım. "Nerede?" diye sordum muhafızlara. Derisi pörsümüş kemikli uzun parmaklarıyla pencereleri işaret ettiler. "Benimle gelin." Arkamda dört muhafızla sarayın koridorlarını hızla geçtik. Yolda karşılaştığımız diğer muhafızlara kapılara savunma yerleştirmelerini söyledim. "Saldırı altında olabiliriz. Zindanları kilitleyin. Dört cepheye de ikişer bölük asker yerleştirin. Kanatlılar çatıya çıksın."

Ana girişin kapısının açılması için işaret verdim. İki kapı muhafızı dev kapıyı çekerek açtılar. Güneş ışığı adımlarıma, oradan saçlarıma çarparken derin bir nefes aldım. Gelen konusunda derin bir yanılgıya düşmüştüm. Yanılgı dev bir atmosfere dönüşmüş, ben de kafa bulana kadar onu solumuştum. Öncelikle gelen tek kişi değildi, üç kişilerdi. Hapa'nın dediği varlık kelimesi ise onları tanımlamaya çalışırken acizce kırılıp büzülüyor ve yanılgı atmosferine karışıyordu.

Işığı ise şıp diye anlamıştım. İkiz güneşten gelmiyordu ışık. Yo, hayır, ışık bambaşka bir şeyden geliyordu. Işık bu üç herifin içinden geliyordu. Boğazlarındaki derinin içinde gizlenmiş alev topu vardı. Alev topu damarlarla yayılarak adamların elmacık kemiklerini çevreliyordu. Acaba adam kelimesi doğru bir seçim miydi?

"Majeste, ne yapalım?" diye sordu Hapa hemen arkamdayken. Endişeli nefesi omzuma çarparken yine de kendini korkusuz göstermeye çalışıyordu.

"Siz bir şey yapmayın," dedim muhafızların duyabileceği kadar yüksek sesle. Sonrasındaysa hançeri daha sıkı tutarak mermer merdivenleri geçip taş meydana ulaştım. Koyu deri çizmelerim taşların üzerinde her bir adımla yabancılara yaklaşırken auramı kontrol altına almaya çalıştım.

Ben Kralım, beni korkutmak öyle kolay değil.

Ben onlara yaklaşırken havada süzülen yabancılar yavaşça zemine alçaldılar. Bir kanatları ya da görünürde uçmalarını sağlayan ışıltılı sinir bozucu tozlardan yoktu. Öyle havada asılılardı ve hiçbir gayret göstermeden hareket edebiliyorlardı. Aramıza akla mantığa uygun birkaç metre mesafe koyarak meydanın hemen bitiminde durdum.

Üçü de toprağa inince ayaklarımın altındaki zemin bir kez daha sallandı. Neydi bunlar, büyücü mü?

"Kötü bir ev sahibi olmak istemem beyler ama şu an benim topraklarıma izinsiz girdiniz." Hançerin ucunu ayaklarını gösterecek şekilde salladım. "Yine de gösterişli gelişiniz hoşuma gitti. Kimsiniz siz?" Yabancılar yüzüme bakıyorlardı ama ifadeleri binlerce yıl önce uçup gitmiş gibiydi. Her neylerse ve ne kadar normal bir bedene sahipmiş gibi görünseler de bir şeyler fena hâlde tersti. Melekler dışında her varlığın aurasını görebilme yetisiyle kutsanmış olsam dahi renkleri tam ayırt edemiyordum ama bu adamlarda aura falan yoktu. Bir bulut çevrelerini sarmıyordu. Oysa ruhu olan her varlığın aurası olurdu.

Gözlerimi sımsıkı kapatıp nefesimi bıkkınca bıraktım. "Hiç derdim yokmuş gibi üç dilsizle uğraşacağım. Gerçekten sınanıyorum." Gözlerimi tekrar açtığımda ortadaki adam sağ elini yavaşça yukarı kaldırdı. Sonrasındaysa koyu renkli dudaklarını araladı. Söylediği şey dudaklarından fısıltı gibi çıkıp havaya karıştı. Ben duyamadım ama anlaşılan duyması gereken duymuştu. Gökyüzü yırtılıyor gibi bir ses çıkarınca başımı geriye atıp neler olduğuna bakmaya çalıştım.

Dev bir arı sürüsü gibiydi. Uğultu çıkarıp aydınlık gökyüzünü simsiyah bulutlarla kaplıyorlardı. Hızlılardı ve istikametleri de belliydi. Benim kıymetli arazime doğru son sürat ilerliyorlardı. İstemeden de olsa birkaç adım gerileyince arkamdaki biri omzuma dokundu. Omzumun üzerinden bakınca iblisçe Rohan'ın korku dolu gözleriyle karşılaştım. "Majeste," dedi temkinli bir şekilde. "Şu saniyeden sonra lütfen sözlerinizi dikkatli seçin." Sonra çenesini kaldırarak yabancıları işaret etti.

Siyah arı sürüsüne benzer kalabalık yaklaştıkça onların kâinatta arıya en çok benzemeyen şeyler olduklarını fark ettim. Öncelikle arılar ata binmezdi. Ve bir arı büyümc şarabına banıp bir ata binebilseydi bile o atların kanatları olmazdı. Ayrıca bunu koca bir sürü yapmazdı. Rohan kulağıma yaklaşıp isimlerini fısıldayana kadar bu yaratıkları ortaya çıkarabilmek için çiftleşebilecek canlıları zihnimde canlandırıyordum. "Onlar Valkür," dedi yaşlı adam ardından gözlerini tekrar yabancılara çevirdi. "Eski ordu," dedi sanki bu her şeyi açıklarmış gibi.

Gökten bir irin gibi üzerimize akıp çevremizi siyaha boyayan orduyu görmezden gelerek yabancılara döndüm. "Son kez soruyorum. Kimsiniz?"

Yabancılardan ortada duranı diğerlerine kısacık bir bakış attı. Sonraysa tüm hayatım boyunca görebileceğim en ürkütücü şeyi yaptı. Gülümsedi.

Ruhum içimde boynuna bir urgan bağlayıp kendini asmaya çalışınca Rohan'ın kolunu tutup sıktım. "Bunlar kim be adam?" Rohan yaşlı, çelimsiz bedeni sanki ellerimin arasından kayıp gidecekmiş gibi titreyince tutuşumu zayıflattım. "Onlar unutulanlar."

Unutulan mı?

"Tüm evrende en unutulan ve en siktir edilen varlık benim Rohan. Bunlar kim?"

Yaşlı adam konuştuktan sonra evren kavramı üzerine uzun uzun düşünmem gerektiğini anlayacaktım. Evren nasıldı ve ben bu evren diye bildiğim şeyin neresindeydim? Ve çok sevgili atalarım bizlere neden bunu anlatmamışlardı? Bir iblis olarak yapabileceklerimin sınırı vardı, şeytanlar aşkına!

"Onlar," dedi Rohan gözleri bana gülümseyen kahverengi saçlı adamda kilitlenirken. "Unutulmuş yaratıkların en eskileri. Onlar ejderha."

BÖLÜM 9

"Nathaniel ile göreve çıkacaksın. Onun sözünden çıkma." Azrail uzun pelerinini geniş omuzlarından indirip şöminenin hemen yanındaki beyaz deri koltuğun üzerine bıraktı. İnce ve kibar parmaklarını siyah, düz saçları arasından geçirirken huzursuzluğu küçük kulübemin içini tamamen dolduruyordu.

"Bana anlatman gereken şeyler olduğunu söyledin," dedim mutsuzca. "Melekler verdiği sözleri tutmaz mı?" Azrail şimdi masadaki belgelere bakıyor, beni duymazlıktan geliyordu. Kendimi görünür kılmak için yanına gidip ellerimi ahşap masaya koydum. "Evet," dedim sabırsızca. Gözleri hâlâ kâğıtlardayken melek tek düze bir sesle başını dahi kaldırmadan yanıtladı. "Sen de meleksin. Sen söyle."

Bu neydi şimdi? "Saygısızlık etmek istemiyorum. Sorun çıkarmaya da çalışmıyorum, sadece cevaplara ihtiyacım var." İşaret parmağımı şakaklarıma koydum. "Burada bir şeyler eksik ve ben bilinmezliğin içinde sürükleniyor gibiyim."

Azrail masaya doğru eğilerek bir kâğıdın üzerindeki isimlere yoğunlaştı. "Kanatlarının beyaz olması yeterli değil mi?"

Sorduğu sorunun tuhaflığı karşısında duraksadım. "Nasıl yani?"

Melek masada duran kalemi alıp kâğıda artık aşinası olduğum harfleri kullanarak bir şeyler karaladı. "Kanatlarının beyaz olması çoğu ilahi varlık için yeterlidir. Sen neden hep daha fazlasını istiyorsun? Geçmişinin seni etkilemediğini düşündüğüm her seferinde beni yanıltıyorsun. Bu beden," dedi başını hafifçe kaldırıp alnına düşen sarı saçlarının ardından bana bakarken, "Ne kadar ışıktan oluşsa da kan aynı kan işte."

Sözlerini anlamıyordum. Ama Azrail konuşmaya devam etmeyecekti. Bitirdiğini ifade edercesine doğruldu ve masadaki kâğıtları kol altına aldı. "Nathaniel'in talimatlarından çıkma. Eğer her şeyi harfiyen uygularsan gün bitiminde belki de o çok istediğin geçmişini sana veririm." Cümlesini bitirdikten sonra pelerinine bakmadan odayı adımlayıp evden çıktı.

Çatırdayan ateşin gölgesinde kalakalmıştım. İstediğim bilgileri asla alamayacak gibiydim. Ama Azrail yalan söylemezdi, öyle değil mi? Gün biterken her şeyi bana anlatacaktı ve ben ilk defa tamamlanmış hissedecektim.

Kapı gıcırtılar eşliğinde tekrar açılınca gözlerim geleni görmek için eşiğe yöneldi. Nathaniel kolunda evrak çantası ile başını eşikten uzatıp etrafı taradı, beni gördüğünde gülümsedi. "Bugün beraber çalışacakmışız. Çok ilginç şeyler yapacağız, sabırsızlanıyorum." Mavi gözleri parlarken bir kez daha gülümsedi. "Sonsuza dek seni bekleyemem Aidan, hadi ayaklan." Ardından dışarı çıktı. Zihnimdeki soru işaretlerini kilimin altına süpürüp onu izleyerek evden çıktım. Nathaniel avluda durmuş, sırtını esnetiyordu. "Önce ruh çıkaracağız ve ardından onu teslim edeceğiz. Teslimi ilk kez göreceksin değil mi?"

"Teslim ne? Ben genelde belgeleri düzenliyorum ve sadece birkaç kez ruh çıkarmaya gittim. Daha sonra teslim edildiğini bile..." Nathaniel zarif elini kaldırıp beni susturdu. "Anladım anladım. Bebek meleksin daha zaten. Birinin sana bu aşamaları anlatması gerekiyor. Gel benimle, yürü." Onu takip ettim. Beraber avluyu aşıp uçmak için çıktığımız tepeye yürüdük.

"Ruhları kendi bedenimizde muhafaza ederiz, sonra da ruh havuzuna akıtırız. Alırken kullandığımız güçle eşit ama biraz daha farklı. Birinde çekme birinde ise itme kuvveti var. Bugün senin bedenine ruh yüklemeyeceğiz ama nasıl olduğunu beni gözlemleyerek öğrenebilirsin."

Tepeye çıkarken Nathaniel elindeki çantayı bana uzattı. "En öndeki iç gözde liste var. İlk sıraya birazdan gideceğiz. Eğer bir gün için çok fazla olursa ikinci sırayı yarına bırakırız." Bir yandan yürüyor bir yandan da klipsi açıp listeyi çıkarıyordum. İlk sıradaki isme uzun uzun baktım.

"Gitme zamanlarının geldiğini ruhlar biliyor mu?" Nathaniel başını olumsuz anlamda salladı. Hâlâ kâğıda bakarken, "Peki ya," dedim, "biz onların gitme zamanı geldiğini nasıl anlıyoruz?"

Nathaniel kanatları sırtından çıkmadan hemen önce gülümsedi. "Biz de bilemeyiz. İsimler ilahi düzenle bize gelir, biz de sadece işimizi yaparız. Hadi!" İki kez serbest şekilde havayı dövdükten sonra göğe yükseldi. Kâğıdı cüppemin cebine koyup çantayı çapraz takarak kanatlarımı açtım. Birkaç kez hız aldıktan sonra hemen arkasından yükseldim.

Cennetten dünyaya yükseldiğimiz tepe özel bir tepe miydi bilmiyordum. Tek bildiğim biz uçarken zaman ve mekân kavramının önemini yitirdiğiydi. Dünya zamanıyla belki birkaç dakika sürüyordu ama cennetten dünyaya geçiş birkaç yıl yaşlanmışım gibi hissettiriyordu. Cennetin verimli toprakları yerini karanlık bir şehrin arka sokaklarına bırakırken böylesi bir tecrübeyi herkesin kaldıramayacağını düşündüm.

Koyu gri bulutlar kanatlarımın ucundaki tüylere çarparken Nathaniel'i takip etmeye devam ettim. "Yine bir hastane mi?" diye sordum beyaz kanatlarının arasından gittiği binayı görünce.

"Evet," dedi melek sesi rüzgârda kısılırken. "Basit bir iş olacak. Gözlemlemen açısından kolay olur diye düşündüm." Biz yaklaştıkça binanın pencereleri büyüyor, az önce şekilsiz görünen gölgeler yerlerini insan silüetlerine bırakıyordu. Daha fazla yaklaşamaz olduğumuzda Nathaniel beni uyardı. "İnsanlar melekleri her zaman göremez ama iki ışık huzmesinin binaya yaklaştığını görebilirler. Bizi havai fişek ya da kayan yıldız filan sanıyorlar."

Bahsettiği şeyleri bilmesem de başımı salladım. Sonra bunun aptalca geldiğini fark ettim. Zira Nathaniel beni görmüyordu bile. "İşte geldik," dedi pike yaparak çatıya yükseldiğinde. Kenarlardan uzaklaşıp tam ortaya konduk. "Bir kat ineceğiz sadece. Ben yolu gösteririm. Başka hiçbir şey yapma." Kapıyı açıp merdivenlerden aşağı inmeye başladık.

Aklım istemeden hep geçen seferki anıya takılıp gidiyordu. O kızı düşünmeden edemiyordum. Bana seslenmişti, gözleri üzerimde durmuştu, beni görmüştü ve Azrail ondan şeytan diye bahsetmişti. Her şey çok karmaşık geliyordu.

İnsanlarla dolu bir koridorun önünde durduğumuzda aklımı hâlâ o kızdan alamıyordum. Bir daha görmek istiyor muydum? Yanıt evet ise nedendi? Onu tanımıyordum ki.

"İşte şu kapı," dedi Nathaniel beni daldığım düşüncelerden uyandırırken. "Yaşlı bir kadın." Bana hastayla ilgili bilgiler vermek için duraksadığında gözleri bir şeye takıldı. Bahsettiği kapının önünde duvara yaslanmış sarı saçlı bir kız duruyordu. Nathaniel kıza bir faniye baktığından çok daha uzun süre bakınca merakım kabardı.

"O kim?"

Melek hareketlenmeden önce yanıtladı. "Burada olmaması gereken biri." Hiddetli bir nefes meleğin zarif burnundan dışarı çıktı. "Nereden haber alırlar bilmem."

Biz kapıya yaklaşana kadar kız başını kaldırıp bize bakmadı. Nihayet aramızda sadece birkaç santim kalınca başını kaldırdı. Gözlerine değen kâkülleri siyahtı. Sarı saçıyla tuhaf bir tezat oluşturuyordu. Kız bir şey söylemeyip dik dik bakınca melek konuştu.

"Burada olmaman gerekiyor zebani."

"Aynı şeyi senin için de söyleyebilirim." Nathaniel yumruklarını hafifçe sıkınca gözlerim ayrıldı, bir meleğin daha önce sinirlendiğini hiç görmemiştim.

"Benim görevim bu. Ben sizin gibi kendimi doyurmak için ruh emmiyorum." Kız umursamaz tavrını sürdürerek kollarını göğsünde kavuşturdu. "Bu nereden baktığına göre değişir melek. Ruhları topladıktan sonra ne yapıyorsun bilemem."

Melek kızın üzerine yürüyünce kolunu tuttum. "Sence de biraz fazla tepki vermiyor musun?" dedim tereddütle. Sessiz, sakin ve sinir bozucu şekildeki huzurlu hayatıma renk arayışında değildim ama karşıdaki güçsüz görünen bir dişiydi. Ve Nathaniel tanıdığım -Azrail dışındaki- herkesten daha güçlüydü.

"O bir kâfir," dedi mavi gözleri öfkeyle koyulaşırken. Sonra tekrar kıza döndü. "Dünyada dolanmaya doymadınız mı?

Burası benim alanım. Bir ruhu daha kaybetmeye niyetim yok. İçindeki cadıyı çağır ve gidin buradan." Kız hareket etmeyince Nathaniel kızı kenara ittirip kapıyı açtı. Yanından geçerken kızın kâküllerinin ardından gülümsediğini gördüm ama umursamadım. Zebaniler demek ki deliydi, kim bilir.

Ve odaya girdiğim an donup kaldım.

O kız. Yatakta yatan bir kadının üzerine eğilmiş, kadının bedeninden çıkan sarı sisi emiyor gibiydi. Hemen karşısındaysa elindeki eski bir kitaptan sözler okuyan turuncu saçlı bir kız vardı.

"Geç kaldık," dedi Nathaniel kapı aralığında. Sonra odadan çıkıp zebaninin yanına gitti. "Sizi şikâyet edeceğim. Geldiğin yıldırımla Merkür'e göndereceğim seni." Kız yanıt veriyordu ama sözlerini işitemiyordum, zira dikkatim bambaşka bir şeydeydi.

Sedyenin üzerine eğilmiş koyu renk saçlı kıza bakıyordum. Kız bedenini kaplayan sisi, araladığı koyu pembe renkli dudaklarının arasına alırken gözlerini kapamıştı. Yanındakiyse sanki tüm evrenin hayatı buna bağlıymışçasına kitaptan kafayı kaldırmıyordu. Bakışlarım tekrar kıza kayarken kahverengi saçlarından bir tutamı omuzlarına düştü ve ben nefesimi tuttum.

İkisi de aynı anda bana döndü.

Sis hâlâ havada asılı dururken koyu renk saçlı kız doğruldu. Kıpkırmızı gözleri irileşirken bir an için dengesini kaybeder gibi olup yatağa tutundu. Farkında olmadan bir adım daha atmıştım. İçimde bir şeyler beş dakika öncesi gibi değildi. Bir şeyler farklıydı ve ne olduğu hakkında hiçbir fikrim yoktu.

"Aidan?" dedi kız tereddütle. Tekrar doğrulup yanıma gelişini ağır çekimde izledim. "Bu sen misin?" Kızıl gözleri parlamaya başlayınca biriken yaşları fark ettim. Güzel neydi ben güzel miydim bilmiyordum ama bu varlık... Güzel olmalıydı. Büyüleyiciydi.

"Sensin değil mi?" Ben yanıt veremeden turuncu saçlı olan cıyakladı. "Onun bedeninde gizlenen başkası olabilir. Şaşırtmaca iblisleri olabilir Cass."

Bedende gizlenmek mi? Cass mi? Adı bu muydu? Ne tuhaf bir isim diye düşündüm kız elini kaldırıp bana uzatmadan önce. Sonrasındaysa az önce ağır çekime alınan zaman bütünüyle durdu.

Şimdi ne hastanenin uğultusu ne de kapı aralığında kavga eden zebaniyle meleğin hoşnutsuz mırıltılarını duyabiliyordum. Kız zarif ufak parmaklarını yüzüme değirene kadar nefesimi bile tutmuştum.

Parmak uçları yanağıma değince hissettiğim titreşimle kanatlarımın uçları bile kaşındı. "Bu sensin," diye bildirdi sessizce. "Ama seni nasıl görebilirim? Onlar demişti ki..." Cümlesini bitirmeden boynuma sarıldı. İki kolu sırtıma öyle sahiplenici bir şekilde tutundu ki dengemi kaybedecek gibi oldum. Kahverengi saçları çeneme değerken buz kesmiş gibiydim.

Kimse kokuların ve kadın bedeninin bu denli hoş hissettirdiğinden bahsetmemişti. Ya da spesifik bir kadının bedeninin. Cass denilen.

"Sen yok olmuştun. Onlar dedi ki karanlık olanlar... Melekleri... Öyle dediler." Dediklerinden hiçbir şey anlamadım.

"Beni tanıyor musun?" diye sordum nefesim saçlarına çarparken. Sonra kız başını hafifçe yukarı kaldırınca gözleri gözlerimi buldu.

"Ne?"

"Benim hafızam... İyi değil. Ben hatırlamıyorum." Sözcükleri dikkatli seçmek istedim. Çünkü sırtımdaki elleri gitsin istemiyordum. Hoş hissettiriyordu, neredeyse ev gibi, o an bunu kaybetmek istemedim. Kız elektrik verilmiş gibi benden uzaklaşınca kendime kızdım.

"Sen Aidan değil misin?" Şimdi bana öyle şüpheyle bakıyordu ki gözlerindeki yaşlar sanki hiç var olmamış gibi kuruyup buharlaşmıştı.

"Adım Aidan. Ama hafızam iyi değil. Başka bir hayattan beni tanıyor olabilir misin?"

Turuncu saçlı kız elindeki kitabı pat diye kapatıp sinirli bir şekilde güldü. "Başka bir hayat mı? Kız kardeşim sen yaşa diye az daha ölüyordu. Sana diyorum Cass, Aidan hep salaktı ama sanki son gördüğümden bu yana daha bir salaklaşmış."

"Bana neden salak diyorsun?"

Kız yeşil gözlerini kısarak bana baktı. "Bu hafızamı kaybettim ayakları Cass'de işe yarayabilir ama bende yaramaz. Bana işkence ettirip zindanda çürümeye bıraktığın o günleri unutmadım. Ha başka hayatta falan değildi, geçen seneydi." Burnundan soluyordu. İşkence diyordu, zindan diyordu ama sözleri benim için bir anlam ifade etmiyordu.

"Bunu anlamanın bir tek yolu var," dedi esas kız. Sonra üzerime doğru hızla gelip kollarını boynuma doladı. Elleri ensemde, çok iyi hissettiren bir yerde buluştuğunda alnını alnıma yasladı ve sıcak nefesi dudaklarıma çarptı. Bir kalbim olduğunu ve çarpabildiğini o ana kadar nasıl fark etmediğimi anlamaya çalışırken kız kırmızı gözlerini dudaklarıma indirdi ve koyu renk dolgun dudakları dudaklarıma kapandı.

Kokusu burnuma dolarken teninin tenimle temas edişini sindirmeye çalıştım. Başta sadece değiyordu, Tanrım çok yumuşaktı ama sonra... Sonra dudaklarını araladı ve ıslak dili alt dudağıma sürtündü. İstemsizce dudaklarımı açtığımda dili dilime değdi ve ben kıza uzanıp belini tuttum. Nefesime ne olmuştu bilmiyordum. Bu ateş nereden geliyordu onu da bilmiyordum. Dev bir şöminenin başında oturuyormuş gibi kavruluyordum. Kızın bedeni bedenime değerken içimdeki yaşam enerjisi somutlaşmıştı. Doğuyor gibiydim ya da ölüyordum. Bir şeyler değişmişti.

"Burada ne oluyor?"

Nathaniel'in sesini duydum ama ilk kez umurumda olmadı. Kız dudaklarıma nefesini verirken belini daha sıkı kavradım. Evrendeki en mükemmel koku boynundan geliyor olabilir miydi? Bu da neydi böyle?

"Aidan, hemen bırak o kızı." Kızın mükemmel bir hızla hareket eden dudakları birden durdu. Dilini içine çekti ve ılık nefesi dudaklarıma değecek şekilde benden ayrıldı. Alnı alnıma yaslıydı ve gözleri kapalıydı. Göğsü inip kalkarken dudaklarını yaladı. Konuşmak için enerji topluyor gibiydi. Ben ise... Kilitlenmiştim.

"Benim emrimden çıkmaman gerekiyordu." Güçlü bir kol bileğimi yakalayıp kızın belini bıraktırdı. Nathaniel'in gücüyle neredeyse savrulan kıza baktım. "Bir dakika. Bana bir dakika ver Nathaniel."

Melek beni çekip kızdan uzaklaştırınca ona karşı koydum. "Bir dakikamız yok. Gidiyoruz, hem de hemen." Dikkatim hâlâ kızdaydı. Gözleri kapalıydı, tüm enerjisi az önce çekilmiş bir yaprak gibi titriyordu. Bana bakmasını diledim ama bakmadı.

"Lütfen Nathaniel. Bana bir dakika ver." Melek kolumu daha sıkı kavrayınca tekrar kıza baktım. "Sen kimsin ve bana ne yaptın?" Kız gözlerini açmadı. Turuncu saçlı olan hızla yatağın diğer tarafına geçip kızın yanına geldi. Kollarını tutunca Cass denilen kız ona yaslandı. Ayakta duramıyordu.

"Gidiyoruz." Kapıdan zorla çıkarılırken gözlerim hâlâ onlardaydı. Biz kapıdan çıkıp koridora sürüklenirken az önceki Zebani arkamızdan kapıyı kapatarak odaya girdi. "Sözümden çıkmamanı söylemiştim," dedi melek kolumu sımsıkı tutup peşi sıra koridor boyunca beni sürüklerken. Aklım hâlâ beni öpen kızdaydı, meleği duyuyordum ama yanıt vermek istemiyordum. Odaya dönmek istiyordum. "Aklında ne vardı bilmiyorum. Bir şeytanı öpmek... Daha tiksindirici çok az şey gördüm."

Kolumu çekip tutuşundan kurtardım. "Tiksindirici değildi. O kız beni tanıyordu. Geçmişimden biri, öyle değil mi?" Nathaniel gözlerini kaçırdı, adımları eskisinden de hızlıydı. Merdivenleri çıkmaya başladığımızda içimdeki geri dönme dürtüsüne engel olmaya çalışıyordum.

"Bugün başarılı olamadık. Azrail'in verdiği sözden haberim var. Sen başarılı bir iş çıkarsaydın belki o zaman o çok kıymetli geçmişini öğrenebilirdin."

Kulaklarım içimde yeni yeni hissetmeye başladığım, Nathaniel'in az önce zebaniye duyduğu hisler gibi öfkeyle doldu. Çatıya çıktığımızda uçmak için bir hamle yapınca bileğini tuttum. "Azrail bana söz verdi. Ve sözünü tutacak." Melek sanki ben dünyanın en tuhaf şeyini söylemişim gibi şaşkınca yüzüme baktı. Parlak safir rengi gözleri önce yüzümde sonra bileğini tutan elime kaydı. "Sen çıldırmışsın," dedi sadece. Bileğini bıraktığım an bana arkasını dönüp kanatlarını çıkararak göğe yükseldi.

Bir saniyeliğine durduğum yere baktım. O cevapları alacaktım. Ardından kanatlarımı açıp hırsla çarparak yükseldim.

***

Max elinde su dolu bir kovayla odaya girene kadar gözlerimi açmadım. Hissettiğim duyguların yoğunluğu altında ezilmiş, paramparça olmuştum. Önümüzdeki birkaç yüzyıl uykuya dalsam ve bir daha kalkmasam bile dinlenemeyecek gibiydim.

"Onu her getirdiğinde öncekinden daha berbat bir hâlde oluyor. Ve hep iyileştireceğim vaadiyle götürüyorsun Merr. Dev bir sıçan Cassie'nin kafasına sıçmış gibi." Araladığım gözlerimin ardında Max öfkeli bir ifadeyle Meredith'e bakıyordu. Cadıyı kalçasıyla ittirip yatağın sağına yaklaştı. Başucumdaki lambayı açıp koyu mavi, eski kovayı komodine koydu. Üzerime eğilip elinin tersiyle alnıma dokundu. "Yanıyor," dedi ürkekçe. "Şeytanların ateşi çıkar mı?"

Kardeşim gülünce başımı hafifçe diğer tarafa çevirdim. "Ah, o ateşli bir şeytan Max. Birkaç saat önce görmeliydin, bir melekle yiyişirken ateşi falan yoktu." Yine de sesi endişeli geliyordu, klasik Merr.

"Ben burada yokmuşum gibi konuşmaya bayıldığınızı biliyorum. Ama buradayım işte." Max'e döndüm. "Ruhu alamadık. İşler düşündüğümüz gibi gitmedi ve ben... Aidan'ı gördüm."

Max'in lacivert gözleri üzerine vuran loş ışıkta kocaman açıldı. "Yüzyılın en büyük dedikodusunu sona mı sakladınız?" dedi omzumu hafifçe dürterek. "Biri bir şey anlatacak mı yoksa bu buz gibi suyu başınızdan aşağı dökeyim mi istiyorsunuz?" Bileklerinden şıkırtı sesleri gelirken kovayı parmağıyla hafifçe dürttü. Yatakta doğrulup Meredith'in zorla üzerime örttüğü örtüyü tekmeledim. Gücümün yettiği ölçüde hızla olanları anlatıp tekrar sessizliğe gömüldüm. Ben anlatırken Max kovaya eski bir örtüyü zaman zaman daldırıyor, suya buladıktan sonra çıkarıp önce alnıma sonra da boynuma ve daha aşağılara sürtüyordu. O ıslak bez tenime her değdiğinde içimde hâlâ olup olmadığından emin olmadığım ruhumun donduğunu hissediyordum.

"Marcus'a olanları mesaj attım. Sanırım ailenin izini bulmuşlar. Bu arada Urange, Aidan'ı hâlâ sevmediğini belirtmemi istemiş."

Sırıttım. "İyi hissetmiyorum. Çürümüş gibiyim." Çürük meyveler gibiydim, dışım parlak ve güzelken içim kurtlarla kaplıydı. Beynimi kemiren yüzlerce kurtla doluydum.

"Eğer beslenmezsen cehenneme gidemeyeceğiz. Aidan'ı görmek istediğini biliyorum ama bu her şeyi riske atıyor. Sen ve ben bu dünya için yaratılmadık. Görmüyor musun Cass, burada mutlu bile değiliz. Tahtı bıraktın, aileni aramaya çıktın ama bunlar hep bahaneydi. Görmüyor musun, mutsuzsun işte. Yapamadık işte. Buraya uygun değiliz." Cep telefonunu ayakucuma atıp ayağa kalktı. Küçücük odada volta atarken kendi kendine söylenmeye devam ediyordu, benden bir yanıt beklemiyordu bile. "Bu dünyada doğdum. Bebekken öldürüldüm, çocukken işkence edildim, gençken haksızlığa uğradım. Dışlandım. Ailem olmadı, arkadaşlarım olmadı, doğru düzgün bir kardeşim bile olmadı. Şimdiyse senin peşinden sürükleniyorum. Uğruna savaştığım her şey kıçıma kaçmış durumda. Yolun neresindeyim bilmiyorum." İki elini başının yanlarına koyup yürümeyi bıraktı. "Tek amacım kahrolası seni hayatta tutmak ama ona bile izin vermiyorsun." Yeşil gözlerini açıp delici bir öfkeyle bana baktı. "Şu hâline bak. Sana kızamıyorum bile. Bok gibi bir hâldesin. Nihayet şu koskoca kâinatta yalnız kalmadığımı, beni anlayan birinin olduğunu düşündüğüm ilk seferde o biri bencilce hayatını riske atıyor. Hayatta kalmak için çabalamıyorsun bile."

"Sence de biraz fazla üstüne gitmiyor musun?" Max alnımdaki ıslak bezi alıp kovaya atarken Meredith'e bakıyordu. "O sadece genç bir kız, kimse ondan evrenin sırrını çözmesini beklemiyor."

Meredith ellerini indirip sinirle güldü. Sözcükleri histerik kahkahasına karışır hâlde sağlıksız bir şekilde karanlıkta dikiliyordu. "Hayır, bekliyorlar. O cehennemin kraliçesi ya da Draza'ya tacı fırlatıp atmadan önce öyleydi. Safkan bir şeytan. Ondan çok şey bekliyorlar ve o da bunları yapacak. Evrenin kaosa sürüklenmesini istemiyorsa yapacak."

Max bezi sıkıp tekrar alnıma koymak için yanaşınca bileğini tutup başımı iki yana salladım. "Senin göbek adın kaos, Merr. Şimdi bu evreni düzene sokma lafların... İçleri boş geliyor işte." Max vazgeçerek bezi kovaya atıp ayağa kalktı. Kız kardeş tartışmalarına karışmak istemediği her hâlinden belliydi. Çaktırmadan odadan süzülmenin yollarını arıyor gibi huzursuzca ileri geri sallanıyordu.

"Tamam, siktir edelim o hâlde. Evreni de düzeni de ve geri kalan her şeyi de. Güneş batsın, gün doğsun ve umursamamaya etmeye devam edelim. Amaçsızca yaşayalım. Belki sonraki gün ölmezsen de yürüyebilirsen, birinin canını alırız ve kıymetli meleğin Aidan'ını görebilirsin." Ardından birkaç küfür savurduktan sonra odayı terk etti.

Max bu kez yatağıma oturdu. "Ona kızma. O seni düşünüyor," dedi alnımdaki saçları kenarlara iterken. "Senin kendini düşünmediğin zamanlarda bile Meredith seni düşünüyor."

"O haklı. Her neyse Max, sana morgain incilerinden bahsettiğim o geceyi hatırlıyor musun?"

Arkadaşım yavaşça başını salladı. "Sarhoştun ve beni hizmetkârın yapmaya çalışıyordun."

Sırıttım. "Evet. Benim burada ne kadar kalabileceğim muamma. Olur da dayanabilsem bile geri dönmem gerekecek. Burada hayatta kalmaya uygun değilim. Hele şimdi Aidanhell'i görüp ona dokunmuşken... Bir şekilde daha da güçsüzleştim. Sanki bedenim iyi hisleri kaldıramıyor gibi."

Max elini elimin üzerine koyunca başımı kaldırıp insan arkadaşımın endişeli yüzüne baktım. "Her şey için teşekkür ederim. Hayatına bu saçma iblisleri aldığın ve onlarla aklın yokmuşçasına delice şeyler yaptığın için de. Başka kimse bir iblis ve bir cadıya oda vermezdi." Durup başucumdaki kovayı gösterdim. "Kimse bir iblis kızın ateşini düşürmeye çalışmazdı. İnsanların çoğu arkasını dönüp kaçardı ya da kendilerinden farklı bir şeyle karşılaştıkları her seferde yaptıkları gibi ona saldırırlardı." Elini avuçlarımın arasına aldım. "Beni eskiden tanısan daha çok severdin. Daha... İyi biriydim."

Max gülümseyince gözlerinin yanındaki kırışıklıklar belirginleşti. "Sen tanıdığım en iyi insanlardan birisin."

"Bu pek mümkün olamaz," dedim zoraki bir gülümsemeyle. "Şimdi ben daha önce kimseye morgain incisi vermedim. İlk kez sana vereceğim."

Max gözlerini kısıp suratında şapşal bir gülümseme varken başını hafifçe yana yatırdı. "Öyle ciddisin ki, neredeyse bekâretini veriyor gibisin."

Eline vurup tam karşıma gelecek şekilde oturttum onu. "Bileğinde iki tane minik inci oluşacak. Biri bana bir şey olursa yeni yapılmış bir dövme gibi sızlayacak diğeri ise... Eh, onu pek öğrenmeni şimdilik istemem." Bir elimi çekip omuzlarımı işaret ettim. "Sana incileri bırakırken benim de omzumda dövme oluşacak. Bekâreti vermek böyle bir şey mi bilemem ama sonsuza dek ikimiz arasında bir bağ olacak diyelim."

Sonra tekrar ellerini tuttum ve gözlerini kapamasını istedim. Gözleri kapalı birinin elini son tuttuğumda, ruhumdan bir parçayı kaybetmiştim. Sevdiğim adamın yitip gitmesini engellerken kendim yitip gitmiş, kayıp bir ruh olmuştum.

Yoğunlaştıktan sonra ben de gözlerimi kapadım ve hâlâ beni bu diyarda tutan enerjimin kırıntılarıyla ruh diyebileceğim o özü açtım. Öz, göğsümden çıkıp Max ve benim aramda titreşirken daha da yoğunlaştım. Öyle ki bir süre sonra öz, ben ve Max üçümüz bir bütün hâline gelmiştik. Ben nefes alıyordum, Max ise nefes veriyordu ve öz kendinden emin bir şekilde ikimizin ciğerlerini birbirine bağlıyordu. Nihayet birkaç dakikanın sonunda trans artık kaçınılmaz bir hâl aldı, özüm önce büyüyüp parladı, ardından aramızda iki küçük damlaya dönüşene kadar ufaldı. Nihayet gözlerimi açtığımda iki küçük inci havada asılı duruyordu. İnciler Max'in bileğine kazınırken omuzlarımın hemen üzerinde çiziğe benzer ufak bir sızlama oldu. Başımı çevirip baktığımda dövmelerimi gördüm. Max ise ellerimi bırakmış, çoktan bileğinde oluşan taze kızarıklığa bakıyordu.

"Artık senin hizmetkârınım öyleyse," dedi gururlu bir ifadeyle.

Yatakta geriye çekilip sırtımı yatak başlığına dayarken konuştum. "Bugün ve daima sevgili Max, bugün ve daima."

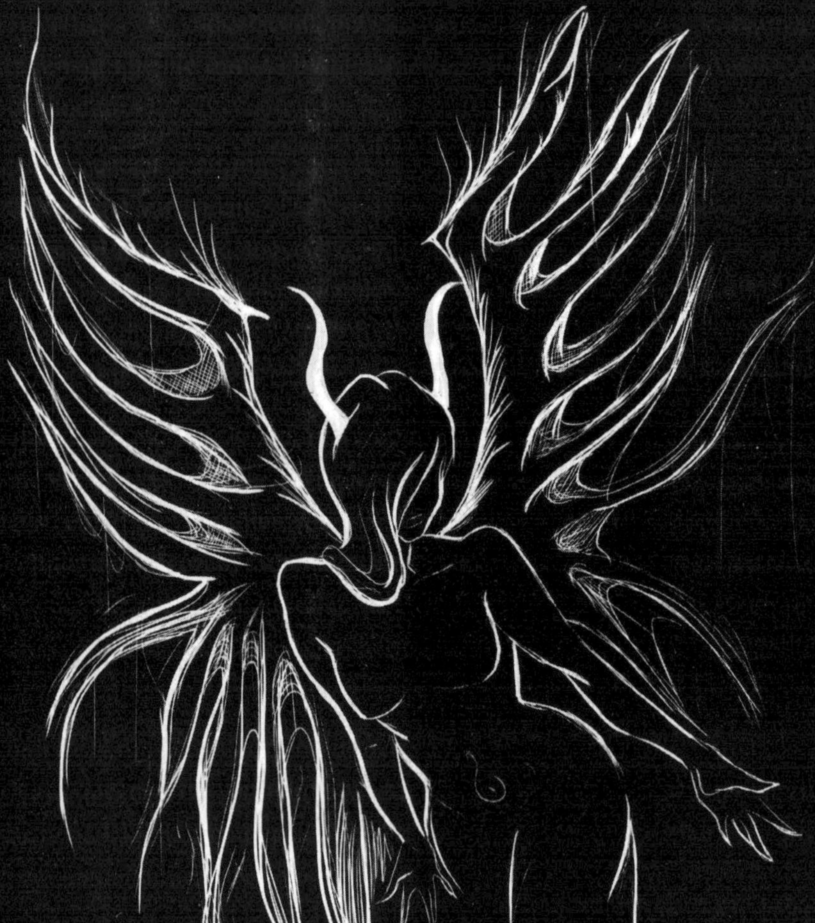

"Ben hayal kırıklığı gibiyim,
hayallerle beslenirim."

BÖLÜM 10

Nathaniel beni bırakıp gittiğinden beri koltukta tek başıma oturmuş düşünüyordum. Ara sıra parmaklarımla dudağıma değiyordum. Çaktırmadan kızın sıcaklığının hâlâ kalıp kalmadığını kontrol ediyordum. Ama dudaklarım aynı gibiydi. Sanki hoş kokulu bir kız onlara yapışmamış, diliyle onları yalamamış ve beni kendine esir etmemiş gibiydi.

Kendine esir etmek... Böyle cümleler zihnime bardaktan boşalırcasına yağan yağmur misali akıyordu. Çıtırdayan odunların sesleri odayı doldururken zihnim Azrail'in telaşlı bekleyişini olabilecek en güzel şekilde renklendiriyordu. Cass'i düşünerek. Elim istemeden tekrar dudaklarıma kayınca canım sıkıldı. Orta boylu, ufak tefek ve fazlasıyla yorgun görünen bir kızın bende bu denli değişikliklere sebep olması saçmaydı. Üstelik kızın gözleri normal bile değildi, kırmızıydı. Ki kırmızı gözlerin de çok eşsiz olabileceğini görmüştüm böylelikle.

Kapı açılınca oturuşumu düzelttim. Nathaniel çoktan gidip rapor vermiş olmalıydı. Bugünkü olaylara verdiği inanılmaz tepki cennete girdiğimiz anda da devam etmişti. Bana kızıyor, zebaniler hakkında sayıp sövüyor, iblislere ise âdeta kan kusuyordu. İki ırk birbirinden tiksiniyorsa neden ben ve Cass birbirimizden tiksinmemiştik?

Azrail, siyah kuzgun rengi pelerinini masanın her yerine saçılmış kâğıtların üstüne bıraktı. Konuşmaya başladığında meleği ilk kez bu kadar yorgun görüyordum. Gözlerinin siyahı bile bir önceki gün gibi değildi, bir şeyler meleği yormuş, tüm yaşam enerjisini çekmiş gibiydi.

"Bu artık çok uzadı. Sana bir şeyler anlatacağım ama baştan uyarayım sevgili Aidan, bu o kadar kolay olmayacak." Melek sandalyeden iki masayı şömineye yaklaştırdıktan sonra birini kendine çekip oturdu. Diğerini eliyle işaret edip, "Gel bakalım Aidan. Kâinat dediğimiz karmaşayı ve senin bu karmaşanın neresinde olduğunu sana anlatayım."

Melek konuşmaya başladığında evren, içinde bulunduğum ev, pelerinimi sıcacık yapan şömineden gelen ateş ve diğer tüm şeyler bir bir önemini yitiyordu. Saniyeler dakikalara karışırken anlatılanlar hep başka saklı bir anıya gebe kalıyordu. Azrail'in tüm yaşamımı anlatması, o konuşmayı sürdürdükçe daha imkânsız gelmeye başlamıştı. Koca bir hayat, onca sene nasıl olur da sözcüklere sığabilirdi ki?

O kızı nasıl tanımazdım? Ona âşık olmuştum. Ve bu her şeyin sonunu getirmişti. Hem de her şeyin. Arasında gezindiğim dünya benim için bitmişti. Onu görmüş ve ölümden çekip almıştım. Sonrası ise tam bir fiyaskoydu. O avcıya âşık olmuştum.

Ve o babamı öldürmüştü.

Azrail, cümlelerin yeterli gelmediği yerde uzun sivri parmaklarıyla alnımın tam ortasındaki noktaya dokunuyor ve zihnime anıları gönderiyordu. Ne kadar zaman geçti bilmiyordum ama bir noktadan sonra kulübenin içinde sinirden kahkahalar atmaya başlamıştım. Başım asla ağrımayacağını düşündüğüm şekillerde acıyordu. "Ah, seni aptal Aidan!" Anılar öyle hop diye gelmiyorlardı. Melek onları bana getirmek için ciddi bir efor sarf ediyordu. Bunca zaman anlatmamasının sebebi ise benim hiçbir şey hatırlamıyor olmamdı.

Eh, artık oldukça çok şey hatırlıyordum.

Draza.

Ölmüştü, hayır hayır dirilmişti, onu geri getirmiştik. Peki sonra... O avcıya bir kez daha âşık olup peşinden dünyaya gitmiştim. TAHTIMI BIRAKMIŞTIM. Ve sonra hastalanmıştım.

Hikâyenin bu bölümü oldukça tuhaftı çünkü şeytanlar hastalanmazdı. Melek, bunun Draza için yaptığım anlaşma ile ilgisi olduğunu söylemişti. Ve Meredith göz önünde bulundurulunca bundan neredeyse emindim. Evet, bir şeyleri feda etmiştim.

Kendimi.

Ama ölmemiştim. Başka birisi de benim için bir şeyleri feda etmişti.

Cassie...

Ve sonunda o şeytan, ben ise melek olmuştum.

İşte tam bu noktada beynim idrak sınırlarının dışına taşıyordu. Kahkahalar atarak masaya vurdum. Cennette sesimi duyan diğer melekler ne düşünüyordu acaba? Gerçi başından beri kimliğimi bilmeden gezindiğim için onlara bir aptal gibi görünmüş olmalıydım, muhtemelen bana gülüyorlardı. Zavallı Aidanhell, Lucifer'ın göz bebeği sonunda kafayı sıyırmış, günahlarından arınmış ve bir melek olmuştu. Hatta sıradan bir melek de değil. Azrail'in çırağı. Kanlarla örülü hayatıma da bu yakışırdı işte. Ölüm. Elbette ki.

Anıları bana gösteriyordu ama her şeyi gösteremezdi öyle değil mi? Sadece önemli şeyler vardı burada. Bana ait, benim olan, ufak tefek ama değerli anıların her biri paramparça bir şekilde evrene yayılmıştı.

Azrail anlatabileceği her şeyi anlattığını söyleyip sandalyesinde huzursuzca geri çekildiğinde aciz ve yorgun beynimde ona soracağım tek bir soru belirdi. "Ne zaman geri döneceğim?" Melek bu sorumu anlamadı. Sanki ben ona hayattaki en saçma şeyi sormuşum gibi bana baktı. EN SAÇMA ŞEY! Biri neden cenneti bıraksın ki?

Melek keskin bir şekilde parlayan gözlerini kısarak şüpheyle baktı. "Bunu soruyorsun çünkü…" diye sordu sakince.

"Çünkü dışarıda bir yerde bana ait olan bir şey var ve ben burada ona sahip değilim."

Melek kendinden emin bir şekilde gülümseyince sorumu yine anlamadığını düşündüm. "Ah sevgili çırak, ihtiyacın olan her şeye sahipsin. Artık sana ait hiçbir şey yok. O başka bir hayattaydı." Sonrasında pelerinini alıp sanki az önce mahvolan hayatımı sözcüklere sığdırmamış gibi bir kayıtsızlıkla evden çıkıp gitti.

Aradan geçen sessiz saatler sonrasında naçizane kulübemin kapısı tekrar açıldı. Gelen Azrail değildi. Nathaniel siyah kukuletalı bir cübbe giymiş, yüzünü ve ellerini de maske ve eldivenle kapatmıştı. Normaldeki tarzından çok daha değişik bir şekilde giyindiğini fark edince yerimde kıpırdandım. Bugün benimle ne yapmak isterse istesin ilgilenmiyordum. Az önce üzerimden yüz melek tepinerek geçmiş gibiydi, hayatın amacını falan sorgulamaya başlamıştım ve şöminenin de bana pek yardımı dokunmamıştı. Şömine sessiz bir oda arkadaşıydı, dertlerimi dinlese bile akıl vermemişti. Öte yandan Nathaniel bir arkadaş değildi. Anılarımın tamamı bende olmasa bile arkadaşın tanımını bilebileceğimi düşündüm.

Elinde Azrail'in olmadığı geceler gezdirdiği kalın deri defteriyle kapıda belirdi. "Çok işimiz var Aidan." Defteri dizimin üzerine bırakınca ona baktım. Buradan gidemeyecektim. Beni bırakmaya niyetleri yoktu. Onlar bana baktığında ne görüyordu bilmiyorum ama ben bir enkaz görüyordum. Bu enkazın parlak, beyaz kanatları olabilirdi ama yine de enkazdı işte.

"Bugün her zamankinden daha az ruh topladım ve normal seyirde gelen birkaç ölümü yerine getiremedim, o yüzden tekrar gitmemiz gerekiyor." Durup onu dinleyip dinlemediğime baktı. "Bak, Azrail'in sana anlattıklarını biliyorum. Sen buraya aitsin. Artık arındın. Burada biz melekler birbirimizi kollar ve ebedi görevlerimizi yerine getiririz. Sen çok kutsal bir işin bir parçası oldun."

İnanamayarak nefesimi bıraktım. "Birilerini öldürmek mi? Eğer bu kutsal ise ben bunu önceden de yapıyordum." Melek defterin yapraklarını gelişigüzel karıştırırken ekledim. "Yapıyormuşum yani. Birileri hafızamı kemirmeden önce."

Bana mı öyle geldi emin değildim ama melek sabırsızlığını ortaya koyan derin bir nefes aldı. "Önceki gibi konuşmaya başladın. Burada ciddi bir problemimiz olabilir. Alaycı konuşmak buraya pek uymuyor."

"Nathaniel, bugün az kalsın bir zebaniyi saçından sürükleyecektin, üstelik yol boyu asla kullanmaman gereken bir ton laf ettin. Burada bana cennetin lügatından ve gerekliliklerinden bahsedecek son melek sensin."

Nathaniel bilgelikle cilalanmış safir gözlerini gözlerime dikti. "Aynı şey değil. Niyetim kötü değildi. Burada kötü yoktur Aidan." Bu dediğine öyle ateşli bir şekilde bağlıydı ki, dünkü hâlini görmesem ona inanabilirdim.

"Daha önce anlatmalıydınız. Bana yalan söylediniz. Hazır konusu geçmişken melekler yalan söyleyebiliyor mu?"

"Hayır," dedi hışımla. Masmavi gözleri öfkeden çakmak çakmak olmuştu. Bakışları çağlayan nehirler gibiydi. "Sana anlatmamayı seçtik çünkü birileri sen şımarıkça geçmişini hatırlayıp ortalarda gezin diye kendini feda etmedi." Ellerini iki omzuma koydu. "Sen bir melek olarak yaşa diye bir melez kendi ruhunu verdi. Bu ne demek biliyor musun?"

Çığlıklar atarak önüme gelen her şeyi devirmek istiyordum.

"Seni iyi bir melek yapacağız demek. Sen artık buraya aitsin." Ardından arkasını dönüp kapıya gitti. "İblisler ve zebaniler işimizi bozuyor olabilir ama onlarla baş etmenin yolunu buldum. Gün batımında artık işimize karışacak pek fazla iblis olacağını sanmıyorum."

Melek kapıyı kapatır kapatmaz önümde duran masaya tekme attım. Masa lambası düşüp camlar etrafa yayıldığında sinirden deliye dönmüştüm.

Çok şeyi hatırlamıyor olabilirdim.

Ama bildiğim bir şey varsa o da hiçbir yere ait olmadığımdı.

Deri kaplı defteri çantama koyup başımdan çapraz bir şekilde geçirdim. Birkaç saat önce yaşadığım anlamsız tuhaf olayı atlatmaya çalışırken içine daha da gömülmüştüm. Az sonra kafamda binbir düşünce cirit atarken Nathaniel ve dev kanatları bana rehberlik edecek, birlikte yükselip cennetin göğü yırttığı eşikten yeryüzüne gidecektik.

Nathaniel'in beyaz kanatları zifiri karanlıkta simsiyah görünecek ve insanlar bizim fazlaca yakından geçen yabani bir kuş olduğumuzu sanacaktı.

Tek bir seferde bunu idrak edebilmiştim. İnsanların yaşadığı şey bir hayattı ama bizimki değildi. Biz onlar için sadece gölgeydik. Oysa Nathaniel bunu yaratılışından beri yapıyordu.

Yaratılış.

Bunu düşününce kaşlarımın tam ortasına bir ağrı saplanıyordu. O ağrı başladığında ise kötü sözler söylemek istiyordum. Ardı ardına gelen bir sürü anlamsız kötü söz. Nathaniel'in bana asla söylemememi tembihlediği ama kendisinin sakınmadan kullandığı sözlerdi bunlar.

Kapı sertçe açılınca başımdaki ağrıyı görmezden gelip ayaklandım. Nathaniel tıpkı az önceki gibi beraberinde cennetin bahçelerindeki asılı kalmış o ferah kokuyu getirip odaya saldı. Fazlasıyla zeki gözleri yüzümde yavaşça gezindi. "Bir sorun mu var?"

"Pek sayılmaz." *Sadece o kızı merak ettim. Ve yaratılışımla ilgili o büyük gizemi çözmek istiyorum, Azrail bana her şeyi anlatmadı ve eğer her şeyi anlatırsa aciz aklımın bunu kaldırabileceğinden de emin değilim.*

"Pekâlâ." Nathaniel uzun kollarını arkasında birleştirip geriniyormuş gibi hareket etti. Gerinmekten kastım o devasa kanatlarının girdiği kaburga kemiklerini ciddi anlamda çıtırdatmıştı.

Elim istemsizce kendi sırtıma gitti. Daha önce sadece üç kez uçmuştum ve daha şimdiden kanatlarımı özlemiştim.

Bu da beni başka bir çıkmaza getirmişti. ÖZLEMEK.

Düşüncelerimi dağıtabilirmişim gibi başımı sağa sola salladım. "Gidiyor muyuz?" Nathaniel yanıt vermeden önce kaslarını esnetmeyi bırakıp bir süre bana baktı. Bende bir değişiklik görüp görmediğini merak ettim. Ama ben ona bunu soramadan, "Hazırlan," deyip odadan çıktı.

Üzerime baktım. Hazırlanmakla ilgili ekstra yapacağım hiçbir şey yoktu. Kıyafetlerim temizdi. Gerekli şeyleri yanıma almıştım, elbette *aklım* dışında. Yapacağım tek şey dışarı çıkıp beklemek olabilirdi. Öyle de yaptım.

Avluya gidip şirin kulübemin rüzgârlığına yaslandım. Bugün oraya yine birilerinin canını almaya gidiyorduk ve aklımdaki tek şey Cassie'yi görüp göremeyeceğimdi. Kalbimde bir şeyler adını içimden söylesem bile şaha kalkıyordu.

"Demek heyecanlısın." Başımı çevirip gelen meleğe baktım. "Bugün senin için özel bir görevim var Aidan. Buna bayılacaksın. Eğer hayatının yolunda gitmediğini düşünüyorsan bu her şeyi yoluna koymak için altın bir fırsat olacak."

Melek yüzünde mağrur bir ifadeyle bana arkasını döndü. Altın sarısı saçları sırtından aniden çıkan kanatlar yüzünden dalgalandı. Bir saniye sonra ise bir insanın yaklaşık altı katı uzunluğundaki dev kanatlarını açtı ve yükseldi. Ben de benzer hareketlerle peşinden gittim.

Cennetin perdesinin inceldiği yere gidip ellerimizi görünmez duvarın içinden geçirdik. Yapış yapış bir duvar bizi sarmalarken geriye dönüp bakmak istedim. İçimde bir yer kulübeye, burada geçirdiğim aylara bir bakmak istedi.

Ama sonra kendimi durdurdum. Artık cennete aittim, bir yere gittiğim yoktu ki.

Cennetin ince zarif perdesi yırtılırken kanatlarımı gerebildiğim kadar gerdim. Perdeyi aşıp dünya atmosferine girdiğimizde kanatlarımdaki tüyler elektrik verilmişçesine diklendiler. Başımı hafifçe yana çevirip değişen hava akımının uğultusundan kurtuldum.

Nathaniel, hemen önümde tüm bu fiziksel şeylerden hiç etkilenmemişçesine, zarafetinden ödün vermeden, kararlı bir şekilde ilerlemeye devam ediyordu. Kaşlarımı çatıp göğsümü şişiren derin bir nefes aldım.

Binalar tıpkı daha önceki gibi içlerindeki insanların yaktıkları ışıklarla yarı yarıya aydınlanmıştı. Başımı kaldırıp binaların ardına, bulutların da üstüne baktım. Yarım kilometre çapında uçan tek canlı bizlerdik.

Gömleğimin yakası boynuma vurunca fazla hızlandığımı fark ettim. Bu hızda devam edersem Nate'e çarpacaktım. Sonunda ne olurdu bilmiyorum ama denememeye kararlıydım.

"Gelmek üzereyiz." Beni görmese de başımla onayladım.

Alçalıp binaların çatısından uçmaya başladık. İnsanların bizi göremeyeceğini biliyordum. Aslında görüyorlardı ama tam olarak değil. Bunu açıklamak zordu. Bizler diğer canlılar gibi değildik. Diğer canlılardan kastım ise Azrail'in anlattığı birkaç şeytan ve insanlardı.

Bir de hayvanlar vardı. Onlar bizi görebilirdi. Kediler ve köpekler bizleri görüyorlardı. Azrail'e onların da bir çeşit melek olup olmadığını sormuştum. Ruhları parlıyordu bizler gibi. O ise gülümsemişti. Reddetmemişti. Bu yüzden uçarken gördüğüm damdaki sarı bir kediye selam verdim. O ise ağzını açarak kocaman esnedi.

Ve bu bugün ikinci kez daha önce hissetmediğim bir şey kalbimin sızlamasına sebep oldu. Mutluluk.

"Hastaneye gidiyoruz." Orayı biliyordum. Onu yakından takip etmeme gerek olmadığı için yükseldim. Hastane binası, devasa ışıklarla hiçlikte var olmuş gibiydi. Bir anlığına yerimde durdum. Kanatlarımı havada asılı kalmak için çırparken hastaneye bakıyordum. Ölüm meleği yavaşça oraya doğru yol alıyordu.

Bir şekilde... Bir şey hissetmiştim. Ve bunu tanımlayamadım. Hayatım dediğim süre boyunca hiç yol ayrımına düşmüş müydüm bilmiyordum. Omzumun üstünden geriye, geldiğim yöne baktım. Birkaç bina ötesindeki sarı kedi gözleri parlarken bana bakıyordu. Tekrar dönüp önümde ilerleyen meleğe baktım.

Tüm bunları neden yapıyordum?

Dünyaya sadece iki kez gelmiştim ve cennetin mükemmelliğine dair kafam sorularla dolmuştu. Ben orayı, bu mükemmelliği hak etmiyordum. Azrail'in anlattıklarına göre ben cehennemdeki en günahkâr varlıktım ve... Hak etmiyordum işte. Derin bir nefes alıp hastane istikametine uçmaya başladım. O kızı tekrar görebilmenin umudu kanatlarıma yepyeni bir güç vermişti.

Birkaç dakikanın sonunda hastaneye varmıştım. Nathaniel kanatlarını içine çekip çatıya bağdaş kurup oturmuştu. Beni bekliyordu. Kuvvetli bir inişten sonra kaburgalarımı gerip beyaz kanatlarımı bedenime çektim.

"Ne düşünüyordun Aidan? Yetişemedin."

Bu soru beni hazırlıksız yakaladı. Ellerimle saçlarımı düzeltip bakışlarımı ondan uzaklaştırdım. "Sadece lüzumsuz şeyler. Seni rahatsız etmeye değecek kadar değerli değiller."

Melek yüzünde sanki bunu asırlardır yapıyormuşçasına antika ve bir o kadar da doğal bir gülümsemeyle yavaşça ayağa kalktı. "Sorular olur. Her sorunun da bir cevabı olur. Cevabını öğrenmek istediğin soruları sorarsın. Ama eğer kendine saklıyorsan... Cevaplardan korktuğun içindir." Yanıma gelip soğuk elini omzuma koydu. Başımı çevirip mavi gözlerine baktım. "Ve kardeşim, senin korkman gereken tek şey yaratıcımız. Geri kalanlar," boşta kalan eli ile dünyayı işaret etti, "senden korkabilir."

Hafif bir meltem saçlarımı uçuştururken yavaşça başımı salladım. Nathaniel mavi gözlerini kapatıp derin bir nefes aldı. "Milyonlarca kez yapsan da alışamıyorsun işte. Bugünkü diğerlerinden daha özel. Daha kutsal bir amaca hizmet ettiğini damarlarında akan melek kanından anlayabilirsin."

Onu sorgulamıyordum. Meleklerin aldıkları emirler kutsaldı. Kafama göre hareket edemeyeceğimi biliyordum. "Gel benimle." Nate çatıdaki kapıyı açıp merdivenleri bana gösterdi. Beraber inerken bedenimdeki ürperti hissinin giderek arttığının farkındaydım.

Dün geceyi unutmamıştım.

O kızın bana bakışı, beni tanıyışı.

Beni öpüşü. Bedenimin ona verdiği tepki.

Ve kızın *iblis* oluşu.

Kalabalık hastane koridorlarında ilerlerken çevreme bakmıyordum. Nathaniel insanlara parlayan ışıklar gibi göründüğümüzü söylemişti. *Parlayan ışıklar...* Faniler bulundukları dünyanın aslında hiç de bildikleri gibi olmadığını öğrenseler kafayı yerlerdi.

Hedefimizdeki odaya vardığımızda melek kaşlarını çattı. "Yine mi?" dedi öfkeli sesiyle. Ardından kapıyı açmak için uzandı. Kilitli olduğu anlaşılınca geriye çekilip sert bir tekme ile açtı.

Menteşeler bağırırken kapı ardındaki gözler önüne serdi. Yine o kız ve yanındaki.

Bir hastanın üzerine eğilmişlerdi. Bir ruhu bedenine aktarır gibiydi. "Bu ne?" Afallayarak onlara doğru davrandım ama melek benden önce odaya girdi. "Durdur çabuk. Seni salak! Ne ile uğraştığın hakkında hiçbir fikrin yok."

Ben ise... Sadece bakıyordum. Hayatımda gördüğüm en güzel şeye.

Turuncu saçlı olan önce bana ardından meleğe baktı. "Lütfen geri çekil. Cassie eğer bu kızı öldürmezse ölecek. Gücü tükendi."

Cassie...

Bir dakika, ölecek miydi?

İçimi kaplayan ürperti dudaklarımı aralattı. "Burada neler oluyor? O neden ölsün ki?" Gözlerimi ondan alamıyordum. O ise benim farkımda değilmiş gibiydi. Oda sanki çevremizde dönüyordu ve bunu sadece ben fark ediyordum. Nate öfkeli bir hâlde elini kaldırınca öne doğru uzandım. "Hey!"

O ise uzandığım elimi itti. "Bu ruh bize ait. İblisini alıp gitmezsen...Boş versene. Çekil."

Sonrası biraz hızlıydı. Turuncu saçlı kız Nate'in önüne çıkınca melek onu itmişti. Ve bunu öyle bir kuvvetle yapmıştı ki kız duvara çarpıp monitörleri devirmişti. Bunun üzerine Cass denilen kız başını kaldırıp bizden tarafa bakmıştı. Nathaniel ise onu görmezden gelip üzerine eğildiği bedene dokundu.

Olanları anladığımda çok geçti. "Hayır!" Onlara koştum. Ruh kutsal parıltı eşliğinde bedenden süzülüp Nate'e geçerken dehşete kapılmıştım. Cassie ise geriye savrulmuştu. Düşüşü derinlerde bir yerimi rahatsız etmişti. Yerde doğal olmayan bir açıyla boylu boyunca uzanmıştı.

Kendimi tutamadan yanına gittim. İki elimi başının yanlarına koyduğumda kalbime bir şey oldu. Yoğun bir elektrik beni çarpmış gibiydi. Aynı anda hem nefes alıp hem nefes vermek gibiydi. Yarım kalmışlık hissi bedenimde her bir hücremi tek tek gezerken kızın yüzüne bakıyordum.

Parmaklarımla önüne gelen koyu kahve saçlarını çekince kızın alnındaki ter damlacıklarını gördüm. Hayır hayır, ölüyor olamazdı değil mi? İblis bile olsa ölmemeliydi. Başımı kaldırıp Nate'e baktım. Çoktan teslim için ruhu emmiş, yüzünde anlaşılmaz bir ifadeyle bizi izliyordu.

"Ona yardım et Nathaniel." Tekrar kıza döndüm. Gözleri kapalıydı. İşaret ve başparmağımla kurumuş dudaklarını aralayınca arasından kırmızı bir sıvı döküldü. Kan. Tekrar Nate'e döndüm. "Neden yardım etmiyorsun? Gelsene!"

Oysa o hâlâ anlamıyordu. "Sen orada ne yapıyorsun? O parmağındaki iblis kanı mı? Buraya gel. Sana bugünün özel bir gün olduğunu söylemiştim."

Kocaman bir saniye boyunca meleğe baktım. Dediklerini anlamlandırmaya çalıştım ama yapamadım. "O ölecek. Eğer sen yardım etmezsen."

Nate sabırsızca kıpırdandı. Yataktan uzaklaşırken bir yandan da defterini çantadan çıkarıyordu. "Şeytanları korumuyoruz Aidan. Onları sevmeyiz. Bir tanesi ölüyorsa kutlama yapmamız gerekir."

Bir tanesi. Oysa bu herhangi bir şeytan değildi. Gözlerimi kısıp omuzlarımı dikleştirdim. "O sıradan biri değil." Melek yanıt vermeyince istemsizce boğazımdan bir hırıltı yükseldi. Bu güzel kokulu kız benim için o kadar önemli olmalıydı ki uğruna tahtı terk edecek, babamı öldürdüğü için onu affedecek ve her seferinde sanki dünyada başka kız yokmuşçasına yeniden ona dönecektim.

Ah lanet...

Sözcüğün yarattığı his içimi ürpertti. Lanet okumaya başlamıştım. Elimi saçlarımın arsından geçirirken dudaklarımı ısırdım. "Görev her neyse yapacağım, sadece ona yardım et." Sözlerim fısıltı gibi çıkmıştı. Bu bir başkaldırı ya da o tarz bir şey değildi, bu gereklilikti. Dizimdeki sıcak başı ve koyu saçları üzerime serpilmiş olan bu kızı bırakamazdım. Kan kokusu güzel kokusuna karışan bu... Bu... Şeytanı.

"Ne olur yardım et Aidan. Lütfen." Turuncu saçlı kız düştüğü yerden hafifçe doğrulup bana doğru emeklemeye başladı. Yanıma gelip iki kolunu da sıkıca sırtıma dolayınca kaskatı kesildim. "Yaptığın tüm zorbalıkları unutacağım." Biraz geri çekilip yaşların biriktiği parlak yeşil gözlerini gözlerime dikti. "Kanatlarım yok, onu cehenneme götüremem. Bu hâlde uçamaz. Senin kanatların var. Ne olur bizi götür." Gözlerinden akan birkaç damla yaş beyaz gömleğimin omuzlarını ıslattı.

Aklımı kaçırıyordum.

Cassie'nin dizimdeki başı sallanınca aklımı kaçırdığımdan emin oldum. Narin bedeni her sarsılışında dudaklarından kanlar dökülüyordu. Ilık kan dizlerimi ıslatırken Nate hiçbir şey yapmadan âdeta bir gösteri izler gibi bizi izliyordu. Başımı kaldırıp onunla iletişim kurmaya çalıştım. "Onu bırakamam. Lütfen onlara yardım etmeme izin ver." Nate gülümsedi. Sadece gülümsedi. Ve bu benim sinirime dokundu. "Ölmesine izin veremem." Şimdi elinde defteri tutuyordu, bir parmağı sayfalardan birindeydi.

"Neden Aidan?"

Bilmiyordum.

"Sadece veremem işte. Bir melek kendine ihtiyacı olana yardım etmeli. Üstelik o beni kurtardı. Sen de biliyorsun, bu kız olmasa ben şu an... Kaybolmuştum."

Melek sabırsızca yerinde kıpırdandı. "Hah. Sen ne istediğinin farkında mısın? Bir şeytana yardım etmek... Bunu bırak bir de cehennem diyorsun. Oraya gidemezsin. Üstelik vereceğim görevi yerine dahi getirmedin."

Görev görev görev.

Bir dakika. Melekler cehenneme gidemez mi?

Cassie bir kez daha öksürünce sarsıldım. "Oraya gidebilirim. Görevini de yapacağım. Sadece şu an eğer önceliğim bu olmazsa beni yaşatan kadın ölecek. Hepsi bu Nate. Hepsi gerçekten bu."

Nathaniel sinirli bir kahkaha atınca turuncu saçlı kız pustu. Dudakları belirli belirsiz hareket ediyor, bir duayı sessizce okuyor gibiydi. Ağlamaktan şişen gözleri ve yüzündeki dehşete kapılmış ifade ile Cassie'ye bakıyordu. Ne dediği hakkında hiçbir fikrim yoktu.

"Eğer cehenneme gidersen Aidan, bir daha cennete dönemezsin. Cehennemin kraliçesini kurtarman kabul edilemez."

O bir kraliçe miydi? Azrail bu ayrıntıyı neden vermemişti ki? Başparmağımı kanlı alt dudağına değirince bir kez daha ürperdim. Bir günah kadar güzeldi.

Tanrım, neler saçmalıyordum? Günah neden güzel olacaktı ki?

"Ben..."

Binbir parçaya ayrılmıştım. Onu kurtarmalıydım. O parlıyordu. O çok güzeldi ve o ölüyordu. Onun kim olduğunu biliyordum ama daha fazlasını bilmeye ihtiyacım vardı. Ölmesine izin veremezdim.

Nathaniel yataktan uzaklaşıp yanıma geldi. Benim hizama eğilip ağzını kapatan maskeyi eldivenli parmağıyla aşağı çekti. Konuşmaya başladığında fısıldıyordu ama zaten diğer kızın -ki bir anıda onun Meredith olduğunu öğrenmiştim- bizi duyacak hâli yoktu. Azrail Meredith'in olduğu tuhaf bir anı göstermişti ama zihnimdeki hiçbir parça Meredith'in neden Cassie'yi kurtarmaya çalıştığını çözemiyordu.

"Aidan, bizler meleğiz. Birbirimizi kollarız. Önceki hayatından parçalar taşıyorsun ve bu senin için her şeyi daha da zorlaştıracak ama sana diyorum, senin ailen artık biziz. Ne bu iblis kız ne de cehennemdeki kara elf senin ailen. Onlar bambaşka hayattan kırıntılar sadece. Sen melek olmadan önce de güçlüydün, yine güçlü olacaksın. Birkaç yıl sonra bu anı belki sana yine acı verecek ama unutup gideceksin." Cassie hareket etmeyi bırakalı birkaç dakika olmuştu. Nefes alışverişi zayıflamıştı. Aralık kalan dudaklarından çıkan kesik ılık nefesler hâlâ bacaklarıma vuruyordu ve bu deli saçması durumda da akıl sağlığımı korumamın yegâne sebebi buydu.

Nathaniel elindeki defteri havaya kaldırıp eldivenli parmaklarıyla defterin yapraklarını açtı. Uzun işaret parmağı sayfada mürekkeple yazılan isimlerin en sonunda durdu. Parmağıyla hafifçe sayfaya vururken doğrudan bana bakıyordu. "Görevin burada adı yazan kişinin ruhunu almak."

İsmi okumaya çalışırken kalbim sıkıştı.

"Hayır," dedim hayal kırıklığı ile. "Cassie yazıyor orada. Onun ruhunu almayacağım." Nathaniel defteri kapatıp kucağımda yatan kızın hemen yanına bıraktı. Konuştuğunda sarkan maskenin kısmen gizlediği yüzünde anlayışlı ama kendinden emin, bilge bir adamın ifadesi kazılıydı. "Bu senin görevin. Düzeni sağlamak için ismi yazılanları götürürüz. Sen ölüm meleğisin Aidanhell ve hilekâr artık ölmeli."

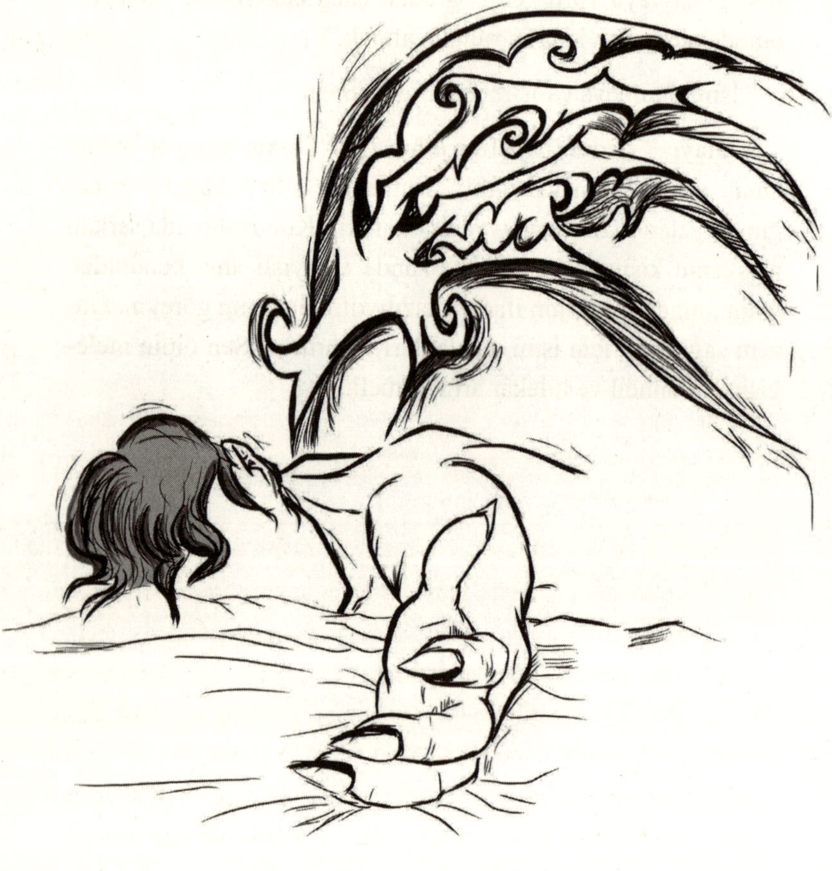

"Bir kız parçaladı kâinatı
ve tüm varoluşlar karıştı birden.
Ve hilekâr bir kez daha ölmeli yeniden."

BÖLÜM 11

Draza

"Ejderhaların soyları tükendi."

Kollarımı göğsümde kavuşturup çenemi meydan okurcasına dikleştirdim. Üç adam bana tepeden bakıyorlardı ve tepeden bakılmasından nefret ederdim. Rohan yanıma gelip bir adamlara bir de bana baktı, sonrasında ellerini huzursuzca önünde birleştirip başını hafifçe eğdi. "Majeste. Öyle biliyorduk lakin onlar *unutulanlar*. Cennet, cehennem, çukur ya da herhangi bir dünya onları kapsamıyor. Dünya milyarlar yaşındaysa ve cehennem ondan daha da yaşlıysa, eh... Karşımızda kâinatta gördüğümüz en yaşlı varlıklar duruyor demektir."

Herifler bizi duyuyorsa bile belli etmiyorlardı, sanki tepki vermenin manasını bilmiyor gibiydiler. "Ürkütücü göründüklerini biliyorum ama hemen koy verme iblisçe. Dik dur. Bu sorunu çözeceğiz." Bir bu eksikti. Her şey tam olmuştu. Yeterince kaos ve sapkın yaratığımız yokmuş gibi. Sanki her sabah yataktan çıktığımda hangi kurdun kıçımı kemireceğini düşünmüyormuşum gibi.

"Onlar ürkütücü zaten Majeste. Sebebi görünüşleri değil. Lütfen onlarla terbiyeli konuşun." Terbiye kelimesi vücudumda bir tiksinti nöbeti geçirmeme sebep oldu.

Terbiye mi? O da ne?

"Rohan, sakin ol ve bana bırak." Hançerimi ayaklarımın dibine bırakıp ejderhalara doğru ağır adımlarla yürüdüm. "Krallığıma ve elbette ki cehenneme hoş geldiniz." Üç adam karşımda hiçbir şey demeden dikilmeye devam ettiler. Kara elflerin konuşkan olmadığını düşünüyorsanız bir de ejderhaları görün.

Ortadaki adam elini tekrar kaldırınca içimdeki kıçımı kollama isteğine karşı gelmeye çalıştım. Karizmayı çizdirmemek adına sakinliğimi korudum. Adamın parmaklarını hayatlarındaki en önemli şeymiş gibi izleyen kanatlı fetiş ordusu, gökyüzünden bir kez daha dalışa geçti. "Beyler, iletişim kurmaya çalışıyorum sadece. Biri benimle konuşursa eğer daha mutlu olacağım." Karşımdaki ateşli ejderha grubunun solisti ortadaki beyaz saçlı herif sanıyordum ama yanındaki adam konuşmaya başlayınca dikkatim onun üzerinde yoğunlaştı. İşte o zaman onların üçüz olduğunu anladım. Öndekinin saçının beyaz arkadakilerin ise kırmızı ve siyahtı.

"White pek konuşmaz," dedi ikizlerden kırmızı takım elbiseli olanı. Öndekinin omzuna elini koyup öne geçti. Bana doğru yaklaşıp elini uzattı.

Pekâlâ, evhamlı olmak hakkında ne derler bilirsiniz. Ama ben dilimden zehir saçabiliyorsam onlar da elleriyle zehri taşıyabilirlerdi. Yine de bu tuhaf durumda -yukarıdaki vızıldayan Valkür ordusu ve karşımdaki suratsız üçüz ejderhalar- elini sıkmaktan başka şansım yoktu. Bu yüzden istemeyerek de olsa ejderha adamla el sıkıştım. "Benim adım Red." Elini tekrar çekip göz alıcı kırmızı takım elbisesinin cebine koydu. "Arkadaki de Black." Takım elbiselerinden ziyade saçları da uyumluydu. Bordo saçları vardı Red'in. Perdeli zarif kulağında ise irili ufaklı küpeler takılıydı. Biraz daha yakından bakınca kaşını da deldirmiş olduğunu gördüm.

"Ben Draza."

O da beni inceliyordu. Yılanı andıran oval irisli gözleri uzunca bir süre yüzümde gezindi. "Kolay bir hayatın olmamış," dedi nihayet inceleme işlemini bitirdiğinde. Boşta kalan elinin işaret parmağı bir ressamınki gibi akıcı bir hareketle yüzümü gösterecek şekilde havada daire çizdi. "Simsiyah gözler... Çok resmedilesi."

Suratına bomboş baktım. Sonra iç sesimin karnına dirseğimi gömdüm ve cılız bir teşekkür mırıldandım. "Ben tahttaki vekil kralım." Ana Saray'ı gösterecek şekilde hafifçe yana kaydım. "Gelme sebebinizi öğrenebilir miyim?" Onlar kadar klas giyinmediğim için kendime sessizce sövmek istedim. Onlar çok şıktı ve ben sadece savaşçı bir elf gibi görünüyordum, gerçi elflerin kanatları olmazdı. Bu yüzden biraz süslü sayılabilirdim ve anlaşılan Red bunu zaten biliyordu. "Ejder uykusundaydık," dedi Red sakince. "Benimle yürür müsün Draza?" Majesteyi tercih ettiğimi söylemek istemiştim ama tepedeki vızıltılı ordunun büyüklüğünü göz önüne alırsak bunu yapamazdım. Onun yerine başımla onayladım ve beraber yürümeye başladık. Arkamda bir yerlerde Rohan'ın yaşlı kalbinin durup durup attığını duyabiliyordum. Bu adama da yazık oluyordu. Padişahla yaşadığı günlerini özlediğinden emindim.

Biz yanlarından geçerken ürkütücü ikizler bize bakmadı bile. Gözlerini kırpmadan Ana Saray'a bakıyorlardı ve bu ensemde ufaktan bir karıncalanmaya sebep olmaya başlamıştı.

Onlarla aramıza birkaç metre mesafe koyduktan sonra ejderha adımlarını yavaşlattı. "Ejder uykusundaydık. Burada huzuru bozuyor gibi bir tablo çiziyor olabiliriz ama biz düzen sağlayıcılarız. Zaman zaman şu an yaptığımızı yapmamız gerekebiliyor." Bir cehennem meşesinin yanında durup uzun ojeli tırnaklarını meşenin üzerinde gezdirdi.

"Şu an yaptığınız ne peki?"

Ejderha adam düşünüyormuş gibi dudaklarını büktü. "Ehh. Darbe gibi bir şey ya da daha dostane bir dille ifade etmek gerekirse otorite değişikliği diyelim."

Buz gibi bir his bedenimde gezinince bir anlığına nefes alamadım, yutkunamadım, sadece baktım. "Bu bir şaka mı?" Ejderha değil anlamında başını sağa sola salladı. "Kulağa kötü geldiğinin farkındayım ama bu herkes için gerekli. Buradaki *herkes* kelimesi cehennem ve dünya sakinlerinden her birini kapsıyor. Hatta cenneti bile. Kâinat bir denge üzerine kuruludur. O dengeyi bozan tek bir zerrecik büyük bir yıkıma yol açar. Sevgili Draza, sen akıllı ve karizmatik bir lidersin ama bu dengeyi sağlamak senin için çok ağır bir yük. Biz bu yükü sırtlanacağız."

"Ben doğduğum andan beri çok yük sırtlandım, ejderha. Ayrıca düşündüğünüz gibi her yere kaos hâkim değil. Her şey kontrolümüz altında." Red tek gözünü kısarak şüpheyle gözlerime baktı. "Cehennemin leydisi cehennemde değil. Sen desek daha yeni hiçbir canlının yaşamaması gereken bir olayı tecrübe ettin. Şu an konuşup gülmen ve normal davranman bile mucize. Dünya ise yıkım getirenlerle ve zincirini kırmış iblislerle dolu. Cennet zebanilerle tartışmaktan kendi işini yapamaz hâlde ve daha bilmediğin pek çok şey de var." Gözlerinin önüne düşen koyu kızıl saçlarını eliyle ittirdi. "Sen buna kontrol altında mı diyorsun? Kontrol her neyse bu değil Draza ve daha kötü günler gelecek. O günler geldiğinde kâinatın bir toz bulutu misali yok olması ise kaçınılmaz."

Hafif ılık bir meltem tenime çarpınca ürperdim. "Tüm her şey boşa mıydı yani? Taht, varis olmam, sonunda kaybettiğimi düşünürken kral olabilmem?"

Red gülünce sinirlerime hâkim olmak beş dakika öncesine nazaran daha da zorlaştı. Komik bir şey demediğimden emindim. Üstten bakılmaktan, bir çocuk gibi görülmekten ve acemi hissettirilmekten nefret ediyordum. Ben Mor Kule Zindanları'nı yönetmiştim, tecrübeliydim. Mantıklı kararlar alabilen bir iblistim, ben doğduğum andan beri bunun için eğitilmiştim. Ve şimdi çıkıp her şeyi halledebileceğimi düşündüğüm ilk anda kızıl saçlı, küpeli, serseri bir ejderha işime el koyacağını söylüyordu.

"Buna izin veremem. Ne kadar yaşlı ya da kadim olduğunuz umurumda değil. Bulunduğum yere kolay gelmedim. Kanla geldim. Şu an olduğum adam olabilmek için döktüğüm kanları bir nehir yapsalar, tüm cehennem her gün o nehirde yıkanırken boğulabilir. Neleri göze aldığımı, nelerden vazgeçtiğimi bilmi-" Red sabırsızca sözümü kesti. "Biliyorum. Başından geçen her olayı biliyorum. Bunları hiç yaşamamalıydın ama seçimlerin seni bu ana getirdi. Şimdi ise elinde bir şekle oturtamayacağın ölçüde taşkın bir kaos var." Bana yaklaşıp elini omzuma koyunca kendimi geri çekerek tutuşundan kurtuldum. "Sonsuza dek kalmak gibi bir niyetimiz yok. İşler düzene girdiğinde yeniden geldiğimiz hiçliğe döneceğiz. Bundan keyif almıyoruz. Ejder uykusundan uyandırılıp görevlendirilmeyi biz de istemedik ama işte buradayız."

"İşleri düzeltmeniz kaç bin yıl alacak peki?" Rohan'ın terbiyeli olmamla ilgili verdiği tüm öğütler kulağımın bir yanından girip diğer yanından çıkıyordu. Bu adamlar eskiydi, onların işleri düzeltme süresi ile bizimkisi bir olamazdı.

"Zaman bile kendini tanımlayamazken benim zamanı tanımlayabilmem mümkün değil." Sonra dönüp hâlâ köprüde bizi bekleyen kardeşlerine baktı. "Eğer karşı çıkarsan hiç gerekmeyen bir savaşın içine düşeceksin. Valkür ordusu kolay kolay pes etmez ve sayıca çok daha üstünler. Biz buraya ait değiliz belki ama bildiğin her şeyden çok daha eski ve tecrübeliyiz. Asla yenemeyeceğin üç krala ve onların konseyindeki komutanlarına, yenilmez ordularına bakıyorsun. Bunu bir iyilik gibi düşün ve yardım etmemize izin ver."

Aklım hâlâ az önceki sözlerindeydi. "Bilmediğim şeyler olduğunu söyledin. Daha farklı ne olmuş olabilir ki? Dünyanın ne kadar boka battığının ben de farkındayım. Ama daha ne olmuş olabilir ki?" Ejderhanın yanıt vermesi için gereken süre sanki saniyeler değil de saatler sürmüş gibiydi. Valkür ordusu uğultuyu kesip kendi içinde bölüklere ayrılmaya başlamıştı. Daha da üstlerinde diğerlerinin aksine beyaz giyinen bir grup kadın atlarıyla inişe geçiyorlardı. Her şeyleriyle orduları, kralları ve komutanlarıyla koca bir krallık buraya taşınmış gibiydi. Olmaması gereken tek şey ise doğum hakkımla aldığım Ana Saray'a çöreklenmeleriydi ve anlaşılan kozmik evrendeki hiçbir güç onları bundan alıkoyamayacaktı.

Çok güçlü olduğumu, kralın oğlu olduğum için yenilmez olduğumu düşünmüştüm. Çukurdan canlı bir şekilde döndüğüm için tüm iblisler tarafından saygı görmüştüm. Bir noktada ben bile içimdeki çürüyen anormal parçamı görmezden gelip kendimle gurur duymuştum ama şimdi her şey önemini yitiriyordu.

"Kötü düşüncelere kapılma genç Draza. Eğer doğru olanı yapmazsan gün geldiğinde ne üzerinde oturacağın bir taht ne de yöneteceğin bir halkın olacak." Red yalan söylemiyordu. Koyu kızılın iç içe geçtiği bordo gözlerindeki bir ifade çok fazla şey görüp bildiğini bangır bangır bağırıyordu.

"Soruma yanıt vermedin," dedim huzursuzca. "Her şey istediğin gibi olacak. Yardımınızı kabul edeceğim ama bana her şeyi anlatacaksın. Bu kez bir şeylerin dışında kalmak istemiyorum."

Red zarif parmaklarını kaldırıp kardeşlerine geldiğimizi işaret etmeden önce gülümsedi. "Dünyayı karıştıran biri daha var Draza. Ve diğerleriyle ilgilendikten sonra sıra ona gelecek. İşler o raddeye vardığında yanında bir ejderha durmasını istersin, güven bana."

Köprüye doğru yürürken can sıkıntım en az benim kadar gerçek bir bedene bürünmüştü. "O kim peki?" diye sordum. Aslında tüm bunlardan sonra bilmek istediğimden bile emin değildim ama kader, tüm zamanların içinde tam da şu an kırmızı saçlı yabancı bir adamdan bu kelimeyi duymamı istiyor gibiydi. Sanki evren bir sarmaldı ve ben kopan ucunu çektikçe dönüyor, dönüyor ve nihai sona, en tepedeki uca ulaşıyordu. Ejderha konuştuğunda nihayet sarmalın sonuna ulaşmıştım ve elimde artık soluk bitik bir ip kalmıştı.

"Keranu," dedi ejderha gözlerime bakmadan. "Annen büyük bir problem olmaya başladı."

* * *

Defter yerde zararsız bir şekilde dururken gözlerimi siyah derinin soluk kıvrımlarından alamıyordum. Bir şey bu kadar zararsız görünüp nasıl bu denli ölümcül olabilirdi?

"Defterde şeytanların ismi yazamaz. Orada sadece insanların adı yazılabilir. Sen söylemiştin, cennet ve cehennem işleri karışmaz diye." Nate yanıt vermeyince bir papağan gibi tekrar ettim. "Sen söylemiştin." Elimle Cassie'nin elini tutup kavradım. Yanıyordu.

Nathaniel göz ucuyla yanında duran, dünyadaki en çatlak cadı olan Meredith'e baktı. Meredith olanları duymuş muydu bilmiyordum ama artık hepten kafayı yemiş gibi bakıyordu. Sağlıksız kocaman gözleri Cassie'nin üzerine sabitlenmişti. Ben ise… Ne hâlde olduğum hakkında hiçbir fikrim yoktu.

"Cassandra yeryüzünde haddinden fazla zaman geçirdi. İblis özellikleri cehennemde olduğu gibi aktif değil. Onun adı deftere bir insanmış gibi yazılabilir."

Bomboş yüzüne baktım. "Deftere yazıların ilahi bir güçle aktarıldığını söylemiştin. Biz yazamayız demiştin. Cassie'nin adını sen yazdın!" Kucağımdaki kızın elini bırakıp başının altına kolumu yerleştirdim, sonrasında ise yavaşça yere bıraktım. Doğrulduğumda Nathaniel yerdeki defteri alıp benden birkaç adım uzaklaşmıştı, *akıllı melek.*

"O deftere daha başka kimlerin adını yazdın? Sırf yazabiliyor olduğun için!"

Nate mavi gözlerinden ateş çıkarabilseydi o an çıkarırdı, bundan emindim. Melek bana öyle nefretle baktı ki bir an için konuşamayacağını düşündüm, birinin nefretini kazanmak bu kadar kolaydı işte. Tek bir kızdırıcı söz ve hoşça kal dostluk.

"Kâfirce sözler etme."

Sinirlerime hâkim olamadım. "Bunu yapmayacağım Nathaniel. O deftere o ismi sen yazdın. Söylediğin kadar iyiysen neden bunu yaptın? Hakir gördüğün bir ırk gibi davranıyorsun."

"Kes sesini!" Nate, defteri çantasına koyup onu da omzuna astı. Sinirden parmakları titriyordu. Sakin olmaya çalışırken neler yapabileceğini kestiremiyordum. O, çok güçlü bir melekti, parmağını kıpırdatmadan pek çok şey yapabilirdi. "Defterdeki isimler boşuna yazılmıyor. Cennetin yasalarına karşı gelemezsin. O kız ölmeli."

"Hayır. Benim elimden olmayacak. Bu benim kararım, beni ilgilendiriyor."

Nathaniel parlak safir gözlerini keskin bir şekilde kıstı. "Sen olmasan bile bir başkası öldürecek. Çünkü zamanı geldi, çok daha önce gelmişti. O uçurumda onun canını almalıydım." Meredith sessiz bir küfür savurdu.

"O sendin." Nate bakışlarını kaçırdı. "Anlaşmayı seninle yapmıştım. Neden daha önce söylemedin? Bu bir tesadüf olamaz, neyin peşindesin Nathaniel?" Üzerine doğru yürüyünce melek geri çekilmedi. Aksine o da bana doğru geldi. Aramızda sadece birkaç santim kalacak şekilde durup gözlerindeki küçümseyen bakışla beni süzdü. "Sen lanetlisin. Senden iyi bir şey olamaz."

"Dövüşecekseniz dövüşün ama sonra gidelim. Cassie cehenneme götürülmeli." Meredith ciyaklarken ne ben ne de Nate başımızı çevirmedik. "Neden Cassandra'yı öldürmeye bu kadar takıntılısın? Bana anlatmadığın şeyler var."

Nathaniel kollarını göğsünde kavuşturup sakinleşmek için derin bir nefes aldı. "Anlamıyorsun değil mi?" dedi sinirden gülerek. "Aşk senin lanetin. Bin kez de yeniden doğsan, yine ona âşık olacaksın. Ve her seferinde cezalandırılacaksın. Bu döngüyü şu an kırabilirsin, eğer benimle cennete gelirsen bir daha lanet için endişelenmene gerek kalmaz. Sen bir meleksin Aidan. Senin yerin benim yanım."

"Sözlerin anlamsız geliyor."

Hem de pek çok açıdan.

Öfkemin beni ele geçirmemesi için çalıştım. "Bak bunun aşk ve lanetlerle ilgisi yok. Bu onu kurtarmakla ilgili."

Meleğin mavi gözleri hüzünle gölgelenince söyleyeceğim diğer şeyleri yuttum. "Her şeyin aşk ile bir ilgisi vardır Aidan."

Sonra ikimiz de sustuk. "O," dedim yerde yatan kıza dönüp, "ölmemeli." Tekrar Nate'e döndüğümde artık bana bakmıyordu. Meredith'e bakıyordu.

"Ben elimden geleni yaptım. Bundan sonra yalnızsınız," dedi. Arkasını dönmeden hemen önce bana son bir kez baktı. "Cennetin emrini yerine getirmedin. Cehenneme gidersen geri dönemezsin. Ve unutma, sen bunu yapmasan bile bir başkası bu görevi yerine getirecek."

Ardından melek kırdığı kapıdan dışarı çıktı. Orada ayakta öylece kaldım. Tüm bu olanların ne anlama geldiğini bilmiyordum. Ve boşluktaydım. Boşluk beni yutmuştu.

Bir şey elime dokunca düşüncelerimden sıyrılıp arkamı döndüm. "Lütfen, fazla zamanı kalmadı. Bizi cehenneme götür Aidan." Meredith yerde oturuyordu, bana uzanan kolu ve darmadağın olmuş saçları ile acınası durumdaydı. Cassie'nin yüzüne baktım. Artık terlemiyordu ve teninin rengi gitgide soluklaşıyordu.

Cennetten atılmıştım. Cehenneme ayak bastığım an bir daha geri dönmem imkânsız olacaktı. Önce emirlerini yerine getirmemiş, şimdi de yasaklanmış bir şeyi yapacaktım. O benim için yapmıştı, bir zamanlar ona âşıktım. O bana âşıktı. Ve benim için her şeyi riske atmıştı, şimdi ben de onun için kendimi yakacaktım. Ve bunun kararını vermek Nathaniel'in düşündüğü gibi çok zor olmamıştı. Cassie'ye bir kez bakmam yetmişti.

Tek bir bakış tüm günahlara bedeldi.

"Pekâlâ," dedim derin bir nefes alıp. "Onu kucaklamam gerekiyor." Ardından Meredith'i kolunu tutarak ayağa kaldırdım. "Yolu sen söylersin."

Cassie'yi kucağıma alıp pencereye yürüdüm. Meredith arkamda hızla eşyalarını toplarken titreyen sesiyle küfürler ediyordu. "Diğerlerine haber vermeliyim," dedi küfürlerinin arasından. Cep telefonunu çıkarıp hızla bir numarayı tuşladı ve odanın bir köşesine gidip fısıltıyla konuşmaya başladı.

Kucağımdaki kıza baktım. Önceki gün dudaklarıma yapışan bu kıza bir zamanlar âşıktım. Azrail tüm anılarımı bana vermemişti. Bu kızla kim bilir neler yaşamıştım. Serçe parmağımla soğuk terlerin damla damla olduğu yanaklarına yapışan koyu kahve saçlarını kulağının arkasına yerleştirdim. Bu kadar güzel bir kız başına nasıl bu denli belâlar açabilmişti? Ayrıca insan ruhlarıyla ne işi vardı ki?

"Geldim. Beni nasıl taşıyacaksın?" Başımı kaldırıp saçlarını hırsla tokalayan cadıya baktım. "Sanırım belime tutunman gerekecek." Meredith'in saçını toplayan elleri havada dondu. Yüzü soluk beyazlığını kaybedip yeşile dönerken gözlerimi kıstım. "Uçmaktan korkmuyorsundur herhâlde?"

Cadı gururlu bir ifadeyle çenesini dikleştirdi. "Asla," dedi. "Sadece... Umarım beni düşürmezsin."

Bundan emin değildim ama ona söylemeyecektim, kaybedilecek bir dakikamız daha yoktu. Meredith perdeleri sökermişçesine iterek pencereyi açtı. Kucağımdaki baygın kıza son bir kez bakıp pervaza adımımı attım. Kendimi bırakmadan önce cadı sımsıkı belime tutundu.

Aşağı atladıktan hemen sonra kanatlarımı açtım. Cadı bir küfür savurup tırnaklarını belime geçirince bir saniyeliğine dengemi kaybettim. Sonrasında tekrar yükseldim.

Yarım saatlik aralıksız bir uçuştan sonra Meredith bağırmaya başladı. "Mola verebiliriz değil mi?"

Başı göğsümde serbestçe duran kıza baktım. "Mola verirsek ölür." Cadı yanıt olarak kollarını daha sıkı sarıp başını sırtımın hemen altına bastırdı. Yolculuk berbattı ama başka çaremiz yoktu. Cehenneme giden yol cadının dediği gibi gökyüzünden geçiyordu ve tek uçabilen bendim. Cassie bırakın kanatlarını çıkarmayı, gözlerini açacak durumda bile değildi.

"Onun tam olarak nesi var?"

Cadı homurdanınca kanatlarımın arasındaki mesafeyi sesini duyabileceğim şekilde hafifçe kıstım. "Seni duyamadım cadı."

Meredith bu kez küfür olduğundan emin olduğum bir sözü bilerek yüksek sesle söyledi, ardından duyabilmem için başını sırtımdan çekip bağırdı. "Yeryüzünde güçleri azalıyor ama sadece bu değil. Hissetmemesi gereken şeyler hissetti. Sanırım kalbi ve damarlarında akan iblis kanı savaş hâlinde."

Sözlerini düşünürken bulutların arasından dikey yükselişe geçtim. Cenneti bile geride bırakmıştık, neredeydi bu cehennem? Yeterince yükseldikten sonra sorularıma devam ettim. "Hissetmemesi gereken hisler derken?"

"Merhamet, sevgi, bağlılık... Ailesine duyduğu sevgi kaynaklı derin endişeler, sana duyduğu aşk... vesaire vesaire."

Cadı kullandığı aşk kelimesinin kalbime oturduğunu fark etmemişti. O aşk deyince dengemin hafifçe bozulduğunu ve karşılığında Cassie'nin dudaklarının boynuma denk geldiğini de bilmiyordu. Kızın nefesi boynuma çarpınca kanatlarımı sıktım. Aşk diyordu herkes, aşk bu kadar kötü bir şeyse neden günah işliyor gibi hissetmiyordum? Tanrım, ben ne yapıyordum? Tövbe edip bu kızları bir tepeciğe bırakarak geri mi dönmeliydim? Cassie'nin yüzüne bakınca bunu bir saniye olsa bile düşündüğüme inanamadım.

"Ayak parmak uçlarımı hissetmiyorum Aidan. Sanırım yaklaştık." Cehennemin sıcak olduğu yanılgısına nereden varmıştım bilmiyordum ama hiç de öyle değildi. Cassie'nin kaşlarının ve başının üzerinde minik buzlar oluşmuştu. Hava iyiden iyiye soğurken ben daha da yükseldim. *Soğuğun dayanılmaz olduğu yerde sıcak bir perde*, demişti cadı yolu tarif ederken.

Ve nihayet o perdeyi gördüm. "Geldik," dedim sırtımdaki cadıya doğru. Ölüp ölmediğinden emin olmak ister gibi hafifçe sağa sola büktüm kendimi. Karşılığında cadıdan homurtular yükselince hâlâ yaşadığını anladım.

Cehennem perdesi dedikleri şey gökdelenler kadar büyük, dev bir yarıktı. Ateş rengi yarığın çevreye yaydığı ışık ise güneş gibi hissettirmişti. Zihnimde sanki yaklaştıkça kanatlarımın ucu yanacak gibi bir düşünce belirmişti. Yarığa olan mesafe azaldıkça perdenin çerçevesi küçülüyor gibiydi. Biz içinden geçmeye başladığımızda perde kıvılcımlar çıkartarak üzerimize devrildi ve geçidin diğer yanına uçarken bize tutundu. Birkaç metre sonra perde bizi bırakıp tekrar eski hâline döndü.

"Gergedan sümüğüne bulanmış gibiyim," dedi cadı bir yandan alev rengi saçındaki akışkan sıvıyı çıkarırken. "Sıkı tutun."

Başımı kaldırıp göğe baktım. İkiz güneşler tıpkı Azrail'in bana verdiği anılardaki gibiydi.

"Ana Saray'a gitmek için şuradaki Mor Kuleleri geçmen lazım. Çok yakın uçma, beyaz kanatlarınla dikkat çekmeni istemeyiz." Dediğini yaptım. Ne kadar zamanımız kaldığını bilmediğimden daha hızlı uçmaya çalıştım. Cassie'nin nefes alışveriş hızı değişmemişti ama bu tuhaf diyarlarda her şey olabilirdi.

"Aidan, doğru yere geldiğimizden emin misin?"

"Ne demek istiyorsun?" Cadı bir elini belimden çekip kulelerin ötesindeki karanlık bir vadiyi işaret etti. Gözlerimi kısıp dikkatli bakınca onun bir vadi olmadığını anladım. "O karaltılar ne?" Yaklaşmasına yaklaşıyorduk ama o kadar fazlalardı ki, ne oldukları hakkında en ufak bir fikrim yoktu. "Bu anılarımda yoktu, belli ki sen de görmedin."

Meredith, sesi rüzgârda kaybolurken beni onayladı. "Onların ne olduğunu bilmiyorum ama Ana Saray'ın, yani senin sarayının üstünde duruyorlar." Cassie'yi göğsüme daha da bastırıp inişe geçtim.

Ben yaklaşıkça karaltılar hareket etmeye başladı. Kayıp giden bulutların arasından onları gördüğüm her seferde şekiller değişiyor gibiydi. "Onlar sanırım at," dedim cadıya emin olamayarak. Daha da yaklaşınca gördüğüm şeyin sadece at olmadığını anladım. Atların üzerinde kanatlı kadınlar oturuyordu. Ellerinde dev altın sarısı mızraklarıyla göğe bakıyorlardı.

Baktıkları şeyin bulanık, ilginç bir üçlü olduğunu anladığımda bunu cadıya söyledim. "Bak burada ne oluyor bilmiyorum ama Cassie'yi şifacılara götürmemiz gerek. Bu kadınlar çok öfkeli bakıyor."

"Onlar Valkür ve burada olmaları da benim kuyruk çıkarmam kadar saçma. Beni indir ve konuşalım." Valkürlerden oluşan dev ordunun üzerine pike yaparak inerken tedbiri elden bırakmamaya çalıştım. Biz onlara yaklaşınca kanatlı atlar çember hâlinde hareket ederek bize yer açtılar.

Zemine indiğim an Meredith benden uzaklaştı ve ben de Cassie'yi taşıyan ellerimin tutuşunu gevşettim.

"Kendinizi tanıtın," dedi gür sarı saçlarının iç içe geçtiği, başında ejder figürlü miğferi olan kadın. Atın üzerinden atlayıp yanımıza gelirken mızrağını zararsız bir nesneymiş gibi gelişi güzel elinde tutuyordu.

Ben bir şey diyemeden Meredith konuşmaya başladı. "Ben Meredith. O," dedi bana bakıp kaşlarını çatarken, "bize yardım eden bir arkadaş. Ve beraberinde taşıdığımız ise cehennemin kraliçesi Cassandra. Ana Saray'a gidiyoruz. Sizi Draza mı görevlendirdi?"

Valkür, cadının sözleri üzerine tüm dikkatini kucağımdaki kıza verdi. Anlaşılmaz delice bakışlarının kızı incelediği birkaç saniyenin sonunda yanıt verdi.

"Cehennemin yönetimi artık o küçük kızda değil. Krallar Ana Saray'da. Sadakatinizi sunduktan sonra onlardan kız için bir şey isteyebilirsiniz."

Meredith gözleri yuvalarında dönerken korkuyla bana baktı. Cehennemin yönetimi Cassie ve Draza'da değilse kimdeydi? Ve bu yeni krallar da kimin nesiydi?

Cennetteki geçitten geçerken son bir kez kulübeme bakmak istediğimi hatırladım. O an başıma gelecekler hakkında en ufak bir fikrim bile yoktu.

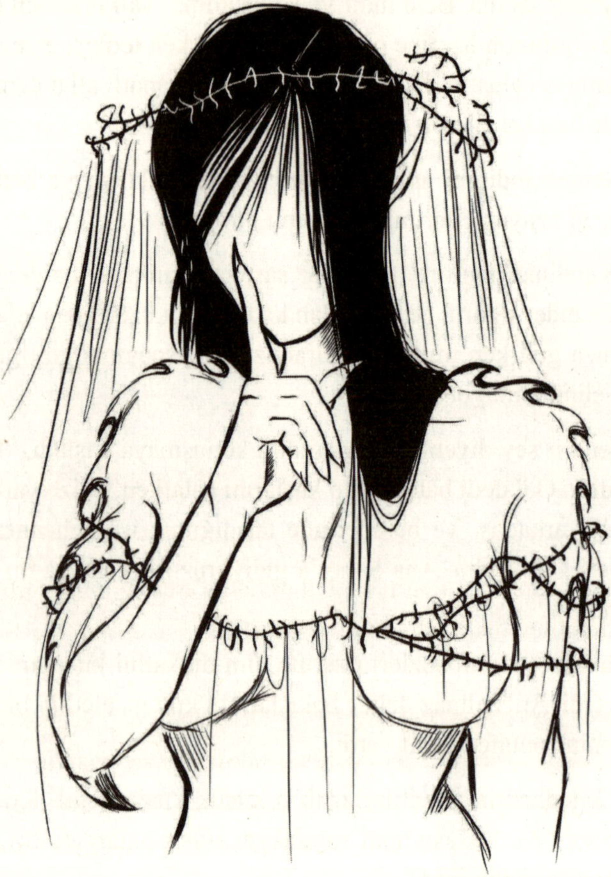

"Lider olamazsa Hilekâr
sonsuza dek kaybolacak
aşklar ve yalanlar."

BÖLÜM 12

Draza

"Pekâlâ Rohan, sanırım tekilayı fazla kaçırdım." Rohan yanı başımda durmuş, masaya yaydığı defterlerle ilgileniyordu. Savaş stratejileri hakkında yüzlerce yıllık arşivi olduğunu biliyordum. Ejderhalar yönetimi devraldığından bu yana, iblisçe yanımda olduğu seneler boyunca hiç olmadığı kadar çalışmak zorunda kalmıştı. Benim görevim ise şimdilik sadece ayak uydurmak ve sarhoş olmaktı. İlkinden her zaman emin olamasam da ikincisi konusunda beklentiyi boşa çıkarmamaya gayret ediyordum.

"Majeste sonunda kabul etti." Rohan, majeste kelimesini sessizce söylemeye gayret etmişti. Esas majesteler üç taneydiler ve tam karşımızda tüm o sinir zıplatan sükûnetleriyle oturuyorlardı. Sırıttığını görebiliyordum ama ben ciddiydim. "Yani baksana artık hayal görüyorum." Bu kez ben de sırıttım. Dudaklarımda zehirle etkileşime giren alkolün tadıyla gördüğüm hayale el sallayıp sallamamak arasında kaldım.

Rohan gözlüğünü çıkarıp altın varaklı masanın üzerine koydu. Endişeli bakışlarını bana yöneltince ona hayal görmemden bahsetmenin iyi bir fikir olmayabileceğini anladım. "Ne hayali?"

Bu kez elimdeki bardağı masaya bırakıp gözlerimi kırptım. Bana doğru hıza yaklaşan hayale baktım. "Ya hiçbir şeye değil de cehennem cadıları bile bana kafayı kırdıramazken sanırım kraliyet işlerinin onların yapamadığını yapmış olmasına gülüyorum." Elimi kaldırıp hayale el salladım. "Aidan kucağında Cassie ile bize doğru geliyor." Ardından kahkahayı bastım.

Aslında sonunda delirmem sağlıklı biri olduğumu gösterirdi değil mi?

Yani düşünsenize, ya her şey normalmiş gibi davransaydım? Bence bu kanatlı bir kara elf olmamdan daha ürkütücü olurdu.

İblisçem elleriyle koltuğun kollarından destek alıp vücudunu yan çevirerek baktığım yöne döndü. Ben ise hâlâ sırıtarak el sallıyordum. Hayalimde Aidan'ın beyaz kanatları vardı ve tıraş olmuştu. Bembeyaz bir takım elbise giyiyordu ki bu bile hayalimin saçma olduğunu gösteriyordu. Beyaz onun rengi değildi.

Ayrıca hayalimdeki Aidan cehennemin kraliçesinin bedenini tutuyordu, ki Cassie kimsenin ona dokunmasına izin vermeyen kaçık bir iblise dönüşmüştü. Ve elbette Aidan, Meredith kaltağını asla sırtında taşımazdı. Tekrar içkiye uzanıp büyük bir yudum aldım.

"Aman Tanrım!" Rohan eski alışkanlıklarını kolay kolay bırakmıyordu.

Başımı sağa sola sallayıp söylediği söze gülecekken durdum. Elimdeki bardak bağımsızlığını ilan edip avucumdan kayarken yerimde sıçradım.

"Hay anasını..." O da benimle aynı şeyi görüyordu.

Yerimden hızla kalkıp Red'in yanına gittim. "Emir yetkimi kullanabilirim değil mi?" Ejderhanın kararsız bakışları önce benim sonra kardeşlerinin üzerinde gezdi. Sonra, "Sadece sınırlı bir yetki alanın var," dedi. Bunun üzerine onu geride bırakıp kapıya koştum. "Kapıları açın! Lanet kapıları açın yoksa elinizde tuttuğunuz mızrakları kıçınıza sokarım!" Kapılar ardı ardına açılınca beni yavaşlatmaması için sırtımdaki pelerini yere bırakıp omuzlarımı oynattım. Birkaç adım sonrasında kanatlarımı açıp havalandım.

Muhafızların açtığı kapıdan çıktıktan sonra kanatlarımı iyice gerip genişleterek hızlandım. Onlara yaklaştıkça hayal gerçekliğini kazanıyordu. Tıpkı Rohan gibi "Aman Tanrım," demek üzereydim ki bu evrende başıma daha fazla şeyin gelmesine sebep olabilecek bir şeydi.

Kanatlarımı hırsla açıp nefes almadan onlara uçtum.

Aramızda sadece birkaç metre kalınca dayanamayıp bağırdım. "Aidan. Bu sensin. Ve Cassie." Meredith ben bağırınca başını Aidan'ın arkasına yaslamıştı. Kafasını kuma gömen bir deve kuşu kadar gizlenebilmişti, ahmak cadı.

Aidan şaşkın gibiydi, uçuşu yavaşlayınca ona yetişmek için hızlandım. Nihayet yanına geldiğimde aramızda sadece iki metre vardı. Ona uzandım. "Döndün." Aidan bana sarılmadı ama geri de çekilmedi. Ona hızlıca sarılıp tekrar uzaklaştım. Geri zekâlıyı bir daha asla göremeyeceğimi düşünmüştüm, buradaki asla kelimesi dört harften oluşabilir ama aslında asır olan dört harfli başka bir kelimeyi niteliyor. "Döndün ama sikik bir robot gibi dikiliyorsun."

Sonra bakışlarımı kucağındaki şeytana yönelttim. "Nesi var?" dedim Cassie'yi almak için uzandığımda.

Kardeşim geriye uçup Cassie'nin bedenini benden uzaklaştırdı. "Ben onu taşırım."

Gözlerimi devirdim. "Seni geri zekâlı, kimse seninkine döşemiyor." Bir an durdum. "Hem onun nesi var?" Meredith'i görmezden gelmek dünyada başarabildiğim en güzel işlerden biriydi, ben onu umursamadığım sürece cadının varlığı önemli değildi. Artık değildi.

Kardeşim yanıt vermeyince gözlerindeki bilinmezliği okudum. Burada bir şey fena hâlde yanlıştı. "Saraya gidelim." Aidan omzumun üzerinden geriye baktı. Sarayın yerini bilmiyor muydu yani?

"Senin neyin var? Melek olunca yaşadığın yeri mi unuttun?" Ona baktığımda kardeşim irkilmişti. Neredeyse Cassie'yi kucağından düşürecekti. "Hey hey, ağır ol! Kızı bana ver. Yorgunsun, hemen yanımda uç."

"Hayır, bende kalsın," deyince ona hırladım. "Onu bana ver Aidan." Ama Aidan dediğimi yapmadı. Yanıt olarak kanatlarını sertçe çırptı. O an onun kardeşim olmaktan ne kadar uzak olduğunun farkına vardım. Görüntü Aidan'dı fakat içi boşaltılmış bir voodoo bebeği gibiydi.

Kaşlarımı çatıp derin bir nefes aldım. Gözlerim Cassie'ye kaydı. Boku yemiş gibi duruyordu. "Onu hemen şifacıların yanına götürmezsen... Bilemiyorum, biraz tiksindirici duruyor." Aidan sözlerimin üzerine kucağında taşıdığı kızın yüzüne baktı. Orada gördüğü şey tiksindirici olmaktan çok uzaktı.

Midemi bulandırıyorlardı.

"Hadi, beni izle!" Arkamı dönüp kanatlarımın dibindeki kaslarımı oynatarak var gücümle çırptım. Rüzgâr tenime setçe vururken başımı yan çevirip kardeşime baktım. Gözlerinde o her zamanki kararlı ifadesiyle Cassie'yi sımsıkı tutmuş, yanı başımda uçuyordu. Beraber, tıpkı hayatımızın sikik bir parodi misali mahvolmasından önceki zamanlarında yaptığımız gibi sarayın görkemli bahçesindeki vahşi ağaçların tepesinden uçuyorduk.

Tabii o zamanlar şu ankiler gibi dertlerimiz yoktu. O zamanlar biz sadece çocuktuk. Şu an ise ne olduğumuz hakkında hiçbir fikrim yoktu.

Sarayın kapılarına geldiğimizde yavaşlamadım. Aidanhell de hemen yanımdan jilet gibi geçti. Nöbetçiler kapıyı kaldırırken onlara bağırıyordum. "Şifacıları çağırın. Hepsini taht odasına istiyorum." Askerler emirlerimi duyuyor ama anında hareket edemiyorlardı. Hepsi manzara karşısında donmuş gibiydi. Eh bu da artık hayal görmediğimin kesin kanıtıydı. Aidan kara askerler taht salonunun kapısını açınca kanatlarını içine çekip ayaklarının üzerinde zarifçe yere indi. Ben de kanatlarımı içime çekip iki insan boyu yükseklikten zemine indim.

Rohan, ortadaki sunağın yanında suratında dehşete kapılmış bir ifadeyle bize bakıyordu. Aidan kucağında Cassie ile hızla yürüyerek yaşlı iblisçenin yanından geçip gitti. Pekâlâ, Aidanhell'in Rohan'ı tanımaması gibi bir durum olamazdı, demek ki bu hâlâ hayal ya da büyü olabilirdi.

"Majesteleri, onlar Lucifer oğlu Aidanhell ve Lilith kızı Cassandra. Bir süredir dünyadaydılar ve açıkçası şu an neden burada olduklarını bilmiyorum, bilhassa Aidanhell'in buraya nasıl ve neden geldiğini bilmiyorum." Rohan, Red'in yanına eğilip ona hızlı bir özet geçerken Aidan bunu sorgulamadı, ejderhaları görmedi bile. Oysa ona dik dik bakan, üçü birbirinin aynı tahta kurulmuş olan Red, White ve Black'i görmemek imkânsızdı.

"Onların kim olduğunu biliyorum. Mevcut karmaşada azımsanamayacak bir payları var. Özellikle kız, kozmik dengelerin altını üstüne getirdi. Yine de şimdilik neler olacağını bekleyip görmek istiyoruz." Red önce gözlerini şüpheyle kıstı, ardından ise bana dönüp hafifçe gülümsedi.

"Biz toplantı odasına geçsek daha iyi olacak," dedim Red'e, sonra kalın kafalı kardeşime yaklaşarak Cassie'yi taşımasını söyledim. Hemen yanımda Rohan, önümüzde Cassie'nin hareketsiz bedenini taşıyan Aidan ve arkamızda yarım düzine askerle taş duvarın içinden geçip toplantı odasına girdik.

Kimse hareket etmiyordu, pek ihtiyaç olmadığını düşünecek olursak nefes alan da yoktu. Bu yüzden yapabileceğim tek şeyi yaparak şifacıların uzak koridorlarda yankılanan adımlarını dinledim. Sesler daha yakından gelmeye başlayınca kapının önünde durduğumu fark edip yana çekildim. İki yanlarında kara bölük askerlerinin eskortluk yaptığı bir düzine kadar şifacı içeri girerken, olanların bir hayalden çok daha ileri olduğunu fark ettim. Benim gördüğümü herkes görüyordu.

Şifacılardan biri gözleriyle beni arayınca boğazımı temizleyip derin bir nefes aldım. Ânı kurtarma işi her zamanki gibi bana kalmıştı. Kollarımı iki yanıma açıp yüzüme her zamanki maskeli ifademi yerleştirip gülümsedim. "Hoş geldiniz. Aklınızda sorular olduğunu biliyorum." İNANIN BANA, BENİM DE SORULARIM VAR!

"Ama," dedim iyice yanlarına yaklaştığımda, "şimdi daha önemli bir şey var. Cassandra'ya müdahale etmeniz gerekiyor." Şifacılardan en yaşlısı -ki kendisi bir peri olan Urange'ın büyükbabasıydı- öne atılıp Aidan'a yaklaştı. "Nesi var?" diye sordu yanında getirdiği sandığın kapağını kaldırırken. Aidan'ın şüphe dolu bakışları şifacı ile benim aramda gidip geldi. Adama güvenemiyormuş gibiydi.

Sağ gözüm sinirden seğirmeye başladı. Derdi neydi bunun?

"Bilmiyorum," dedi nihayet konuştuğunda. "Bir ruhu emiyordu, sonra ben ve ölüm meleği..." Aidan sözlerini tamamlayamadı. Odadaki hayret nidaları pencereleri titretir cinstendi. Birkaç kişi sessizce küfretmişti. Sanırım ben de onlardan biriydim.

Komutanlarımdan biri kapının hemen önünde silahına uzanınca aceleyle gözlerine baktım. "Sorun yok," dedim kendimden emin bir şekilde. Evet, tabii, ne sorun olacaktı ki? Öz kardeşimin Azrail ile kanka olup müstakbel eski kraliçemizi darmaduman etmesi dışında bir sorunumuz yoktu. Neyse ki şeytanlar affedicilikleri ile tanınırlardı. Kimsenin sorun etmeyeceğine emindim.

Ha ha ha!

"O bir hain." Şifacılardan biri -kısa boylu, kirli bir kadın- geriye adım atıp uğursuz suratını ekşitti. "Siz de duydunuz. Melekten söz etti." Kızgın gözlerini Aidanhell'den çekip sinirden tek bir ince çizgiye dönen dudaklarını araladı. Tam yere tükürecekken yanına uçtum. Başını iki elimin arasına alıp boynunu sertçe çevirdim. Kemiğin kırılması tok bir şekilde taht odasında yankılanınca tüm sesler kesildi. Ellerimi çekince şifacının bedeni avuçlarımın arasından kayıp kaygan zemine düştü.

Bir süre kimse konuşmadı.

Sessizliği bozan bendim. "Kullandığınız sözcüklere dikkat edeceksiniz. Aidan ve Cassie bir görevdeydiler." Kararlı görünmeye çalışmakla kabız olduğumu gizlemek arasında gidip gelen bir yüz ifadem olduğundan emindim. Neyse ki kimse içimde kopan kararsızlık fırtınalarından haberdar değildi. Birkaç kişi istemsizce kendi boğazlarını ovuyorlardı.

"Prense hain diyenin sonu böyle olur." Çenemle yerdeki cesedi işaret ettim. "Ee, sorusu olan?" Kimsenin sorusu yoktu. "O zaman şimdi Cassandra'yı alıp revire götürün. Pacos, onlara eşlik edin. Kimsenin haddi olmayan bir şekilde davranmadığından da emin olun." Muhafızım başıyla onaylayıp şifacılara kendisini takip etmeleri gerektiğini söyledi.

Anjoh yanı başımda durup yavaşça kendini Aidanhell'e takdim etti. "Efendim, Kraliçe'yi alıp revire götürmemiz gerekiyor." Kibarca iki elini kardeşime uzattı. Aidanhell ise bir saniye bunu düşündü. "Ben de geliyorum," dedi duruşunu düzeltip Cassie'yi sıkıca tutarken.

"Cık cık cık. Orada dur koca adam. Bırak kızı götürsünler. Sen burada kalıp birkaç soru yanıtlayacaksın." Kardeşim başını onaylamaz bir ifadeyle sallayınca sinirlerime daha fazla hâkim olamadım. Üstüne yürüyüp ona bağırdım. "Seni geri zekâlı! Burada duracaksın ve eğer Cassie'yi onlara vermezsen ölecek." Aidan, gözlerime meydan okurcasına baktı. "Doğruyu söylüyorum Aidan." Bunun üzerine isteksizce kızı kara iblise uzattı. Anjoh iki şekilsiz kanadını sırtında büküp selam vererek yanımızdan gidince kardeşimin koluna sertçe vurdum. "Bana her şeyi anlatacaksın."

Aidan yanıt vermek için dudaklarını açıp sonrasında bir japon balığı gibi tekrar kapattı. Yeni bir küfürle onu konuşmaya şevklendirecekken kibarca susturuldum. "Üzgünüm Draza ama

Aidan sana her şeyi anlatamaz." Kollarını sırtında birleştirmiş bir şekilde etekleri yerleri süpüren sarı beyaz cüppesiyle Rohan yanımıza geldi. Suratında o yine aslında her şeyi biliyorum ifadesi takılı kalmıştı.

Aidan ise onu tanımıyordu, hâlâ.

Gözlerimi devirdim. Başımı kolonlardan birine vurup kırmak istedim. "O nedenmiş?" dedim dişlerimin arasından. Meredith bedenini Rohan'ın arkasında gizlerken kaçamak bakışları üzerimdeydi.

"Çünkü," dedi yaşlı iblisçe şefkatli bir şekilde kolunu Aidanhell'in omzuna koyarken, "O da bilmiyor. O artık cennetin bir meleği değil."

***

Önümdeki kırmızı parlak elmalardan oluşan büyük tabağı izliyordum. İçimde her saniyeyle adını koyamadığım, katlanarak artan bir öfke vardı. Ve ben sebebini bilmiyordum.

Bildiğim şeyler de zaten sınırlıydı. Örneğin Cassie'yi alınıp götürüleli saatler olmuştu, bunu biliyordum ama Cassie'nin iyi olup olmadığını bilmiyordum. Gözlerimi kapatıp başımı beyaz masa örtüsüne yasladım. Ne yaptığım hakkında hiçbir fikrim yoktu.

"Melekler meyve yemiyor mu?" Başımı kaldırıp sesin kaynağına baktım. Tombul yanaklı bir kadın yanı başımda durmuş, ela gözleriyle beni izliyordu. Üzerinde beyaz bir önlük vardı.

"Yiyor ama iştahım yok."

Bu yanıt kadını tatmin etmedi. "Eskiden severdiniz."

Bu da başımın daha çok ağrımasına sebep oldu. İçleri boşaltılmış kabuktan ibaret bir sürü boş anı. Hatırlanmayan ve asla hatırlanamayacak olan.

"Onunla konuşma Katja, kafası çok karışık." Rohan bahçe kapısında belirince adı Katja olan kadın meyve kâsesini tombul kollarının altına sıkıştırıp gitti. O ayrılırken yaşlı adam içeri girmeden bekledi. Beni inceliyordu. Kendimi deneyde gibi hissediyordum. Bir şekilde yanlış bir diyarda oluğumu hissediyorum.

Buraya ait değildim.

Oysa çevremdeki herkes buraya aitti. O beyaz saçlı kaçık erkek kardeşim Draza, kucağımdaki kız, hatta bu tombul kadın da dâhil herkes. Bir tek ben bu büyülü diyarın içinde aidiyet duygusunu yitirmiş, acınası bir ruhtum.

Güçlüydüm ama fiziksel olarak güç hiçbir anlam ifade etmiyordu. Aksine kollarım ve bacaklarım, hatta kanatlarımın köklerini tutan kaslarım ne kadar gelişmiş ve sağlam ise aklım o kadar boştu, ruhum bomboştu.

Ne yapacağımı bilmiyordum.

Yerimden kalktım. Bir şeyler yapmaya karar falan vermemiştim, sadece artık daha fazla oturmak istemiyordum. Doğrulduğumda gözlerimi kapayıp yüzüme çarpan cehennemin nemli, rutubetli havasından derin bir nefes aldım.

Arkamı dönüp öğlen güneşlerinin yansıdığı beyaz merdivenleri tırmandım. Sarayın bahçeye açılan kapısından geçtim. Birkaç kara iblis beni görünce başlarını öne eğip selam vermişlerdi. Karanlık gözlerinden ne düşündüklerini anlayamamıştım ama ben de onlara selam vermiştim. En azından burada birileri bana saygı duyuyordu. Nathaniel'e selam verseydim bana hareket çekebilirdi. Sahi ne demişti güzel melek, *bir daha buraya dönemezsin.*

Geniş koridorda yürürken havayı kokladım. Daha önce koklayarak yön bulmuş muydum bilmiyordum ama o an bu çok normal gelmişti. İçime derin bir nefes çekip cehennem sarayının koridorlarını kokladım. Bir koku hepsini bastırıp hücrelerime doluşunca birden durdum. Kızın kokusuydu bu.

Şu kız.

En yakın duvara yaslanıp kaşlarımı çattım. Şuurum neredeydi benim?

"Bir yere mi gidiyordun?" Başımı kaldırıp gelene baktım. Beyaz saçlı şeytan tam karşımda duruyordu. Üzerinde tıpkı benim giydiğim gibi beyaz takım elbise vardı. O güzeldi. Ama benim kadar değil.

Derinlerde, çok derinlerde, belki kutsal kumlarla örtülü toprağın altında bir yerde, içimdeki şey hafifçe güldü.

"Ee, nasılsın?"

"Hmm." Kızın kokusu tekrar burnuma dolunca ne diyeceğimi unuttum. Bakışlarım istemsizce yukarılara kaymıştı. Sarayın tavanı çok yükseklerdeydi ve diğer katlara erişim için merdivenler yoktu.

Ki kanatlı yaratıklar için merdivenlere ihtiyaç da yoktu.

"O, yukarıda Aidan." Tekrar beyaz saçlı iblise döndüm. "Cassie mi?" Başını evet anlamında salladı. Dudaklarımı neredeyse parçalayacak kadar ısırıyordum. Kararsızlık ve bilinmezlik beni alt etmişti. "Onun yukarıda olması beni ilgilendiriyor mu?"

Aslında bunu umursamıyor gibi söylemeye çalışmıştım ama beyaz saçlı iblis sanki ben yüzyılın en saçma şeyini söylemişim gibi çekik gözlerini kocaman açmıştı. O gülmeye başladığında bozulduğumu belli etmemeye çalıştım. Gözlerim istemeden de olsa hâlâ yukarı kayıyordu ve ben... Oraya gitmek için içimde dayanılmaz bir çekim duyuyordum.

Daha önce hiçbir şeye çekim duyduğum olmamıştı.

"Ben sanırım..." Elimle yukarıyı gösterip ardından saçımı karıştırdım. "Bilirsin." Draza ben sanki ilginç bir şeymişim gibi yan yan bana baktı. Ellerini pantolonunun ceplerine koyup öne doğru eğildi. Saçlarından birkaçı kulağının arkasından kurtulup simsiyah gözlerinin önüne düştü. "Cassandra'ya baktıktan sonra yanıma gel. Seni birkaç şifacıya göstermek istiyorum." Katran karası gözlerini gözlerimden ayırıp sırtıma dikti. "O iğrenç, beyaz kanatlarını da göstermek istiyorum, belki karartmak için seni biraz kızartırız." Ona baktım. Şaka yapmıyordu.

"Pekâlâ, ben gitsem iyi olacak." Yanından hızlı adımlarla uzaklaşıp koridorda -sanki nereye gideceğimi çok biliyormuş gibi- yürümeye devam ettim. Beyaz iblisle arama gerekli mesafeyi koyduktan sonra omzumun üzerinden yukarı baktım. Kanatlarımı açmak için kürek kemiklerimi hareket ettirdim.

Kanatlarım sivri birer ok gibi sırtımdan fırlayınca derin bir nefes aldım. Sanki onlara hem hep başından beri sahipmiş hem de ilk defa taşıyormuş gibiydim.

Kafam pek çok yönden karmakarışıktı. Ama bir şey netti. Yukarı kata yükselirken net olduğunu düşündüğüm şeyi de sorgulamaya başlamıştım. Adımlarım yeniden yere değdiğinde karşımdaki kara askerler önlerinde durdukları kapıdan ayrıldılar. Yine bana selam veriyorlardı. Bu biraz ürperticiydi çünkü daha önce burada pek çok kez bulunmuşum gibi hissettiriyordu.

Yanlarından geçip kapı koluna uzandığımda bir iblis önümde belirdi. "Efendim, özür dilerim ama kraliçe yatıyor. Onu uyandırmamalıyız. Ejderha kralların talimatı bu yönde."

Ejderha krallar mı? O da nesiydi ki? Gitgide Azrail'in bana anılarımın en gereksiz olanlarını gösterdiğine emin oluyordum.

Elimi kapı kolundan çekmedim. "Uyandırmayacağım zaten." Ardından kapıyı açıp tek adımda içeri girdim. Arkamdan tekrar kapatıp sırtımı kapıya yasladım. Tanrım... O heriflerde yolunda olmayan bir şeyler vardı.

Nihayet kapıdan uzaklaştığımda onu gördüm. Yüzyıllıkmış gibi duran dev bir yatağın üzerinde yatıyordu. Kıza yaklaşırken birilerinin onu temizlediğini ve yıkadığını fark ettim. Güzelliğini gölgeleyen kandan nihayet arınmıştı. Saçları güzelce taranmış, kar beyaz yastığa serilmişti. Bembeyaz bir gecelik giyiyordu. Görüntüsü kalbimi acıtıyordu.

Kimsin sen? Neden benim için her şeyden vazgeçtin? Ve ben neden seni görünce bir saniye bile tereddüt etmeden cenneti terk ettim?

Yatağının yanındaki komodine döndüm. Üzerinden çıkan kıyafetleri dürüp kaldırmışlardı. Bir tanesini alıp elimin içinde yuvarladım. Ondan yayılan koku muazzamdı. Dizlerimi titretiyordu. Yumru yaptığım kumaşı burnuma götürünce dudaklarımı ısırdım. Tanrım... Sarsılmıştım.

Kumaş hâlâ burnumdayken yeniden ona baktım. Ölü gibi yatıyordu. Bu düşünce beni aniden afallattı, elimdeki giysiyi yere düşürüp iki elimle yatağının başlığını tuttum. Başımı göğüs hizasına eğip yan çevirdim. Göğsü kıpırdamayınca biraz daha yukarı kaldırıp kulağımı dudaklarının hizasına çektim. Cılız, belli belirsiz ılık bir hava kulağıma çarpında rahatlayarak gözlerimi kapadım. Yaşıyordu.

Ve mükemmel kokuyordu. Ona bu kadar yakınken dokunmamak çok zordu. Biraz geri çekilip kapalı gözlerine baktım. Hiç açacakmış gibi durmuyordu. Bakışlarımı dudaklarına indirdim.

Bu çok doğru geliyordu.

Ama bir o kadar da yanlış.

Dudaklarımı ısırdım, hatta neredeyse kanattım. Hâlâ onun dudaklarına bakıyordum. Kırmızı bir elma gibiydi. En kırmızısı, en lezzetlisi ve en bana ait olan. Ve ben artık tatlarını biliyordum.

"Bana mı ait?" Kaşlarımı çatıp geri çekildim. Uyuyan kızlara sapıklık yapan, kafayı yemiş elma düşkünü bir salak mıydım ben? Ya da onları koklayan.

Ama kız güzel kokuyordu. Ve o an gerçekten tek doğru buymuş gibi geldi.

Yeniden ona yaklaştım. Elimle yanağının üzerindeki kumral saç telini çektim. Parmağıma dolanan kokusu kalbimde bir yerleri eritti. "Ah..." Ardından belki de bu kaçık hayatım için bile aşırı olan bir şey yaptım. Eğilip onu öptüm.

Ölümün birçok efsanede pek çok karşılığı vardır. Bazıları ölürken insanların affedildiğini bazıları ise cezalandırıldığını söyler. Bazıları ise o ceza ya da ödülden önce sonsuz karanlığa teslim olmadan hemen önce, nefesin bedenden ayrılırken verdiği savaşın içinde yaşadıklarını gördüğünü iddia eder. Yaşananlar bir film şeridi gibi gözlerinin önünden geçer. Sanki veda ediyormuş gibi. Ya da belki sanki... Yeniden canlanıyormuş gibi.

O an pek çok şey oldu. Bu, hayatımın geri kalanı boyunca sorumlu olacağım bir şeydi. Onu öperken tüm ebedi yaşamımın seçimini yaptığımı anlamıştım. Kader, sizi pek çok yoldan kıstırır, kendi istediği yere getirirdi. Kader bizi başka diyarlara, başka ailelere, bambaşka birer canlıya çevirmişti.

Ama ben tüm kaderlerin arasından yine ona gelmiştim.

Kader ve hayat, bana asla güzel mutlu bir gelecek vaat etmemişlerdi. Onlar bana geleceğimin yağmur bulutları arasında kararıp solduğunu, lanetlendiğini ve yıldırımlarla kül edileceğini söylemişlerdi. Ama ben gelecekten küllerin içinden doğan bir şey beklemiştim, onu.

Gözlerini yavaşça açan minik melezimi.

Belki o henüz bilmiyordu ama ben lanetli ve acınası tüm hayatım boyunca onu beklemiştim. O da beni.

Kader sizin için farklı şeyler yazıp çizebilir ama eğer beğenmiyorsanız siz de onu baştan yazın.

***

Aşk için söylenen pek çok şey ölüm için de söylenir. Örneğin sadece bir kez ölürsünüz ve bir kez âşık olursunuz. Sadece bir kez kendinizi ölüme ve aşka bırakırsınız.

Ölüm, çoğu zaman siz onu seçemeden gelir, aşk da öyle. Öyle birden başınıza konuverir. Ve asla da gitmez.

"Güzel görünüyorsun." Gözlerimi hafifçe aralarken sesi tanımaya çalışıyordum. Ilık bahar gecesi rüzgârı gibi tenimi gıdıklayan o erkeksi sesi. Görüntü, başta odama sızan ışığın altındaki buğulu silüetten ibaretti. Birkaç kez gözlerimi kırpınca karşımda daha fazla şey olduğunu anladım. İlk olarak tek bir silüet değildi. En az üç kafa vardı ve bir de parıldayan başka bir şey.

"Urange?" Parıldayan şey başını salladı. "Ah, beni hatırladı."

Az önce duyduğum bahar esintisi genizden gelen öfkeli bir ses çıkardı. "İlk olarak beni hatırlamasını beklerdim." Sesindeki kıskançlık beni neredeyse güldürecekti. Kulağıma çarpan her bir sözle kafama balyozlar iniyordu.

Beyni yerinden çekiliyormuş gibi ağrıyan bir ben miydim?

Peri'nin kaygısız sesi tekrar duyulduğunda yüzümü ekşittim. "Senin burada olmaman gerekiyor. Gidip dinlenmelisin, bok gibi görünüyorsun."

"Teşekkürler."

Beyni ağrıyan kesinlikle bendim, geri kalanlar şakalaşıp kahkaha atarken yatakta tetanos olmuş trol gibi yatıyordum ki troller tetanos olmazdı. Eh, bu bilgi de içinde bulunduğum ânı kolaylaştırmıyordu.

Gözlerimi kapatıp derin nefes almaya çalışınca kaburgalarım yerinden oynadı. "Aahh!" Gözlerim ardına kadar güneş ışığının aydınlattığı turuncu beyaz odaya açıldı. Ama yine de hiçbir şey net değildi. "Sırtım," diyebildim sadece.

"Hey hey, ağır ol!" Nahif bir kız sesi odayı doldurunca diğerleri sustular. "Bence hepiniz çıkın," dedi kız ardından başımı kaldırıp altına bir yastık daha koydu. "Ayrıca Aidan, sen de git, gerçekten de bok gibi görünüyorsun."

Aidan…

Aidan…

"Ai…" Odada bir kıpırtı oldu. Birkaç fısıltı duyuldu ardından bahar esintisi üzerime doğru eğildi. Gözlerimi açmaya çalıştıysam da olmadı.

Yaşlı bir adam boğazını temizledi. "Biraz dinlensin. Sonuçta her gün dönüşüm geçirmiyor. Ayrıca Aidan'ı şifacılara götürün, dün her ne olduysa beyaz kanatların dibinde siyah tüyler çıkmaya başlamış. Bana öyle geliyor ki gün doğumu olmadan önce tüm eski kanadı dökülüp yerine yenisi çıkacak."

Duyduğum şeylerin saçmalığı uykuma dalmamı kolaylaştırdı.

Kanatlar, dönüşüm ya da başka bir şey dinlemek istemiyordum. Bahar esintisi kokusunu içime çekmek ve... Peynirli cips yemek istiyordum.

Ağzım sulanırken uykuya daldım.

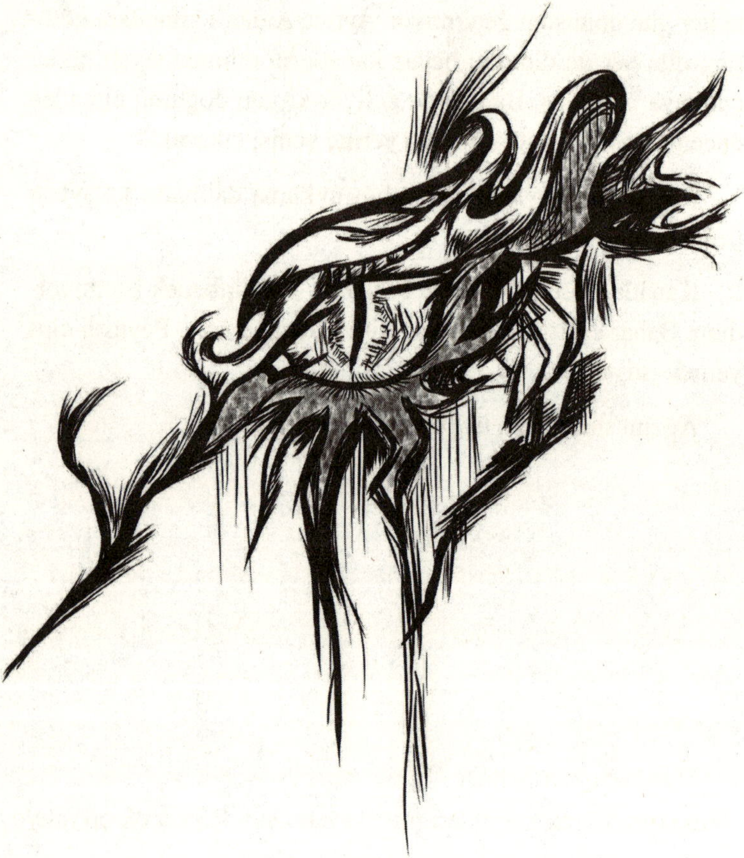

"Gerçekler dirildiğinde yalanlar,
sonsuz uykuya yatar."

BÖLÜM 13

Yemin ederim hepiniz delisiniz. Ama bu hoşuma gidiyor.

Belimin üstündeki kolun ağırlığı böğrümü deliyor gibiydi. Uyku zihnimin ücra köşelerinden bir bir çekilirken gerçeklik gelgit zamanındaki bir dalga hareketi gibi anılarımı yıkadı.

Doğdum, avcı oldum, büyüdüm, şeytan oldum, melez oldum sonra tekrar şeytan oldum ve şimdi yeniden farklı hissediyordum.

Gözlerimi açmadan boştaki elimle sırtımı yokladım. Parmaklarım kürek kemiklerimin aşağısındaki iki küçük çıkıntıya değince rahatladım. Hâlâ oradaydılar.

Bir şey daha oradaydı. Varlığını hissediyor ama gözlerimi açmaya korkuyordum. Ya gerçek değilse? Ya her şey dev bir şakaysa ve birazdan Max ve Meredith gelip bana eşek şakası yapmak için birkaç faninin ruhunu perilere sattıklarını söylerlerse? Onları öldürürdüm. Ah, evet, bunu yapardım!

"Cesur ol ve uyan." Derin bir nefesle ciğerlerimi güçlendirip gözlerimi araladım.

Kalbim tekledi.

Yerimden nasıl kalktım bilmiyorum ama birkaç saniye içinde üzerindeydim. Bacaklarımı iki yanına koyup ellerimle yüzündeki kömür karası saçları çektim. Ölü müydü? Hayır hayır, bu saçma olurdu. Yanımda neden ölü bir hâlde yatıyor olsundu ki?

Gözyaşlarım gözlerimi yakarken bağırmaya başladım. "Hayır hayır, uyan, ölmedin değil mi? Öldüysen seni öldürürüm!"

Şeytan o kadifemsi kahverengi kirpiklerini oynattı.

Ve ben neredeyse üzerinden devrilecektim. Göz kapakları yavaşça yukarı kalkarken kolumla burnumdan akan sümüklerimi sildim. Şeytan kahverengi bal gözlerini gözlerime dikince dengemi bütünüyle kaybedip üzerine kapandım. Şimdi hıçkırıyordum. "Sen gittin. Ben seni aradım ama melekler... Seni bulamadım."

"Şşş, Cass! Buradayım, sakin ol." Güçlü elini ensemde hissettim, saçlarımı okşuyor gibiydi. Beni sakinleştirmeye çalışıyordu ama ben konuşmaya devam ettim, ona her şeyi anlatmam gerekiyordu. "Ben birilerini öldürdüm ama çok öldürdüm. Ah, Aidan, ben artık ben değilim." Ve tekrar hıçkırıklara gömüldüm.

Gerçek, pek çok şekilde beynime üşüşürken güçlü kalmak imkânsızdı. Aidan gittikten sonra tamamen karanlık tarafa geçmiştim. Lilith'in kuklası olmuş, avcıları öldürmüş, bir av köpeği gibi sevdiklerimin bile peşine düşmüştüm.

Kalbimdeki tüm iyilik Aidan ile ölmüştü.

Gözyaşlarım şeytanımın güzel kokulu yanaklarını ıslatırken ağlamaya devam ettim. Sesim ağzına mendil sokulup konuşmaya çalıştırılan insanlar gibiydi. "Seni aradım. Göremeyeceğimi bilsem de aradım. Ama aşkımdan değil. Rüyalarımda kafamı karıştırıyordun, seni öldürmek için aradım."

Ondan ayrılıp vereceği tepkiyi görmek için gözlerine bakamadım. Orada öylece durmaya devam ettim. Dizlerim bükülü kalmanın verdiği etkiyle acımaya başlamış olsa da duruşumu bozmadım. Acıyı neden hissettiğimi bilmeden ağlayarak konuşmaya çalıştım. "Sonra dünyaya indim... Jo. Onu bulmam lazım."

Şeytanımla aramızda tek bir santim bile kalmadan nefeslerimiz birbirine karışırken birbirimize baktık. Şişmiş bir kurbağa gibiydim. "Her şey için özür dilerim." Aidan işaret parmağıyla dudaklarıma hafifçe dokundu.

"Seni öptüm."

Sözcüğün yarattığı sarhoş etki ile sendeledim. Ne alakaydı ki şimdi bu?

Aidan dudaklarıma bakarak konuşmaya devam etti. "Ve artık melek değilim. O yanımı tam olarak nasıl yaptığımı anlayamasam da sana geri verdim. Sen de artık eskisi gibi melezsin. Bu ağlama krizleri de devam edecek. Duyguların geri geldi Cass."

Sözlerini anlamaya çalışırken gözlerimdeki yaşlar durdu. "Beni öptüğün için mi oldu tüm bunlar?" Şeytanım, kahverengi gözleri hâlâ dudaklarımdayken başını salladı.

Ve o an ciddi anlamda çıldırdım.

Gözlerimi bürüyen anlamsız öfke ruhumu titretirken ayağa kalktım. Elime ilk gelen şeyi -başucumda duran eski bir şamdanlıktı bu- çevirip Aidan'ın kafasına attım. İblis, eşya daha havada uçarken yakaladı.

Tanıdık tiksindirici bir koku burnuma dolunca donakaldım.

Draza.

Arkamı dönüp ahmaklar sürüsünün beni izlediğini gördüm. Onlara tısladım. Öfke bedenimi kavururken hepsinden nefret ettiğimi düşündüm. Hepsi ölmeyi hak ediyordu. Onlar mide bulandırıcıydı!

"Bunun olabileceğini biliyorduk," dedi arkalarda hüzünlü, oldukça yaşlı bir ses. Draza'nın hemen arkasından kısa boylu iblisçe başını uzattı. Bir eliyle Aidan'ın omzunu tutuyordu. Aidan'ın ise başı öne düşmüştü.

"Senin de sıran gelecek ihtiyar. Hepinizi kazığa oturtacağım." Kollarım pörsümüş derili parmaklar tarafından zapt edildi. İki yanımda kara asker beni tutup götürmeye çalışıyordu. "Beni bırak! Bırakın beni!" Kanatlarımı açıp onları savuşturmaya çalıştım. Kanatlarımdan birinin kavisi kara askerin gözüne saplanınca neşeyle kahkaha attım.

"Çekilin. Uyu seni şapşal kız." Parıltılı tozlar üzerime yağarken son duyduğum şey Meredith'in bana doğru yürürken fısıldadığı sözleri oldu.

***

Cassie aşağıda bir yerde bağlı hâlde yatıyordu. Odama sızan ay ışığı tavanımı aydınlatıyor, duvarlardaki nesnelerin alışılmadık gölgeleri yatağımın üzerine vuruyordu.

Kafamı dağıtmaya çalışıyordum.

Hiçbir şey yolunda değildi. Cassie'nin kaybettiği tüm o duygular bir anda bedenine doluşmuştu ve o da dâhil hiçbirimiz bununla ne yapacağımızı bilmiyorduk. Bir an kahkahalar atarak ne kadar mutlu olduğunu anlatıyor, sonra ise deliriyordu.

Dün geceden beri iki kez kendini öldürmeye çalışmıştı. Bu yüzden artık onu bağlıyorduk. Meredith ise ejderhaları hadım ederken kullanılan eski bir yatıştırıcıyla onu uyutmuştu. Ejderhalar demişken... İşler tam da çığırından daha fazla çıkamaz derken yine kader yapacağını yapmıştı. Kendi sarayımda bir misafir gibi kalıyordum. Ejderha krallar sıçma demezlerse sıçmayacaktım, gerçi sıçmaya çok ihtiyacım olduğu da söylenemezdi ama işte. Onların komutası altındaydım ve her hareketimi izliyorlardı. Eskiden benden emir alan kara iblisler şimdi bana gardiyanlık yapıyordu.

Kolumla gözlerimi kapayıp daha net düşünebilmek için kendimi karanlığa bıraktım.

Artık bir melek değildim. Ve bu pek çok açıdan tuhaftı. Cassie için cennetten vazgeçmiştim. Tıpkı babamın Lilith için cenneti bıraktığı gibi.

"Eğer yaşasaydın benimle gurur duyardın baba."

Kapım yavaşça açılırken kolumu gözlerimin üzerinden indirdim. "Evet, sana bayılırdı. Bu dönüştüğün şeye." Draza elinde eski bir çanta ile kapımın pervazına yaslandı. Umursamaz görünmeye çalışan, doğum zamanı gelmiş kadınlar gibiydi.

Onu anlıyordum.

"Esprilerin alt katta hepimizi kazığa oturtup yakmak isteyen bir kız olduğu gerçeğini değiştirmeyecek."

Bunun üzerine kardeşim kaşlarını çattı. "Önce yakacağını söylediğini sanıyordum. Hcy hcy, şunu dinle!" Kapıyı tekmesiyle kapatıp çantayı kolunun altına sıkıştırdı. "Meredith'e göğüslerindeki silikonları yutturacağını söylemiş." Bembeyaz dişleri neredeyse tüm yüzünü kaplarken kardeşim kahkahalar atıyordu. Ben ise artık tepki veremiyordum.

Yanıma gelip yatağıma oturduğunda hafifçe geriye kaykılıp sırtımı geniş yatak başlığına yasladım. Başımı pencereye çevirdim. Gözlerim görünenin ötesinde, çok uzaklardaydı.

"Sen nasılsın?"

Berbat, bok gibi.

"Şahane."

Draza güldü. Ben de başımı ona çevirdim. Gözleri geçen bir seneye rağmen hâlâ simsiyahtı. "Başına gelenler hakkında konuşmak istersen..."

Neredeyse boğuluyordum. "Seninle mi konuşacağım?"

Draza bozulmuş gibiydi. "Hayır, seni salak. Konuşmak istersen kendine bir terapist bul diyecektim."

Suratımı ekşittim. "Evet, tabii, sağ ol."

Ama Draza gitmedi. "Baksana," dedi. Tekrar dikkatimi ona verirken kollarımı göğsümde birleştirdim. "Şu cennet. Nasıl bir yer?"

"Hmm." Merakla kara gözleri gözlerime dikmişti. Onun gibi umursamaz bir herifin cenneti neden merak ettiğini anlayamadım. "Güzeldi sanırım." Aklım karışmıştı. Parmağımın tersiyle burnumu kaşıdım. "Sanırım unutuyorum. Bir yerlere not almalıyım."

Bu ani farkındalık tuhaftı. Şimdiden bazı küçük şeyleri hatırlayamamaya başlamıştım.

Acaba onları bir daha görebilecek miydim? Azrail beni gördüğünde ne yapacaktı? Eh, bu bir sır değildi.

"Anladım," dedi Draza kucağında tuttuğu çantasını açarken. Uzun, beyaz parmaklarını içine daldırdığında camların birbirine vururken çıkardığı seslerden çıktı. "Bunları güçlenmen için getirdim." Çantadan iki büyük cam şişe çıkardı.

Kırmızı günahkâr bir sıvı camın iç yüzeyinde oynaşırken ay ışığı şişenin kapağını aydınlattı.

Kapağın üzerindeki ay taşı yanmaya başlayınca kollarımı çözdüm. "Bunlar düşündüğüm şey mi?"

"Düşündüğün şeyin ne olduğunu bilemem." Draza ile keyifli sohbetlere hoş geldiniz. Şişelerden nispeten daha süslü olanını işaret ettim. "O annemin mi?" Kardeşim diğer şişeyi göz hizama kaldırıp hafifçe salladı. "Bu da babamın."

Yutkundum. "Bunca zaman neredelerdi?" Kardeşim bir an bunu düşündü. Gözlerini kırpıp o ünlü düşünen Draza hareketlerinden birini yaptı. "Bahçedeki erik ağacının altındaydı."

"Ha?"

"Öküz gibi sesler çıkarma lütfen."

"Pardon."

Anneme ait olan şişeyi yavaşça kucağıma bıraktı. "Hiç bu kadar acil bir durum yaşanmamıştı. Ben de onları orada tuttum. Anneminkinden takviye alman lazım." Şişeye uzanıp ellerimin arasına aldım. Kan tembelce hareket ederken, "Teşekkür ederim," dedim.

Draza ayaklanırken çantayı yatağımın yanına bıraktı. "İşin bittiğinde onları çantaya koyup bana geri ver. Gömeceğim." Ardından kardeşim odadan çıktı.

Elimde annemin kanının dolu olduğu şişeyle baş başa kaldım. Ebeveynlerinizin ruhu, bedeni ve kanı sizi şekillendirirdi. Yani tüm o aslında çevresel faktörlere göre şekilleniriz saçmalığı yalandı. Üç altın parametre vardı iblislerin dünyasında. Ve şeytan aileler sadece sizi çok seviyorlarsa kanlarını saklayıp miras bırakırlardı. Her iblis, ailesinden kalan yadigâr kanı içmenin kendini yenilediğini bilirdi.

Şişenin kapağını çevirirken yaptığım seçimleri düşündüm.

Cassie'yi öperek şeytanlığa tek yönlü bilet almış olmak tam olarak suçum sayılmazdı ama annemin kanını içmek kesinlikle iblisçe bir şeydi.

Kan dudaklarımda sıcak bir his bırakırken bu kez yapmaktan kaçındığım seçimleri düşündüm. "Eh, sanırım artık geri dönülmez bir yoldayım." Ardından şişenin ağzını kapattım.

❄❄❄

Uykudan uyanmak için pek çok yol vardır ama ben, firari Aidanhell, şu an en tatlısını yaşadığıma yemin edebilirdim. Sıcak bir beden üzerimdeydi. Elimi oynatınca parmaklarım ipeksi bir şeylerin içinden geçti.

Saçlar.

Gözlerimi araladım. Görüntü başta odaya hâlâ vurmakta olan loş ay ışığından ibaretti. Daha sonra ışığın vurduğu nesnelerin gölgelerini görmeye başladım. Sonrasında parmaklarıma baktım. Koyu renkli ipeksi saçların içinden geçmişlerdi. Cassie... Neredeyse yarı çıplak bir şekilde üzerimde yatıyordu.

Bir an için kan beynimde dolanmayı bıraktı.

Kıpırdamadan, nefes dahi almadan durdum. Minik melezim her nasıl olduysa gece onu tuttukları yerden kaçıp yanıma gelmiş, yatağıma girmişti. Onu uyandırmamak için başımı hafifçe kaldırıp karşı karşıya kaldığım güzel manzaraya baktım.

Bu kadar mükemmel olması haksızlıktı. Saçları, göğsümün yarısına gelişigüzel dağılmıştı. Yüzünü göremiyordum ama ılık nefesi pazılarıma çarpıyordu. Üzerinde, gece sandalyenin üzerine attığım gömlek vardı. Üstüne benim gömleğimi giymişti ama alt tarafında ne vardı? Tanrım... Orada ciddi anlamda bir şey yok gibiydi. Kalçasının yarısı bacağımın üzerine kapanmıştı ve arası oldukça sıcaktı.

Dişlerimi sıkarak boşta kalan elimi yumruk yaptım. Bu nasıl bir sınanmaydı böyle? Cennetten gidişimin cezası fazla ironik olmamış mıydı? Ayrıca Cassie uyandığından beri bir tuhaf davranmıyor muydu? Bir yerlerimi kesmezdi, öyle değil mi?

"Mmm."

Lucifer'ın kara gözleri aşkına! Bir heykel gibi nefes almadan durmaya devam ettim. Üzerimdeki tatlı melez, kafasını tembelce sağa sola oynattı. Ardından başını hafifçe kaldırıp direkt olarak gözlerime baktı. Ergenliğe yeni girmiş bir çocuk gibi bedenimi bir titreme aldı.

Onu özlemiştim.

"Aidan, seni özledim." Cassie doğrularak karnımla bacaklarımın başladığı o yere oturdu. Ben ise dehşete kapılmış bir hâlde onu izliyordum. Ben yanıt vermeyince yaramaz melezim, "Seni ne kadar özlediğim hakkında bir fikrin yok," dedi. Uzanıp ellerimle yüzüne dokundum. Sol elimle ensesindeki kıvrılmış saçları okşarken sağ elimin başparmağı alt dudağını keşfe çıkmıştı. Yumuşacıktı. *Tıpkı son bıraktığımdaki gibi.*

Bedenimde uzun zamandır olmayan o şey canlanmaya başladı. Gözlerimi dudaklarından alıp kızıl irislere çevirdiğimde... Bana bakışı başımı döndürüyordu. "Seni istiyorum."

Daha fazla bir şey demesine gerek yoktu. İki elimle belini kavrayarak onu havaya kaldırdıktan sonra yatağa yatırıp dirseklerimden destek alarak üzerine çıktım.

Kokusu haksızlıktı. "Öyle güzel kokuyorsun ki." Burnumu boynuna sürtüp kokusunu içime çektim. Cassie iki eliyle saçlarımı karıştırıp çok ama çok derin nefesler almaya başladı. Her nefes alışında göğsü yükselip göğsüme çarpıyor, beni âdeta tahrik ediyordu.

Bana değen her yerinin yumuşak olmasına bayılıyordum.

"O karanlık zamanlarda seni bir daha göremeyeceğimi düşündüm." Dudaklarımla yanaklarını okşarken durup göz hizasına kalktım. Bakışları uzaklarda bir anıda kaybolmuş gibiydi. "Ben de." Dalgın gözleri benimkilerle buluştu. Ardından Cassie o dolgun, ufacık alt dudağını ısırdı. İstemsizce üzerine kapanıp bedenimi ileri hareket ettirdim.

Cassie gözlerini kapayıp bacaklarını aralayınca dengemi kaybedecek gibi oldum. Başımı hemen yanındaki yastığa gömdüm. "Cass, Cass, benim güzel Cassie'im. Ben iyi bir adam değilim."

Eğer iyi kalpli bir prens olsaydım, sevdiğim kızı bırakmam gerekirdi ama değildim. Hiçbir zaman iyi bir adam olma iddiası da taşımamıştım. İyi biri benimle aynı sokağa girse bir piç olarak çıkardı. İyi olmaya en çok yaklaştığım konu Cassie'ye olan aşkımdı. Geri kalan her şeyimle ben bir şeytandım.

Nefesim düzensizleşti. Bacaklarımın arasında kocaman bir gerçeklik vardı. Tüm evren şu an ikimiz arasında akışkan bir hâlde hareketlenip kaynıyordu. Onu istiyordum. Her bir hücresi için kıvranıyordum.

Yastıkları ısırmak üzereyken Cassie konuştu. "İyi biri olmanı istemiyorum." Ardından başımı kaldırıp dudaklarımı dudaklarına bastırdım. Onu öyle sert öptüm ki, saniyeler sonra bıraktığımda ufacık bir pişmanlık duydum. "Öpmeyi bırakma," dedi küçük melezim. Sonra beni sırtüstü yatırıp kucağıma çıktı. Onu öpmek için doğrulduğumda bacaklarını belime doladı.

Öpüşürken dudaklarıma bir inilti bıraktı. Aygırlaşmak ve aygırlaşmamak arasındaki o ince çizgide kendimi bulmaya çalışıyordum.

Bunun iyi olmasını sağmalıyım çünkü bu önemliydi, ah ona tapıyordum.

Ellerimle kalçalarını sıkıp kulağına fısıldadım. "Sana tapıyorum." Cassie hâlinden memnun bir inilti daha çıkarıp kalçalarını bütünüyle bana bastırdı. Sırtındaki elimle gömleğini sertçe çekip parçaladım. "Sana aidim," diye mırladı güzel melezim. Bir yandan öpüşüme karşılık verirken iki eliyle alt tarafımda kalan giysileri çıkardı.

Tamamen çıplak olduğumda ben bedenine aç bir şekilde bakamadan kucağımda yükseldi. Göz göze geldiğimizde yeniden oturmaya hazırlanıyordu. Atmayı unutan kalbim ve ben gözlerinde hapsolduk. Onun arzularının esiriydim. Ve ne olursa olsun, ne yaşanırsa yaşansın ona doyamayacaktım.

Cassie yavaşça kucağıma yerleşecekken nefesimi tuttum.

Kapı sert bir gıcırtı eşliğinde açılırken gerçekliğim binbir parçaya bölündü.

Aynı anda pek çok şey oldu. Pekâlâ, ilki biri beni dövmüş gibi hissediyordum. Bir anlığına kıpırdayamamıştım. Sonra altımdaki çarşafı Cassie'nin üzerine atıp onu yatağa itmiştim. Sonra ise pantolonumla malûm bölgeyi saklamıştım.

Ama net düşünemiyordum, bunlar otomatik ani tepkilerdi. Beynimde yeterince kan yoktu.

"Seni salak!" Bu yüzden beynim karşımda duran öfkeli cadıyı anında tanıyamadı. "Seni mal!" Öfkeli cadı, kafama çizmesini atınca beynime kan hücum etti ve kafamdaki dişliler yeniden çalışmaya başladı.

"Meredith," dedim kucağıma düşen çizmeyi tutup kaldırırken. "Neler oluyor?" Bacaklarımın arası zonkluyordu. Arkamda Cassie'nin çarşafın içinde büzüştüğünü hissedebiliyordum. Ona bakmaya cesaretim yoktu. Az önce biz tam da...

"Sana sormalı!" Ardından Meredith diğer çizmeyi de kafama geçirdi. Reflekslerimin yavaşlığını arkamda duran çıplak melezime bağlıyordum. Ah sahi, hâlâ çıplak ve sıcaktı.

"Burada biraz mahremiyete ihtiyacımız var." Ona sinirleniyordum. "Gitsene... Sonunda kafayı yedin. Git odamdan!" Onu dünyaya kadar kovalamak istiyordum, neyi mahvettiğinden haberi bile yoktu. Cadı gülümseyince suratı az öncekinden daha korkunç bir hâl aldı. Sağ gözüm öfkeden seğiriyordu.

"Cassie uyandığından beri her şeyi daha yoğun hissediyor. Üzüntüyü, öfkeyi, neşeyi, siniri ve arzuyu. Şu an tam fullenmiş şehvet makinesi gibi. Ondan faydalanıyordun seni moron!"

Kafama balyozlar art arda iniyor gibiydi. Ve bunun Meredith'in giydiği kırk numara çizmelerle ilgisi yoktu. "O kendinde değil miydi?" Şehvet, ardında devasa bir utanç duygusu bırakarak bedenimden gitmeye hazırlanıyordu.

"Ben burada yokmuşum gibi konuşmayı kesin." Bunun üzerine ikimiz de ona döndük. Saçları darmaduman olmuş, boynuna kadar çarşafı çekmiş, sinirli gözleriyle çakmak çakmak bize bakıyordu.

Onu bir kez daha istedim.

Sonra sessizce kendime sövdüm. Ondan aşırı yüklenmiş duygu durumunda faydalanamazdım. Elimi yumruk yapıp alnıma bir tane patlattım. "Meredith, Cassie'yi hemen götürür müsün? Eğer çabuk olmazsan olacakları garanti edemem." Meredith aceleyle yanımızda bitip kız kardeşini yataktan kaldırdı. Bir kolunu kolunun altına alıp kapıya doğru onu ilerletirken başımı kaldırıp Cassie'ye baktım.

Öpmekten şişirdiğim alt dudağını yuvarlatarak gördüğüm en seksi şekilde bana bir öpücük yolladı. "Yine geleceğim." Ardından diliyle alt dudağını yaladı.

Kapıyı kapattıklarında bedenim sızlıyordu. Kendimi sırtüstü yatağa bırakıp derin, acılı bir nefes aldım. "Uzun bir gece olacak."

***

Yaşadığım en uzun gece oldu. Aylar sonra rüya gördüm. Hepsi de Cassie'li, aşırı terli, fazlaca sıcak ve son derece mutlu biten rüyalardı.

Onun eksikliğini daha önce hiç bu kadar yoğun hissetmemiştim. Avuç içlerim karıncalanıyordu. İçimdeki çok vahşi bir yanım Cassie'yi ziyaret etmem gerektiğini söylüyordu. Onunla yarım kalan işimizi halledersem hayatıma kaldığım yerden devam edebilirdim.

İşin kötü yanı onunla yarım kalan işim tek seferle hallolacak bir şey değildi.

"Ooo, azgın prensimiz, günaydın." Kendi nefesim beni boğarken öksürdüm. Dalgınca gezerken mutfağa girmiştim. Ve mutfak olmaması gereken heriflerle doluydu. En başta da kardeşim. "Gidip beyaz kıçını başka bir yerde dinlendirir misin?"

Draza gerçek, tok bir kahkaha attı. "Kıçlardan bahsetmişken senin bronz kıçın hakkında birkaç ilginç şey duydum."

Gözlerimi devirdim. "Ah, kapa çeneni. Bir yerlerde işkence edeceğin birileri yok mu senin?" Lavabonun üzerindeki geniş kaselerden birine uzandım. Açlıktan ölemezdim ama o an ölüyor gibiydim. Ağzıma aynı anda üç kurabiye birden soktum.

Başımın üzerinden gelen *fiyuu* sesi ile doğruldum. Hâlâ ağzımdakileri çiğniyordum. Urange havada bağdaş kurmuş bir şekilde oturuyordu. O bayılarak giydiği eski püskü taytıyla dizlerinin üzerine yaydığı kâğıtları okuyordu. "Sohbetiniz çok eğlenceli ama bugün yapmamız gereken şeyler var. Dünyada herkes kafayı yemiş durumda. Sanırım bir görevlendirme olacak."

"Bogogohoıı gık."

İkisi de bana döndü. "Üzgünüm, çiftleşen mamut dilinden anlamıyorum," dedi uyuz kardeşim. Ağzımdakini yutup bir kez daha denedim." Dünyayı siktir edip kendi kıçımızı kurtardığımız bölüme geçebilir miyiz? Her gün bir saldırı oluyor ve koltuğun kimde olduğu belli değil."

Urange hoşnutsuzca yüzünü ekşitti. "Şeytanlığa bu kadar hızlı dönmeni beklemiyordum. Üstelik ejderhalar gitseler bile leydimiz var."

"Evet, leydin gece Aidan'ın odasında yarı çıplak bir şekilde geziniyormuş," dedi Draza dudakları keyifle kıvrılırken. İki adımda yanına varıp elimle sertçe göğsünü ittim. "Boş konuşma, kendinde değildi." Draza ellerini kaldırıp son derece masum bir şekilde gözlerini kocaman açtı. "Kötü bir şey demeyecektim ki satranç oynuyorsunuz diye duydum. Meredith için ne derler bilirsin? Çok dürüsttür."

Başımı eğip yere tükürdüm. "Bu konu açılmayacak." Sonra kardeşimin beyaz ipek göleğinin büzüştürdüğüm yakasını bıraktım. "Odama gidiyorum, Rohan'ı odama gönderin." Ardından mutfaktan çıktım.

Adımlarımı hızlandırırken başımı öne eğdim. Urange ve Draza'nın suratlarındaki aptal ifade tüm saraya bulaşmış gibiydi. Sanki şeytanlar sarayının yapacağı başka hiçbir işi kalmamış gibi.

Koridordan sola dönünce taht odasının ağır ahşap kapılarını gördüm. Rohan, babamın sarayı düzenlerken Osmanlı süsleme sanatından esinlendiğini söylemişti. Babam aslında söylenilenlerin aksine güzel şeyleri takdir ederdi. Mimariye her zaman hassas bir yapısı olmuştu.

Yine de toplantı odasında yerlerin kanla yıkanmasını hangi mimari akımdan aldığını anlamaya çalışıyordum. Kazıklı voyvoda mı?

Elimle kapıyı ittirirken derin bir nefes aldım. Giriş odanın üç bir yanından gelen büyü ile aydınlanıyordu. İçeride ilerledikçe görüşüme daha fazla şey girmeye başladı. Ben buralarda olmayalı birkaç şey değişmişti.

Taht artık tek değildi. Üç taht yan yanaydı.

Tahtların rengi de değişmişti, ki pembe kesinlikle böyle durumlar için tercih edeceğim bir şey değildi. Tahtın hemen iki yanına genişçe koltuklar yerleştirilmişti ve onlar da pembenin tonlarına degrade biçimleriyle eşik ediyorlardı.

Zemin artık kan yerine gül suyuyla yıkanıyordu, ki bu insanın içini ferahlatan bir yenilikti. Başımı çevirerek duvarları incelediğimde ise neredeyse düşüyordum. Gelmiş geçmiş en güçlü liderlerin resimleri duvarları boydan boya kaplamıştı.

"Burada biraz feminen bir hava hâkim." Bir kıkırtı duyulunca durup sesin geldiği yöne baktım. Lilith'in kızları pencerenin önünde bahçeyi izliyorlardı.

Cassie'nin üzerinde dün gece giydiğim gömlek yerine uzun, siyah bir cübbe vardı. Bu kıvrımlarını saklıyor olsa da ona daha asil bir hava katmıştı. Saçları birkaç siyah inciyle başının tepesinde toplanmış, boynuna ise parıltısı bir insanı kör edecek şekilde elmaslar yerleştirilmişti.

Dizlerimin bağının dün kopmayacaksa bile bugün kopacağından emin oldum.

Ve olabilecek en saçma şeyi söyledim. "Selam." İki kadın da bana dönünce içimden kendime sessizce küfrettim. Cassie'nin bakışları beni tepeden tırnağa sarınca vücudumda açıklayamayacağım bir kasılma oldu. Dün gece aramızda her ne alev aldıysa hâlâ oradaydı. Bunu, beni tepeden tırnağa süzen ve sonra da gözlerime kilitlenen aç bakışlarında görmüştüm. "Meredith, bize biraz izin verir misin?" Gözlerimi melezimden zor belâ alıp deliler delisi ahmak kız kardeşine çevirdim. O da bu durumdan benim kadar hoşnutsuzdu. "Kapının dışında olacağım." Söylediği şey yüzünden ondan nefret mi etsem ona gülsem mi bilemedim. Sanki Cassie yardım için çağırdığında ben ona sahip olmadan buraya yetişebilirmiş gibi.

Meredith elbisesinin etekleri yerleri süpürürken topuklarını sinirli sinirli zemine vurarak odadan çıktı. Son bir kez kapıyı gümletmekten de geri durmadı.

O odadan çıkar çıkmaz Cassie'ye koştum. İki elimle onu öyle sıkı sardım ki tüm bedenini avuçlarımda ve kol içlerimde hissedebiliyordum. Zeminden gelen kokuyu onun seçtiğini biliyordum çünkü Cassie dikenli bir gül gibiydi. Tanrım, her yerime dikeni batsa da onu istiyordum. Her zaman onu isteyecektim.

Sarılmayı bırakamadığım için dudaklarım saçlarındayken konuştum. "Dün gece için..." Cassie başını hafifçe geriye çekip ince, zarif parmaklarıyla dudağıma dokundu. "Düzeldim." İyiden iyiye uzaklaşıp iki elimle yuvarlak omuzlarını tuttum. "Nasıl?"

Melezim -BUNU GERÇEKTEN ÖZLEMİŞTİM- yanakları kızarırken bakışlarını indirdi. "Rohan ve şifacılar tüm gücümün dün gece emildiğini söyledi." Bir eliyle kendi dudaklarına dokundu. Ah, evet, dün gece o dudakları bayağı bir emmiştim.

Odaklan seni hıyar, odaklan.

Gözlerimi birkaç kez kırptım. "Yani dün gece yorulduğun için düzeldin."

Bu kez Cassie kendini ellerimle ona ördüğüm hapishaneden kurtardı. "Sonsuza dek beni kurtarmaktan hiç vazgeçmeyeceksin, şeytan." Birkaç adım ilerleyip omzunun üzerinden bana baktı. Göz bebekleri kızıllaşırken bakışlarımı onlardan alamadım. "Belki de tam kurtulamamışımdır. Yani bir denemek istersen diye diyorum." Cassie sağ elinin işaret parmağı ile boynunun hemen altındaki korsesinin iplerinden birini gevşetti.

Saniyesinde ellerine uzanıp vücudumu ona yasladım. Kalbi karnımın hemen üzerinde kalp krizi geçiren bir serçe gibi tekliyordu. "Cass, ateşle oynuyorsun." Çenesine dokunup bana bakmasını sağladım. "Bu bedenin ne kadardır sana hasret olduğunu biliyor musun?" Melezim ellerimin altında titreyince gözlerimi kızıla çevirdim. "Dün başladığımız şey..."

"Aidan, Cassie! Hemen buraya gelmeniz gerekiyor!" Bu kez kapı açılmadı. Kapının ardından Meredith avazı çıktığı kadar bize bağırıyordu. Ben onu bırakmak üzereyken Cassie parmak uçlarında kalkıp dudaklarıma bir öpücük kondurdu.

Ardından beni orada bırakıp çıkışa yöneldi. Kendime geldiğimde benden birkaç adım ilerideydi. Gerçekten kendimi tutabileceğimi ona düşündüren neydi? Onun için cenneti bırakmıştım. Ölümden dönmüştüm. Asla kendimi tutmayacaktım. Bulduğum ilk fırsatta ona sahip olacaktım.

Melezim kapıyı açınca düşüncelerim yarıda kesildi. Kapının önünde bekleyen kalabalığı gördüğümde ise tüm seks hayallerim suya düşmüştü.

İki süvari başlıklarını geriye atmış, Rohan ile koyu bir sohbete tutuşmuştu. Onları tanımıyordum ama zaten Araf Süvarileri ünlü kimseler değillerdi. Ayrıca başlıklarının gri oluşundan onların elçi olduğunu anlamıştım.

Ben yanlarına geldiğimde Rohan başıyla beni selamlayıp ikisine döndü. "Dünyadan haber var. Yardıma ihtiyaçları var." Ben bir şey diyemeden ekledi. "Sana hızlı bir özet geçeyim. Kurt adamlar vampirlerin peşinden dünyaya indiler. Eğer bir şeyler yapmazsak dünya çok yakında ya vampirlerin olacak ya da kurtların. Hangisi daha kötü bilmiyorum. Yer konusunda kendi bölgelerine nasıl düşkün olduklarını bilirsin."

Kollarımı göğsümde kavuşturup yanlarına sokuldum. Göz ucumla Cassie'nin gelen kurt adamlarla gittiğini görebiliyordum. Bu da daha da canımı sıkmıştı. Bana gerek duymuyordu, bir süredir buranın leydisi oydu.

Aklımı ondan alıp içinde bulunduğum ana verdim. "Draza nerede?" Süvarilerden biri nihayet başını kaldırıp bana baktı. Bakışlarının selam veya kibarlıkla yakından ilgisi yoktu. "Az önce gelen vampirlerle gitti." Ardından tekrar önüne döndü.

Elindeki dolma kalemle diğerinin dedikleri doğrultusunda haritada işaretleme yapıyordu. "Tüm vampirler inmedi mi?" Rohan başını sağa sola salladı. "Yönetim değişikliğinden memnun olmayanlar yeryüzüne indiler. Hırsızlar da onlarla birlikte. Gerçekten işler sarpa sarmış durumda. Fanilerin bir tuhaflık olduğunu anlaması çok uzun sürmeyecek. Dün farklı ülkelerde on üç tane ölüm oldu. Hepsi de aynı şekilde." Elindeki kâğıdı bana uzattı. Birkaç fotoğraf, on üç tane isim ve ölüm sebepleri yazıyordu.

"Eğer bu salaklar buna devam ederse hepimizi ifşa etmiş olacaklar." Kâğıdı tekrar ona verdim. "Nuh'un zamanında neler oldu biliyorsun. İnsanlar bizi bilmemeli." Ah, Nuh'un zamanı her yerde anlatılırdı. Şeytan ırkının nasıl yok olduğunu, insanların nasıl kazandığını hepimiz okumuştuk. Bu biz iblisleri yüzlerce yıl geriye götürmüştü, hâlâ daha toparlanamayan kastlar vardı.

Ejderha Krallar tebaalarıyla odaya girince bir sessizlik çöktü. Red ile tanıştırılmıştım ama diğerleriyle aramdaki tek muhabbet selamlaşmak olabilmişti. Onun dışında Draza'nın onlara Cassie durumunu anlattığından emindim. Nedense ona yanaşmamışlardı. Ondan uzak durmaya dikkat ediyor gibiydiler. Bir defasında White'ın Cassie'ye, o sanki egzotik bir böcekmiş gibi baktığını görmüştüm ama yine de ikisi henüz konuşmamışlardı.

"Toplantıya bizsiz başlamışsınız," dedi Red ortadaki tahta doğru basamakları ağır ağır çıkarken. "Eh, eski alışkanlıklar kolay kaybedilmiyor olsa gerek," dedi Rohan kibarca. Göz ucumla Cassie'ye baktım. Kurtlarla konuşmayı bırakmış ejderhalara bakıyordu. Küçük ela gözlerinde anlamadığım bir ifade vardı. Red tahtına kurulunca dikkatim tekrar renkli takım elbiseler içindeki üç ejderhaya kaydı. "Valkürler Ana Saray'da kalacak. Draza sayesinde Mor Kule zindanları için küçük çaplı bir af çıkardık. Çok yakında saray kara elfle dolacak. Yani şimdilik burası için endişelenmeye gerek yok."

Yeni bilgileri sessizce idrar ederken Black boğazını temizleyerek sessizliği bozdu. "Aidanhell gelmeden önce cenneti karıştırmış. Meleklerle aramızda hiç olmaması gereken bir anlaşmazlık çıktı. Ama bu başka bir zamanın problemi, şimdi sadece dünyadaki kaosa odaklanmalıyız. Diyarlar arası bir perde var ve o perdenin de orada olmasının iyi bir sebebi var." Durup kendisi dışındaki her şeyi hakir gören soğuk bakışlarını hepimizin üzerinde tek tek gezdirdi. "İnsanlar ve iblisler bir arada yaşayamaz. Bu iki türden birinin sonu olur."

"Tüm cehennemin kenetleneceğinden emin misin Majeste?" dedim kendimi tutamadan. "İblisler bırakın başkalarıyla beraber hareket etmeyi, kendi ırklarıyla bile birlik olamazlar. Birini kafalamamız hepsini ikna ettiğimiz anlamına gelmiyor. Kurtlar farklıdır."

Cassie soru soran gözlerle Black'e baktı. "Kurt adamlar bize yardım mı edecekler?" dedi inanamayarak. Red gülümsedi. "Birkaç atlımızı onlara ödünç verdik, şafak sökmeden dünyada olacaklar."

"Onları korunmasız göndermek aptalca değil mi? Yeni dönüşmüş vampirlerin ne kadar yıkıcı olabildiğini unuttunuz mu?" Cassie'nin bakışları bir an eski hatıralarla karardı. Aloha'yı düşündüğünü anlamıştım.

Red umursamaz bir tavırla yakasını düzeltir gibi yaptı. "Yalnız değiller ki, cehennemin leydisi onlara eşlik edecek."

BÖLÜM 14

"O bensiz bir yere gidemez." Güneşler gökyüzünde tembelce hareket etmiş, saati ittirerek öğleden sonraya getirmişlerdi. Süvariler yapılan aralıksız toplantılar sonucu gitmiş, kurt adamlar ise yarın sabah yola çıkmak üzere misafir odalarına yerleştirilmişti. Sarayın içinde tam bir koşuşturma hâkimdi. Meredith oradan oraya âdeta uçarcasına gidiyor, çalışanlara emirler yağdırıyordu. Ejderler nedense Meredith'e bayılmışlardı, utanmasalar ona da pembe görkemli bir taht ayıracaklardı. Yine de ben Ana Saray'dakilerin ona katlanamadığını biliyordum. Katja'nın bir yerlerde o salak kızdan sıkılıp bileklerini kestiğini tahmin edebiliyordum.

Rohan koltuğuna kurulmuştu. Yaşlı beyninin her şeyi bu kadar hızlı idrak edip kabullenmesi büyüleyiciydi. Ben hâlâ yeniden şeytan olmak ve üç ejderha tarafından yönetilme düşünceleriyle kafayı yememeye çalışıyordum. "Üzgünüm Aidan. Ona güveniyorlar. Cassandra hazırlanıp gidecek."

"Ben de gidiyorum o hâlde." Yerimden kalkıp oturduğum koltuğu tekmeledim. Kimse benden uslu bir çocuk olmamı beklemiyorsa ben de istediğim gibi her yeri tekmeleyebilirdim.

Kendim olmadan geçirdiğim sürelerin acısını çıkarmak istiyordum. Kaybettiğim bir senem vardı değil mi? Başımı iki elimin arasına alıp gözlerimi sımsıkı kapadım.

Bu hayata, ağabeyim Draza bir piliç için tahtı bıraktığından bu yana kral olmaya hazırlanmak için doğmuştum. Bazı sebeplerle herkes bunun için biçilmiş kaftan olduğumu düşünmüştü. Fakat kimse bunak bir kâhinin hayatımı değiştireceğini söylememişti. Her şey Cassie'nin uçurumdan aşağı itilmesiyle başlamıştı.

"Ejderhalar zeki olabilir, bilgili ve tecrübeli de olabilirler ama Valkürler dünyada ne yapacaklarını bilmiyorlar. Hele kurtlar? Rohan, kurt adamlar dünyaya inse bir arabanın altında can verirler. Dünya sen görmediğinden bu yana çok değişti. Bana güven. Tek başlarına halledemezler. Bana ihtiyaçları var." Hâlâ ellerimin arasında tuttuğum başımı kaldırdım. Rohan'ı ikna etme çabalarım bir trole bale yapmayı öğretmek kadar faydasızdı. O yeşil, kırışmış, derin gözlerinin altından bana bakıyor, zaten diyeceğim her şeyi önceden tahmin ediyordu. Onu o bulduğum savaş alanında öldürmeliydim, bir milenyum gibi hissettiren seneler önce.

Rohan, başını sağa sola salladı. Aurası, *lanet olsun, hepiniz geberin de biraz rahatlayayım,* grisine bürünmüştü. Omuzlarında taşıdığı yük görmeyeli onu biraz kamburlaştırmıştı. "Halkının sana ihtiyacı var."

Kıçımla güldüm.

Ciddi anlamda sıkı kalçalarım ve ben güldük.

"Sanki halk beni istermiş gibi. Herkes bakir bir melek olduğuma inanıyor." Sırtımdaki beyaz kanatların hafifçe ucunu çıkardım. Rohan onlara bakmadan konuşmaya devam etti. Neredeyse yekpare olacak beyaz kaşları çatıktı.

"O hâlde onları daha iyi yönet."

"İyi de nasıl? Zaten ejderhalar var. Ve dürüst olalım, gerçekten bu işi biliyorlar."

"Ejderhalar sonsuza dek cehennemde kalmayacaklar. Onlarınki gibi kadim ruhlar uzun süre aynı yerde barınamazlar. Öte yandan sen işe baban gibi kaçmamakla başlayabilirsin." Abartılı bir nefes verip kendimi koltuğa bıraktım. "Diyelim ki burada kalıyorum..." İki elimle koltuğun kenarlarını okşadım. Kadife elime yumuşacık geliyordu neredeyse cennetteki çimler gibi. *Neredeyse.* "Herkes savaş alanında birbirinin bağırsaklarını deşerken burada ne yapacağım?" Gerçek anlamda bağırsaklar deşilecek, gözler çıkartılacak ve belki de o çıkarılan gözleri birileri yiyecekti. Yeme kısmı hiçbir zaman ilgimi çekmemişti ama... Her neyse.

Rohan da karşımdaki koltuğa geçti. Bacak bacak üstüne atıp çenesindeki beyaz sakalları kaşıdı. "Herkes gitmiyor, sadece üç bölük asker gidiyor. Bahaneler üretmeyi kes. Yarın sabah Cassandra ve diğerleri gitmiş olacak. Sen de yapman gerektiği gibi zamanı geldiğinde tahtına sahip çıkacaksın."

"Tahtımı siksinler. Bir tahtım bile yok. Üç alevli kıç o tahtlarda kurulmuş oturuyor. Ben ise... Cennetten kovuldum, cehennemden azat edildim. Ait olduğum, benim diyebileceğim tek bir yer var. O da o kızın yanı." Yerimden kalkıp hızlı adımlarla odayı ilerleyip geçtim. Kapıyı ardımdan kapattığımda birkaç yüzyıldır yerlerinden kıpırdamayan menteşeler yere saçılmıştı.

Bir kez daha kaybetmeden önce melezimi görmeliydim.

***

Dizlerim titriyordu.

Ve bunun sebebi yorgunluk, uykusuzluk ya da hastalık değildi. Evet, yeniden hastalanabiliyordum. Melezliğe geri dönüş, beraberinde stabil olmayan durumları da getirmişti. Bunlar ani patlamalar, kafayı yemeler, kâbuslar, auralardaki sapmalar ve hastalık gibi şeylerdi. Kanatlarımın grileşmesi ise beni dehşete düşürüyordu. Urange köklerinden pembe ve neon mavi renkler çıkarsa Unicorn'a dönüşeceğimi söyleyip dalga geçiyordu.

Unicornları severdim. Ama onlardan biri olmak istemiyordum.

Tanrım… Hâlâ bana bakıyordu!

Şeytanım aramızdaki metrelerce mesafeden dizlerimi titretiyordu. Tüm bu çılgınlığın içinde kucağına atlayıp bu diyarlardan gitme arzum istemsizce filizleniyordu. Şu an bile o kızıl irisleri geri gelmiş, hafif çekik sürmeli gözlerinin içinde yanan birer kor gibi bana doğrultulmuştu. Ne düşündüğünü anlayabiliyordum. Dudakları hafif aralıktı ve kıpkırmızıydılar. O dudakları ısırmak istiyordum. Özellikle de Aidan'ın gülerken köşeli bir hâle gelen o dolgun alt dudağını dişlerimin arasına alıp emmek istiyordum.

"Dikkatini ver Cass. Delege Maun, eğer kuzey yolunu seçersek daha az kayıp vereceğimizi düşünüyor."

Hönk!

Aidan uzaktan hafifçe kıkırdayınca gerçekliğe döndüm. Düşüncelerimi okumuştu. *Ah Tanrım, bu yetmez! Lütfen biraz daha rezil olayım.*

"Cassie!"

Yanımdaki kardeşime döndüm. "Ne dedin?" Meredith abartılı bir tavırla gözlerini devirdi. O öyle yaptığında bir şeyleri yanlış yaptığımı biliyordum. Ama Aidan buradayken ve ben ona kavuşamazken... Her şey önemini yitirmişti.

Dikkatimi toplamak adına derin bir nefes aldım. Gözlerimi zorlukla Aidan'ın bedeninden alıp delegeye bakmaya çalıştım. Maun otuzlu yaşların başında gibi görünen iyi huylu bir hizmetkârdı. Vampirlerin onu birkaç bin senedir yanlarında tuttuklarını biliyordum. "Leydim, eğer kuzey yolunu tercih edersek orada daha az insan yaşıyor. İnsanlara görünmeden şehri gece vakti geçebiliriz. Periler bir kısmımızın uçmasını sağlar, ayrıca süvarilerin atları fanilerin dünyasında arabalara dönüşebiliyor."

"Hmm." Aslında son günlerde herkesin bir fikri vardı ve bu artık can sıkıcı olmaya başlamıştı. Bu yüzden biraz öne eğilip dirseklerimi dizime yasladım. "Gece vakti bir kişi bile bizi görse ne olur biliyor musun?" Delege gözlerime baktı. "Birine anlatmaması için onu öldürmek zorunda kalırız."

"Ya da," dedi kız kardeşim araya girerek, "ona hafıza büyüsü yaparız."

"Evet, tabii. En son yaptığında neler olduğunu saymazsak bayağı işe yarayan bir büyü." Kız kardeşimin o kalkık küçük burnundan neredeyse alevler çıktı. Bir kişiye daha hafıza büyüsü denemeyecektik. Anılarla oynamayacaktık. Birini öldürmeyecektim.

"Sabaha karşı gidelim. Kuzeyde eski bir otoyol var, orayı takip edelim. Kimse uçmasın, birilerinin görmesi riskini alamayız. Periler gelmeye çok heveslilerse arafın sınırında durup o salak cadıları diyarımızdan atabilirler." Durup bir an için Meredith'e baktım. "Üstüne alınma."

Elini önemsemediğini işaret eder gibi havada salladı. Tekrar delegeye döndüm. "Dolunay vakti geldiğinde kurtların dünyada olmasını istemiyorum. Marcus dışında hiçbir kurt gelmeyecek. Ayrıca Aloha'yı zincirleyecek bile olsanız yanımda istiyorum. Strigoi olduktan sonra tehlike alarmı gibi yanıp sönmeye başladı." Bu doğruydu. Aloha artık bizim sigortamızdı. Bir şekilde her şey olup biterken sessiz sedasız zindanında ona bir çeşit yaratık güncellemesi gelmişti. Düşman, kurnaz ve güçlüydü ama radarlı olan biz olacaktık.

"Efendim, Aloha hakkında..." Elimle onu susturdum. "Gurur duymayacağı şeyler yaptı." Gözlerinin içine bakıp anlaması için tane tane konuştum. "Hepimiz gibi. Hiçbirimiz masum değiliz."

Kalbimde hâlâ insanımsı kalan ufacık yanım, ciğerlerimi yırtıp içimden bağırıyordu. *Sen hâlâ on sekiz yaşındasın, masumsun, çok can almadın.* Ama almıştım. Kendimde olup olmaması önemli değildi. Ben de diğerleri gibiydim, özel değildim.

"Pekâlâ, notlarımı aldım. Birkaç saat sonra on askerle burada olacağım. Süvariler silahlı gelecekler. Umarım buna gerek kalmaz." Başımla onayladım. Delege ayağa kalkıp selam verdikten sonra yanımızdan uzaklaştı. Aidan odada değildi. Meredith ise dalgın bir şekilde arkasından bakıyordu.

Dirseğimle onu hafifçe dürttüm. "Aslında sen yeterince güçlü olsaydın askerlere ihtiyacımız olmazdı. Bana söylemediğin şeyler olduğunu fark etmedim mi sanıyorsun?" Kız kardeşim yanıt vermeden önce gözlerini odada gezdirdi. "Burayı kanla kazandılar, kanla kaybettiler, sen de kanla kazandın ve kaybetmek umurunda bile değil. Bu tahtı hak etmiyor olabilirsin."

Bla bla.

"Bak içini rahatlatır mı bilmiyorum ama tek derdim..." Aniden durdum. Tek derdim neydi? Kafayı yediğim o karanlık zamanda tek derdim güçtü. Ama şu an neydi? Ailemi yaşatıp güvene almak, Aidan'a sarılıp sonsuz kadar bir döngü oluşturup içinde hapsolmak istiyordum. Evet, derdim buydu. Dertlerimin arasında taht yoktu. Bu gerçek bir balyoz gibi zihnime çarpmıştı. Durgunluğum Meredith'in dikkatini çekince ifademi değiştirdim. "Aidan'ı görmem lazım." Ardından kaçarcasına uzaklaştım. Kimsenin sorularına yanıt verecek bir havada değildim.

Adımlarım beni sarayın içinde yaklaşık yarım saat süren anlamsız bir yolculuğa çıkarmıştı. Herkese Aidan'ı sormuş ama bulamamıştım. Artık ciddi anlamda canım sıkılmaya başladığında ikinci katın terasına varmıştım. Başımı duvarların arasından hafifçe uzatıp rüzgârın tenimi yalamasına izin verdim. Öğleden sonra güneşi tüm terası aydınlatıyordu. Ve Aidan orada da değildi.

Çünkü arkamdaydı.

Eliyle ağzımı kapadığı an o taze çim kokusunu hissettim. Sıcak, güçlü parmakları dudaklarımın hemen üzerinde dururken onları hafifçe okşuyordu. Diğer eli omuzlarımdan aşağı, kolumun iç yüzüne kayarken kendimi ona bırakmamak için direndim. Tüm benliğimle bedenimi ona bastırmamak için savaşıyordum.

"Ellerimin altında eriyorsun."

Ve Aidan, Aidan'dı işte. Elini tutup dudaklarımdan çekerek karşısına geçtim. "Hava çok sıcak, biliyorsun." Oysa hava sıcak falan değildi. Bedenimdeki, bacaklarımın arasındaki o ateşin sebebi hava değildi. Ve Aidan bunu biliyordu.

Aptal lanet bariyerler! Hemen zihnime onları ördüm.

Şeytanım bana laf sokup aşağılamadı, bir adımda yanıma gelerek bana sarıldı. Boynuma etli sıcak dudaklarını dokundurdu. "Seninle çok işim olacak Cassandra. Ama şu an sadece sana kavuşmanın mutluluğunu yaşıyorum." Az önce erimediyse bile şimdi kalbim eriyordu işte. Gözlerim dolmasın diye onları kocaman açtım. *Ne olur ağlamayayım!*

Aidan eliyle saçlarımı okşarken içim titriyordu. Onunla dünyada geçirdiğim zamanı düşünüyordum. Onunla dans etmeyi özlemiştim. Sonra anılar değişiyordu ve yerini onun ölürkenki hâli alıyordu.

Korkudan dilim tutulur gibi oldu. Şu an kollarımdaydı, o yüzden hâlâ yapabiliyorken ben de ona sıkıca sarıldım. Ellerimle sırtını yokladıktan sonra dalgalı siyah saçlarına dokundum. O artık benimleydi, ölmemişti, gelmişti. Ellerimin arasından kayıp giderken onu kaybetmemiştim.

Onu asla bırakmayacaktım. Birazcık geri çekilip aniden dudaklarına yapıştım. Aidan, bir an için şaşırmış olsa da ardından öpüşüme daha şiddetli bir şekilde yanıt verdi. Sıcak dili dilime değince içimde bir şeyler kopar gibi oldu. Dudakları alev alevdi ve tek sıcak yer orası da değildi. Aidan iki elini sırtıma kaydırıp belimi kavrayınca ona daha sıkı tutundum. Bir an için dudaklarımı bırakıp burnunu boynuma sürttü. Nefesi boynumun altına vururken bacaklarımın arası zonklamaya başladı.

Bana neler oluyordu böyle?

"Ah Cassie." Aidan'ın dudaklarından adımı duymak paha biçilemezdi. Elimle başını tutup yeniden öptüm. Bu dünyanın en güzel şeyini yalamak gibiydi. Onları sonsuza dek yalayabilirdim. Ve öyle yaptım. Bu da Aidan'ı daha çok çıldırttı. Göğsünden gelen erkeksi bir gürlemeyle şaşkınlık içinde dudaklarını bıraktım.

Gözleri kırmızıydı. Ve bu sadece daha fazla ısınmama sebep oldu.

"Dudaklarını ısırıp bana bakıyorsun."

Ah, evet! Bunu daha önce de demişti. "Kasten yapmıyorum." Şeytanımın gözleri büyülenmiş gibi dudaklarıma kayarken bu kez kasti olarak onları ısırdım.

Bakışları gözlerime sabitlendi. Artık kasten onu baştan çıkarıyordum ve DÜNYANIN CANI CEHENNEME!

Öyle sık nefesler alıyordum ki göğsüm Aidan'ın göğsüyle birleşmiş gibiydi. Her nefes verişimde tişörtüm gömleğine sürtünüyordu. Bu yüzden Aidan gömleğini tek koluyla yırtarak çekip çıkarttığında şaşırmadım, şikâyet etmedim, sadece ona daha fazla sokuldum. Parmaklarımı boynundan köprücük kemiklerine, oradan da geniş göğsüne indirdim. Büyülenmiştim. Her yerine dokunmak istiyordum. Bu sanki sonunda hak ettiğim bir ödül gibiydi. O benimdi.

Ellerim hâlâ üzerindeyken bakışlarımı kaslarından kaldırıp gözlerine kaydırdım. Nutkum tutulmuştu. Bana beni yiyecek gibi bakıyordu. O güzel ağzıyla beni çiğneyip yutacak gibiydi. Tanrım... Kavruluyordum! "Kucağıma yerleş Cassie." Ağzımın içi kupkuru oldu.

Dediğini yapmak için hafifçe yukarı çıkınca Aidan erkeksi bir şekilde inledi. Bacaklarımı beline sımsıkı sarıp kendimi yeniden onun kucağına bıraktım. Bu kez inleme sırası bendeydi. Altımdaki o baskıya dayanamıyordum. Bu çok hoştu, karşı konulmazdı.

"Cassie," dedi Aidan nefesini saçlarıma üflerken. "Kendini bana bastır." Bunu yaptım. Aidan iki eliyle kalçalarımı tutup bedenimi kendi bedenine bastırdı ve bu sesli bir şekilde inlememe sebep oldu. “Ahh,” dedim. Dağılıyordum, binbir parçaya ayrılıyordum. Sanki hayatımdaki en doğal şeyi yapıyordum.

“Iyy, bu iğrenç!”

Aidan’ın bacaklarımın arasındaki sert gerçekliği aniden dondu. Ben de dondum. Sırtımdaki soğuk terler bile dondu. Ürperti, omurgam boyunca gezinirken gözlerim kocaman açılmıştı. “Odanız yok mu be?”

Saniyeler içinde Aidan beni kucağından indirip terasın tek kapısından çıkarak gözden kayboldu. Bunu o klasik doğaüstü hızıyla yapmıştı. Tişörtümü aşağı indirip kâküllerimi yüzümden çekerken arkamı döndüm.

Bu sesi tanıyordum. Ama emin olmalıydım.

Ve kız gülümsedi.

Kendimi yabancının kollarına atıp kahkahalarla gülmeye başladım. “Seni pembe saçlı sürtük. Zaten senden başkası olamazdı. Her ânı berbat ediyorsun değil mi?” Katze iki eliyle beni sımsıkı sardı. En iyi arkadaş gibi kokuyordu ve ben onu çok özlemiştim. “Az önce bekâretini kurtardığım için bana teşekkür ediyorsun herhâlde.”

Ya, ne demezsin. Ona daha sıkı sarıldım. Ardından biraz uzaklaşırken hâlâ iki elimle ellerini tutuyordum. “Son bir sene hakkında söylemek istediğim şeyler var.”

“Şşş, şimdi bunu konuşmaya gerek yok,” dedi vampir.

Başımı net bir şekilde sağa sola salladım. “Hayır, var.” Suçluluk duygusu beni alaşağı etmeden önce birilerinden özür dilemeliydim, yaptıklarım ve yapmadıklarım için. “Üzgünüm, ben kendimde değildim. Sanki kontrolü deli bir sürtük almıştı ve ben bilmiyorum, her şey çok hızlı gelişti." Arkadaşım tekrar bana sarıldı.

O, en zor anlarımın destekçisi olmuştu. Beni ilk gördüğünde öldürmemişti, ki bunu yapabilirdi. Öte yandan dünyada onunla yaşamış, omuz omuza savaşmıştım. Ona kendi kanımı vermiştim ve bu diğer pek çok şeyden daha mahrem bir şeydi.

Elimle kısacık dalgalı saçlarını dağıttım. Hâlâ bana sarılı hâldeyken kahkaha atıyordu. "Aidan'la o hâliniz neydi öyle? Tavşanlar gibiydiniz." Biraz uzaklaşıp yüzüme baktı. "Hâlâ kızarıyorsun." Bu kez somurttum.

"Hepimiz senin gibi değiliz Katze. Bazılarımız hâlâ bakire." Bu kez arkadaşımın gülüşü tüm yüzüne yayılırken kolumu çimdikledi. "Seni kötü, çok kötü kraliçe."

"Kötü kısmına katılıyorum ama kraliçe kısmına... Eh, artık değil." Vampir anlamayan gözlerini gözlerime dikti. "Gel, sana göstermem gerekenler var." Elini tutup onu terastan çıkardım. Evi ilk kez görmeye gelen misafir çocuğunu gezdirir gibiydim. Beraber mermer basamaklardan atlayıp taht odasına yöneldik. Zaman kaybetmemek için ona anlatmaya çoktan başladım. "Aloha iyi."

Daha fazlasını söylemek istemiştim ama olmadı.

"Önce onu görebilir miyim?" Yavaşlayıp onu diğer koridora yönlendirdim. "Tabii ki. Eşlik etmemi ister misin?"

"Hayır, kendim yapsam daha rahat olurum."

"Pekâlâ. Koridorun sonundaki oda. Kapıda iki kara asker var, aldırış etme, sana karışmazlar." Vampir dostum başıyla onaylayıp dediğim istikamete gitmeden önce derin bir nefes aldı.

Hepimizin şeytanları vardı. Ben benimkileri öldürüp yerlerine geçmiştim. Katze ise kendi şeytanını yaratmıştı.

Kimse bir vampirin bir iblisçeyi strigoiye dönüştürebileceğini düşünemezdi. Öte yandan kimse bir melezin şeytana dönüşüp bir başka şeytanın affedileceğini de bilemezdi. O affedilmişti. Benim durumum ise belirsizliğini koruyordu.

"Birinin yanıtlaması gereken sorular var." Nereye gideceğimi biliyordum.

***

Lilith ile son iletişimim avcılardan en azılı olanını öldürmemle sonlanmıştı. Karanlık zamanlarımda elimde bir liste vardı. Lilith ve ben o listeyi hazırlamak için neredeyse bir ay döngüsünün tüm günlerinde çalışmıştık. O zamanlar bu kulağa komik geliyordu ama şimdi sadece tiksindiriciydi. Listenin adı ölüler listesiydi. O listede olması gereken neredeyse herkes ölmüştü... *Neredeyse.*

Bir kraliçe olup halkımı yönetmem gerekiyordu ve zarar veremediğim tek kişi, aynı zamanda bana her şeyi öğretebilecek tek kişiydi. En iyi zamanınızda bile Lilith'i dinlemek istemezdiniz. Oysa ben elimde yakıcı bir cehennem gücü olduğunda Lilith'in öğretilerini dinlemiştim.

Beni anlamıştı. İhtiyaçlarımı biliyordu. Tanıdığım herkesten daha fazla biliyordu kâinatı, kuralları ve acımasızlığı. Bana bir liderin acımasız olması gerektiğini söylemişti, acımasız olursanız insanlar sizi dinlerdi. Sizi sevmelerine gerek yoktu. Sevgi zayıflıktı ve şeytanların kalbinde sevgi olmazdı. Sadece korku barınabilirdi bu parçalanmış ruhlarda. Sadece korku var olabiliyordu kalp diyebildikleri o çürümüş yerlerinde. Ve ben de en iyi hocadan öğrenmiştim korkuyu kullanmayı.

Ağlayan tepelere öğleden sonra güneşleri hâlâ tepedeyken uçtum. Bir cadı değildim, büyü yapamıyordum, aslında Aidan gibi ufak tefek şeyler yapabiliyordum ama hiçbiri büyü değildi. Melez de olsam bu konuda eğitilmemiştim. Hem ışınlanmayı yapabilen varsa bile kendini henüz açık etmemişti zaten. Akıllıca bir seçim.

Rüzgâr burun deliklerimi gıdıklarken içimde bir şeyler oynamaya devam ediyordu. Bir gün önce bokun tekiydim. Kimsesiz, sevgisiz, karanlık bir çamurun içindeydim. Ve kurtulmaya çalıştıkça çamur beni daha da içeri çekiyordu. Bir zaman sonra sadece çamurlaşmıştım.

Ta ki o gelene kadar.

Ne gelmişti ama... Onsuz nasıl nefes alabildiğimi hatırlamıyordum bile. Aidan, yaşamımdaki tüm önce ve sonraların sınır çizgisiydi.

Tepeler menzilime girince kanatlarımı bükerek hafifçe alçaldım, aklımda hâlâ Aidan vardı. Yeniden sahip olduğum bu mükemmel şeyle ne yapacaktım? Bu acınası çer çöp döngümde sahip olduğum en iyi iki şeyden biri Aidan'dı, diğeri ise kardeşim.

Jo, iyiydi. Şimdilik. Öte yandan Aidan iyi olmaktan çok uzaktı. Her şey yolundaymış gibi davranmasına rağmen kafasının karışık olduğunu bir aptal bile anlayabilirdi. Ne yaptığını bilmiyor gibiydi ve bu anlaşılabilirdi. Zaten kan banyosundan henüz çıkmış biri olarak onu yargılayamazdım.

Zagros Dağı'nı görünce kanatlarımı iyiden iyiye büzüp bedenimi yan çevirdim. Sivri uçlu tepelerden herhangi birinin bedenimde şenlenmesini istemiyorsam dikkatli uçmalıydım. Bu yüzden kendi akımımı üretmek yerine rüzgâra sırtımı vererek daireler çizdim. Dairelerimin yörüngesi artıp hızım yavaşlarken tepenin altındaki ahşap evi görebilmiştim.

Adımlarım toprağa değer değmez kanatlarımı silkeleyip bedenime çektim. Lilith yılın annesi ödülünü alacak tiplerden değildi. O yılın en kötü annesi ya da katil anne gibi ödülleri alabilecek biriydi. Öte yandan bilinmeze karşı olan o tuhaf merakı bazı durumlarda işime yarıyordu.

Rüzgârdan arkası katlanan tişörtümü indirip saçlarımı düzelttim. Dağ, arkasındaki tüm pisliği gizler gibi enine doğru yayılmıştı. Belki de tarihin en eski tepelerinden biriydi. Ama Zagros bile Lilith'in inini gözlerden uzun süre saklayamazdı. Lilith, geçtiği her yerdeki canlıları etkilerdi. Bitkileri çürütür, hayvanları zehirlerdi. İşin kötü yanı bunu yaptığından bile haberi olmayışıydı. O zararsız bir şekilde kâinatta var olabildiğini sanıyordu.

Derin bir nefes alıp son bir kez karşımdaki manzaraya baktım. Burada kendi küçük, sapkın sarayını ahşaptan inşa etmişti. Kara sarayın tıpatıp aynı olmasının kurt kocasına bir atıf olabileceğinden şüpheleniyordum.

Her neyse.

Adımlarımı olabildiğince sıklaştırarak annemin sarayına doğru yol aldım. Toprak zemin kendini taş kaldırımlarına bırakınca gözlerimle stratejik bölgelere baktım. Hiçbir nöbetçi yoktu. Lilith'in nöbetçiye ihtiyacı da yoktu. Kim Lilith'i ziyaret edecek kadar geri zekâlı olabilirdi ki?

Benim dışımda tabi ki.

Kapıya ulaşınca ağır sürgüyü ellerimle ittirdim. "Eğer yakınlardaysan lütfen daha fazla yaklaşma." Gözlerimi sımsıkı kapayıp beni vuracak olan acıya hazırlandım. Ama öyle bir şey olmadı. Temkinli bir şekilde gözlerimi açıp kapıyı arkamdan kapadım. Lilith ile aynı odada bulunmak nükleer enerji lolipopunu yalamak gibiydi. Bu kadar güç barındırmama rağmen asla onun kadar olamıyordum.

"Hoş geldin."

Benden uzaktaydı. Sesi fısıltı gibi geliyordu ama bu yine de bu gözlerimi acıyla sımsıkı kapamama sebep olmuştu. "Sana sormam gerekenler var." Bunun üzerine Lilith ilerideki geniş koridorun ucunda göründü. Göz alıcı kızıl saçları her zamanki gibi görkemliydi. O güzel başının çevresini canlı parlak yılanlar gibi süslemişti. Kan rengi gözleri ise Tanrı'nın bahşettiği en güzel mücevher olabilirdi. Bazen onu kıskanıyordum. Ben asla onun kadar güzel değildim. Aslında Lilith'in yanında biraz çapulcuydum.

Ardından öldürücü güzellikteki kadın kahkaha attı. Şimdi görüş açıma daha fazlası giriyordu. O yaklaşmaya başlayınca eklem yerlerimin kaşındığını hissedebiliyordum. Bedenimdeki tüm kemikler kırılmadan biyolojik annemle sohbet edememek üzücüydü.

"Beni güzel bulmana sevindim. Aslında çocuklarım arasında bana en çok benzeyen sensin. Tabii bu seni rahatlatacaksa." Başıma saplanan ağrıdan sözlerini zar zor duyabiliyordum.

"Evet, bayağı rahatlatıcı. Teşekkürler."

Lilith geniş salona girince baş ağrısı yavaşça boynuma yayıldı. Bu bedenime en fazla birkaç dakika daha dayanabileceğini gösteren alarmın ta kendisiydi. "Gelişmiş iblis radarın sayesinde olanları biliyorsundur." Lilith aramıza bana zarar vermeyecek şekilde emniyetli bir mesafe yerleştirip sırtını tam karşımdaki taş duvara yasladı. Top modelleri andıran muhteşem fiziği ve podyumda dikiliyormuş edasıyla Lilith, yaşayan herkese üstten bakardı. Günahların en saklısı kibirle örülüydü içi boşaltmış ruhsuz güzel kabuğu.

"Biliyorum. Yeniden melez olmuşsun. Bunun olacağını tahmin etmezdim."

Ondan daha da uzaklaşmak adına geri adım attım ve sırtıma değen soğuk duvarla karşılaştım. "Bir şeyleri hâlâ tahmin edemiyor olman hakkında ne düşünmeliyim?"

Lilith mükemmel beyazlıktaki göz alıcı dişlerini gösterecek şekilde güldü. "İnsan olduğumu." İşte buna gülerdim. Annem pek çok şey olabilirdi ama insan sıfatı bunlardan biri değildi. Bir zamanlar insan olması hâlâ fazlasıyla kafa karıştırıcıydı. "Ejderhaların var olduğunu bilmiyordum."

"Sen kızım, pek çok şeyi zaten bilmiyorsun." Kızım dediğindeki ses tonu kollarımdaki tüyleri diken diken etti. Lilith bu kelimeyi öyle sıradan söylüyordu ki, onunla ölüler listesi hazırlamamış olsam sıradan bir anne kız muhabbetimiz olduğunu düşünürdüm. Hey anne, az kalsın yok oluyordum ama sevmediğin erkek arkadaşım beni kurtardı. Görüşmeyeli ölümlülerin ruhlarını toplamayı öğrendim ve cehennemi de artık üç yakışıklı ejderha yönetiyor. Ve tüm bunlar olurken kardeşlerim de bana destek oluyor.

"Ejderhalar yönetimi ele geçirdi," dedim sıkıntıyla.

"Şeytanların kanları yeniden alev aldı." Cümlenin tanıdıklığı bir an duraksamama sebep oldu. "Hatırlıyorum bu cümleyi," dedim mırıldanarak. Ardından gözlerine baktım. İki kızıl iris benimkilere çarpınca yutkundum. Kehanetteki cümleydi bu. Hiçbir şey yaşanmamışken, dünyam raydan çıkan çılgın bir tren değilken yazılmış kehanetteki anlayamadığım cümleydi. Ejderhaların geleceğinin habercisiydi, sadece biz anlamamıştık.

Ben konuşmayınca annem zarif elini kaldırıp ince, uzun, kibar parmaklarını oynattı. Konuşmaya başladığında parmak uçlarından minik yeşil kıvılcımlar çıkıyordu. "Ejderhalar ve Valkürler eski tanrıların zamanından kalma kadim yaratıklar. Cehennem diyarına indilerse sorun bizlerin gördüğünden daha büyük olmalı. Öte yandan bunun hiçbir önemi yok, çok yakında her şey değişecek zaten." Kıvılcımlar renklerini solgun turunculara bırakırken annem havadan sudan konuşur gibi konuşmasını devam ettirdi. "Neden geldin?"

İçimi kaplayan huzursuzluk duygusunu yutup belli etmemeye çalıştım. "Aidan artık melek değil."

Lilith'in havadaki eli durdu. Gözleri yavaşça kıvılcımlardan bana kaydı. "Zamanla kanatları da kararacak. Lucifer'ın oğlu eskiden nasıl ise öyle olacak."

İçim içimi kemiriyordu. "Ben ne olacağım peki? Güçlerim ne olacak?" Sırtımdan destek alarak duvardan uzaklaştım. "Değişime ayak uydurmaya çalışırken aklımı kaçırmaktan korkuyorum. Eğer bir aklım varsa tabii. Üstelik ben bir şeyler hissediyorum ve sen hissedemeyeceğimi söylemiştin."

"Neden aşkının sınandığı ve sonucunda başardığını kabul edip hayatına devam etmiyorsun? Her şeyi irdelemen faydasız. Gerçi bu özelliğini benden almışsın." Kıvılcımlar sönüp tırnaklarının içinden cılız dumanlar yükselirken Lilith gülümsedi. "Ben de her şeyi zor yoldan öğrendim." Lilith bana gerekli yanıtları vermemek için her zaman bu üstü kapalı bilmecevari sözlerine gömülürdü.

"Pekâlâ, sorularım bitmedi. Bir savaş var ve sonucunda ne olacağını bilmek istiyorum." Fark etmeden acıdan iki büklüm olmuştum, bu yüzden tekrar doğruldum. Annemin kızıl, çekik gözlerinde saf bir kötülük vardı. Korkutucuydu, benim için bile. "Çocuklarının başına ne geleceği umurunda değil, değil mi?" Lilith bir şey demedi. Bunun yerine bana bakmayı sürdürdü.

Dişi şeytan ürkütücü gözlerini kırpmadığı için bu bakışma korkutucu bir hâle gelmeye başlamıştı. Bir an sonra gözlerini kıstı. "Bu çok ilginç. Yeni bir kehanet geliyor." Bakışları gözlerimden karnıma kadar indi. Baktığı her yerde bedenime saplanan sancıları görmezden gelmeye çalıştım. Yanağımın içini öyle sert ısırıyordum ki ağzıma kan tadı gelmeye başladı.

"Bu yeni kehanet sevdiklerimi nasıl hayatta tutacağımla ilgili mucizevi bilgiler içeriyor mu?" Annem gülümsedi ve bu karnımda acıdan daha farklı bir duygunun oynaşmasına sebep oldu. Tabii bu sadece birkaç salise sürmüştü. O Lilith'di, başka bir şey olamayacak kadar şeytandı.

Aidan gibi.

"Kendine güven Cassandra. Sevdiklerini korumak için bilmen gereken yeni hiçbir şey yok. Sen her duruma uygun yaratıldın."

Bir dejavu hissi zihnimde oynaşırken ona bakmaya devam ettim. "Kardeşim peki? O da dayanıklı mı?" Lilith o zarif başını yavaşça salladı. Daha iyi hissetmiştim, içimdeki çarpık bir nokta ona bir sebepten ötürü güveniyordu.

O çarpık noktam başıma hep belâ oluyordu.

Burnumdan ılık bir damla süzülünce parmaklarımla dudağımın üzerine dokundum. Pekâlâ, kanıyordum. Yani gitme vaktim gelmişti. "Gitmem gerekiyor."

"Burada kalabilmek için tek yapman gereken..."

Elimi kaldırıp onu susturmaya çalıştım. "Daha fazla kara büyüyle ilgilenmiyorum. Ömrümün sonuna kadar yetecek şekilde aldım zaten." Gitmek üzere arkamı döndüm ama aniden durdum. Omzumun üzerinden oradaki tüm mükemmelliğiyle göz dolduran mistik kadına baktım. "Kehanet ne ile ilgili? Sonunda birileri ölüyor mu?"

Bunun yanıtını duymak istediğimden emin değildim. Lilith de zaten bana yanıtı verecek gibi değildi. Tek bir zarif kaşı yavaşça yukarı kalktı. Gülümsüyor gibiydi. "Ölümler hep olur. Bu doğmak kadar doğaldır. Hayatın malzemesi budur, buna alış kızım." Tamamdır, buradaki işim resmi olarak bitmişti.

"Teşekkürler." Gitmeden önce dönüp bir kez daha ona baktım. Hâlâ parlıyordu, hâlâ taze bir gül gibiydi ama kanıyordu. Şeytan böyleydi, sizi güzel kokularla bezeyerek ta içinize işler, sizi kanatırdı.

Arkamı dönüp kapıya yöneldim. Avuçlarımda bilinmezlik, sırtımda taşıyamayacağım bir yük ve yaralı ruhumla evimize dönüyorduk.

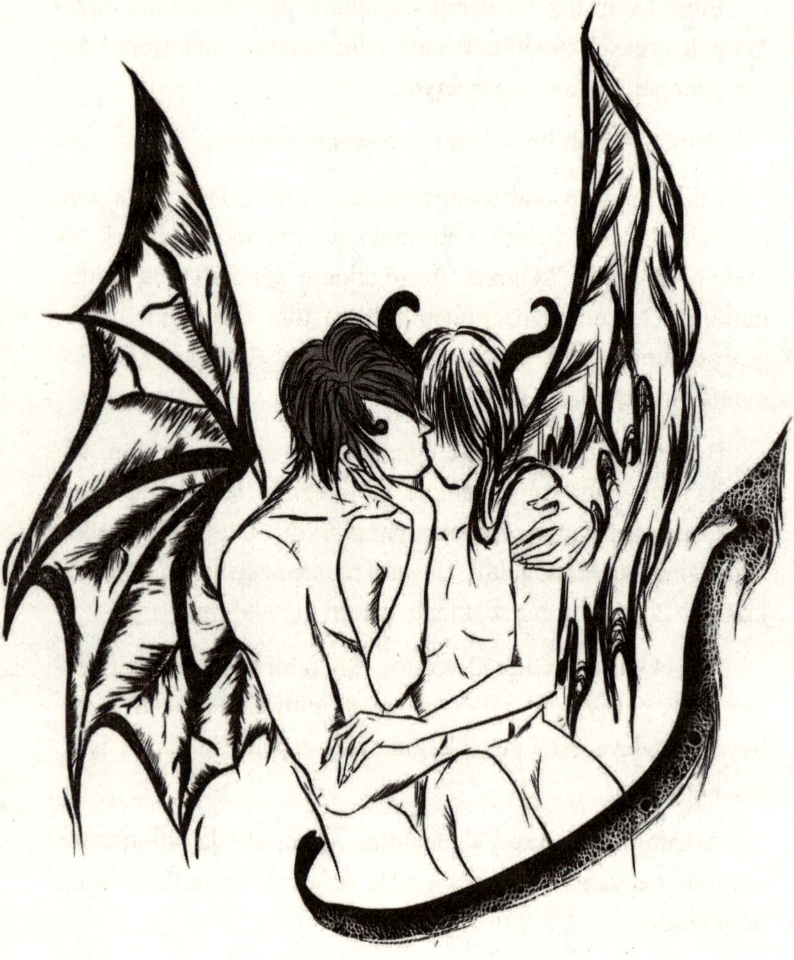

"Yalnızca aşk,
sonsuzluğu katlanılabilir kılar."

BÖLÜM 15

Şeytan hakkında pek çok şey söylenir.

En bilineni, şeytan hilekârdır. Sözleri kalbinizi zehirler ama kimse beni gözleri konusunda uyarmamıştı. Burada durmuş şeytanımın tatlı kahverengi gözlerine bakarken düşündüklerim buydu. Benim için cenneti bırakmıştı ve bu kulağa pek çok açıdan mantık dışı geliyordu. Küçük zararsız bir eylem gibi değildi, bir şeyleri kökünden değiştiren bir karardı.

"Ne düşünüyorsun?" Parmağım Aidan'ın o en çok sevdiğim, kemirilesi dolgun alt dudağında geziniyordu. Evrendeki yakışıklı erkekler pastasındaki en kremalı dilimi benim alacağımı kim bilebilirdi ki?

"Hiç." Bunun üzerine şeytanım güldü ve parmaklarım bembeyaz dişlerine değdi. Onunla ilgili her şey inanılmaz derecede güzeldi. Zihnimde Aidan'ın bana kötü geldiği bir ânı var mı diye aradım. Öldüğü gün… Ölürken bile kusursuzdu.

"Ah, ne oldu?" Aidanhell'in dövüşmekten nasırlaşmış avuç içi yanağımda gezinip gözlerimin hemen altında durdu. "O kadar çirkin miyim? Bana bakınca ağlamak mı istiyorsun?" Şaka yapıyor olmalıydı. Ne söylediği hakkında hiçbir fikri yoktu ama yine de sözleri üzerimdeki umutsuz auramı dağıtmama yardımcı oldu.

Kendimi bedeninde biraz yukarı çekip gözlerine daha dikkatli baktım. "Gözlerini kırmızı yapsana." Aidan kahkaha atmak için başını geriye atınca siyah kâkülleri uçuştu. Kalbim hızlanıyordu. Ona bayılıyordum. Ona bu kadar bayılırken kaç defa öpüşmüş olabileceğimizi düşündüm. Beş on… Bu kadardı. Tüm bu çılgınca koşturmacalar arasında onu öpemiyordum bile. Onunla öpüşemeden yaşlanıyordum.

"Şimdi de somurtuyorsun. Düşünceli Cassie ifadesi." Boşta kalan elimi tutup işaret parmağımı hafifçe ısırdı. "Hey! Daha zor yolculuklarımız olmuştu. Marcus'un üzerimize kustuğu yolculuğumuzu hatırlıyor musun? Tanrım, ne yemişti o herif?" Kıkırdadım. "Asla bir kurda pizza yedirme." Gülerken kirpiklerinin dağılmasını izledim. Bu kadar zahmetsiz bir şekilde böyle mükemmel görünebilmesi kalbimi acıtıyordu. Yaşadığımız tüm o çılgın şeylerden sonra yeniden bir araya gelmiştik. Ona onu sevdiğimi söylemiştim, o ise…

Aidanhell gülümsemeyi bırakıp derin bakışlarıyla beni taradı. Ona âşıktım. Ve bu muhtemelen sonumu getirecekti. Derin bir nefes alıp alnımı alnına yasladım. Gözlerimi kapattım. "Kardeşimi Bethany'den alacağız. Hırsızları şişleyeceğiz ve vampirleri toplayıp geleceğiz." Kraliçeleri olduğum için bir ırkı yok edemezdim, bu beni şeytanların gözünde faşist yapardı ama eğer direnirlerse başka şansımız kalmayacaktı. "Vampirleri öldürmemiz gerekirse Katze'nin suratına nasıl bakacağımı bilmiyorum."

Aidan alnı alnımdayken hafifçe başını salladı. "Beraber üstesinden geleceğiz." Tuttuğum nefesimi bıraktım. Keşke evren şu gözlerimi kapadığım birkaç saniye için var olsaydı. "Aidan," dedim içinde bulunduğum ânı uzatmaya çalışarak. "Bana bir söz verir misin?" Bunun üzerine Aidan alnını çekip kulak mememi hafifçe dişledi. Gözlerimi açıp kucağında zıpladım. "Hey, ciddi bir şey söylemeye çalışıyorum." Ama şeytanım hiç benim havamda değildi. Üzerinden buram buram tatlı kokular yayılırken muziplik peşindeki gözlerini deviriyordu.

"Sözler ve yeminlerle aram pekiyi değil, biliyorsun."

Haklıydı.

Direttim. "Bu çok önemli." Ciddi görünmeye çalışırken kollarından ayrılmak için yeltendim ama Aidan kaşlarını çatıp beni sımsıkı kenetledi. "Pekâlâ, o zaman söz." Şaşkınlıkla açılan ağzımı kapadım. Öküzüm yontuluyordu!

Boğazımı temizledim. "Pekâlâ, orada, yani savaş alanında bir karar vermen gerekirse eğer beni değil Jo'yu seç, tamam mı?" Şeytanım hâlâ aynı ifade ile bana bakıyordu. Anlamamıştı. "Beni değil Jo'yu kurtar. Eğer onu geride bırakıp beni kurtarırsan... Öyle bir hayatı yaşamak istemiyorum, önceliğin o olacak, anlaştık mı?"

Aidan yanıt vermek yerine beni itti. Yatağın ucuna kadar sertçe itildim, öyle ki neredeyse düşüyordum. O ise kalkıp bir elini yumruk yaparak komodinin yanındaki duvara geçirdi. Alçı parçaları yere dökülürken sessizce onu izlemeye devam ettim. Bir yanıt vermesine gerek yoktu. Aidan, Aidanlık yapıyordu.

Yataktan kalkıp ona gidemeden Aidan odadan çıkıp kapıyı beraberinde sertçe kapattı. Dünyaya gitmeden önceki son anlarımızı berbat etmiştim. Derin bir pişmanlık duygusu tam kalbimin ortasına taş yığını gibi çöktü. Aniden kendimi çok güçsüz hissettim, tüm o sorumluluklarımı sırtıma yüklemiş sürünüyordum ve beni mutlu eden tek şey az önce duvarı yumruklayan öfkeli iblisti. O da çekip gitmişti.

Yataktan zorla kalkıp az önce çarpılan kapıyı açarken dağılan sinirlerimi toparlamaya çalışıyordum. Bu hayatı ben seçmemiştim.

Kapıyı açınca kahverengi bir çift gözle karşılaştım. Aidan gitmemişti, kapının hemen önünde kalçasını duvara yaslamış, kollarını göğsünde kavuşturmuş bir şekilde duruyordu. Beni görünce başını indirip alnına düşen siyah kıvır kıvır saçlarıyla gözlerini kapadı. Ona ihtiyacım varken neden göt gibi davranıyordu ki?

"Bu hayatta beni en çok kızdıran sensin." Bir şey demedim. Öfkeli ses tonunu tüm hücrelerime sindirmekle meşguldüm. Onu sinir etmeye bayılmıyordum, ben sadece kendim gibi davranıyordum ve o hep sinirleniyordu.

Şeytanım gözlerini saçları ardına gizlemiş bir şekilde konuşmaya devam etti. "Sen ya da bir başkası ölmeyecek. Gitmene izin vermem." Çenesini hafifçe sağa yatırıp karanlık saçlarının ardından bana baktı. Kızıl gözleri öfkenin en içlisine bürünmüştü. Öyle ki insanda bir adım gerileme arzusu uyandırıyordu ama ben orada durmaya devam ettim.

"Neler yaşadığımı biliyor musun Cassandra?" Göğüs kafesimde bir yerlerin sıkıştığını hissettim. Şeytan kapıyı arkasından kapatıp tekrar bana döndü. Aramızda kalan acınası mesafeyi ne o ne ben geçebiliyorduk. Aidan duygusal konulara girerken böyle yapardı, mesafeyi bir kalkan gibi kullanırdı. Ben ise… Eh, ben duygusal ya da değil hiçbir konuda becerikli olduğumu sanmıyordum.

"Neler yaşadığını bilemem," dedim o konuşmaya devam etmeyince. Bir kolumla diğerini huzursuzca sıvazlarken gözlerimi kaçırdım. "Ama ben de zor zamanlar yaşadım." Gözlerimi kapayıp sızlayan göğsümü şişirecek kadar derin bir nefes aldım. Göz kapaklarım açıldığında Aidan tapılası yüzünde hüzünlü bir ifade gezinirken bana bakıyordu. "Cennetteydim. Kim olduğumu bilmiyordum." Dirseğimi tutan elime uzandı. Parmaklarımı avucunun içine alıp hafifçe üzerime eğildi. "Kim olduğumu bilmeden aylar geçirdim. Azrail ve Nathaniel dışında konuşabilecek kimsem yoktu. Sadece koca bir hiçlik ve hiçlikten daha büyük tek şey ise her yeri aydınlatan bir ışık." Parmaklarım avucunda terliyordu. Beraber savaşmış, beraber yemiş, uyumuş, birlikte gözyaşı dökmüştük. Aidan bu dünyadan bir diğerine giderken, gözlerinden akan birkaç damla yaşta ıslanıp boğulmuştum.

Bir ürperti bedenimi sararken anıları geldiği yere göndermeye çalıştım. Bu çok çok uzun zaman önceydi ve biz bunu aştık. Öyle değil mi?

"Aydınlıkta insan yolunu bulabilirmiş gibi geliyor ama hayır Cassie. Aydınlıkta insan kayboluyor. Düşünemiyor, göremiyor, sadece var olabiliyor. Ve ben o hiçliğin yuttuğu yerde neden var olduğumu bilmeden nefes aldım." Başımı hafifçe kaldırıp gözlerine baktım. Şeytan anlaşılmak için kıvranıyor gibiydi ama ben onu zaten anlıyordum. Ben de karanlıkta kaybolmuştum ve hiçlik dediği şeyin içinde de değildim, ben hiçliğe dönüşmüştüm.

Konuşmak için dudaklarımı aralayınca Aidan boşta kalan elinin işaret parmağını dudağıma koydu. "Kimliğimin olmadığı tüm o zaman boyunca bana mantıklı gelen tek şey, ruhlarını topladığımız insanların asla gerçekleşmeyecek olan hayalleriydi. Sadece o hayallere bakarken ben, içimdeki o derin boşluğu hissettim. Benim neden anılarım yoktu? Ben hiç ölümle yüzleşmiş miydim? Faniler gibi yitip giderken ruhum, sevdiğim birini düşünmüş müydüm?" Gözlerim yanarken daha fazla dayanamadım. Pınarlarda yaşlar toplanırken kirpiklerimi kırpmamaya çalıştım, akmayacaktı gözyaşım. Önce Aidanhell'in sözlerini içecektim, sonra ağlayacaktım. Çok sonra yine ağlayacaktım çünkü ilk defa şu an Aidanhell'in beni sevdiğinden emindim.

O da beni sevmişti. Bu çılgın, raylardan çıkıp duran dünyada bir şekilde buluşmuştu ruhlarımız. Ben onu kabul etmiştim o da beni. O yitip giderken bana tutunmuştu, ben de ölürsem eğer onu düşünecektim. Çünkü benim tüm hayallerimde Aidan vardı. Tek bir hayal seçip alabilseydik zihnimden, içinde Aidanhell olurdu. Başka türlüsü imkânsızdı.

Karşımda duran adamın acı çeken güzel yüzüne bakarken nefes almayı unuttum. Yaşlar gözlerimi kaplayıp yakışıklı üzgün yüzünü bulanıklaştırırken kıpırdamadan onu izlemeye devam ettim. "Sonra seni gördüm," dedi şeytanım fısıldar gibi bir sesle. "Ve tüm dünyam anlam kazandı."

Ne zaman ıslattığımı anlamadığım yanağımı parmağıyla silip hüzünlü bir şekilde gülümsedi. "Bu kadar lafı sümüğünü görmek için anlatmıyorum Cassie." Ve kirpiklerim art arda kapandı, esaretten fırlayan damlalar yanaklarımı daha çok ıslattı. Elimi avucundan çekip koluna yumruk attım. "Seni öküz." Sonrasında güldüm ve Aidan tekrar elime uzandı. "Eğer aynı şeyleri tekrar yaşama şansımız olsaydı, ben yine seni seçerdim. Yine bırakırdım cenneti ve sana gelirdim. Sonsuzluk ve ötesinde ne olursa olsun bu kalp," dedi kendi göğsünü işaret ederek, "her zaman bir şekilde bu fareye dönecek." Sonra beni kendine çekti ve güçlü kollarını sırtıma doladı. Sahiplenircesine sımsıkı tuttu beni.

"Ben fare değilim," dedim dudaklarım göğsüne değerken. Duyup duymadığından emin değildim çünkü sesim kasları arasında boğulup kaybolmuştu. Ama önemli de değildi. Aidan, seni seviyorum demeden sevmişti beni. Hatta öyle güzel sevmişti ki, birkaç ömür boyunca seni seviyorum demese de olurdu.

"Madem gerek yok, demem ben de."

Gözlerim kocaman açılırken tutuşu arasından sıyrılmaya çalıştım. "Böylesi bir anda bile düşüncelerimi mi okuyorsun?"

Şeytanım sırıtıyordu. Az önceki ifadesi tamamen silinmemişti ama mutluluğu aurasından taşıyor, benim aurama karışıyordu. "Senin zihnini okumaktan daha keyif verici tek şey Draza'yı direk dansı yaparken seyretmek olabilir."

Bu kez kahkahayı bastım. Hâlâ ağlıyordum ama gülmeye başlamıştım. Şeytan böyleydi işte, ağlarken güldürürdü sizi. Siz tam öldüm derken çekip çıkarır, yaşadığınızı fark ettirene kadar sarsardı sizi. "Draza'yı öyle görmedim ama hayali bile insanı dehşete düşürüyor."

Aidan'ın eli saçlarımda gezinirken başımı tekrar göğsüne yaslayıp gözlerimi kapadım. Bir senedir hiç uyumamış gibi tutundum alnıma değen sıcak nefesine. Şu girintide biraz uyusam ve gözlerimi açtığımda her şey yoluna girseydi keşke.

Ben huzurlu bir ifadeyle şeytanımın göğsünde mırlarken Aidan havadan sudan bahseder gibi konuşmasını sürdürdü. "Sen direk dansından bahsetmişken," dedi ciddi bir sesle. Başımı kaldırıp ifadesini görmeye çalıştım. "Ben direk dansı demedim. Sen söyledin." Aidan saçımı okşayan parmaklarını kaldırıp havayı dövdü. "Her neyse işte," dedi çabucak. "Bu bana bir şeyi hatırlattı. Seninle kapanmamış bir hesabım var." Kızıl gözleri dudaklarıma inip bir süre orada durunca yutkundum. Kendime gelmeye çalışırken farklı bir şeyler düşünmek istedim ama gözlerinin etkisinden kurtulmak kolay değildi.

"Kes şunu. Çıplak hissediyorum." Bedeninden birazcık uzaklaşırken kollarımla göğsümü kapayıp kendimi sıvazladım. Meme uçlarım karıncalanıyordu. Aidan orada sadece gözleriyle beni soyuyor ve fantezisine uygun şekilde hayal ediyordu. Bunu görebiliyordum. Açlığı bedenimi sararken ürperiyordum. Duygu durumlarım düzeldiği için artık azgın bir melez değildim ama söz konusu Aidan olunca bacaklarımı kapalı tutmak zorlaşıyordu.

Bir kez daha yutkundum. Boynumdan ince bir damla ter yavaşça köprücük kemiğime, oradan göğüslerimin arasına aktı. "Git Cassandra." Aidan'ın gözleri artık dudaklarımda değildi, her yerdeydiler. Titriyordum. Tam dediğine uyup yanından geçip gidecekken kavuşturduğu kollarına dokunup üzerine eğildim. Öpmek için dudaklarına yaklaşırken Aidan beni kollarımdan yakaladı. "Aşağıdalar, yanımıza gelecekler. Otuz saniyemiz var. Sana hemen burada otuz saniye içinde sahip olabilirim." Dudakları saçlarıma sürtünürken kontrolü kaybetmiştim, dizlerimin üzerinde duramıyordum.

"Otuz saniye ateşini biraz söndürmeme yardım edebilir." Dudağı kulağıma sürtünürken dudaklarımı yaladım. "Ama benimkini söndürmez. İstersen onlara yarım saat sonra geleceğimizi söyle ve seninle istediğin her şekilde…" Yanıyordum. Kurumuş dudaklarımdan ses çıkarabilmek için birkaç kez kendimi zorlamam gerekti. "Hayır. Döndüğümüzde."

Ve şeytanımın gözlerinde müthiş bir parıltı koptu. O an Aidan'a sevişme sözü verdiğimi anlamıştım.

***

Fanilerin dünyasına uçarak gidecektik. Bazılarımızın aksine diğerlerinde kanatlar yoktu, bu yüzden uçuş tozu gerekliydi. Urange bu sebeple dün gece çıkıp sabahın erken saatlerinde beraberinde iki peri ve kocaman bir çuvalla gelmişti. Orada bir krallığı beraber uçuracak kadar toz vardı.

Sırt çantamı hazırlamak için odama uçtuğumda kapımdaki kara askerlerin tartışmada olduklarını duydum. "Neler oluyor?" Ben ikisine baktığımda tedirgin bir hâlde sessizleştiler. Bir tanesi dibi görünmeyen karanlık gözlerini önce yere dikse de ardından bana döndü. "Efendimisss, biz de size katılmak istiyorusss." Hmm. Devam etmesi için elimle işaret yapıp odanın kapısını açtım. Kara bölük askeri peşimden odaya girdi. "Bu hâlimizde bizi tanırlar ama cadı büyü yapabilir." Hmm. Çantamı dolabın üzerinden alıp yatağa koydum. "Konuşmanız normal insanlar gibi değil, bu da büyük bir problem." Dolabı açıp iki kot pantolonu çantama tıktım.

"Sizi kollayacak birilerine ihtiyacınız olabilir. Vampir siz arkanızı döndüğünüz an tüyecektir," dedi kara iblis terslenerek.

Eh, biraz haklıydı. "Aloha'yı diyorsunuz." Üst çekmeceden iç çamaşırlarımı alıp yatağın altındaki bıçakları da çantamın içine attım. Ardından yatağa oturup bacak bacak üstüne attım. "Pekâlâ, iki asker fazla. Sen de geliyorsun ama bizimle değil, delegenin de katıldığı süvarilerle geleceksin. Seni haberci olarak kullanacağız." İblis başını eğip selam vererek odadan çıktı. Diğerine döndüm. "Meredith'e o askere gerekli büyüleri yapması gerektiğini söyle. Konuşmasını düzeltsin." Diğer asker de odadan çıkınca bir süre arkalarından kapıya baktım. Alınması gereken her şeyi almıştım. Ufak tefek şeyler dışında. Elimle yeniden yatağın altındaki kutuya uzandım. İçini açıp buralarda çalışmayan cep telefonumu ve şarj aletini aldım. Ardından sırt çantamı sırtıma takıp odadan çıktım.

Aidanhell'in nerede olabileceğini merak ediyordum. Kanatlarımı açıp tırabzandan atladım. Aşağı yavaşça indiğimde dağılan kâküllerimi düzeltip misafir odalarına giden yola koyuldum.

Adımlarım mermer zeminde tok sesler çıkarırken ortamın olması gerekenden daha sessiz olduğunu fark etmiştim.

Bir gargoyle heykeli kıpırdanınca gözlerimi adımlarımdan kaldırdım. Duvarlardaki meşaleler gölgemi oynatarak zemine akıtmaya başlayınca zindan yoluna girdiğimi fark ettim. Biraz dalgındım ve bu anlaşılabilirdi.

Koridordan dönünce bekçiler beni görüp selamladılar. Hemen arkalarındaki kalabalığa nefesimi bıkkın bir şekilde verip giriştim. "Selam beyler." Aloha diğerlerinin elinden kurtulup iki kolunu yukarı kaldırdı. Gözlerimi devirdim. Yanlarına gidip diğerlerine tasvip etmeyen bakışımı attım, bana gösterdiği gümüş kelepçelerine baktım. "Açın." Bir iblis hemen sessizce anahtarı kilide sokup Aloha'yı kelepçelerden kurtardı.

"Sağ ol." Aloha bileklerini ovalarken çevresine ürkütücü bakışlar atıyordu. Bir katliamla arasında duran tek şeyin ben olduğumu hissedebiliyordum. Ama kaybetmeyecektim hayatımdaki kazanımlarımı arttırdığım dönemlerden birindeydim.

Kalabalığa baktım. Aidan aralarında yoktu. Bu canımı sıkmamış gibi davranmaya çalıştım. "Herkes hazır mı?" İblis yanımızdan çekilince tabureye oturan Rohan'la bakıştık.

"Herkes değil. Meredith ondan istediğin büyüyü yapıyor."

"Katze, Marcus ve Urange aşağıdalar. Draza, sen ve Aidan hazır olduğunuzda yola çıkacaksınız."

Aloha gıcık bir kahkaha atınca sohbetimiz bölündü. "Sizinle gelmemin iyi bir fikir olduğunu düşünen sikik beyinli hanginizdi?"

Omzumu silktim. "Bendim, ne olmuş?"

Strigoi gülmeye devam etti. "Hiç."

Kaşlarımı endişe ile çatmamaya çalıştım. "Her neyse, iletişim hâlinde olabilmemiz için Urange'ı birkaç günde bir göndereceğim," dedim iblisçeye. Rohan yerinden kalkıp yanıma gelince Aloha'yı geride bıraktık. Omzumun üzerinden baktığımda bizi takip ettiğini görüp konuşmamı sürdürdüm. "Bir şeyler ters giderse eğer... Olur da birimiz dönmezsek, süvarilerden en güvendiklerini yolla. Orada bir savaş çıkarma niyetinde değilim ama hırsızlar ve vampirler yollarından dönmezlerse yapacak başka bir şeyim yok. Senden başka kimseye güvenemem Rohan." İblisçem başını salladı. Hissettiği endişeler ve aklında gezinen sayısız kötü olasılık yüzünden keyfi kaçmıştı. Olduğundan daha yaşlı görünüyordu. "Sen nasıl istersen."

Durup elimi omzuna koydum. Gözlerimle yeşil yorgun gözlerini buldum. "Dert etme, atlatırız." İblisçem buruşmuş elini elimin üzerine koyup zoraki bir şekilde gülümsedi.

"Ağlayacağım sanırım." İkimiz de sesin geldiği yere baktık. Draza duvara yaslanmış bizi izliyordu. Gözlerimi devirdim. "Ne zamandır oradasın?" Gümüş saçlı iblis bunu düşünüyormuş gibi yaptı. "Sümüğün akmaya başladığından beri." Keyfim o kadar kaçmıştı ki Draza'nın daha da kaçırabilmesine imkân yoktu. Bu yüzden yanından geçerken omzumla omzuna vurmaktan geri durmadım. Bu onu oldukça keyiflendirdi. "Hâlâ ergen gibi davranıyorsun."

Evet, bla bla.

"Sen de göt gibi davranıyorsun ama kimse bunu sorgulamıyor." Vampirin sesini duyunca kendimi az öncekinden daha az umutsuz hissetmeye başladım. Katze elinde birkaç torba ile görüş açımıza girdiğinde sırıttım. "Hey, yabancı." Vampir sivri dişleri görünecek şekilde gülümsedi.

Draza ise umursamamış gibiydi. "Burada sadece kraliyetten olanlar konuşabilir. Varoşlar için aşağı katlar daha uygun," dedi vampir ardından keyifli bir şekilde bana göz kırparken. Draza ise o uğursuz gözleriyle Katze'ye tepeden baktı. "Halkını kontrol edemeyen bir kraliçe de bana göre kraliçe değil. Olsa olsa şey olur. Hımmm, ne diyordunuz şu kurt adamlarla yatanlara? Kurt artığı mı?"

Ve ittifakımız o an son bulmuştu. Katze elindekileri bırakıp çevik bir hareketle Draza'nın suratına yumruğunu indirmişti. Tanrım, beraber takılabilmemiz kaç saniye sürmüştü? Üç mü?

Elimle Katze'nin kolunu tutmaya çalıştım ama Draza çoktan dilini çıkarıp dudaklarını yalamaya başlamıştı. "Ah, hayır, panzehir hazırlayacak vaktimiz yok." Katze'yi sertçe ittim. Vampir yere kapaklanınca işaret parmağımla Draza'nın göğsünü dürttüm. "Zehirli tükürüğünü gerçekten hak edenlere sakla. O bizden biri, tamam mı? Ayrıca dünyada böyle sululuklar yapamazsın." Elf hâlâ derin derin nefes alıyordu. Beyaz göğsü hızla inip kalkarken öfkeyle yerden kalkan arkadaşıma bakıyordu.

"Artık fahişelerle aynı tarafta mı yer alıyoruz?"

Katze çığlık atıp ona doğru koşunca kendimi Draza'ya siper ettim. "Hey hey, sakin ol! Onu takma, tamam mı? Sakin ol. Hadi ama Katze, sonsuza dek aranızda duramam. Evet, böyle tamam, sağ ol." Katze geri çekilirken burnundan soluyordu. Bu hâlini biliyordum. Kurt adamları öldürürken takındığı o ruh hâli içindeydi. Ama bilmediği şey Draza'yı öldürmek kolay değildi. Bir şekilde hep geri gelirdi.

"Sen de uslu dur." Dönüp gözlerimi elfin gözlerine diktim. "Ciddiyim, saçını atkuyruğu yap ve şu kulaklarını kapat. Dünyada insanların senin gibi kulakları yok."

Elf zarif parmaklarıyla yüzünü işaret etti. "Peki gözlerimi ne yapacağız?" Bana sorgulayan bir ifade ile bakan beyazı olmayan simsiyah gözlerine baktım. "Sanırım gözlük takacaksın." Elf bir şey demedi.

Ufak çaplı krizimizden sonra Katze geldiği yoldan gitmişti. Koridorda bıraktığı torbaları Aloha almış, içlerine bakıyordu. "Kan stoğu yapmış baksana, 0 rh bile var. Hey Draza, senin kan grubun neydi?"

Draza umursamaz bir tavırla orta parmağını gösterince Aloha sesli bir kahkaha attı. Bu aslında bana bir çeşit alarm olmalıydı, şey gibi, *sakın şu iki salağı dünyaya götürme*! Ama kalın kafalının tekiydim, bu yüzden ikisine de beni takip etmelerini söyleyip avluya çıktım.

İşte oradaydı.

Dünyada giydiği gibi siyah tişörtü ve siyah deri pantolonuyla orada duruyordu. Ayaklarının dibinde koyu mat bir sırt çantası vardı. Dirseğini ağaca yaslamış, hararetli bir şekilde Marcus'la konuşuyordu. Uzun zamandır görmediğim kadar sakin duruyordu. En son ne zaman gerginliğini kapıda bırakıp sadece genç bir erkek olarak yaşamıştı ki? Tam şu an gülmüştü ve erkek kardeşim de elini Aidan'ın omzuna koyup katıla katıla gülmeye başlamıştı. Bu sahneyi Boston'da görseydiniz iki yakışıklı erkeğin şakalaşması olarak yorumlayabilirdiniz. Ama şimdi büyük bir savaşa girmeden hemen öncesinde, ejderhaların yönettiği cehennem krallığında bir kurt ve iblisin konuşmasıydı bu. Ve açıkça görülüyor ki filizlenen yeni dostluklarının bir nişanesi olan şey de kahkahalarıydı. Onlara bakarken tüm gerginliğim uçup gitti.

Hemen yanlarında Meredith kara iblise doğru eğilmiş bir şeyler yapıyordu. Büyüyü henüz bitirememişti. Çatık kaşlarından memnuniyetsizliği belli oluyordu. Yine en zor işler ona kaldı diye düşünüp kendine acıdığından yüzde bin emindim. Bir yerlerde bir çınlama sesi duyunca Urange'ın konuştuğunu anlayıp başımı geriye çevirdim. Orada durmuş Katze'ye elindeki belgeleri okutmaya çalışıyordu. Dudaklarından "Yaprak Taht," kelimesini seçebilmiştim. Vampir dostumun ise dünya umurunda değil gibiydi. Benim yanımda da Draza ve Aloha vardı, ikisi de burada olmaktan memnun değillerdi.

Kafileye son bir kez bakıp derin bir nefes çektim. O an şeytanımın gözleri gözlerimi buldu. Onunla güvendeydim. Onunla savaşacaktım, yorulduğumda başımı onun omzuna yaslayacaktım ve yeri gelecek, verdiği nefesi ben alacaktım. Artık ona sahiptim, artık lanetlenmiş yalnız bir ruh değildim. Terk edilmiştim, itilmiştim ve kayıp ruhlar dehlizinde çürümeye bırakılmıştım. Ve Aidan ışığım olmuştu. Aidan gülümseyince ben de karşılık verdim. Zihnimi okumuş muydu bilmiyordum ama önemli değildi. Peri dövmecisindeki kör kâhin kadın bile bize kilometrelerce öteden baksa Aidanhell'e âşık olduğumu anlardı.

Derin bir nefes alıp sırt çantamı taktıktan sonra Urange'a işaret verdim. İşaretimi görenler yanımıza yaklaştı. Ardından Urange çuvalı getirdi ve herkes avucuna biraz uçuş tozu aldı. Kanadı olmayanlar burnuna çekmeye başlayınca son bir kez şeytanımın gözlerine baktım.

Aidan bana göz kırpınca tekrar gülümsedim.

Güvendesin, ilk kez gerçekten sevdiklerinle berabersin ve onlarla birlikte güvendesin.

"Pekâlâ, herkes kıçını kaldırsın, şov başlıyor!" Ardından kanatlarımı açıp bilinmezliğe doğru yükseldim.

BÖLÜM 16

İtiraf etmeliyim ki dünya son geldiğimdeki gibi değildi. Öncelikle sokakları çiş kokmuyordu ve her yerde şu parlak telefonlardan yoktu. Bir hafta içinde insanlık kafayı yemiş gibi telefon satın almış olmalıydı. Her yerdeydiler ve bu durum hepimiz için aşırı can sıkıcı bir hâl almıştı. Kimseye görünmeden geçip gitmek fikri o telefonlar sayesinde mümkün değildi.

Yine de uğraştık. İlk olarak Draza'ya gözlük taktık ve Meredith bunun her anından aşırı keyif aldı. O ve elf arasında hesabı görülmeyen şeyler vardı ve bu canımızı tehlikeye atmadığı sürece umursamayacaktım. İkinci olarak gördüğümüz vampirleri boğazlamadan önce onlardan bilgi almaya başlamıştık, ki bu da Marcus ve Katze'nin arasının açılmasına sebep olmuştu. Ama o kavganın da ortasında kalmak istemiyordum.

Benim derdim daha büyüktü. Kasları vardı ve hoş kokuyordu. Derdimi öldürmek ya da kollarına atılmak arasında gidip geliyordum çünkü Aidan sizde böyle duygular uyandırırdı. Sadece yakışıklı olması için böbreğimi verebilirdim ama o sadece yakışıklı değildi. O pek çok anlamda *sadece* olmayacak her şeydi. Neyse, sanırım anladınız.

Akşamüstü güneşi tepeden sanki biri eziyormuş gibi kayarken ekibin geri kalanına baktım. Bugün için hazırlanmışlardı. Urange peri muhbirlerinden büyük bir konvoyun karşımıza çıkacağı haberini alalı yirmi dört saat olmuştu ve o yirmi dört saat boyunca plan yapmıştık.

"Vampirleri korumak görevimizdi." Katze mırıldanıyordu. Yere çömelmiş, henüz birkaç saat önce oraya atılmış olan pis bir mendili izliyordu. İz sürdüğünü anlamak için deha olmama gerek yoktu. Cevap veremedim. O haklıydı, bir şekilde bu görevimizdi. Ama bazılarını kurtaramazdınız.

"Hepimizi tehlikeye attılar. Yüzyıllardır güvende olan sırrımızı ifşa ediyorlar."

"Binler," diye düzeltti Draza.

"Hepimiz enkaz değiliz. Bazılarımız birkaç yüzyıldır burada." Marcus meydan okurcasına elfe baktı. Draza konuşmak için zehirli dudaklarını araladı fakat vazgeçti. "Yüzyıllardır zevk ve sefa içinde hayatımızı sürdürmemizin sebebi iki ayaklı felaketlerin bizim var olduğumuzu bilmemesi," dedi elf sakince.

Kıçımla güldüm. "Sanki bilseler bir şey değişecekti. Ayrıca zevk ve sefa mı? Her gün yattığım yerde biri boğazımı kesmeye çalışıyor." Kardeşim omuz silkti. O da ben de haklı gibiydik.

"Dinozorları bile yendiler. Hatta bana sorarsanız yemiş bile olabilirler." Bunu düşündüm. Marcus insanlarla ilgili oldukça değişik teorilere sahipti. Gözlerimin önüne altlarındaki bezle dinozorun tepesine çıkmış vahşi insanlar geldi. "Olabilir." Oturduğum pozisyonu değiştirdim, eğer konuşmazsak beklemekten çıldıracağımızı düşünmüştüm ama konuşmak da pekiyi gelmemişti. Kafam hâlâ malûm olaylardan dolayı yerinde değildi. Öldürme eyleminden bahsetmek ve onu gerçekleştirmek arasında ciddi bir fark vardı. Özellikle de yeniden bir kısmımın melek olduğu düşünülürse.

Kendimi yabancı biri gibi hissediyordum. Bazı anlar durup içim çıkana dek ağlamak isterken bazı anlar ise kontrolü kaybediyordum, herkesin ölmesini diliyordum. Ölümde diğer hiçbir şeyde olmayan imrenilesi bir huzur vardı.

"Hey, midesi olanlar acıktıysa gidip pizza alabilirim." Urange'ın sesi içimdeki karamsarlıktan beni uyandırdı. Başımı kaldırıp periye bakacakken gözlerim şeytanıma kaydı. Konuşmuyordu. Ne düşündüğünü de bilmiyordum. Düşünüyor muydu emin de değildim. Zihin kalkanları öyle sık örülmüştü ki arasından bir ışık gibi sızamıyordum. Koca bir bilinmezlikti Aidan ve buradaki kocaman kelimesinin altını birkaç kez çizmek istiyorum.

"Ben acıktım," dedim elimi kaldırırken. "Yeniden ucube olunca böyle oluyor." Melez olmamın beni insanlaştırdığı gerçeği ile baş etmem biraz zamanımı almıştı. İnsan daha kompleks bir hâle dönüşünce benliğini kaybettiğini sanıyordu ama işte. Yeniden bendim. Acıkan ve acı yiyince tuvalete koşan Cassie. Aidan ise yeniden şeytandı. Sadece dünyada olduğu için biraz besleniyor ve birkaç dakika uyuyordu. Katze gibiler ise eh, biliyorsunuz.

"Marcus'a da al. Katze için ise bir tavuk yakalayabilirsin." Katze sesini çıkarmadan çömeldiği yerden göz ucuyla bana bakmakla yetindi. Vampirleri avladığımız için üzgün hissettiğini biliyordum ama kriz anlarını yönetmek sanıldığı kadar kolay değildi. Bazen sonuçları keskin olan güçlü kararlar almak gerekiyordu ve bu kararlar da sorun çıkaranları yok etmek olabiliyordu. Melekleri bulsunlar diye gönderdiğim hırsızlar başıma belâ olmuştu.

İç çekmekten kendimi alamıyordum. Bir şeyler kötü giderse bunun tek suçlusu bendim. Başımı kaldırıp ekibime baktım. Onlar ve peşimizden gelen üç bölük asker benim için kendilerini ölüme bile atardı. Ejderhaların gönderdiği süvariler gökyüzünde gizlenerek bizi kolluyorlardı, olası bir tehlikede ölmek için emir almışlardı ve korkusuz bakışlarının süslediği çelik gibi iradeleriyle Valkürler bunu yapardı. Peki ben ne yapardım? Muhtemelen saçma çocukça kararlar verip herkesin ölümüne sebep olurdum.

Yine kendimden nefret ediyordum. Meredith'in yardımcı büyüleri sayesinde aralarında stabil bir manyak gibi dolaşıyordum, ki bu diğer hâllerimden daha iyiydi.

Diğer hâllerim ise birilerinin boğazındaki atar damarın parçalanması ile sonuçlanıyordu. Böyle durumlarda Aidan beni alıp uzaklara uçuruyor ve yeniden Cassie olana kadar getirmiyordu. Yeniden Cassie olma anlarımda fırsattan istifa ederek Aidan'ın kucağına yerleşiyor ve çektiğim ıstırabı ona da tattırıyordum. Birileri kafayı yiyecekse bu tek ben olmayacaktım.

Urange elinde pizzalarla gelene kadar Katze ile oturup saldırı planımızı konuştuk. Katze elimle havaya çizdiğim isten izlere bakıyor, bir yandan da dudağını dişliyordu. "Yaşayanların kaderini çoktan ölmüş üç ejderhaya bırakmak iyi bir fikir mi acaba?" Yüzümü buruşturdum. "İyiden daha farklı bir kelime kullanırdım sanırım." Gözlerim hâlâ pizza kutularındayken ekledim. "Gerisi için endişelenmek istemiyorum, yapacak çok işim var. Ejderhalar hangi ilahi kararla gönderilmiş olursa olsun bana emanet edilen sadece o taht değil. Ailem var. Jo ve diğerleri."

Katze yetmiş yaşındaki bir vampir gibi görmüş geçirmiş bir ifade ile gözlerime baktı. "Artık yeni bir ailen var. Kızıl kafayı pek sevmiyorum ama şu iri kıyım hiç de fena değil." Urange elinde cılız bir fareyle kalabalıktan uzaklaşırken Katze kalkık ufak burnuyla pizzaları parçalayan sarışın adamı işaret etti. Marcus onu izlediğimizden haberdar değildi. "Evet, şu iştahı kardeş olmamızı haklı çıkarıyor."

İkimiz de sırıttık. Ama sonra Katze vampirlere özgü o içi boş surat ifadesini takındı. "Diğer vampirleri avlamak hoşuma gitmiyor. Biliyorum suçlular ama..." Cümlesini tamamlayamadı.

Elimi dizinin üzerinde gergince tuttuğu siyah ojeli parmaklarının üstüne koydum. Teni buz gibiydi. "Biliyorum. Ben de artık birilerini öldürmek istemiyorum." İçimden sessizce ekledim, *çoğu zaman*.

Katze elini yavaşça elimden çekti. "Hadi ama Cass, cehennem kafayı yemişti. Onları suçlayamayız." Haklıydı. Gergince iç çektim. "Aldığımız duyumlara göre birçoğu çoktan insanları strigoiye dönüştürmüş. Durdurulmaları gerekiyor. Marr ve Anton hep insanlarla bir anlaşma içinde olduğumuzu söylerdi. Bilirsin."

"Neyden bahsediyorsun? İnsanlar uyuyan bir mamut kadar şapşallar. Kıçlarından haberleri yok. Orada duruyor ve sosyal medyaya giriyorlar, tek yaptıkları bu." Hmm. Ben burada yokken sosyal medya daha da popülerleşmişti demek.

"Hayır," dedi iblisçe birden. Başımı kaldırdım. Aloha yanımıza gelmişti ve bunu ne ben ne de Katze fark edebilmiştik. Katze'nin omuzlarını gergince kıpırdattığını görebiliyordum. Bu kadar sessiz olması strigoilere has doğal olmayan bir şeydi, memelilerin böylesi bir yırtıcıya karşı hiç şansları yoktu.

"Ne demek istiyorsun?"

Durup kocaman yeşil gözlerini tepemizde dikilen iblisçeye çevirdi. Katze'nin bakışları buz ise Aloha'nınkiler buzuldu.

İçinde bir şeyler fena hâlde yanlıştı. Ve bunu anlamak için insana dehşet veren o ruhsuz kızıl gözlerine bakmaya gerek yoktu. O farklı kokuyordu.

"İnsanlar ve diğer dünyalar bir anlaşma içindeler. Bu yaradılıştan sonraki en eski kuraldır. Bunu herkes bilir." Herkesin buradaki hiç kimseyi kapsadığını sanmıyordum. Belki Meredith biliyor olabilirdi, eh o da burada değildi. Sahi nereye kaybolmuştu?

"Ne çeşit bir kural?" diye sordu Marcus ağzının içindeki pizza ile sekerek yanımıza gelirken. Kol altında ısısı bir metreden hissedilen kocaman bir paket sıcak pizza vardı. Aidan'a teklif ettiğinden şüpheliydim.

"Pekâlâ, çaylaklar toplanın size bir hikâye anlatacağım." Urange, Aloha'nın sesini duyunca yüzünü ekşitse de bize yaklaştı. Elinde kuyruğundan tuttuğu fareyi, Katze'ye kibarca vermenin yollarını arıyor gibiydi. Anlaşılan tavuk bulamamıştı. Vampir, perinin elinden fareyi alırken hayvan tüyleri diken diken edecek şekilde viyakladı. Aidan ve Draza duymamış gibi uzakta konuşmaya devam ediyorlardı. Draza öfkeli görünüyordu, Aidan'ın ise arkası dönüktü. Çıkık kürek kemiklerinden başka bir şey göremiyordum, eğilmişti.

Herkes yanımıza doluşunca Aloha da yere çöktü. Urange, Katze ile aramıza oturmuş, Marcus'tan belki de böbreğini vererek aldığı pizza kutusunu önümüze açmıştı. Katze'nin ilgilendiği yoktu ama ben bir dilim yiyebilirdim. Kutunun kapağını kaldırdığımda strigoi konuşmaya başladı.

"Sizin atalarınız henüz bu diyarlarda yokken insanlar vardı." Bir sosis parçası ciğerime kaçacakken öksürdüm.

"Ah, evet sevgili Cassie, iblisler ve melekler dünyaya uzun yıllar gelmediler. Dünya değerli insanoğlu için yaratıldı. Çok sonra melekler, en son da şeytanlar yeryüzüne indi." Çıkan tek ses ağzımı şapırdattığım için çıkan sesti. Bu yüzden kocaman bir lokma yutup kutuyu kapattım. "İnsanlar melekler indiğinde onların küçük heykellerini yaptı. Onları sevdiler, ta ki melekler onların canını alana kadar." Uzaktaki uğultu susunca Aidan ve Draza'nın da bizi dinlediğini anladım. "Melekler, insan soyunun son bulmaması için çabalıyorlardı, bu yüzden bir çeşit düzen geliştirdiler. Bu düzene göre insanlardan kötü kalpli olanlar doğduktan sonra fark ediliyordu, onlar da bu sorunlar büyümeden çözmenin bir yolunu buldu."

"Onların bebeklerini mi öldürdük?" Urange dehşete kapılmıştı.

Biz de öyle. Pekâlâ, belki Katze dehşete kapılmamıştı, güzel yüzü farenin kaburga kemiklerinin arasında kırmızıya bulanmakla meşguldü.

"Evet. Melekler, bu düzenin işleyeceğini düşündü. Çünkü onlar auraları görebiliyorlardı ve aurasında kötülük olan her bebeği öldürdüler. Böylelikle sadece iyi olanlar kalacaktı."

Kimse konuşmaya cesaret edemiyordu. Hepimiz Aloha'ya bakıyorduk. "Ya sonra?" diye sordum dizlerimi toplayıp karnıma yaslayarak.

"Melekler, bu düzene bir süre devam etti. İnsanoğlunun sayısı azaldıkça doğa güzelleşti, kaynaklar sınırsızlaştı ve kötülük kayboldu. Melekler bu düzene *Diriliş* dediler. Onlara göre bu insanoğlunun *dirilişiydi.*" Kimse cevap vermeyince Aloha tembelce esnedi. Gerindi ve tekrar devam etti. "Ama tabii ki bu çok da uzun süremdi. Bebeklerinin kaçırılmasından rahatsız olan ebeveynlerin auraları kararmaya başladı. Kimse insanların sonradan kötüleşeceğini bilememişti. İnsanlar melekleri başlarından atmak için çareler aramaya başladılar ve buldular da. O zamanlar kendilerine Diablo derlerdi." Kızıl gözleri Draza ve Aidan'ın üzerinde durdu. "Nam-ı değer şeytanlar."

Aidan'a baktım. Beni izliyordu. Bakışlarımı kaçırdım.

"Ve şeytanlar meleklerle savaşıp onları ait oldukları yere gönderdi. Böylelikle diriliş de meleklerin gidişiyle son buldu."

Hikâyenin bu kadar temiz bir son içermediğini hissedebiliyordum. Benim hikâyelerim kanlı olurdu, bu anlatı da fazlasıyla temizdi. İnanmıyordum. "Ee, peki insanlara ne oldu?"

"Anlaşma yaptılar." Sesin geldiği yöne doğru başımı kaldırdım. Meredith gölgelerin arasından sıyrılırken ellerini sanki toza bulanmışlar gibi pantolonuna siliyordu. Ne zaman kaybolduğu ve nereye gittiği hakkında hiçbir fikrim yoktu ama acıkmışsa hemen buraya gelmesi gerekiyordu, Marcus tüm insanlığın kalan son pizzalarını bile kemiriyor olabilirdi.

"Ne anlaşması bu?" diye sordu vampir nihayet iri dolgun bir yudum daha içip içi boşaltılmış faresini boş bir karton pizza kutusuna koyarken. Aloha gözlerini farenin cesedinden ayırmadan yanıtladı. "Melekler ve şeytanlarla. İşlerine karışılmayacaktı. Taraflar kabul etti ve diriliş toprağın en derin katmanına gömüldü." Kelimenin yarattığı ürpertici etki pizza kutusunun üzerinde somutlaşıyordu. Uzanıp dokunabilirdim. Hatta altında ezilebilirdim. Kötüydük ve kötü olmamızın tek açıklaması iyi olmaya çalışmaktı. Bu saf, katıksız iyilik barındıran kanlı gerçek bana iyiyi ve kötüyü sorgulatmıştı.

Bir yanım iyiyken diğer yanım değildi. Evet, bir yanım kötüydü, iblisti ve affedilemezdi, oysa diğer yanım saf bir iyilik-ten meydana gelmiyordu. Herkesin kendi doğruları vardı ve bu doğruların yükünü omuzlarımdaki iki kanat misali taşıyordum.

İç çektim. "Acıkan yemeğini yesin, yarın büyük bir gün."

Urange hemen beni susturdu. İri gözleriyle iblisçeye bakıyordu. "İnsanlar pes mi etti yani? Böyle bir tehlike bir daha olur diye endişelenmediler mi?" Anlaşılan perinin bu gece hikâye dinleyesi vardı.

Uzakta bir yerde parlayan ışık gözlerimi aldı. Tekrar baktığımda sokak karanlıktı. Evhamlı yapıma sessizce küfretmek istedim.

"İnsanlar aptaldır peri. Yüzyıllar önce verdikleri savaşı çoktan unuttular." Aloha kendini zemine sırtüstü bırakıp kızıl gözlerini kapattı. Ayağa kalkıp cebimdeki saati çıkardım. "Bir şeyler yiyin ve dinlenin, dört saat sonra vampirler buradan geçecek, onlar gelmeden kokumuzu silelim." Herkes ayaklanmaya başlayınca kalabalıktan faydalanıp Aidan'a doğru yürüdüm.

Draza erkek kardeşinin yanında dururken bir şeyler düşünür gibi uzaklara bakıyordu. "Ne diyordunuz?"

Elf bana bakmadı. Bazen ona seslendiğimde beni duymuyormuş gibi yapıyordu ve beyaz kıçını ona yedirmek istiyordum. Oysa iblisim yumuşak bir ifadeyle yanıtladı. Kahverengi sıcacık gözleri gözlerime indi. "Sizi dinledik."

İçimdeki çiftleşen kelebekleri yutup ona bakmaya devam ettim. "Güzel bir hikâyeydi. İnsanların aptal olduğunu sanmıyorum ama belki onları yönetenler aptaldır."

Draza uyuz kahkahasını bastı. "Evet, aptal yöneticiler ile ilgili birkaç şey biliyorum." Zehirli siyah gözleriyle yan yan bana baktı. Yanıt vermem için kışkırtılmıştım ama takmadım. "Dünya seni güçsüzleştirdi mi?"

Aidan bir an için bunu düşünmüş gibi dolgun alt dudağını dişleri arasına aldı. Bu hareketinin dünyadaki kadın nüfusu için biyolojik bir silah olabileceğinden haberi yoktu. Gözlerimi dudaklarından alıp gözlerine çevirdim ve anında pişman oldum, beni açık bir kitap gibi okuyordu. Bundan zevk alıyordu. Hafifçe gülümsedi.

"Belirli belirsiz bir his sadece. Güçsüzlük denemez."

"Kıç gıdıklanması gibi mi?" İkimiz de Draza'nın tuhaf yorumuna gözlerimizi devirdik. "Sen nasıl hissediyorsun?" dedi şeytanım endişe ile yüzüme bakarken.

"Deve boku gibi.

"İyi." Şüpheli erkeksi bakışları yüzümü taradı. "Hadi, gidelim artık buradan." İçimde bir savaş vererek elini tutmayı düşündüm ama yapamadım. Korkuluk gibi dikiliyordum. Kollarım aniden sanki o an var olmuşlar gibi bir yere sığamıyordu.

Saniyeler geçip gidince aptalca dikildiğimi fark edip kulaklarım yanarken arkamı döndüm. Ne beklemiştim? Aidan ile el ele tutuşmayı mı? Vampir kalbi kazıklarken birbirimize *aşkım* mı diyecektik?

Ben birine aşkım diyebilme şansını üç yaşında elimde hançerle gezerken kaybetmiştim. Sikik bir dünyadaki şaşkın avcı kızdım ben.

İki adım anca atabilmiştim ki parmaklarım sıcacık bir el tarafından kuşatıldı. Aciz kalbim atmayı unutup öylece kalakaldı. Aidan elimi tutuyordu.

Ve bu bütün düşlerimden daha güzel, daha sıcak bir şeydi.

Bu kez terk edilmiş, yarım kalmış hissetmiyordum.

Elimi tutan eline baktım ve istemeden de olsa aptalca gülümsedim.

Ah ahhh, bu kız fena bir âşıktı.

Ah aptal Cassie.

***

"Vampirler sıçıyor mu?"

"Haydaaaa!" Oturduğum yerde sırtımı dikleştirdim. Yaklaşık yarım saattir sekiz katlı bir binanın tepesine tünemiş hâlde kafileyi gözlüyorduk. Urange peri tozuyla bizden on dakika uzaklıktaki bir tepede komut vermek için hazır bekliyordu.

"Ne var bu soruda?" dedi Draza. Neredeyse yerinden düşecekmiş gibi duran Katze yanıt vermekle vermemek arasında kaldı.

"Kan içiyorsunuz sonuçta, yani kan mı çıkıyor alttan? Ne var?" Aidan kardeşinin karnına dirseğini bastırıyordu ama Draza sorusunda ısrarcıydı. "Bulmuşken sorayım dedim. Yani bir vampir bizi ısırmadan kaç dakika adam akıllı konuşabiliyoruz ki?"

Marcus, elfe öldürücü bakışlar atınca sonumun bu ikisinden mi yoksa aşağıdakilerin elinden mi geleceği konusunda karar vermeye çalışıyordum.

"Sıkıntıdan saçmalıyorsun," dedim sadece.

Draza hepimizi şaşırtan bir sakinlikle üstelemekten vazgeçti. Katze'nin ise tepesi atmıştı. Başının üstünden hayali dumanlar çıkarıyor gibiydi vampir. Aslında bu soruyu ben de merak ediyordum ama fazlasıyla özel bir konuydu arkadaşıma soramamıştım. İnsanın başında bu kadar belâ varken bile çocuklaşması komikti. Bu bir yanımın tamamen ele geçirilmediğinin tek kanıtı olabilirdi. Ucubeydim ama yüzde yüz değildim.

Aidan derin, bıkkın bir iç çekince boğulduğum düşüncelerimden sıyrılıp ona döndüm. Draza'nın gitmesini istiyordu ama burada hepimiz dizlerimizin üzerinde oturmuş aşağıya bakarken bu pek olası değildi. Bir baskın yapmak üzereydik ve duruşumuzu değiştiremezdik.

Bir ıslık sesi duyunca gözlerimi kırptım. Urange'nın çınlayan ıslığı üzerine göğsümü şişirerek derin bir nefes aldım. "Üç deyince," dedim fısıldayarak.

Vampirlerin rüzgârı yaran hızlı adımları melez kulaklarıma dolarken saymaya başladım. "Bir."

Aidan birden doğrulup sırtını gerdi. "Ben gidiyorum." Ardından o kadar hızlı zıpladı ki kanatlarını açıp havada süzülmesi nerdeyse beş saniyesini almıştı. Şaşkınlık ve sinir krizi arasındaki ince çizgide gidip geldikten sonra kaşlarımı çatıp ben de doğruldum. "Onu takip edin."

Ve hepimiz bir bir parapetlerden aşağı atlamaya başladık. Kanatlarımı açmadan yere indiğimde yanı başımda Katze'nin belindeki hançerleri çıkardığını gördüm. Parlak dişleri dudağının üzerinde öldürücü bir şekilde parlarken bana gülümsedi.

Diğer tarafımda ise Aloha avına atlamak üzere olan bir goril gibiydi. İblisçenin elleri sanki gitgide büyüyordu, sırtını kamburlaştırıp dizlerini bükmüştü. Tepemde bir yerlerde Urange'ın büyü keselerini fırlatmak için hazırlandığını biliyordum, üzerime şapşal parlak tozlarından döküyordu. Ama kalbimi esas zıplatan bunlar değildi.

Oydu.

Yer yer siyahın bulaştığı beyaz kanatları havada zarifçe süzülürken Aidan bacaklarını geriyordu. Kahverengi saçları akımla uçuşarak gözlerini kapatıyordu, çevresine yaydığı güçlü aura her kanat darbesinde atmosfere yayılıyor; burnuma, dudaklarıma ve vücuduma ulaşıyordu.

Öyle zarafetli bir şekilde çıldırmıştı ki ona bakarak ağlayabilirdim. Onun her şeyi bir yana, bu gücünü özlemiştim. Onun şeytanlığını özlemiştim.

Ve bu farkındalık ellerimin titremesine sebep olarak beni bir adım geriye atmıştı. Bu farkındalık bilincimin tüm aralık kalmış kapaklarını sertçe kapatınca kendime geldim. Onu öyle çok istiyordum ki bu sadece kişiliği, bedeni, hatta duygularıyla ilgili değildi, ben ondaki vahşiliği ve kötülüğü de seviyordum.

Aidan'a dönülemez bir şekilde vurulmuştum. Ve bu vurgun şu an kalbimin tam üstüne oturmuştu. Onun iyi olması âşık olmamı sağlamamıştı, ona ilk gördüğüm andan beri aşıktım.

Bir şeytan olması bunu azaltmamıştı. Onun şeytanlığını bile seviyordum.

Şeytanım yavaşça yere konup o dev, gür kanatları sırtının içine çekerken gri tişörtü parçalar hâlinde yere düştü.

"Ağzının suyunu sil." İrkildim. Draza onaylamayan bir bakışla üstten bana bakıyordu. Gözlüklerini çıkarmıştı. Derin bir nefes alıp vampirlere odaklanmaya çalıştım.

Boynumu önce sağa sonra sola çevirip kıtırdattım. Pekâlâ, sivri dişli sürtüklerle uğraştıktan sonra umutsuz aşk hayatımla ilgilenecektim.

İlk darbe en sesli olanıydı. Aidan siyah saçlı bir vampiri yere serip deri çizmeleriyle kafasını eziyordu. Başka bir tanesi sırtına yapışınca ona doğru koşup kılıcımı vampirin boğazına bastırdım. Sivri ucu vampirin atar damarına gömülünce sapını çevirip boynunun diğer tarafından çıkmasını sağladım. Yüzüme fışkıran kan gözlerimi yakarken kılıcı çıkarıp vampiri tekmeleyerek yere serdim. Bir el beni saçımdan yakalayınca çığlığı bastım.

Acı gözlerimi kör ederken boşta kalan elimle beni tutan kişiye vurmaya çalıştım. "Kes şunu!" Katze arkamdaki vampiri yere serince kafamdaki birkaç saç teliyle beraber o çekici güç de kayboldu. Arkamı dönüp acıdan yaşaran gözlerimi yerdeki vampire diktim. Kılıcı var gücümle kaldırdım, tam indirecekken vampir dostum elimi tuttu. "Bekle." Bir an için beynim bu komutu algılayamadı. Kılıç ellerimden kaydı ve vampirin karnına saplandı. Acı içinde yerde kıvranan vampir küfretmeye başladı.

Soru soran gözlerle Katze'ye baktım. Artık bana bakmıyordu, yerdeki vampire eğilmişti. Anlamıyordum. Başımı kaldırdığımda Aidan'ın iki vampirle dövüştüğünü gördüm. Düşünmeden yere düşen kılıcımı alıp ona katılmak için koştum.

Bir tanesinin gırtlağını kesip hız kesmeden arkamı dönerek Aloha'nın yanına gittim, ona ulaşmaya çalışan iki vampirin üzerine atladım. Birinin boynunu kırmak için sırtına oturduğumda diğeri beni üzerinden indirmeye çalışıyordu.

"Üç tane daha geliyor!" dedi Urange'ın çınlayan sesi. Arkamdaki vampirin gözlerine tırnaklarımı geçirirken altımdaki beni üstünden atmak için âdeta zıplıyordu. Tırnaklarımda yumuşak ve kaygan göz yuvarlağını hissedince vampir acı içinde bağırarak geri çekildi. Kanlı ellerimle sırtında oturduğum vampirin boynunu tutup çevirdim. Tok bir ses kulağıma dolarken altımdaki vampir pelte gibi yere yığıldı. Diz kapaklarım yere değdiğinde bir an için çevremdeki kargaşaya baktım. Deli bir vampir kızıl gözlerinde aç bir ifadeyle bana doğru koşarken zeminden zıplayıp kolumu önüme siper ettim. Tırnaklarını gelişigüzel savururken kolumu tırmaladı. Ama bu yaptığı son şeydi. Urange vampirin tepesinden ona iri bir büyü torbası atınca vampir patlayarak yok oldu. Şimdi üzerimdeki tek şey kan değildi, vampirin asitleşmiş organları bedenimi yakıyordu. Bütünüyle kırmızıydım. "Bu şey yakıyor."

"Bedava solaryum." Draza bir vampirin üzerine tükürdü. Tükürükten çıkan dumanlar vampirin zıplamasına sebep oldu. "Bu ne? Bu ucube ağzından ne çıkardı?" Vampir koşarak uzaklaşmaya çalıştı. Draza gülümsüyordu. Tek yapması gereken o uğursuz dudaklarını aralamaktı. Böylelikle kara elf zehri dudaklarından süzülebilecekti. Basit ama etkili bir çözümdü.

Aidan bir vampiri tam yanı başıma fırlatınca kılıcımı yere atıp belimdeki hançerimi çıkardım. Yanıma düşen vampirin gırtlağını kesip doğruldum. Sadece iki vampir kalmıştı. Marcus dönüşmeden bir tanesini parçalamıştı. Aloha ise elinde kesik bir kolla bale yapıyor gibiydi, kimse ona böyle bir gerekliliğinin olduğunu söylememesine rağmen.

Yaklaşık yarım saat sonra sokağın ortasında kanlar içinde nefes nefese duruyordum. Cildim artık yanmıyordu ve bunun ne anlama geldiğinden tam olarak tam emin değildim. Kül başımın üzerinden yağmur misali yağarken hançerimi pantolonuma silip belime yerleştirdim.

Draza cesetleri ayaklarından çekip götürürken Aloha da ona yardım ediyordu. Marcus ve Urange, delegelere bilgi vermek için şehir merkezine gitmişlerdi. Aidan yanıma gelirken gözlerim vampir dostumu arıyordu. "Katze nerede?"

Aidan sorum üzerine çevresine baktı. Sağ gözünün üzeri patlamıştı, kanı akıyordu. "Bilmiyorum, onu göremedim."

"Ben de." Kılıcımı yerden alıp kınına yerleştirirken gözlerime yapışan kanlı kâkülleri arkaya attım. "Herhâlde Marcus'un yanındadır." Aidan yanıt vermedi, bunun yerine elini omzuma koydu. "Kan içindesin, tek görünen yerin gözlerin." Elinin tersiyle burnumu silmeye çalıştı. Elinin nasırlaşmış derisi burnumu bir zımpara gibi temizlerken ona baktım.

"Orada iyi iş çıkardın."

"Hmm."

"O hareketleri yaparken... Güzel görünüyordun." Kana bulanan yanaklarım için şükrettim. Aidan iltifat ederken kızarmak hâlâ aptalca geliyordu ama oluyordu işte. Kendisinin bir savaş tanrısı gibi göründüğünü bilmiyor muydu acaba?

"Sen, ben ve toprakla ilgili olan lafımı hatırlıyorsun değil mi?" Gözlerimi kapatan saçlarımı kulağımın arkasına attı. Ilık nefesi yüzüme çarparken dediklerini anlamaya çalıştım.

Sonra anladım.

Aidan yüzünü yüzüme yaklaştırınca nefesim kesildi. "Şu," dedi fısıldarken, "seni toprağın üzerine yatırmakla ilgili olan." Gözlerimi kapatıp anın tadını çıkardım. "Sen o vampiri yere sererken seni alıp buradan götürmemek için kendimi zor tuttum." O kısık sesinde kontrolü eline almaya çalışan bir boğa gizliydi ve derinlerde bir yanım o boğaya zincirlerinden kurtulması için meydan okuyordu.

Yutkunarak sınırları zorladım. "Ormana götürsen ne olacaktı ki?" dedim bağırmaktan kısılmış çatallaşan sesimle.

Ve Aidan dudaklarını kulaklarımdan çekip gözlerime bakarken öldürücü bir şekilde gülümsedi. "Ne yapacağımı biliyorsun." Gözleri kahverengiden sıyrılıp kızıla dönerken bacaklarımın arsında bir korun yandığını hissedebiliyordum. Bazı şeylerin sırası değildi ama o sıra hiç gelemiyordu ki. Bu yüzden parmak uçlarımda kalkıp dudaklarımı dudaklarına sürdüm.

Yapış yapış kirli kan tadı benden ona geçerken Aidan elini belime attı. Konuşmak için aramıza bir nefeslik mesafe bıraktığında, "Bana hayran hayran bakman beni deli ediyor. Beni çıldırtıyor. Bu asla vazgeçemeyeceğim bir şey," dedi erkeksi sesiyle fısıldayarak. Konuşurken dudaklarıma bakıyordu. "Bana bir sözün var sevgili Cassandra." İşaret parmağını öperek temizlediği alt dudağıma sürdü. "Bu sözü en can alıcı şekilde alacağım." Dizlerim tutmuyordu, ona yaslandım. Kaslı karnıma değen şeyi başta kılıcı sanmıştım ama sonra Aidan'ın kılıç kullanmadığı aklıma gelmişti.

Göz bebeklerim büyüdü. "Beni zorluyorsun," dedim neredeyse mırıldanarak. Gözlerimi kapadım. "Hançerin bedenime batıyor." Aidan öyle içten, öyle sıcak güldü ki bedenimde ıslanmayan tek bir nokta kalmadı.

"Ben ne kılıç ne hançer kullanıyorum, benim güzel melezim."

Başım dönüyordu. Ve bunun öldürdüğüm o vampirlerle ilgisi yoktu.

"Siz ikiniz kendinize bir köşe bulun. İştahımı kaçırıyorsunuz." Aloha görüş alanıma girerken kafamı Aidan'ın kollarına daha da gömdüm. Bazen gerçek dünyadan ışınlanarak kurtulabilmek istiyordum.

Aidan başımı yavaşça tutup bedeninden ayırırken hissettiğim hayal kırıklığıyla kaşlarımı çattım. "Hepsi bitti mi? Diğerleri nerede?" diye sordum strigoiye. Artık aramızda bir metre vardı ama gözleri hâlâ kızıldı, demek ki hâlâ o da beni hissediyordu, bunu bilmenin verdiği rahatlık omuzlarıma çökerken sırtımı esnettim.

"Geliyorlar. Ha bu arada, Katze'yi sordular." Draza, uzun sivri ellerini kotuna silerek yanımıza yaklaştı. Üzerindeki ceset kokusunun geçmesi için onu çitilemek gerekecekti. Burnum sızlıyordu.

"Onlarla değil mi?" İki adam birbirine baktı. Verecek cevapları yoktu. "Aidan onu en son ne zaman gördün?"

Şeytanım bunu düşündü. "Seni haklamaya çalışan vampirin başına çökmüştü." Bir şeyler anlamsız geliyordu.

"Ne yani? Kaçırıldı mı? Katze?"

"Hayır, sanmıyorum," dedi Aloha. "Katze'yi kaçıracak kadar güçlü biri yoktu aralarında. Aslında buna biraz şaşırdım. Kuzeni Ryan'nın orada olmasını beklemiyordum."

Beynime ağrılar saplanıyordu. "Kim kim? Ne diyorsun?"

Aloha gözlerini devirdi. "Bu cehaletle nasıl hayatta kalıyorsunuz? Kraliyet ailesinden olanlarda dövme olur. Katze ile konuşan vampirin kolunda aile sembolleri vardı. Kuzeni Ryan olması muhtemel çünkü o da esmerdi. Yani biraz şu omuzlarınızın üzerindeki şeyi çalıştırsanız diyorum."

Aklımdan geçen sözler Draza'nın dudaklarından akan komik aksanıyla aramızda inledi. "Katze kaçırılmadı çünkü kendi gitti. Sanırım bir firarimiz var."

BÖLÜM 17

Max'in barındaydık.

Morgain incilerinden birini taşıdığı için artık hizmetkârım olan Max, gecenin bir vakti uykusundan uyandırılıp arka sokağa açılan kapıda karşısında kana bulanmış bir grup deliyle karşılaşmıştı. Aklını kaçırmasına tek engel olan şey ise bu delilerin içinde benim ve Meredith'in oluşuydu. Üzerindeki bisiklet desenli mavi pijamasıyla uykulu bir şekilde kapı aralığında belirdiğinde tek diyebildiği şey "Vay!" olmuştu. Sonrasındaysa kapıyı ardına kadar açıp içeri yerleşmemize izin verdi.

Aidan ve Draza insanlıktan uzaktan yakından nasibini almamış iki öküz kardeş oldukları için Max'e selam dahi vermeden barın tezgâhına yol aldılar. Max ise boynuna indirdiği tavşanlı mavi göz bandını yukarı çıkarıp dağınık sarı saçlarının ardına itti. Konuşmaya başladığında sesi uykudan kalkan herhangi sıradan bir fani gibiydi.

"Dönüşünüzün bu kadar çabuk olmasını beklemiyordum." Sarılmak için Meredith'e hamle yapınca kız kardeşim geri çekildi. Kanların kurumaya başladığını tişörtünü parmağıyla çekiştirip, "Vampir pisliğine bulanmak istemiyorsan bence bana dokunma," dedi zoraki bir gülümsemeyle. Max iki elini teslim olmuş gibi kaldırdı. "Hepiniz saatlerce yıkanmaya ihtiyacınız var gibi görünüyorsunuz. Bir tek şu çocuk temiz." Manikürlü tırnaklarıyla odanın bir köşesinde Marcus'a çantasından çıkardığı eşyaları veren Urange'ı işaret etti. Haklıydı, peri gerçekten de tertemizdi.

"O tüm aksiyon boyunca tepede durup büyü kesesi fırlattı. Ama kese derken sevimli bir şey bekleme. Vampirlerin üzerine düştüğü an organlarını eritip patlatıyor." Ağzımı açıp parmağımı sokar gibi yaptım. Yüzüm şekilden şekle girerken Max'in bir gözü seğirir gibi oldu.

"Şu ufak şey mi insanları patlattı. Psikopat bir civciv ha?"

Meredith tezgâhtan aldığı havluya saçlarını siliyordu. "Civciv, periler için kullanmayı seçtiğimiz sözcüklerden biri değil. Parlak diyebilirsin. Bu onlara nedense küfür gibi geliyor." Durup kendi kişisel zorbalığına güldü. "Öte yandan kafileyi tanıtayım sana. Şu hâlâ kapı aralığında duran sessiz herif var ya, o Aloha. İçeri davet edilmeden giremez ve açıkçası davet etmesek daha iyi olur." Dirseğimle Meredith'in yumuşak karnına vurdum. "Zorbalığını başkalarında kullan. Aloha bizden biri. Ve Max onu içeri davet edecek."

Max'in kararsız mavi gözleri benim ile kapı aralığındaki gölge arasında gidip geldi. "Öyle mi yapacağım? Biraz tekinsiz duruyor Cass." Omuz silktim. "Geri kalanımız da rahibeler topluluğu değil, ayrıca sen benim hizmetkârımsın falan, bu yüzden hadi git ve davet et onu." Max bir kez daha kapıya bakınca kaşlarımı çattım. "Max, hadi. İnan bana o çok değer verdiğin şehrinde sokaklarda başıboş yarı deli bir strigoinin gezmesini istemezsin." Max aurası kararmış bir hâlde sırtını kamburlaştırarak kapıya yöneldiğinde Meredith'e döndüm.

"Kendini çok zeki sanıyorsun değil mi?" Kız kardeşim sorumu duymazdan gelerek turuncu saçlarına yapışmış parçalı kan öbeklerini havluya silmeye devam etti. Kollarımı göğsümde kavuşturup gözlerimi kısarak onu süzmeye başladım. "Neredeydin?" Meredith saçlarının yarısı artık rengi bombok olan sarı havlunun içindeyken başını kaldırıp bana baktı. Yeşil gözlerinde bir şeyler mi titreşmişti yoksa ben artık halüsinasyonlar da mı görüyordum emin değildim. "Ne demek neredeydin? Sizinleydim." Arkamda bir hareketlilik olunca omzumun üzerinden gelenlere baktım. Max, Aloha'yı içeri davet etmiş, sahnenin hemen önündeki masaya yönlendirmişti. Oturması için masanın üzerindeki ters dönmüş sandalyeleri indirmeye başladığında tekrar cadıya döndüm. "Bak, kız kardeş. Burada kıçını tek kollayan benim. İnsanlar sana güvenmiyor ve onları suçlayamazsın bile. Şu an hayatta sana güvenen tek kıza bakıyorsun ve yalan söylüyorsun. Bana yalan söylersen sana nasıl güvenmeye devam edebilirim?"

Kız kardeşim sözümü kesmedi. Hareketleri konuşmamın sonuna geldiğimde yavaşlayıp durmuştu. Kararsız bakışlarında titreşen belirli belirsiz korku beni durduğum yere mıhladı. Meredith çok hayat yaşamıştı, belki bu diyarda değil ama başka diyarlarda seneleri devirmişti ve tecrübelerime dayanarak söylüyorum söz konusu şey benim vereceğim son nefes değilse Meredith'i hiçbir şey kolay kolay korkutamazdı. "Bak, bana güven, tamam mı? Evet, bu belki zor bir şey ama şu kalın kafalılar beni anlamaz." Durup diğerlerine baktı. "Ama sen anlarsın," dedi tekrar bana döndüğünde. "Her anlamda yanındaydım, sadece bu kez bana güven. Kötü bir şeyler yapmıyorum Cass."

Başparmağımla kendi gözlerimi oymak istediğim nadide anlardan birini yaşıyordum.

"İyi de kime göre kötü Merr? Durduğumuz şu noktaya bir bak. Bana iyinin ve kötünün net bir tanımını yapabilir misin?" Kardeşim yanıt vermek için kan kırmızısı dudaklarını yavaşça araladı. Sonra vazgeçti. Tekrar konuşmaya karar vermeden önce kanlı tişörtünün göğsünü şişirerek oldukça bıkkın, derin bir nefes aldı. "Bilmesen daha iyi. Dertlerine bir yenisini daha eklemek istemiyorum. Hem çok yakında kaçınılmaz bir şekilde öğreneceksin, şu an için sadece işimize odaklanalım, sonra..." Sözünü bitiremeden dirseğini tuttum. Kendime bakmaya zorlarken hafifçe sarstım onu. "Birilerinin hayatı tehlikede mi?" Bilmecelerden de söz oyunlarından da ve altüst olmuş dünyamın karanlık gizemli olaylarından da bıkmıştım. Artık karşıma bir dinozor çıkacak olsa bile bunu bilmek istiyordum. Birilerinin bana, "Hey Cass, arkanda bir Tiranozor var ve oldukça aç görünüyor," deyip beni uyarmasını istiyordum. Korku filmlerinin klasik sahnelerindeki şapşal kızlar gibi tehlike kıçımda, bitene kadar arkamı dönmeyip son saniye biri tarafından dişlenerek can vermek istemiyordum.

Kardeşim hızla başını sağa sola salladı. "Hayır. Öyle olsa sana söylerdim. Bana güven, nasıl olsa her şeyin masaya yatırılacağı o gün gelecek. Şimdilik sadece kız kardeşine güven ve bırak kendi kontrolümde olan şeylerle ben ilgileneyim." Parmaklarını kolunu kavrayan elimin üzerine koydu. Konuşmaya başladığında gözlerinde anlayışlı bir ifade geziniyordu. "Kendini çok fazla yoruyorsun. Artık kraliçe değilsin. Her şeyi sen düzene sokamazsın Cassie. Evren düşündüğün kadar basit işlemiyor. Biraz mola ver." O an onunla konuşmayı özlediğimi fark ettim. Bu kulağa ne kadar normal geliyordu bilmiyordum ama onunla geçirdiğim zaman boyunca Meredith benim en yakın değil tek dostum olmuştu. Ve bu beni başka bir probleme taşıdı.

"Sayımızda bir eksiklik göze çarpıyor mu?" diye sordum en yakındaki sandalyeye kendimi bırakırken. Bir bacağımı diğerinin üzerine koyup çizmemin iplerini çözmeye başladım. Cadı tam karşıma yerleşirken başını salyangoz gibi uzatıp kafilemizi inceledi. "Hayır, tüm kaçıklar burada gibi. Hey, bekle. Benim ezeli rakibim dışındaki herkes burada." Çizmemin birini çıkarıp ayak parmaklarımı oynatırken ne dediğini anlamaya çalıştım. "Urange'ı mı diyorsun? O da şurada." Meredith başını sağa sola sallayıp kendini beğenmiş bir ifadeyle dirseklerini arkasındaki masaya koyarak gerindi. "Bir peri benim rakibim olamaz. Vampiri diyorum. Senin arkadaşlığın söz konusu olduğunda benimle ciddi bir rekabete giriyor."

Kahkaha ağzımdan kaçarken onu tutmaya çalıştım ama çok geçti. Ben boğulur gibi sesler çıkarırken Aidan bana bakıyordu. Bu mesafeden ne düşündüğünü anlamak zordu ama muhtemelen balataları sıyırdığıma kanaat getiriyordu.

"Yani Merr, nasıl desem bilemedim. Ben öyle arkadaşlığı için rekabete tutulacak bir insan değilim." Diğer ayakkabıyı da çıkarıp çoraplı parmaklarımı zeminde yan yana getirip hareket ettirerek esnettim. Meredith nihayet havluyu masaya koyarken suratındaki o kendini beğenmiş ifade olduğu gibi duruyordu. "Kendini kıymetli bir şey sanma. Neyse, bu ego sana birkaç gün yeter. Yenilemek istediğinde haber verirsin." Sırıttım. Belimdeki hançeri çıkarıp sonra temizlenmek üzere masaya koydum. "Katze çatışmanın ortasında kayboldu. Sen de görmedin değil mi?"

Kız kardeşim, "Hayır," dedi tereddütle, sonrasında dirseğini dizine koyup başını ellerine yasladı. "Onu düşündüğümden değil ama ortalık fena hâlde karışacak gibi."

"Eğer yarına kadar ortaya çıkmazsa endişelenmeye başlayacağım. Şimdilik sadece dinleneceğim. O büyük bir kız. Başının çaresine bakabilir." Kendimi sandalyemde geriye itip gözlerimi kapadım. Beynimin içini yoğurmuşlar, üstüne limonu sıkmışlar, sonra da limonun yeterli gelmeyeceğini düşünüp dev bir ayvayı püre yapıp ezmişler gibi hissediyordum. Ağrıyan uzuvlarıma mı yoksa bunu daha ne kadar devam ettireceğimizin kesin olmayışına mı yanmalıydım, bilmiyordum. Tek bildiğim artık eskisi gibi hissetmediğimdi. Yaşlanıyordum, yorgundum. Uyumama gerek olmamasına rağmen uyuyordum ve yorgunluğum asla geçmiyordu. Bu ruh yorulmuştu işte, kim ne derse desin.

Marcus ve Urange cesetleri toplayıp ıssız bir yerde yakmaya götüreli birkaç saat geçmişti. Bu süre boyunca Aloha'yı, Katze'yi araması için dışarı yollamıştık ama bulamamıştı. Marcus'a ise söylememiştik. Sinir krizi geçirip bizi deşmesi riskini göze alamamıştık. Şimdilik kız arkadaşının döneceğini beklediğimize inanması gerekiyordu.

Sıcak bir duş alıp saçlarımı tarayarak daha normal birine benzemek için biraz çabalamıştım. Diğerleri de benzer şeyler yaptıktan sonra aşağıda, Max'in tezgâhında buluşmuştuk. Barmen her birimize dörder shot koymuştu.

Elime bardaklardan birini alıp çevirirken Katze'nin nereye gidebileceğini düşünüyordum.

"Onu içmeyeceksen alabilir miyim?"

"Al senin olsun." Draza elimdeki bardağı alıp kafasına dikti. Aidan da bardaklarına dokunmamıştı, düşünceli bir ifadeyle tezgâhtaki yansımasına bakıyordu. Henüz birkaç saat önce kucağına atlamak üzere olduğum gerçeği ile saç diplerim alev alıyordu.

"Eee Max," dedi başını daldığı düşüncelerden kaldırıp, "dünyada işler nasıl?" Barmen Aidan'ın bu sıradan sorusunu yanıtlamak için düşünmedi. "Süper. Müşteriler iyi. Her zamankinden daha doluyuz."

"Diğer çalışanlar nerede?" Sorumu sorduktan sonra kalkıp Aidan'ın yanındaki bar taburesine oturdum. Şeytanım ben yanına oturunca kolunu omzuma attı. Ondan yayılan güven verici ısı sayesinde istemeden de olsa sırttım.

"Sen ve Meredith gittikten sonra ne bok yediğimi bilmek istiyorsun herhâlde. İki yeni çocuğu işe aldım. Bugünlük yoklar, gönderdim. Senin aksine ben çalışanlarımın canına değer veriyorum." Mavi gözleri memnuniyetsizce etrafta gezdirdi. "Kaç gün kalacaksınız burada?"

"Misafirperverliğin için teşekkürler Max." Sesimdeki alaycılığa gözlerini devirdi. Aidan'ın kolunun bedenimi daha sert sarması ona bakmama sebep oldu. İfadesi değişmişti, biraz öfkeli gibiydi. Yakıcı bakışları altında ezilip büzülmemeye çalıştım. Kafam karışmıştı. Max'in ise bir şeyden haberi yoktu. Elindeki viski bardağını kurulamak için takıntılı bir şekilde bezi tekrar tekrar çeviriyordu. "Yanlış anlamayın, size bayılıyorum, sadece burası böyle leş gibi kan koktuğu sürece müşterilerim ardına bakmadan kaçar. Ve ben de aç kalırım. Birilerinin hâlâ para kazanması lazım." Parlak bir gülümseme sunduktan sonra arkasını dönüp kaldığı yerden işe koyuldu.

Aidan hâlâ yüzüme bakıyordu. Kolumdaki sıcak tutuşu birazcık daha sertleşmişti ama yüzünde öyle bir ifade vardı ki ne yaptığını bildiğinden emin değildim. Şaşkınlıkla ona bakarken şeytanım hafifçe üzerime eğildi. Boynundan yayılan baharat kokusu hücrelerime dolarken sadece kokusuyla bile sarhoş olabildiğimi fark ettim. "Ben yokken Max ile neler yaptınız?" diye sordu fısıltı hâlinde.

Vay canına! Şeytanım beni kıskanmıştı.

Bu öyle absürt bir soruydu ki suratına bakmaktan başka yanıt veremedim.

Oysa Max güldü.

Ve bu Aidan için hiç iyi olmadı. Kolunu sırtımdan çekip Max'in boğazına sarıldı. Yere düşen bardaklar büyük bir şangırtı koparırken arkada bir yerlerde Draza'nın memnun kahkahası yankılandı. Kaotik herif!

Yerimden fırlayarak araya girmeye çalıştım. "Dur! Ne yapıyorsun? Aidan, çek elini." Ama Aidan çekmedi. Max yanıt veremiyordu çünkü nefesi kesiliyordu. Barmeni tezgâha dayamış boynunu sıkıyordu. Bedeninden öyle bir öfke akıyordu ki ne yapacağımı bilemedim.

"Ben cennette melekçilik oynarken sen gördüğün her erkeğin kucağına mı atlıyordun?"

"Saçmalama!" Nasıl böyle düşünürdü? Aidan bir şey söylemeden barmenin boğazını sıkmaya devam etti. Elimle koluna dokunarak onu Max'den ayırmaya çalıştım. "Çek elini dedim."

"Gel de dene," dedi iblis sıkılı dişleri arasından. Ve denedim. Var gücümle onu itip Max'i tezgâhın diğer tarafına yuvarladım. "Kendine gel iblis!" Önüne geçip ona bağırdım. "Kimsenin kucağına çıkmadım seni salak! Sen tam bir aptalsın."

Aidan kızgın bir boğa gibi nefes alıyordu. Gözleri hâlâ toparlanmaya çalışan Max'teydi. "Dünyada ne halt ettiğini kim bilir? Çok uzun bir süre yoktum. Bu salakla neler yaptın? Sen bir şeytansın. İhtiyaçların olmuştur ve elbette onları karşılayacak birileri." Yumruk yaptığı elini tezgâha vurunca tezgâhın zemini çıtırdadı. Kocaman bir yarık oluşup üzerindeki votka şişesini devirdi. Şimdi bir kez daha büyük bir şangırtı kopmuştu. Evrende hâlâ bizi duymayan birkaç fani varsa bile çoktan uykuyu bırakıp ayaklanmışlardı.

Aidan yere tükürdü. Ben de sövdüm. "Kimseyle bir şey yapmadım! Senden nefret ediyorum." İki elimle göğsünü itip arkamı döndüm. Merdivenleri uçarak çıkarken gözlerim yanıyordu. Aptal kızlar gibi ağlamayacaktım. Ağlamayacaktım. Ama yukarı varıp kapıyı arkamdan kapattığımda sırtımı kapıya yaslayıp gözlerimi kapadım.

Akmayacağından emin olduğum bir damla yaş yanaklarımı ıslatınca sessizce sövdüm. Nasıl böyle düşünürdü?

***

Avucuma aldığım kırık camı sımsıkı tuttum. Sıcak kan, parmaklarımın arasından parke zemine damlarken huzuru bulmaya çalıştım ama bu imkânsızdı. Cassie yukarıdaydı ve yanına gidemezdim. Aptalca bir şey yapmamaya çalışırken aptalca şeyler yapmıştım. Her zamanki ben.

Barmen saklandığı yerden yavaşça başını çıkarınca göz göze geldik. "O haklı. O benim kardeşim gibi," dedi kekeleyerek. Ve bu daha iyi hissettirse de bir yandan her şeyi bombok ettiğimi kanıtlıyordu. Max yakışıklıydı ve benim Cassie'nin bir erkekte aradığı özellikler hakkında hiçbir fikrim yoktu. Onu sadece benimleyken tanıyabilmiştim ve bu kaderin enteresan ağları yüzünden bölünüp durmuştu. Yine de ben burada yokken Cassie'nin dünyada gezinmiş olma fikri kanıma dokunuyordu.

"Siktir git!"

Barmen ikiletmedi. Saklandığı yerden kalkıp tökezleyerek de olsa kendini dışarı attı. Başımı kaldırıp yukarı baktım. Üst kattaydı. Onu tutup zorla getirip ve tokatlayarak kendimi dinletebilirdim. Tabii bu melezim dışında herkeste işi yarayabilirdi, onda değil. O lanet bir kızdı. Dinlemek istemezse dinlemezdi işte, ölmek üzereyken karşımda güçsüz bir şekilde ödünç nefesiyle bile dikilirken çenesini yukarıda tutmuştu Cassie. "Bana fare deme şeytan," demişti gururlu bir ifadeyle. Midem düğümleniyor gibiydi ve bu çok boktan bir histi.

Draza boğazını temizleyince tek kaşımı kaldırıp ona baktım. İki elini kaldırıp masumca konuşmaya başladı. "Yanlış anlama kızı sevdiğimden değil ama o, böyle biri değil." Draza'nın Cassie'yi savunmasına mı yoksa onun bile sevdiğim kızı tanırken benim tanımayışıma mı yanmalıydım bilemiyordum.

Elf kalçasını masaya yaslayıp kibar elindeki parmaklarına baktı. O kadar kaygısız görünüyordu ki onu kıskandım. "Yani sen olsan boş durmazdın ama o senin kadar şerefsiz değil."

"Teşekkürler Draza. Beni utandırıyorsun." Cassie bana öküz diyordu ama ben öküzsem Draza'yı tanımlayacak kelime ne olabilirdi? O beyaz suratındaki morarmış elf dudaklarından hayırlı bir kelimeyi ne zaman duyacaktım ben?

"Kendine acı diye demedim Aidan. Gönül işlerin ayak bağı olmasın bize. Sen burada evcilik oynarken ejderhalar orada başarısız olursak bizi nasıl ejder çorbası yapacaklarını konuşuyorlar. Git bir yer bul ve çiftleş. Sen de o da rahatlasın."

Tek kaşımı kaldırarak soluk renkli suratına baktım. "Ejder çorbası diye bir şey yok. Ayrıca sırf ben istiyorum diye sevişemeyiz. Onun da istemesi… Ya ben neden seninle bunu konuşuyorum ki?" Bir küfür savurup başımı ellerimin arasına aldım.

Düşünceler birbiri ardına zehirli bir yılan gibi zihnime kıvrılarak buldukları her oyuğa doluyorlardı. Bir çuval incir ve berbat etme deyimi benim için bulunmuştu. Kardeşim gerinirken gözlerim masanın iç karartıcı deseninden Draza'nın karanlık dipsiz kuyuyu andıran gözlerine kaydı. "Çünkü ben Draza'yım. Herkes Draza'yı sever. Draza akıllıdır. Sizin gibi sikik romantik şeylerin peşinde koşmaz. Draza kadınların bir yanılsamadan ibaret olduğunu bilir. Pipisini alıp yollara düşmez."

Ona tam en güzelinden bir yanıt vermek için ağzımı açtığımda iri yarı kurt ve peri içeri girdi. Yağmura yakalanmış komik tipleri ile barmenin az önce deli gibi sildiği yerleri çamurladılar. Bundan sapıkça bir zevk aldım.

"Katze nerede?" Marcus yerdeki cam kırıklarına bakıp gür sarı kaşlarını çattı. Onunla Cassie arasında bir benzerlik bulma çalışmalarım tüylerinin sarılığını görünce sonlanıyordu. Lilith'deki yumurtalıkların saklanması gerekiyordu, bir kızıl bir siyah bir de sarışın doğurmuştu. Kadın sürprizlerle doluydu.

"Konuşmalıyız." Elimin tersiyle yanımdaki taburenin üzerindeki cam kırıklarını silkeledim. Oturmasını işaret ettim. Kurt tereddütlü bir ifadeyle yaklaşıp yanıma oturdu. Peri ise yukarı çıkmaya başlamıştı. Gözlerim merdivenleri çıkan perideyken konuşmaya başladım. "Katze'nin geri döneceğini umut ediyorduk ama gelmedi. Aloha şu an onu arıyor. Biri sana bahsetti mi bilmiyorum ama savaş alanında neredeyse Ryan adında bir çocuğun bağırsaklarından kolye yapacaktık ve öğrendik ki Katze'nin kuzeniymiş." Herhangi bir yanıt vermeyince konuşmaya devam ettim. "Yine de Aloha bugün onu bulamazsa yarın geleceğini düşünüyoruz. Kuzeni bir strigoi. Bir yerde ona yardım etmeye çalıştığından eminim."

Marcus sessizdi. Fazla sessizdi.

Sonra kurt derin bir nefes alıp sertçe tezgâha vurdu. Hızla ayağa kalkıp taburesini tekmeledi ve bir hışım bardan çıktı.

Az önce mağara adamı edasıyla tepinirken ben de böyle budala gibi mi görünmüştüm?

***

Urange odama girip kapıyı arkasından kilitlediğinde yere çömelmiş kendime üzülüyordum. Bir melez ya da insan, birinin bazen içinde sürüklendiği bilinmezlikte kaybolup kendine acıması doğaldı. Urange'ın düzensiz nefes sesleri odada yankılanırken varoluşsal sancılarımdan arınmaya çalıştım. Peri çocuk kilitlediği kapının önünde yüzünde gergin bir ifadeyle dikiliyordu. Sırılsıklamdı.

"Selam," dedim elimi kaldırıp gelmesini işaret ederek. Urange kıpırdamadı. Aksine diyeceği şeyi düşünüyor gibiydi. "Cassie, fazla zamanımız yok. Başımız belâda." Elini artık ıslandığı için çok daha koyu olan yeşil ceketinin cebine atıp bir kâğıt çıkardı. Yanıma gelerek kâğıdı uzattı. Yerimden kalkıp eline uzandım. "Bu nedir?"

"Okusan iyi olur." Kâğıtta kocaman harflerle tek bir sözcük yazıyordu. "Kaçın!"

"Bunu kim verdi?"

Peri çocuk ince dudaklarını büzdü. "Sanırım Katze verdi. Emin değilim. Savaş alnındayken biri cebime sıkıştırdı. Ama o vermiş olmalı. O hengâmede bana tek değen oydu."

Kaçın...

İyi de neden? "Yani Katze kaçmamızı istiyor ama sebep belirtmiyor."

"Belki de sebep belirtecek vakti yoktu." İri yeşil gözlerini gözlerime dikti. Katze bizim fark edemediğimiz neyi fark etmiş olabilirdi ki?

"Buradan gitmemiz gerekiyor, herkesi toplayalım." Kilitlediği kapıyı açıp kendimi merdivenlere attım. Duvarın bittiği yerde gözlerim ilk Aidan'ı gördü, bana bakıyordu. Bakışlarımı kaçırdım ve Draza'nın yanına doğru yol aldım. Sesli bir şekilde olanları anlattım. Marcus ses çıkarmadan dış kapının aralığından beni dinlemişti. Canı sıkkındı, benim de canım sıkkındı, en yakın zamanda dostumdan haber almak istiyordum. "Max nerede?" Aidan sanki bu önemsizmiş gibi eli ile havayı yokladı. "Bir süre buralara uğrayacağını sanmıyorum."

"Yine de ona bir not bırakmalıyım." Tam kalem kâğıt arayacakken cep telefonu olduğunu hatırladım ama Max'in bende numarası yoktu, bu yüzden tekrar kalem aramaya koyuldum. Tezgâhın üzerine kâğıdı yapıştırarak üzerine kocaman harflerle '*Kaç ve sakın gelme! Tatil yap.*' yazdım.

Yanıma alacağım pek eşyam yoktu, buraya avlanmaya gelmiştik ama av olacaktık ve kim bizi avlayacaktı bilmiyordum.

"Hadi hazırlanın gidelim." Marcus istifini bozmadı, Urange ise aceleyle üstünü değiştirmek için tuvalete doğru giden koridorda gözden kayboldu. Aloha, Draza ve Aidan ise hareketlenmişlerdi. Meredith sırt çantasını hazırlayıp sırtına geçirdikten sonra saçlarını ensesinde topladı. "O Valkürler şimdi işimize yarayabilirdi. Neden ormanda bıraktık ki?" Bir yandan kemerindeki küçük iksir şişelerinin kapaklarını kontrol ediyor, diğer yandan bana vızıldıyordu. "Onlar savaşçı. Bir kemirgen ordusu karşısında onlara ihtiyacımız var."

Elime geçen gerekli gereksiz her şeyi çantamın içine sığsınlar diye bastırarak tıkıyordum. "Toprağa yakın olmak istediler. Bu beton yığınlarının içinde o kadınları düşünemiyorum. Ayrıca kanatlı atlarını da unutma. Düşünsene, şu arka sokakta o kanatlı atı gören her fani altına yapardı ve şehir boktan geçilmezdi." Meredith umursamazca omuz silkti.

Marcus hırlayınca hepimiz kapıya döndük. Barın dörtte üçü sayısız çirkin sticker yapıştırılmış, camlı, eski kapısı açılırken üzerindeki zil öttü. Gelenin Max olduğunu görünce ayaklandım. Elinde az önce kapıya yapıştırdığım, üzerinde sarı bandıyla yazdığım not vardı. Notu çantamın durduğu masaya bırakırken mavi gözlerini kocaman açtı. "Gerçekten mi? Tatil mi?" dedi hayretler içinde. Rahatsızca kıpırdandım. "Seni tehlikeye atamam Max. Çok yakında burası kafayı yemiş vampirlerle dolacak. Zaten yeterince bu işin içindesin, hem biraz ara vermiş olursun."

Max sinirli bir şekilde güldü. Konuşmadan önce içini henüz doldurduğum çantanın kollarından birini parmağına doluyordu. Bakışları bende değildi, bilerek temas kurmuyordu. "Buranın kirasını cehennemdeki iblisler ya da cennetin melekleri ödemeyecek, öyle kafama her estiğinde tatile ayrılamam, ayrıca dediğin gibi bu işin içindeyim. Bana sadece kendimi nasıl koruyacağımı söyle. Ben de burada kalayım. Zamanı geldiğinde gelip kalabilmeniz için burayı koruyayım Cass."

Tuttuğu nefesini yorgunlukla bıraktı. "Sana kendini korumayı bu kadar kısa zamanda öğretemem. Ben bile bazen yapamıyorum." Max'in bakışları diğerlerine kayınca aceleyle ekledim. "Onlar daha yaşlı olabilir ama inan bana onlar da bazen kendilerini koruyamıyor." Arkamda bir yerden öfkeli bir hırıltı duyunca Marcus olduğunu anladım.

"Bu inciler beni korumaz mı?" Dövmesini gösterecek şekilde içini çevirdiği bileğine baktım. Uzanıp dövmesine dokunurken boşta kalan elimi omzuna yerleştirdim. "Bu seni ölümsüze yakın bir şey yapıyor. Onun dışında başın belâya girerse dövmelerim canıma okuyarak senin başının belâda olduğunu hissettirecekler. Unutma, gördüğün en ufak tehlikeli şeyde buradan tüy, tamam mı?"

Max parmaklarımın altındaki kolunu hızla çekip koşar adım tezgâhına gitti. Üzerinden uzanıp bir şey aldı. Kâğıda numarasını yazıp elime tutuşturdu. "Pekâlâ. Eski usul şeyleri sevdiğinizi biliyorum, şu dövme yanması filan ama artık teknoloji gelişti ve… Her neyse işte, beni ara. Burada sizi bekliyor olacağım," dedi aceleyle. Telefonumu arka cebimden çıkarıp çantama atarak fermuarı çektim. Sırtıma taktından sonra Max'in karşısında üzgünce durdum. Vedalardan nefret etmeme rağmen neden hep başıma geliyordu? Vedalaşmak için özel olarak lanetlenmiş miydim? Lilith böyle bir şey yapsaydı hiç şaşırmazdım.

Hizmetkârım boynuma sarılınca ben de kollarımı sırtına doladım. "Üstümü başımı sümük etme. Belki yarın gece dönmüş oluruz. Tehlikeyi öğrenelim de önce." Max bedenimden yavaşça ayrılırken üzgün gözlerini birkaç kez kırptı. "Düşündüğünden güçlüyüm," dedi üzgün bir tebessümle. "Hadi gidin ve dünyayı kurtarın. Ben burada olacağım." Ondan uzaklaşıp kafileme seslendim, hepimiz kapıdan art arda çıkıp sokağın karşısına geçtik.

"Bir koku alıyorum," dedi Marcus şok tabancısıyla dürtülmüş gibi aniden dururken. Draza da havayı koklamaya başlayınca belimdeki hançeri çıkardım. "Arkamda dur," dedim Meredith'e. Cadı ikiletmeden arkama geçti. Aidan ise bir anda önümde bitmişti. "Bir koku var," dedi o da tıpkı Marcus gibi robotik bir sesle. Urange burnuna biraz toz çekip yerden birkaç metre havalandı. Duvara yakın duruyor, sürünerek ilerliyordu. Bir dakika sonra kaybolduğu karanlıktan geri geldi. "Bize notu yazan kişiyi buldum sanırım," dedi eliyle karanlığı gösterirken. Sonra tepeden Marcus'a baktı. "Hayır, Katze değil, üzgünüm." Erkek kardeşimin omuzları hayal kırıklığıyla çökerken elimi koluna koydum. "Halledeceğiz. Biliyorsun, hep hallettik." Marcus yanıtlamadı.

"Ee, kimmiş peki? Ya da neymiş? Araftaki devlerden biri deme sakın, gerçekten artık kalbim bu tempoyu kaldıramıyor." Urange yanımıza doğru hafifçe süzülürken yüzündeki ifadeyi çözmeye çalıştım. "Emin değilim. Bir insan sanırım." Sonra adımları yere değdi. Omzunun üzerinden karanlığa bakıp, "Öğrenmenin tek bir yolu var," dedi.

En önde ben ve Aidan, hemen arkamızda birbiriyle çok iyi anlaştıkları için Draza ve Meredith. Güvenli bir mesafeden çember oluşturabilelim diye yanlarda Aloha ve Marcus ile ilerliyorduk. Urange, az önceki gibi duvarların dibinden kayarak ilerliyordu.

Perinin bahsettiği yere gelince Meredith sırt çantasından fenerini çıkarıp tam karşımıza tuttu. Işık gözlerine değince bir kız elini kahverengi saçlarının önüne siper etti. "Yüzüme tutmasan olur mu Meredith?" Cadı şaşkınlıktan neredeyse feneri düşürecekti. Işığı kapatıp koluma yapıştı. "Kim olduğunu bilen var mı?" diye sordu sessizce. Kafileden yanıt gelmeyince karşımızdaki kız konuştu. Endişeden büyümüş ela gözleri üzerimde gezinirken elinin tersiyle burnunu kaşıdı. "Beni tanımıyorsunuz ama ben hepinizi tanıyorum. Sizi uyarmaya geldim."

Arkamda bir yerlerde Draza gülünce kızın endişeli ifadesi silindi. "Tanımadığımız birine güvenmeye bayılırız. Bak Aloha'ya sor. En son tanımadığı birine güvendiğinde her şey ne kadar da yolunda gitti, değil mi?" dedi alayla. Yanıt olarak Aloha sertçe hırladı ve karşımdaki kız tıpkı benim yapacağımı yapıp gözlerini devirdi.

"Pekâlâ, gençler. Gün batımına kadar hayatta kalmak istiyorsanız beni dinleyeceksiniz."

Çenemi dikleştirdim. "Sen kimsin ki seni dinleyelim?" Kahverengi saçlı kız çapraz taktığı çantasını düzeltip kibarca gülümsedi. Gözlerindeki bir şey beni biraz tedirgin etmişti. O her kimse bir kurdun, perinin, iblislerin ve siyah gözlü kara elfin karşısında durmasından korkmuyor gibiydi. Deli gibi bir şey olmalıydı ve deli birini görünce tedirgin olmak doğaldı.

"Ben Gaye," dedi ela gözlü kız. "Sizinle tanıştığıma çok memnun oldum."

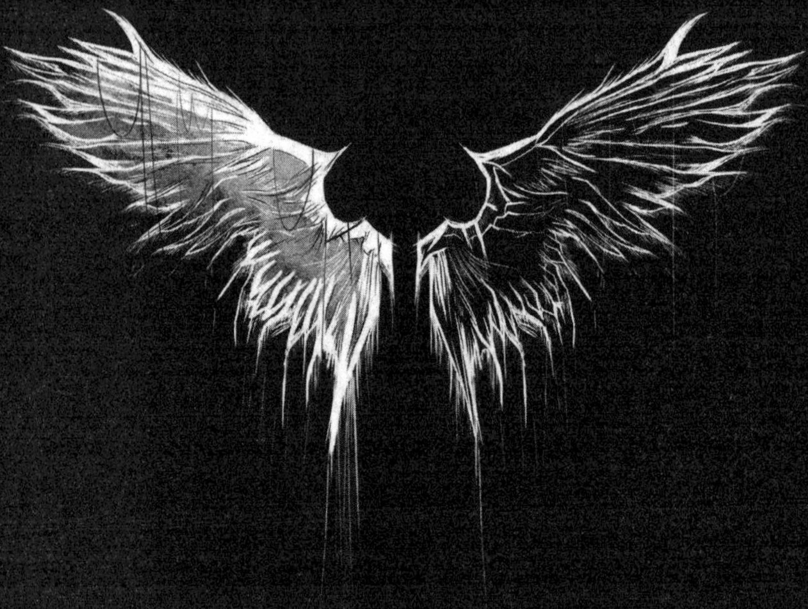

"Bir kız ağladı, bir kurt uludu
ve bir çocuk doğdu hiçlikten.
Ve hile yaptı ait olmayan kişi
saklandığı yerden."

BÖLÜM 18

Bir süre kimse konuşmadı.

Karşımızdaki kız, küçük ela gözlerini tek tek üzerimizde gezdirirken hepimiz egzotik bir hayvanmışçasına onu inceliyorduk. Gaye'nin meraklı bakışları her saniye odağını değiştiriyordu. Hangimizin daha tehlikeli olduğunu kavramaya çalışır gibiydi, aurası tedirginlikle dolup taşmıştı.

"Bunun bizim için bir anlam mı ifade etmesi gerekiyor?" Konuşan Draza olmuştu. Her zamanki gibi o soluk uğursuz dudaklarını aralamış ve insanı sinir eden kayıtsızlığıyla konuşmaya başlamıştı. Eğer bir şirketseniz ve halkla ilişkiler uzmanınız Draza ise, şirket daha açılmadan batardı. Net.

"Bence öldürelim gitsin." Kara elf arkamdan sıyrılıp bir anda önüme geçti. Kızın bakışlarında bir değişiklik olmayınca uzanıp elfin koluna dokundum. "Bekle. Bize yardımcı olacağını söyledi. Dinlemekten zarar gelmez." Kız hâlâ bize bakarken diğerlerine döndüm. "Aidan da benimle gelsin, avcıyla konuşacağız. Geri kalanınız beklesin. Urange, sen Draza ile çatıya çık, gelen giden için gözcülük yapın." Draza bir an karşı çıkacak gibi olduysa da bir şey demedi. Arkasını dönüp gruptan birkaç adım uzaklaştıktan sonra kanatlarını açıp göğe yükseldi. Meredith ve Marcus hoşnutsuz bakışlarını gizlemeden dikilmeye devam ettiler. Marcus'un aklındaki tek şey Katze'ydi ve onu suçlayamazdım. Sabırsızlığını anlıyordum.

Tekrar önüme döndüğümde Aidan'ın kızı incelediğini gördüm. Aidan'ı artık tanıyordum, Gaye'den hoşlanmamıştı. Ve ben tam bu durum için çıkarım yapacakken zihnime konuştu.

Onda yolunda olmayan bir şeyler var.

Diğer avcılar kadar kaçık. Avcıların genelinde yolunda olmayan şeyler var Aidan.

Hayır, dedi iblisim. *Onda farklı bir şey var.*

Derin bir nefes alıp kıza baktım. "Gel, beraber yürüyelim." Gaye başını yavaşça sallayıp ellerini belinde birleştirdi. "Çok vaktim yok. Buraya gizli geldim. Hemen dönmem gerekiyor." Aidan'dan hoş olmayan bir homurtu yükselince gözlerimi devirdim. *Biraz daha medeni ol.* Şeytanım omuz silkmekle yetindi.

Avcının yanına yaklaşıp üzerini koklamaya çalıştım. Aşinası olduğum kokularla karşılaşamayınca kafam karıştı. "Burnundan çıkan nefesi hissediyorum Cassandra ve evet, ben normal kokmuyorum."

"Tam adımı nereden biliyorsun?" Varlıkların içinde insan ya da değil, kendinden olmayanlara karşı bir tepki oluşurdu. Sizden farklı bir canlı gördüğünüzde ilk tepkiniz onu bağrınıza basmak değil, boğazını parçalamak oluyordu. Bu yüzden kimsenin doğru düzgün bilmediği tam adımı söyleyen yabancı kıza kötü kötü bakıyordum.

"Pek çok şey biliyorum," dedi kız net bir dille. Gözleri şeytanıma kaydı. "Onun hakkında da oldukça şey biliyorum. Sorun şu ki bunları benim bilmemin pek bir önemi yok. Ben size zarar vermem ama herkes böyle düşünmüyor olabilir." Aidan alaylı bir şekilde gülünce kız ona döndü. "İnanmıyor olabilirsin ama sizin hayatlarınıza değer veriyorum." Aidan'ın bembeyaz dişleri dudaklarını süslerken iblis bir kez daha alayla güldü. Bu seferki kahkahası diğerinden daha sivriydi.

"Bir avcı bizim hayatımızı önemsemez, küçük kız. Zamanın olmadığını söylüyorsun, o hâlde anlatmaya başla."

Gaye tıpkı benim gün içinde çevremdeki deliler yüzünden bin kez yaptığım gibi gözlerini devirdi. "Aranızdaki en iyi konuşmacının Aidanhell olduğunu söyleyemem," dedikten sonra bana daha da yaklaştı. "Yıkım getirenler eskisinden daha güçlü. Kibirli olup görmezden gelebilirsin ama yerinde olsam bunun önemli olduğunu düşünürdüm. Avcılar dinlerini değiştiriyorlar, artık herkes yıkım getiren oluyor. Dinlerin insan beyni için ne denli etkili olduğunu bilirsin." Durup ela gözlerini kocaman açarak bana baktı. İfadesindeki çaresizlik, Aidan ve Draza'nın alaylı sözcüklerini yutup gidiyordu. Kız sözlerine derinden inanıyordu ve annemin henüz küçük bir kızken bana dediği gibi *-benim küçük kâhinim-* hislerim doğru söylediği yönündeydi.

"Herkes yıkım getiren olamaz. Ayrıca kimse onlara demiyor mu? Dünya onların çöplüğü değil. Buraya uygun yaratılmadılar. Arafa dönmeleri gerekiyor. Düzeni bozuyorlar." Avcı başıyla onayladı. "Onlar düzeni şeytanların bozduğundan emin. Yaratılış gayemiz dengeyi korumak ama onlar bunu kötülüğü tamamen yok etmek olarak algılıyor."

Gözlerimi şüpheyle kıstım. "Sen öyle düşünmüyor musun yani?"

"Benim ne düşündüğümün bir önemi yok." Aidan ileri atılıp kızın kolunu tuttu. Dirseğinin hemen üzerinden iyice kavrayıp onu sarsmaya başladı. "Sen bizi salak mı sanıyorsun? Hiçlikten çıkıp muhbirlik yapıyorsun ve sana inanmamızı bekliyorsun. Senin damarlarında akan kan bile bize düşman." Kız kolunu sertçe çekip Aidan'ın barbar tutuşundan kurtardı. "Bana inanma, iblis. Ama o inanıyor çünkü doğru olduğunu biliyor." Şimdi ikisi de bana bakıyordu.

Yalanlarla çevrili on yedi yıllık hayatım sonucunda, uzun soluklu bir rüyadan uyanmış ve kendimi bu kez de bir kâbusun içinde bulmuştum. İyi ve kötü üzerine düşünecek çok vaktim olmuştu ve ben her seferinde kâinattaki dengeyi çözmeye ne kadar yakın hissetsem de aslında bir bok bilmediğim gerçeğiyle yüzleşiyordum.

"Pekâlâ, bize söylemek istediğin şeyler nedir?" Gaye durup derin bir nefes aldı. Onu bu kadar gerenin söyleyecekleri mi yoksa yakalanma korkusu mu olup olmadığını anlayamıyordum. Avcının dudakları adrenalinden kurumuştu ve konuştuğunda sesi çok alçaktan geliyordu. "Sizlerin ve onların işleri yoluna koyma düşünceleri paralel değil. Eğer iki ekip de burnunun dikine giderse korkarım bu işin sonunda avlananlar sizler olacaksınız. Yoldan çıkan iblislerinizle kendiniz ilgilenmek istiyorsunuz ama bunu yıkım getirenlere de bırakabilirsiniz."

Aidan kollarını göğsünde birleştirip Gaye'ye oldukça tepeden baktı. Aurasındaki kibir dolup taşarken şeytanımın koyu saçları kahverengi-kızıl bakışlarını gölgeledi. "Cehennemde olan cehennemde kalır. Siz insanlar bizim işlerimizle ilgilenemezsiniz."

"Ayrıca," dedim sözlerine ekleyerek. "Yönetim değişti. Kutsal Krallar bu işi halletmemizi istiyor, eğer daha büyük kozmik bir kaos istemiyorsanız onların emirlerini uygulamamız gerek." Gaye sözlerimi düşünüyormuş gibi dudaklarını büzdü. Bir cehennem cadısı olmadığı aşikârdı ama düşüncelerini yine de okuyamıyordum.

Avcının eli belindeki kemere gitti. Yan yana sıralanmış küçük cam şişelerin takılı olduğu bağı parmağıyla işaret etti. "Tehlikenin derecesini anlamadınız galiba," dedi tırnağıyla hafifçe şişelerin üzerine vururken. "Bu şişeler senin bildiğin zehirlerle dolu değil Cassie. Ayrıca Meredith'in ürettiği, Bethany'nin kara elfi vururken kullandığı zehir de değil. Bunlar çok daha başka bir şey. Keşke daha fazla şey söyleyebilseydim. Ama tek diyebileceğim kanınızda bunların dolaşmasını istemezsiniz. Bazı şeyler geri alınabilir, bu filmi hepimiz daha önce izledik ama geri alınamayacak şeyler de var." Ceketini düzeltip tehlikeli kemerini gizledi. "Cassie, bana güven. Bu diyarda kalmak istemezsin."

Gözlerindeki bir şey ona inanmamı sağlıyordu. Gecenin soğuk rüzgârı tenime çarparken riske atılabilecek şeyleri düşündüm. Dostlarım, riske atılacaklar bölümünde değildi.

"Ailemle görüşme talep ediyorum," dedim sonra net bir şekilde. "Hepsiyle. Jo'nun yerini bilmiyoruz deme. Bildiğinizi biliyorum." Gaye ellerini teslim olmuş gibi havaya kaldırdı. "Öncesinde biriyle konuşman gerekecek." Üstünü başını düzeltip son bir kez bana baktı. "Umarım her şey bitip de tekrar karşılaştığımızda şartlar daha güzel olur. Kendine iyi bak Cassie." Başını eğip koşar adımlarla karanlık sokağın içinde gözden kayboldu.

Aidan'ın elini omzumda hissedince daldığım transtan zıplayıp gerçeğe döndüm. "Ona güvenmediğini söyle." Şeytanım sorgularcasına yüzüme bakarken onu tatmin edecek herhangi bir yanıtım olmadığını düşündüm. "Sen benden çok daha önce var oldun. Bazı şeyleri hissedebilmen lazım. Doğruları söylediğini sen de biliyorsun." Aidan yanıt vermek yerine omzumdaki elini kolumu okşayarak indirip elimi tuttu. Parmaklarımı avucunun içine alırken kızıl bakışları üzerimdeydi. "Bizi alt etmek öyle kolay değil. Hem birilerinden korkma şansımız varsa bunlar bu bir grup dindar insan değil, üç büyük ejderha olurdu."

Gülümsedim. "İnsanları küçümsüyorsun. Bu hataya çok sık düşüyorsun. Öfkeli ve bir amaç uğruna toplanan insanların ne kadar ürkütücü olabileceğini bilmiyorsun."

"Cass haklı Aidan." Bir kız sesi kulaklarıma dolunca irkildim. Kukuletalı bir yabancı karanlıkta belirirken gözlerim istemsizce arkasındaki üç gölgeye kaydı.

Tanıdık kokular benliğime çarpınca birçok duyguyu aynı anda hissettim. Öfke miydi bu kadere karşı ve özlem miydi asla kavuşulamayana duyulan. Ve en çok hüzün müydü kalbimi sıkıştıran, kaybettiğim zamana, yitip gidenlere karşı.

Yabancı yaklaşırken Meredith ve Marcus iki yanıma geçtiler. Tek bir hareketle başlıklı kızı öldürebileceklerini biliyordum. Ama onlar da diğer iblislerin düştüğü yanılgıya düşüyorlardı. Kukuletalı kız da onları öldürürdü.

"Seni yeniden görmek çok güzel," dedi Bethany eklemleri siyaha boyanmış parmaklarıyla kukuletasını indirirken. "Sana bir hediye getirdim." Ve gölgelerdeki yabancılar, ben sokak lambası altında yüzlerini görene kadar öne çıktılar.

***

Gölgelerden biri, lambalar bedenini aydınlatmaya başladıktan sonra gölge olmayı bıraktı. Jo, koşar adım yanıma gelirken zaman yavaşladı, yavaşladı ve en sonunda neredeyse durdu.

Kardeşim boynuma atlarken hâlâ mantıklı ve soğukkanlı olabilen bir yanım varsa bile tuz buz olarak havaya karışarak yok oldu. "Neredeydin seni küçük böcek?" Gözyaşlarım gözlerimi yakarken yutkunmaya çalıştım. "Burada olduğuna inanamıyorum," dedi Jo. Normalde erkeklere has olan, şu karizmayı çizdirmemek için duygulanmama durumunu kapıda bırakmıştı. Kardeşime olabildiği kadar çok sarılıp neredeyse kemiklerini kırarken Jo, ağlama ile gülme arası karışık bir sesle, "Gel. Seni bekleyen iki kişi daha var," dedi. Kollarını sırtımdan çekip eliyle Bethany'nin hemen yanında duran gölgeleri işaret etti.

Jo tam gidecekken kolunu tutup durdurdum. Kendime çevirdikten sonra iki elimi omzuna yerleştirip, "Önce ben de seni iki kişiyle tanıştırayım," dedim. Başımızın üzerinde son derece keskin bir kader kılıcı sallanıp duruyor, ancak kılıcın gölgesi üzerimize vurduğunda rahat nefes alabiliyorduk. Hayatın bize ne zaman kılıcın keskin tarafını saplayacağının garantisi yoktu. Hâlâ yapabiliyorken tüm belirsizliklerin kalkmasını istiyordum.

Jo, suratıma merakla bakarken Marcus ve Meredith'e döndüm. "Gelsenize sizi ahmaklar." Kardeşlerim bocalasalar da yanıma geldiler. Biri kanlı bir cadı diğeri ise gözü dönmüş bir kurttu ama söz konusu şey aile bağları olunca herkes böyle şapşallaşabiliyordu.

Marcus Jo'nun yanına geldi. "Seni hatırlıyorum," dedi Jo ela gözlerini şüpheyle kısarak. "Beni kaçırmaya çalışmıştınız." Marcus zoraki bir ifadeyle sırıttı. "O aslında seni kurtarmak içindi ama evet. Şey, resmi olarak tanışalım. Ben Marcus." İri elini Jo'ya uzattı. Jo benim aksime sıcakkanlılıktan ölmüyordu, o ailenin yabani oğluydu. Gerçi aile kavramımız genişlediğine göre yabani sıfatını artık gönül rahatlığıyla Marcus taşıyabilirdi. Her neyse.

Jo, yüzüme ne yapayım dercesine bakınca güven verici bir şekilde gülümsedim. Bunun üzerine Jo, Marcus'un elini sıktı. Marcus bir eliyle tokalaşırken diğer eliyle kardeşimi işaret etti. "Tutuşu sıkı. Sevdim bu çocuğu. Hem burnu da bana benziyor." Eliyle burnunun ucunu dürtünce Meredith boğuluyor gibi bir ses çıkardı. "Bu pek mümkün değil. Senin burnun onlarca kez kırıldı. Oysa o daha taze. Bu arada ben Meredith." El sallamakla yetindi cadı. Ailenin yabani olanı sıfatı hızla yer değiştiriyordu.

"Biz kardeşiz," dedi Meredith kibar parmaklarını dördümüz üzerinde kaydırırken. "Hepimiz anlamında. Annelerimiz ortak, Lilith. Gerçi sen ve Cass'in babası da ortak. Yani işler biraz karışık, küçük melezcik." Meredith'in boşboğazlığının yarattığı yıkıcı etkiyi görmek için Jo'ya baktığımda sırıttığını gördüm. Pekâlâ, ağır gelmişti işte. O da balataları sıyırmıştı.

"Başka kardeşlerimiz olduğunu söylemiştin. Ama bu ikisi kadar deli olmalarını beklemiyordum," dedi hâlâ gülerken. "Sizinle tanışmak çok güzel." Parlayan gözleri iki deli arasında gidip geldi. "Hep bir ağabeyim olsun istemiştim," dedi nihayet gözleri Marcus'ta sabitlenirken. "Seninle çok iyi anlaşacağız iri çocuk." Marcus şaşkınlıktan ağzını açıp yanıt veremedi. Jo'nun laf ebeliğini bile özlemiştim. Bu yüzden ileri atılıp bir kez daha sarıldım. "Evet, belki sonra. Her şey bittikten sonra hep beraber takılacağımız bir gün gelecek." Ensesindeki saçları karıştırıp darmadağın ederken gülümsüyordum. Uzun zamandır hissetmediğim kadar huzurluydum.

"Şimdi seni, bekleyenlere götürme vakti," dedi kardeşim saçlarımın arasından. "Uzun zamandır bunu bekliyorlardı Cass." Bakışlarım yere düştü. Ayakkabılarıma bakıyordum. Güvende olmalarını istemek başka şeydi, onlarla yeniden konuşmak başka şey. Ayakkabılarımın bağcıklarına bakmak daha kolaydı. Hem bağcıklar daha gerçekti. İpler başka bir hayatta bana yalanlar söyleyerek beni büyüten ailemden daha gerçekti işte.

"Bilmiyorum," diyebildim mırıldanarak. "Belki de zamanı değildir. Şu an başımız hiç olmadığı kadar belâda zaten." Ama kardeşimin pes etmeye pek niyeti yoktu. "Ailen için her zaman doğru zamandır."

"Onu görebilmek için bir kez bile uğraşmayan ailesi mi?" İkimiz de arkamızı dönüp öfkeli gözlerle gölgeleri izleyen Aidan'a baktık. Öfkesini gizlemeye gerek bile duymuyordu. Aidan'ın aile ve güven kavramları üzerine ciddi problemleri olduğunu biliyordum ve belki de kendi ailesi olana kadar bu problemleri hiç çözemeyecekti. Kendi ailesi mi?

Beynimin içi asla yaşanmayacak saçma sapan hayallerle dolarken onlardan kurtulabilmek için gözlerimi birkaç kez kırptım.

"Sen kimsin?" dedi Jo onu tutan ellerimden sıyrılıp Aidan'ın karşısına dikilirken. "Ablamı devamlı üzen şu dangalak mı?" Üstümüzde bir yerlerden Draza'nın altına yaparcasına güldüğünden emindim.

"Ben..." dedi Aidan ne diyeceğini bilemez hâlde yardım için bana bakarken. Ama o cümlesini bitiremeden kardeşim şeytanımın yüzüne okkalı bir yumruk attı. Aidan yumruğun ani gelişiyle geriye yalpalarken Meredith tıksırıyor gibi bir ses çıkardı.

Yerimden fırlayıp Jo'nun önüne geçtim. "Ne yapıyorsun? O bizden biri." Jo az önce Aidan'ın yüzüne damga yapan yumruğunu sıvazladı. "Bunu hak etmişti. Beth her şeyi anlatmıyor ama anlattığı kadarıyla bile bunu hak etti. Seni sahipsiz sanmalarına izin vermem."

Meredith suskunluğunu bozdu. "Sevdim bu çocuğu." Gözlerimi devirdim. Omzumun üzerinden Aidan'a baktım. Yanağını tutuyordu, bakışları öyle şaşkındı ki irisler yeniden kahverengi olmuştu. Benim yakışıklı, şaşkın erkeğim.

O daha küçük bir çocuk Aidan.

Biliyorum.

"Hadi Cass. Bekliyorlar." Jo beni çekiştirince doğrulup sokak lambasının ardındaki gölgelere baktım. Sadece Bethany onlardan çok daha önde duruyor, temkinli bakışlarla beni izliyordu. Göz göze gelince arkadaşım gülümsedi. Derin bir nefes alıp adımlarım beni geri götürmeye çalışırken gölgelere doğru ilerledim.

Bethany'nin yanından geçip gidecekken vazgeçtim. "Onlarla olan konuşmam bitsin seninle görüşeceğim, olur mu?" Arkadaşım koluma sevgiyle dokunurken başıyla onayladı.

Annem ve babam ben onlara yaklaşırken karanlıktan çıktılar. Tam karşılarına gelecek şekilde durduğumda hafif bir rüzgâr saçlarımı karıştırdı. Ve bu Marr'in gözlerinin aniden dolmasına sebep oldu. "Hâlâ aynı Cassie gibi duruyorsun." Gözlerinden yaşlar akarken ellerini bana doğru uzattı. "Sana sarılabilir miyim?" Babam homurdanarak yerinde rahatsızca kıpırdandı. "O senin kızın. Tabii ki sarılabilirsin," dedi sertçe. Ve ben yanıt veremeden Marr boynuma atıldı.

İlk başta ağlayanın sadece o olduğunu sanmıştım ama sonra yanaklarımın ıslak olduğunu ve üzerimize yağmur yağmadığını fark ettim. İnsan farkında olmadan ağlayabilir miydi? Ağlıyormuş demek ki. Annemin eli saçlarımda gezinirken gözlerimi kapadım ve sarılışına karşılık verdim. "Ah, benim küçük avcım." Annem hâlâ ağlamaya devam ederken babam öksürerek boğazını temizledi. "Kız biraz nefes alsın Marrland." Gözlerimi açıp babama baktım. Yüzünde hüzünlü bir ifadeyle bizi izliyordu, Anton duygularını kolayca gösterebilen adamlardan değildi. "Sorun değil," dedim mırıldanarak. Sonrasında annem elleri hâlâ omzumdayken geri çekildi. Bu kadar yakından tüm yaşantım boyunca milyarlarca kez baktığım yüze bakıp da nasıl olurdu da önceden benzemediğimizi anlayamadığımı düşündüm.

"Sana her şeyi daha önce anlatmamız gerekiyordu," dedi annem sesi üzüntüden kısılırken. "Ama doğru zamanı beklerken seneler geçti. Üstelik Jo da büyüyordu ve doğru zaman bir türlü gelmedi işte." Anton yanımıza gelip Marr'ın omzumdaki elinin üzerine kendi iri elini koydu. Siyah gözleri sulanmış mıydı kafayı mı yiyordum, emin değildim.

"Sizi ilk aldığımız gün bir şeyleri hatırlıyordun, bu yüzden cadılardan sana büyü yapmasını istedik. Böylece önceki hayatını sormayacaktın." Anton'un olayları sanki dün olmuşçasına anlatışı tüylerimi ürpertti. "Ama sen yine de hatırladın. Evde mobilyaların üzerine çıkıp atlamaya çalışıyordun. Kanatlarını bastırıcılarla bastırıyorduk ve böylece hep yere çakılıyordun işte."

Kaşlarımı çattım. Belki aptalca bir öfkeydi ama haklıydım. "Sırf bu yüzden dudağımı kaç kez patlatmama sebep oldunuz." Çocukluk anılarımdaki sızı aklıma dolunca gözlerimi birkaç kez kırptım.

"Böylesi daha güvenliydi. Sizi almadan önce başka bir kafiledeydik ve bir gece elimizde iki çocukla dönemezdik. Bu yüzden sizi aldığımız gün bizim hayatımız da sonsuza dek değişti. Bildiğimiz, tanıdığımız her şeyden uzaklaştık."

"Son bir senem âdeta, kelimenin tam anlamıyla cehennem gibi geçmemiş olsa size üzülebilirdim baba." Son söylediğim sözcük havaya karışırken kimse ses çıkarmadı. Arkamda bir yerlerde kardeşlerimin kaynaştığını duyabiliyordum.

“Annenin o deli kadın olması önemli değil.” Marr’ın sıcacık avuçları iki yanağımı kavradı. “Seni doğurmamış olabilirim ama ben büyüttüm. Kanında neler dolanıyor bilemem ama,” bir elini indirip işaret parmağını kalbimin üzerine koydu, “burada sevgi olduğunu biliyorum. Sen ve Jo hayat boyu başımıza gelen en güzel şeylersiniz. Babana bakma, o da aynı düşünüyor.” Ama ben babama bakıyordum. Gözleri dolmuştu, az önceki kendine güvenen sert aurası buharlaşıp gitmiş, yerine zar zor ayakta durabilen kamburu çıkmış bir adam gelmişti. İhtiyacı olan şeyin sarılmam olduğunu biliyordum, bu yüzden öyle de yaptım. Annemden uzaklaşıp Anton’un boynuna sarıldım ve içimde tuttuğum hıçkırıklar ciğerimi kazırken ağlamaya başladım.

Belki özlemden döküyordum gözyaşını ya da yitip giden zamanıma ağlıyordum. Belki sadece ihanete uğramama, defalarca öldürülmeye çalışılmama ağlıyordum. Belki tüm bu olanlardan sonra kavuştuğum için ağlıyordum. Esas olarak sebebini bilmiyordum ama içimde tuttuğum ne varsa gözyaşı pınarlarımdan akmaya niyetliydi ve ben de bıraktım.

Temkinli olmaya ne oldu bilmiyordum. Temkinli olmayı barda Max ile bırakmış olmalıydım ama an itibariyle anne ve babama sarılmışken temkinli olmanın canı cehennemeydi.

Dakikalar sonra sümük sesleri karanlık sokakta yankılanırken annem ve babam yanaklarını sildiler. Ben ise hâlâ bir rakun gibi şişmiş gözlerle onlara bakmaya devam ettim. “Bizim için artık avcılarla beraber bir hayat yok. Uzun zaman önce bırakmalıydık. Aileyi her şeyin üzerinde tutmalıydık. Yaptığımız her şey için üzgünüm. Sizi böyle yetiştirmemeliydik Cass.” Annem yeniden ellerimi tuttu. “Keşke sizi aldığımız o karlı kış gecesine dönebilsek. Olayların böyle olmaması için elimden geleni yapardım." Ona inanıyordum. Ama inanmak bir şeyi değiştiremezdi. Zaman öyle gerçek, öyle zalim bir kavramdı ki siz ne yaparsanız yapın yolundan dönmez, daima ileri giderdi.

"Nerede kalacaksınız?"

Anton elini sallayarak soruyu geçiştirdi. "Bir yer bulduk. Basit işlerde çalışacağız ve hayata tutunacağız. Jo da bizimle gelecek. Belâdan onu uzak tutacağız. Sen ise... Seni vazgeçirmeyi umuyordum aslında kızım."

Bir şey söylemeden önce derin bir nefes aldığımda Aidan'ın hoş sesi zihnime doldu.

Onlara nişanlandığımızı söyle.

Ürperti bedenimde kanımla gezintiye çıkıp kalbime âdeta gümleyerek vurdu. Doğru mu duyuyordum?

Biz nişanlanmadık ki.

Aidan yanıt vermeyince omzumun üzerinden ona baktım. Bizi izliyordu.

Sen öyle diyorsan, dedi huysuzca. Ve ben aklımı tepetaklak ettiği için içimden sessizce sövdüm. Tam mantık çerçevesinde bir şeyleri yoluna koymaya çalışırken Aidan ve mükemmel derecede işlevli hormonları aniden çıkageliyor, ortalığı dağıtıyor ve ardında şuuru alınmış kuş gibi bırakıyordu beni.

"Cassie?"

"Hmm."

Anton elini kâküllerimin hemen üzerine koydu. "Bizimle gel. Basit bir hayatımız olur. Burada, dünyada yaşarız. Belki yaşıtların gibi okula gidersin. Başka bir geleceğin olur. Mutlu oluruz Cassie ve beraber oluruz. Geçirdiğim kan kokulu senelerden sonra kızım, önemli olan tek şeyin aile olduğunu biliyorum." İri eli kâküllerimden kulaklarıma kayınca kulak mememi çekiştirip güldü. "Şarkı söylemeyi severdin. Belki müzik okursun. Gençlerin kullandığı enstrümanlardan sende de olur ve Jo da bizimle güvende kalır. İnsanlardan saklarız sizi. Bir yolu hep bulunur."

Kalbim sancıyordu. Babamın anlattığı hayaller hem gerçek dışı hem de kolayca ulaşabilecek şeylerdi ve kalbimi en çok ulaşılabilir olması yakıyordu. İnsanlığın kaderini siktir edebilseydim keşke. Keşke böyle büyük bir sorumluluk benim yaşımdaki bir kıza kalmasaydı. Keşke her şeyi değiştirebilseydim. Basit bir hayatım olsaydı, bir keman çalıp Max'in barında şarkı söyleyen şu metalcilere solist olabilseydim. Aidan da benimle kalsaydı ve evlenebilseydik. Ama kaderin bizim için başka planları vardı.

Yine öldürecek ve belki öldürülecektim.

Yine sevdiğim insanları tehlikeye atacaktım ve onlar tehlikedeyken çaresizce onları izleyecektim. Yapabileceklerim sınırlıydı ve yine elimden geleni yapacaktım. Ve elimden gelen yetmezse de... Daha önce yaptığım gibi fedakârlık yapacaktım. Ve şu anki fedakârlık ailemle mutlu bir hayata hayır demek olacaktı. Bazı kapılar sonsuza dek kapanırdı, Lucifer'ın katran karası kalbine melek kılıcını sokup çevirirken o kapılardan en güzel ve parlak olanını sonsuza dek kapatmıştım. Anahtarı da cehennemin en dibine atmıştım. Benim için kaygısız, mutlu bir hayat asla olamazdı. Ben kaosun içinde açan bir çiçektim, kaosun dışında solar giderdim. Kendimi sorunsuz bir diyarda hayal dahi edemiyordum.

"Konuşmuyorsun çünkü bizimle gelmeyeceksin," dedi annem. Acı acı gülerken bir elimle onun, diğer elimle de babamın elini tuttum. "Cep numaralarınızı bana vereceksiniz ve her şey bittiğinde yanınıza geleceğim. O zamana kadar birbirinize sahip çıkın." Babam tekrar sarılınca elimle hafifçe sırtına vurdum. "Siz beni güçlü yetiştirdiniz. Bana güvenin, buna ihtiyacım var, lütfen." Üçümüz birkaç saniye birbirimize kenetlenmiş hâlde kaldıktan sonra nihayet telefon numaralarımızı kaydettik. Son bir kez daha sarıldıktan sonra annem ve babam arka tarafa, Jo'nun yanına gittiler ve böylece en yakın arkadaşım ve ben yalnız kaldık.

"Hepsi sivri kulaklarını bize dikmiş dinliyorlar değil mi?"

Sırıttım. "Yalan mı söyleyeyim yoksa gerçeği mi?" Bethany kukuletasını omuzlarının arkasına attı. "Önemi yok." Çenesiyle ailemi işaret etti. "Merak etme, güvenli bir yere gittiklerinden emin olacağım." Sonrasındaysa bakışlarını kaçırdı. Ne düşündüğünü anlamak için zihnine girmeyi aklımdan bir saniye de olsa geçirdim ama hemen vazgeçtim, bunu yapmayı sevemiyordum.

"Zihin okumuyorum Beth. Ve karın ağrını anlamak için aurana bakmama da gerek yok. Söyle hadi. Beni ne şaşırtabilir ki?"

Bethany kolları ile kendini sardı. "Keşke bunu demeseydin, seni şaşırtacak milyarlarca şey sayabilirim. Ama en güzeli, artık annem bir yıkım getiren."

Gözlerimin kafamı kapladığından emin bir hâlde, "Nasıl yani? Din mi değiştirdi?" diye sordum. Bethany'nin annesi tanıdığım en sert şeytan avcılarından biriydi. İşine tutkuyla bağlı oluşu da onu çok iyi bir avcı yapıyordu. Hatta fazla iyi. Ne taraftan baktığınıza göre değişir.

Beth başıyla onayladı. "Ve bir seçim oldu. Joan artık sadece konseyde. Başımızda artık annem var Cassie." Az önce kurduğum saçma cümle için bana birkaç yüz kişi küfredebilirdi ve ben her bir küfür zerreciğini bile fazlasıyla hak etmiştim. *Beni ne şaşırtırdı, öyle mi?*

"Daha başka şeyler var mı?"

Eskiden en yakın arkadaşım olan ve artık karşı taraflarda yer aldığımız dostum bir kez daha bakışlarını kaçırdı. "Rüzgârın yönü değişecek Cass. Bu diyarı terk etmeniz gerekiyor. Bilhassa senin. Hayat amacı sadece senin öldüğünü görmek olan avcılar ve yıkım getirenler var. Üstelik artık karşında aşinası olduğun o avcılar da yok. Bir şeyler değişti ve ben senin bu değişimle yüzleşmeni istemeyecek kadar seni önemsiyorum."

Başıma ağrılar giriyordu. "Beth, burada söz konusu olan dostlarımın hayatı. Ne ile karşılaşacaklarını bilmeleri gerekiyor. Bu eğer gerçekten önemli ise bana yardım et." Beth benden hafifçe uzaklaşınca kalbimde bir yerlerde bir sızı oluştu. Bakışlarında kararsız bir ifade gezinirken arkadaşım gözlerime baktı. "Sana bilgi verirsem sizinkiler de benim halkımı öldürür. Bunu onlarla paylaşırsın çünkü onlar da senin halkın. Beni anlamalısın Cassie. Sen nasıl insanlarını koruyorsan ben de benimkileri koruyorum." Elini cebine atıp küçük cılız bir fular çıkardı. Beyaz-mavi fuları nerede görsem tanırdım. Bu Bethany'nin en sevdiği fulardı.

Arkadaşım kumaşı elinin içinde biraz yuvarladıktan sonra bana uzattı. "Al. Veda hediyesi olarak gör. Savaş alanında seninle karşılaşmak istemiyorum. Gidin. Uzaklara gidin." Gözleri içime işlerken, "Lütfen," dedi Bethany. "Karşı karşıya gelmeyelim Cass."

Ona ne sorarsam sorayım yanıt vermeyecekti. Kalbimin içine batan iğneler canımı yakıyordu, ona küsmek, düşman olmak basit olandı ama onu anlamaya çalıştıkça ruhumun bir kısmı çürüyor gibi hissetmiştim. Onu anlıyordum. Maalesef ki anlıyordum, halkını koruyordu, ben de öyle. O ya da bu şekilde artık biz karşı taraflardaydık.

Sonsuzluk gibi süren birkaç dakikanın sonunda fuları alıp kemerime bağladım. *Bir hediye* diye düşündüm, en kıymetlilerinden değerli bir hediye.

"Katze sizinle mi? Pembe saçlı vampir kız." Bethany'nin gözlerinden anlık değişik bir ifade geçti. Öyle hızlı geçti ki karanlığın gözlerime oynadığı bir oyun gibiydi. "Hayır," dedi dostum kesin bir dille. "Şimdi vedalaşın. Onları güvenli eve götürüyorum. Söylediklerimi düşün, olur mu?" Onaylar hâlde mırıldanıp ailemin yanına koştum. Her birine tek tek sarılıp öptüm. Konuşamadığımız konular, paylaşamadığımız olaylarla ailem giderken arkalarından bakıyordum. Bir dakika sonra görüş açımdan çıktılar ve ben yeniden kendimi çılgın ekibimle buldum.

Bir el omzuma dokununca Aidan sanıp hevesle döndüm ama Marcus'tu. "Üzülme Cassie. Bir kurdun sözleri ne denli değerli olabilir bilmem ama onları tekrar göreceksin." Elimi elinin üzerine koyup üzgün gözlerle gülümsedim. "Kurdun dediği şeyler deli saçması olabilir ama bir cadı doğrusunu bilir. O baş belâsı kardeşini tekrar göreceksin," dedi cadı sırıtırken. "Ama önce şu sokağın başındaki misafirlerle ilgilenmemiz lazım." O daha cümlesini bitiremeden Draza yıldırım gibi tepemize indi. Kanatlarını sırtına çekerken nefes nefeseydi. "İki kişi geliyor ve nabız hissetmiyorum."

Çevreme bakınıp Aidan'ı görmeye çalıştım. Çoktan gölgeleri fark etmiş, onlara doğru emin adımlarla ilerlemeye başlamıştı. Diğerlerini ittirip koşar adım peşine düştüm.

Ne yaptığını sanıyorsun? Kahraman mı olmaya çalışıyorsun?

Aidan yanıt vermedi. Aurası öfkeyle kaynıyordu. Ondan bedenime akan tüm hisler iç karartıcı ve düşmancaydı.

Konuş Aidan.

Aidan durdu. Gölgeler hâlâ bize doğru gelirken bana döndü. Konuştuğunda çehresi kararmıştı. "Herkesi hayatta tutmak için gözünü kırpmadan ölüme koşarsın ama ben yapınca kahraman oluyorum öyle mi? Orada hissettiklerini biliyorum. Kendini feda etmekten asla çekinmezsin. Sen busun. Peki o hâlde. O beynin alıyor mu sen gidersen bana ne olacağını?"

Kendimi savunmak için söyleyeceğim sözler de bedenim gibi donakalmıştı. Sadece Aidan'a, haklı sözlerine ve arkasında durmadan bize yaklaşan gölgelere bakabiliyordum.

"Bunu sonra konuşacağız Cassandra." Ve Aidan tekrar gölgelere döndü. Gölgelerden birinin başı diğerinin omzuna düşünce adımlarım yavaşladı. Işığın altına gelene kadar aklımdan geçenin olmamış olmasını diledim.

Hayır, hayır hayır, yine olmaz. Hayır!

Işık gölgelerden birinin pembe saçına vurunca yutkundum. Arkamda bir yerden Marcus'un bağrışını duydum. "Katze," dedi kurt feryat eder gibi.

Draza nabız almamıştı, alamazdı, çünkü Katze ölmüştü.

BÖLÜM 19

Kader, ben ve sevdiklerim için ağlarını örerken oldukça cömert davranmıştı. Diğer yaşayanlara harcanan keratinin çok daha fazlasını bana harcanmıştı. Çünkü şu an içinde yaşadığım durumun başka bir izahı yoktu.

Burada durmuş, Marcus omzuma vurup beni geçerken, ayaklarım bir anda onlarca ağırlığı kaldıramıyormuş gibi yere yapışmışken, kaderin ağlarını düşünüyordum. Belki kader bana tek bir ağ bırakmıştı ve bir cambaz gibi üzerinde yürümemi istemişti. Ölüm ya da yaşam. Düştüğün an kaybedersin Cassie.

Ve ben durmadan düşüyordum. Tam yüzeye çıktığım anda ağ beni üstünden atıyor ve ben yuvarlanarak kaderimin karanlık köşelerine sürükleniyordum. "Ona ne oldu?" Aloha'nın sesi kulaklarıma yoğun bir sis bulutunun ardından ulaşıyor gibiydi. Her şeyi yutan bir çınlama, rüzgârın, dostlarımın nefeslerinin sesini dâhil kapatmış ve ne kadar odaklanmaya çalışırsam çalışayım başka bir şey duymamı imkânsız hâle getirmişti. "Toparlan," dedi Meredith kolumu tutup beni hafifçe sarsarak. Bir robot gibi suratına baktım. "Hadi Cass."

"Bana bırak," dedi Aidan iki kolumdan tutarak hiç ağırlığım yokmuşçasına beni kaldırıp kendine bakmaya zorlarken. Meredith de diğerlerine katılıp Katze'ye bakmak için gözden kayboldu. Ben ise Aidan'ın çenesine bakıyordum. Sanki kıpırdamak ve odaklanmak tüm hayatıma mâl olacakmış gibi hissediyordum. O yüzden hafif hafif çıkmaya başlamış kirli sakallarında karar kıldı gözlerim.

"Benim yüzümden öldü. Dostum... Benim yüzümden..." Aidan ağır çekimde başını alnıma yasladı. Şimdi az önce baktığım çenesi alnımdaydı ve ufak sakalları tenimi çiziyordu. Kulaklarımda hâlâ uğultu vardı ama açıkçası ses duymak da istemiyordum. Ne duyacaktım? Marcus'un eşleştiği ruhu kaybetmesinin ağıdını mı? Lnn'e ne diyecektim? Katze neden gitmişti?

"Şşhh," dedi Aidan teskin eden sesiyle. Dudakları kâküllerime değerken ılık nefesi alnıma çarpıyordu. "Bunu çözeceğiz. Şimdi tek yapman gereken koy vermemek. Bunu yapabilir misin?" Milyarlarca ton ağırlığındaki başımı salladım. "Evet mi, hayır mı?" diye üsteledi şeytanım. Güçlü kollarıyla beni sıkı sıkı sarmıştı.

"Evet," dedim neredeyse fısıltı gibi. Sonra gözlerimi kapayıp dünyadaki tüm oksijeni âdeta içime çektim. Ciğerlerim başka bir kaybın kokusunu hücrelerime gönderirken güçlü durmaya çalıştım. Herkes için güçlü durmalıydım. "Oraya gidelim," dedim neredeyse saatler gibi geçen bir yarım dakikanın sonunda. Aidan başını sallayınca alnımdaki dağılan saçlar gözlerime girdi. Kırpmadım bile. Gözlerime bırakın saçlarımı, koca koca iğneler soksalardı bile şu an hissettiğim acı dışında bir şey hissedebilir miydim emin değildim.

Aidan'ın güven verici sıcak bedeni beni yavaşça terk ederken görüş açım genişledi. Marcus ve Aloha kavga ediyorlardı.

İyi de bu çok saçmaydı? Yoksa değil miydi? Şeytanım elimi tutup beni sürüklercesine kaosa götürürken gözlerim hâlâ o ikisinin üzerindeydi. "Ondan uzak dur," diyordu kurt strigoiye. "Çek o pis ellerini vampir." Aloha ise umursamıyordu. Katze'nin hareketsiz bedeninin üzerine eğilmişti hemen dibinde ayakta tırnaklarını yerken ağlayan bir Ryan duruyordu. Mavi saçları dağılmıştı. Gözaltları öyle çok morarmıştı ki sanki az önce biri onu mezarından kaldırıp zorla buraya getirmiş gibiydi. Ki aslında bu oldukça olasıydı.

Yanlarına vardığımda Aidan elimi bıraktı ve ben dizlerimin üzerinde yere oturdum. Aloha'yı ittirip Katze'ye baktım. Arkadaşım hareket etmiyordu. Arkamda Marcus Aloha'nın boğazına pençesini geçirip sıkıyordu ve benim artık bu saçma kavgalara ayıracak sabrım kalmamıştı. "Sizin neyiniz var be? Marcus bırak onu. Yanıma gelin." Arkadaşımın solgun kolunu alıp ön tarafını çevirerek bileğine baktım. Siyah, güz dallarını andıran damarlardan yoktu. Bakışlarım bu kez Ryan'a kaydı. Yoksunluk sendromu çeken eroinman gibi sallanıyordu. İri mavi gözlerinden durmadan kanla karışık yaşlar akıyor, parçaladığı tırnaklarını yemeye çalışıyordu. Kolları kan içindeydi. "Şimdi dikkatini bana ver olur mu? Biliyorum bu çok zor. İnan biliyorum." Ellerim Katze'nin soğuk bedenindeyken başımı kaldırıp neredeyse yalvarırcasına Ryan'a bakıyordum. "Sen onun kuzenisin, değil mi?" Ryan başıyla onayladı. Kaçamak bakışları Aloha ile Marcus arasında gidip geliyordu. "Onları dert etme," dedim sesimin normal çıkmasına çalışarak.

Katze'nin üzerine pembe peri tozları düşünce başımı kaldırıp göğe baktım. "Cassie, iki sokak ötede bir hareketlilik var. Yine strigoiler." Urange havadaydı. Bakışları sadece bir an için yerde hareketsiz yatan kıza takıldı, sonrasında o da yukarı baktı. Draza'nın verdiği işareti görememiştim ama Urange tekrar bana baktığında, "Buraya sıçramayacak gibi. Yani her ne yapıyorsanız vaktiniz var. Meredith buraya gizleme büyüsü yaparsa faniler de bu sokağı görmeden geçip giderler." Peri hızla yukarı uçunca birkaç toz daha üstümüze düştü. Meredith yanıma oturdu. "Burayı gizleyebilirim. Ama yine de bizi görürler, sadece gördüklerini anlamayacaklar." Elini teskin edercesine koluma koydu. "Çok şey atlattık. Bunu da atlatırız. Ölüm bir son değil Cass." Güzel yeşil gözlerinden birini kırpıp ellerinden destek alarak ayağa kalktı.

Göğsümü şişirerek derin bir nefes aldım. "Şimdi bana neler olduğunu anlat. Kuzenin dün gece hayattaydı." Ryan'ın ürkek mavi bakışları Marcus'un üzerindeydi. "Bana odaklan Ryan."

"Neden ki?" dedi vampir sesi titreyip soğuk kış gecesine karışırken. "Artık yapılacak bir şey yok." Ardından yenecek tek bir zerresi kalmayan tırnaklarını dudaklarına götürdü. Ve dudakları kana boyanana kadar tırnaklarını yemeye başladı.

"Ne olduğunu anlat." Marcus ileri doğru atılınca Aidan onu tuttu. Şeytanımla göz göze geldik. *Teşekkür ederim.* Aidan omuz silkip Marcus'u tutan ellerini sıkılaştırdı. Marcus bu kez çaresizlikle hırlamaya başladı. "Anlat dedim, seni gerzek vampir. Ona ne oldu?" Ryan bakışlarını güçlükle yanı başındaki kızgın kurttan alıp Katze'ye indirdi. "Bana yardım etmeye çalışıyordu. Daha önce bir strigoiye yardım ettiğini söyledi." Yanımdaki Aloha'dan belirli belirsiz bir iç çekiş duyuldu. Ryan devam ettiğinde artık dudaklarını dişlemeye başlamıştı. Kan sızıntılar şeklinde çenesine, oradan da üzerindeki tişörtüne akıyordu. "Bana kendi kanını verdi. Fanilere zarar vermemem için." Odağını şaşıran parlak gözleri Katze'nin üzerindeydi. "Fanilere zarar verirsem beni koruyamazmış, ben de bu yüzden onun kanını içtim." Kırık kanlı tırnağıyla Katze'nin kolunu işaret etti. Çevirdiğimde bahsettiği iki minik diş izini gördüm. "Bedenindeki tüm kanı mı emdin Ryan?" Vampir bakışlarını kaçırdı. Marcus'un mantıklı düşünen son zerreciğinin de kül olup gittiğini hissettim.

Kurt öyle güçlü uludu ki, üstünde oturduğum zemin titredi. "Onu öldürdün," dedi Marcus sıkılı dişleri arasından. "Ve senin sefil hayatını almam bir şeyi değiştirmeyecek. Dengi bile olmaz senin alıp verdiğin o pis nefes." Aidan koluna asılınca Marcus savrularak geriye düştü.

Gözlerimi kapayıp iki elimle başımın yanlarına bastırdım. Düşünmeye çalıştım. "Vampirler kafaları kopmadan ya da kazıkla kalpleri delinmeden nasıl ölebilirler?" Kimseden ses gelmeyince bu kez bağırdım. "Bilen biri aydınlatabilir mi acaba?"

Meredith sokağın caddeye açıldığı yoldan bana doğru koşar adımlarla gelirken seslendi. "Ölmezler." Gözlerimi devirdim ve bu anında beynime daha fazla acının saplanmasına sebep oldu. "İyi. Gel de bunu şu nefes almayan kıza anlat. Duydun mu Katze? Ölmemen gerekiyormuş." Arkadaşımın uğursuz soğukluktaki elini avucumun içine aldım. Meredith hemen yanı başıma çökerken gözlerimi kırpmadan yerde yatan dostuma bakıyordum.

Onca hikâye ve yaşamın ardından Katze burada ölecek miydi yani? Meredith elinin tersiyle kızın yanaklarına dokundu. Pembe saçlarını yüzünden çekti. Uzun, kibar parmaklarını vampirin aralık kalmış dudaklarının arasına soktu ve azı dişlerini görecek şekilde dudağını yukarı çekiştirdi. Mistik muayenesi bitmiş olacak ki sonrasında ellerini dizlerine koyup bıkkınca nefesini bıraktı. "Vampirler bu şekilde ölmez. Ona ne oldu bilmiyorum." Bakışları her an sinir krizi geçirecekmiş gibi duran Ryan'a kaydı. "Siz safkanlar ne oldu da strigoi oldunuz?" Ardından bana dönüp hızlıca ekledi. "Eğer bunu bilirsek Katze'nin başına geleni de anlayabiliriz. Sadece insanlar vampire dönüştüklerinde strigoi olabilirler. İblis dünyasında Draza haricinde hiçbir iblis lanetlenmediği sürece bir alt kasta düşürülmez. Ve Katze lanetli değil." Avuç içleri vampirin bedenini gösterecek şekilde hızla üzerinde gezdirdi. Meredith'in parmaklarından mavi parıltılı bir sis bulutu vampirin bedeninde usulca gezindi. "Bak," dedi Meredith hâlâ parmak uçlarından mavi dumanlar çıkarken onları şaklatarak, "Eğer bir lanet ya da büyü olsaydı maviler rengini kırmızıya bırakırdı. Her ne olmuşsa daha önce karşılaşmadığımız bir şey."

Harika... Yine oradaydım. İhtimaller denizinde. Ve artık eskisi kadar iyi bir yüzücü olduğumdan emin değildim. Yüzeye çıkmaya çalıştıkça boğuluyordum. Meredith irisin renkten renge girdiği parlak gözlerini kısarak Katze'yi incelemeyi sürdürdü. Ryan ise ne cevap vereceğinden emin değildi. "İnsanlar," dedi çoktan kırdığı tırnaklarını koparmaya çalışırken sivri dişleriyle parmak uçlarını parçaladığından habersiz. "Onlar yaptı."

Marcus nihayet debelenmeyi bırakmıştı. "Avcılar mı?" diye sordu sıkılı dişlerinin arasından. Ryan sanki birileri onu duyabilirmiş gibi korkuyla çevresine bakındı. Safkan bir vampiri neyin bu denli ürkütebildiğini anlamaya çalışıyordum ama bulamıyordum.

"Bilmiyorum," dedi vampir kollarını bedeni etrafına dolayıp yere çökerken. Bedenine doladığı kollarıyla dizlerini sardı. İleri geri sallanırken kanlı yaşlarla yıkanmış gözleri Katze'nin üzerindeydi. "Bana bir şeyler yaptılar ve ben değiştim. Belki Katze'nin kanını değiştiren budur." Kurumuş kan lekeli parmaklarından birini kendi azı dişine sürttü. "Ben kanını emerken onu zehirlemiş olmalıyım."

Anlatılanların saçmalığı karşısında beynim hata veriyordu. "Onun bir strigoi olmasına imkân yok. Kimsenin kanını emmedi. Birine kanını vermesi de onu strigoi yapmaz." Katze'nin bedeninde damarların koyulaştığı tek bir yer yoktu. Ne ile karşı karşıya olduğumuzu bilmiyordum ama Ryan saçmalıyordu.

"Hayır," dedi vampir dizlerinin üzerine yaydığı mavi saçları havaya kalkarken. "O manyak insanlar bana bir şey yaptılar." İri gözleri korkuyla açılmıştı.

"Hep mi deliydin yoksa orada olanlardan sonra mı oldu?" Konuşan Draza'ydı. Çatıdan inmişti. Ne kadar süredir buradaydı bilmiyordum. Ryan kara elfe bomboş gözlerle baktı. Draza'nın çukurda olduğu zaman boyunca işkenceye uğradığını duymuştum ama açıkçası elfi öncesinde de tanıyordum, o her zaman şu birkaç tahtası eksik olan tiplerden biriydi.

"Açık konuşayım gençler, bu çocuk deli." Kara elf kollarını bilgiç bir edayla göğsünde kavuşturduktan sonra ciddiyetini güçlendiren açık gri kaşlarını çattı. "Ama insanlar gerektiğinde psikopatlaşabiliyorlar. Bu çocuğa birileri bir şey yapmış." Ryan başını yeniden dizlerine gömüp mırıldanarak sallanmaya başladı. Bu kez çıldırma sırası bendeydi. Kimseye bir faydam dokunamıyordu. Ne yapmam gerektiğini bilmiyordum. Kendimi bıçaklamak istedim.

Aniden zihnimde minik bir ampul yandı. Bu öyle belirsiz cılız ışıklı bir ampuldü ki odaklanmazsam hemen unutabilirdim. Bu yüzden düşüncelerime sıkı sıkıya tutundum. "Bir kadın vardı. Delinin teki ama kâhin. Ona sorabiliriz. O böyle şeyleri bilebilir."

"Sonunda mantıklı bir fikir," dedi Marcus kendisini tutan Aidan'ın koluna vururken. "Kendini bana çiğnetme Aidan."

Şeytanım Marcus'un pençesi havayı yarmadan önce yakalayıp geri itti. "Sanki yapabilirsin de." Marcus göğsünü şişirerek şeytanımın üzerine yürüdü. "Dene hadi beni."

Ayağa kalktım. "Kesin şunu," dedim öfkeyle. "Siz burada sidik yarıştırırken kim bilir Katze'ye neler oluyor." Hırlayan iki adamın arasında kalmıştım. Ellerimi iki yana açıp bu saçma yükselişten kimseye zarar gelmemesi için uğraştım. "Hazırlanın. Urange'ı çağır Draza. Perilere gidiyoruz."

***

Meredith'in yaptığı yer bulucu sayesinde perilerin takıldığı dövmeci dükkânını bulmuştuk. Yaklaşık beş dakikadır sokağın ucundaki çöp kutularının arkasında pozisyon almıştık. "İçeri sadece iki kişi gideceğiz. Ben ve Meredith. Eğer Katze'ye ihtiyaç duyulursa Meredith size haber verir ve getirirsiniz. O zamana kadar Urange ve Draza çatıda kalacaklar. Aidan ile Aloha da kapıyı gözleyecek. Ryan, sakın Katze'nin yanından ayrılma, tamam mı?"

Draza sinir bozucu bir şekilde güldü. "Sanki Katze bir yere gidebilirmiş gibi," dedi alayla. Gözlerimi devirdim. Belki de Draza'yı dünyaya getirmek düşündüğüm kadar iyi bir fikir değildi.

"Ben ne yapacağım?" diye sordu Marcus. "Bir şey yapmadan duramıyorum. Ya sizi ya kendimi parçalayacağım."

Her şeyi düşündüğümü sandığım ilk seferde en önemli şeyleri unutuyordum. "İnan bunu düşünmedim."

Marcus burnundan öfkeyle nefes verdi. "Ben alfa kurdum Cassie. Bir sürüm olmasa bile alfayım ve sevdiğim kadın yaşam ile ölüm arasındaki o sikik çizgide gezinirken sen burada durmuş ve yapacağım hiçbir şey olmayacağını söylüyorsun bana. Sizinle geliyorum."

İtiraz etmek için saklandığım yerden çıktım. Marcus da gizlendiği yerden çıkıp heybetli gövdesiyle bana kafa tuttu. Aidan'ın kendini tutmak için insanüstü bir çaba sarf ettiğini biliyordum. "Tamam, bizimle gel." Bu saçma başkaldırısı için o altın sarısı saçlarını yolmak istedim ama onu anlıyordum. Aidan da tehlikede olsaydı ve birileri bana uzak durmam gerektiğini söyleseydi, o birilerini cehennemdeki sıcak su kuyularında boğardım.

Meredith, Marcus ve ben tüm anlaşmazlıklarımızı kapıda bırakıp kendimizi soğuk ve uğursuz gecenin karanlık kaldırımlarına bıraktık. Aslında üç kişiymişiz gibi hissetmiyordum. Biz dört kişiydik, endişelerimiz de bir insana dönüşüp peşimiz sıra bizi takip ediyordu.

Dükkânın önüne gelene kadar küçük kardeşler grubumuzdan çıt bile çıkmadı. Kapının önündeki gülüşen serseri perileri görünce Marcus sessizce sordu. "Eğer kâhin bize yardım etmezse ona işkence ederek bilgi alabiliriz değil mi?" Meredith boğuluyor gibi bir ses çıkardı. "Hayır, Marcus. Bir kâhini kendimize düşman etmeyeceğiz. Hem içimdeki bir his bize yardım edeceğini söylüyor."

Bu kez kurdun yüzünde son derece tehlikeli, öfkeli bir sırıtış belirdi. Adımlarını daha da hızlandırırken gözleri birkaç metre ötemizdeki perilerdeydi. "Nesin sen, kâhin mi? İçine doğuyormuş," dedi ters ters. Hızlanarak ona yetiştim. "Aslında seni kendini zeki sanan kurt, evet, ben bir kâhinim. Yani annem ben küçükken öyle diyordu. Adımın anlamı da bu seni moron. Cassandra."

Meredith koluma girince dikkatim dağıldı. "Annem derken Lilith'i kastediyorsun değil mi? Ona güvenme. Pek çok şey söyler. Sözleri hilelerle süslüdür. Zehirli olsa bile sana bal gibi gelir." Marcus kız kardeşime yanıt vermedi, ben de sustum.

Yan yana dizilmiş parıldayan motorlar dükkânın girişini neredeyse kapatmıştı. Çocuklardan birkaçı üzerlerindeki parlayan dövmelerle gerçekten dünya dışı duruyorlardı ama ben kimdim ki dünyayı ve dışını sorgulayabiliyordum.

"Selam, gençler. Kâhin için geldik." Marcus elbette planladığımız gibi davranmak yerine bodoslama dalmıştı. Şapkalı, zayıf, ince ve uzun bir çocuk sırtını kapının hemen yanındaki duvara yasladı, gölgede kalan gözlerini kısarak bize baktı. "Kim soruyor kâhini?"

Kardeşimin kolunu tuttum. "Belki de konuşmaları ben yapmalıyım." Marcus anlamayan gözlerle bana baktı. "Güven bana," dedim telkin edercesine yumuşak bir sesle. Sonra şapkalı çocuğa döndüm. "Hilekâr ve arkadaşları." Peri yavaşça doğrulup hemen yanındaki başka bir perinin kulağına eğilip fısıldadı. Birkaç saniye içinde boş muhabbet çeviren kim varsa motoruna doğru yola koyulmuştu. Motorların çalışırken çıkardıkları sesler kulağımıza dolarken peri çocuk kapıyı sırtıyla açıp bize gelmemiz için işaret verdi. Önde ben, arkamda kardeşlerim kapıdan geçip gittik.

"Normalde kâhin her talep edenle görüşmez ama seni zaten bekliyordu." Omzunun üzerinden geriye baktığında gözlerimiz buluştu. İrisler hızla renk değiştirince perilerin nefes alıp vermek kadar sık bir şekilde büyü yaptıklarını hatırladım.

Tütsü dumanı havasız dükkânda hapsolmuştu. Sırasıyla adaçayı, karabiber ve adını bilmediğim hâlde çocukluğumdan beri aşina olduğum otların kokuları ciğerlerime doldu. Göz ucumla Marcus'a baktım. *Umarım otlardan biri kurtboğan değildir. İşte tam o zaman her şey şenlik olur.*

Daha önce gördüğüm kapının önünde durduğunda peri son bir kez bize baktı. "İyi şanslar," dedi kapıyı açıp karanlık odaya bizi alırken. Arkamızdan kapıyı kapatıp bizi yerde oturan kör kâhinle yalnız bıraktı.

"Yine geleceğini biliyordum. Tam vaktinde, evet." Beyaz saçları yerde bir güneş oluşturacak şekilde parça parça ayrılmıştı. Çapraz yerleştirdiği bacaklarının hemen önünde büyük bir taş yığını vardı. Hiçbiri de kristal küre falan değildi, o tarz şeyler fanilerin uydurduğu peri masallarında olurdu.

"Kiminle konuşuyor?" dedi Meredith kulağıma usulca eğilirken. Sonra bir elini kaldırıp başının hemen yanında daire çizdi. Elini hızla indirdim. "O tam olarak kör değil." Sonra bir adım öne çıktım. "Yardımın için geldik."

Kâhin eliyle karşısına oturmamı buyurdu. Yavaşça tam karşısına gelecek şekilde dizlerimin üzerinde oturdum.

"Buraya geliyorsun ama hiç hediye vermiyorsun. İsteklerin de öyle karşılıksız yapılabilecek şeyler olmuyor, lider." Dişlerinin içine gömüldüğü, yarığı andıran ürkütücü dudakları tuhaf bir gülümsemeyle iki yana açıldı. Kâhin elini kaldırıp kardeşlerimi işaret etti. "Ve hep tuhaf misafirler getiriyorsun." Sonrasındaysa başını kaldırıp bir köpek gibi havayı kokladı. "Mmm," dedi kendi kendine mırıldanırken. "Aynı kan fakat farklı bedenler. Bu üç ruh bu diyarda sonunda birbirlerini buldular demek." Marcus'un gözünün sinirden seğirdiğine emindim ama sessizce oturmaya devam ettim.

"Geçen sefer yanımda gelen kız," dedim topuklarım kalçama batarken. Öyle rahatsız bir oturuş seçmiştim ki kendime küfürler ediyordum. "O kızın başı belâda." Ve olanları akla mantığa ve herhangi bir canlının kulağına deli saçması gelmeyecek şekilde açıklamaya çalıştım. Ben anlattıkça kâhin önündeki taşları domino misali dizmeye devam ediyordu. "Şimdi de onu kurtarmanın bir yolunu bulmalıyız," dedim konuşmamı noktalarken. Ve kâhin de biten cümlemle beraber son taşı koydu.

Muhtemelen Marcus'a sonsuzluk gibi gelen birkaç saniye boyunca odada kimse konuşmadı. Bu boşluktan faydalanıp oturuşumu değiştirince yaşlı peri güldü. "Sen daha bir çocuksun ama tüm dünyanın yükü senin şu küçük yuvarlak omuzlarında. Öyle değil mi kızım?" Ne diyeceğimi bilemedim. "Bu uğursuz ruh, peşindekilere de acı getiriyor. Bir sonraki gelişinde bu kadar şanslı olmayacaksınız." Şimdi görmeyen gözleriyle bana bakıyordu. Ruhumun dibinde, karanlık kuyuların ardında bir yerde bir ürperti filizlendi. Ben uğursuzdum. Ve peşimdeki herkese zarar veriyordum, bunu bilmek için bir kâhin olmaya gerek bile yoktu. Sadece bana bakmak yeterdi.

"Hilekâr, kehanetini ben yazmadım," dedi yaşlı kadın birden. Omzumun üzerinden kardeşlerime baktım. Az öncekinden daha şaşkın bir hâlde bizi izliyorlardı. "Sonradan melek olan şeytanına verdiğim kâğıttaki sözler benim değil." Aidanhell'den bahsediyordu. "Lilith kehaneti mi?" diye sordum merakla. Bu hayatımı değiştiren şeydi. Ne ile karşı karşıya olduğumu bilmek istiyordum. Beni şu ana getiren o sözler kimden çıkmıştı?

Kâhin sadece güldü. Saçlarından bir tanesi çivilendiği yerden kurtulup havaya yükselirken yaşlı kadın konuşmaya başladı.

Şeytanların kanları yeniden alev aldı.

Unutulmayanlar bir bir akıllara kazındı.

Dirilenler mezarlarından çıktı.

Bir kız ağladı, bir kurt uludu ve bir çocuk doğdu hiçlikten.

Ve hile yaptı ait olmayan kişi saklandığı yerden.

Kükredi güneş ve yaktı cehennem tüm uğursuz ruhları.

Geldi o güzel son, tüm kâinatların kurtuluşu ve nihai yok oluşu.

Bir kız parçaladı kâinatı ve tüm varoluşlar karıştı birden.

Ve hilekâr, bir kez daha ölmeli yeniden.

Kâhin gözlerini açtı. Ve ben kapalı hâlinde çok daha iyi olduklarına kanaat getirdim. Sözlerinden tek bir tanesini bile anlamamıştım ama kehanetlerin meselesi de buydu zaten. Biz anlamayalım diye yazılıyorlardı. "Bu bir kehanet mi?" Kâhin yavaşça başını salladı. Taşları bir bir yan yatırıp ortaya topluyordu. "Sen mi yazdın?"

Yaşlı kadının eli pembe bir kuvars taşının üzerinde durdu. "Bunu da pek çoğu gibi ben yazmadım," dedi sadece. Ardından tüm taşları toplayıp bej rengi bir çuvalın içine attı. Havadaki saçları bir bir yere düşerken çiviler hayali çekiçler tarafından yeri dövmeye başlamıştı.

"Peki Katze'nin tüm bunlarla ne alakası var?" Marcus kendini tutamamıştı. Gerçi o sormasa benim bir sonraki sorum bu olacaktı. Dışarıda son nefesine tutunan bir dostum vardı ve ben burada deli bir kadının manasız sözlerini analiz etmeye çalışıyordum.

Kâhin sanki bugünkü konuşmanın en aptalca olanı buymuş gibi önemsiz bir edada yanıtladı. "Ha o mu? O kolay. Şeytanların kanları yeniden alev aldı. Tanıdık geldi mi?"

"Kendimi s-" Meredith'e öyle bir baktım ki cadı sus pus oldu. "Evet, kehanette geçiyordu," dedim tüm hanımefendiliğimle.

Kâhin, kırışmış kuru dudaklarını şaklattı. "O ejderhayı temsil eden bir cümle."

"Kralları mı diyorsunuz?" diye sordu Meredith ve kâhin o odaya girdiğinden beri ilk kez kız kardeşime baktı. Sadece onu mu yoksa ona ait olan koca bir evreni mi görüyordu emin değildim.

"Hayır. Onlar unutulanlar. Kanları bir işe yaramaz. Bedenen zaten var olmadılar. Gerçek bir ejderhadan bahsediyorum. Burada, Boston'da yaşayan. Onun kanı, kurdun eşleştiği vampiri kurtarabilir." Bacaklarını tekrar çapraz yapıp cılız kollarını üzerlerine yerleştirdi. Gözünü kapatıp huzurlu bir ifadeyle başını kaldırdığında kapı açıldı. Kâhin çoktan meditasyonuna dönmüştü. "Gitmeniz gerekiyor," dedi kapıdaki peri. Hayır hayır, işimiz bitmedi ki!

"Ama bir ejderhayı nereden bulacağız?" Kâhin yanıt vermeyince onu omuzlarından tutup sarsmak istedim. Seni çılgın kadın! Buradan elimiz boş dönemeyiz!

"Cadı biliyor," dedi kâhin aniden gözlerini açıp. Sonra tekrar eski pozisyonuna döndü. "Cadı en başından beri biliyordu."

Gözlerim Meredith'deyken sordum. "Cadı neyi biliyordu?"

Kâhin derin bir nefesin ardından dudaklarını daire şekline getirerek aldığı havayı geri üfledi. "Aidanhell ve Draza'nın ejderha kardeşinin en başından beri yaşadığını tabii."

BÖLÜM 20

Dükkândan çıkıp diğerlerinin yanına dönerken Meredith ile konuşmadım. Oysa cadı kapıyı kapatıp kâhini geride bıraktığımız andan itibaren hiç susmadan kendini açıklamaya çalışmıştı. En çok Meredith biliyordu bir şeylerin gizlenmesinden ne kadar nefret ettiğimi ve yine de gizlemişti.

Cadı, ben kaldırımları hızla adımlarken arkamdan yaklaşıp bileğimi tutmaya çalıştı. "Haklı sebeplerim vardı," dedi milyonuncu kez. Elimi çekip tutuşundan kurtardım. Marcus başparmağını havaya kaldırarak gölgelerde gizlenen ekibimize işaret verdi. Meredith ise hâlâ benimle konuşmaya çalışıyordu.

"Yanlarına gitmeden önce bir dinlesen olmaz mı?" Olmazdı. Az önce kız kardeşlik imtiyazını kaybetmişti.

"Belki de onu dinlemelisin," dedi Marcus kulağıma eğilerek. "Meredith akıllı bir kızdır. Eğer saklamayı tercih ettiyse mantıklı bir sebebi olmalı." Sinirle güldüm. "Bir saat önce herkese hırlıyordun. Ne oldu da hemen yumuşadın?" Marcus kısık sesle sövünce çenemi dikleştirerek adımlarımı hızlandırdım.

Kardeşlerimle arama birkaç metre mesafe koyup sokağın karşısına geçtim.

Aidan duvarın arkasındaki gölgelerden çıkıp beni karşıladı. "Az öncekinden daha beter hâlde geldiniz," dedi gözleri benden arkamda bize doğru yaklaşan kardeşlerime kayarken.

Öfke ruhumu kemirirken sakin kalmaya çalışıyordum. "Katze'yi kurtarabilirmişiz." Başımı kaldırıp gözlerine baktım. Aidan böyle güzel bir haberi tekdüze bir sesle vermemin sebebini anlayamamış gibiydi. "Ee, o hâlde sorun ne?" Uzanıp koluna dokunarak kendimi sakinleştirmeye çalıştım. "Sorun," dedim henüz yanıma varmış kız kardeşime bakarken. "Meredith'in değişmemiş olması."

"Yapma Cass," dedi kız kardeşim haksızlığa uğramış bir surat ifadesi ile. Bir şeyler gizleyen oydu ama haksızlığa uğrayan da oydu, öyle mi? Kollarımı göğsümde birleştirip en gıcık yüzümü takındım. "Neden iblis kardeşlere gizlediğin şeyleri anlatmıyorsun? Hepimiz seni bekliyoruz." Draza kendisinden bahsedildiğini duymuş gibi binanın yangın merdiveninden başını sarkıttı. Beyaz saçları yerçekimine yenik düşerken karanlık gözleri cadıda sabitlenmişti. Ne düşündüğünü anlayabiliyordum. Onu tanıdığım tüm bu süre boyunca elf durmadan Meredith'in güvenilmez olduğunu söylemişti ama aptal ben her seferinde kulaklarımı gerçeklere tıkamıştım.

Meredith meraklı birçok çift göze maruz kalınca bir an için ne diyeceğini bilemedi. Parlak yeşil gözleri mahcup bir ifadeyle yüzlerimizde dolanırken ellerini kucağında birleştirdi. Eğer Marcus imdadına yetişmeseydi kız kardeşimin konuşması bir asır sürebilirdi. "Katze'yi kurtarabilmek için ejderha kanına ihtiyacımız var. Siz sormadan söyleyeyim, kralların kanı olmazmış. Yaşayan kanlı canlı bir ejderha gerekiyor ve o ejderha da Aidan ve Draza'nın öz kardeşi." Marcus konuşmasına bir nefesçik mola verirken bana döndü. "Gördün mü bak? Çok kolay. Her şeyi dramatikleştirmeye gerek yok. Dan diye söyleyin gitsin." Draza ile Aidan'ı gösterip alaylı bir şekilde dudaklarını büktü. "Sence o ikisinin bozulacak sağlam bir psikolojileri var mı?" Haklıydı. İblis kardeşler yaşamları boyunca öyle tuhaf şeylerle karşılaşmıştı ki ejderha bir kardeş onları çok da şaşırtamazdı.

Aidan'ın sıcak kahverengiye dönerken irileşen gözleri son cümlemi yutmama sebep oldu. "Kardeşimiz yaşıyor mu?" Ellerimi bırakıp Meredith'in yanına gitti. "Bunun seninle ne ilgisi var? Sen biliyor muydun?" Cadı çevresine kaçamak bakışlar atarak huzursuzca yerinde kıpırdandı. "Anlatacaktım ama daha önemli dertlerimiz vardı." Tam üstümüzden bir ıslık sesi gelince yukarı baktık. Draza sarktığı tırabzanlardan birine otururken sesini duyurmak için bağırmaktan çekinmiyordu. "Öyle bir kadın o. Alışın artık. Yılanı boynunda gezdirip sonra seni sokunca ağlamaman lazım Cassie. Yılan bu, tabiatı nasılsa öyle davranır."

Urange baş aşağı bir şekilde yangın merdivenine inişe geçti. Draza'nın hemen yanında durduğunda gözlerinde hoşnutsuz bir ifadeyle, "Biraz daha bağır elf. Henüz duymayan birkaç blok kaldı," dedi. Bunun üzerine Draza uğursuz koca çenesini kapattı.

Küçük kaçık grubumuzda bir uğultu başlamıştı. Mevcut yeni bilgiyle ne yapacağımız ve yerine getirmemiz gereken tonla görev varken Katze'yi nasıl kurtaracağımız konusunda herkes fikrini belirtiyordu. Can sıkıntısı tüm hücrelerime dolarken Meredith'den tarafa bakmamaya çalışıyordum. Beni izlediğini fark etmem için çok da akıllı olmama gerek yoktu.

Aidan'ın parmakları bileklerime sürtününce bakışlarımı şeytanımın şaşkın, tatlı gözlerine kaldırdım. "Meredith her ne biliyorsa bana anlatmaz ama sana anlatacaktır. O çürük kalbinde hangi sapkın nokta buna hükmediyor bilmiyorum ama kendince seni seviyor." Acı acı güldüm. "Evet, çok seviyor. Koskoca bir kehaneti benden gizlemiş. Oradaki maddeleri duymalısın." Gözlerimi kısarak son derece üzgün görünen kız kardeşime baktım. "Daha neler gizlediğini ancak tahmin edebiliriz." Aidan'ın eli çenemi kibarca kavrayıp beni kendine çevirince gözlerim cadıdan tekrar ona kaydı. "Bu sevdiklerinin ilk kez senden bir şey sakladığı an değil. İnan bana iyi biliyorum. Bir zamanlar kalbimi verdiğim baş belâsı bir avcı başından beri babamı öldürmesi gerektiğini benden gizlemişti."

Utanç ayak parmak uçlarımdan yanaklarıma fırlayınca gözlerimi kaçırmaya çalıştım ama Aidan çenemi tekrar sıkıca tuttu. "Kızgın değilim Cassie. Bu çok uzun zaman önceydi ve sebeplerin vardı." Durup meraklı bir ifadeyle cadıya baktı. "Onun da haklı sebepleri olabilir."

Aidan'ın haklı olmasından nefret ediyordum. Şeytanımın karşısında inadımın birkaç saniye içinde tuz buz olmasından da nefret ediyordum. Şımarık kızlar gibi ayağımı yere vurup bağıra çağıra ortalığı birbirine katmak istedim ama bunun yerine gözlerimi kapatıp derin bir nefes aldım. "Onunla konuşalım öyleyse." Aidan bir şey söylemek için dudaklarını aralayınca elimle ağzını kapattım. "Ama sadece sen böyle sevimli bir şekilde istediğin için. Bana kalsaydı onunla bir milenyum boyunca konuşmazdım." Aidan ağzına kapanan parmaklarımı tutup indirirken bembeyaz dişlerinin süslediği dudakları keyifle kıvrıldı. "Kâinatta beni sevimli bulan tek yaratık sensin." Omuz silktim. Geri kalan beş milyar insanın Aidan'ı ürkütücü bulması benim sorunum değildi.

Aidan'ın kolları sırtımda bana güç verircesine gezinirken kız kardeşimin yanına gittim. "En başından itibaren anlatmazsan yemin ederim herkese aslında saçlarının siyah olduğunu söylerim." Meredith'in yeşil gözleri ardına kadar açılırken Aidan öksürüyor gibi bir ses çıkardı. "Saçlarım aslen siyah değil ki." Gözlerimi devirdim. "Benim sözüme karşılık seninki. Sence hangimize inanırlar?" Gergin ortamları anında yumuşatabilen gıcık espri yeteneğim için kendimle sessizce gurur duydum. Oysa Aidan iç sesimi duyabildiği için ben kafayı yemişim gibi beni izliyordu. Bazen bu kadar deli bir kızı neden sevdiğini anlamaya çalışıyordum.

Cadı o ana kadar kendini zor tutmuş gibi yakınındaki bir çöp kovasına sırtını yaslarken biriktirdiği nefesleri ardı ardına verdi. Kızıl saçları tokasından kurtulup gelişigüzel bir şekilde omuzlarına dökülürken, "Tamam, anlatacağım," dedi yorgun çıkan sesiyle.

***

Valkürlerin takıldığı parktaydık. Meredith Marcus'un tüm ısrarlarına rağmen anlatma işini erteleyebildiği kadar geciktirmişti. Kanatlı komutanlarla görüşmem bittiğinde Meredith'i bir bankta yalnız otururken yakaladım. Dalgın yeşil gözleri uzaklardaki su birikintisinde sabitlenmişti. Yanına oturmadan önce çevreme bakındım. Ben cehennem delegeleriyle görüşürken Urange, "Aç iblisler oynamaz," diyerek favori yiyeceğimizi almaya gitmişti. Gerçi kimsede iştah olduğunu sanmıyordum.

Kendimi dikkatlice ahşap banka bırakırken cadı gözlerini kırpmadı bile. İzlediği sıkıcı gölete çevirdim gözlerimi. "Daha fazla erteleyemezsin, biliyorsun. Marcus seni boğar, daha önce yapmadı da değil üstelik." Marcus henüz küçük bir çocukken dönüşüm geçirerek Meredith'in boğazını boydan boya yarmıştı. O zamanlar Merr henüz bir bebekti ama annemiz Lilith, onu kurtarmak için çukura gitmeden önce kız kardeşim orada haddinden fazla kalmıştı. Çocukluk travmaları yaptıklarını bir yere kadar açıklayabiliyordu tabii.

"Senden özellikle bir şey saklamak istemedim," dedi kız kardeşim gözlerini birkaç kez kırptıktan sonra bana dönerek. "Ama zaten çok doluydun ve dertlerine yenilerini eklemek istemedim. Aslında bu biraz komik çünkü tüm hayatımda ilk kez birini *gerçekten* düşünerek hareket ediyorum ve sonucunda suçlanıyorum."

Sinirli bir şekilde güldüm. "Merr, hadi ama! Suçlanmanın sebebi iyi niyetin falan değil. Kehaneti biliyordun ve tek kelime etmedin. Kör kadının sözlerini hatırlıyor musun? Benimle ilgili olanı. Onu da biliyor muydun?" Kardeşim sessizce başını salladı. "Ama önemsiz olduğunu düşündüm. Belki bir söz aldatmacasıdır dedim. İblisler diyarında her şey mantıklı olmuyor zaten. Bunu ciddiye alacağını biliyordum." Konuşmak için ağzımı açınca üzgün yeşil gözlerine baktım, ardından sustum. İblise dönüştüğümde bana koşulsuz şartsız yardım eden kız duruyordu karşımda.

Nefesimi bıkkınca bıraktım. "Elbette kehanetleri ciddiye alacağım. O kâğıtta yazılanlar yüzünden sevdiklerimi aylarca göremedim, iki kez ölümden döndüm ve kalpsiz bir katile dönüştüm." Konuyu daha fazla uzatmak istemedim. Geçmiş üzerinde konuşulmayacak kadar karanlık ve boktandı. Gerçi şimdi, kimsenin uğramadığı ıssız bir parkta otururken geleceğin de en az geçmişim kadar boktan olduğunu düşünmeye başlamıştım.

Arkamızdan yaklaşan adım seslerini duyunca Meredith ve ben oturuşumuzu düzelttik. Gelenler Aidan ve Draza'ydı. Aidan bankın ucuna yerleşip beni belimden çekerek dizine oturttu. Draza ise ayakta durmayı tercih etti, zarif kollarını göğsünde kavuşturup ifadesiz, dipsiz kuyular misali kapkaranlık gözlerini cadıya sabitledi. Draza'nın hayatını mahveden kadınla aynı ortamda bulunmasının ne kadar zor olabileceğini fark ettim.

Meredith konuşmaya başlamadan önce başını geriye atıp abartılı derin bir nefes aldı. "Aidanhell melek olduğunda," dedi gözleri beni kavrayan iblisime kayarken, "Cassandra Ana Saray'da kafayı yemişti." Pekâlâ, bunlar bir sır değildi. Hayatımın o partını derin bir çukur kazıp gömdükten sonra üstüne işeyerek kapatmak istiyordum. "Sorun şu ki," dedi cadı devam ederek. "Ona nasıl yardım edebileceğimi bilmiyordum, bu yüzden ben de tanıdığım iblislik konusunda her şeyi bilen tek kişiye gittim."

"Annemize," dedim cümlesini tamamlayarak. Meredith başıyla onaylayınca Draza'nın soğuk suratında ürkütücü bir tebessüm belirdi. "Lilith her şeyi bilir," dedi dalga geçer gibi. Cadı onu umursamadan kaldığı yerden devam etti. "Annem o zaman bana kehanetten bahsetti. Ve kehanetteki alev alan şeytan kanı kardeşiniz Diego'ydu." Tepkilerini görmek istercesine iblis kardeşlere baktı. Aidan'ın ifadesi dalgalı siyah saçlarının ardında gizliydi, Draza ise bir tepki verecekse bile bunu Meredith'in karşısında yapmayacaktı.

"Lilith bana anneniz Keranu'dan bahsetti ve elbette ki Diego'dan. Ejderha oğlunu yeryüzüne gönderip nasıl saklamayı başardığını anlattı. Zamanı geldiğinde Diego ile yollarımızın kesişeceğini söyledi ama bu olduğunda her şey o kadar boktan bir hâlde olacakmış ki, hiç olmamasını diledim." Kendi kendine acır gibi güldü cadı. "Ama şu işe bakın, her şey gerçekten de boktan bir hâlde ve bizim o çocuğa ihtiyacımız var." Kimse konuşmuyordu, kulaklarıma gelen tek şey Valkürlerin uzaklardaki atlarının çırptıkları kanatlarının sesiydi.

"Peki bu Diego'yu nerede bulacağız?" Aidan sessizliğini nihayet bozduğunda çenemi yumuşacık, mis kokulu saçlarının üzerine koydum. Meredith bize doğru gelen Urange'ın elindeki pizza poşetlerine baktı. Çenesiyle işaret ederken, "Adres şu an yürüyerek size geliyor," dedi. Omzumun üzerinden perinin elindeki poşete baktım. Meredith yerinden kalkıp kot pantolonunun kalçasındaki tozları temizledi. "Kardeşiniz bir pizzacıda çalışıyor. Urange'ın günde neredeyse üç defa gittiği pizzacıda."

***

Urange uçuş tozunu baygın vampirin üzerine olabildiğince serptikten sonra kızı sırtına aldı. "Max seni bekliyor," dedim perinin sırtında hareketsiz duran arkadaşımın pembe saçlarını yüzünden çekerken. "Çatı katındaki odaya yatır onu. Zamanı geldiğinde Max aracılığıyla sana ulaşırım."

Peri çocuk sırtında Katze ile havalanırken Ryan da yaya olarak onların peşine takıldı. Hemen yanımda Marcus, perinin gökyüzünde giderek küçülen silüetini yüzünde büyük bir acıyla izliyordu. Kolumla hafifçe dürtüp, "Sakin ol alfa," dedim. Kardeşim üzgün kehribar gözlerini bana çevirince güven verici bir şekilde gülümsemeye çalıştım. "Ejderha, Katze'nin ilacı. Güven bana, bunu halledeceğiz." Marcus zoraki bir şekilde gülümserken Meredith elindeki parlayan zincirli nesneyi sallıyordu. "Hadi gelin," dedi boştaki eliyle işaret ederken. Daha dikkatli bakınca zincirin ucundaki madalyonu gördüm.

"O madalyon düşündüğüm şey mi?" Kız kardeşim gözlerini yuvarlak kolye ucunun üzerindeki yanıp sönen taşlardan ayırmadan başını salladı. "O bir ejderha bulucu mu?" diye sordum şaşırarak.

Aloha aniden başını omzumun arkasından geçirince zıpladım. "Hayır, o bir her şey bulucu. İstediğin kişiyi onunla bulabilirsin. Beni asla şaşırtmıyor bu kadın." Cadıya çekici olduğunu düşündüğü ürkütücü bir ifadeyle gülümsemişti ama Meredith ona bakmadı bile.

Meredith'in önderliğinde birlikte parkı geçtikten sonra cadı aydınlık bir caddenin tam ortasında durdu. Başını kaldırıp çevreyi hızla taradıktan sonra, "Şu taraftan," dedi sakince. Aidan elini belime koyunca atacağım adımı unutup istemeden tökezledim. İblisin yakınlığı motor fonksiyonlarımı bile etkiliyordu. Sadece Aidan tüm evren yanıp kül olsa bile bana bir şeyler hissettirebilecek olan tek erkekti.

Hemen solumda Aloha alaylı bir ifadeyle konuşunca düşüncelerim yakışıklı şeytanımdan uzaklaştı. "Ben de Draza'ya mı sarılayım?" dedi Aloha. Sonra kendi yaptığı tuhaf esprisine güldü. Aidan sıcacık ellerini belimden çekince öldürücü gözlerle strigoiye baktım. Sadece iki dakika mutlu olmam bile herkese batıyordu değil mi?

"Geldik," diye bildirdi cadı ışıklarının neredeyse tüm caddeyi aydınlattığı dükkânın önünde durduğunda. Yan yana sıralanıp camın ardından içeriye bakmaya çalıştık. Merr'in elindeki kolye deli gibi parlıyordu. "Orada bir çocuk var," dedi elf uzun tırnaklarıyla kasayı işaret ederken. Dükkânın içinde görebildiğim kadarıyla beş dikdörtgen masa, girişe yakın bir kasa ve arkalarında tezgâh penceresinin olduğu mutfak vardı. Kasanın arkasındaki koridorda iki çalışan şakalaşarak gözden kayboldular.

"İçeride çok kişi var. Hangisi olduğu nereden anlayacağız?" Aidan'ın sorusu üzerine gözler Meredith'e çevrildi. Ve cadı nihayet gülümsüyordu. Kendini herkesten çok daha zeki gördüğü zamanlarda yaptığı şu gülümsemelerden biriydi. "Bana bırakın," dedi kendinden emin bir şekilde, sonrasında bizleri beklemeden kapıyı iterek pizzacıya girdi.

Peşi sıra dükkâna girdiğimizde ekipteki kaslı oğlanlar sağ olsun neredeyse nefes alacak yer kalmamış gibiydi. Masalar bile bizimkileri görünce kıskanıp küçülmüşlerdi sanki. Kasadaki şapkalı çocuk başını kaldırmadan, "Hoş geldiniz," dedi. Eliyle panoyu işaret ederek, "İndirimli menülerden mi alırsınız yoksa ben öneri mi yapayım?" Meredith bankonun üzerine eğilip elindeki parlayan madalyonu salladı. "Ben bir ejderhalı menü istiyorum," dedi sinsice, ardından ekledi: "Alevlerde çok kalmış olması tercihim." Bunun üzerine şapkalı çocuk âdeta dondu. Başını kaldırıp önce cadıya sonra arkasındaki bizlere baktı. Meredith anlık boşluktan faydalanarak çocuğun eline uzandı ve madalyonu avuçlarına bıraktı.

Kolye dumanlar çıkarınca cadı arkasını dönüp bize seslendi. "Bu o." Şapkalı çocuk elindeki madalyonu zehirli bir yılanmış gibi fırlatıp geri çekildi. Aidan ve Draza ona doğru ilerleyince çocuğun endişe dolu kahverengi gözleri mutfağın arkasındaki kapıya kaydı. "Kaçacak!" dedim kasaya doğru hızla ilerlerken ve öyle de oldu. Çocuk öyle şaşkındı ki sandalyesini devirip eşyalarını etrafa saçarak mutfağa doğru gözden kayboldu. Peşinden gidip arka sokağa açılan kapıyı tekmeleyerek açtık. Henüz birkaç metre ilerlemişti ki ona seslendik.

"Kaçmana gerek yok. Neden kaçıyorsun?" Bunun üzerine Diego titreyen elleriyle başındaki şapkayı çıkarıp yere attı. Gri saçları dudaklarından çıkan sıcak bir esintiyle havalanırken boğuk bir şekilde konuştu. "Beni ele geçiremeyeceksiniz sizi gerzek insanlar!" İki elini yanlara açarak sokaktaki oksijeni âdeta emercesine içine çekti. Ardından dudaklarını araladı ve ben dişlerinin hemen altındaki parlayan alevleri gördüm. Bizi alevlere boğacağını anladığımda dehşete kapıldım ama Aidan çoktan kanatlanıp gökyüzünde takla açarak çocuğun tam arkasına geçmişti. Diego ağzından henüz birkaç santim alev çıkarabilmişti ki Aidan kardeşinin ensesine dirseğini sertçe geçirdi. Ejderha çocuk yere yığılırken arkamda bir yerde Marcus'un küfrünü işittim. "Baygın bir ejderhanın bize çok yardımı olacak," dedi kurt yanımdan geçip Aidan'a doğru yürümeden hemen önce.

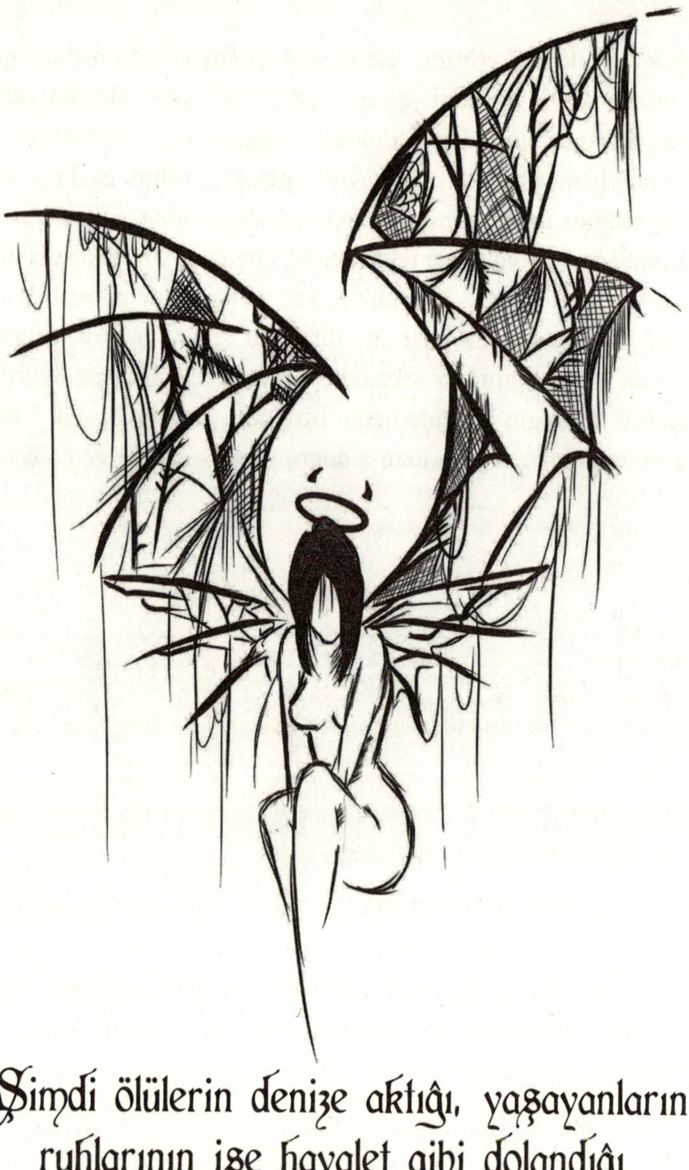

"Şimdi ölülerin denize aktığı, yaşayanların
ruhlarının ise hayalet gibi dolandığı
o yerdeyim, cehennemdeyim."

BÖLÜM 21

Diego

"Burnu annemi andırıyor."

"Hayır, burnunda kavis var. Lucifer'ın burnu bu."

Sesler tanıdık değildi. Evimde, sıcacık yatağımda dinlenirken tanımadığım heriflerin neden odamda, başımın dibinde bağırdığını anlamaya çalıştım. Onları içeri kim almıştı ve bahsettikleri burun kimin burnuydu?

"Ayılıyor galiba," dedi bir kız sesi, ardından belime sertçe çarpan şeyle yüzümü buruşturdum. "Yabani misin Meredith? Çocuğu neden tekmeledin ki şimdi?" Başka bir kızın öfkeli sesi beynime doluşunca gözlerimi açmaya karar verdim. Evime zorla girmenin bedelini bu serserilere ödetecektim.

Başımı oynatınca keskin bir ağrı ensemden şakaklarıma saplandı ve inleyerek elimi gözlerime götürdüm. Ağrı gözlerimde değil, başımın hemen arkasındaydı. Acı saniyelerle artarken yüzümü kapayan parmaklarımı indirip göz kapaklarımı araladım.

Bir grup insanın başımda toplandığı doğruydu ama mekân yanlıştı. Evimdeki sıcacık yatağımda değildim, dükkânın arkasındaki çöp kovalarından birine yaslanmıştım. Beynim bir an için gördüklerini idrak edemeyince gözlerimi tekrar tekrar kapatıp açtım. Yabancılar hâlâ karşımdaydılar, simsiyah gözleri olan gümüş saçlı bir tanesi üzerime eğilince kaçmak için kendimi geri çektim.

Sırtım teneke kovaya sertçe çarpınca başımdaki ağrı yeniden hortladı ve bu kez sövdüm.

"O kesinlikle senin kardeşin Draza," dedi kız. Sesi keyifliydi. Ben burada ruhumu teslim ederken o gülüyor muydu yani? Gözlerimi açmadan elimi havada rastgele salladım. "Pekâlâ, kimsiniz bilmiyorum ama inanın bende isteyeceğiniz hiçbir şey yok. Param yok." Elimi pantolonumun ön cebine atıp cep telefonumu çıkardım. Gözlerim hâlâ kapalıyken telefonumu bilinmezliğe uzatıp, "Tek sahip olduğum bu. Taksitlerini hâlâ ödüyorum ama alın sizin olsun," dedim. Biri elime vurunca telefonum sokağın karanlık asfaltına sertçe çarptı.

"Gözünü aç ejderha." Güçlü bir erkek sesi konuşunca diğerleri sessizliğe gömüldü. İçimdeki ateşi çağırmayı düşündüm ama yeterince güçlü hissetmiyordum ki. Alevli nefesi çağırmak oldukça büyük bir güç gerektiriyordu.

"Yüzlerinizi görmedim, yani beni bırakın ve hayatlarınıza geri dönün. Sizi yetkililere teslim etmem." Oysa über mükemmel çalışan altıncı hissim bu insanların yetkilerle işi olmadığını söylüyordu.

Ya Diego... İşte böyle. Onca yıllık ejder uykusu, sosyal hizmetler kâbusu, sayısız koruyucu aile ve asla güldürmeyen kız arkadaşlardan sonra sonun bu bok kokulu çöplerin arasında can vermek olacak.

Elimi enseme götürüp acının kaynağına parmaklarımla dokundum. Diklemesine bir bıçak beynimin içine giriyor gibi hissettirirken daha fazla dayanamayıp gözlerimi açtım.

Haklıydım, bu insanların yetkililerle işi olamazdı çünkü öncelikle onlar insan değillerdi. Beyaz saçları neredeyse beline kadar uzanan zarif bir adam suratında kuşku dolu bir ifadeyle beni izliyordu. Karanlıktan mı öyle görüyordum yoksa bu herifin göz bebekleri yok muydu, emin olamıyordum. Hemen yanında başka bir adam iri kollarını göğsünde kavuşturup merakla yüzüme bakıyordu. Kafamı artık nasıl sert çarptıysam adamın arkasında uzanan dev alacalı kanatlar görüyordum. Kızlarsa iki kişiydiler. Biri oldukça sıradan ama güzeldi. Ela gözlerini kocaman açarak üzerime eğilmiş yüzümü inceliyordu, hemen yanındaki kızıl ise bankoda memelerini masaya yayıp elime yakıcı bir kolye fırlatan kızdı.

"Selam," dedim kimse konuşmayınca. Oğlanlar anlamayan dümdüz suratlarıyla birbirine bakarken arkada bir kahkaha duyuldu. Kahkahanın sahibi gölgelerin arasından çıkıp gelerek kızların tam ortasında durdu. Kıpkırmızı gözleri ve son bir aydır yemek yememiş gibi duran solgun cildiyle bir zombi olabileceğini düşündüm. Adam diğerlerine dönüp hâlâ gülerken, "Bu gezintilerimiz çok keyifli olmaya başladı, lütfen sık sık yapalım," dedi. Kahverengi saçlı kız gözlerini devirince zombi kılıklı herif sustu.

"Konuşmamız gerek," dedi sonra kız. Yanıma yaklaşıp elini uzatırken kendini tanıttı. "Ben Cassie. Yanımdaki kız kardeşim Meredith ve şunlar da Aidan ile Draza." Beyaz saçlı tuhaf yaratık Draza ismi geçtiğinde elini kaldırıp selamladı. Uzattığı elini sıkarken, "Ben de Diego. Şu kim?" dedim tekrar gölgelere dönen zombi adamı işaret ettim. "O da Aloha," dedi kız bu kez. Dizlerini büküp ellerini onların üzerine yerleştirdi. Konuştuğunda gözleri gri saçlarımdaydı. "Kafan nasıl?" Elimi istemsizce enseme götürdüm ve anında pişman oldum. "Mükemmel," dedim sinirle. Sonra adı Aidan olan adama baktım. "Seni kanatla üzerimde takla atarken hatırlıyorum." Adam yanıt vermek yerine omuz silkti. "Beyin travması için teşekkürler." Aidan suskunluğunu korudu.

Cassie yeniden doğrulurken yanındaki kızıl konuşmaya başladı. "Ne kadarını bildiğini bilmiyorum ama biz cehennemden geliyoruz. Ben cadıyım. Cassie melez. Aloha'nın işi biraz karışık. Şu ikisi de iblis. Beyaz saçlı olan aynı zamanda kara elf ama sen bunları düşünme. Esas olay bu değil."

Ellerimle yerden destek alarak ayağa kalktım. Dünya aldığım darbe ile dönerken dengemi sağlamak için duvara tutundum. "Siz bir sirkten falan mı geliyorsunuz? Animatör müsünüz?" Kız ağzını açtı fakat sonra hemen geri kapattı. Sonra tekrar açtı. "Buna zaman yok," dedi bıkkınca. Ardından sırtını hafifçe kamburlaştırıp bükerek sırtından jilet gibi fırlayan gri kanatlarını çıkardı.

Geçmişi hatırlarken açık kalan ağzımı kapamaya çalıştım. Demek ki kızılderili koruyucu ailelerimin uyku öncesi anlattığı hikâyeler gerçekti. İblisler gerçekten varlardı. "Bir saniye," dedim parmağımı havaya kaldırarak. Ardından elimi cebime atıp sigara paketimi çıkardım. Sigarayı dudaklarımın arasına yerleştirip nefesimle yaktım.

"Sigara içen bir ejderha," dedi beyaz saçlı ürkütücü herif. Onu umursamadım. "Anladığım kadarıyla sizler ciddisiniz. Şu insan örgütünden değilsiniz değil mi?" Dumanı içime çekerken tek tek yüzlerine baktım. Örgüt kelimesini ömürlerinde ilk defa duymuş gibi bir ifadeleri vardı. "Hangi insan örgütü?" dedi Aidan ilk kez konuştuğunda. Ağzımdaki dumanı üflerken, "Şu ceketlerinde *D* harfi kazılı bir arma taşıyan ucubeleri diyorum. Peşimdeler ve bir kez beni yakalamaya gerçekten yaklaştılar," dedim.

Kızıl cadı anlamaz bakışlarla yüzümü taradı. "Avcıları mı diyorsun?" Bir elimle ensemdeki saçları karıştırırken yerdeki çöp torbalarını tekmeledim. "Yani ben avcılar mı bilemem. Ama ömrümde hiç o kadar güzel kadın tarafından aynı anda kovalanmamıştım." Durup sırıttım. Ve benim dışımda herkes cenazede gibi dikilmeye devam etti. Anlaşılan şeytanlar espriden anlamıyordu, kendi kayıpları. "Neden buradasınız? Yani benden ne istiyorsunuz?" Sigarayı tutan parmaklarımla yerde zararsız bir hâlde yatan gariban cep telefonumu işaret ettim. "Belli ki derdiniz para değil. O hâlde ne?" Kaçıklar grubu sessizliğini koruyunca kendimi tutamadım. "Hadi ama söyleyin. Bunun için dayak yedim." Elimle ensemi işaret ettim. "Bana borçlu sayılırsınız."

Cadı bir adım öne çıktı. "Bunu güvenli bir yerde konuşabilir miyiz?" dedi gözleri sokağın iki girişini tararken. "Ben ajan değilim. Güvenli yerim yok, sadece evim var. Eğer organlarımı kaçırıp mafyaya satmayacaksanız sizi götürürüm." Tanımadığınız iblisleri evinize götürmeniz hakkında ne derler bilirsiniz, ya da bilmezsiniz. Kim bir iblisi yolda görüp evine alırdı ki? Benim dışımda tabii.

"Şu insanlar," dedi kanatlı adam yanıma yaklaşırken. "Neden senin peşindeler?"

İki kolumu yanlara açarak, "Bilmiyorum," diyebildim. "Sanırım beni kaçırıp üzerimde deney yapmak istiyorlar." Ardından hâlâ yanan izmariti yere atıp keten ayakkabımla ezdim.

***

Ejderhanın evi düşündüğüm gibi bir yer değildi. Draza ve ben nasıl rezil bir hayatımız olduğuyla ilgili hayıflanırken bunca zaman aslında zengin bir hayatı yaşadığımızın farkında bile değildik.

Çocuğun evinde sadece iki oda ve bir mutfak vardı. Eşikten geçince tam karşınızdaki oda içinde iblisürüngenlerin bile anca yaşayacağı türden ufacık bir yerdi. İki tane birbirinden uyumsuz koltuk, eski bir televizyon ve nota kâğıtlarıyla doluydu oda. Gerçi odayı küçülten şeylerden biri de köşede devasa bir ucube gibi dikilen bateri takımıydı.

Diego, her şeyiyle bizden çok farklı bir hayat yaşamıştı. Gözlerim salon duvarına asılı çerçevelerde gezinirken onun gerçekten bir hayat yaşadığını anlamıştım. Bizimkisi ise son bir sene hariç bomboş bir yaşamdı. Benim diyebileceğim tek bir fotoğrafım yoktu. Göz ucuyla Draza'ya baktım. Onun da bir fotoğraf albümü olduğundan şüpheliydim.

"Demek vampir arkadaşınız kanımı emecek ve *bumm*, iyileşecek öyle mi?" Bir yandan bizimle konuşuyor bir yandan da oturabilelim diye koltukların üzerindeki kâğıtları topluyordu. "Bunu umuyoruz, evet," dedi Cassie. Sonra benim sevimli melezim Max'i arayarak Katze'yi getirmeleri için adresi verdi. "Üzgünüm, ev biraz dağınık. Cehennemden birkaç kaçığın uğramasını beklemiyordum." Ejderha elinde kâğıtlarla doğrulurken sırıttı. Fazla mı neşeliydi bana mı öyle geliyordu?

Draza kendini koltuklardan birine bırakırken Aloha duvardaki çerçeveleri yakından incelemeye başladı. İçeride bir yerlerde Meredith yiyecek bir şey olup olmadığına bakmaya gitmişti. Diego temkinli bir ifadeyle Draza'ya bakarak koltuğun diğer ucuna yerleşti. "Dokuz koruyucu aileden sonra insan ilişkilerinde tecrübeli olacağını sanıyorsun ama hayır. Hâlâ böyle uyumsuzum," dedi ejderha gülümseyerek.

"Bu zamana kadar nasıl dünyada barınabildin?" Cassie hâlâ telefonda konuşurken tam karşılarına gelecek şekilde diğer koltuğa oturdum. "Cadının dediği gibi annem seni dünyaya getirdiyse bile şimdiye kadar birileri senin farkında olmalıydı. Ayrıca cehennem ve dünyada zaman aynı ilerlemiyor. Çok daha yaşlı olmalıydın." Ejderha çocuk, gri dalgalı saçları gözlerinin önüne düşünce başını geriye yasladı. "Beni kızılderililer büyüttü. Yani beni doğuran bir kadın varsa bile ben hiç görmedim." Dudaklarını bir şeyi hatırlamaya çalışıyor gibi büktü. "Bebeklikten beri kabilelerdeyim. Ejderhalar ejder uykusu denilen bir uykuya yatıyorlar. Her on yılda bir uyanabiliyorum sadece. Uyanalı bir hafta oldu, bir zaman sonra tekrar uykuya dalacağım ve *bumm*! On yıl geçecek." Elleriyle kafasının üzerinde bir kuş yuvası gibi dağınık duran saçlarını karıştırdı. "Her uyandığımda bana bakan ailem yaşlanıyor. Birkaç kez öldüler. Ve kabile beni kendi içinde başka bir ailenin himayesine verdi. Yaşantım boyunca onlarca annem ve babam oldu. Bir kısmını ben gömdüm bir kısmının ise cenazesine bile yetişemedim, lanet ejder uykusu."

Az önce ona imrenen parçamı yakalayıp sağlam bir şekilde tokatladıktan sonra bıçağı alıp parçalara ayırmak istedim. Diego'nun bir hayat yaşadığını düşünmüştüm ve bir bakıma haklıydım ama o hayat düşündüğümün aksine acılarla doluydu. O kadar ölümden ve yer değiştirmeden sonra ejderhanın akıl sağlığını koruyabilmesi bile tuhaftı. Gözlerim kendi saçlarıyla savaşan yeni kardeşime kayınca bu düşüncem buharlaşıp havaya karıştı. Gülüp duruyordu, bir noktada akıl sağlığını yitirmişti demek ki.

Ben orada durup analizler yaparken Diego ayaklarını ortadaki ahşap masaya uzatıp anlatmaya devam etti. "Gerçi bir kadın var. O da insan değil ama ne olduğunu bilmiyorum. Son birkaç uyanışımda bana hep yardımcı oldu. Sosyal hizmetlerde çalışıyor. İnsan aileler bulmam konusunda yardımcı oluyor, genç görünüyorum. Devlet kendi başıma yaşayamayacağımı düşünüyor." Tekrar sırıtıp meraklı parlak kahverengi gözleriyle önce bana sonra Draza'ya baktı. "Sizlerin hayatı nasıldı? Sen elf uykusuna, o da iblis uykusuna yattı mı?" Aloha hemen arkalarında boğulur gibi bir ses çıkardı. Meredith başını kapı aralığından uzatıp, "Kimse uykuya yatmadı. Bunu ilk kez senden duyuyoruz," dedi ve sonrasında tekrar kayboldu. Ocağın açıldığını duyduğumda şaşkınlıktan neredeyse küçük dilimi yutacaktım. Cadı yemek yapmayı biliyor muydu? Eğer biliyorsa onun uğursuz parmaklarından yemek yiyeceğimizi ona düşündüren şey neydi?

Güzel bir koku burnuma dolarken arkamdan yaklaşan iki kol boynuma sarıldı. Yumuşacık teni çeneme sürtünürken Cassie başını boynuma yaslayıp derin bir nefes aldı. "Katze'yi getiriyorlar. İlk kez bir şeyler yolunda gidiyor," dedi dudakları bir fısıltı eşliğinde kulağıma değerken. Ardından kollarını çekip kız kardeşinin peşinden gitti.

Aloha duvardaki tablolardan birini çekip çıkarınca zaten olmayan dikkatimiz hepten dağıldı. Strigoi kızıl gözleri çerçevenin içinde hapsolmuş bir şekilde yanımıza gelip Draza ile Diego'nun tam arasına oturdu. "Sana yardım eden kadın bu muydu?" diye sordu çerçeveyi Diego'ya uzatırken. Ejderha çocuk başıyla onaylayınca Draza sessizce sövdü. Ayağa kalkıp fotoğrafı strigoinin elinden aldım. Resimde bir kadın ve küçük bir çocuk kol kola poz vermiş gülümsüyorlardı. Tarih ise elli sene öncesiydi. Gözlerim kadının aşina olduğum yüz hatlarında gezinirken içimde kabaran öfkeye hâkim olmaya çalıştım.

"Bu kadın sosyal hizmetler görevlisi falan değil Diego. Bu kadın annemiz." Fotoğrafı göreceği şekilde ona çevirdim. Keranu sanılanın aksine kaybolmamış, ölmemiş, sadece bizi terk edip kaçarak dünyaya yerleşmişti.

***

Kapı çaldığında kardeşler odanın ortasında duran dev fili sindirmeye çalışıyordu. Onca şeyden sonra anneleri onlarla olmamayı tercih etmişti. Onun yerine bu gri saçlı ejderhayı büyütmüştü.

"İnsanları gızlice dinleme Cass," dedi Meredith büyük bir noodle paketini suyun kaynadığı tencereye dökerken. "Şşhh, sessiz ol!" Tekrar baktığımda ejder odadan çıkıyordu. Sonrasında koridordan geçerek kapıyı açtı. Arkadaşlarımı karşılamak için Meredith'i mutfakta bırakıp girişe yöneldim. Urange, üzerinden bunaltıcı bir yorgunluk akarken içeri girip salona adımladı. Marcus ise kucağında Katze ile kapıda dikiliyordu. "Ben Marcus. Yardımların için şimdiden teşekkür ederim," dedi kibarca. Sonrasında Diego onu yatak odasına yönlendirdi. Ben de peşlerinden gittim.

Marcus, Katze'yi Diego'nun tek kişilik yatağının üzerine yavaşça bıraktıktan sonra bir ölü kadar hareketsiz yatan vampir kızın yüzündeki pembe saçları kulaklarının ardına aldı. Diego kollarıyla ne yapacağını bilemeyen ergen çocuklar gibi odanın bir köşesinde sessizce bize bakıyordu. Kurt, ejderhaya dönerek keskin bir şeyi olup olmadığını sordu. Bunun üzerine Diego yatağın altındaki çekmeceden küçük, beyaz bir bıçak çıkardı.

"Aldığımdan beri bilemedim, hâlâ keskin mi bilmiyorum," dedi kurda uzatırken. Sonrasında Marcus alkol getirmesini rica etti.

Gri saçlı genç ejderha, mini boy bir votka şişesiyle odaya geldiğinde yatakta Katze'nin yanına oturmuş uyuyormuş hissi veren huzurlu yüzünü izliyordum. "Bileğini çok derin olmayacak şekilde kesmen gerekiyor ama önce bıçağı alkolle dezenfekte et." Ejderha bileğini kesmeye pek hevesli değildi ama yine de yüzünde kaygılı bir ifade asılıyken şişeyi açıp bıçağa boca etti. Ardından bıçağı tenine değdirmeden önce bana baktı. "Başlıyorum," diye bildirdi nefes alışverişi hızlanırken. Sonra bileğini kesiverdi. Marcus hızla ejderhanın koluna uzanıp tutarak kan damlayan yeri Katze'nin dudaklarının üstüne getirdi.

Bordo renkli kanın damlalar hâlinde Katze'nin solgun dudaklarına akışını izlerken Marcus Diego'nun bileğini tutan elini sıkılaştırdı. "Üzgünüm. Sadece biraz daha," dedi endişeli kehribar rengi gözleri ejderhanın acıdan buruşan yüzüne odaklanırken.

Ve tam o an içeriden kulakları inletecek büyük bir şangırtı koptu. Üçümüz birden kapıya bakınca, bilekten akan kan yönünü şaşırıp Katze'nin boynuna damlamaya başladı. "Siz devam edin ben gidip bakayım," dedim hızla. Kapıyı arkamdan kapatırken elim çoktan belimdeki hançerime gitmişti.

Odaya girdiğimde pencereler bir kez daha patladı. Solgun bir el kırık pencereden içeri uzanınca bağırdım. "Vampirler!

Çabuk toplanın!" Ben elin sahibini göremeden çevik bir vampir alttakini ezerek penceredeki açıklıktan içeri fırladı. Hemen yanında teras kapısını tekmeleyerek kıran başka bir vampir vardı. Aidan baterinin zillerinden birini çekip çıkararak terastaki vampirin boğazına sapladı. Vampir ölmeyince onlara doğru koşup hançeri ensesinden içeri soktum. Hançer yaratığın etine gömülünce vampir feryatlar ederek acıdan göremeyen gözlerle debelenmeye başladı. Hançeri almak için uzanırken sağ yanımda bir hareketlenme oldu.

Az önce elini gördüğüm kız, uzun saplı bir bıçağı kavrayıp gülümserken bana bakıyordu. Kirden keçeleşmiş sarı saçları tüm yüzüne yapışmış, çıkık elmacık kemiklerinin üzerindeki damarlar zehirden çürüyüp siyaha dönüşmüştü. "Sizi öldüremeyiz belki ama canınızı yakabiliriz," dedi neredeyse kara askerler gibi tıslayarak. Bana doğru hamle yapınca Draza kızın üstüne çıkıp boynunu kırdı ama öfkesini alamamış olacak ki kırdığı boynunun ucunda pelte gibi sallanan başı savaş narası atarak yerinden söküp çıkardı.

Geriye kalan tek strigoi elinde acınası bir bıçakla pencerenin önünde dikiliyordu. Rengârenk saçlarının gölgelediği korku dolu kızıl gözleri her birimizin üzerinde öyle hızlı dolanıyordu ki ne yapacağını kestirmek imkânsızdı. Aidan ani bir hareketle resim çerçevesini korkak vampire fırlatınca vampir geri geri giderek denizliğe ulaştı, dengesini sağlamak için kollarını açarken pencereden aşağı yuvarlandı. Bir parçalanma sesi duyulunca kırık camlara dokunmamaya özen göstererek aşağı sarktım. Elektrik direği vampirin kalbinin tam ortasından geçerek onu pörsümüş üç büyük parçaya ayırmıştı.

Diego bileği sarılı hâlde odaya girerken gözleri her gördüğü şeyle daha da irileşti. Önce bize, sonra etrafa en son da yerdeki cesetlere baktı ejderha. Ardından artık daha fazla büyüyemeyeceğini düşündüğüm gözleri parçalanmış baterisine kaydı. "Harika," dedi sinirle. "Onu almak için kaç ay çalıştım biliyor musunuz?" Arkasını döndüğünde yanlışlıkla yerdeki vampirin eline bastı sonrasında sayıp söverek odadan çıktı. Suçlu birer çocukmuş gibi birbirimize baktık. "Sadece üç kişiydiler," dedi Aidan az önce vampirin ensesine sapladığım bıçağı çekmek için ayağıyla cesedin sırtına bastırırken. "Kafayı yemiş olmalılar. Yani amaç bizi tanımak değilse düşmanına bu kadar az askerle gelmezsin," diye ekledi. Bulamaca dönmüş hançerin keskin yerlerini koltuktaki kırlente sildikten sonra bana uzattı.

Zil çalınca elimdeki bıçağı neredeyse düşürüyordum. "Ben bakarım," dedi Diego sesi yan odadan gelirken. *Sanki herhangi birimiz bakmaya yeltenecekmişiz gibi.*

Sonrasındaysa arkasında iki Valkür kadınıyla salonun girişinde belirdi. "Sanırım bu misafirler sana."

BÖLÜM 22

Valkür komutanının soğuk gözleri karşısındaki manzara karşısında yavaşça kısıldı. Hemen arkasında duran askerlerine elini kaldırarak kapıyı gösterdi. Askerler başlarıyla selam verip ellerindeki altın sarısı mızraklarıyla salonu terk ederken kadın, mızrağını duvara yaslayıp yavaşça miğferini çıkardı. Ejderha desenli dev miğferi kol altına koyup bana döndü. "Acilen cehenneme dönüp rapor vermemiz emredildi. İki gün doğumu sonra tekrar geleceğiz."

Onlarla birlikte kapıya yürüyüp gönderdikten sonra sırtımı ahşaba yaslayıp bedenimi kaydırarak yere oturdum. Ani adrenalin düşüşü eşliğinde gözlerimi tam karşımda duran ayakkabılığa diktim. Nihayet her şey yoluna girmeye başlamıştı. Katze yaşayacak, ailem güvende olacak ve cehennemin sorumluluğu da işini bilen üç ejderhada olacaktı. Geriye tek bir şey kalıyordu, o da vampir sorununu kökünden çözmek. *Ama*, dedi zihnim uyuşuk bir şekilde, *bu başka bir günün problemi olacak.*

Meredith, Draza ve Aloha salondaki cesetleri Diego'nun verdiği büyük çöp poşetlerine koyarken orada oturmaya devam edip gözlerimle Aidan'ı aradım. Şeytanım ortalarda yoktu. Ayağa kalkıp yatak odasına gittiğimde Marcus ve Katze'yi gördüm. Kurt alnını vampirin alnına dayamış bir şeyler söylüyordu, Katze'nin onu duyduğundan şüpheliydim çünkü vampir gözlerini açmamıştı. Odanın kapısını sessizce kapatıp koridoru adımladım.

İşte tam o zaman fısıltıları duydum.

Aidan ve başka birinin bir fısıltıdan ibaret sohbetiydi bu ve banyodan geliyordu. Karanlık koridordaki kitaplığın yanına gizlenerek seslere kulak kabarttım.

"Bu işin peşini bırak Nathaniel. O defterde adı bin kez yazılmış olsa da Cassie'yi öldürmeyeceğim." Dizlerim boşalınca düşmemek için duvara tutundum. Az önce doğru mu duymuştum?

Diğer ses konuşunca ruhumda fokurdayan hisleri bastırmaya çalıştım. "Sen ya da bir başkası bunu zaten yapacak. Eğer bu sen olursan cennete geri dönebileceksin. Hayatının aciz ve amaçsız olduğunu düşünüyordun Aidan. Şimdi sana bir amaç veriyorum." Daha fazlasını duymak istemedim. Göremeyen gözlerle koridorda ilerlerken bir şeye çarpıp geriye savruldum.

Meredith elinde kocaman su dolu bir kovayla bana çarpmıştı, ya da şaşkınca bakışından anladığım kadarıyla ben ona çarpmıştım. Cadı beni görünce durdu. Geçip gitmek üzereyken kolumdan yakaladı ve karın hizasında kucakladığı kovayı yere bıraktı. "Ne oldu Cass? Yüzünün rengi Draza'nın saçlarından bile daha beyaz." Kıvrak zekâsının yansıması olan yeşil gözleri yüzümde gezinip sorunun kaynağını anlamaya çalıştı, oysa ben kendimi cümle kuracak kadar iyi hissetmiyordum. Beynimin içinde bir yer uğulduyordu. Aidan neden bana bunu anlatmamıştı? Anlatabileceği öyle çok fırsatı olmuştu ki.

"Cassie?" Şeytanımın soru soran güzel sesini arkamda duyunca gözlerimi sımsıkı kapadım. Harika! Kimseye çaktırmadan bir metre bile ilerleyemiyordum. "Bir sıkıntı mı var?" diye sordu iblis ben yanıt vermeyince Meredith'e. Kız kardeşimin gözleri Aidan ile benim aramda gidip geldi. Sonra Aidan'da karar kıldı. İncecik koyu kızıl kaşları hafifçe çatılırken cadı yere bıraktığı kovayı tekrar kucakladı. "Bir öküzlük yaptın değil mi?" diye tersledi Aidan'ı. Göz göze geldiğimizde bakışlarımı okumuş olacak ki tekrar iblise dönüp söylendi. "Ne halt ettiysen çöz çabuk." Sonrasında telkin edici bir şekilde kolumu sıvazlayıp kanla yıkanan cam parçalarının iç içe geçtiği salona yöneldi.

Kendimi daha fazla güçlü gibi gösteremedim. Öfkeden mi yoksa hayal kırıklığından mı yanıyordu gözlerim, emin değildim, emin olduğum tek şey vardı o da yanan gözlerimin ağlamamın habercisi olduğuydu. Bu yüzden alnımı duvara yaslayıp Aidan'ın bana uzanan elinden kurtuldum. Sadece gitsin istiyordum.

"Cassie, neyin var?"

"Beni rahat bırak." Omzuma konan elinden kurtulmak için omuzlarımı oynattım. Komik hayvan videolarındaki küskün yavru köpekler gibiydim ama umurumda değildi. Sevdiğim herkes benden bir şey saklıyordu; ailem, arkadaşlarım ve şimdi de o. Kendimi kandırılmış hissediyordum.

Aidan kolumdan tutup beni kendine çevirdiğinde bile bakışlarımı yerden kaldırmadım. Bu kez şeytan çeneme uzanıp beni kendine bakmaya zorladı. Öfkeyle ıslak gözlerimi açıp gözlerine baktım. "Seni duydum. Biriyle konuşuyordun. Sadece bir melek o şekilde gelip gidebilir." Yanıt vermesi için ona biraz zaman tanıdım ama şeytanım konuşmadı. Acının yansıdığı hüzünlü kahverengi gözleriyle bana baktı. Canımın daha fazla yanamayacağını düşündüğüm sırada şeytan konuşmaya başladı. "O Nathaniel'di. Azrail'in başçırağı. Hastanede seni alıp cehenneme götürmeye karar verdiğim gün, o da oradaydı."

Aidan alnını alnıma yaslayıp kıvrımlı gür kirpiklerinin ardından bana baktı. "Azrail'in canını alacağı insanların adlarıyla dolu bir defteri var. Ölüm sırası o defterde beliren isimlere göre işliyor." Susup ılık nefesini dudaklarıma verdikten sonra devam etti. "O gün defterde senin adın yazıyordu ve melek seni öldürmemi emretti." Bunu konuşmak canını yakıyormuş gibi aniden sustu. Elimi kaldırıp şeytanımın yanağına dokundum. "Bu yüzden mi cennetten kovuldun?" Aidan yanıt vermek yerine başını hafifçe çevirerek yanağındaki avuç içimi öptü. "Eğer," dedim sesim hissettiğim umutsuzlukla gittikçe kısılırken, "doğru olan oysa? Ya ölmem gerekiyorsa?" Aidan gözlerini açtı fakat yanıt vermedi.

Zihnimde tek bir cümle tekrar tekrar yankılanırken şeytanımın güzel yüzüne baktım.

Ve hilekâr ölmeli yeniden.

Dudaklarımı Aidan'ın dudağına bastırırken kehanetteki başka bir cümle sızdı zihnime.

Bir kız parçaladı kâinatı ve tüm varoluşlar karıştı birden.

Ve hilekâr, bir kez daha ölmeli yeniden.

***

Aidan'a doyamıyordum.

Kehanet zihnimde tekrar tekrar uğursuz bir şekilde dolanırken tüm düşünme yetimi kapının ardında bırakıp sadece onunla olmak istiyordum çünkü Aidan varken dünya siliniyordu. Tüm kehanetler, öngörüler, can yakıcı tüm o hisler önemini yitiriyordu.

"Yalnız kalacağımız bir yere gitmek istiyorum," dedim dudaklarından ayrılırken fısıltıyla. Aidan tekrar dudaklarıma yapışınca bu kez iki elimle göğsünü ittim. Ben kendimi anlatmaya çalıştıkça Aidan boynuma art arda öpücükler konduruyor, konuşmama fırsat vermeden şapşal şapşal gülmeme sebep oluyordu. "Ben ciddiyim," dedim ılık nefesi boynumda gezinirken. Şeytanım bir an için başını benden uzaklaştırıp omzumun arkasından geriye baktı. "Bu evde iki oda var sadece. Birinde vampir bağırsakları var, diğerindeyse Marcus ve Katze." Gözleri yeniden gözlerimi bulduğunda keyfi biraz kaçmıştı. Bu duruma nasıl bir çözüm bulacağımızı bilmiyordum, tek bildiğim Aidan'ı istediğimdi. Dünyam yine uğursuz bir kehanetle sarsılmadan önce ona sımsıkı tutunmalıydım. Aidan, meleğin arzusunu önemsememişti ama ben bir şeylerin yolunda olmadığını biliyordum. Sonuçta ölmem gerektiğini tek söyleyen o değildi, kör kâhin de kehanetinde bahsetmişti.

Sözleri tekrar hatırlayınca bir kez daha içim ürperdi.

Diego'nun yatak odasının kapısı açılınca bedenimi Aidan'ın bedeninden elektrik verilmişçesine ayırdım. Önce Marcus, ardından ona tutunarak ilerleyen Katze'ye ilişti gözlerim. Vampir dostum sonunda uyanmıştı. "İşte bu!" diye bağırdım vampirin boynuna atlarken. Katze hoş, cılız bir kahkaha atarken erkek kardeşim beni çekmeye çalıştı. "Daha gücü yerine gelmedi Cass." Ama onu dinlemedim. "Seni kaybedeceğim diye çok korktum," dedim hâlâ sarılırken. Katze kurt adama tutunmadığı diğer kolunu belime sardı. "Benden bu kadar çabuk kurtulabileceğini düşünüyorsan ya deli olmalısın ya da çok saf." Kıkırdadım.

"Hadi Cass! Kızı rahat bırak." Marcus kurt adamlara has o kocaman ellerini omuzlarıma koydu. "Yarın ve diğer gün de burada olacak. Güçlendiğinde bol bol sarılırsın." Beni ikna etmeye çalışırken çıkardığı kibar ses tonuna kahkaha attım. Vampirden ayrılırken hâlâ Marcus'a gülüyordum. Kurt yeniden kadınını kolları altına alıp pembe saçlarına bir öpücük kondurdu. "İstediğinde," dedim sağ elimin işaret parmağını sallayıp gözlerimi kısarak, "kibarlaşabiliyormuşsun." Bu kez Marcus da sırıttı. "Annemden aldığımız güzel genlerden olsa gerek. İstediğimizi almanın hep bir yolunu buluyoruz." Ona katılıyordum. Göz ucumla koridorda duran yakışıklı adama baktım. İstediğim oydu ve alacaktım, Lilith'in kızı olayım ya da olmayayım.

Katze konuşunca dikkatim iblisten uzaklaştı. "Bu havasız odada ölümü bekleyerek geçirdiğim saatlerin acısını çıkarmalıyım. Çekilin, bu kız biraz hava alsın." Odadan çıkıp koridora ilerlediklerinde arkalarından seslendim. "Bizim Aidan ile konuşmamız gereken şeyler var. Bir süre kimse bu odaya gelmesin lütfen." Kıkırtılar kulağıma ulaşınca Aidan ile göz göze geldik ve ben utançtan kızarırken gülmeye başladım.

Kaybedecek bir dakikam daha yoktu.

Kâhinin sözleri kulaklarımda yankılanırken iblisime uzandım. Kana bulanmış tişörtünün yakalarını çekiştirerek geri geri odaya sürüklüyordum Aidan'ı. Şeytanın gözlerinde öyle çapkın bir ifade vardı ki, böyle bakmaya devam ederse evde alevlerle uğraşan tek kişi Diego olmayacaktı, kapıyı tekmeleyerek kapatırken ben de alev almak üzereydim.

Aidan, Katze'nin yattığı çarşafları tek hamlede çekip atarken botlarımı çıkarmaya başladım. Şeytanımın tek kaşı şaşkınlıkla yukarı kalkınca içimde bir yerler o yakışıklı yüzünü ısırmak istedi. "Konuşacağımız şeyler var sanıyordum," dedi

Aidan alayla. Ardından gözleri yukarı sıyırmakta olduğum tişörtüme kaydı. "Öyle," dedim tişörtü başımdan tutup çıkarırken. "Ama önce yapmamız gereken başka bir şey var." Atletim de ayaklarımın dibindeki giysi öbeğine katılırken Aidan'ın bakışları yavaş yavaş berraklığını kaybetti. Hançerimin takılı olduğu kemeri çözüp pantolonumun düğmelerini tek tek açmaya başladım.

Şeytanın gözleri sanki sihirli bir değnek tarafından kutsanmışçasına bir anda kızıllaşmaya başladığında pantolonumu dizlerime kadar indirmiştim. "Ah Cassie," dedi Aidan fısıltıyı andıran o baştan çıkarıcı sesiyle. "Ne kadar seksi olduğunu biliyor musun?" Pantolonu çıkarıp atarken kızarmamaya çalıştım. Aidan'ın bakışlarındaki bir şey sizi dünyanın en seksi dişisi gibi hissettiriyordu ve bu his müptelası olunacak kadar zevkli bir şeydi.

Nihayet üzerimde sadece iç çamaşırlarım kaldığında şeytan elime uzanıp beni yatağa çekti. "Sen çıkarmayacak mısın?" diye sordum tişörtünün kollarını yukarı doğru sıvayıp pazılarını okşarken. İblis gülünce ılık nefesi yüzümü yaladı. "O kadar azgınsın ki senin yırtıp atmanı umuyordum." Gözlerinin önüne düşen dalgalı bir tutamı çekince Aidan parmağımı ısırdı. "Ah!"

"Sen başlattın," dedi şeytan, sonra ısırdığı parmağımı öperek bedenini geriye doğru esnetti. Kana bulanmış tişörtünü çıkarıp atınca tekrar üzerime uzandı. Parmaklarım karın kaslarında gezinirken büyüleyici kokusu beni hapsetmişti. "Bunlara dokunmaya bayılıyorum," dedim kendimden geçmiş hâlde. Aidan'ın beni kucağına aldığı her seferde karnındaki kasların kasılışına bayılıyordum. Şeytan kendini tamamen üzerime bırakıp başını başımın yanına koydu. Elleri alt tarafa kayınca ürpererek nefesimi tuttum. Sonrasında pantolonunu çıkarmaya çalıştığını fark ederek bir kez daha utandım. Bana dokunmasını öyle çaresizce istiyordum ki, artık bunu saklayacak gücü ve iradeyi kendimde bulamıyordum. Ben kimdim ki arzunun karşısında duracaktım?

İkimiz de iç çamaşırlarımızla kaldığımızda Aidan çenesini alnıma yasladı. Kaslı göğsü inip kalkarken bedenimi saklamakta acınası şekilde yetersiz olan sütyenime çarpıyordu. Şeytan bir eliyle alt dudağımla oynarken diğer eliyle boynumu okşuyordu. "Seninle sevişmeyi bir ömür bekledim gibi." Sözleri karnımda yanan ateşi bedenime dalga dalga yayarken gözlerimi kapattım. Tüm yaşantım boyunca mutlu olduğum her ânı düşündüm ansızın. Hiçbirinde şu anki kadar mutlu olmadığımı fark ettim.

"Cassie," dedi Aidan neredeyse inler gibi. "Ah, benim güzel melezim." Başımı hafifçe kaldırıp dudaklarımı dudaklarına bastırdım. Soluklanmak için geri çekildiğimde, "Aidan," dedim bedenim arzudan kıvranırken. "Öp beni." Ve şeytan isteğimi ikiletmedi. Güçlü kollarını sırtımda birleştirip beni kucağına oturttu.

Aşinası olduğum o sertlik bacaklarımın arasındaki katlanan iç çamaşırıma çarpınca dudaklarına inledim. Aidan bir elini belime indirip kalçamı sabitlerken diğerini saçlarıma kaydırdı. Öpüşmemiz daha şiddetli bir hâl alırken iblis dudaklarımı bir saniyeliğine bırakıp başını boynuma gömdü. Minik dil darbeleri boynumdan köprücük kemiğime kayarken beni sıkan bir şeylerin artık üzerimde olmadığını fark ettim. Aidan ben fark edemeden sütyenimin kopçasını çözüp çıkarmıştı. Şimdi göğüslerim ona değerken şeytanım kalçamdaki elini çekip aramıza düşen sütyeni alarak fırlattı. Tekrar dudaklarına yapışmak için ileri atılınca beni durdurdu.

Gözleri göğüslerime kenetlenmişti. "Çok güzelsin," dedi bakışları arzudan kararırken. Parmağını göğüslerimin üzerinde okşar gibi gezdirince dudaklarımdan zevkli bir inilti koptu. "Aidan," dedim nefes nefese. Sırtım bir yay gibi geriye bükülürken Aidan'ın bir eli göğüslerimden birini tutmuştu. Diğer eli kalçamı bacaklarının arasındaki sertliğe bastırırken zevkten ağlayabileceğimi fark ettim.

"Ben artık dayanamıyorum," dedi erkeksi sesiyle üzerime atılmadan önce. Bedenimi kendisiyle yatağın arasına hapsederken bacaklarımı kalçasına doladım. İleri geri hareket etmeye başladığında aklımı yitirdiğimi düşündüm. Ona tapıyordum. Ona bayılıyordum. Ve bakışlarındaki karanlık ifadeye bakılırsa aynı şeyleri o da hissediyordu.

Aidan ellerini göğsümden çekip dirseklerinden destek alarak bedeninin üst tarafını hafifçe yukarı kaldırdı. Kalçası aynı ritimde hareket ederken gözlerime baktı. Genizden gelen boğuk bir sesle, "Seni inlerken görmek istiyorum," dedi. Ve ben daha fazla dayanamayacağımı düşünüp zevkten inlerken elimle bir şeylere tutunmaya çalıştım. Bir elimle yatağa tutunuyor, diğer elimle duvarda tutunacak bir şey arıyordum. Ve şeytan aklımı bedenimden uçururcasına bir hızla ritmini arttırdığında tırnaklarımla duvarı tırmaladım.

Şeytanımın bakışları bir an için göğüslerimden duvara değen parmaklarıma kaydı. Ve yavaşlayarak durdu. "Ne oldu?" dedim nefes nefese bir hâlde kurumuş dudaklarımı yalarken. Gözlerinin durduğu yöne başımı çevirdim. Elimi kaldırınca duvardaki koyu lekeye ilişti gözlerim.

"Tırnak diplerin kanamış," dedi şeytan yüzünde dalgın bir ifadeyle. Yatakta doğrulurken elimi açıp kanayan yaralara baktım. "Ne olmuş?" dedim anlamayarak. Kalbim ritmini şaşırmışken ve beynimdeki mantıklı tüm hücreler orgazmla meşgulken neden buna takıldığını anlamaya çalıştım.

Şeytan aniden kendi elini kaldırıp dişlerini avuç içlerine geçirince şaşkınlıkla yerimde zıpladım. Kan avucunda ince bir sızı şeklinde akarken Aidan boşta kalan eliyle elime uzandı. Avucumu açıp tırnağıyla derimi kesince ufak bir sızı hissettim. Bir saniye sonrasında ise şeytanım kanayan avucunu benimkine kapattı.

"Bu kan yemini," dedi kendinden emin bir sesle. Gözlerim birbirine kapanan kanlı ellerimiz ve şeytanımın aşk dolu kahverengi gözleri arasında gidip geldi. "Biz bu diyardan yok olana dek bu yeminimiz geçerli olacak." Ben sözlerinin ağırlığıyla nefes alamazken o çevresine bakınıp yatağın yanına devrilmiş duran pet şişeyi eline aldı. Tek eliyle açıp kapaktaki mavi plastik halkayı tutarken gözleri zaferle parlıyordu.

Nereden geldiğini anlamadığım yaşlar yanaklarıma akmaya başladığında görüşüm bulanıklaştı. "Ah Aidan," dedim sesim kaybolup giderken. Aidan diğer elime uzanıp yüzük parmağıma mavi plastik halkayı taktı. Bu ana net şahit olabilmek için gözlerimi art arda kırpıp yaşları yanaklarıma gönderdim.

"Sonsuzluk ve ötesinde," dedi Aidan ellerimizin içindeki kanlar birbirine karışırken. "Sonsuzluk ve ötesinde," dedim sevinçten ağlarken.

Ve içimizden sessizce ekledik.

Seni hep seveceğim.

❋❋❋

Mutfak masasında ekibimle beraber oturuyordum. Bir şeyler planlar gibi heyecanla mırıldanan seslerini duyuyordum ama anlayamıyordum. Aklım hâlâ dün gecedeydi. Masanın altından diğer elimin parmaklarıyla sağ elimdeki plastik halkaya dokundum, bir rüya değildi. Bu yüzük bizim nişanımızdı.

Bir el görüş alanıma girince gözlerimi kırpıp çevreme bakındım. "Daldın gittin. Bizi dinliyor muydun?" diye sordu sallanan elin sahibi cadı. Yüzünde meraklı bir ifadeyle bana bakıyordu. Ne diyebilirdim ki? Ne konuştukları hakkında hiçbir fikrim yoktu. Meredith gözlerini devirip bıkkın bir şekilde ofladı. "Vampirlerin inini basacağız," dedi sabırsızca. Boş gözlerle suratına baktım.

"Dün gece iyi uyumadın galiba," dedi tam karşımda oturan vampir. Katze sırıtıyordu, ayağımla bacağına vurunca acıdan yüzünü ekşitti. Dudaklarını kıpırdatarak *dün gece ne oldu,* diye sordu. Sanki söylerdim de.

Mutfak kapısı açıldığında soluğunu tutan sadece bendim. Diğerleri gelenin farkına bile varmadan planları hakkında konuşmaya devam ederken ben odaya giren adamın son derece farkındaydım. Aidan uyku sersemi dağınık saçlarıyla mutfağa girdiğinde gözleri hızla çevreyi taradı, nihayet beni bulduğunda sıcacık bir şekilde gülümsedi. Utancımdan sandalyemi eritirken bakışlarımı kaçırdım.

Meredith kaba bir şekilde saçımı çekince bir kez daha yerimde sıçradım. "Salondaki kırlente bir vampirin kanı bulanmış. Madalyonu kullanarak yerini saptadım. İnlerini biliyoruz. Urange, kurt adam sürüsünü oraya gönderiyor şimdi. Biz gelene kadar saklanacaklar."

Kafam karışmıştı. "Bunları kim komuta etti peki?" diye sordum masadaki yüzlere bakarken. "Urange, sabaha karşı ejder krallardan haber getirdi. Vampir sorununu kökten çözmemizi istiyorlar. Sorunu halledip yuvayı temizledikten sonra cehenneme geri döneceğiz." Yeşil gözleri heyecanla parlarken elinde tuttuğu tavayı hareket ettirdi. "Şimdi, kim omlet yemek istiyor?"

Kahvaltıdan sonra herkes hazırlanmaya başladı. Katze'yi burada Diego ile beraber kalmaya ikna etmek, dün gece kanla kirlenen kılıçlarımızı temizlemekten daha zordu. Keşke herkesin silahını ben temizleseydim ama Katze'yle başkası uğraşsaydı diye geçirdim içimden.

"Strigoi tekmeleyecek kadar güçlüyüm," dedi vampir milyonuncu kez onu yatırdığım koltuktan kalkmaya çalışırken. "Üstüne alınma Aloha," diye ekledi. Aloha umursamadığını belli eder cinsten gülümsedi ya da sadece delirdiğinden gülümsüyordu. Artık aradaki farkı ayırt edemiyordum.

"Gün batmadan dönmüş olacağız. Şu an gelirsen bize sadece ayak bağı olursun." Vampir dostum dişlerini göstererek öfkeyle hırladı. "O geliyor ama," dedi odaya giren Meredith'i gösterirken. "Dövüşmeyi bile bilmiyor, asıl ayak bağı o." Gözlerimi devirdim. "Hadi ama," dedim sıkılmış gibi. "Akşam döneceğiz." Ve vampir orta parmağını son kez gösterdikten sonra koltukta geri yaslanıp başını diğer tarafa çevirdi. Sonunda ikna olmuştu.

"Oyalanmayın," dedi Draza koridordan bağırıp sesini herkese duyurmaya çalışırken. Son bir kez kendime çeki düzen verip parmağımdaki yüzükle oynayarak odadan çıktım.

Merdivenlerden inerken Aidan yavaşça yanıma sokuldu. Tatlı baharat kokusu ciğerlerime dolarken şeytanım gülümsedi. "Seni özledim," dedi neredeyse fısıldar gibi. Karnımdaki çiftleşen kelebekleri kovalayıp ben de ona gülümsedim. *Ben senin için ölüyorum, bir bilsen.*

Cilveleşerek merdivenleri inerken Diego'nun bağırtısıyla adımlarımız durdu. Ejderha evden çıkıp merdiven boşluğuna gelerek, "Geldiler! Tanrım, geldiler!" dedi. Gözleri ardına kadar ayrılmış, teni ise birkaç ton daha açılmıştı. Başımızı kaldırıp çıldırmış gibi davranan ejderhaya baktık. "Kim geldi?" diye sordu Draza eli temkinli bir biçimde belindeki kılıcı kavrarken.

Diego cevap vermeden önce boğazından histerik bir hıçkırık duyuldu. "D." Olanlardan habersiz Meredith, binanın dış kapısını açarken gözlerim kapının önüne park eden birbiri ardına sıralanmış, üzerlerinde D harfi kazılı siyah ciplere kaydı. Meredith donakalmış bir ifadeyle aralıkta dikilirken kardeşime seslendim. "Merr. Çabuk buraya gel!"

Ve arabalardan birinin ön kapısı açıldı.

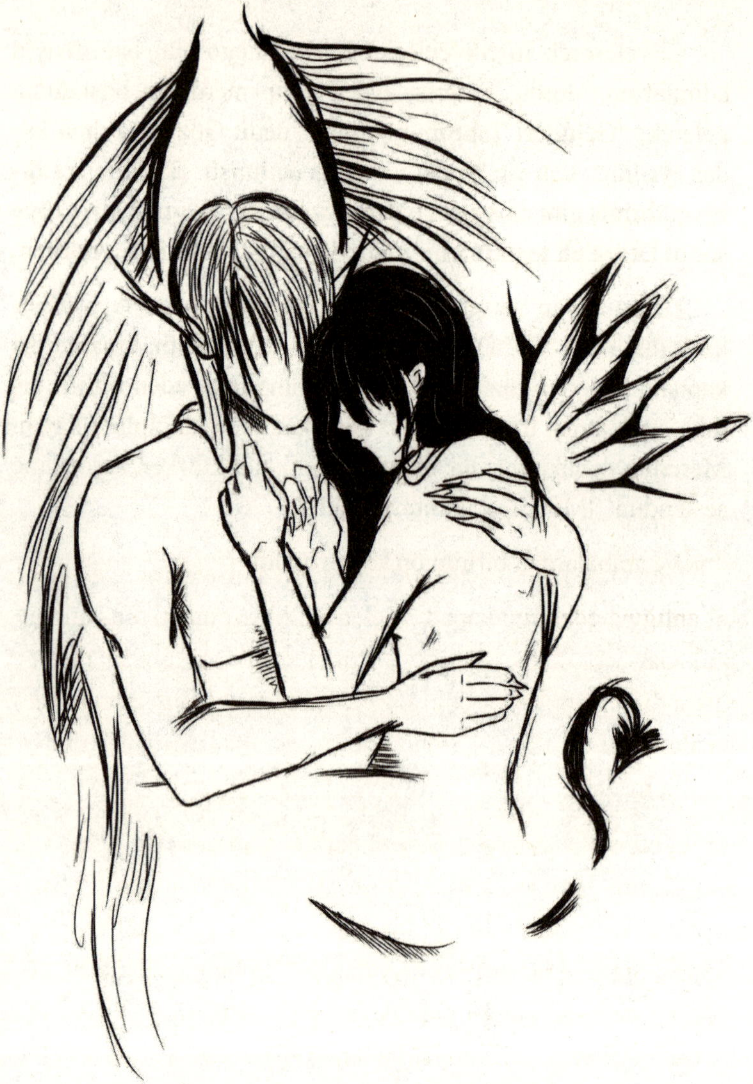

"Ya ben ölecektim ya o.
İkimizin de yaşayacağı alternatif
bir gelecek yok."

BÖLÜM 23

Lucifer, bekliyordu.

Şeytan, çukurun kül kokulu atmosferini içine çekerken bir anlığına gözlerini kapadı. Geleceğini hissetmişti ama bunun bu kadar çabuk olacağını hiç düşünmemişti. Onca zaman sonra şimdi sevdiği kadın onu görmek için unutulmuş toprakların da altına, yeryüzünün bir diğerine bağlandığı o karanlık dipsiz çukura inecekti.

Lucifer gözlerini açıp bir çift parlak boynuzun süslediği başını yukarı, göğe kaldırdı. Çukuru tasarlarken öyle derin olsun istemişti ki, buradan bakan bir ruh bir daha asla güneşi göremezdi. Şimdi Lucifer, kendi yarattığı cehennemde tutsak olmuşken bir daha güneşi göremeyeceğini düşündü, istemiyordu da zaten. Güneş, Tanrının harikalarından biriydi. Şeytan için bu aydınlıktan bile daha beterdi.

Ayaklarının altındaki zemin titreyince iblis omuzlarını süsleyen, daha önce kimsenin görmediği büyüklükteki dev kanatlarını sırtının içine çekti. Gelene bakmak için yavaşça arkasını döndüğünde cennetten kovulduğundan beri atmayan kalbinde bir sıcaklık filizlendi. Lucifer tutkuyla sevgiyi bilirdi, insanlık tarihinin en büyük manipülatörü, hilekârların atasıydı. Ama aşk bile Lucifer'ın iyi olduğu konulardan biri değildi.

Yaratılanların en ateşlisi, heybetinin yansıması olan ağır adımlarla çukurun kan kokulu zemininde yürüyordu. Buraya gelmeyi hiç istememişti ama geçen onca seneden sonra artık buna mecburdu. Hiç yüzleşemediği o acımasız adamın gözlerine bakmaya mecburdu.

İki kutsal varlık karşılaştığında, zamanın çarklarından biri durdu. Yelkovan akreple çarpıştı ve saatin yay tamburu yörüngesinden çıkıp daireler çizerek sonsuzluğun içinde kayboldu.

Ne kötü bir adam, diye düşündü Lilith.

Ne güzel bir kadın, dedi Lucifer.

Ve bir araya asla gelmemesi gereken iki varlık, aynı kül kokulu havayı solumaya başladı.

"Buraya bir daha gelmezsin sanıyordum," dedi Işık Taşıyan Başmeleklerin en eskisi Lucifer, gözleri hâlâ dişi şeytanın üzerindeyken. Lilith'den ayrı kaldığı asırlar boyunca hep onunla karşılaşacağı ânı düşünmüştü. Ne diyecekti? Özür mü dileyecekti? Tüm yaptıkları için. Lilith onu asla affetmezdi. Lucifer, yaratılanların en kurnazı da bunu zaten biliyordu. Aşkı bildiğini sanıyorlar, dedi oğullarını düşünerek. Aşk... Lilith demekti.

"Buraya bir daha gelemem sanıyordum," dedi Lilith. Kızıl gözleri çukurun her bir zerresinde oyalanırken Lucifer'a bakmamaya çalıştı. "Bir baba olarak oğullarının canı senin için önemli değil mi?"

Lucifer'ın dudakları keyifle yukarı kıvrıldı. Konuşmaya başladığında en az boynuzları kadar keskin olan gözlerinde karanlık bir ifade vardı. "Ya sen? Kızının canının değeri yok mu?" Bakışlar öldürebilseydi eğer, Lilith şeytanı küle çevirirdi. Hiddetli bir nefes dişi şeytanın zarif burnundan süzülürken, "Bunu tüm varlıklar içinde kızımı benden alan adam mı söylüyor?" dedi.

Lucifer bir an için karşısındaki kadının gözlerine bakakaldı. Ve o bir an yapabilseydi eğer, parçalara ayrılan *zamanı* tamir eder ve bu ânı sonsuzluğa hapsederdi. Ama sonra kadının eğer ilgisini yitirirse yine çekip gideceğini düşündü.

"Kâhinin kim olduğunu hâlâ bilmiyorlar," dedi birden. Maksadı saniyeler bile olsa o kadını biraz daha görebilmekti. Tok sesi çukurun taş duvarlarından onlarca eko yaparak dağılırken ekledi. "Eğer söyleseydin bu her şeyi kolaylaştırırdı." Lilith kibar, uzun parmaklarını kızıl ışıkların oynaştığı gür saçlarının arasından geçirirken sinirli bir kahkaha attı. "Bunu konuşmaya sadece sen cüret edebilirdin zaten." Dişi şeytan buraya gelmenin bir hata olduğunu anlamıştı. Bu adam ebediyette çürüse bile onu bir daha asla görmek istemiyordu. Onunla hiç tanışmamış, onu baştan çıkarmamış ve cennetten sürdürmemiş olmayı diledi.

"Değdi mi Lilian?" dedi Lucifer çaresizce. Tüm söz oyunlarına ve gizemli kalma çabalarına rağmen dişi şeytanın kalbinde tek bir zerre yoktu Lucifer'a ilgi duyan. Şeytan bu çaresizliği tüm bedeninde hissetti. "Azrail için beni bırakmana değdi mi?"

Kadının zeminde yankılanan adımları durdu. Tekrar şeytana döndüğünde öfke kulaklarında yankılanan bir uğultu misali tüm duyularını kapatmıştı. "Sen," dedi Lucifer'ın üzerine yürüyecekken, sonra söyleyeceği tüm sözleri yuttu. "Değmezsin," dedi sadece ve geriye bir adım atarak son bir kez şeytana baktı.

"Kızın sonunda kâhinin kim olduğunu öğrenecek. O zaman geldiğinde ne yapacaksın? Kaçtığım için bana bakan hakir gözlerin utanmayacak mı? Ne yapacaksın Lilian?"

"O benim kızım değil!" Lilith'in öfkeli çığlığı çukurun taş duvarlarını yerinden oynattı. Milyarlarca toz havaya dağılırken Lilith bağırmaya devam etti. "Sen öldürdün! Senin o lanetli uğursuz kıskançlığın öldürdü onu! Cassandra gibi konuşup görünebilir, hatta onun gibi kokabilir de ama o benim kızım değil. Benim kızım bir avuç toprak şimdi."

Tüm yaratılışı boyunca hiç ağlamamış olan Lilith'in günahkâr gözlerinden akan bir damla yaş, çukurun kül ve kan kaplı zeminine düştü.

***

Meredith açtığı kapıyı tekrar kapatmak isteyince eşikte iki silahlı adam belirdi. Biri kapıyı açıp binaya girerken diğeri ucunda tel olan uzun metal sopasını kız kardeşime çevirdi. Meredith adamla boğuşurken hançerimi çıkarıp onlara doğru koştum. Eşikten içeri giren adam ben son hız üzerine gelirken elini *D* armalı ceketinin iç cebine atıp gri renkli bir sprey şişesi çıkardı. Tam yüzüme gelecek şekilde püskürtünce dengemi kaybederek sendeledim.

Arkamda bir yerlerde Aidan'ın bağırtısını duyuyordum. Yarı kısık gözlerimin arasından içeri art arda silahlı adamların girdiğini gördüm. Marcus'un hırıltısı apartmanı inletirken adamlardan biri sessizce küfretti. "Kurt adamın da burada olduğu söylenmemişti," dedi diğerlerine.

"Göremiyorum," dedim bağırarak. Hançerimi gelişigüzel sallıyor, adamlardan birinin bedenine isabet etmesi için dua ediyordum. Kanatlarımı açsam bile gidecek yerim yoktu. "Meredith," dedim kız kardeşimin sesini duyabilmek için çaresizce bağırırken.

Aidan'ın zihnine ulaşmaya çalıştım ama başaramadım. Nihayet sağ gözümü açtığımda gördüğüm manzara sebebiyle donakaldım. Adam sopanın ucundaki teli kız kardeşimin boğazına geçirmişti. Cadı beceriksiz ellerle adamın yüzünü tırmalamaya çalışırken adam sopayı tüm gücüyle çeviriyordu. Bir an sonra Meredith adamı bırakıp boynundaki tellere uzandı. "Onu boğuyorsun kahrolası piç!" O an neden onlara doğru gidemediğimi fark ettim. Ellerim ve ayaklarımda gümüş kelepçeler vardı. Farkındalık öyle ağır bir balyoz gibi tepeme indi ki bir an yutkunamadım.

Var gücümle kollarımı ayırmaya çalışıyor, deli gibi çığlık atıyordum ama ne yaparsam yapayım kelepçeler bir milim bile oynamıyordu. Sol gözüm kapalı, sağ gözümden yaşlar akar hâlde yardım için çevreme bakındım. *Birisi lütfen Meredith'e yardım etsin!*

Adamlardan üçü Aidan'ı merdivende sıkıştırıp ucundan kıvılcım çıkaran sopalarla o yabani bir hayvanmışçasına canını yakıyorlardı. Kıvılcımlı bir sopa Aidan'ın karnına değince şeytanım dişlerini sıkarak iki büklüm bir şekilde yere eğildi. Hemen yanında Draza ve Aloha tıpkı benim gibi kelepçelerini kırmaya çalışıyorlardı.

"Kızıl olanı alacağız sadece," dedi kapının önünde duran takım elbiseli bir adam. Sulanan gözlerimle ona baktığımda yakasındaki *D* armasını görebildim. "Kız kardeşimi bırakın sizi şerefsiz domuzlar!" Ama adam bana bakmadı bile. Elini kaldırıp Meredith'i boynundan sürükleyen adamı çağırdı. "Bindirin kızı," dedi soğuk bir dille.

Aidan'a işkence yapan adamlardan biri kapıdaki takım elbiseliye seslendi. "Efendim, diğerlerini ne yapalım?" Adamın karanlık gözlüklerinin ardında gizlenen gözleri bir an için acı içinde kıvranan bize kaydı, sonrasında tekdüze bir sesle, "Gazla bayıltın," dedi. Meredith'in turuncu saçlarını hâlâ görebiliyorken emeklemeye çalıştım. "Lütfen," diyordum kime yalvardığımı bile bilmeden. "Lütfen." Kapıya doğru emeklerden gözlerim arabaya zorla bindirilen Merr'deydi.

"Meredith!" dedim çığlığım boğazımı yırtarken. Sonrasında ise görüntüm sadece bir çift siyah bottan ibaretti. Adamlardan biri benim hizama eğilip siyah gözlüklerinin ardından yüzüme baktı. Dudakları keyifle kıvrılırken elindeki yuvarlak topu işaret etti. "İyi uykular sürtük," dedi başparmağı düğmenin üzerine kapanmadan hemen önce. Ardından topu bina girişine fırlatıp dış kapıyı arkalarından kapatarak gözden kayboldular.

Toptan çıkan gaz bulutu etrafı sararken şişmiş gözlerimle Aidan'ı görmeye çalıştım. Ama göz kapaklarım öyle ağırlaştı ki bunu yapamadım.

***

Masmavi safir gözler.

Tıpkı bakir bir gölün ışıklı, büyüleyici, pürüzsüz yüzeyi gibi.

Gözlerim yavaşça açılırken az önce yaşananların bir kâbus olmasını diledim. Ölüm meleğinin mavi gözleri kasvetle koyulaşırken gözlerimi kocaman açtım. "Ah, hayır," dedim inleyerek. Her şey gerçekti. Kelepçeli ayaklarımı birleştirip dizimi bükerek alnımı yasladım. *Gerçekmiş, hepsi.*

Ölüm meleğinin ılık elini saçlarımda hissedince yaşlı gözlerimle başımı kaldırıp ona baktım. Meleğin mavi gözleri bileklerimi tutan kelepçeye kaydı. Avuçlarını kelepçeye kapatarak bir dua okudu melek. Ve çelik zımbırtı melek daha konuşmasını bitirmeden çatlayıverdi birkaç yerinden. Aynısını ayaklarımdaki kelepçeye yaptıktan sonra diğerlerinin yanına gitti.

Az önce Meredith'in zorla sürüklendiği yere geldim. Gözyaşlarım gözlerimi yakarken küfrederek ayağımı sertçe yere vurdum. "Lanet olsun!" Ayağımın altında bir şey ses çıkarınca şiş gözlerimle yere baktım. Madalyondu bu. Kız kardeşimin madalyonu. Eğilip kolyeyi aldım, avucumun içinde sertçe sıktım.

"Hepsi iyi olacaklar," dedi melek yeniden yanıma geldiğinde. "Başın belâdan çıkmıyor, öyle değil mi?" Hâlâ şiş olan gözlerimle meleğin parıltılı güzel yüzüne baktım. "Birkaç dakika önce gelseydin kız kardeşimi de kurtarabilirdin," dedim sessizce.

Melek gülümsedi. "İblisten teşekkür beklemek fazla iyimser olurdu, şeytan her zaman talepkârdır." Araladığım sokak kapısından dışarı baktı melek. Omzumun üzerinden arkamda duran dostlarıma baktım. Ağır aksak adımlarımla şeytanımın yanına varıp yüzüstü duracak şekilde gövdesini çevirdim. Aidanhell'in tişörtü yer yer yanmış deliklerle doluydu. Kumaşı sıyırınca cildindeki derin yanık izlerini gördüm. Dehşete kapılmıştım. "O neden iyileşmiyor?" diye sordum hâlâ ayakta duran meleğe.

Melek peşi sıra bir pelerin gibi sürüklediği beyaz kanatlarını hafifçe oynatıp sırtının içine aldı. "O insanlar normal avcılardan değiller," dedi sadece. Gözleri arkadaşlarımın baygın bedenlerinde usul usul gezindi. Ellerimle Aidan'ın saçlarını düzeltirken bakışlarımı meleğe çevirdim. "Sen Nathaniel misin?"

Safir gözlü melek gülümsedi. "Yoksa beni hatırladın mı?" dedi muzip bir gülüşle güzel yüzü aydınlanırken. "Ölüm meleği," diye mırıldandım ruhsuzca. Dün geceyi ve bir de içinde bulunduğum şu anı düşündüm. Adamlar ellerindeki son model silahlarla ruhumu da çıkarmış olmalılardı, öyle uyuşmuştum ki şoku sindiremiyordum bile.

"Herkesi kurtarmanın bir yolu var Cassandra," dedi ölüm meleği. Aidan ile sohbeti zihnime doluşunca kaşlarımı çattım. "Ben herkesi kurtarabilirim," dedim kendimden emin bir sesle. Şimdiye kadar öyle yapmamış mıydım? Sevdiklerim için yapamayacağım herhangi bir fedakârlık kalmış mıydı? Aidanhell'in başını kaldırıp dizimin üzerine koydum.

Nathaniel yüzünde her şeyi bildiğini söyleyen bir ifadeyle merdivenin ilk basamağına oturdu. "Bu kez," değil dedi aniden. Dirseğini bacağına yerleştirip çenesini ellerine koydu. Parlak gözleri Aidan'da sabitlenmişti. "Çukur hakkında bilmen gereken bir şey var. O tarafa giden kapı sonsuza dek kapandı."

Sözlerini anlamlandırmaya çalışırken beynimin sağlıklı kalan tek tük hücreleri de yanmaya başladı. "Teklifin ne o hâlde melek?" Kaybedecek tek bir saniyem bile yoktu. Bir an önce toparlanıp üzerimdeki ölü toprağını atarak harekete geçmeliydim.

"Hilekâr ölmeli Cassandra, artık vakit geldi."

Sözler zararsız birer fısıltı gibi çıkmıştı meleğin incecik biçimli dudaklarından. Ölmeli diyordu herkes, şu kahrolası hilekâr ölmeli.

"Ve bu her şeyi düzeltecek mi?" Nathaniel başıyla onayladı. "Sen gittikten sonra onlarla ilgileneceğim. Meredith ile bile. Kimse için endişelenmen gerekmeyecek." Nathaniel öyle psikopatça ölmemi istemiyordu, hayır, onun bakışlarında daha farklı bir duygu gizliydi. Meleğin safir gözleri âdeta yalvarıyordu. *Lütfen öl,* diye.

Ellerim hâlâ Aidan'ın kömür karası saçlarını okşarken, "Neden sana güveneyim?" diye sordum. "Ben siktir olup gittikten sonra sevdiklerimi kurtaracağının bir garantisi var mı?" Ve o an Nathaniel hiç düşünmediğim bir şey yaptı. Uzanıp Aidan'ın başındaki parmaklarımın üzerine elini koydu. "Çünkü biz kardeşiz. Bir kardeş diğerine bir söz verirse bunu yapar."

Daha önceleri evrenin espri anlayışının komik olduğunu düşünürdüm, oysa şimdi hayatımdaki en komik varlığı bulmuştum. O Nathaniel'di. Histerik bir gülme krizi bedenimi ele geçirirken meleğin tuttuğu elimi çekip kurtarmaya çalıştım. Ama Nathaniel daha sıkı tuttu. Şimdi az önceki nahif ifadesinin yerini kararlılık almıştı. "İkimiz de Azrail'in çocuklarıyız Cassandra. Tek fark, ben şeytan bir anadan doğmadım. Annem de melekti benim."

Bir melez olduğum tüm aylar boyunca umutsuzca biyolojik babamı merak ettiğim anılarım geldi aklıma. Annem şeytansa ve ben bir melezsem babam melek olmalıydı ama kimdi? Neden beni görmeye gelmemişti? Neden içinde bulunduğum çıkılması imkânsız gibi görünen hiçbir durumdan beni kurtarmamıştı? *Benden o kadar mı nefret ediyordu?*

Daha fazla akamayacağını düşündüğüm yaşlar gazın tahriş edip şişirdiği gözlerimden dökülürken meleğin avucundaki elimi çekip yanaklarımı sildim. "Bunu babam istiyor değil mi? Ölmemi?" Nathaniel başıyla onayladı.

Sonrasında üzgün mavi gözlerini yere dikti.

"Sen aslında hiç var olmamalıydın."

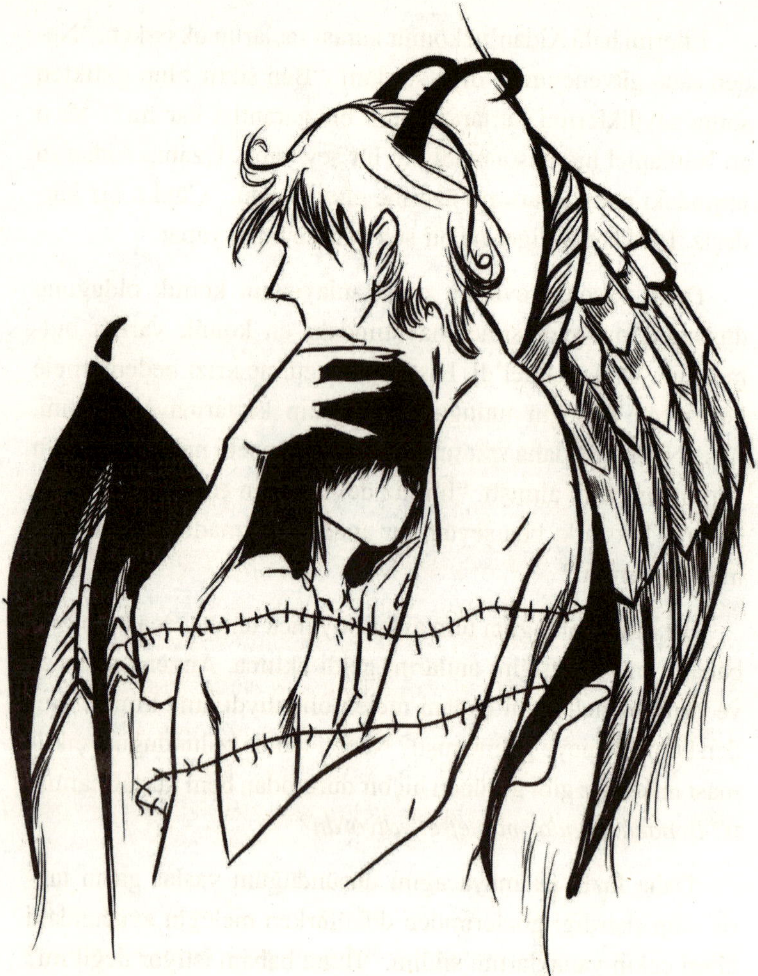

"Çünkü gözlerim ben yaşadığım süre
boyunca sana hep aynı bakacak."

BÖLÜM 24

Gözlerimi açtığımda Diego'nun koltuğundaydım.

Hava aydınlıktı ve sanki bayılmadan önce yaşadığım şeyler hiç olmamış gibiydi. Koltukta doğrulurken üzerimdeki tişörte baktım. Yanık izlerinin çevresine yayılan koyu kan lekeleri gözüme sokarcasına gerçeği haykırdı, saldırıya uğramıştık. Yerimden hızla kalkarak Cassie'ye seslendim. Salondaki diğer koltukta Draza, yerde de Aloha yatıyordu. Cassie görünürlerde yoktu. Kalbim göğüs kafesimi delmeye çalışırken bir kez daha bağırdım. "Cassie?"

Melezim mutfak kapısının ardından o güzel öpülesi başını uzattı. Tek adımda yanına giderek boynuna sarıldım. "Neredeydin seni aptal fare?" Saçlarının kokusunu içime çektim. Elleri ve kolları bağlı yerde sürünürken birkaç piçin ona yaklaştığını görmüştüm, sonra mı? Sonrası karanlık.

Cassie kollarını sırtıma dolayıp başını göğsüme bastırınca hissettiğim huzuru ifade edemezdim. İyi olduğu için öyle çok sevinmiştim ki dizlerimin bağı çözülmüştü. Nihayet gözlerimi açıp başımı saçlarından çekince mutfak masasındaki kalabalığı gördüm. Marcus da en az benim kadar bok gibi görünüyordu, hemen yanında Katze kurdun patlamış dudağına ıslak bir bez sürüyordu. Lavabonun üzerinde ise elinde Meredith'in madalyonu ile duran Urange vardı.

"Konuşmamız gerek," dedi Cassie çenesi hâlâ göğsümdeyken gözlerini yukarı kaldırarak. "Bundan hiç hoşlanmadım," dedim tereddütle ama çoktan kolumu tutan minik, güçlü parmaklar tarafından yönlendirilip sandalyelerden birine oturmuştum. Oturacak yer kalmadığı için de Cassie ayakta duruyordu. "Size anlattıklarımı ona da anlatacağım," dedi melezim sakin bir şekilde. Gözlerinde öyle mutsuz bir ifade vardı ki içinin sesi kadar sakin olmadığından emindim.

"Adamların giderken attığı gaz bombasını hatırlıyorsundur," dedi melezim. Bir gözü şişmişti ve nasıl olmuştu da düzelmediğini aklım idrak edemedi. "Bayıldıktan sonra Nathaniel geldi." Öfke kalbimin içinde patlarken yumruğumu masaya vurdum. "Sana bir şey yapmadı değil mi?" Melezim başını sağa sola salladı. "Benimle konuştu." Ve sonra Cassie'nin o güzel dudakları birbiri ardına açılıp kapanırken melezim olanları anlattı. Azrail'in babası oluşunu, kör perinin okuduğu kehaneti ve herkesi kurtarmak için ölmesi gerektiğini söyleyen Nathaniel'i. Konuşmasını bitirdiğinde sandalyelere oranla bodur olan taburelerden birini çekip oturdu.

Melezim kollarını masaya koyup ellerini iç içe geçirdi. Bana beklentiyle baktığını fark edince şaşırdım. "Ee? Yani?" dedim anlamayarak. Hemen yanımdaki pembe saçlı vampir gözlerini devirerek suskunluğunu bozdu. "Ölürse bizi kurtaracağını sanıyor, en başta Meredith cadısını elbette."

Sinirim şakaklarımda dolanırken başparmaklarımı kapalı göz kapaklarıma bastırdım. Sıkılı dişlerimin arasından, "Cassie," dedim. "Nathaniel'e güveniyor olamazsın. Azrail ile aylarca beraberdim, bir kez bile seninle ilgili bir şey söylemedi bana." Melezimin acı gülüşü yüzünü kaplarken hemen dediklerimi düzelttim. "Yani seni önemsemediğinden değil, gerçekten böyle bir şey olmadığı için. Ona inanıyor olamazsın."

"Sorun inanmak ya da inanmamak değil," dedi melezim yerinde rahatsızca hareket ederken. "Bu kez sevdiklerimden bir şey saklamak istemedim. Hep beraber karar verelim dedim." Bakışlarını masada birleştirdiği parmaklarına indirdi. Arkada bir yerden peri çocuk elinde madalyonu zafer kazanmış bir edayla havaya kaldırıp salladı. "Oyum Cassie'nin gitmemesi yönünde," dedi sırıtırken, sonra ekledi. "Kendini öldürmesine izin vermeyeceğimiz için madalyonu kullanarak Meredith'in yerini saptamaya çalıştık. Sonunda o uğursuz heriflerin kaldığı yeri biliyoruz."

Masanın üzerinden melezimin ellerine uzandım. İç içe geçirdiği parmaklarını ellerimin arasına alırken avucuma değen plastiği hissettim. "Bu işte beraberiz," dedim âşık olduğum kadının gözlerine bakarken.

***

Ayaklarım toprağa değdiği an taşımakta olduğum vampiri bıraktım. Katze düşüşün yarattığı ani şokla mücadele ederken bir dizi hoş olmayan küfür savurdu. Hemen yanımda Draza alçalıp Marcus'u zemine bırakırken arkamda da Aidan Aloha'yı yere indirdi. Urange bizden saniyeler önce varmış, son derece keskin gören büyülü peri gözleriyle bomboş arazideki tek yapıya bakıyordu. Bir hapishaneye benzeyen, kocaman duvarlarla örtülü bir yapıydı bu.

Urange'ın büyülü gözleri araziyi tararken bir yandan da gördüklerini aktarıyordu. Odaklanmış hâlde tekdüze bir sesle konuşuyordu turuncu saçlı peri dostum. "Güvenlik oldukça fazla. Adamlar devriyeler halinde geziyor. İçeride her ne yapıyorlarsa çok gizli ve önemli olmalı. Ayrıca binanın hemen her yerinde kocaman *D* harfleri kazılı."

Baktığı yere bakınca sadece dev yükseklikteki gri duvarları görebilmiştim.

"Her iki dakikada bir, yer altındaki kapı açılıyor ve kapalı otoparktan siyah cipler çıkıyor." Peri büyüyle neredeyse avuç içim büyüklüğündeki merceğe benzeyen gözlerini birkaç kez kırpıp bize döndü. "O kapıya hiç bulaşmadan üstten saldıralım," dedi. Aloha gülmemek için boğuluyor gibi sesler çıkarıyordu.

"Neyin var?" dedi peri kafa tutar gibi. "Bunu akıl edemeyenler olabilir. Mesela sen." Kollarını göğsünde kavuşturup çenesini dikleştirdi. Parmaklarının arasından aşağı sarkan madalyonu görünce yaklaşıp eline uzandım. Madalyonun zinciri avuçlarının arasından kayarken peri bir an için şaşkınca yüzüme baktı. Ardından kolyeyi almam için elini açtı.

Madalyonu boynumdan geçirip uğurlu sütyenimin içine sarkıttım. Meredith'in yaşadığını biliyordum. Nasıl bildiğimden tam olarak emin olamasam da biliyordum işte. Belki de bu kardeşlere has şu özel hislerden biriydi.

Ama daha net bildiğim bir şey varsa o da cadının yerimde olduğu takdirde beni kurtarmak için elinden geleni yapacağıydı. Bir iblis olarak kendimi dünyada, neredeyse ölüme terk ettiğim pek çok seferde, Meredith beni kurtarmak için hep yanı başımda durmuştu. Kustuğumda ensemde saçlarımı tutan, ağladığımda omuzlarına sümüklerimi silmeme izin veren bir kız kardeşe dönüşmüştü son bir senede. Benim için insanların boğazlarını keserek ruhlarını bedenlerinden çıkarmış, onu bulduğu yerde öldürmek isteyen Draza'ya dayanmıştı. Hatta sırf ben üzülüp kendimi herkes için feda etmeyeyim diye kehaneti bana yalan söylemek pahasına da olsa saklamıştı. Ve ben bunun için onu cezalandırmıştım.

Aklıma dolan utanç dolu hallerim yüzümü ekşitmeme sebep oldu. Bazen kendimden nefret ediyordum, bu da o anlardan biriydi işte.

Şeytanımın sıcak parmakları elime değerken içinde bulunduğum karamsar ruh halinden uyandım. Orada duruyor, tüm yakışıklılığı ve güven verici aurasıyla beni tekrar tekrar kendine âşık ediyordu. Aidanhell tatlı kahverengi gözleri parlarken yüzüme baktı. "Beraberiz," dedi kendinden emin bir sesle. "Sonsuzluk ve ötesinde." Parmak uçlarımda kalkıp yanağını öptüm.

Yeniden ayrıldığımızda arkadaşlarıma seslendim. "Öldürmeden bir diğerine geçmek yok. Bu piçler kaybın acısını iliklerinde hissedecekler." Ardından biz üç kanatlılar diğerlerini alarak havalandık. Urange tozlar içinde uçuşurken yaklaşık otuz metre yüksekliğindeki dev duvarlara yaklaşıyorduk. Kanatlarımı daha sert çırpınca Katze, pembe saçlı vampir başını karnıma gömdü. Sesinin bir kısmı rüzgârın arasında boğulurken bağırdı vampir. "Dejavu yaşıyor gibiyim. Kurtların sarayına girdiğimiz o günü hatırlıyor musun?" Sırıttım. "Nasıl unutabilirim seni çılgın vampir?"

Bir dakika sonrasında nihayet hedefimize ulaşmıştık. Canla başla korudukları binaya hızla yaklaşan kanatlıları gördüklerinde kulak zarını patlatacak kadar yüksek bir siren sesi havayı doldurdu. Duvarların üzerinden uçarken kapıdaki güvenlikler ellerindeki silahlarla bizi hedef alıyorlardı. "Zik zak çizin," diye bağırdım iblis kardeşlere. Böylelikle beyinsizlerin attığı tek bir kurşun bile bize isabet etmeden avluya indik.

"Kelepçelenmeyin. Gazı atarlarsa bile kanatlarımızla havayı dağıtırız, açık havadayız." Arkadaşlarım ve sevgilimle bir daire oluşturup, binanın kapısından avluya bir hamam böceği sürüsü gibi akan insanlara meydan okuduk. Gözümün önünden Meredith'in boynundaki ince telle sürüklenişi geçince, "Affetmek yok," dedim sıkılı dişlerimin arasından.

Sonrasında kaos başladı.

Gözüm dönmüştü. Gözlerim çok uzun zaman önce dönmüştü ama artık içimdeki öfke hapsolduğum bedenime dar geliyordu. Kanatlarımı bir an bile kapatmadan avluda uçup duruyor, adamlar nereden geldiğimi anlayamadan sırtlarına konuyor, ellerindeki acınası silahlarını kırıp paramparça ediyordum. Sıra kendilerine geldiğinde ise hançeri boğazlarına sokup artı şeklinde yarıyor, onlar kendi kanları içinde boğulurlarken bir diğerine geçiyordum.

Göz ucuyla bizimkilere denk geldiğim zamanlarda, onların da benzer hareketlerle adamları parçaladıklarını gördüm. Katze önüne gelen her insanın boynuna dişlerini geçirip atar damarını deldikten sonra bir diğerine geçiyordu. Aidan ise Savaş Tanrısı gibiydi. Eğer onu izlemeye kalkarsam öldürülmem iki saniye sürerdi, bu yüzden dikkatimi tam şu anda gözlerine parmaklarımı soktuğum adama verdim. Adam beni üstünden atmaya çalışınca boynunu kırıp tekrar göğe yükseldim.

Hamam böceği sürüsü bitmiyordu. Tam ortadaki binanın iki kollu giriş kapısından bardaktan boşanırcasına akıyorlardı. Gözlerimi kısıp daha dikkatli baktığımda yeni gelenlerden birkaçının ellerinde ok ve yay gördüm.

Bunlar avcıydı. Diğerleri de insan. Ve görünen o ki göğüslerinin üzerindeki büyük *D* harfi onları birleştirmişti. "Lanet olsun!"

Bir çığlık beynimin içine işleyince sesin kaynağını bulmak için deli gibi aşağı bakındım. Çığlık tekrar havayı delince kaynağı buldum. İki adam ellerindeki kocaman silindir silahlarıyla alev çıkarıyorlardı. Alevler öyle hızlı ve büyüktü ki kendilerinden birkaç metre uzağa bile sıçrayabiliyordu. Daha dikkatli bakınca ateşin odağındaki ufak figürü gördüm.

Peri çığlık çığlığa bağırarak koşturuyordu. "Hayır!" dedim gürleyerek. "Hayır! Olamaz!" Tam üzerlerine doğru inişe geçerken bir kurşun karnıma saplandı.

Şaşkınlıkla karışık bir acı belimi hissizleştirirken bakışlarımı eğerek kanayan yaraya baktım. Bu sıradan bir kurşun olamazdı, sıradan kurşunlar bizlerin canını yakmazdı. Yo, hayır, burada her ne oluyorsa bunun sıradanlıkla alakası yoktu. Ellerimle yaramı kapatmaya çalışırken dengemi kaybettim.

Aşağıda bir yerde, "Cassie," diyordu Aidan. Şeytanımın kızıl gözleri onca kalabalığın arasından bulmuştu beni. Ve gizlemeye çalışsam da parmaklarımın arasından sızan kana gitti gözleri. Ağrı dayanılmaz bir hâl aldığında daha fazla havada kalamayacağımı anlamıştım.

Aidan bana ulaşmak için yükselince, "Hayır," demek istedim. "Kaçın, gidin. Geri çekilelim!" Ama tüm bunlar birer fısıltı gibi dökülmüştü aralık kalan güçsüz dudaklarımdan. Şeytanım yüzünde acı çeken bir ifadeyle bana yaklaşırken kâhinin sözleri geldi aklıma.

Bu uğursuz ruh peşindekilere de acı getiriyor. Bir sonraki gelişinde bu kadar şanslı olmayacaksınız.

Kanayan yarama tampon yapmayı bırakıp Aidan'a doğru uçtum. Bu uğursuz ruh bir kaybı daha kaldırmayacaktı.

Ama kaderin benim için başka planları vardı. Kanlı parmak uçlarım Aidan'ın uzattığı eline değer değmez bir şey beni geri çekti. Bu öyle bir şeydi ki kanatlarımla beraber aşağı çekilirken karşı dahi koyamadım. Aidan'ın güzel yüzü hayretler içinde kararırken ona uzanmaya çalıştım.

Ucu çengelli başka bir halat başımın hemen yanından geçince omzumun üstünden geriye baktım. Dev gümüş bir çengel sağ kanadımın içinden geçmişti. Ucundaki halatı tutan insanlar da var güçleriyle asılıyorlardı. Kurtulmak için yaptığım her hamlede kanadımdaki kaslardan birinin yırtıldığını hissediyordum. Artık savaşamayacağımı anladığım sırada şeytanımın kanatları bedenimi sardı. Aidan var gücüyle bağırarak çengelin ucunu kanadımdan çıkardı. Beni kucağına alıp göğe yükselmeye çalıştığında ise birkaç el silah sesi duyuldu.

"Cassie," dedi Aidan acıyla büktüğü dudaklarının arasından kanlar akarken. "Sonsuzluk ve ötes..." Devamını tamamlayamadan düşüşe geçtik. Ellerimle yüzüne dokunuyor, bana tepki vermesi için gözlerini açmaya çalışıyordum. "Aidan, gör beni lütfen!" Ama şeytanım gözlerini açamadı. Kırık kanadım acınası bir şekilde sırtımdan çıkarken geç kaldığımı anlamıştım. Beraber beton zemine çakıldığımızda tek yaptığım neden hâlâ ölmediğim için ağlamaktı.

Başımıza üşüşen adamlar Aidan'ın bedenini tekmeleriyle hareket ettirdiklerinde vücudumda kalan son canımla onlara saldırdım. "Sizi lanetler! Onu öldürdünüz! Rahat bırakın!" Adamlar benden uzaklaşınca başka bir çengel kanadıma saplandı. Ardından bir tane daha. Üç kalın halat kanatlarımı yırtarak bedenimi geri büküp sürüklerken Aidan'ın elini tutmaya çalıştım.

"Aidan, ah Aidan!" Çengelin biri kanadımı boydan boya yardığında bile acı ulaşamıyordu beynime. Zeminde değersiz bir eşyaymış gibi sürüklenirken adamların yeniden Aidanhell'in bedeninin başına toplandığını gördüm. İri kıyım bir tanesi yanındakilere tutunup ayağıyla var gücüyle şeytanımın güzel yüzüne bastığında kalbim paramparça oldu.

Aidanhell'in dokunmaya kıyamadığım kömür karası saçları aldığı darbelerle dağılırken son gücümle bağırdım.

"Keşke hiç var olmasaydım!"

Ardından kendimi halatlara bırakıp bedenim bir pelte haline gelene kadar beni ölüme sürüklemelerine izin verdim.

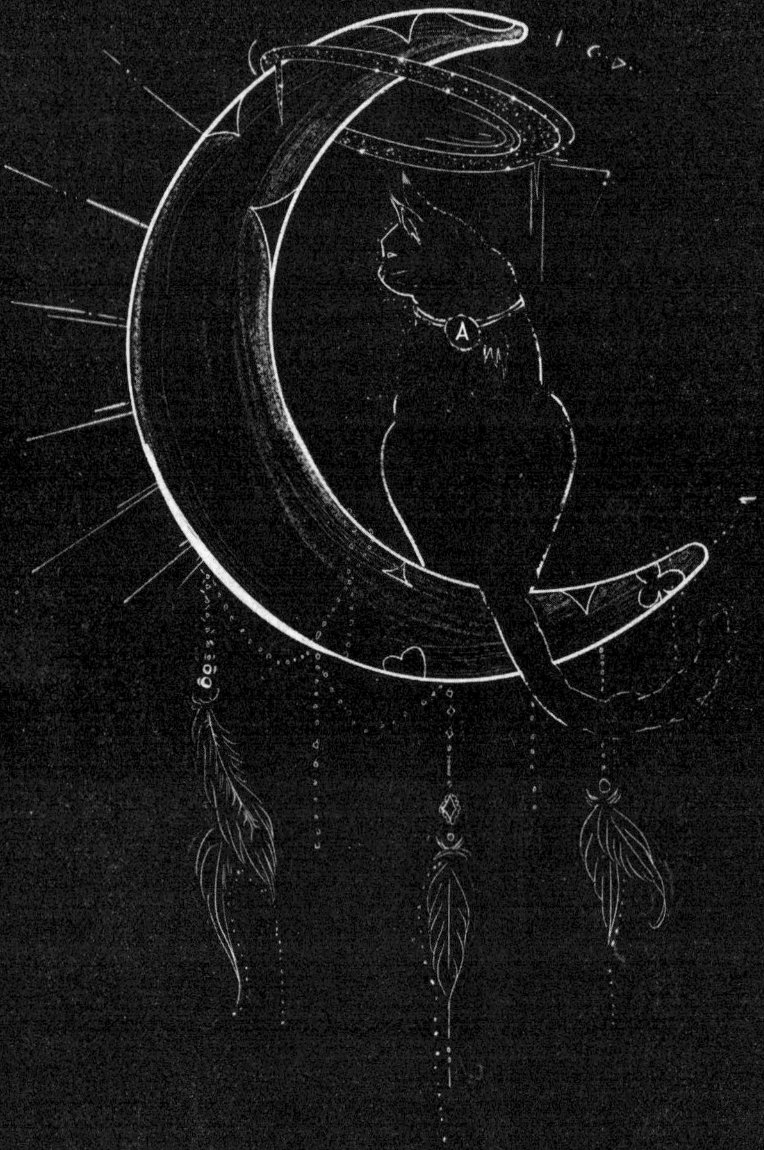

"Yıldızlar bile benim kadar yalnız değil."

Bilinmesi Gerekenler

Avcılar : İnsanlarla beraber yaratılan, şeytanı alt etmek için savaşan, birtakım güçleri olan insan sınıfı.

Aidanhell : Şeytanın ikinci oğlu.

Araf Süvarileri : Arafı gezen, bir yere ait olamayan süvari ruhlar.

Cehennem Cadıları : Cehennemde zulüm vermek için yaratılan cadılar. İleride onlardan birini tanıyacağız.

Çukur : İblislerin öldükten sonra gittiği varsayılan karanlık mezar. Neye benzediği henüz bilinmiyor.

Draza : Şeytanın büyük oğlu. Sürgüne gönderilip kara elfe dönüştü, şu an için türü bilinmiyor.

Devler : Trol sınıfından düşük iblis kastları.

Ejderhalar	: Soylarının tükendiği varsayılan eski iblis sınıfı.
Hırsız	: Ölümlülerin -tercihen güç sahibi olanların- bedenlerine yerleşen şeytani ruhlar.
İblisçe	: Şeytanın oğullarını yetiştiren öğretmenlere verilen ad.
İblisürüngenler	: En düşük iblis kastı.
İblis Öldüren	: İblisleri kısa süreliğine bayıltan minik hançerler.
Kabul Kitap	: Son kutsal kitap.
Kanlı Görü	: Şeytan tarafından gösterilen, haberleşmek için kullanılan eski, kanlı bir yol.
Kâhin	: Her yüzyılda bir kehanette bulunan ölümsüz varlık.
Kara Elf	: İblis kastlarında şeytandan hemen sonra gelen sınıf. Rivayete göre kötülük barındıran ilk elf Kahirsifin'in cezalandırılmasıyla ortaya çıkan tür.
Kara Saray	: Kurtların hanedanlığının diğer bir adı. Şehir ve kralın yaşadığı sarayla aynı ismi taşımaktadır.
Lilith	: Çukurda var olduğu sanılan dişi şeytan. Haber alınamamaktadır.
Melekler	: Yeterli bilgi bulunmamaktadır.
Morgain İncisi	: Şeytanın hizmetkârı olan kimselerin taşıdığı varsayılan, deriye kazınmış görünmez dövme.

Periler : Arafın diğer misafirleri. Zaman zaman iyi olmakla beraber kötücül sihirli yaratıklar.

Periotrus : Araf Ormanı'nın içinde ustalıkla gizlenmiş cadıların yaşadığı karanlık orman.

Şeytan : Cennetten kovulan. İtaatsiz. Cehennemdeki ana kral.

Şeytan Savaşları : Dünya Savaşları ile aynı anda başlayan, bitmeyen karanlık süreç.

Valkür : İskandinav mitolojisinde, miğfer ve mızrakla silahlanmış genç ve güzel bakirelerdir.

Vanelia : Merkezinde kral ve kraliçenin yaşadığı karanlık şato olan üst sınıf, soylu vampirlerin yaşadığı şehir.

Vampirler : Diabloların en itaatsiz vahşi sınıfı.

Yıkım Getiren : Milattan önce yaşamış, kana susamış feminist kadın avcı grubu.

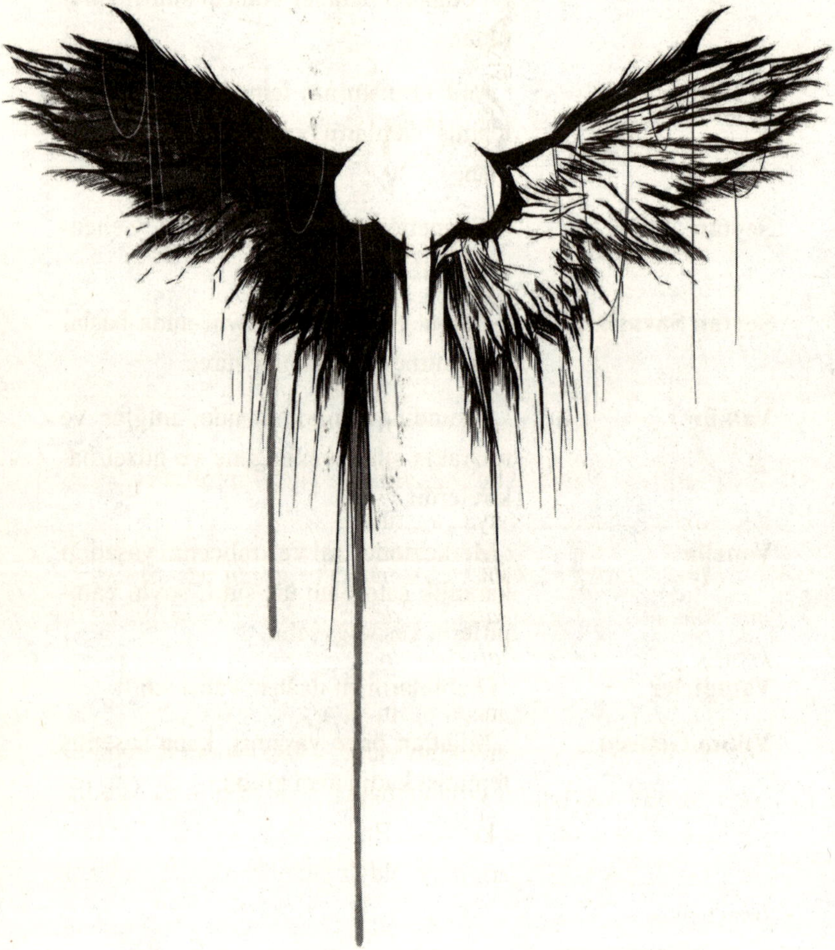

"Beni soluyana ölüm hediye ederim.
Ben gölgemi, beni önemseyenlere
bırakır da giderim."

KÂHİN

Her şey mahvolmadan önce mutlu bir insan mıydım?

Bir anı... Belirli belirsiz silik bir anı zihnime çöreklenirken gözlerimi açık tutmaya çalıştım.

Bir ev. Ahşap kapısındaki menteşeler geçen yaz savaştığımız iblisürüngenler tarafından darbe almış. Her açıldığında kemiğe değen bıçak misali çıkardığı gıcırtılar.

Bir insan sesi düşüncelerimin arasından kulağıma süzüldü. "Diriliş'e hoş geldin kadim varlık." Gözlerimi açamadım. Sesin nereden geldiğini de anlamadım. Anıya gitmek istedim yeniden. Ama ses tekrar konuştu. Bu kez benimle değildi. "Onu mahzene kapatın. Güçlerinin ne olduğunu bilmiyoruz. Yalıtımlı odaya alın."

Güçler… Oysa ben anıma gitmek istiyordum.

Ailemle beraber bıçaklarımızı temizlerken kardeşim Jo'nun bıçağı elinden düşürüp bağırmasını hatırlıyordum. Öyle içten ve acıyla bağırmıştı ki, Marr elini kesmiş olabileceğini düşünmüştü. Çekmeceden oksijenli su alıp kardeşimi yanına çağırmıştı.

"Kanatlarından biri kötü durumda. Bu şekilde kaçabileceğini sanmıyorum."

Sesler konuşuyordu. Öldükten sonra cennete gitmeyeceğimi bilecek kadar akıllıydım. Ama cehennemi görmüş, bizzat hükmetmiştim. Orada da değildim. Nerede olduğum hakkında bir fikrim yoktu. Zihnim salonumuzun loş ışığı altında kalan ceketlerimizin atıldığı eski mobilyalarımızda takılı kalmıştı. *Marr, Jo'nun parmağına suyu dökerken kardeşim zıplamıştı.*

Ben ise gülmüştüm. Babama erkek bir oğlu olduğu için sevinmesinin saçma olduğunu hatırlatmıştım gururla. Babamsa sadece gülümsemişti.

"Kanatları kökünden ayıralım o hâlde. Doktor Hilda ve Grey halleder. Çağırın onları."

Diğer ses bir süre yanıt vermeyince anılarıma geri döneceğim için sevindim.

"Efendim, kızın omurgası ile kanatlar birlikteyse sakat bırakabiliriz." Diğer ses bu kez güldü. Ama bu kahkaha babamınki gibi değildi. Draza bile hiç böyle gülmemişti. Sevgili cadı kardeşim Meredith bile ölümümüze sebep olabilecek bir olay tezgâhladığında böyle gülmemişti.

"O bir kız değil," dedi sesi yaşlı ve kendinden emin olan. Sesi az önceki sahte kahkahasının tınısından sıyrılmıştı. Sakindi. Ürkütücü bir sakinlik perdesine gizlenmiş gibiydi.

"Sakat kalsa bile bizimle konuşabilir. Tek istediğimiz bilgi."

Bilgi, güç demekti. İşte buna gülmek istedim. Ama yapamadım. Kıpırdayamadan o çok sevdiğim sevgili ölümün beni yutmasını bekledim.

İnsan ne zaman ölürdü?

Son nefesim kaç saniye sürerdi? Nefesimi tutsam sonuma daha hızlı gider miydim?

Sonumda değil miydim?

"Eğer onları sökersek acıdan ölebilir." Toy olan kim için üzülüyordu? Benim için mi? Ben bir insanın benim için üzülmesine layık değildim ki. Varlığım zehirliydi benim. Beni soluyana ölüm hediye ederdim. Ben gölgemi beni önemseyen insanlara bırakır da giderdim. Ben buydum. Bir yıkım getiren. Yıkıp geçerdim, ta ki ardımda bir şey kalmayana dek.

Gaddar olan bileğime dokundu. Acı ufak parçalar halinde tenimi dağlarken gözlerimden minik, ufacık, belki bir kar zerresi kadar bir parça yaş doğdu. Damla akamadan buharlaştı gözlerimde. Gölgeme karıştı, oradan da ruhuma aktı. Ağlayamamıştım bile.

"Karnındaki çizgilere bak. Bu varlık acıyı biliyor. Bizim yapacağımız şeylerin canını yakacağını sanmıyorum." Sivri soğuk bir el karnıma değdi. Bu kez genç olan telaşlı gibi öksürdü. "Efendim, üstüne bir şey örtelim, en azından doktorlar gelene kadar."

Yaşlı adam gülünce içimde minik bir parça ezildi. Çıplaktım. Kıyafetlerim, uğurlu savaş sütyenim üzerimde değildi. Göğüslerime düşen soğuk madalyon bedenimde öylece duruyordu.

"Çıplaklık insanlara özgü bir şey David. O, bir insan değil. Bir hayvan nasıl çıplak sayılmazsa o da sayılmaz."

Bir hayvan.

Zihnimde bir kurt uludu. Diğer tüm uğultular sustu. Kurdun acı dolu sesi kulaklarıma doldu.

Bir tek ben duyuyordum kurdu. Belki de kurt bendim. Bilmiyorum.

"Geldiler," dedi ses tekrar. Ben ise ailemi düşünmeye geri döndüm. Ama yapamadım, aklım Aidan'a kaydı. Aidan'ın bakışlarına kaydı zihnim. Ve sonra o kahverengiler beni yuttu. Yine olsaydı bana ne derdi? Kendimi bu durumda bıraktığım için bana ne söylerdi? Bana kızar mıydı? Muhtemelen canıma okurdu. O kendini beğenmiş çarpık gülümsemesi ile belki de dalga geçerdi. "Cassandra," dedi o boğuk, genizden gelen güçlü sesiyle. "Yine başını belâya soktun." Ben de kendimi savunurdum hemen. "Hayır, şeytan. Bu kez benim hiçbir suçum yok."

Bilmediğim bir kadın sesi konuştu. Biri kanadımı kaldırıyordu. Yabancı bir el kanadımın ucuna dokunup oradan bir tüyü çekip çıkardı.

"Bu zaten kullanılmaz hâlde. Diğerini ameliyatla alırız ama bunu zaten incecik bir kas tutuyor. Bakın." Bu kez birden fazla el kanadımı kaldırdı.

Hissizlik üzerime yoğun bir gece yarısı gibi çöktü. Hissedemiyordum. Az önce tüyleri hissetmiştim ama şimdi birileri kanadımı büküyordu ve hissedemiyordum.

"Biri yardım etsin." Ardından hissizlik sessizce kayıplara karıştı ve yakın dostu acı geldi. Acı önce beni selamladı. Sonra parmağını dudaklarına götürüp *sessiz ol*, dedi usulca. *Her şey bitecek.*

"Diğerini zaten kaybettik, bu seferki ölmesin."

Ardından kanadımı tuttular. Kalbimden bir parça kopup gözlerime hükmetti. Savaş seni kahrolası, savaş! Uyan.

Gözlerimi açmaya çalıştım.

Çalıştım.

Dişlerimi gıcırdattım.

Ama gözlerim...

En sonunda açtım.

Karşımda beyaz saçlı bir kadın duruyordu. Gözlerimi açtığımı fark etmişti. "Durun," dedi bana bakarak. Ardından üzerime eğildi. Beyaz cansız saç uçları alnıma değdi. Naneli nefesi yüzüme çarparken, "Merhaba varlık," dedi usulca. "Diriliş örgütüne hoş geldin." Ardından elini kaldırıp diğerlerine döndü. Kanlı göz bebeklerim havada hareket eden parmağına takıldı.

Eli yavaşça yere inerken zaman dondu.

Bir çatırt sesi ruhumu bedenimden ayırdı.

Acı yanı başımda durmuş ağlıyordu. Kurt bile ulumayı bırakmıştı.

Kanadım bedenimden kopup giderken çığlık atamadım. Sonra ellerinde beyaz siyah tüylerine kan bulanmış çarpık kanadımı gördüm. Bedenimden ayırıp yanıma koydular. Gereksiz bir parçaymış gibi.

Uzanıp ona sarılmak istedim ama kıpırdayamadım. Kanadım çoktan ölüm kokmaya başlamıştı sanki. Ölüm kokar mıydı ki? Bilmiyordum.

Gözlerimden kaçıp saklanmak isteyen taneler yanaklarıma dökülürken çürümeye bırakılan kanadıma dokunmak istedim.

Ölmek bu değildi. Ölmeyi bile beceremedim. Aidan yapabildi. Ben yapamadım. Ben ölümü bile hak edemedim.

Kadın boynuma bir şırınga saplayınca gözlerimi kapadım. Sırtımdaki ıslak soğukluk sancıyordu. Artık yalnızdım.

Acı bile kurdu kucaklayıp gitmişti.

Ay, bulutları toplayıp göğü terk etmiş, yıldızlar üstlerine kara çuvallar giyip gizlenmişti.

Herkes gitti.

Yalnızım.

Bu kez tamamen yalnız.

-TAKİP EDİN-

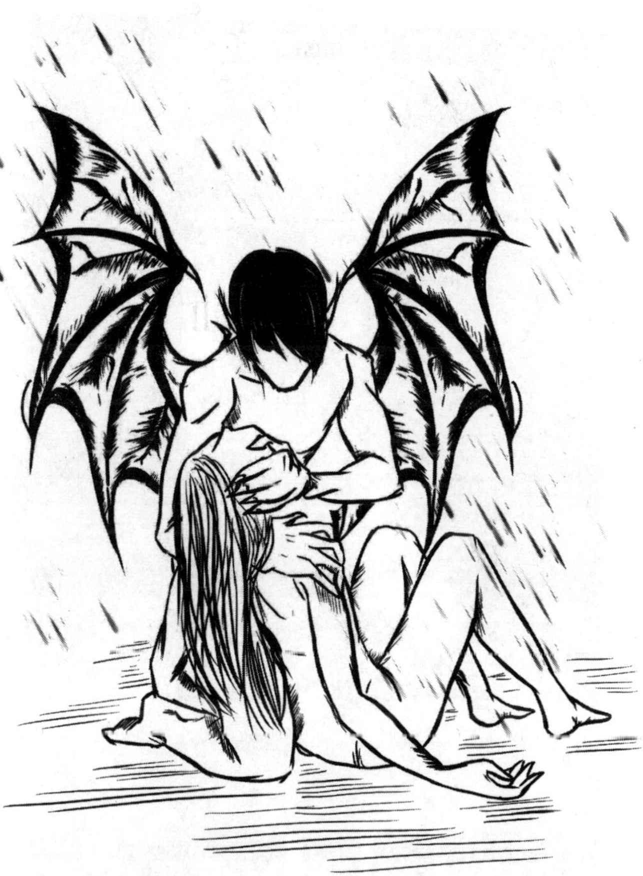

"Bir melek olarak aldığım
ilk nefes senin."

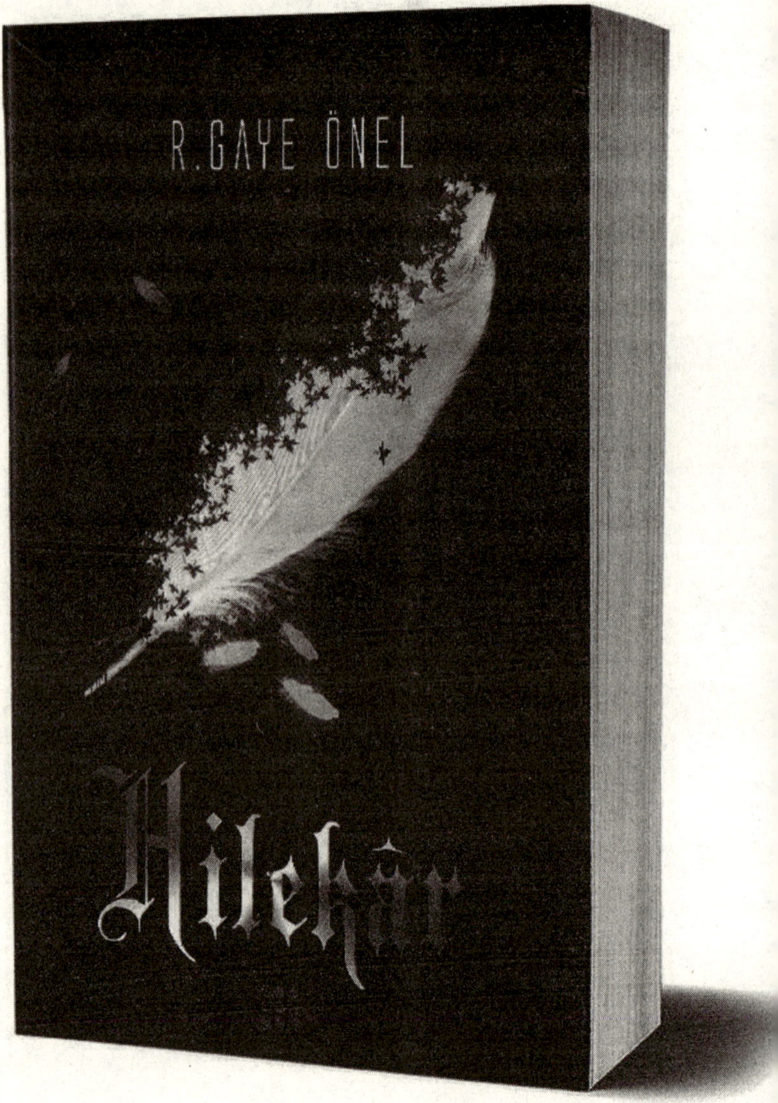
R. GAYE ÖNEL
Hilekâr

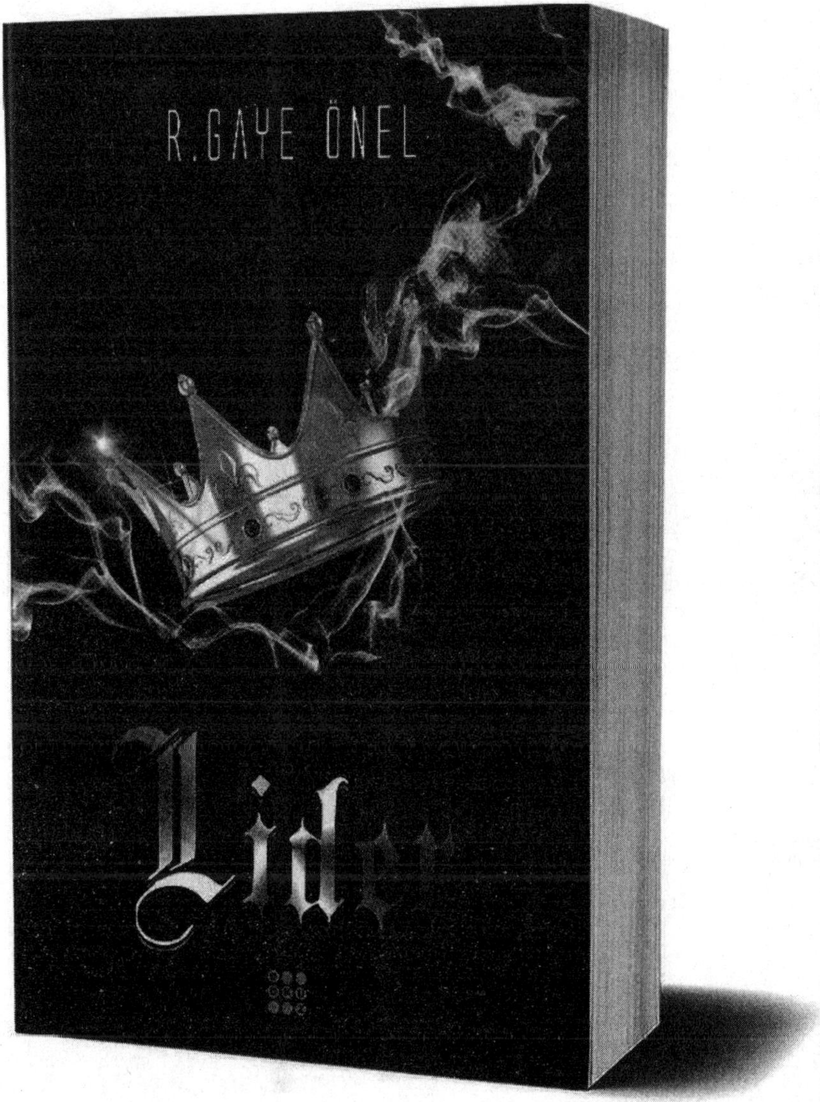
R.GAYE ÖNEL

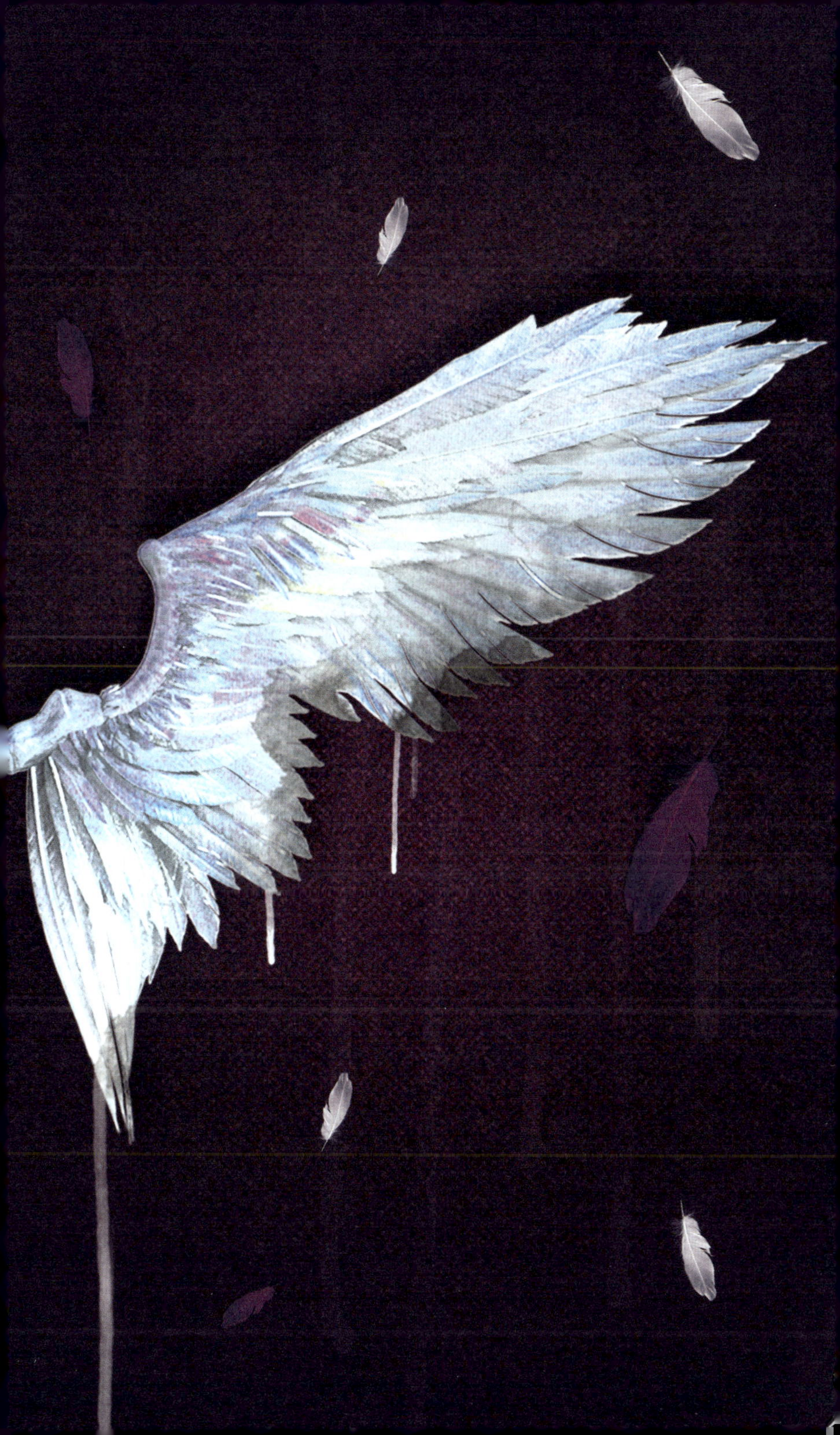

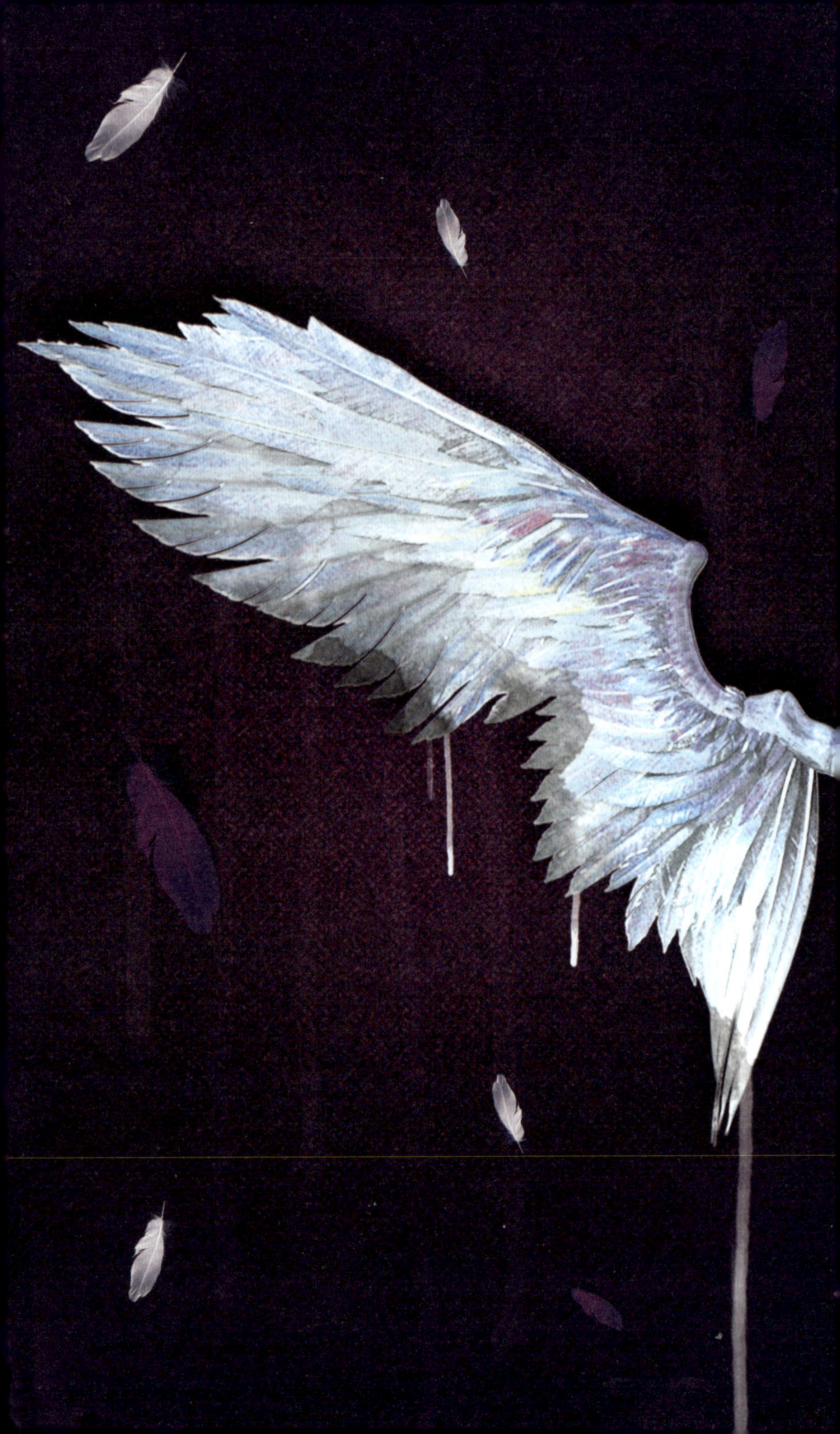